Maria Coif
2010

PARIS

Capital of the World

PARIS

CAPITAL OF THE WORLD

PATRICE HIGONNET

Translated by Arthur Goldhammer

——— THE BELKNAP PRESS OF ———
HARVARD UNIVERSITY PRESS
Cambridge, Massachusetts
London, England
2002

The endpapers reproduce two views of Paris, courtesy of the
Harvard Map Collection, Harvard College Library.
Front: *Panorama de Paris, vue pris Place de la Concorde.*
Paris: Lemercier & Cie [1875].
A detail of this panorama appears on page ix.
Back: *Nouveau Plan de Paris monumental.*
Paris: L. Guilman [1900].

Designed by Gwen Nefsky Frankfeldt

Library of Congress Cataloging-in-Publication Data
Higonnet, Patrice L. R.
Paris : capital of the world / Patrice Higonnet ;
translated by Arthur Goldhammer.
p.   cm.
Includes bibliographical references and index.
ISBN 0-674-00887-1 (alk. paper)
1. Paris (France)—History. I. Tirle.
DC707 .H585 2002
944'.361—dc21
2002071216

Margaret

---

a gift
this book of Paris
which I could never have written
without you

Contents

1

A City of Myths

THE HISTORY OF PARIS reaches back to Roman and even Neolithic times. Visitors often have the impression that the city has always been there, and always had to be there. To move from one of its monuments to another is to walk through history. Goethe—though he never visited Paris—called it the universal city, and over the centuries the resonances of the place have been rich and varied. Its native sons and daughters have achieved great things, as have the visitors who chose to live there for brief periods or a lifetime—from John Adams and Ben Franklin to Gertrude Stein and James Baldwin, to name only a few who came from the United States. And unlike Venice or Florence, contemporary Paris is not just a center of world tourism with a glorious past. It remains a vibrant and modern city whose influence extends through time and space.

How can we attempt to understand Paris, both historically and emotionally? And how can we write a history of this great city that will not just rehearse material that many fine historians have already made familiar to us? The approach taken here is to give an account of its myths, a history not of factual events but of the way in which the city has been perceived, conceived, and dreamed—Paris as the capital of modernity, or mystery, or tradition; Paris as the capital of art and fashion; Paris as the capital of world revolution; Paris as the capital of pleasure, crime, sex, science.

This choice of method is not without problems, the most obvious being that it is very hard to say what a "myth" might be. It often seems as if the number of definitions bears a direct correlation to the number of scholars who have written on the subject. Enlightenment thinkers, for example, generally viewed myth as the (confused) recollection of events that had actually occurred; thus the biblical myth of a great flood was attributed to the hazy remembrance of some ancient catastrophe. Others have proposed anthropomorphic definitions, seeing myth as the stylization of lived experience; on this reasoning, Apollo is the Greek god of the sun and Chac is the Mayan god of rain because the individual yearns to connect the essential aspects of his daily life and being to such deities, whose good will he can implore and whose deeds and voices can be fitted into vast celestial schemes. The German scholar Hans Blumenberg, in his book *Arbeit am Mythos* (Work on Myth; 1979), took issue with Descartes's view of myths as useless and deleterious prejudice and suggested that they are, instead, useful explanations of inexplicable mystery. In this context, myths (that is, the myths that manage to endure) are the survivors of a war of words—a Darwinian struggle in which useless myths inevitably die. A myth expresses a need, old or new, and myths are made by those who need them. Thus the fall of the Bastille, built to defend and then oppress Paris, became a myth because human beings needed—and no doubt still need—this symbol of liberty.

There are also structural explanations of myth. In the writings of Claude Lévi-Strauss, myths are imaginary constructs that enable us to understand what might otherwise seem to defy common sense and lived experience. Hence the myth of Paris as "the capital of the nineteenth century"—a concept which originated with Karl Ludwig Börne (1786–1837) and which was taken up, famously, by Walter Benjamin (1892–1940). This compelling idea helps us to "understand" the extraordinary assemblage of talented individuals—poets, novelists, painters, composers, statesmen, philosophers, scientists—that inhabited the city in those days, especially in the 1840s.

Yet the definition of myth that best fits the history of Paris is simpler and plainer (too plain, no doubt!). For the purposes of this book, we shall view myths as life stories, each of which has a beginning, a trajectory, and a conclusion—stories that all societies elaborate to explain to themselves the rise and sometimes the fall of their collective enterprise. The story of Genesis served this function for ancient Israel, just as the tale of the birth, death, and apotheosis of Christ does within the Christian worldview. All peoples—from the Mayans, with their Popol Vuh, to the Russian Soviets, with their Marxist tracts—have evolved cosmogonic myths of creation, becoming, and decline.

Universality is the primary characteristic of such myths. The story of Romulus and Remus concerns the origin of the entire Roman people; it does not distinguish between the plebs and the equestrian class. Its selfless heroes express the aspirations of the society as a whole—they have no private goals or flaws. A myth of this type is, in Nietzsche's phrase, an "orgiastische Selbstvernichtung"—a festive and even orgiastic self-nullification.[1] In ancient Rome, as anterior founding myths became less and less credible, it was precisely their universality that made possible the shift from comprehensive myths to comprehensive histories of the city. Similarly, the history of Paris in the nineteenth century—or from the middle decades of the eighteenth century to the early middle decades of the twentieth—can be imagined as the universalizing and secularized sequel to collective religious myths that had begun to die.

This definition of myth, which will be central to the following pages, derives in no small measure from the work of the linguist and philosopher Roland Barthes. In his view, the purpose of *modern* mythologies is to deform, diminish, and even destroy our understanding of lived experience by altering the expected relation of the sign (any element that represents) to the signified (that which is represented). Contemporary myth, he thought, turns a meaningful sign—which bespeaks an enriching exchange or correlation—into a static, artificial, and arbitrary fabrication. Instead of conceptualizing the object or situation it describes, it ignores the origin and true purpose of the signified. The modern myth is deception.

In *Mythologies* (1957), Barthes clarified his argument with a photograph from a popular illustrated French weekly, *Paris Match*. The photo showed a very black soldier, dressed in a French uniform and saluting

or maybe just give to meaning

the tricolor national flag. How would average Frenchmen in the 1950s have reacted to this image? They would no doubt have felt deep pride. They would have seen in this "text" yet one more proof—if proof were needed—of France's civilizing mission and of French culture's ability to transform potential (or even practicing) cannibals into law-abiding citizens. This cultural musing would have led such viewers to the thought that France's colonialism was justified: other countries had acquired colonies for profit or strategic gain, but France—or so the photo implied—was more selfless.

More sophisticated viewers, however, might have seen this military image as validating their belief that France, weakened by self-indulgence and a reluctance to endure sacrifice, needed colonial troops to defend itself against envious or malicious neighbors. On such a reading, this carefully staged photograph concealed the true nature of French and European colonialism. Its image was a "myth" in the ordinary sense of that word today—meaning that it was a fabrication, a false rendering of some person or situation. Indeed, as Barthes argued, the photo, like most modern myths, was a conservative or even reactionary fabrication because it aimed to structure the worldview of the spectator: on the one side was Africa, sorely in need of European-style civilizing; on the other was France, modern, generous, internally consistent and homogeneous. Whatever differences might have existed within French society were ignored. Such modern mythologies, in Barthes's sense, are still being created today. They are essentially engineered by manipulative governments and avaricious corporations that wish to foist onto a nation's citizens many policies and consumer goods they do not need or even truly want.

We seem to encounter a contradiction here: cosmogonic myths are in some deep sense true, but Barthes's myths are manifestly false. How can the two be reconciled? The answer given here is that they are compatible if properly historicized. Myths—in particular, the myths of Paris—are not uniform over time. The modern phenomenon that Barthes described should be termed not a myth but a *phantasmagoria*.

A cosmogonic myth explains the profane by reference to what is sacred and eternal. For example, in 1871 the Parisian Communards un-

4

derstood their lives by placing them in a universal context: their struggle, however local it might have seemed, was that of an ecumenical and
enduring proletariat struggling throughout the world to be free. What
a dangerous but exciting dream it is, wrote the critic Claude Pichois in
1938, ⟨to find traces of eternity in the fleetingness of life that Paris offers to those who observe its spectacle."⟩

Phantasmagoria, in contrast, inverts the purpose of cosmogonic
myth. It deforms the past in a self-justifying way by drastically simpli-
fying it to accord with a superficial and even selfish need. This process
can be viewed in a positive light, as the Surrealists of the 1920s viewed
it when they described phantasmagoria as a world where "beings and
things assume unexpected forms and bedeck themselves in dreamlike
color." But in this book we will take phantasmagoria to be a self-delud-
ing and self-indulgent fantasy, shallow and deceptive. "There is no place
in the world like Paris," wrote Mozart to his father in 1778; Parisians,
he thought, "are and always will be asses." Fashion and appearance mattered more to them than real life, a harsh judgment, no doubt, but one
that fits nicely here: whereas myths enable us to understand, phantasmagorias help us merely to deceive. Advertisements therefore often have a
phantasmagoric purpose, taking a reference that we know (such as a
brand name) and combining it with false promises. In Barthes's words,
the "erosion" effected by such a phantasmagoria is "directly proportional
to the arbitrariness of its meaning."

But why use the term "phantasmagoria" rather than the simpler
"phantasm" or even "fantasy"? First, and most literally, because phantasmagorias (though, alas, invented in London) were an authentically Parisian phenomenon. These enormously popular nineteenth-century enter-
tainments consisted of images projected from a lantern onto a screen,
which was set between the lantern and the spectators. The inventor of
the process, a professor of physics named Etienne Robert (later Robert-
son), born in Belgium but buried at Père-Lachaise Cemetery in 1837,
claimed that phantasmagorias were so lifelike that through them it was
possible "to make the dead speak."[2]

Second, and more important, is the metaphorical meaning of the
word. Marx, a historian of Parisian politics (all his historical writings re-

late to Paris), often used the term "phantasmagoria" in a very precise way that is directly relevant here. For him the word denoted an illusion—or better, a self-delusion—that would have us believe that universalist relations of love or equality (which are a kind of transcendence) can exist in a hierarchical society where some people brutally command and others abjectly obey. On this definition, Edmund Burke's eighteenth-century ideal of noble-minded landowners who cared deeply about their loyal peasants is a phantasmagoria. As is the American South's antebellum ideal of the benevolent plantation owner who was generous to his slaves and was loved by them in turn. A related variant is Walter Benjamin's "phantasmagoria of the interior": the delusion of the wealthy private art collector who is shocked by the materialism of the system that feeds him and who seeks, out of obtuseness and perverted self-love, to create a beneficent and noncapitalist universe within the confines of his own home.[3]

Phantasmagorias of all types, like collections, can make for visual and intellectual pleasure. They are often ingeniously, even elegantly disguised, especially on the television or movie screen. Many TV programs are dull and mediocre, but the advertisements that frame them—and that are their economic raison d'être—can be highly entertaining and cleverly conceived. In Paris, the Pompidou Center, with its fake, neo-industrial design, is an architectural phantasmagoria—intelligent, quite useful, and intended as a complex, crowd-pleasing phantasmagoric joke, both mocking and ironic.

MYTHS AND PHANTASMAGORIAS, then, display essential differences. But both can be periodized historically. Although some scholars consider myths, like fairy tales, to be structured explanations of reality that are drawn from the vast, common, and unchanging human unconscious, others see myths as changing from zeitgeist to zeitgeist, even at times from one moment to the next. In the case of Paris, myths have indeed changed over time, and three dates can serve as thresholds: 1750, when the first secularized myths of Paris appeared; 1830, the point at which they started to flower; and 1889, when they began to atrophy. It is at this last juncture that the term "phantasmagoria" comes into its own.

To be sure, medieval Paris had its myths—notably its patron saints, such as Joan of Arc, wounded before its walls in 1429, and the martyred early Christian Saint Denis, who allegedly carried his own severed head from Notre Dame to the site of the modern Church of Saint Denis. But these Parisian religious figures acquired mythic significance only within the larger context of Christian cosmology. Indeed, one is tempted to suppose that it was precisely the decline of that God-centered world-view and the rise of the Enlightenment that made possible the emergence of a specifically secularized Parisian mythology. It is this secular mythologized Paris—the city that around 1750 became the capital of the Republic of Letters and the temporary or permanent home for many distinguished foreigners from the four corners of the globe—that will serve as our starting point.

It was a beginning that soon fulfilled its initial promise. Curiously, the Revolution of 1789—by far the most meaningful of the numerous political upheavals that Paris witnessed over the centuries—was not initially perceived, either in France or abroad, as proof that the city had become the mythical capital of world politics. This came only after 1830. Paris was basically quiescent during the reigns of Napoleon and his Bourbon successors (Louis XVIII to 1824, and Charles X to 1830, both of them younger brothers of Louis XVI, who had been executed in January 1793 on what is now the Place de la Concorde). One of Napoleon's goals—or so he claimed in his tendentious *Mémorial*—was to make Paris "the true capital of Europe . . . something fabulous and colossal, the likes of which have been unknown until today." But he did very little to bring this about. Thus the first important scholarly study of a mythified Paris, written by Pierre Citron, begins in earnest in 1830—which is curious, because the revolution of that year was, of all the Parisian insurrections of the nineteenth century, the least dramatic.[4] Nonetheless, that moment marks the beginning of a wave of secularized Parisian mythology that crested in the 1860s with Baron Haussmann's astounding reconstruction of the city. No other place has ever transformed itself so boldly and so quickly.

The mythology of the city was still vibrant in 1889, as was evident in the creation of Gustave Eiffel's thousand-foot tower (which, though subsequently used for radio transmission, was completely useless at the time and thus stood as a splendid rebuke to the utilitarian myths of its day). Yet the year was a turning point: a decade later the image of Paris had become less myth than phantasmagoria. We sense this immediately when we compare the Eiffel Tower with the Alexander III Bridge, built over the Seine in 1900, and likewise of metal but decidedly reactionary in its neo-Baroque design. In the 1920s the Surrealists brought the cycle of phantasmagoria to a close. For them, Paris was still a unique city, unpredictable and mysterious; by wandering through its streets, they believed, the sensitive observer could better read his own hopes and fears. But they felt profound disdain for Haussmann's Paris (echoed in many respects by Walter Benjamin, a Marxist critic, whose anticapitalist hero, the poet Baudelaire, was Haussmann's antithesis). In their eyes, the myths of bourgeois Paris were no more than alienating obfuscation.

HOW CAN WE EXPLAIN the rise and fall of the myths of Paris? And why are 1750, 1830, and 1889 the crucial years? One might approach this problem by looking at the political context. In the mid-eighteenth century the prestige of the French monarchy began to crumble. In 1774 Louis XV, who had been much loved in 1745, died in disgrace. Religious controversies (Gallicans and Jansenists versus the more orthodox Catholics) now became politicized as never before. Here we see the first phase of a secularizing cycle that would end eighty years later, with the fall of Charles X in 1830—a moment that marked the definitive collapse of political traditionalism, the rise of republicanism, and the resurgence of communist ideas (which had been prefigured in 1795–1796). Further on, the year 1889 would see the first premonitions of twentieth-century fascism, the rise of anti-Semitism, and the apogee of European imperialism.

Yet another approach to the problem would be to look at it in economic terms. The eighteenth century was a period of unprecedented prosperity in the history of France. Paris became, along with Amster-

not even industrialized yet

dam and London, one of the great financial centers of Europe. In 1750 the Industrial Revolution still lay in the future, but in both France and England a commercial revolution, complete with a building boom and land speculation, was already transforming the face and purpose of their respective capitals. Similarly, when seen in an economic context the Revolution of 1830 signals the triumph of bourgeois life and entrepreneurial capitalism, with Louis Philippe as the citizen-king of France and Queen Victoria as the matriarchal symbol of middle-class masculinist respectability. And at the end of this mythic cycle, in the 1890s, came a new economic phase, with technological advances (electricity, rubber, oil, the nascent automobile industry), a shift from entrepreneurial builders to organization men, and the growth of banks, corporations, and cartels.

These factors will be assessed differently depending on one's perspective, but the common lesson here is that myths do not arise in a social void. Nineteenth-century Parisians saw myth as a key not just to their dreams but to their lives as well. Roger Caillois has insightfully described this relationship: "From a psychological point of view, mythology . . . exerts its hold over people by virtue of its ability to explain individually or collectively structured tensions, which it also promises to resolve." Both Marx and Haussmann understood this. Jules Michelet, too, thought of the history of Paris as his personal history: "I have identified myself too closely with this city . . . As History universalized my private condition, I have lived through that greater life . . . I have recognized my own heart in its monuments . . . I have felt in myself not its vices, but all of its destructive passions; I have contained its riots in my own heart." In 1838 the young Michelet, on taking up his new post at the Collège de France, chose the history of Paris as the topic of his first lectures. And nearly half a century later, as an exile in Florence, Michelet died of a stroke when told about the burning of the Paris City Hall during the last days of the Commune. Goethe's dictum "Es ist der Geist der sich den Körper baut" ("It is the spirit that constructs the body") reminds us that although material life all too often shapes our worldview, from time to time our spirit and imagination—our *Geist*— can also reshape our earthly life to suit itself. It is through myth that we often understand the nature of our existential situation. As Caillois wrote, with reference to Paris: "It is in myth that we best grasp, with unrivaled immediacy, the collusion that binds the most violent impulses of the individual psyche and the most troubling impositions of the social order."[5]

The case of Haussmann, who rightly described himself as a "demolition artist," illustrates this relationship of myth to fact. On the face of it, his originality was (to say the least) circumscribed, as his associate Adolphe Alphand made clear in an ambiguous eulogy in 1891, shortly after Haussmann's death. Alphand "observed that Haussmann had an amazing faculty for assimilation and 'often took as his own, with the greatest good faith, the ideas he had once adopted' from others."[6] But this is also to say that Haussmann unconsciously understood to perfection his era's idea of modernity, as it had been dreamed and imagined by countless urbanists, civil servants, and writers, from Jean-Baptiste Colbert to Victor Hugo. Though even he himself did not realize it, Haussmann's practical remaking of Paris was a dream made real.

Myth has structured the lived experience of generations of Parisians. "Thinkers mold the common herd," wrote Baudelaire in *L'Art romantique.* "It is the visionaries who create the real." Testifying to the truth of this is the (imagined) history of the city's celebrated sewers. The subject captured Parisians' interest in the 1840s (though it had been of little interest thirty years before), and henceforth everything changed in the way underground Paris was imagined. As Alain Corbin explains, in 1850 Parisian sewage was reconceived as that which had to be rejected for the social order to exist: "The reassuring victory of hygiene and blandness underscored the stability of the social order." That reconceptualization of the subterranean world of Paris was even described in gendered terms. The ineffective sewers of premodern Paris were now imagined to have been somehow feminized as part of a larger system of which prostitution was a symbol—a deplorable state of affairs happily superseded by the masculinized, efficient, and cleanly designed Haussmannian sewers, themselves part of a new system which battled crime and diseased sexuality: a victory of the pure over the impure.

Myths shape life, but everyday life also shapes myth in turn. It seems self-evident that the Paris of Baudelaire's *Les Fleurs du mal* (Flowers of Evil), the first capital of world alienation, is in no small measure an effect whose cause lies in Haussmann's rebuilding of Paris. "Societal beliefs," wrote the French sociologist Maurice Halbwachs, "are in some respects the expression of traditions or collective memories, . . . but they are also conventions that come from our understanding of the present."

What is more, myths have a life of their own. Myths, which extend the past into the present, can beget other myths which bring new complexities into sharper focus. For example, the Haussmannian myth that Paris's boulevards are the highest expression of urban modernity engendered the counter-myth of a beloved, ancient, precapitalist Paris—a counter-myth that was itself schizophrenic, since its evocation of the past underscored the hybrid nature of the Paris of yore, at once full of life and prone to criminality. In the words once again of Roger Caillois, who was surely the most perceptive student of Parisian myths, we can easily identify the external frame of myths, but (he wisely adds) "myths are also driven from within by a specific dialectic of self-propagation and self-crystallization, which has its own specificity and syntax."[7] The Parisian myth of modernity and public health defined itself in 1850 in contradistinction to the older, Christian myth of the respect owed to tradition, just as in 1880 the counter-myth of Old Paris was rife with ambiguities. A perfect illustration of these is Balzac's Vautrin, who first appears as a master criminal and later becomes head of the Paris police.

SOME MYTHS, then, flow from quotidian life as we live it day by day; others originate in our imagined life as we would like to live it; and still others emerge, as it were, by parthenogenesis. In contrast, phantasmagorias spring from clearer sources. Barthes gives us a starting point when he notes that phantasmagorias "are politically to the right." The modern phantasmagoria, as he sees it, is a pitiable "deus ex machina." It is a fiction produced by bourgeois industrialism, or, in the jargon of his time (the 1960s and 1970s), by the "ideological apparatus of the state"—that is, by formal or informal social and political mechanisms—whose invidious purpose is to deceive a credulous and exploited public by erasing history and truncating the public's ability to understand and to judge. For Barthes (and for Guy Debord after him), a "society of spectacle" founded on sterile and bloated consumerism has been imposed on society by the right—by a conservative, obscurantist state bureaucracy and entrepreneurial class. Myths expand our sense of self, as they did for nineteenth-century Parisians; phantasmagorias shrink it, as they did for the Parisians of the Belle Epoque.

Yet what we see today, of course, is that falsely mythical phantasmagorias can serve the interests of either the left or the right. Indeed, they are the expression of the late twentieth and early twenty-first centuries in general, just as encyclopedias spoke for the eighteenth century and as novels of education *(Bildungsromane)* spoke for the nineteenth century. For Paris, the varied origins of phantasmagoria can perhaps best be traced in the history of representations of the Parisian working class, in both print and film.

As Louis Chevalier pointed out so brilliantly, in the Paris of the 1830s and 1840s an analogy was often drawn between the "working classes" and the "dangerous classes," between workers and ordinary criminals. Unable to understand the rise of a new industrial proletariat, the Parisian bourgeoisie in the second quarter of the nineteenth century chose to identify it with a social class that had long been familiar: the city's floating criminal population. Despite innumerable tales about the virtues of the city's street urchins, the capital's proprietor class at mid-century (after the Revolution of 1848, especially) had a very dim and largely illusory view of their working-class neighbors and compatriots.

This negative image slowly shifted. As the century progressed, the working classes became more familiar and seemed less threatening. Bohemian life, always quasi-proletarian in character, was an unknown quantity in 1830, but by 1840 it had become the stuff of popular literature, and the death in 1861 of Henri Murger, whose book *Scènes de la vie de bohème* (Scenes of Bohemian Life) had codified it in the public mind, was a signal event. The haves were less and less fearful of the have-nots; even during the violent months of the Commune in 1871, most bohemians remained politically disengaged. In this connection, 1889 was yet another turning point, if not in the daily reality of the working classes, at least in the perception of what that reality was supposed to be: in that year the cabaret singer and songwriter Aristide Bruant made bohemian life a commercial item. And the poet Paul Verlaine, with his melancholy verses, soon became the incarnation of this phantasmagoria. In record time, his bust would grace the Luxembourg Gardens, just a stone's throw from his slum home on the rue Descartes.

What Bruant had begun—the reshaping of the image of the Parisian proletarian intellectual—movies would soon accomplish for proletarians generally. The history of film in Paris is of ancient and noble vintage. As early as 1895 the brothers Louis and Auguste Lumière were charging admission to a film in a movie house on the boulevard des Capucines. And in 1897 it was, sadly, a cinema projection booth that was the origin of the disastrous fire at the Charity Bazaar, when elegant Parisian gentlemen were seen frantically slashing their way to safety by knocking down wives, mothers, and mistresses with their canes. Then, in 1913, Paris movie screens first presented the great and mysterious arch-criminal Fantômas, a peerless mythological figure and symbol of human evil, whose praises the Surrealist poet Robert Desnos would sing in mock-heroic verse:

> From the Dome of the Invalides
> The gold leaf was stolen every night.
> But who was the culprit? It was he . . .
> His shadow was everywhere,
> On the world, and on Paris too.
> Who is this predatory gray-eyed specter
> Whose stealthy footsteps none can trace?
> Fantômas, are you the one
> Ruling the rooftops of our Parisian sea?[8]

In the 1930s the Paris film industry went even further. Compared with American movies, which dealt with the mores of the middle class, the best French films of that decade were resolutely populist. After the introduction of sound in cinema, the Parisian poor became a subject of choice for French directors. Jean Renoir's *Toni* (1935) was the first great French film, which was born from news items about working-class life.

13

As the filmmaker Marcel Carné explained, populism was a natural theme for the cinema: "Neither the word nor the thing frightens us. Describing the simple life of humble people, laying out their hardworking life—isn't that more worthwhile than one more depiction of an overheated dance hall?" Renoir's celebrated film *La Marseillaise,* paid for by a popular subscription that had been endorsed by the Communist Party, was similarly inspired. "Of course," Renoir explained in 1936, "the best subject would have been our own daily life, the electoral victory of the Popular Front in May, the strikes in June . . . It would have been wonderful, but it would have taken too long to make. So we fell back on the historical epoch that was most like ours: the French Revolution."

These well-intentioned films aimed to create, or at least express, a myth: that of a proletariat which had moved from a mere "class in itself" to a self-assured "class for itself" (as Hegel might have said). But in truth they are merely phantasmagoric, and far closer in spirit to the fantasies of left-wing Parisian intellectuals than to the lived experience of the working people. The choice of settings for these films is revealing. Historically, the Parisian poor had actually lived in the heart of the city, near the church and cloister of Saint Merri, a rough and menacing neighborhood. But in the phantasmagoric cinema of populist directors, the working people of Paris, tamed and deodorized, lived where one would now wish them to be: not outside Paris altogether (else how could they have been Parisian?) but picturesquely on its fringes—in Montmartre or, as in Carné's film *Hôtel du Nord,* on a bridge over the Saint Martin Canal (a bridge that was reproduced down to the last detail in a film studio at Boulogne)—safely removed from the heart of the city.

The result was a curious case of divergent perspectives. For the French proprietor class, educated into a historicizing mode, the sit-down strikes of 1936 were one more chapter in the long domestic war of left versus right that had begun in 1789 and that has raged up to the twenty-first century. In that imagined frame, the victory of the Popular Front was, in the eyes of the middle class, a catastrophe: for the first time ever, the French working classes (dangerous classes) had taken control not just of Paris, as in 1871, but of the nation's government. Yet for the artisans and working people of Paris, who had learned to see themselves as populist films had depicted them, these same strikes were a kind of popular rejoicing. Thus were born two views of Paris, two manufactured phantasmagorias, which by the late 1930s did not have much to do with life "as it really was" but which nonetheless determined the way people thought.

Universalizing myths that arise spontaneously; artificial phantasmagorias that represent rather than explain. It is in this dual context, incorporating two stages, that the history of Paris will be presented here. In the first stage, which began in 1750, the city became the capital of a reshaped Republic of Letters; the capital of politics, science, and modernity; and, with Baudelaire and Manet, the capital of world alienation. In the second stage, inaugurated in 1889, the year of the Eiffel Tower, Paris became the phantasmagoric, falsely mythical capital of pleasure, sex, and (in 1931) European colonialism.

Of course, these myths and counter-myths did not always march to orders. Paris did not change overnight in 1750, or even in 1830—though the "three glorious days" of the 1830 Revolution (July 26, 27, and 28) were as rapid and clear a break between a neo-medieval past and the birth of modernity as one could hope to find. Nor did the myths of Paris die overnight on December 31, 1889; indeed, the myth of Paris as the capital of world art survived for another half-century. Loose ends abound everywhere. The eclectic Paris Opera, designed by the architect Charles Garnier and begun in the 1860s, prefigured the phantasmagorias of later decades. Likewise, Manet's *Olympia* of 1863, with its defiant representation of commercial sex, prefigured the commodification of twenty-first-century Western life, as did the invention in Paris, at about the same time, of the modern department store. These signs are mixed, but they nonetheless structure the history of Paris, which for more than a century was truly the capital of the world.

From the work of Northrop Frye and Hayden White, we know that historians—consciously or not—"emplot" their narratives. For Karl Marx, as White explained, the history of France (or of Paris, one should say, since that is what Marx really cared about) was a tragedy, marked by the fall of the city's proletarians in June 1848 and by the brutal suppression of the Commune in 1871—but a tragedy that would be reversed, in a not-too-distant future, by their redemption and the consequent end of history (a trajectory that, because of its happy ending, might best be described as a "divine comedy"). Alexis de Tocqueville, in contrast, saw these same events as ironic: France, destined by historical experience to suffer political convulsions, was driven to abolish centralized government in 1789 and then to restore it in 1799 (the year Napoleon seized power) as the only alternative to revolutionary chaos. Thomas Carlyle's romantic, racist, and organicist version represented yet another genre: in his eyes, the French Revolution was like some "black World-tornado" or some "black *Dream become real,*" a phenomenon of nature, fated to unravel disastrously and destined never to be replicated or even truly understood.[9] And Michelet, finally, saw this same revolutionary trajectory as a romance—as the miraculous intersection of what is now called *le roman national français* (the national French novel) with the eternal values of struggling, Sisyphean humanity, yearning to find its liberty, equality, and fraternity.

In a similar mode, we see the modern history of Paris in terms that would be familiar to those philosophers—that is to say, as a romance with dramatic chiaroscuro, as a universalizing quest with a clear beginning (1750), a middle (1830), and a sense of closure (1889). It is in this quasi-literary context that I have tried to frame the salient facts of the case. In these pages, the history of Paris in modern times is not viewed as a tragedy: the older social divisions in the city have been definitively resolved, and it was spared destruction during the Second World War. Nor is this history to be seen as a comedy, because it has *not* looped around and returned, after much travail, to its starting point; the history of Paris is not one of much ado about nothing. It is instead a history of constant change, restlessness, and becoming, and might best be termed a *romance*—a tale of imaginary characters involved in heroic or mysterious adventures. To paraphrase Michelet, the heroic and mythologized history of Paris lies at the intersection between the lives of millions and the salient cultural values of their age—namely, modernity and alienation, the primacy of reason, and the crucial centrality of art.

A romance, then—albeit an ironic or at least an autumnal one, as often happens to romances when they reach their bittersweet or even dark conclusion. Gawain the Green Knight did not end his days as a "parfit knight," nor did Ahab slay the Great White Whale. Paris was—but is not now, and never again will be (as it was for Chateaubriand in 1840)—"the capital of the civilized world." Its municipal politics today are at times farcical. In short, to paraphrase Simone Signoret, Paris, like nostalgia, is not what it used to be. But then, neither is our disenchanted world as a whole. And although Paris is no longer a fabled blueprint for our future, who could, in our culturally unanchored world, imagine life without this city?

2

Capital of the Modern Self

"THIS CITY," wrote Louis-Sébastien Mercier in 1799 in *Le Tableau de Paris*, one of the most curious of the 10,000 books of one sort or another devoted to Paris, "eternally rivets the gaze of the entire world."[1] It was not ordained by nature that this should be so, however. In order for a myth of Paris to take shape, two conditions had to be met. First, there had to exist, in the real world, an imposing metropolis of more than half a million people (quite a large population in Mercier's time); and second, there also had to exist, in the world of ideas, a hunger for modernity and individualism, of which Paris would then become the mythical capital. That revolution of the mind did not begin to take place until late in the seventeenth century and did not reach full fruition until the Enlightenment. Only then, from the middle decades of the Enlightenment onward, was the image of Paris presented in salons and academies as part of a vast and noble "outline of the progress of the human spirit" (to borrow the title that the philosophe and politician Antoine-Nicolas de Condorcet—under a death sentence at the time—gave to his account of progress in history, literature, and science).

Paris had not always had this pride of place: before 1750 and for about a century, from the time of Louis XIV, the city had not even been the capital of France and its Bourbon monarchy. Indeed, politically, Paris did not take center stage until October 5, 1789, when a mob forced "the baker, the baker's wife, and the baker's boy" (the king, the queen, and the heir apparent) to return from Versailles to Paris. Only then did Paris once again become the capital of the French nation, even though the city had long outshone Versailles thanks to its new renown as the capital of letters and modernity. It was as Versailles sank that Paris rose. *Opportunity*

B<small>UT WHAT DID</small> people in Paris in the eighteenth and nineteenth centuries mean by the term "modernity" and later by the term "individualism"? Paris, capital of the modern self: but what self? In our present postmodern condition, the definition of what is modern is no longer obvious, and for us the early modernity of the Enlightenment is simultaneously present and remote.

How then to define the modernity of which Paris was to be the first capital after 1750? To put it in a nutshell: a blend of meliorism, rationality, individualism, and scientism. This is the answer most philosophes would have given (though in different terms, of course, since little of our historical and sociological jargon existed at the time). A comprehensive definition, to which the Jacobins of Year II (1793) added a concern for morality, secularism, sacrifice, civic pride, and nation.

This definition of "modern" differs strikingly from our own. For us, the meaning of modernity lies in a series of themes that run directly counter to those of modernity as it was understood in the Enlightenment: for us, what matters (inter alia) is multiculturalism, revival of religious sentiment, and a rejection of meta-narratives, all of which imply an end to many forms of ideology and even teleology. Nor can we forget the transformation of our notion of the "self," which now is defined as much in opposition to civil society (in feminism) as in opposition to the state (in leftism), whereas the "self" of the Enlightenment and the Jacobins was defined through a civil society in the process of emancipation and, simultaneously, through participation in the government of a state that had at last become "national" and "regenerated."[2]

In the history of what is, or was, modern (that is, of what stood in opposition to the Christian traditionalism of the Middle Ages and to the Renaissance emphasis on pagan antiquity), therefore, we need to distinguish three principal stages in the history of the self in Paris. Here we will proceed backwards in time, beginning with the past thirty or forty years of postmodernism, of a fluid society of technology and consumption, derided by some of its critics as a factitious "society of spectacle." (It is, incidentally, in Paris more than in any other place that this concept has been elaborated.)

Moving further back, from 1960 to 1890, we have modernism: Freud and the unconscious; Proust, Bergson, and the burden of time; Picasso and the *Demoiselles d'Avignon* of 1907. Here we also have the discovery of the irrational, along with anti-Semitism, non-European cultures, and primitive art. (The English critic Roger Fry, also a great admirer of Cézanne, praised the "Douanier" Rousseau as "a neolithic artist.") Scientists might add non-Euclidean geometry and the principle of relativity, de Broglie and Einstein, and the Heisenberg uncertainty principle. (Paris and Vienna were the cities where this intellectual movement began.)

So, postmodernism today, modernism before that, and, earlier still, especially in Paris, the epoch of Enlightenment modernity: rational, scientific, and predictable. A complex cultural stratification and one that was made more so by geography: this eighteenth-century "modernity" was of course interpreted in different ways depending on where one happened to be. Paris was one of many variants: in Berlin, until 1840 at any rate, political modernity meant Hohenzollern absolutism and enlightened despotism in the manner of Frederick the Great. In that Prussian context the concept of popular sovereignty was understood indirectly and was essentially defined, as Frederick himself explained, by the willingness of the functionary-king to think of himself as "first servant of the people." (It was Louis XVI's inability, despite the urging of the economist and finance minister Turgot, to give this kind of inflection to the French monarchy that sealed its doom.)

And in London after the Glorious Revolution of 1688, political modernity meant a curious mixture of monarchy with a parliamentary system that was to some extent representative, and whose forms (the House of Lords, Anglo-Norman legal dialect, strange costumes) were rhetorical survivals of the old regime—a bizarre amalgam capable of tolerating many curious anachronisms. (England's Queen Anne, at her coronation in 1702, still laid hands on the scrofulous to cure them with her healing touch, as would Charles X when he was crowned at Rheims in 1825.)

In North America, between 1776 and 1787, Thomas Jefferson and his friends elaborated yet another form of political modernity, in which the cult of the yeoman and the survival of slavery might both be fitted into the ideal of a classical, universalist republic.

All of these eighteenth-century variants of modernity did share an obvious family resemblance, but it is important to bear in mind that the family was a large one. David Hume and Thomas Paine, Benjamin Franklin and Thomas Jefferson, E. M. Forster and Alexander von Humboldt were all Parisians, but each in his own manner. Paris and London were the capitals of a new mode of thinking set between tradition and modernism, and each of these cities had its preferences and specificities.

PARIS, THEN, to be great, needed to be modern, if in its own way, different from that of its neighbors or our own. We shall return to this vast theme, but first it is important to note that Paris, in order to become the capital of the modern self, also had to acquire a commensurate physical and material presence. Only by binding these two themes together could it become, in the words of Anarcharsis Clootz, a Jacobin and a former Prussian baron who would die on the guillotine, the "commune centrale du globe."

A first step in the consideration of that second and more material subject—the physical expansion of the city—will be to consider the city's gender and reputation. For before Paris became the masculinized capital of the Republic of Letters, the city was—so to speak—a woman, so that  its name was for many centuries considered to be a feminine noun. It was not until around the sixteenth century that people stopped referring to "Paris l'ancienne," as Gilles Corrozet had it in a poem written in 1532 (in French one still says *la Rome ancienne*). Nowadays, of course, Paris is masculine: one says *le vieux Paris, le nouveau Paris, le tout Paris,* and so on; but this masculinization came about only gradually. The pace of change in this as in many other domains did not begin to accelerate until the Revolution of 1830, and even after that some writers, such as

Baudelaire and Marx, continued to refer to the city indifferently as masculine or feminine. Mythology often insists on masculinity: the common sort—*la populace, la foule, la plèbe, la canaille*—did not become a mythological entity until it became *le Peuple,* and Paris followed a similar course.[3] In French, that is, but not in English: thus Alice Kaplan, the author of *French Lessons,* translates as "Paris has been broken, Paris has been martyred, but Paris has been liberated by herself" General de Gaulle's eloquent but outrageous statement of August 1944: "Paris brisé, Paris martyrisé, mais Paris libéré par lui-même" (that is to say, "himself").[4]

Gender, then, is a clue that reminds us of the fact that there was nothing mythological or magical about medieval or Renaissance Paris, not even for those who, as far back as the twelfth century, claimed that the city had been founded by Trojans: these defeated warriors, it was then suggested, had taken several centuries to make their way through Germania to the banks of the Seine, which they reached in 376 A.D., when they changed the name of their new home from the Latin Lutetia to Paris in honor of the Trojan prince.[5]

To be sure, with its population of more than 200,000, medieval Paris was perhaps the largest city in Europe. Administratively, however, the city was only the capital of the kingdom for brief periods. The Bourbons bestowed that honor on Versailles; before them, the Valois preferred Chinon, Loches, Amboise, Blois, and Fontainebleau; and for the Carolingians there had been other places as well, such as Aix-la-Chapelle and Laon.

Nor was any poem devoted to Paris before the end of the fourteenth century, even though Paris-Lutetia had by then existed for more than a millennium. Eustace Deschamps (1346–1406) was the first poet to sing the praises of the capital; but it was a merely local form of patriotism that moved his pen: for him, Paris would have been a city like any other city had he not lived there. The first text devoted exclusively to Paris was Jean de Jandun's *Louanges de Paris* (In Praise of Paris; 1323). François Villon was the first great Parisian poet, but one would search his poems in vain for "any expression of sentiment—love, hate, amazement, or fatigue—in regard to Paris," which in any case he refused to personify.[6]

The Renaissance was more generous, but only grudgingly. For Pierre de Ronsard, Paris was "The Glory of the Muses." Joachim Du Bellay said the capital was "en savoir une Grèce féconde" (in knowledge a fertile Greece). And Montaigne went further: for him the city was "the glory of France and one of the world's noblest ornaments." Ludovico Ariosto (1474–1533) also praised Paris, but his vision of the city remained rather vague since it largely figured in a description of an imaginary battle fought outside its walls by Charlemagne, "per ogni porta fuore / da san Germano in fino a san Vittore" (from Saint-Germain round to Saint Victor's gate, / King Charles his forces placed as for checkmate).[7]

In its essence this Renaissance Paris, by its size, gender, and reputation, was still a city much like any other. What struck the authors of the *Satire Ménippée* (1594), who were subjects of Henri III and Henri IV and enemies of the Ligueurs, was not so much the theme of Paris itself as the sudden rise of an anti-Paris, a Paris that had become, as they put it, "a den of wild beasts, a citadel of Spaniards, Walloons, and Neapolitans."

And although by the sixteenth and seventeenth centuries poems about Paris were becoming more numerous, they were still not especially approving: in 1532 Corrozet did offer his readers a *Fleur des antiquitez de Paris,* followed in 1550 by his *Antiquitez, histoires, croniques et singularitez de la grande & excellente ville de Paris, ville capitalle & chef du Rouyaume de France,* dedicated to the city's noble and illustrious families. But his purpose was no more than to reproach those families for not taking their city seriously. Nicolas Boileau (1636–1711), who was born and died in Paris, also left us a description of the city, but one that comments frequently on its "embarras," or difficulties. Thus in 1650 Paris was not yet a mythic or even a monumental city, and it was not until 1701, when Germain Brice published his *Description nouvelle de ce qu'il y a de plus remarquable dans la ville de Paris,* that it became possible to read a panegyric devoted to contemporary Paris rather than to the Paris of the past.[8]

It is fair to conclude that, in these first centuries of the city's history, it was not the literary imagination that most fully revealed the first flourishing of Paris but rather the city's gradually changing and concrete presence; and on that score, by 1700, Paris was indeed more important than it had ever been. As early as 1560, in fact, Ronsard had celebrated its "hundred thousand artisans in a hundred thousand ways." Paris grew in these early centuries, albeit slowly. The number of its artisans swelled steadily, even if their tapestries and furniture usually wound up in Versailles. By 1700 Paris was already home to the artisans of the Gobelins in the Faubourg Saint-Marcel as well as to Boulle and his furniture makers in the Faubourg Saint-Antoine.

Ludovician Paris, then, while not yet a mythical city, was already a place of some size, and it would not be surpassed by London until 1702, after which London in turn took second place to New York, which itself was outstripped first by Tokyo in 1980 and then, in the 1990s, by various Third World capitals such as São Paolo, Bombay, and Mexico City, a large population being today a symbol of disorder rather than, as in the previous three centuries, a sign of modernity.

growing

Despite what has been called "the crisis of the seventeenth century," Paris continued to develop in the reign of the Sun King, and in the eighteenth century that growth accelerated. The Paris of Louis XV and Louis XVI was already a great financial center, and from the time of the financier John Law to that of Terray, Turgot, and Calonne, the "tremors" that began in Paris gradually became the earthquakes that shook the whole economy of France.

Paris in 1700 was thus far more visible than it had been, and—more critically—its relation to the French crown, ensconced at Versailles, was also changing. In some ways Louis XIV, or at any rate certain of his ministers, did work diligently to enhance the splendor of the first city of the realm. The Sun King's finance minister Jean-Baptiste Colbert had ambitious plans for Paris, including the creation of a "grand Louvre" with the help of the Italian architect Bernini, "le cavalier Bernin," who came and just as quickly went. The city's *places royales* continue to attest to the scope of those ambitions. To be sure, the Place de France of which Henri IV dreamed was never built, and all that remains of it today is the rue de Turenne and adjacent streets, which were to have been its antennae. But the Place des Vosges, inaugurated by the young Louis XIII, was the first of a series of marvelous achievements culminating in the Place de la Concorde (at the time called Place Louis XV). This was "begun in 1757, inaugurated in 1763, and completed in 1772."⁹ When Louis XV congratulated the Abbé Galiani, the Neapolitan ambassador—a friend of Mme d'Epinay, an enemy of the economists, and a consummate courtier—on having been awarded the "place" of viceroy of Sicily, one of "the most beautiful places in Europe," Galiani replied without missing a beat, "Sire, the most beautiful place in Europe is the Place Vendôme"—and indeed it is the most elegant and classical (that is, the chilliest and most regular) of the capital's *places royales.*

Clearly, then, the monarchy did not wholly neglect Paris, which was an important place materially; but the fact remains that with the Sun King in the seventeenth century French ideological and intellectual modernity was not yet centered in the capital. It had instead taken up residence, rebellious and bellicose, in Holland (where the king's Protestant enemies sought refuge); or settled peacefully into royal service in palaces scattered throughout what are today the suburbs of "greater Paris": Versailles, Saint-Cloud, Saint-Germain, Marly, Vincennes, Fontainebleau. The historian Ernest Lavisse would dub the latter migration "the royal secession."

Henri IV, known as Le Vert Galant for his amorous adventures, famously said that Paris was well worth a Mass, and called it his "great city." But in the forty-four years from 1671 to 1715 his grandson Louis XIV would visit Paris only twenty-four times, usually for just a few hours because he didn't like to spend the night there. To woo him, the city in 1672 struck a medal celebrating him as "Louis le Grand." To no avail, however. When the city proposed that he make a solemn entry in 1678, the king rejected "cet embarras"; not until 1687 did he accede to the city's wishes. It is of symbolic significance that it was also at this time that the Bastille, formerly a defensive fortress, became a state prison for Parisians such as Voltaire, Diderot, and Sade, who had the misfortune to displease the sovereign or one of his servants.

Thus, while Le Grand Roi was staging extraordinary pageants on that "Enchanted Isle," Versailles, the bourgeois of Paris made themselves quite scarce. In Versailles, Molière (1622–1673) made fun of them, much to the delight of the courtiers of a monarch scornful and suspicious of the *grand'ville* (this, when you think about it, was rather ungrateful of Molière, who after all was born in Paris as Jean-Baptiste Poquelin). In the work of Jean de La Bruyère, too, Paris was nothing more than a foil for the court: the nobility of Versailles and the bourgeoisie of Paris were poles apart, much to the detriment of the latter. What was worthwhile or great was to be sought in Versailles, La Bruyère believed, whereas in Paris people were steeped in "sumptuousness and magnificence in splendor, dissipation, folly, and ineptitude in private [ineptie dans le particulier]." The Parisian spirit was parochial: "They know the world . . . through what is least beautiful and least attractive about it. They are ignorant of nature, of its beginnings, its progress, its gifts, and its largesse. Often their ignorance is voluntary, and based on the esteem they feel for their profession and their talents." Paris, moreover, "usually apes the court and is not always clever at imitating it."[10] In 1666 Antoine Furetière, though Paris-born, made a similar observation in the *Roman bourgeois* (Bourgeois Novel): Paris, he alleged, either imitates the manners of the court or sinks to the level of the rustic. Monsieur Jourdain, Molière's *bourgeois gentilhomme,* would have understood this distressing dilemma perfectly.

ALL THIS BEGAN to change radically in about 1750, and probably even earlier in certain areas of culture, such as music. Now the fame of Paris began to parallel its material growth. There is no article on Paris in Diderot's *Encyclopedia.* Yet by the second half of the eighteenth century Paris was truly in a category of its own, different from every other French city not only because of its vast size but also, indeed primarily, because of its cultural modernity. Of the 147 guides to Paris published in the seventeenth and eighteenth centuries, most date from the last fifty years of the Century of Enlightenment. This was also when the first foreign tourist guides to Paris began to appear; an English example was *The Gentleman's Guide in His Tour through France,* by a former army officer, John Millard Thickness.

In 1660 cultural modernity had abandoned Paris for Versailles, the headquarters of absolutism, with its bureaus, its mercantilism, and its administrative centralism—the first modern form of government. But in the 1750s and 1760s the current began to flow in the opposite direction. This is a crucial indicator, an early sign of the advent of a new Parisian mythology and modernity.

The Sun King of Versailles had done everything he could to ensure that his Apollonian reign would attain the dignity of myth, that he would be known as the greatest king in the world, and perhaps as the greatest king of all time. By contrast, his successor, Louis XV, though he bore at first the epithet "le Bien-aimé," or "well-loved by his subjects," was by the end of his reign not loved at all, and neither was his court. By the time of his death in 1774 Versailles had been dethroned by Paris not only in the cultural domain but in the political as well. After 1750 any number of events may be taken as precursors of the king's eventual forced return to Paris in October 1789. In the struggle, for example, between the episcopacy allied to the more or less pro-Jesuit monarchy and, on the other side, the Parisian men of law, it was the largely Gallican and Jansenist Parlement of Paris that emerged victorious with the expulsion of the Jesuits in 1762. And the distant crown was again defeated in 1774 when the parlements were reconvened and the monarchist but reform-minded ministers Maupeou and Terray were dismissed in disgrace. And Versailles bowed yet again in 1776, when shrewdly orchestrated crowds of Parisians and peasants blocked Turgot's pre-capitalist legislation, whose modernizing thrust had become impossible to implement because of its association with Versailles.

THUS BY THE late eighteenth century the place of Paris in the world was quite different from what it had been a century before. Economically, culturally, the city's role had broadened, and its ensuing fame was bolstered yet further by a substantial change in the way Europeans perceived the shifting balance between town and country.

For the Physiocrats Dr. Quesnay and Mirabeau *père* (the "Friend of Man" who was also the scourge of his nearest and dearest, sending his son to the Bastille and his daughter to a convent), *labourage et pâturage*, the production of grain and livestock, remained *les deux mamelles*, the twin teats, *de la France.* In 1776, however, Adam Smith published *The*

Wealth of Nations, which advanced a very different view of the modern economy. Diderot's *Encyclopedia* (59 percent of whose contributors resided in the capital) likewise celebrated mankind's Promethean ingenuity, and Diderot, though he claimed to be celebrating the ingenuity of the whole of mankind, was in fact far more interested in urban than in rural man. A few years later the Jacobins, who dreamed of a nation of republican farmers, belonged to clubs whose membership was overwhelmingly urban.

Looking forward a bit, it matters that by the time of Karl Marx and Jules Michelet the primacy of the city was no longer a hypothesis at all but an incontrovertible fact. It was in the great cities of Europe (and Paris in particular) that the destiny of *la France éternelle* would be decided, or so Michelet imagined; just as Marx assumed that Paris, Berlin, or Manchester would be the place where the destiny of suffering proletarianized humanity would soon be resolved. Balzac, who thought of himself as a royalist, had only a very rough idea of peasant life in France despite *Le Lys dans la vallée* (The Lily of the Valley), despite his extended sojourns in rural Touraine, and despite *Le Médecin de campagne* (The Country Doctor); and he had even less of an idea of the lives of the peasants on the estates of his rich and noble Polish wife.

B Y 1750, then, Paris was fast becoming the world capital of modernity, and we can gauge that shift by considering once again, in a completely new context, the transformation of the city's relationship to Versailles and its absolutist court. On the eve of the Revolution, Mercier, adopting a prosecutorial tone, commented on this unprecedented change:

> The word "court" no longer impresses us as it did in the time of Louis XIV. The Court no longer decides which opinions will prevail or which reputations will be highest in any genre. No one any longer utters the ridiculously pretentious phrase "Such is the judgment of the Court." We overturn the Court's judgments. We say flatly, "The Court understands nothing, it has no ideas on that subject, it is incapable of having ideas, it lacks the proper point of view."

The Court itself, not unaware of the change, no longer dares to pro-
nounce upon a book, a play, a new masterpiece, or a singular or extraordinary event. It awaits the declaration of the capital. It even goes to great
lengths to find out what the capital thinks, so as not to run the risk of ut-
tering an opinion that would be tossed out of court at once, with assess-
ment of costs . . . The Court holds its tongue. Paris talks.[11]

In other words, by the mid-eighteenth century Paris was already seen
as the capital of what Mikhail Bakhtin would call heteroglossia. Thus
Rousseau in book IV of *Emile* (1762) tells us that "few books are published in Europe whose authors have not gone to Paris to educate themselves," a statement that can of course be applied to Rousseau himself.
And as for Nicolas Restif de la Bretonne (1734–1806), "le Rousseau du
ruisseau," or the Rousseau of the gutter, Paris was "liberty's divine
dwelling place." Restif, who had a genius for neologism, invented the
word "pornography" as well as another term, "inconnussion" or "state of
being unknown," a word intended, he explained, to describe the condition of the Parisian:

> Each person, whose business is unknown, as are his relations, his faults,
> and his weaknesses, acts with complete freedom and full human dignity.
> He exhibits himself with the grandeur . . . that was once the distinctive
> possession of the Great . . . "No man is a prophet in his own land," says
> the proverb . . . It should, however, be extended to say, "No man is
> a prophet in an immense city," where not only is no one universally
> known, but to be universally known would be inconceivable.

In short, it was to Paris that one had to go to learn how to talk, even if
what one learned to talk about was, as we shall see, alienation and anti-
Parisianism.[12]

Also characteristic of the new era was the presence in Paris of distinguished foreigners, if I may put it that way: not just artisans from Italy
and Germany, soldiers from Ireland, or 350 English and Irish nuns
(some 5,000 people in all in 1789), but men of letters, nobles, and even
foreign monarchs, such as Gustavus III of Sweden and of course the king
of Poland, who became an intimate of Mme Geoffrin, whom he called
"Maman." Mention should also be made of the many prominent Eng-

lish visitors to Paris, including James Boswell, Dr. Samuel Johnson, the fabulously wealthy Horace Walpole, inventor of the "gothic novel" and intimate of Mme du Deffand, and Quentin Craufurd, whose lover, the elegant Eleonora Sullivan, had once been the mistress of the duke—virtually king—of Württemberg. Pitt the Younger also spent time in Paris, and the philosopher David Hume briefly thought of "settling there for life" because of the "great number of sensible, knowing, and polite company with which that city abounds above all places in the universe." Deluxe cultural tourism also began at this time: it has been estimated that some 5,000 English "visitors" (who would not be called tourists until the 1840s) crossed the Channel annually before the Revolution, a number that doubled after the Battle of Waterloo in 1815.[13]

Important changes, and all of them interconnected. For just as modernity shifted from Versailles to Paris, so did the city's center of gravity move from the Pont-Neuf to the Palais Royal, the new headquarters of "public opinion" and of men of letters. (It was also in the Palais Royal that Rameau's nephew, a professional idler, played chess at the Café de la Régence.) Speaking of the Parisian men of letters who were now assembling there, Chrétien Lamoignon de Malesherbes, Louis XVI's minister, said that they were "to the people dispersed what the orators of Rome and Athens had been to the people assembled."[14]

Of course, we must distinguish here between different streams of opinion, between the legitimacy that flowed from what was said in the café or the street and the accolades that were bestowed by the salons and the women who managed these informal institutions, the *salonnières*. But the Parisian philosophes benefited from both of these two currents. From the point of view of Antoine de Rivarol, a grammarian and conservative journalist, Mercier's *Tableau de Paris*—an illegal text that was widely read—was both vulgar in its style and false in its premises precisely because it had been praised "in the cellars and the attics, but not in the intermediate salons." This was a doubly deficient judgment. To be sure, what was said in the salons often differed drastically from popular rumor, but the two could overlap and both differed from what was thought at Versailles.

In this unprecedented context, the philosophes wielded a renewed cultural power in the French capital, and so did the booksellers, about whom Mercier made the ironic comment that they "take themselves for men of consequence because they stock their shops with other people's wit and sometimes venture to judge what they print. There is nothing more comical than the timid but proud beginning of a poet who, burning to be thrust into the limelight, approaches for the first time a bookseller on the rue Saint-Jacques, who will suddenly stick out his chest and present himself as a judge of literary merit."[15]

What was at stake was the novel power in Paris of the printed word, of books and of periodicals (Hegel would say that newspaper reading was for modern man a quasi-religious act), as well as the importance of the sites where books were read or conceived: cafés like Procope, which still exists in Paris today; reading rooms and lending libraries (Paris counted about fifty such); and masonic lodges. Similarly critical were the academies, of which Benjamin Constant, who was as unacademic a politician as a politician could be, was soon to write that they should be models for the nation's new political assemblies: long before the Revolution, their learned rites, the eulogies they made on the occasions of deaths and new memberships, were closely followed by the public.

But it was in the salons of the capital that the new spirit of the age was really forged. Parisian salons were famous throughout Europe, renowned for their mixing of social ranks, their wit, the exchange of ideas, and the charm of conversation.

Salons were not specific to the second half of the eighteenth century. Seventeenth-century Parisian salons had already become sites of urban and apolitical civility; and these assemblies would remain in the nineteenth century as social and exclusive entities. But in the pre-revolutionary age the Parisian salons took on a more active look: at that point these informal institutions were intellectually ecumenical and therefore, without too much exaggeration, "quasi-republican."

Traditional French and especially Parisian corporatist society had been based on principles of exclusion and stratification, with a hierarchy of corporations ranging from the *grands corps* of the state down to the capital's various *corps de métiers,* or trade guilds. By contrast, the Enlightenment salon, that archetypal—and new—Parisian institution, prided itself on the presence of distinguished foreigners (such as Benjamin Franklin, a guest of Mme Helvétius, and Vittorio Alfieri, a guest of Mme d'Epinay). Their presence highlighted the role of the salons as places for international exchange. In the seventeenth century the phrase "republic of letters" referred to small groups of scholars who communicated in Latin, and it applied mainly to Holland, to the exclusion of other countries. In Paris after 1750, however, the Republic of Letters came to encompass civilized men and women from all over the world who came to France and spoke French. The old corporations had been part of the ancien régime; the new salons were the prologue to political upheavals.

And the emphasis here must indeed be on speaking, because a key component of this new Parisian way of life was, as has been mentioned, conversation. For it was at this time that the myth of Parisian *savoir-faire* and *savoir-parler* took shape. "You ask me," Diderot wrote, "if I've read Abbé Raynal. No. But why? Because I no longer have the time for reading, nor the taste. To read by oneself, without anyone to talk to, argue with, shine in the presence of, listen to, or command the attention of, is impossible." And in *Emile* Rousseau wrote that "if a man of influence makes a serious proposal" in a Parisian salon, "everyone's attention immediately focuses on this new object: men, women, old folks, children—everyone considers it from every angle, and people are astonished at the sense and reason that seem to gush forth from so many playful heads. A question of ethics would not be more fully dissected by a society of philosophers than by the society gathered around a pretty woman in Paris." Mme de Staël went even further: for the French, as she saw it, conversation was not a way of communicating ideas, feelings, and affairs but "an instrument that people like to play and that revives the spirit, as music does for some nations and strong liquor for others." (Here it was the Germans she had in mind.) Conversation, she thought, engendered physical well-being. It must conform to certain rules, which made it "a studied form of spontaneity."[16]

"You talk, you talk, that's all you know how to do," says the (Parisian) parrot in Raymond Queneau's novel *Zazie dans le Métro*. Voltaire did not share this pessimistic view of oral exchange. For him, as he explained in his article on wit in the *Dictionnaire philosophique,* conversation, like wit, could be enchanting if unexpected and original; and it was in Voltaire's period that the equation France = Paris = conversation was firmly established in all minds with a few exceptions like the bilious Louis de Bonald, Mme de Staël's enemy. To be Parisian meant to converse. Not to be in Paris meant to pine for good conversation. After eight years as an émigré in America and England, the young Chateaubriand was shocked by the dirtiness of Parisian houses and by the filth and noise of the capital. What appealed to him, though, was "the sociability that sets us apart, the charming, easy, rapid commerce of intelligence . . . the natural leveling of all ranks, the equality of mind that makes French society incomparable and redeems our faults. After a few months living in our midst, a person feels that he can no longer live anywhere but in Paris."[17]

And curiously enough, although Paris as world capital of letters belongs to a bygone era, the myth of Parisian conversation, like many Parisian myths, still persists vestigially: in this capital, to be worldly, to be intelligent, has always meant and still means to speak elegantly. To this day, the manipulation of the pluperfect subjunctive is an unfailing signifier of social rank. Nearly a century ago Theodor Herzl, the founder of Zionism, made an observation that retains its validity today: "Nowhere else is the spoken word as prestigious as it is here. Hence nowhere else are there as many talkers, speakers, lecturers, rhetoricians, and orators of such quality among the people. In the afternoon, when the weather outside is marvelous, the most distinguished people will crowd into a dank Sorbonne amphitheater to savor a 'lecture' of some sort."[18]

For Sartre a conversation about ideas was a deadly thing. But his fellow Parisians did not share his opinion then and do not share it now.

FROM MYTH TO FANTASY: looking forward from the eighteenth century to our own day, what laws and signs govern this evolution, this rise and decay of myth, regardless of its specific content? One law might be that the concrete, material underpinnings of myth refuse to die even when their deeper meaning has vanished or been stood on its head. For instance, Parisian arcades were the *ne plus ultra* of commerce in

1825. By 1840 this was no longer the case, yet the arcades still exist to-day. (In a similar vein, by 1850 Paris was no longer the capital of crime, but the "Apaches" of 1890 were still attracting tourists.)

To continue this thought (and to finish with the history of the Parisian salons), although the Revolution of 1789 reduced the political and ideological importance of the salons, these worldly gatherings did survive until the Second World War, but in a different mode: in 1850, for example, Mme de Girardin estimated that there were still twenty or so fashionable salons in the capital.[19]

As has been mentioned, however, the nineteenth-century Parisian salons did not have much in common with those of the previous century, and this matters for an understanding of how Enlightenment Paris worked. In those pre-revolutionary salons *grands seigneurs* could hobnob with the philosophe du jour. By contrast, the *salonnières* of the next century would pride themselves on their exclusivity, as was the case with the very "select" salon of Mme de Beauséant in Balzac's *Père Goriot,* to which the ambitious baronne de Nucingen, wife of an oafish banker, dreamed of being invited. Indeed, some of the later Parisian salons were little more than appendages of the stock exchange: witness Mme Dambreuse's salon in Flaubert's *L'Education sentimentale.* Admittedly, the salons of the Princesse de Guermantes, Mme de Villeparisis, and Mme Verdurin (in Proust's *A la recherche du temps perdu*) retained a vaguely cultural tinge, but the conversations there were often astonishing in their banality, and little of moment was decided in these places other than the election of men like the baron de Norpois to the Académie Française.

In essence, then, after the Revolution of 1830, Parisian salons really mattered only to young women for whom husbands were being sought and to the close friends of some wealthy or titled patrons like Princess Mathilde. A young American, George Ticknor, described them condescendingly: "They are the most rational form of society I have ever yet seen . . . You come in without ceremony, talk as long as you find persons you like and go away without taking leave, to repeat the same process in another salon . . . the general tone of these societies . . . is brilliant, graceful, superficial and hollow."[20] Their shift from inclusiveness to exclusiveness parallels the creation of the blueblood Cercle de l'Union in 1828 and the even more stylish and racy Jockey Club in 1833.

Under the Third Republic, even first-rank political salons such as that of Léon Gambetta's patron Mme Adam were much less important than political parties, circles, newspapers, and the Bourse. Edmond and Jules de Goncourt complained about the dearth of salons open to men of letters. In the Paris of the 1860s there were really only two salons frequented by the literary set, one sponsored by Princess Mathilde, the other by Mme Païva, a Russian by birth and a woman of somewhat dubious reputation, part princess and part adventuress.

In 1855 Théophile Gautier sang the praises of the Café Tortoni, "where guests seated on upholstered couches in private rooms delight in bandying witticisms back and forth, for salons do still exist, despite what people say."[21] What is striking about this sentence is its implication that people went to the Tortoni because salons were no longer what they used to be.

And, strangely enough, the last important incarnation of the ancien régime salon in Paris would be the salons presided over by American women such as Natalie Barney, Edith Wharton, and Gertrude Stein in the 1920s and 1930s, along with the celebrated Shakespeare and Company bookstore run by Sylvia Beach. Each of these women exemplified a certain social style and a new sexual style as well.

BUT TO MOVE BACK from the human avatars of the salons and return to Paris in the eighteenth century, what we see after 1750 is the decline of Versailles and the rise of a newly prestigious Paris, with its cafés and salons and its celebrated conversational style. But why did these changes take place? The explanations that are current today would have surprised yesterday's *marxisant* historians of the period as well as the nationalist historians who preceded them. Today's explanations reflect a new sociological worldview, as elaborated in the work of German sociologists such as Reinhardt Koselleck and Jürgen Habermas.

In the opinion of Mme de Staël, salon conversation was merely "a liberal art that has no purpose and no result," and half a century ago Norbert Elias could have accepted her interpretation, since he imagined these bourgeois institutions (salons and conversation) as imitations of the all-powerful absolutist court.[22] Elias was a "non-Marxist," for whom

culture proceeded from the top down. By contrast, for the new generation of neo-Marxist German sociologists, whose ideas have shaped much
recent French and Anglo-American thinking about the Enlightenment,
the Paris salon was not a courtly offshoot but the premier raw material
out of which the eighteenth century built an altogether new public
space, a new tribunal of public opinion, which was in turn a new source
of sovereignty, the essence of a new modernity, which proceeded from
the bottom up.

Much is at stake in this formulation: where our understanding of pre-
revolutionary French social history was once centered either on class rivalries between nobility and bourgeoisie or on the purely heuristic intellectual origins of 1789 (the influence of Rousseau on Robespierre),
the new approach posits a protean system to which a new social elite
that was simultaneously noble and bourgeois contributed mightily. To
think about eighteenth-century Paris in contemporary scholarly terms is
therefore to *re*think the entire method of the social sciences as they have
been practiced for a century.

What the new historiography sees in the decline of Versailles and the
rise of Paris is the emergence of an utterly new phenomenon in world
history, namely public opinion, which before 1789 was headquartered
in the salons of Paris, only to move after 1789 into the political assemblies of the Revolution, also located in Paris. Robespierre was no doubt
sincere when he declared in November 1792: "Despite Louis XVI and
his allies, the opinion of the Jacobins and of the popular societies was
that of the French nation. No citizen created or dominated it, and all I
have done is to see that it was shared."[23]

In the old Marxist mode of thinking, culture was often no more than
a superstructure. In the new mode of seeing, the changing culture of
Paris in the late Enlightenment is presented as the starting point of
world change. The salons and the salonnières who once were mere curiosities are now the subjects of learned dissertations.

The debate focuses in large part on the measure of autonomy that historians are prepared to ascribe to cultural phenomena now taken as
causes of the upheaval of 1789. The new approach also leads us to rein-
terpret (as both cause and effect) all of Parisian musical, literary, and

artistic life in its various and increasingly politicized phases. The argument here must be that Parisian literary opinion—and conversation—mattered, because public opinion did not at first dare to venture onto political terrain, which the absolutist state had occupied since the 1660s. It was after it had honed its skills on neutral and seemingly apolitical subjects such as music, painting, and dance that it could move on to politics. But, in the new scheme of things, it did move on.

The influence of this Habermasian interpretation of the causes and antecedents of the French Revolution on the historiography of the eighteenth century can hardly be exaggerated. It has also transformed our sense of the history of the city: where Marxist historians once spoke of Parisian commerce, industry, manufacturing, proletariats, and accumulation, contemporary historians now speak of cultural sites, books, and theater.

That is to say, topics such as Parisian salons and conversation are now seen as having been important not only in themselves but above all else, as the prologue to the political struggles of the Revolution. For once they had ventured to criticize art—or so runs the Habermasian argument—Parisians soon felt free to judge the actions of the monarch as well: Jacques-Louis David's painting *Oath of the Horatii* (depicting three martial brothers who joined forces for the common good) was exhibited four years before 1789, and his *Lictors Bringing Brutus the Bodies of His Sons* (in which Brutus has condemned his own sons to death for plotting to restore the Roman monarchy) four years before the terroristic judgments of the unforgiving Revolutionary Tribunal.

In this frame, also, we can now step back to consider, for example, the remarkable career—heretofore ignored—of La Font de Saint-Yenne, a Parisian who has lately been celebrated as the inventor of a neo-political genre of writing, namely, art criticism. His Paris-born antagonist the painter Charles-Antoine Coypel (1694–1752) was shocked that visitors to the Salons (public exhibitions of painting—not to be confused with the salons famous for their conversation) dared to express judgments of the paintings on display. The crowds in the galleries were constantly changing, and to Coypel they seemed more like a mob than a jury; he refused to accept their judgments as valid. History did not agree with him, however. The opinions of those visitors, sharpened by La Font and his emulators, were what really mattered: ominous aesthetic judgments would soon be politicized. The capital's spectators had become a thinking public that talked not only about plays and paintings but also about privileges and constitutions. The painter ceased to be an artisan and became something quite the opposite: a quasi-political artist, and often a wealthy one to boot. Jean-Louis Carra, a critique of the salons in 1788 and a Girondin journalist in 1792 (guillotined in 1793), is a figure one might cite as illustrative of the transition from the arts to political engagement.

This transition may well have taken place across Europe, but it was a Parisian phenomenon above all, as we can verify by considering the one exception to the rule of Parisian cultural and pre-political domination: music. For music, the center of the new modernity, of the new "publicity," if I may put it that way, was London. The young Mozart, a prodigy who was exhibited to princes and royal courts, did pass through Paris (which he did not much like) in 1763 and spend several months there in 1778. But it was to the London audience that Haydn went in the 1790s—Haydn the erstwhile musical artisan who became the first of the great musical geniuses of the nineteenth century, the precursor of Beethoven and a mythical, as well as well-remunerated, personage, universally admired. When the Abbé Barthélemy teased Mme du Deffand for using the word "energy," the lady called upon the duchesse de Choiseul for her expert opinion. "You ask me if I am familiar with the word 'energy,'" the duchess responded. "Of course I am. I can even fix the time of its birth. It was sometime after people began having convulsions while listening to music."[24] She might have added that such convulsions first became fashionable in London.

Music was a mere exception, however, because long before the Revolution, Paris had become the world capital of the Republic of Letters and the capital of public opinion, and for that reason it would soon become the capital of world revolution.

Important changes, then, if still incomplete: in 1789 pre-revolutionary Paris was not yet fully mythical, but was poised to be so. By the closing decades of the eighteenth century Paris was no longer a big city like other cities. It had become, as Montesquieu had put it earlier in the century in his *Persian Letters,* "the seat of the European empire, the proud rival of the City of the Sun."

"PARIS CHANGE! mais rien dans ma mélancolie / N'a bougé" (Paris changes! but without altering my melancholy one whit): so said Baudelaire in *Les Fleurs du mal* (Flowers of Evil). But in the new Paris that Charles de Peysonnel described in 1789 as "the Epitome of the Universe, a vast and shapeless city, full of marvels, virtues, vices, and foolishness,"[25] some Parisians and their visitors already found the experience of modern life melancholic. Indeed, the capital of France—now become the capital of the Republic of Letters—was for some a sad or even depressing city.

By 1900, amid the phantasmagorias of fin-de-siècle Paris, the Belle Epoque's capital of pleasure, the Parisian was in principle a happy man, and foreigners the world over dreamed of "Gay Paree." Think of the familiar American tune of 1918: "How ya gonna keep 'em down on the farm after they've seen Paree?" Having glimpsed Paris, would the American doughboy be willing to return to the old homestead? It is in the nature of fantasies to substitute a virtual reality of pure joy and happiness for the reality of actual experience.

On the eve of the Revolution, however, the nascent myth of modern Paris was more demanding, more unyielding. To the new theme of Paris as alternative to and replacement for the moribund court was soon added a second theme, seemingly unrelated to the first but in fact closely intertwined with it: the theme of Paris as a place where everyday life was attended by astonishing and novel psychological miseries. Well before the Revolution Paris was being described as the capital of wickedness and artificiality; for some, there was nothing "universalizing" about the salons, which exemplified, rather, the "abuse of language" that Rousseau detested and in which hatred he would be joined by the Jacobins of Year II.

Indeed, can one imagine a novel like Pierre Choderlos de Laclos's *Liaisons dangereuses* (1782) with predatory characters like Valmont and the marquise de Merteuil set anywhere other than in this capital of elegance and perversity? For many commentators, the new "post-Versailles" Paris could be characterized in moral terms as a "swamp" or a "wasteland." In *La Vie de Marianne,* Pierre de Marivaux has his heroine say this: "The more I saw of society and change in the prodigious city that is Paris, the more I discovered of silence and solitude for myself. A forest would have seemed less deserted to me. There I would have felt less alone, less lost." Even Voltaire wrote to the comte de Caylus in 1739: "Paris is like the statue of Nebuchadnezzar, part gold and part muck." The Faubourg Saint-Marcel reminded Candide of "the vilest village in Westphalia." Voltaire, though a Parisian native, born there in 1694, had recently been living the life of a Helvetic lord in Ferney, and he now found the center of the French capital "dark, cramped, and ugly, typical of the most shameful age of barbarism . . . We blush to see public markets set up in narrow streets, spewing filth, spreading infection, and occasioning constant disorder."[26]

And for Rousseau, inevitably, Paris was "perhaps the city in the world where fortunes are most unequal, and where the most sumptuous opulence reigns alongside the most deplorable misery." True, the Parisian success of *La Nouvelle Héloïse* would diminish Jean-Jacques's animosity somewhat. "Contrary to my expectations," he wrote in the *Confessions,* the book was

> least successful in Switzerland and most successful in Paris. Are friendship, love, and virtue therefore more prevalent in Paris than elsewhere? Certainly not, but what does prevail there is an exquisite sensibility, which causes the heart to leap at the image of these good things and makes people cherish in others the pure, tender, decent feelings they no longer feel themselves. Corruption is the same everywhere. Morality and virtue no longer exist in Europe, but if some vestige of love for them survives, it is in Paris that it is to be sought.[27]

Ordinarily, however, for Rousseau Paris was a "human wasteland." It struck him in 1731 as less beautiful than Turin: "Upon entering by way of the Faubourg Saint-Marceau [thus by the rue Mouffetard], I saw nothing but filthy, stinking little streets, wretched, dark houses, and the look of uncleanliness, poverty, beggars, carters, seamstresses, and women hawking tisanes and old hats. So powerful was this first impression that all the real splendor of Paris I have seen since has not been able to overcome it, and a secret distaste for this capital has stayed with me." Certainly for Rousseau Paris was a place where it was possible to become more intelligent—but generally only at the cost of unhappiness. Saint-Preux, the hero of *La Nouvelle Héloïse,* describes the capital as a "désert du monde." And in *Emile* Rousseau wrote: "Farewell, then, Paris, celebrated city, city of noise, smoke, and filth, in which women no longer believe in honor nor men in virtue. Farewell, Paris: we seek love, happiness, innocence. We can never get far enough away from you."[28]

On the eve of the Revolution, Paris may well have become the site of a new sociability, of a new "mood," as Oswald Spengler put it; but at times this new city, in which mobility was everything and corporatist ties were crumbling, could also seem brutal and devouring. The young Chateaubriand found Paris "unbearable" and "disgusting." In August 1788 Vittorio Alfieri wrote of being "sucked into a fetid sewer." And in 1790 the young Russian N. M. Karamzin confided that in Paris he felt he was "but a grain of sand in a dizzying torrent or whirlwind."[29]

Suddenly there were vivid descriptions of malodorous corners of the capital, from the Bicêtre prison to the Saint-Gervais cloister. For Mercier it was the sounds of the city that were disturbing, for "there is no city in the world where the voices of the hawkers, male and female alike, are sharper or more piercing . . . [These voices] fly across rooftops" and could be heard even above the din of busy intersections. The capital, the historian Daniel Roche tells us, was seen as "necrophiliac and coprophagous." There was fear that buildings might collapse, as happened in Ménilmontant in July 1778 when an entire building vanished into a quarry from which gypsum (used in making plaster of Paris) had been extracted. Charles-Axel Guillaumot, whose job was to inspect these gypsum quarries, explained the problem: "The temples, palaces, dwellings and public streets in several quarters of Paris and its environs [are] in danger of being swallowed up by sinkholes as deep as they are wide."[30]

How can we reconcile these two fundamentally different attitudes, both of them modern, but one positive and the other surprisingly nega-tive? Paris of the salons, and Paris of loneliness and the detached modern self? One way to answer this question might be to look again at the his-torical development of the concepts of modernity, modernism, and post-modernism, but now from a different angle, focusing this time on the concepts of individuality, individualism, and alienation.

In everyday practice, Paris on the eve of the Revolution was still a "hyper-corporatist" city, wholly communitarian in its social organiza-tion. Individualism was not its actuating principle. But the key event of the 1770s in Paris was Turgot's (unsuccessful) attack on corporate privi-leges, conducted under the banner of the more individualistic market economy that this neo-Physiocrat hoped to create. In Paris communi-tarianism still ruled, even if among the elites nascent public opinion had already been won over to the new view.

In this bipolar cultural ambiance, in the lived social experience of late eighteenth-century Paris, these two extremes—individuated and com-munitarian—defined the limits of possibility. Two systems confronted each other. In one, which might be described as neo-medieval cor-poratism, Parisian individuality expressed itself (in principle) in the context of a group. In the other, the system of Turgot and the Le Chapelier Law of June 1791, which made labor a commodity, individu-ality would be obliged to find its own direct means of expression. (This was also the system favored by the Abbé Sieyès, a reader of Adam Smith, who called in his world-famous pamphlet *What Is the Third Estate?* for the creation of a fully sovereign individual in a nation that was also to be fully sovereign.)

And between these two poles—the anti-individualist corporatism of the ancien régime and the individualism of the Enlightenment and the bourgeois revolution—was an empty area, a kind of vacuum mitigated for some but not all Parisians by the new sociability of shared readings, salons, cafés, and masonic lodges. To be sure, the individualism of the salons was for those who frequented them like a first glimpse of liberal nirvana, but not everyone in Paris felt at home in this setting. (Recall Rousseau and his "abuse of language" allegation.) But many Parisians, among the literate as well as among the common sort, rejected the new worldview, and by reaction to the new individualistic ethos many residents, of all social ranks, would soon become enthusiastic supporters of enemies of capitalism and economic individualism, as did the utopian socialists Fourier, Saint-Simon, Comte, and Considérant. This notion of rejection, in some cases unconscious, of the new individualism can also be used to account for the many vivid and heartfelt descriptions of Paris in the 1780s as a city that was not just a physically deleterious place but also an emotional wasteland and a prison of solitude.

This critical shift was ominous for Western culture, because Paris in this domain was to be a model—or perhaps an anti-model—for the rest of the world, at a time when the entire North Atlantic world was desperately trying to resolve these same antinomies between citizen and nation, individual and society. In the English-speaking world, the home of the Scottish Enlightenment and the economic system of Adam Smith, this led to the "invisible hand," Smith's ingenious mechanism for reconciling the interests of the individual producer (seeking to maximize his profits and undercut the competition) with those of society at large, conceived as an aggregate of consumers pleased to be offered better value for less money. More nobly, the French Revolution and Parisian Jacobinism would seek to achieve similar ecumenical goals but by way of politics rather than economics. The French revolutionary hero, be he legislator, member of the Convention, or Parisian militant, spoke not for himself but in the name of the entire city, nation, or people, for his section of Paris or for all mankind. Though fiercely sectarian in practice, the Jacobin was in principle conciliatory and mild. The Jacobin fête was in every way inclusive. And both of these models spoke to a new consciousness of self that was characteristic of social life in the pre-revolutionary capital.

WITH AN EYE to the future, let me add at once that the notion of Paris as the capital of an individualistic modernity would later develop many variants and go through ups and downs which we shall have occasion to follow in these pages. From 1750 until about 1830 the ideal of triumphant individuality remained alive in Paris, but within a series of constantly shifting forms.

especially of all revolutions

For the philosophes and Jacobins, as has been said, the new libertarian and communitarian values still seemed complementary. For Balzac, whose novels came as a riposte not only to Constant's *Adolphe,* Chateaubriand's *René,* and Senancour's *Obermann* but also to the "feminine novels" of Mme de Staël, Mme de Genlis, and Mme de Souza (not to be confused with the feminist novels of George Sand),[31] a second version of the self took shape after the bourgeois revolution of 1830: individualism as it was experienced by the capital's elites now became more extreme, verging on solipsism. This affected politics, property rights, and even the ambitions of every person of sensibility. As Balzac was to explain in 1839, "everyone interprets music in relation to his own private pain or joy, his own hopes and despairs." After the pre-republican philosophe of the Enlightenment and the Jacobin-republican hero of Year II who fulfilled himself through love of country, a new hero appeared on the scene around 1820. (The lugubriously inclined will see this Parisian version of the triumphant self as the forerunner of the fascist hero of 1922–1945: the man who defined himself not through but in opposition to and by domination of the masses.) "The destiny of a strong man is despotism," Balzac explained. For Gautier, "every soul" in Balzac's Human Comedy "is charged with will through and through. So is Balzac himself." And as the Surrealist critic Roger Caillois so shrewdly observed, both Baudelaire and Balzac were admirers of the Jesuits.[32]

And in that second view, Paris seemed fated to have become the capital of knowledge, power, and the power of ideas, as well as the capital of unbridled individualism. This was also the Paris in which the naive egoism of young Rastignac (in Balzac's *Père Goriot*) would flourish to the full. (Indeed Rastignac became such a well-known figure in the French cultural universe that no one in France missed General de Gaulle's meaning when he referred to François Mitterrand as "the Rastignac of the Nièvre.")

Rastignac in Paris, and innocence in the provinces: to the contemporaries of Balzac it seemed obvious that the communal spirit so dead in Paris remained alive and well in the provinces, a leitmotiv that would continue to develop throughout the nineteenth century. As the Goncourt brothers put it, "Dogs in the provinces know a very different kind of happiness from the dogs of Paris. In Paris a dog is a passerby. He is alone. Here I see dogs on the square: they form a society."[33] (As it happens, the Goncourts may well have been right, given the solitary habits not so much of the dogs of Paris as of their masters.)

PUBLIC OPINION, academies, salons, and sometimes solitude: these were the things that shaped the new conception that Parisians formed of living in a city that, as Mercier said, "eternally rivets the gaze of the entire world."

Roger Caillois has given us an excellent description of the change from community and self to mere self in the decades from 1750 to 1850. "The conversion was total," he wrote of the difference between the ancient and the modern and post-Christian: "The world of sublime grandeurs and inexpiable failures, of unbroken violence and mystery, where at any moment . . . anything is possible anywhere because the imagination has lavished upon and invested in it the most extraordinary attention—that world was no longer remote, inaccessible, and autonomous; it was the world in which everyone spends his life."[34] What had previously been the heroic stuff of legend now became the daily life and struggle of embattled individuals. Indeed, and even before 1789, if one wanted to be able to live in that new and open-ended world, one had to go to Paris to experience its possibilities.

45

3

Capital of Revolution

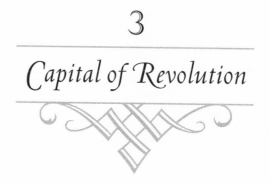

IN A CARTOON published in *Le Canard enchaîné* shortly after the Liberation but before the end of the Second World War, Philippe Pétain, head of the erstwhile Vichy government and now a captive in forced German exile, speaks to his former prime minister: "Tell me, Laval, have the Gaullists chosen a provisional capital?" "Yes," Laval answers. "Paris."

Since the time of the Capetians, of the Battle of Bouvines in 1214, of Philip Augustus and his wall (parts of which still stand), Paris has been the heart of the French nation. The monarchy claimed to rule by divine right, but one might almost say that its right to exist was guaranteed by Paris. The great kings, the ones whose memory has survived in the minds of the French people, are for the most part the ones who trusted in their capital: Philip Augustus and the Louvre in 1204, Saint Louis and his oak, Francis I (founder in 1530 of the Collège de France), Henri IV on his equestrian statue, which became a fetish.[1] We no longer remember the great painted wooden equestrian statue of Philip the Fair, which stood inside Notre Dame until 1792, but in its day this too was a mythical effigy. The monarchical idea foundered in France only when it was vetoed by Paris, in 1792, in 1848, and in the 1870s.

France has been far more closely identified with its capital over the course of its history than have other nations, such as Germany (which only recently chose Berlin over Bonn and its predecessor Weimar); Italy with its intransigent Lombards; Switzerland, Belgium, Holland, and

Canada; and, even more tellingly, the United States, Australia, and Brazil, whose capitals were, initially at least, artificial, planned cities. "I have two loves," sang the expatriate American performer Josephine Baker in 1931, "my country and Paris"—by which she meant, or so we can presume, Paris as the capital of her adopted country.

Politically, however, as opposed to emotionally, the relation between Paris and France, symbolized by the presence of the Parisian blue and red among the three colors of the French flag, has been more complex. Is it accurate to say, for instance, that Paris was the capital of the Republic—or, better, the republican spirit—from 1870 to 1940? Albert Bayet often resided in Paris, but his newspaper was published in Toulouse. Edouard Herriot, that very epitome of the Third Republic, was noted first and foremost as mayor of Lyons. There has often been reason to doubt the firmness of Parisian support for the Republic, as during the period of General Boulanger's popularity in the capital in 1889 or during the riots of February 1934. Paris and France seemed to march in lockstep in Year II, but nearly all the leading Jacobins hailed from the provinces, even if several of them had come to know the "commune centrale du Globe" quite well (Danton settled in the city in 1780, and Robespierre and Desmoulins studied there at the Collège Louis le Grand). Although it was Paris that elected them, their support came from the sansculottes and not from the bourgeoisie, which may have been Jacobin in the provinces but was relatively conservative in Paris. More typical of the Parisian deputies was Louis-Sébastien Mercier, a notorious anti-Jacobin despite his hostility to the ancien régime, a man who was close to the Girondins and an enemy of the Montagnards.

Paradoxically, then, Paris was more the capital of populist revolution than it was of any of France's five centrist republics, even though the republics were born there, and even though the government formed after the fall of Napoleon III included only Parisian republicans among its ministers. Whether monarchical or republican, the state in France has often suspected Paris of being too far to either the right or the left. From the Directory (1795–1799) until the presidency of Valéry Giscard d'Estaing in the 1970s, the city paid a heavy price for its special status:

the post of mayor was abolished. From the time of the Revolution, when Jean-Sylvain Bailly and Jérôme Pétion (who both died violently in 1793–1794) had the misfortune to serve in that position, the capital, except for two brief interludes in 1848–1851 and 1870–1871, had no mayor until recently. (Once restored, the office was first occupied by Jacques Chirac, who later became president of France.)

If we wish to understand the myth of Parisian politics, we therefore need to examine the revolutionary spirit of the city's working people rather than the republicanism of its bourgeoisie; and the crux of that history lies, first, in the associationist proclivities of the "petites gens" of the capital between 1789 and 1795; and, second, in the way those proclivities were later co-opted and in some sense betrayed by universalist ideologists, often Marxist in tendency and extra-Parisian in origin.

In other words, from 1792 to 1795, for example, Parisian and associationist sansculottism was a reality, but its memory was subsequently transformed and politicized in the work of revolutionary socialist theoreticians ranging from Gracchus Babeuf in 1796 to Karl Marx after the Paris Commune of 1871. Nor did much of this associationism survive in the propaganda of Marx's twentieth-century followers, some of them ideologized historians, and others Stalinist politicians. (A few managed to compound these two debilitating roles.) For nearly two centuries the memory of the Parisian popular spirit during the Revolution was thus set in one deforming ideological perspective or another, culminating in the Marxism-Leninism through which Parisian workers, and especially those of the city's "Red Belt," were required to speak their grievances.

It was in the conjunction, or rather the uneasy coexistence, of these two strands—the genuinely populist and the artificially ideological—that the constructed myth of Paris, capital of revolution, was elaborated in the nineteenth century and, in denatured form, extended to the world at large: to the Soviet Union from 1917 until 1989, and from there, after the Second World War, to the Third World. Indeed, critics of the city's past might take this line of argument further still. The myth of the revolutionary populace, of total redemption through total struggle—the Parisian myth as extended by the Soviet Union—might then be said to have found its ultimate avatar in the self-destruction of the Cambodian people under Pol Pot, a revolutionary socialist and an erstwhile Parisian. (As were also, by the way, Zhou Enlai, Deng Xiaoping, and before him Ho Chi Minh, who did not yet go by that name, which means "he who enlightens," and who lived in Paris on what he could earn by selling genuine photographic portraits and fake antiques at the Marché des Patriarches in the Fifth Arrondissement.)

THE PRE-REPUBLICAN PARISIAN and revolutionary traditions obviously go back to 1789, and we have all internalized the equation Paris = revolution to such a degree that it is hard for us to imagine eighteenth-century Paris as anything other than the breeding ground of revolutionary ideology. Nevertheless, historians of the pre-1789 Parisian populace agree that the people of what would soon become sans-culotte Paris were a variegated, pro-monarchy, but still largely apolitical population quite unlike the London populace of the same period, which by contrast was hyper-politicized. To make the comparison of turbulent London with this politically inert Paris more vivid, consider this: despite the carnage of the better-known Parisian episodes of the revolutionary period (July 14, 1789; August 10, 1792, which left hundreds dead; 9 Thermidor), the Gordon Riots of 1780 in London, which lasted just one week, did more damage to property than all the revolutionary violence in Paris from the fall of the Bastille to the joyous advent of the First Consul in November 1799.

To get a better idea of the surprising political passivity of the *petit peuple parisien,* let us briefly recall two texts, Daniel Roche's *Le Peuple de Paris: Essai sur la culture populaire au XVIIIe siècle* (The People of Paris: Essay on Eighteenth-Century Popular Culture) and Arlette Farge and Jacques Revel's *The Vanishing Children of Paris.* Roche's argument is partly quantitative. He begins his study of popular and bourgeois attitudes in pre-revolutionary Paris with statistics that reveal a wide range of ways of living. Some residents of the capital were very wealthy, others less so, and still others were desperately poor. Each group had its own distinctive style: some loved cafés, others congregated in taverns. (In 1850 Alexis de Tocqueville observed that people tended to prefer salons, cafés, or cabarets according to their political predilections.)[2] Ninety percent of domestic servants in the capital were "immigrants" from the

49

provinces. Every occupation had its own distinctive peculiarities, privileges, rules, habits, and sociology, and people tended to marry within their own occupational groups.

Urban life was thus fluid and variable, and different observers were apt to see the city in different ways. The administrator, the police officer, and the constable—each saw a Paris of his own. Paris was for them a city without a center, a city in flux. As well as a city that was being socially transformed: as Roche explains, "even in the eyes of its most tenacious defender, Roland Mousnier, the rigid class structure [of Paris] was [in the later decades of the eighteenth century] breaking up into a multiplicity of 'strata' in which hierarchy depended on the possibility of accumulating capital by controlling the work of others and profiting from the market."[3]

Arlette Farge and Jacques Revel pursue a related though different strategy to understand pre-revolutionary Paris. These two historians focus not on numbers but on what they call the "logic of the crowd." They look at a particular riot, which took place in Paris in 1750, and try to explain its course in terms of popular attitudes conditioned by new cultural and social instincts. In those attitudes they see something that historians now call a "mauvais discours," that is to say, a running critique of the monarchy that would ultimately sap its prestige. Like Roche, Farge and Revel stress the importance of social ties, ties not to the city but to the neighborhood, to that small part of Paris where everyone knew everyone else. Despite their differences of method, these three historians agree that the Paris crowd of the 1750s was socially diverse and politically monarchist, and for these reasons radically different from the sansculottes of a later period.

One might of course take a different approach. Where one historian sees a break, another might prefer to look for continuities. One could, it is true, look for the origins of revolutionary Paris in the city's age-old predilection for riots and other forms of social disturbance. As far back as the Middle Ages, the term "Parisian" was synonymous with both *trublion* (troublemaker) and *maillotin* (war hammer, a name applied to insurgent Parisians in 1382). The Parisians of the sixteenth century backed the rebellious Catholic Ligue; in the century after that they joined the Fronde, and some people have seen all these forms of popular

M. Thibault, *Barricades before the Attack, rue Saint-Maur, June 25, 1848, 7:30 A.M.* This daguerreotype is ominously prophetic. The length of the shutter time precluded the inclusion of moving human subjects, but this image also foreshadows the imminent decimation of Parisian working people, which Marx would hail as a great step forward in the creation of a Parisian—and therefore a world-historical—proletarian consciousness. Musée Carnavalet. © Photothèque des musées de la ville de Paris / 87 CAR 6559: Briant.

protest as precursors of the sansculottes of the eighteenth century, the Communards of the nineteenth, and the May 1968 protesters of more recent memory.[4] In this view, at every stage the Parisian has been a rather tough customer.

But it makes more sense to look at the question in another light. What differentiates pre-1789 Paris from post-1789 Paris far outweighs what connects the two periods, and this despite the emotional investment in certain traditions, such as the erecting of barricades. (The word, incidentally, comes from *barriques,* the earth-filled barrels that were assembled into defensive bulwarks in the days of the sixteenth-century

Ligue.) The P<u>aris crow</u>d set off in a new direction in the spring of 1789, as the monarchy began to crumble. It was then, and not in the days of the fourteenth-century mayor Etienne Marcel or even in the days of Jacques Clément, who murdered Henri III in 1589, that the once ideologically passive Parisians began their long revolutionary march.

How can we explain the shift in the allegiance of the *petit peuple* of Paris to sansculottism in 1789–1793? How can we account for the extraordinarily rapid rise of the sansculotte spirit in 1791? Why did a politicized movement grow out of the infusion of revolutionary energy into an ancient and traditionalist popular sensibility? What stages mark the transition from the decaying hierarchical society to the anti-absolutist mob of 1789 and the revolutionary sansculottes of 1792? Some Jacobins may have read Rousseau, but the sansculottes surely did not do so.

The answers to these questions are complex, and here I shall limit myself to three key points. First, popular Paris before the Revolution was, if not precisely anti-monarchy, not pro-monarchy either. Second, the institutions of professional corporatism no longer enjoyed the emotional backing of the *petit peuple*. Nevertheless—my third point—the common man's sensibility remained basically traditionalist. Hence ordinary Parisians were in a very special situation: although hostile to the individualistic modernity of the new Enlightenment (that is, to the Parisian sense of self described in the previous chapter), they were nonetheless ideologically available and therefore eminently susceptible to the universalist principles of the left-wing bourgeoisie, whether Jacobin or democratic, Parisian or provincial.

In 1789, then, the *petit peuple* of Paris was a group comprising artisans (many of whom owned their own small businesses) as well as some 200,000 other Parisians who lived on the edge of misery and in fear of hunger, and who were more or less communitarian and associationist in their attitudes. But disenchanted by the structure of the guilds, put off by the discredit of the monarchy, they were ready to embark on a great new political adventure, which, like ancient Gaul, can be divided into three parts.

First, by the spring of 1789 these Parisians were ready to move on, caught up as they were in the excitement surrounding the election of deputies of the Third Estate, the formal submission of grievances, or *ca-hiers de doléances,* to the king, and the self-proclamation of the National Assembly. They were also impressed in 1789–1791 by what one might call a revolutionary discourse, soon to become a Jacobin discourse. Their ideological biases in these first months of the Revolution were at once indigenous and mimetic, but also practical: they felt stymied by the corporate structures of Parisian life.

Then, in a second phase, toward the end of 1791 and into 1792, Parisian sansculottism acquired much greater consistency in response to the events of the Revolution itself, events that were amplified by the theater of the streets, newspapers, revolutionary festivals, executions, rumors, and crises. In a strange, even bizarre way, the events and institutions of the Revolution created sansculottism, which in turn accelerated the pace of the Revolution, whose dramatic episodes reinforced the sansculotte ideology—a perfect circle, or a vicious one, depending on one's point of view.

Finally, this cycle collapsed in the months between the execution of the sansculotte Hébertistes (March 1794) and the populist *journées* of Germinal and Prairial (spring 1795). From then until the Revolution of July 1830, the Parisian populace would basically remain politically inert.

What, then, was a Parisian sansculotte in the period 1791–1793? To begin with, one should distinguish between the sansculotte and the Jacobin—his inspiration and ally but soon to become his enemy. The Jacobin was a petit bourgeois, a bourgeois, or even a noble such as Lepeletier, Condorcet, Barras, or Bonaparte (who belonged to a Jacobin club in Valence-sur-Rhône). Seventeen percent of Parisian Jacobin club members were aristocrats.[5] The sansculotte, by contrast, was not a proletarian, but neither was he a bourgeois or even a petit bourgeois, even if he was materially well off. His thinking was radically different from that of the average Jacobin.

The sansculottes of the capital were more direct and bloodthirsty than the Jacobins, less literary, and more violent, both in the streets and at home. The average sansculotte in the capital was decidedly of the capital: there were isolated sansculottes in the provinces and even in the countryside, but the typical sansculotte lived by the banks of the Seine, though he may not have lived there very long (roughly a third of Paris's 600,000 or so residents were migrants from the provinces). He took his liquor straight and was proud of it. His pike symbolized his fondness for direct action.

Communitarian though the Parisian sansculotte might be, he was not an enemy of private property. (This is a critical factor.) He was more likely to be an artisan than a worker. Critically, he was motivated more by fear of scarcity than by hatred of the rich, for he had always rubbed shoulders with the wealthy and was resigned to their existence. When the republican militant Vingternier asked "What is a sansculotte?" in 1793, his answer had little to do with social origins but a great deal to do with morality, modesty, willingness to sacrifice, and family feeling.

Where in the capital might one have found a sansculotte? More or less everywhere, it seems, but above all in the old faubourgs (Saint-Antoine and Saint-Marcel), which had been integral parts of the city since the beginning of the eighteenth century and therefore lay within the "tax wall" maintained by the farmers general and designed by Claude-Nicolas Ledoux ("le mur murant Paris qui rend Paris murmurant"—the wall that surrounds Paris makes Paris murmur—as the saying went).[6] Twenty percent of those who lived in these Paris faubourgs were indigent, but among the leaders of the sansculottes skilled craftsmen predominated by a large margin. Bear in mind that nearly 50,000 Parisians were self-employed, and many of these artists/artisans were moderately well-to-do (including Maurice Duplay, who gave Robespierre a room in his house on the rue Saint-Honoré in a building that is now a restaurant). Parisian artisans were skilled at many things. Was there anything that could not be made in Paris, and made better than anywhere else? The city was internationally renowned for its goldsmiths (there were more than six hundred jewelers in the capital), as well as for its cabinetmakers, gilders, metalworkers, grocers, bakers, textile makers, and printers.

What images filled the mind of the Parisian sansculotte? Some were distorted versions of works of the French and English Enlightenment, along with borrowings from Rousseau, of whom many sansculottes

Eugène Delacroix, *Liberty Leading the People, July 28, 1830*. Paris in myth and in modern history: no work of art represents these two themes better than this one. Clambering over a stone barricade and fallen heroes, the Goddess of Liberty, with her tricolor flag, itself born of Revolution, leads Parisians of all social classes to freedom. Paris, once a capital of Christendom—as witnessed by the towers of Notre Dame in the background—has now become the capital of revolutionary modernity.

Eugène Grasset, *View of Paris.* Myth and phantasmagoria: after the myths of Paris from 1750 to 1889 comes the phantasmagoria of Paris, capital of pleasure, classless, familiar, and tranquil, as in this view of the Seine and Notre Dame from the Pont-Sully by an artist who also designed printed cloth, porcelain, and postage stamps.

Musées des Arts Décoratifs, Paris. Photo: Laurent-Sully Jaulmes. All rights reserved.

Anicet Charles G. Lemonnier, *A Lecture at Mme Geoffrin's House,* 1755. Louis XIV had made Versailles the capital of the Bourbon monarchy. In the Age of Enlightenment, a newly created Republic of Letters worked to make Paris the capital of the world and of the French nation as well. In this painting the habitués of Mme Geoffrin's salon listen respectfully to a reading of *The Orphan of China* by Voltaire, whose bust presides over this Areopagus.

Charles Giraud, *Salon of the Princesse Mathilde, Rue de Courcelles,* 1859. This painting of the salon of the Princesse Mathilde, a cousin of Napoleon III, hangs as it should in the Napoleonic chateau of Compiègne rather than in the more ecumenical Louvre. Giraud's canvas shows us a salon very different from Mme Geoffrin's. This interior, at once princely and bourgeois, is a machine of exclusion and a refuge from modernity, rather than, like the great Parisian salons before 1789, an agent of inclusion and change.

Emile Quetier, *The Colonne Vendôme Overturned*, 1871. In 1793–94 Parisian sansculottes acceded to political consciousness, but on terms set (more or less) by provincial bourgeois Jacobins. After the "bourgeois" revolutions of July 1830 and February 1848 came the spontaneous and untheorized workers' insurrection of June 1848. And next in Marxist eschatology came the "Civil War in France" between the murderous troops of "Monsieur Thiers" and the workers' state of the Paris Commune, whose purpose was symbolized by the toppling of Napoleon's column on the barricaded Place Vendôme.

Musée d'Orsay. Photo: Michelle Bellot. Réunion des Musées Nationaux/Art Resource, NY.

René Magritte, *The Return of the Flame,* 1943. Paris was the capital of world revolution for the left, but also the capital of crime for the Parisian bourgeoisie, which had been revolutionary in 1789 and 1830 but by the 1920s had long ceased to be so. Vestigially, however, over the skyline of the city loomed the ghostly presence of the arch-criminal Fantômas, much to the delight of Surrealists like the poet Robert Desnos, who thrived on the survivals in twentieth-century Paris of neo-medieval oddity, coincidence, and mysterious crime.

Giuseppe de Nittis, *The Place des Pyramides, Paris,* 1875. This work by an Italian-born painter is eloquent in its purposeful detail. At the right of this anecdotal street scene is the newly erected statue of Joan of Arc, the perfect Frenchwoman, a daughter of provincial Lorraine. Behind the statue stand the ruins of the Tuileries, a memorial to the evil ways of the Parisian pétroleuses, the most imperfect women of any country, who were thought to have set that palace on fire.

Musée d'Orsay. Photo: Hervé Lewandowski. Réunion des Musées Nationaux /Art Resource, NY.

Luis Jiménez Aranda, *Lady at the Paris Exposition,* 1899. This lady portrayed by the Spanish-born Aranda stands against the background of the new Eiffel Tower. The colors of her clothing are those of the libertarian French flag of 1789. After Joan of Arc, a model of Christian womanhood, we have here the young bourgeois woman destined soon to be a Republican mother. She is at once stylish (she leans on the balustrade of a terraced café), dignified, intensely respectable, and thoroughly informed (as we can see from the newspaper she has been reading).

Meadows Museum, Southern Methodist University, Dallas, Algur H. Meadows Collection, 69.24

knew little more than the name (but did all of yesterday's Marxists read Marx?). At the same time, many other tendencies were also at play, cultural residues, some of them quite ancient. For example, the quasi-mystical vocabulary of sansculottism owed much to Catholic sensibility. Why not suppose that a fair proportion of the thousand people who stormed the Bastille in 1789 also marched in 1785 in processions in honor of Sainte Geneviève, the capital's patron saint, to pray for the end of drought and famine?

Last but not least, Parisian sansculottism was also influenced by the middlebrow and highbrow culture of the capital. Think of the way it drew on the theatrical vocabulary of the 1780s. Some sansculottes no doubt first had their suspicions of dark and political intrigue aroused by the stage, on which private good and evil were likely to be clearly differentiated. The sansculotte of Year II was often a spectator at plays, parades, and vaudevilles. The scatological vocabulary favored by Jacques-René Hébert and his factitiously populist newspaper *Père Duchesne* simply recycled an old tradition of the Parisian stage. Hébert and Jean-Marie Collot d'Herbois had been men of the theater before the Revolution.

"Spectacular" and literary unities, then, but the soon-to-be sansculottes also socialized in more mundane settings; and of all the occupations in which sansculottes engaged, the most important to the formation of the popular Parisian ethos was that of tavernkeeper. There were some 3,000 taverns of one sort or another in the city, and it was in these various "saloons," which together constituted the kind of "public space" that Jürgen Habermas has theorized—a popular equivalent of the salons, circles, and academies of the bourgeoisie—that the sansculotte spirit took shape. When supplies of food arrived or failed to arrive at the central market, it was in the taverns that the news was spread.

Thus we come to what neo-Marxists used to call "revolutionary praxis," the process whereby "sociopolitical" groups organize themselves as politics evolve; which is to say that the Parisian sansculotte was an artisan whose political thinking was shaped and radicalized by discussions of the events of the Revolution as they unfolded. The sansculotte played the leading role in revolutionary *journées* whose fame further unleashed the city's collective energies.

THIS GENUINE TRANSFORMATION, however, was just one aspect of popular Parisian "revolutionism." There was also another influence, far more artificial, which ran counter to this authentically popular and populist tradition, namely a constructed memory of who the sansculottes had been and what they had wanted. From 1795 onward, and for more than a century, the indigenous and truly popular associationist tendencies of the Parisian populace would be relentlessly reinterpreted, deformed, and co-opted by a thoroughly ideological interpretation of popular and revolutionary Paris.

The sansculotte had stood for direct action and the protection of private property. In 1795 and 1796, however, Gracchus Babeuf worked to alter this Parisian attitude in a direction that was less communitarian and more collectivist. And his "communist" view of what sansculottism should have been later became the basis of a scholarly, intellectual, and phantasmagorically inauthentic interpretation of events, which would eventually obliterate all memory of the "participationist" revolutionism of an earlier era.

That is, the universalizing zeal of this socialist revolutionary, and of Marxist intellectuals after him, eventually transformed the memory of the popular Parisian past. And decades later, in the last years of the nineteenth century, this ideologized appropriation gradually became the accepted model of popular action in the capital. In the battle of ideas, the more indigenous and anarchistic Proudhonism of the cooperativist journeymen lost ground to the "constructed" Marxist discourse of universal proletarianism. Parisian sansculottism had been and long remained communitarian and associationist, but it would be remembered otherwise.

This means, again, that Marxist historians (relying on Babeuf's life and work) transformed the Parisian sansculotte into the prototype of the modern proletarian. In retrospect, we can see that the myth of Paris as the capital of world socialist revolution was constructed in several stages, beginning with the work of this "first revolutionary communist" in 1796. Or, more precisely, with the communist orator's followers and historians, most notably Filippo Buonarroti, who counted Michelangelo among his remote ancestors and who, in 1828, published *La Conspi-*

ration pour l'égalité ou des égaux (The Conspiracy of Equality or of Equals), from which, as it happens, we derive most of the information we have about Babeuf's conspiracy of 1795.

Babeuf was not a Parisian at all (he was born in Saint-Quentin). Before the Revolution he had worked as a recorder of feudal deeds; in 1795 he took it upon himself to effect an ideological transformation of Parisian sansculottism. Babeuf frowned on spontaneous and direct political action. For him, the goal was to organize a conspiracy of militant activists. (Lenin was to take an intense interest in this aspect of Babeuf's thinking.) Babeuf hoped to transform the Parisian communitarians into genuine communists. No longer was the purpose of political action simply to obtain bread. Property had to be abolished, Babeuf insisted, and land nationalized. In the end the Babouvist conspiracy failed (one of its leaders was a government agent), and Babeuf, after bungling a suicide attempt, was guillotined in Vendôme in 1797 at the age of thirty-seven.

For some historians, such as Oxford's Richard Cobb, Babouvism was of no significance whatsoever. To a dyed-in-the-wool empiricist like Cobb, Rousseau (whose work did not interest him either) "had no more to do with sansculottism than did Babeuf." The Conspiracy of Equals had been a curse on the history profession, Cobb argued in 1970, and it "has never ceased to plague and bore historians right up to the present day."[7] In some respects, of course, he is quite right: Babouvism did stand sansculottism on its head, for the sansculotte, while communitarian and gregarious, also defended private property and remained firmly attached to his neighborhood; he was brutal but good-natured.

And yet Cobb radically underestimates the force of Babouvism's appeal to leftist theorizers. For the Parisian revolutionary tradition of the nineteenth century operated in two different time frames. There was of course the actual experience of the sansculottes and their descendants, as Cobb recognized. But there was also the politically correct, at first Babouvist and later Marxist interpretation of what had happened. Babouvism, though perhaps only remotely related to what the sansculottes actually thought and did at the time, was very relevant to the later *perception* of what they had thought and done.

The key moment in *The Hound of the Baskervilles* comes when Sherlock

Holmes realizes the significance of the vigilant watchdog's failure to bark. The hiatus in the political activity of the *petit peuple* of Paris between 1796 and 1830 is similarly important: it provided the void in which the ideological adaptation of popular communitarianism, and ultimately its incorporation into what would become the dominant socialist ideology, came into effect. These silent years are at once an extension and a denial of a genuine revolutionary tradition, because, startlingly, Parisian revolutionism all but evaporated for more than thirty years: from 1796 to 1830 there were no real riots in Paris, and it was in an atmosphere of indifference, or at least of nearly perfect Parisian calm, that Louis XVIII succeeded Napoleon in the capital in 1814, only to be succeeded in turn, on March 20, 1815, by none other than the emperor, who, a hundred days later, would again relinquish his place in the Tuileries.

The Babouvo-Marxist historiographical adaptation of revolutionary reality would begin in this vacuum, and at this point we would do well to remind ourselves of Buonarroti's dates: born in 1761, this patriarchal ancestor of Parisian communism did not publish his book until 1828. Most of the revolutionaries whose great deeds he recounted had long since died, and their silence was essential to the success of the nineteenth-century communist narrative. Before long, the Marxist-inspired history of what happened in Paris during the Revolution, an interpretation that picked up where Buonarroti had left off, would come to seem truer and more real than the ephemeral and vague memories of the participants themselves—and that was possible only because the tradition of revolution in Paris had been interrupted for so long.

Juy 1830 marked a renaissance of populist politics in the capital. The city, rising as one against the desultory political maneuvering of Charles X (whom the Parisian poet Pierre-Jean de Béranger derided as "Charles the Simple"), became overnight the mythical capital of world revolution, and this time the myth had a long life.

Of course, the political myth of Paris had its antecedents in the events of 1789, and many people at that time had been troubled by the

thought of Paris in the grip of revolution. In both the capital and the provinces, the main issue in the struggle between Montagnards and Girondins had revolved around the revolutionary role of the capital and its sansculottes: Robespierre had been in favor of enlisting the support of the Parisian crowd, which Jacques-Pierre Brissot opposed. The deputies of first the Constituent Assembly and later the Convention had been fascinated by what the gifted historian Marcel Reinhard has called "the twin faces of Paris," the one seductive, the other hideous. Already, Reinhard pointed out, the myth of Paris had obsessed these political minds.[8]

It was not until 1830, however, that this initial bourgeois apprehension became an integral part of the image of Paris. The Restoration in 1815–1830 had frankly attempted to "royalize" Paris with its ceremonials and its sanctification of the royal victims of the Revolution (the king, the queen, their son the dauphin, and their cousin the hapless duc d'Enghien, who was shot in Vincennes in 1804), but nothing, or almost nothing, survived the regime's fall. By contrast, the July Revolution would establish Paris in memory as the world capital of revolution for more than a century to come. For Pétrus Borel, a "frenetic" poet and novelist, Paris "on the nights of July 28–30" became "a crater" in which "a new moonlight" revealed the atrocities of clericalism. This new Paris was "like a lion [sprung] from its cage," and in those days lions were not always gentle: when the poet-statesman Alphonse de Lamartine was asked why he refused to intercede on behalf of the ousted ministers of Charles X, he answered with a question: "Does the lion grant pardon / when his tongue has tasted blood?" Victor Hugo, in his "Ode à la Colonne" (Ode to the Column), hailed "this potent Paris, which boils and seethes." (In 1851 Herman Melville described the statue of Napoleon on that self-same column as watching those who ruled below, "whether Louis-Philippe, Louis Blanc, or Louis the Devil.")[9]

For several decades thereafter, Paris, "revolutionized" and thoroughly "de-Bourbonized," became "a rolling sea," a hydra, a giant, a lion, a furious torrent, a "roaring abyss," a human river, an oven, a brazier, a source of energy, a volcano. For the Pole Karol Frankowski (1795–1846), Paris was a meteor. For Hugo, all the world's kings watched in terror as "the lava of events bubbled up from this human Vesuvius." Now, he added, "Paris is holding the Bastille in prison." From Germany Heinrich Heine hastened to Paris as to a new Jerusalem. Paris was to the sun what Venice was to the sea: "Drunk on sunlight," wrote Heine, "the people of Paris rose up against crumbling Bastilles and the dictates of slavery. The sun and the city studied each other and fell in love. At night, as the sun sinks into the sea, its eye dwells fondly on the beautiful city of Paris, and with its last rays it caresses the tricolor flags that wave from the city's towers."[10]

The identification of Paris with freedom was felt everywhere in those days: an ironic Alexander Herzen wrote of "the respect, the veneration, the adulation, the admiration that young Russians felt upon arriving in Paris." These young noblemen, who even in Germany, the antechamber to Paris, had felt no need to hold their violence in check, no sooner passed the city's customs barrier "than they began saying *vous* to the same servants they used to whip in Moscow."[11] And for Arnold Ruge, writing in 1841, in all Europe only France stood for the idea of liberty, and Paris was the heart of France.

Liberty, revolution, and of course the association of Paris with barricades, which from then until May 30, 1968, were part of the Parisian landscape. Everyone got used to them: Hugo tells the story of an old man on the rue Saint-Martin who, in May 1839, "went back and forth" with a wagon "from the barricade to the soldiers and from the soldiers to the barricade, impartially serving glasses of coconut milk now to the government, now to anarchy." In 1830 there were said to have been 4,054 barricades comprising some 812,500 cobblestones,[12] which, in turn, had a life of their own: after 1830 the cobblestone, especially the bloody cobblestone, became one of the most eloquent symbols of the Parisian revolutionary spirit. The republican politician and journalist Godefroy Cavaignac would look back on this as the period when someone had the idea of honoring Paris with a statue whose pedestal was to consist entirely of cobblestones. Hugo paid more succinct homage to the revolutionary cobblestone: "The quintessential symbol of the people is the paving stone. You tread upon it until it falls on your head."[13]

The bloody pavement also captivated the attention of poets, Auguste

[handwritten margin note: Makes sense why Hugo wrote the novel]

Barthélemy in particular. And in this respect the artisans of revolution followed the lead of the literati: the Parisian cobbler Edouard Roulier, who served as what one might call minister of political education during the Commune, said, "I cobble people's shoes and uncobble the city's streets."[14] By 1850 the Parisian barricades were famous the world over, and it is interesting to note that the newspaper of the Nicaraguan Sandinistas was called *La Barricada.*

The Citizen-King, Louis Philippe, who was at once (as he had to be) progressive and conservative, tried in the 1830s and 1840s to soften the image of Paris as the capital of revolution. On the one hand he paid homage with the July Column on the site of the destroyed Bastille (revolution deserved its due). On the other hand, symbolically, in some places he had the usual cobblestones replaced by wooden blocks, which were presumably less useful for building barricades. (One novel consequence of this was that, when the city flooded in 1910, entire streets were washed away; in 1968 the cobblestones were again removed from the boulevards of the Latin Quarter, this time to be permanently replaced by asphalt.) "Boulevard," Edouard Fournier remarked in 1864. "I've long wondered where the word comes from, but now I have settled its etymology to my own satisfaction once and for all: it is simply a variant of the word *bouleversement* [upheaval]."[15]

Equally revealing of the July Monarchy's moderation was the renovation of what had been the Place Louis XV, then the Place de la Révolution (Chateaubriand referred to it as a "field of blood"), and then, under Charles X, the Place Louis XVI. From 1830 it was to be known as the Place de la Concorde. The goal of the new name and the new contour was to erase the memory of the Revolution, as is attested by the placement there of the Obelisk of Luxor, which immediately became, as humorists pointed out, the oldest monument in Paris, and which can be seen as a conservative response to Colonne de la Bastille.

Why an Egyptian monument? But what French monument could possibly have been found without political significance and without religious, monarchical, aristocratic, democratic, or out-and-out socialist connotations? How fortunate, then, that in 1828 Mehemet Ali, khedive of Egypt and favorite Middle Eastern son of La Grande Nation, made

61

France a gift of the obelisk. It arrived in Marseilles in 1833 and from there made its way to Paris, where it was dedicated at noon on October 25, 1836, as the royal family and 200,000 spectators looked on—much to the dismay, incidentally, of the Romantic historian Jules Michelet, who in his book *Les Soldats de la Révolution,* written in 1848 but not published until 1878, proposed that this foreign block of stone be moved to (or, rather, hidden in) one of the courtyards of the Louvre. The obelisk of the pharaohs would be more at home, he argued, in the palace of the kings than on the premier *place* of the people of Paris. It must be remembered here that although today the Louvre is universally beloved, in those days this temple of culture was reviled by some progressives as a "lair of tyrants" and of the king's freedom-hating and mercenary Swiss Guards, whom the young author of the heroic revolutionary epic *Les Trois journées* vilified as "the degenerate sons of William Tell."

In 1830, then, the Parisian revolutionary spirit asserted itself, but its resurgence was followed by attempts to tone it down or make it bourgeois, leading to complaints from erstwhile revolutionaries shocked at the conservative evolution of a regime increasingly obsessed with the *juste milieu.* Auguste Barbier, in his poem *La Curée* (The Entrails of the Beast), invoked what would become one of the great themes of the dynastic and republican left: the corruption of Louis Philippe's July Monarchy and the competition for preferment. Paris, in this case the Paris of the bourgeoisie, was now described by this leftist poet as a sewer, a bilge, a slum, and a market. Barthélémy liked to contrast the glorious July Revolution with the ignominious regime it produced:

> Oh! si devant le Louvre ou sur le Pont d'Arcole
> Amis, nous fussions morts avec nôtre auréole,
>   Nul de nous n'aurait vu monter sur l'horizon
> L'astre du déshonneur et de la trahison.
> (O! If, before the Louvre or on the bridge at Arcola
> We had died, friends, in our glory,
>   None of us would have seen the star of dishonor
> And treason rise above the horizon.)

The reasons for this sudden rise after 1830 of the myth of Paris as capital of revolution were diverse. No doubt the prevailing climate of

Romanticism played a large part, but so did the Parisians' sense that they were watching history in the making, and that with the fall of Charles X (Louis XVI's youngest brother) they had witnessed the final collapse of the ancien régime, a turning point in world history marking the advent of democracy. Tocqueville's *Democracy in America* would not appear until 1835, but the voyage into the future on which he based that work took place in 1831.

Note too that the Revolution of 1830, like that of 1789 in its first phase, was in some respects ecumenical. Everyone—moderates, democrats, socialists—was able to find something good in it, as we can see in the celebrated painting *Liberty Leading the People* by Eugène Delacroix (who in his politics was a proponent of the *juste milieu*): in the background, along with the towers of Notre Dame, we find a man of the people, a bourgeois in a top hat, and of course a street urchin. As Tocqueville rather sententiously noted in 1850, "it is usually the urchins of Paris who begin insurrections, and generally they go about it gleefully, like schoolboys on vacation."[16] The Revolution of 1830 was thus the ideal embodiment of the Parisian revolutionary myth in its gentlest form, the triumph of the general will, for once united.

By 1830 people had largely forgotten about the excesses that had occurred in Year II. Alfred de Vigny, for example, would describe Paris as a holy and unified city: his verses eulogize the entire city and not just the *petit peuple.* If Paris were destroyed, he wrote,

> L'ange exterminateur frapperait à genoux
> Et sa main, à la fois flamboyant et timide
> Tremblerait de commettre un second déicide.
> (The exterminating angel would strike while kneeling,
> and his hand, at once fiery and timid,
> would tremble at the thought of committing a second deicide.)

THIS VISION of unity was illusory, however, and from 1830 to 1880 the trajectory of Parisian politics would in fact be the history of an ever-widening gap between artisans who were becoming communistic and a bourgeoisie that was to some degree democratic but that was socially conservative as well. It was this split, clearly, that led to the barricades of June 1848 and 1871, dates that marked, in Paris and in France, the moments when the city's bourgeoisie, horrified by the ever more dangerous turns that this Franco-French conflict was taking, moved away from the sentimental myth of revolutionary Paris that it had accepted in 1830 and engendered in 1789.

In 1830 Tocqueville had bowed to the verdict of history: the Western world, he believed, was proceeding ineluctably toward democracy; this fact might in some respects be deplorable, but it was also ordained by Providence and therefore not to be resisted. By contrast, 1848 was to be resisted at all cost. True enough, the workers' insurrection of June 1848 was for Tocqueville "the greatest and most singular [revolution] in our history and perhaps in all history." (Curiously, his words echoed those of Marx, who wrote in his *Eighteenth Brumaire of Louis Bonaparte* that these same "June days" had been "the most colossal event in the history of European civil war.") For Tocqueville, the difference was that the revolution of 1848 was not providential but demonic, a horrifying proletarian echo of the Great Bourgeois Revolution of 1789, which in retrospect became demonic and mythic as well. What had been a linear progression until February 1848 suddenly became in June of that year a lamentable circularity.[17]

The year 1848 was a threshold not only for Tocqueville but also for the Parisian *grande bourgeoisie:* it had withdrawn its support from Jacobinism in 1792, and so did it subsequently withdraw from the Parisian revolutionary consensus, gradually from 1832 until February 1848, and then very rapidly from February to June of that year. In 1789 the Parisian bourgeois had still thought of himself as living in a mixed neighborhood of some kind. In 1793, however, he began to see himself in a much larger, socially embattled context, and by 1848 this expansion of his horizons was complete and permanent. The Parisian bourgeois now thought in terms not just of the city as a whole but of his social class, which had triumphed in 1830 but felt itself increasingly threatened, perhaps even in mortal peril, in the riots and revolutions of 1832, 1839, and 1848. Writing of Paris in the spring of 1848, Tocqueville said that he saw "society" (but what he meant was Paris) "severed in two: on one side those who owned nothing, united by all they coveted in common, on the other side those who owned everything, united by their common anxiety."[18] Now the time was ripe for the development of an ideological reinterpretation of Parisian history.

From 1850 to 1880, therefore, the new political scenario very much resembled—but in accentuated form—the script of the Great Revolution in Year II as it had been rehearsed by Buonarroti, the disciple of Babeuf. Under the Second Empire a familiar set of factors came together: the indigenous revolutionary associationism of the populace of Parisian artisans, a tradition that had little to do with Babouvist collectivism; the growing tension between the *petit peuple* of Paris and the democratic left; and, especially after the Commune, the co-optation of popular, communitarian, and Parisian traditions by socialist theoreticians. The constellation of forces in 1871 recalls that of Year II: in place of the sansculottes there were Communards; in place of Robespierre and his bourgeois Jacobins there was Léon Gambetta; and in place of Babeuf there was Marx. Gone in that analysis was the sentimentalism of 1848, and in its place was the inflexible analysis of scientific socialism, for which Babeuf was a "grand ancêtre."

This Marxist and communist adaptation of the popular Parisian myth of the Revolution is important in a number of ways. For one, it helps to explain the prestige and development of the communist movement in the twentieth century, as François Furet showed so well in *Le Passé d'une illusion.* For another, it marks an important shift in the development of Marxist thinking.

After being expelled from Prussia, where his brother-in-law, a Rhenish noble, held an important post, Karl Marx lived in Paris at 38, rue Vanneau, from November 1843 until February 1845. The young Hegelian in search of refuge arrived in the city when its intellectual prestige as the "new capital of a new world" was at its zenith. There he met Friedrich Engels for the first time at the Café de la Régence in the Palais Royal, then a Mecca for the city's chess players.

At the age of twenty-five, Marx had the idea of creating in Paris a *Deutsch-Französisches Jahrbuch,* whose purpose would be to "demystify" bourgeois ideology. His contemporary Heinrich Heine had fashioned for himself the role of cultural mediator between two audiences, one

French, the other German; and Marx, similarly, came to Paris seeking a way to reconcile the three distinct strands of his thinking: German philosophy, English political economy, and the French revolutionary experience, or French "revolutionism."[19]

In 1844 Marx's aim was to integrate lived experience with abstract thought, and he made fun of the excessive abstraction in the work of the German critic Szeliga. If he wished to understand the working class, Marx gibed, Szeliga would do better to go to Paris and watch people dance the polka at the Bal de la Chaumière, as Marx himself did from time to time. There he would discover the sensuality, joie de vivre, and humanity of the *petit peuple*. (It is an entertaining thought to imagine Marx, who was an avid reader of Eugène Sue, skipping to a polka in a Parisian dance hall, as if Marcel Carné had filmed a sentimental Marx seated at a table in the Rouge Gorge discussing Hegel with Jean Renoir, Arletty, and Pierre Brasseur.) From Paris Marx wrote to Ludwig Feuerbach, "You would have to attend a meeting of French workers [he meant Parisian workers] to appreciate the untainted vitality and nobility of these men, despite the oppressiveness of their work."[20] For Balzac—that reactionary genius—popular neighborhoods like the Faubourg Saint-Marcel, not far from the Pension Vauquer on the rue Tournefort where Père Goriot dies, were filthy places. Marx was more generous.

Marx's affinity for Paris at this stage of his life was profound, and when we read the manuscripts he wrote then, we get the impression that it was during his stay in Paris that Marx crystallized his materialist theory of history without abandoning his philosophical and voluntaristic commitments.[21] For in this Parisian and humane period of Marx's thought ideas no longer unfolded, as in Hegel, in a material void. On the one hand Marx at this juncture wanted above all to historicize and "materialize" the influence of the Enlightenment. But in this phase of his thinking he also wanted to hold on to a principle that many people today would agree with: that we understand facts not empirically but indirectly, through the ideas we form or the representations we make of those facts. Class consciousness, as Marx imagined it during his early years in Paris, was born of social fact, obviously, but also of cultural ex-

The Place Vendôme during the Commune, 1871. Posing next to the toppled statue of Napoleon are uniformed soldiers and top-hatted officials of the Paris Commune, proud of their place in the history of liberty—as they saw it—and of their city's place in that modern saga. Copyright: Collection Viollet.

perience as it was understood from one historical moment to the next, and not as a pious attitude dictated by abstraction or unquestioning materialism. In brief, in his first Parisian years Marx parted company with Hegel but did not sink into vulgar materialism.

So for Marx in the 1840s Paris was the capital of revolution not only because of its place in the world economy but above all because of its unique political character. If there was a revolution in Paris in 1848, it was not just because Europe was experiencing an industrial revolution but also because Paris had something that London or Berlin did not have, namely a living memory of other revolutions, those of 1830 and 1789.

IT IS FAR MORE DIFFICULT, however, to be so positive about the second Parisian Marx, the older Marx of 1871, the communist historian of the Paris Commune. In 1844 Marx knew and loved, or at any rate admired, the Parisian artisan, whose patience and resignation had been sorely tried by misery and disease. Thirty years later, however, the historian of the Commune overlooked important details and neglected the complexities of the capital's political aspirations. He did so, obviously, in order to present the Parisians as the politically correct harbingers of the universal class, as the vanguard of a proletariat that as he had predicted would soon take over the world; and what was true of Marx in 1871 was even more true of his disciples—especially of Lenin, who lived in Paris from July 1909 to June 1912 (he thought it a "foul hole" and much preferred London),[22] enjoyed having a drink now and then at the Closerie des Lilas, and admired bad art.

In this second Marxist perspective, the defeated Commune of 1871 ceased to be a characteristically Parisian phenomenon. It was denied its historical—and Parisian—specificity, only to become, in Marxist-Leninist dialect, little more than a stage in the irresistible rise of the working class. (In the Soviet Union people joked about the cavemen who, having read Marx, unfurled at the mouths of their caves red banners on which was written, in golden letters, "Long live slavery, an inevitable stage in the progress of the proletariat.") For the Marxist and Soviet historian, the heroes of the Commune had died for a cause they were ill-equipped to understand but for which the advent of Marxism-Leninism at last provided a full explanation.

Some facts about the Paris Commune of 1871 are therefore worth recounting. The vast majority, roughly two-thirds, of the Communards were not Marxists or even socialists: typically, when the writer Jules Vallès reproached the "historic" but nonetheless representative Charles Delescluze for his rampant and humanistic universalism, the journalist sighed that Vallès was no doubt right: "I represent the ideas of another century." The ideal of the Parisian Communards, like that of the prerevolutionary *petit peuple* and the sansculottes, was associationist and socialistic but not collectivist, a point that cannot be overemphasized, and one that can be explained in large part by the social composition of the capital at the time: out of a population of 2 million, 102,000 owned their own businesses (and 62,000 of them worked alone); an additional 27,000 were subcontractors; and only 5 percent were illiterate.[23]

To be sure, as sincere democrats, the Communards believed that the workers, being most numerous, ought to control the government of the city. But the Proudhonians who dominated the Paris Commune also understood that they would have to govern in concert with other citizens. For Delescluze, who had been a prefect in 1848, the socialists, whom he did not like at all, would have turned France into "a convent or a barracks."[24]

I do not mean to portray the Commune as a political phenomenon without a social component. The Communards were not, as some have argued, nationalist petits-bourgeois exasperated by France's defeat at the hands of the Germans and by the end of the moratorium on the payment of debts and rent that had been allowed during the siege of the city. On the contrary, the Commune was a commune of citizens, but of Parisian citizens anchored in their *quartier* rather than of mere proletarians. It encouraged participation and federative organization, and it was also Proudhonian in its emphasis on free individual expression and on the recognition of a diverse institutional structure that involved clubs and federations of both sexes, national guards, workers' associations, professional associations, and neighborhood associations. It is also of interest that many of the Communards were organized around *caisses populaires,* or credit unions, such as the Caisse d'Escompte des Associations Populaires.

And, rather curiously, the genuine proletarians of Paris, that is, the newly recruited factory workers, were on the whole less demanding politically than were the technologically old-fashioned artisans. In fact, the slaughterhouse workers of La Villette even went on strike against the administrator sent by the Commune to supervise their work.[25]

In brief, then, the typical Communard was a Parisian artisan who became an insurrectionist, but not a communist. The enthusiasm and dignity of such men, men like Eugène Varlin, who looked after the Commune's financial affairs, lent a real grandeur to an exercise that, when measured in military or political terms, often seems chaotic. But Marx was to such men as Babeuf had been to the Parisian sansculottes of 1793–1794.

MARX'S THINKING about the Commune was highly malleable. In September 1870, six months before the insurgency began, Marx himself intervened directly to prevent a Parisian insurrection—and in 1881, two years before his death, Marx even told one of his correspondents that the "Commune was not and could not be socialist."

His earlier reticence is easy to understand. Two important events of the 1860s had made an impression on Marx: the victory of the North over the South in the American Civil War and the Second Reform Bill of 1867, which extended the right to vote to most English workers. In such a political context, why have a revolution at all, and especially one that might fail? In an interview he granted to an American newspaper in August 1871, Marx opined that a popular insurrection in London would be "folly." In September 1872, in Amsterdam, he returned to this subject: the proletariat would emerge victorious everywhere, but in different ways. In America, in England, "and if I understand your institutions correctly, in Holland," there would be no revolution.

Privately, therefore, in 1870–1871 Marx believed that an insurrectionary Paris Commune would be neither necessary nor desirable. By 1871 he was in any case more of a Germanophile than a Germanophobe and more of a democrat than a revolutionary. "The French need to take a beating," he wrote to Engels on July 20, 1870. "If the Prussians win, the centralization of state power will help to concentrate the German working class. Furthermore, the preponderance of Germany will shift the center of gravity of the working-class movement away from France, and it suffices to compare the movements in the two countries since 1866 to see that the German working class is superior to the French from the standpoint of theory as well as organization."

And yet, in writing about the Paris Commune, Marx worked hard to present it as an inevitable phase of his social-political teleology, and to do this he did not hesitate to twist the facts or to ignore his own spotted record. In his *Eighteenth Brumaire* Marx had given a brilliant analysis of events from 1848 to 1851, but his book on the Commune was less a work of detached analysis than one of propaganda, which he revealingly entitled *The Civil War in France* in order to emphasize that this was an armed conflict between two governments and not a clash of political factions as in 1830 or of social factions as in 1848. His aim, all too obviously, was to assimilate the Communards' experience into the Marxist system of scientific socialism, and to achieve this end he made abundant use of the conditional: if the Commune had survived, Marx speculated, anything might have happened; it might even "have taken on a proletarian character." It is also revealing that Marx almost never alluded to the major role played by women in the Commune and, when he did touch on the subject, said nothing about its feminist aspect. Nor did he mention men like Raoul Rigault or Jules Vallès, prominent figures of bohemian Paris who were more anarchistic than they were socialist, and whom Marx despised.

Civil war there may have been, but it is important to remember that in its actual workings the Paris Commune was very mild, and far more humane in its treatment of prisoners, for example, than were the Versaillais. Economically, the Commune's most audacious act was to prohibit night work by apprentice bakers. Likewise, the Communard government did not confiscate the gold in the Banque de France—reasoning that if the rest of the nation had become the enemy of the capital, its gold did not belong to the city of Paris. These "unproletarian" acts were well known, but Marx chose to ignore that side of the issue completely. It did not fit into the abstract view that he wished to establish.

Bᴜᴛ ᴡʜʏ ꜰᴀʟꜱɪꜰʏ the Paris Commune as an instance of proletarian revolution? At the most basic level, the answer is that Marx had no choice but to try to incorporate this crucial event into his history of the period. What good would an explanation of the nineteenth century have been that didn't include the Commune?

There is a more interesting response, however: Marx was an assiduous reader of Shakespeare and Sophocles, an amateur of epic drama, and as such eager to hitch the star of Marxism to the myth of Paris, the world capital of revolution since 1789 and 1830. "Paris armed was the Revolution armed," he wrote in *The Civil War in France.* "A Parisian victory over the Prussian aggressor would have been a victory for the French worker over the French capitalist and his parasites in the state."

Within weeks of the Commune's end, Marx was writing derisively that the daily press and the telegraph were making "more myths in a single day than were created over the entire previous century." True enough, but what Marx fails to say is that in 1871 he, too, had ceased to be the philosophical historian of 1844 and had become a journalist and a fabricator. The Commune was for its participants a genuinely mythical event. But the Marxist explanation of this moment in the history of Paris was a fantasy, a calculated strategy.

FOR MORE THAN A CENTURY NOW, Paris has been situated somewhat more to the right politically than to the left. The events of 1968 were essentially the work of a student movement, hence of provincials living in Paris rather than native Parisians. The bastions of French communism were to be found not among the artisans and small shopkeepers of Paris but in the heavy industrial regions of the north and in the underdeveloped and impoverished agricultural regions of the center and the southeast, as well as in the capital's grim industrial suburbs.

Since the days of General Boulanger and his abortive coup (if such it can be called) of 1889, Paris has been on the right. In the last decades of the nineteenth century, moreover, the leading lights of the Parisian extreme left were anarchistic loners rather than socialist politicians. The leftist insurrectionist Auguste Blanqui's true successor was not the pacific socialist Jean Jaurès but Ravachol the anarchist, who was guillotined in 1892. So completely, however, did socialism and Marxism co-opt the Parisian revolutionary tradition that this is no longer easy to see.

At the same time, despite this swerve to the right and the exile of its workers to a "red belt," Paris has retained a modern and even contemporary revolutionary presence, albeit one that is *gauchiste* more than it is Marxist, especially in the usual sense of that term. Here one has to look at the ideological continuity linking what Marx wrote about *Warenfetichismus,* or commodity fetishism, with the Situationists of 1968, symbolized by Guy Debord's *Société de spectacle.*

The concept of commodity fetishism is central to our understanding of Marxist theory: as he explained in 1844, in a capitalist system (or, as we would now say, in a market economy), the exchange value of an object becomes divorced from its actual or use value. In the Middle Ages (at least in theory), an object was worth more or less what it was useful for in practice; but in modern capitalist society, where anything can be bought and sold, commodities have no intrinsic value. Their price inexplicably fluctuates from one moment to the next. Today goods are like fetishes, which have an arbitrary value that is often determined by advertisement. (The contemporary value of diamonds, for example, is in direct proportion to the efficacy of the advertising campaigns that proclaim their worth.) In this context, the price of a commodity no longer reflects the labor value that created it. Hence also, according to Walter Benjamin, the cultural significance of the collector, who can be defined as someone who struggles mightily (but vainly) against the dehumanizing anonymity of capitalism by taking the divorce between the thing and its original function to one of its logical conclusions: in Benjaminian perspective, the collector's goal is "to enter into the closest possible relation with objects that reflect the person he is. The criterion of judgment is diametrically opposed to utility and may be defined, interestingly enough, as one of completeness."[26] In other words, the collector's ideal is to collect objects which, though once useful, have become totally useless and therefore invaluable, as fetishes are.

This Marxist way of thinking, which of course ignores the positive cultural and practical effect of collecting, was an important touchstone for the Situationists, and in the 1960s they struggled to fit it in with many other (Parisian) themes such as facticity/inauthenticity, a society of spectacle, a breakdown of urban sociability, and a conversion of the producer into a consumer. It is more than a coincidence that the Situationists' view of the Paris Commune of 1871 was diametrically opposed to what the older Marx, along with Engels and Lenin, had argued.

For the rebels of 1968 the essence of the Commune of 1871 had not been its pre-proletarian aspect at all, but its spontaneity and popular involvement. For the instrumentalizing, older Marx, Paris in 1871 was a prefiguration of violent revolution. For the Situationists, Paris in 1871 was a prefiguration of Woodstock and the 1960s.

N̲O ONE IN PARIS in 1788 believed that the city could become a revolutionary center, as the Gordon riots had recently proved London to be. Mercier wrote in 1783: "A riot that could degenerate into sedition has become [in Paris] a moral impossibility." Likewise, after the failure of May 1968, it was possible to believe that Paris had sobered up once and for all.

But isn't the inauthenticity of our contemporary modernity one of our greatest woes, and especially in Paris, which is, alas, at its cutting edge? Is there anyone who does not long for greater transparency in social life and more communal feeling in social relations? It would be a strange revenge of the sansculottes and Communards, an unanticipated irony of history, a genuine but welcome surprise, if the "situation" that Debord and his followers longed for did somehow come to pass, and not just anywhere, but in Paris. In such a moment everything might be called into question, but in a peaceful, liberal-minded way. Paris might then quietly and nonviolently reconnect with its past—not in its ideological, Babouvian, and Stalinist form, but in the spirit of humane and popular associationism that once existed in both revolutionary and pre-revolutionary times.

4

Mysterious Capital of Crime

MYTHS DO NOT function in isolation. They give birth to other myths which they nurture or deny. So it was that the eighteenth-century myths of Paris as capital of the revolutionary spirit and as capital of the Republic of Letters engendered, especially after the Revolution of 1830, conservative fears of another mythical Paris characterized in negative terms as outmoded, dirty, decrepit, and criminal. If Paris, capital of revolution, was for some the wave of the future, criminal Paris was for others its fatal undertow: mythical thesis to mythical antithesis, as it were.

This "dialectic of myth" is of course reminiscent of the Marxist explanation for the emergence of new social stratifications. In this abstract realm, social classes never traveled alone: the aristocracy went with the bourgeoisie, the bourgeoisie with the proletariat. In the end it was impossible to think of one without the other. As E. P. Thompson, the Oxford Marxist and author of *The Making of the English Working Class,* once pointed out, to say "bourgeoisie" is to say "working class" as well: before there could be an English working class, there first had to be an English middle class, which defined itself in opposition to the British aristocracy, indeed in opposition to traditional society as a whole. Applied to Paris, this dualistic reasoning likewise implied in 1793 that if there were sansculottes there also had to be *honnêtes gens,* or respectable citizens, to borrow the vocabulary of the time. And this rule (dare I say structural rule?) of social duality also applies to the genesis of Parisian myths. The myth of Paris, capital of crime, of "laboring classes/dangerous classes," was a side effect of the myth of Paris, capital of modernity and of the modern self. Myths, like genders, come in twos (at least). "Anyone at all familiar with myths," Roger Caillois wrote, must see that "they develop from within, through a distinctive dialectic of auto-proliferation and auto-crystallization, which generates its own power and its own syntax."[1]

In Paris this structural process begins with the myth of Paris, capital of the Republic of Letters, to which revolutionary Paris brought even greater prestige. Around 1830, however, a parallel myth of a decaying Paris began to emerge, a myth of Paris as the reverse of modernity, of Paris beset by epidemic disease, inadequate sewers, foul odors, prostitution, and crime. This was the Paris of tainted liquids, of the polluted Seine—an affront to the cosmogonic myth of modernity, a countervailing myth, which was to be countered in turn, in the 1850s and 1880s, when this myth of decadent Paris would generate its own antithesis, the myth of Haussmannized modernity, which would in turn give rise to a new fantasy, that of antiquated, familiar, comforting old Paris.

PARIS NOW BECAME, for conservatives, a capital of crime. For the capital's bourgeoisie, the hyper-politicized Paris of 1840 was an alarming place, a hotbed of revolution and criminality, a smoldering volcano. When France sneezes, Metternich said, Europe catches pneumonia—and Paris was the center of these contagions. It would take a shrewd statesman, Metternich believed, to cling to power in such a wretched capital. The fact that Louis Philippe was able to do just that—despite being a mere citizen-king and the son of that guillotined Montagnard Conventionnel, the duc d'Orléans—won him the esteem even of Czar Nicholas I, the fallen archangel of European reaction.

The classic explanation of this reactionary anti-Parisian sentiment comes from Louis Chevalier, who argues that demographics are the key to understanding the history of Paris from 1789 to 1850. And, indeed, the evolution of the city's population during the July Monarchy *was* rather unusual. In the 1840s there were on average 18,000 deaths each

year in the city, compared with just 14,000 births. Death came easily in
Paris as it did in most large cities at the time. It also came early: the life
expectancy of a newborn in 1840 was roughly thirty years. The two-
thirds of newborns who survived the first year could expect to live to
roughly the age of 40.[2] These are the kinds of figures we associate with
the Third World today.

But despite this startling rate of mortality, Paris seemed—and actually was—woefully overpopulated. It is difficult to know precisely
what its population was: perhaps as high as 600,000 under Louis XVI,
700,000–800,000 in 1831, and over a million in 1846, an increase of
some 16,000–25,000 new residents each year from 1830 to 1840. In
this situation, as one can readily imagine, housing steadily deteriorated,
and Chevalier is at his best in describing the unhealthy conditions that
were to be found in most Parisian dwellings. During the cholera epidemic of 1832 the *Journal des débats* summed up the situation of the
poorest immigrants from the provinces, which was far worse than that of
foreign immigrants today: "A fifth [of the area of the capital] is home to
half the population. In the Arcis quarter, each person has only seven
square meters of living space, . . . and there are neighborhoods where
the typical building houses thirty, forty, or even sixty people." One
Fourierist observed that a tenth of the city's population (indigents and
unemployed workers) lived literally from the crumbs that fell from rich
men's tables. A pound of stale, second-hand bread was worth five sous in
Paris: "These crusts, mixed with pieces of meat that indigents find in
garbage heaps and with peelings from cabbages and potatoes that they
pick up here and there, form their ordinary fare."[3]

It was a dismal situation, and the better-off Parisians reacted to it,
as Chevalier notes, in two ways: first, by elaborating a theory of criminality, and second, with renewed fear of these quasi-aliens. (It was at
about this time, incidentally, that the Parisian press invented the imaginary figure known as Private Chauvin, nationalist soldier, citizen, and
farmer.) In those days most immigrants still came from northern France
(Lorraine, Brittany, Normandy), and many had blue eyes and blond hair;
nevertheless, Parisians treated them as virtual foreigners. For the Breton
novelist Emile Souvestre, the newcomers constituted a "floating popula-

tion drawn from all over Europe, people who treat our French Babylon as the continent's caravansary." Others viewed the Parisian worker as a sort of savage. The new Paris was a moral wasteland, and its proletarians were "Bedouins." For the minor but unequivocal poet J.-F. Destigny, Paris was nothing but

> un réservoir immonde
> Où viennent s'engouffrer de tous les points du monde,
> Mille torrents divers, mille fleuves de corps.
> C'est de la vase au fond, et de l'écume aux bords.
> (a filthy reservoir
> fed by a thousand torrents from every point of the globe,
> a thousand rivers of bodies,
> with muck from the bottom and scum from the fringes.)[4]

In the pages of Eugène Sue's *Mystères de Paris* one finds, among other characters, an Italian abortionist and poisoner, an English tutor, Hungarian servants, and a Creole courtesan. There are also wandering Jews, Hindus such as Prince Djalma and his faithful servant Faringhea, and the horrifying strangler, whose identity and nationality will forever remain a mystery.

And for Sue—as for many others—the "foreign-born" Parisian proletarian was also a cultural alien: "We will attempt to depict for the reader episodes from the lives of barbarians," he wrote, "as far removed from civilization as the savage tribes depicted by [James Fennimore] Cooper. But the barbarians we speak of live among us." There was no doubt about the savagery of these Parisians in the mind of another writer, the political scientist Eugène Buret, who noted "the fervor with which the most degraded segment of the poorer classes [devotes itself] to its passion for drink." The only parallel was to be found "among the savage peoples. The Negro of the coast of Africa will sell his children and even himself for a bottle of liquor. Drunkenness has done more than systematic massacres and famine to exterminate the indigenous races of North America." In Paris the working class seemed a state within a state and an arrogant one at that: for Victor Fournel, ragpickers were "disdainful of the bourgeois. They keep to themselves and form a society apart with its own customs, language, and neighborhoods, which can only be com-

pared to the foul and hideous streets where the sinister Jewish population used to huddle in the Middle Ages."[5]

In Chevalier's view, however, it was not so much xenophobia—strong
though it may have been—as the fear of Parisian criminality that shaped
the attitude of the French, and indeed the European, ruling class toward
the city's proletariat. That is why he entitled his book *Classes laborieuses,
classes dangereuses.* Since bourgeois observers of the new industrial society
had not yet read the books that Marx had not yet written, they could not
understand the workforce engendered by industry. Hence in trying to
describe these new workers, Chevalier argues, commentators tended to
fall back on the familiar vocabulary of Parisian criminality, an identification of workers with criminals that was made all the more plausible by
the fact that the two groups lived in the same neighborhoods, mired in
the same misery. To be sure, this supposed criminality was in no small
part imaginary—to judge by the statistics of the time, the fear of crime
far outpaced its reality—but that did not prevent the idea of rampant
criminality from taking hold.

On this point literature and sociology converged, if one can apply the
term "sociology" to the work of contemporaries of Auguste Comte such
as H.-A. Frégier, whose celebrated book *Des classes dangereuses* (1840)
contained descriptions of 63,000 criminals residing in the capital. Literature was not far behind, as shown both by Balzac's *Code pour les honnêtes
hommes* and by a genre that this age raised to new heights: melodrama.

René-Charles Guilbert de Pixérécourt (1773–1844), the Corneille of
the Parisian boulevard, was the hero here, since he single-handedly
wrote more than 120 plays of this type. Other writers such as Auguste
Anicet-Bourgeois, Adolphe Dennery, and Félix Pyat, the evil genius of
the Commune in 1871, likewise produced plays and novels focused on
poverty, crime, concubinage, illegitimacy, and exploitation.[6] The pulp
newspapers and, after 1850, the even more popular scandal sheets promoted by press barons such as Emile de Girardin reinforced this half-
sociological, half-literary obsession with crime. Two million readers hung
on every word written by the satirist Louis Reybaud (the inventor of
Jérôme Paturot, who was forever on the lookout for an improved "position sociale") about the provenance of a decapitated head found in Paris.

Medicine also entered into this literary and sociological obsession.

In a century that would deify science (see Chapter 6), Paris was the birthplace of a mythologized "physiology of crime." It was in that frame, for example, that Dr. Lachaise confidently explained in 1822 that "the perpetual mental labor, the constant moral effort" required by living in Paris "necessarily gives rise to a nervous susceptibility, an encephalic predominance that the physician must always bear in mind."[7] Sad to say, it is all too easy to trace a direct link between the horrors of the twentieth century and this nineteenth-century "medicalization" of Parisian criminality, which was passed on via the more or less racist pseudo-scientific work of Cesare Lombroso in Italy and Charles Perrier in France (Perrier's *Les Criminels* was published in 1900).

This vision of Paris as a cauldron of criminality reached its zenith (or nadir) in mythical accounts of the lives of great criminals, a genuine sub-genre of romantic literature. In the Paris of the 1840s, Talleyrand was seen as a diplomat of genius, Napoleon as a general of genius, Chateaubriand as a memoirist of genius (as he himself was wont to remind his readers), Delacroix as a painter of genius, Hugo as a poet of genius—and with his pen as well as his actions Pierre-François Lacenaire attempted (unsuccessfully) to position himself as the greatest and most talented literary criminal of them all. Vautrin, the antihero of Balzac's *Père Goriot,* likewise possessed all the essential traits of the proscribed genius. Was he not only an escaped convict but a homosexual, in love with young Rastignac? Nicknamed Trompe-la-Mort (Death-Deceiver), Vautrin was a diabolically clever murderer and a master criminal even more threatening because of the underground gang he led. In subsequent novels he would reappear as a Jesuit and, ultimately, as the head of the Paris police.

In 1840, then, Paris was synonymous—in life up to a point and especially in letters—with illicit violence and crime. Delphine Gay, the wife of the press baron Girardin, whose newspapers spewed forth a flood of vulgar myths and fantasies, spoke for her time when she complained in 1844 that "for the past month I've heard about nothing but nighttime assaults, muggings, and audacious robberies." What frightened her most of all, perhaps, was the "noble impartiality" of the assailants, who attacked rich and poor alike.[8]

Ever present in the Paris of the day, the obsession with criminality traveled through time as well. In the future, Paris was certain to become an unlivable city, because there would be criminals everywhere. And as for the past, hadn't the capital's *cours des miracles,* or dens of thieves, always been threatening places? Never mind that by the eighteenth century these medieval assemblies no longer existed except in legend; Elie Berthet's *Catacombes de Paris* (1854) described them in all their horror: set in the period 1770–1775, the book recounts the crimes of an anti-hero by the name of Médard Pernet, a monster blessed with the ability to see in the dark, who dreams of destroying all the monuments of Paris in order to avenge his father, who was put to the wheel in the Place de Grève years earlier. The diabolically clever Pernet manages to kidnap the novel's heroine, who is rescued in the nick of time, just as her captor is preparing to blow up the Val de Grâce Hospital (a particularly splendid example of seventeenth-century Baroque) and leave her buried in its ruins.

SPREAD BY LITERATURE and no doubt by conversation, the myth of criminal Paris changed the way wealthy Parisians saw both their city and the rest of France. In the eighteenth century people had thought of the capital as an ordinarily well-run place, more or less adequately self-managed by its corporatist institutions, so that the police of the day, although they did take a keen interest in theft and related crimes, scarcely bothered with assault and other violent acts (short of murder), leaving those for the interested parties to resolve. The streets of the capital, however dangerous, seemed safer than the highways outside the city or indeed the countryside as a whole, which were seen as extremely dangerous.[9] Paris had the bandit Cartouche (1693–1721) and his accomplices, but in the provinces there were notorious highwaymen like Mandrin (1724–1755); and it should come as no surprise that in 1789 frightened aristocrats fled from the provinces to Paris. Although the capital was actually more revolutionary at the time than the countryside, that was not the way the nobles saw their problem.

By 1840, however, the myth of Parisian crime had stood this image on its head. Now the highway was a pleasing adventure, a way out, while the country had become a refuge and the city a hotbed of crime. One consequence of this change was that Parisians—and their painters—once again saw the country, with its open spaces, beaches, and mountains, in a positive light. If Paris was the capital of crime, open spaces were, by antithesis, synonymous with innocence and happiness. Here the myth of Paris as capital of modernity had engendered the counter-myth of Paris as capital of crime, which in turn gave rise to an idyllic, George Sandesque image of the countryside, which people had previously looked down upon—and which the unrepentant Baudelaire continued to detest: "The countryside is odious to me," he wrote.[10]

But Baudelaire failed to convince anyone. Parisians now dreamed of escaping from the miasmas of the city into the great outdoors, which would soon become the promised land of migratory Impressionists. In the 1840s a vast network of railroads was designed to link the capital to its far-flung suburbs: in Flaubert's *L'Education sentimentale,* Frédéric Moreau and Rosanette are in Fontainebleau when the June 1848 uprising takes place.

As the urban equivalent of this newfound passion for the outdoors, there was also a revival of interest in the Paris garden—that is to say, in the garden that was sited within an urban conundrum that was by its very nature antithetical to gardens. The Bois de Boulogne and the English garden of the Parc Monceau (where several hundred Communards would be buried) thus stood out from the city's miasmas as visible exceptions. To be sure, the ideas of the garden as refuge and of the countryside as blessed were both very old and ubiquitous: we find them in England in the writings of Alexander Pope and in France in the work of writers from Nicolas Boileau to Jean-Jacques Rousseau, the citizen-botanist. But they gained new vigor in 1830.

Balzac's Rastignac and Stendhal's Julien Sorel were two ambitious country boys who made good in Paris. When they wanted to replenish their energy, though, they went back to the country, to Angoulême or Besançon. A Romantic poet may have longed to be applauded in Paris, but for having grasped the deeper meaning of the countryside. "Don't worry about my Village," the painter Théodore Rousseau wrote to a friend. "Even if I put the finishing touches on it in Paris, I still will have painted virginal impressions of nature. They go way back and can never be erased."[11]

How widespread was this bourgeois and Manichaean vision of a largely criminalized capital? How many Parisians thought this way? An impossible question to answer. But the fear of the urban poor was sufficiently widespread to affect the bourgeoisie's understanding of the city's social geography. For example, the people who in 1850 despised the laboring/dangerous classes had a hard time seeing a contrast within Paris that had still been quite vivid on the eve of the Revolution, namely, the contrast between the medieval neighborhoods of old Paris and the new look of the modernized capital, born of the Enlightenment and of the real estate speculation of the 1760s and 1770s.

For subjects of Louis XVI such as Louis-Sébastien Mercier, the author of *Le Tableau de Paris,* this intra-urban boundary had been perfectly plain to see: in 1789 the population density in the old centers of the capital (around Saint-Germain l'Auxerrois and Saint-André-des-Arts) stood at around a thousand people per hectare, but in the new neighborhoods it was rarely more than a hundred.[12] But this difference between medieval Paris and the newly rebuilt city of Louis XV had faded from people's minds by 1840. Théophile Gautier's contemporaries rarely spoke of eighteenth-century Paris. The Paris that had seemed so modern to Mercier in 1780 now seemed rather old-fashioned. Although Haussmann's contemporaries did not criticize Enlightenment Paris, neither did they sing its praises, because for them only two possibilities existed: Haussmann's Paris, which they fervently hoped would become a reality, and the old Paris, the existing Paris, of which they no longer wanted any part. Between these two alternatives there was no longer room for the Paris of 1760–1780.

Perhaps we will never reach agreement about the deep roots of such changes in attitude, or the source of the moral and ideological gap that separated bourgeois from proletarian in the Paris of 1840. Knowing more about the relevant statistics concerning material and social factors is an obvious first step toward solving this mystery. But we must bear in mind that the bureaucracy that assembled the facts we use to understand Paris sociologically had relatively little use for culture or psychology. It generally gathered information for some specific purpose, usually fiscal, and that information is often irrelevant to our concern. It was because Emile Durkheim failed to understand this that his research into the causes of suicide went awry. His conclusions would have been quite different if the administration had gathered data about the states of mind of desperate individuals rather than about the quantifiable aspects of their social existence.

There are, however, other ways to learn more about these changes, and Chevalier himself mentions a number of them. Why did the bourgeois of 1840 look askance at the worker? Not just because the worker was poor or even criminal but because of a clash of lifestyles: the bourgeois way of life of an earlier generation had been left behind by the bourgeoisie of 1840 but lived on in the working class.

For instance, Chevalier notes the raw language in *Les Caquets de l'accouchée* (The New Mother's Tittle-Tattle), an anonymous work that appeared in Paris in the early seventeenth century: "It is astonishing to read, especially when one thinks of the (prim) way in which the daughters and great-granddaughters of these women expressed themselves. Was there anything these contemporaries of Vert-Galant [Henri IV] and Louis XIII could not say without blushing?"[13] Might it be, then, that the Paris proletariat of 1840 still had roots in a culture that the bourgeoisie had long since dismissed as outmoded? In this context, the bourgeois would have been suspicious of the worker because the worker's thinking resembled that of the bourgeois of an earlier period, when in the meantime the bourgeois had learned to think differently. In 1730 religious faith was nearly universal; everyone, rich or poor, was more or less a believer. In 1930 few people were still religious; unanimity had thus been restored, if in a different key. In 1830, though, opinions were still divided on religion and many other points (even if they were to narrow once again during the Third Republic, owing to the "Frenchification" of the peasant masses and of immigrants to Paris from rural France, as well as to better education, improved hygiene and standards of living, national military service, and the eradication of illiteracy).

Indeed, the same argument of cultural relevance and distance can be applied further back to explain the relationship of Jacobinism to the sansculottes. For Robespierre, the sansculotte was still a potential Jacobin. There were differences, of course, but there was no insuperable cultural gap between the Club des Jacobins and the Clubs des Cordeliers. Hébert was a Cordelier who attended meetings with Jacobins. Collot d'Herbois and Billaud were Jacobins who had friends among the Cordeliers. Between the stylized bourgeois violence of the guillotine and the popular massacres of September 1792, was the gap really so wide?

For Marx and his contemporaries, however, these social continuities had been stretched to the breaking point. In Marx's moral framework (which replicated in inverted form François Guizot's bourgeois model), the working class of Paris was radically different from the bourgeoisie, even if that middle-class bourgeoisie saw itself as radical, left wing, and obedient to the dyed-in-the-wool republican Alexandre-Auguste Ledru-Rollin. For Marx, only the workers were truly on the left; and as we saw in the previous chapter, the author of *The Eighteenth Brumaire* had no sympathy for social marginals (many of them Bonapartists) or bohemians, who stood between the bourgeoisie and the new proletariat.

In the Paris of 1840, then, in the capital of modernity, only two alternatives were available: the largely criminal masses on the left; and on the right the triumphant *juste milieu*, which was rationalist, even positivist, vaguely anticlerical, hostile to public violence, and above all modern in its outlook, oriented toward the future. This was the "fragrant" Paris of Alain Corbin's *The Foul and the Fragrant*. As for the foul, there was the myth of the lower classes: turbulent, decadent, violent, and criminal.

To borrow the terms of Michel Foucault's history of medical discourse in *La Naissance de la clinique* (The Birth of the Clinic)—which Foucault himself borrowed from Georges Canguillem—there now existed a pathological Paris and a normal Paris. And the irony of it all is that the normative, modern, and sanitized Paris barely existed in 1840. It would not really come into being until the time of Haussmann.

IN 1851 Théophile Gautier railed against the vestiges of medieval Paris: "Three-quarters of the streets are nothing but rivers of black and putrid muck, as in the days of outright barbarity." What most struck him about the demolition work undertaken by Haussmann was "all the ugliness" it revealed: "One had no idea how hideous Paris was, for so much was carefully hidden away behind its boulevards, its river, and its fine streets. It is only after visiting the cesspools laid bare by the new construction that one becomes convinced of the need for all this work, which is turning the city upside down to good purpose and making a home for civilization."[14]

Within thirty years, however, a reaction would set in (and I use the word "reaction" advisedly): a new myth of Paris would overturn the modernizing myth that had shaped Gautier's perception. Arrayed against the liberal, Haussmannian myth of Paris, capital of modernity and of crime, there now arose the counter-myth of "old Paris." In 1840 old Paris seemed repellent. By 1890 it had become quite charming, rather surprising everyone, including Haussmann, who said of this new mood and of its votaries that "it is now fashionable to admire old Paris, which they know only from books"—a point of view that surprises us today, in turn, because we too are moved by the Paris of the past that Haussmann so disdained. We are glad that of all the cities of the world, old and new, Paris is the one that has taken the best care of its architectural and monumental past.

For in that context we must remember that the traces of pre-modernity are much more present in today's Paris than they are in other European capitals. Compare Paris with Berlin, for example, which has always portrayed itself as essentially cosmopolitan (Huguenot and Jewish) and modern, in ideological principle during the nineteenth century and from material necessity since 1945. As early as 1804 Mme de Staël expressed her surprise at the strange look of this modern Prussian city, which was cleverly designed but without roots and almost deliberately artificial. After years of extraordinary growth as an imperial capital, Berlin only seemed to confirm that impression. Then, during World War II, the bombing of the city and especially the siege of April 1945 destroyed much of bourgeois, "Wilhelminian" Berlin, a city that had been as imposing as it was arrogant. Postwar reconstruction then oblit-erated the city's Nazi past, just as further rebuilding since the fall of the Berlin Wall is even now effacing the last vestiges of "East German-ness." *Rote* (Red) Berlin is constantly rewriting its history: what Walter Rathenau in 1922 still called Athens on the Spree now looks more like Chicago on the Spree. And Germans seem only mildly surprised by all this. By contrast with Berlin, the image of Paris, the myth of Paris, is far more ambiguous, combining elements of ancientness with elements of novelty. Today the city does proudly display a glass pyramid, but one that sits in the courtyard of the Louvre, an ancient palace.

Of course, as in many domains of Parisian life, the origins of the reac-tion to Haussmann's modernization came more than a century before Haussmann began to wield his pickax. Mercier in the 1770s had already shown interest in the city's ancient monuments: "I infinitely prefer Gothic architecture. It is boldly svelte, and it astonishes me . . . This is an architecture of strong sensations, which strike the imagination."[15] Think, too, of Alexandre Lenoir, a Parisian by birth and an enemy of revolutionary vandalism, who in 1794 created the Musée des Antiquités Françaises. And yet most neoclassical writers had little feeling for the Gothic, and it was not until 1830 and Victor Hugo that the cult of old Paris truly blossomed into a new mythology which would soon bloom in reaction to the Haussmannian myth.

When André Gide was asked to name the greatest French poet, he re-plied with a pained look, "Victor Hugo, alas." An admirable response, and one that applies equally well to Hugo's contribution to the history of Paris. No other poet has written as much or as memorably about the city. He is the literary embodiment of France's capital, and the play-wright Auguste Vacquerie rightly quipped that the towers of Notre Dame form an H in Hugo's honor.[16] At one time or another Hugo man-aged to pluck every string of the Parisian harp: after producing a pan-orama of Paris in 1828, he became the bard of *Les Trois Glorieuses,* the three glorious days of the Revolution of 1830. Later, after styling him-self Victor, comte Hugo, and being named counselor to Louis Philippe in 1834, he wrote a panegyric to the emperor when Napoleon's ashes were returned to Paris in 1840. Still later Hugo celebrated the capital's gardens, statues, skies, and music,[17] and in 1871 he wept for the city in its year of torment.

These were great achievements, but Hugo's premier contribution to the history of the city was the reinvention of its past when he published his first great novel, *Notre-Dame de Paris* (1831). Old Paris was not just a setting for Hugo's novel. He now made of it an organic entity, a living organism, whose future should be a function of its past, an idea that he illustrated with a profusion of Parisian metaphors: the city was a "forest of steeples, of turrets, of chimneys"; in Paris, "buildings . . . have their own way of growing and spreading . . . they shoot up like pressurized sap."

Notre-Dame de Paris was an event in the history of the city, and in its wake a host of neo-Romantic writers set out to counter the rival myth of "laboring classes/dangerous classes." Instead of a Paris beset by crime and wallowing in filth, one now had a picturesque Paris, a city that was a work of art or at any rate a strange and wonderful thing, an organic whole; and Hugo's use of such metaphors proved contagious.

Alexandre Dumas, for example, in his *Isabelle de Bavière,* has two characters contemplate the city from atop a tower of the Bastille. They see "an indistinct mass of houses stretching from east to west, whose roofs seemed to run together in the dark like the shields of an army on the march."[18] In his *Fragments de Nicolas Flamel: Drame chronique,* Gérard de Nerval climbs the Tour Saint-Jacques in order to take in all of Paris at a glance: "How high this tower is! The higher I climb, the more the things of the earth seem to fall away like mist. Paris . . . all Paris is there, with its dais of haze ripped by a thousand needles . . . And what if I were to dive from here into those waves of roofs and belfries?" Sue's derogatory *Mystères de Paris* may have aroused the fears of the bourgeoisie, but in 1854 Pierre Zaccone countered that work with his own *Mystères du vieux Paris,* which painted a fictional but flattering portrait of Paris in 1547.

Many other writers, such as Alfred des Essarts, Louis Bouilhet, and Victor Fournel, followed suit and wrote copiously not only about the charms of old Paris but also about the brutality of Haussmann's project. Haussmann here was a kind of villain; in 1856 a German observer by the name of Adolf Stahr accused "the new master of Paris" of wanting to destroy the old city altogether, and in that same year the poet Charles Valette called Haussmann a "cruel demolisher":

> Je cherche Paris en vain
> Je me cherche moi-même . . .
> (I search in vain for Paris
> I am searching for myself . . .)[19]

And for Baudelaire, in a poem entitled "The Swan":

> Le vieux Paris n'est plus. La forme d'une ville
> Change plus vite hélas, que le coeur d'un mortel.
> (Old Paris is no more. The shape of a city
> changes more quickly, alas, than the heart of a mortal.)

Charles Meryon (1821–1868), whose engravings Baudelaire admired enormously, expressed this new sentiment, as Walter Benjamin saw clearly.[20]

From year to year, more and more Parisians were moved by this new nostalgia. Now people began to weep for old Paris, with its placarded walls and noise-filled streets, which Edmé Bouchardon had captured in his eighteenth-century engravings. They sighed for Paris as a whole and for each of its neighborhoods taken one by one, forgetting even then what we still forget today: that compared with the great cities of northern Europe, the four arrondissements of central Paris had suffered relatively little. For many, each neighborhood became a city unto itself, indeed a separate country, with its own customs, manners, languages, signs, and markets. Balzac's character Augustine Guillaume lives happily as a lark on the rue Saint-Denis until she decides to move to the rue du Vieux-Colombier, where she dies of boredom. Another Balzac character, Esther Gobseck, is a prostitute who becomes a saint when she moves from a bad neighborhood to a good one. In 1854 the writer Alexandre Privat d'Anglemont declared: "What is wonderful about Paris is that the customs of the people who live on one street are no more like the customs of the people who live on the next street than the customs of

Lapland resemble those of South America . . . It is this constant kaleido-scope that is so charming to observe."[21]

In 1868 Victor Fournel would say, with a tinge of nostalgia, in his *Paris nouveau et Paris futur:* "Modern Paris is a parvenu that insists it was born yesterday." In the eighteenth century, however, in the old days, to go

> from the Faubourg Saint-Germain to the Faubourg Saint-Honoré, from the Latin Quarter to the neighborhood of the Palais Royal, from the Faubourg Saint-Denis to the Chaussée d'Antin, from the boulevard des Italiens to the boulevard du Temple, was to travel from one continent to another. Then the capital was nothing but a series of distinct little villages, one for study, one for business, one for luxury, one for retirement, one for recreation and shared pleasures, yet each linked to the others by a host of subtle gradations and transitions. All this is in the process of being erased.[22]

"If no other city offers more striking or more agitated lives," explains Emile Souvestre in *Un Philosophe sous les toits* (A Philosopher in the Attic), a work to which the Académie awarded a prize in 1851, "neither does any other city offer lives more obscure or unperturbed. Big cities are like the sea: as you descend toward the bottom, you come upon a region inaccessible to bustle and noise."[23]

A T FIRST this counter-myth of old Paris was politically innocuous. For writers like Hugo and Nerval, the defense of old Paris was a literary phenomenon, even an emotional necessity, but not a political or sociological issue. Things stayed that way until about 1880, when suddenly everything changed.

Now everyone came to understand that the real Paris, the Paris of Haussmann or the revolutionaries, had been the ideologized expression of a political will to change, to modernize, to "Americanize," to accept a bourgeois present and perhaps also a mildly democratic future. The demolition of an aging, sordid city had represented—they now understood—the "irresistible march of progress." Once upon a time, Frédéric Soulié wrote in 1860, "when there were feudal nobles and suzerain lords, peasants and serfs, we had walled castles, grand palaces, tumbledown cottages, and cesspits. Today, the towers and the privileges are in ruins." And Charles Delon wrote in 1885: "The Parisian does not have a home anymore. Everyone behaves as if he lived in a cheap hotel." Liberty, equality, modernity, in other words.[24]

After 1880, however, public opinion shifted somewhat in the opposite direction. For a new Parisian right, which was soon to become populist or Boulangist and which in some respects was the precursor of twentieth-century fascism, the cult of old Paris ceased to be merely a romantic gesture, as it had been for Hugo, the apostle of progress and republicanism. Henceforth the nostalgia for old Paris was to be one of the new right's most powerful weapons in the war against the party (or parties) of the Enlightenment—parties of the revolutionary or socialist left and the capitalist, Haussmannian center.

Haussmann and modernization: for some these terms now became synonymous with capitalism, Jews, and money: "The more I study the eighteenth century," Jules de Goncourt wrote in 1861, "the more I see that its principle and purpose was amusement, pleasure, just as the principle and purpose of our century is enrichment, money . . . Life in the eighteenth century was for spending money. Modern life is for amassing it."

The great predecessor of this new sensibility was undoubtedly Balzac, the inspired—and reactionary—enemy of modernity and industry. "In working for the masses," he wrote, "modern Industry goes about destroying the creations of ancient Art, whose works were as personal to the consumer as they were to the artisan."[25]

Then, in 1867, came Louis Veuillot, an ultra-Catholic pamphleteer and an unconditional admirer of Pope Pius IX. What did modern Paris—or, to borrow the title of Emile de Labédollière's 1861 guidebook, "the new Paris"—mean to a man like Veuillot? The answer is clear:

> City without a past, full of minds without memories, hearts without sorrows, souls without love! City of uprooted multitudes, shifting piles of human dust, you can grow to become the capital of the world, [but] you will never have citizens . . . Who will live in his father's house? Who will pray in the church where he was baptized? Who will know the room in

which he first heard a child's cry or gathered in a final sigh? . . . My house has been torn down, and the earth has swallowed it up . . . The ignoble pavement has covered everything.[26]

And after these premonitory signs came a flood that began with Edouard Drumont, one of the prime movers behind populist anti-Semitism in France. (During the Occupation the boulevard du Quatre Septembre—the day on which the Republic was proclaimed in 1870 and the street where he once lived—was renamed the boulevard Edouard Drumont.) Drumont's book *Mon vieux Paris,* first published in 1878, was quite restrained. In it Drumont presented himself not as an innovator but as a follower of Gilles Corrozet, who wrote *Les Antiquités de Paris* in 1532. He even had nice things to say about Mlle de Lespinasse, the votive saint of the Enlightenment ("What prodigies of intelligence were expended in the home of this woman, who was almost poor"), and about Robespierre's close friend Camille Desmoulins ("an exquisite writer"). Drumont intended this early text to be an exercise in nostalgia, devoid of all violence, and in consequence he expressed his views mildly: "Our contemporary time, in which things pass quickly, cannot conceive of . . . duration, and it takes a few moments' thought to have any clear notion of such changelessness and stability." There is nothing very harsh in that, and many of today's futurists would agree.

By contrast, the 1893 edition of the same book was ferocious. The myth of old Paris was no longer just a pleasant dream: it had become a political weapon. What was modern, Haussmannian Paris? The distillation of a poison called the "Parisine," an "exquisite and lethal essence . . . a subtle poison." Drumont had recast his argument in resolutely anti-Semitic, xenophobic terms. Paris was a new Babylon, the capital of "European interlopism." It stood for rootlessness, noxious foreigners, and "Jewry." The Montagne Sainte-Geneviève, site of the Pantheon, which had been in such a state of decay that even Balzac found it intolerable, had now become for Drumont the epitome of Frenchness, once again under threat. Drumont saw Haussmann as a Jacobin, himself as a champion of the Vendéens. Each camp had a distinct and uncompromising image of what the capital ought to be, and in their fratricidal struggle a lamentation on the fate of old Paris could be an effective weapon. After all, as Drumont explained in 1893, "nowadays civil wars are no longer fought with rifles"—a quotation that is worth pondering by anyone who cares to retrace the stages of the often violent Franco-French War that ran from 1789 to 1944.

Of course the theme of old Paris is not and never was the exclusive province of the right. Think of the work of the Surrealists and of the photographer Eugène Atget, an admirer of working-class Paris and a socialist, perhaps even a communist sympathizer. Broadly speaking, however, it is accurate to say that the political content of the myth of old Paris shifted very sharply to the right after 1880.

Another sign of incipient fascist tendencies in Drumont is the fact that, although a personage of the right, he nevertheless admired the immanent morality of the Parisian working class, which, though temporarily seduced by the left, remained in his eyes fundamentally noble: Paris, he thought, was a city "where everyone works and where the general moral level is far higher than it is in London or Berlin."

And we find the same reactionary idea—that Parisian "Frenchness" was essentially working class and would be restored to its Gallic and noble origins if fascism miraculously triumphed—in the writing of Léon Daudet, the son of Alphonse Daudet and a convinced anti-Semite though a close friend of Proust, an even greater friend of Charles Maurras, and the number-two man in the Action Française. Daudet's *Paris vécu* (Paris from Day to Day) is a vibrant, well-written book, and one finds in it, alongside expressions of hatred for liberalism and modernity, an eloquent paean to old Paris, workaday Paris, and its quintessential citizen, the Paris worker:

> It is worth noting that the peasant, winnowing in the open air, is far more corruptible than the worker through his contacts in Suburre, the slum of ancient Rome. The working man of Paris, even if he is a boozer or a communist or a believer in neither God nor the Devil, has a traditional morality, a family morality, which protects him from the ambient rot. His irony also shields him. He makes fun of vice. He is jealous by nature and often has more respect for his own home and his neighbor's than does a bourgeois who goes to Mass and has received an education.[27]

Sad to say, two extremes were joined in their opposition to Hauss-mannian liberalism, and it is distressing to note that *Paris vécu,* the work of a man who was among the first to throw in his lot with Marshal Pétain, was a favorite book of Walter Benjamin, a German Jewish refugee and self-professed Marxist. Both the Marxist and the neo-fascist found sustenance in the cult of what they believed to be the antithesis of moneyed Paris. And so did that indefatigable allegorist Baudelaire, at once the prophet and the mortal enemy of modern life, because he was too fascinated by any reminder of the presence of evil in modernity, itself the ultimate incarnation of an eternal evil: "The Jews," wrote the author of *Les Fleurs du mal,* "those bookworms and witnesses to the Redemption . . . What a fine conspiracy it would be to organize the extermination of the Jewish race." "Céline continued in this vein," Walter Benjamin added when he annotated this passage in 1937 for a work he hoped to write about "Paris, capital of the nineteenth century," but only to conclude his note with the comment, "Facetious murderers!"[28]

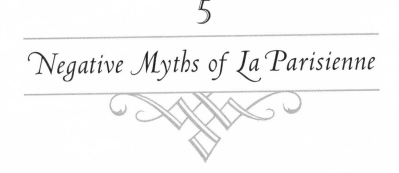

5

Negative Myths of La Parisienne

MEMORIES OF THE Paris Universal Exposition of 1900 feed our nostalgia. It seems to mark the apogee of what would soon be called La Belle Epoque, which for many people may not have been all that *belle* but which seems quite luminous when compared with what came later: the Great War; Bolshevism and its aftershocks, fascism and Nazism; the economic crisis that began in 1929; the Second World War; and the camps.

In particular, we feel nostalgia for all that was symbolized by the imposing statue by René Binet that stood at the entrance to the exposition: *La Parisienne* was the figure of a Parisian woman wrapped in drapery and portrayed in such a way as to seem chic, bold, intelligent, superficial perhaps, but free and incomparably alive, the very image of any number of heroines in the work of Anatole France, the writer everyone in Paris was reading at the time. Binet's statue was nothing less than the embodiment of a certain idea of Paris, which like so many myths of origin needed a feminine incarnation.

France's national and revolutionary saga, for example, often seemed to echo the feminized rhetoric of eighteenth-century sentimental novels bathed in tormented passion: what the suicidal Jacobin "martyrs of Prairial" felt for the Republic in 1795, Saint-Preux had felt for Julie in 1761 (in Rousseau's *La Nouvelle Heloïse*). The republicans' love of country can also be seen as a transposition of literature to another key: after Chateaubriand's *Atala*, as it were, came the republican *Marianne*. In the nineteenth century the nations of Europe often understood themselves in terms of female representations borrowed from literature. And not only nations: with the statue of La Parisienne, the city of Paris also acquired its female symbol. (At the Gare du Nord, the statue of Paris is surrounded, on lower tiers, by female statues of other cities: London is on the second tier; Berlin, on a par with Cologne, is on the third.)

A very powerful symbol it was, but a symbol of a specific kind, a stage in a complex process of elaboration and evolution, by which an often negative myth of woman evolved as the obverse of positive and masculinized myths. In the masculine world of modernity, socialist or bourgeois, the function of Parisian myths of woman was frequently to recall the ineluctable presence of superficiality, and perhaps even of malevolence. The mythical appreciation of woman in Paris, especially at mid-century, was undoubtedly linked to the imposing image of the capital, but with woman cast as the source of confusion, as the "other" to the masculine, Parisian, and modern self.

MAZARIN'S DEATH and the beginning of Louis XIV's personal reign in 1661 marked the advent in France of a first form of political modernity, or at any rate a partial secularization of sovereignty. Kings of France, "Most Christian Kings," as they were called in international treaties of the time, had always reigned by the will of God and would continue to do so, at least in theory, until June 17, 1789, when the Estates General, newly convened in Versailles, proclaimed themselves to be a sovereign and national assembly representing the sovereign people of France. As early as 1661, however, the Most Christian King, served by his grands commis, intendants, and conseillers d'Etat (many of whom were Parisians, incidentally), was not just a quasi-religious figure but also an absolute monarch, a "functionary king" or "royal machine," and as such the supreme head of a new, efficient, and rationalizing bureaucracy. The king defended the Church, but the Church from then on would even more desperately defend a state that often treated it shabbily.

Hence 1661 marks a turning point in the history of French, and Parisian, modernity. And there was a second modernization of mores in 1671, less well known than the first but perhaps just as important, which took place not in Versailles but in Paris: I am thinking of the publication of François Poullain de la Barre's *De l'éducation des dames,* which he followed in 1673 by another text entitled *De l'égalité des deux sexes.*

Poullain de la Barre, whose dates (1647–1723) are close to those of Louis XIV (1638–1715) as well as to those of other modernizers like the philosopher Malebranche (1638–1715) and Dom Pérignon (1639–1715), the inventor of champagne, was initially a Cartesian priest and, as a graduate of the Sorbonne, a Parisian to the core, who would later convert to Protestantism and end his days as a pastor in Geneva. His books, which were immediately translated into English, would inspire Condorcet, the most feminist of the great revolutionaries; John Stuart Mill in the nineteenth century; and Simone de Beauvoir of more recent memory.

Poullain's texts are a point of departure for the history of women in Paris, or at any rate for the history of the perception of Parisian femininity. For him, the inequality of the sexes was ordained not by nature at all but by the arbitrariness of custom, by religious teaching, and by habit. Women, he said, were feminine because in this world they were taught to be. God's will had little to do with it, but the will of His ministers was decisive.

In subsequent decades the thought of this modernizer influenced some but, alas, not all Enlightenment and Parisian thinkers: as is well known, the Parisian philosophes were rather divided on the question of what women were and ought to be. In the *Persian Letters,* Montesquieu, who had read Poullain, gives us a strong heroine, Roxanne, who deceives her master, a polygamous Persian fascinated by Paris. She chooses suicide over humiliation. Voltaire took a rather neutral stand on the subject of women, admiring but mocking. Diderot, on the left, was more sympathetic, especially toward women of a certain age: Antoine Thomas was somewhat less so and Rousseau, of course, much less.

On the theory of feminism, then, the Enlightenment was not of a single mind, and a similar ambivalence can be seen in Parisian *practice* during the Enlightenment, especially regarding the social and personal situation of the *salonnières* from about 1750 to 1780: Mme Geoffrin, Mme Necker, Mme de Tencin, and Mme du Deffand were prudent; Mlle de Lespinasse was passionate. The role of these women was at once crucial and circumscribed.

Strong women abounded in eighteenth-century Europe and America, from Abigail Adams in Boston to Catherine, empress of all the Russias. Women were artists of the first rank: on the right were Angelica Kauffman and Elizabeth Vigée-Lebrun, whose portraits of Marie Antoinette were widely known, as were the works (on the left) of Adélaide Labille-Guiard, who painted a likeness of Robespierre. The salonnières of Paris fit in that Promethean frame, but on a somewhat humbler level because their task was not to create but to facilitate the expression of (masculine) public opinion, opinion newly conceived as the emanation of a newfound popular sovereignty, whose relation to women would remain ambiguous for a long time to come. (In this context it is well to remember that Parisian women, though celebrated for their intelligence, vivacity, and resourcefulness, did not win the right to vote until 1944, nearly three-quarters of a century after their less sophisticated and less widely praised sister-citizens in the American state of Wyoming.)

That said, it remains true that the salonnières of 1770 no longer occupied the same position as the women of Poullain de la Barre's time. Even if the pre-revolutionary salonnière was more a communicator than a creator, she now defined herself in terms of this world rather than the next. This Parisian woman existed in her own right and not simply as someone's daughter, wife, or mother. She no longer saw herself in relation to religion, biblical narrative, or religious mythology. Mme du Deffand and Mme de Tencin were neither Christians nor *précieuses*. They were modern Diotimas, organizers, not to say Stakhanovites, of a newly politicized sensibility, as were Mlle de Lespinasse, who for twelve years received guests every day from five in the afternoon until nine at night, and Mme Geoffrin, whose indefatigable assiduousness (and ineradicable vulgarity) call to mind Proust's ineffable if less appealing Mme Verdurin—also a Parisian.

In this literary domain, then, we find a partial secularization of the female Parisian role and only a partial emancipation of women. The history of Parisian prostitution reveals a similarly mixed pattern of change. Clearly, prostitution in Paris was not peculiar to the eighteenth century or any other period, as we know from the work of Bronislaw Geremek, long the most Parisian of Polish historians and more recently the Polish minister of foreign affairs, who reminds us that Saint Louis outlawed prostitution in 1254 on the grounds that it posed a threat to Christendom.[1]

It was difficult in the eighteenth century to draw a precise line between libertinage and prostitution, but by some estimates there were as many as 20,000 prostitutes in Paris in the final decades of the ancien régime, a figure that amounts to 13 percent of the city's female population, and one which suggests that of women between the ages of 15 and 35 living in the capital in 1780, at least 25 percent worked at least part of the time as prostitutes. The average age of a Paris streetwalker in the era of Louis le Bien-Aimé was 26. Many were very young.

The late Erica-Marie Benabou has left us an excellent book about prostitution in Paris and how it was perceived before the Revolution. It is worth dwelling a moment on what she has to say, because the evolution of views on prostitution before 1789 stands in sharp contrast to the demonization and mythification of the Paris prostitute in the period 1830–1880.

In 1789 sex was for sale everywhere in Paris, but especially on the Right Bank. One possible explanation for this is the religious and celibate vocation of the Left Bank, which at that time was still significant. Large numbers of prostitutes were found in only two places on the southern side of the Seine: around the Place Maubert and in the Grenelle plain near the Ecole Militaire.

To some extent, pre-revolutionary Parisians were already terrified of prostitution in the city, but—and this is crucial—because of its physical consequences rather than its effect on morals. The "venereal danger," which Benabou calls a "collective myth," did evoke "the terrifying image of the hospital," but the prostitute was seen more as a carrier of disease than as a corrupter of bourgeois principle. The apprentice statisticians of the day applied their learned skills learnedly to measure the relationship between prostitution and disease.

In moral terms, however, Parisian prostitution in the eighteenth century still shocked relatively few people. It was part of life for men of all stations. The *femme galante* was often a woman of elegance, her home a social gathering place. It was, Benabou explains, a "meeting ground for people who very likely had nothing else in common." The *soupers galants* or *soupers de débauches* were often refined dinners attended by members of both nobilities, that of the court and that of the gown. The philosophes, though often critical of prostitution, nevertheless availed themselves of it. "When we were young," Diderot wrote in 1784, "Montesquieu, le président [Charles de Brosses, 1709–1777], and I occasionally visited the bordello. Of the three of us, le président, if adequately prepared, was the one who cut the most imposing figure."[2]

And at the other end of the social spectrum, Jacques Ménétra, that stalwart glazier and author of a diary that has since become celebrated, also liked to boast of his supposed relations with any number of "girls" (*fille,* or *fille publique,* was the preferred term for a prostitute at the time). He even thought of marrying one. And as regards the *juste milieu,* Louis-Sébastien Mercier explained that many bourgeois men went to prostitutes out of "fear of fathering an heir."[3]

Prostitution was therefore a formidable presence in pre-revolutionary Paris, but no one claimed it was a distinctive feature of the capital. On the contrary, it was seen as part of the urban condition in general. Louis-Charles Fougeret de Montbron made this point clearly despite the title of the book in which he did so, *La Capitale des Gaules ou la nouvelle Babylone* (1759): "All big cities currently suffer from the same difficulty, and one sees *filles libertines* everywhere in frightening numbers."[4] Everyone agreed, moreover, that poverty rather than bad morals was the primary cause of prostitution. Most prostitutes were thought to be young servant women of peasant origin who had lost their jobs, and prostitution was often linked to the depopulation of the countryside.

Deplorable as it might seem, then, Parisian prostitution seemed inevitable as well, and Nicolas Restif de la Bretonne, who liked to wander the streets of the capital by night, called not for abolishing prostitution but for regulating it through the establishment of "Parthenions," perhaps modeled on the municipal brothels found in southern Europe in the fifteenth and sixteenth centuries. The architect Claude-Nicolas

Ledoux gave architectural substance to these ideas in his proposed Oikema, or house of pleasure, which Benabou describes as a "gigantic bordello . . . in the service of virtue."[5] The building was to have had the form of an immense phallus, and its use was to have been reserved for unmarried youths. And to the extent that prostitution was viewed figuratively at all, it was usually seen as a symbol of political decadence: witness the notoriety of Louis XV's so-called Deer Park in Versailles (a private royal brothel) and the execrable reputation of the former prostitute Mme du Barry, who ended her days on the scaffold.

In this same register, Denis Turmeau de la Morandière, a keen observer of popular life, believed that Paris ought to be purged of prostitution, but for him this was primarily an affair of state. The Genevans had eliminated prostitution, and so had Empress Catherine: it was thanks to her, he rather oddly thought, that Russia had rid itself of the scourge of remunerated lovemaking.[6]

IN REVOLUTIONARY PARIS opinion on this issue had already begun to change. Everything was now subject to moral judgment, and we here stand clearly on the threshold of modern (and negative) mythology.

Pre-revolutionary Parisian *cahiers de doléances* (or books of grievances, drawn up by loyal subjects to draw the attention of a father king to the problems of his wards) clearly exhibited an interest in prostitution: "All the filles de joie should be driven from Paris," says one, "or, if it is felt that some must be retained, special streets and houses should be set aside for them, and special laws prescribed, from which they should not be allowed to deviate without severe punishment. They should also be subject to inspection to ensure their good health."[7]

After 1789 hard-core Jacobins were likewise deeply shocked by prostitution, especially the blatantly commercial prostitution of the Palais Royal. Pierre-Gaspard Chaumette, the prosecutor for the Hébertist Commune of Paris, a newcomer to the capital who had lived in Nevers until 1789, was particularly hard on prostitution, perhaps because his political allies suspected him of being homosexual.

This early and politicized criminalization of the profession, like revolutionary Paris itself, did not acquire its definitive form until the nineteenth century. Only during the Second Empire did it gradually become commonplace to compare the turpitude of Paris during the "imperial feast" of the 1850s to an earlier time of presumed innocence. For enlightenment on this point we can turn to the brothers Edmond and Jules de Goncourt, whose twofold literary mission was to establish the legitimacy of literary naturalism (hence the many stories they tell of contemporary prostitution) while at the same time reviving the study of the eighteenth century and especially of that century's women (three of their favorite subjects were Mme de Pompadour, Mme du Barry, and Marie Antoinette).

In 1863 the brothers ventured out to the Bois de Boulogne, where they had the opportunity to admire "toute la haute bicherie de Paris" (a description best left untranslated). "People talk about the eighteenth century," they wrote, "but in those days there were only ten famous prostitutes. Nowadays there's a whole host of people, a monde, that will devour—that is even now devouring—the (respectable) ladies of the other monde."[8]

There was also a transition at the semiological level. It was an age fertile in neologisms, which in August 1794 produced the locution "terrorism" and in 1797 gave us the word "nationalist" as it soon would give us "socialism" and "feminism"; and in Paris the harsh word *prostituée* now replaced the lighter, more neutral, more eighteenth-century term *fille*. It is said that Eskimos have many words for what we call simply "snow." Similarly, in the Paris of the 1830s and 1840s, one finds prostitutes referred to as "inchworms of love," "les Phrynées subalternes," "sirens," "infamous priestesses of the night" (Alfred de Musset), "filthy specters," "she-wolves," and "the phallophile squadron" (Auguste Barthélemy).[9]

Paris now became known as "Sodom and Gomorrah" or "Babylon," the center of world prostitution and the prime destination of the sex tourists of the day. (For comparison, note that London counted 24,000 prostitutes in 1855 compared with 34,000 for Paris, whose population was half that of the English capital. The number increased as the population of Paris and its suburbs grew: in 1925 there were some 70,000 prostitutes in the city.)[10] Indeed, the city's reputation was such that Paris itself began to be characterized as a prostitute, the greatest prostitute of all. Pierre Citron has traced the stages of this evolution. In 1832 Alexandre Dumas *père* referred to Paris as a "capricious courtesan." In 1833 Balzac in *Ferragus* called it a "great courtesan." In 1835 Victor Hugo became the first to put the image in verse:

> Ce Paris qui querelle et qui pleure
> Et qui chante ébloui par mille visions
> Comme une courtisane aux folles passions.
> (This Paris, which quarrels and weeps
> And, dazzled by a thousand visions, sings
> Like a courtesan in the grip of mad passions.)[11]

In 1833 Michel Chevalier, by then already a Saint-Simonian socialist (who later became the architect of the 1860 free trade agreement with England), apostrophized "this Babel, this Babylon, this Nineveh, this great beast of the Apocalypse, this tawdry, speckled, hoarse-voiced, slovenly prostitute . . . this great whore."[12] Finally, to round out this sample, in 1838 J.-D. Rességuier described Paris in no uncertain terms as a prostituted city, a not very flattering description that soon became a commonplace. Chancellor Bismarck, contemplating the war tax to be levied on the nation and the capital, echoed this theme: "She's a rather wealthy little lady and kept handsomely enough to pay her ransom."[13]

WHY THIS SUDDEN identification of woman, Paris, and prostitution? In all likelihood the reality of Parisian prostitution was no more sordid or depressing than before. What had changed was the perception of commercial sex. How and why did this dark myth arise?

A clue can be found in the cultural context of this issue, for it is quite striking that the equation which instinctively sprang to mind by 1850 was no longer poverty = prostitution, but prostitution = commercialization, capitalism, objectification, and alienation. For those on the left, prostitution had become the inverse of a truly natural life. In this view, bodily freedom (that is, the freedom *not* to be a prostitute) was for women what the freedom to dispose of the fruits of one's labor was for men in the work of Marx.

Olympia in Manet's 1863 painting of that name is a key. The woman in question is by no means poor. Like the respectable Mme Arnoux in *L'Education sentimentale* (whom Flaubert's misguided hero, Frédéric, took to be a "Creole," but who turned out to have been born in Chartres), Olympia employs a servant of color. But she is nonetheless herself an object, a thing: some even ascribed to her a cadaverous, greenish pallor. Having become an object, and accepting herself as such, she exhibits herself, utterly without illusions, simultaneously to her client and to the spectator. Paul Valéry would later write that she represented "the quintessence of the Impure . . . [She] arouses dreams of all that is hidden, all that survives of primitive barbarity and ritual animality, in the customs and exertions of big-city prostitution."[14]

Prostitution was no longer a diversion or an amusement, as it had been for Diderot. It was now a business, and a capitalist one at that, which the Goncourts in their novel *La Fille Elisa* aptly described: "A climb at random . . . up a stairway that beckons in the night . . . Contact . . . between two bodies that will never again touch. Rage."[15] In an 1853 letter to Louise Colet, Flaubert confessed his fascination with prostitution, which seemed to him to exist at the intersection of desire, the emptiness of human relations, and money.[16] In *L'Education sentimentale,* the great novel of the failure of a whole generation of Parisians, Rosanette, the *lorette* and mistress of Frédéric Moreau, a young man of fashion who has inherited a fortune from his uncle, is a woman born in poverty but beyond that corrupted by Parisian low life: having been sold by her mother to a bourgeois from Lyons and being suicidal, she is a pitiful character. But she is above all a luxury object, a fetish, at once the victim and the symbol of a certain type of society. Although sometimes appealing, she is more often repellent: on the Champ de Mars she eats "a slice of foie gras with affected gluttony." Her baby is stillborn, symbolizing the maternal and social disability of a woman whose life is to be bought and sold.

THE ACTUAL HISTORY of the commercialization of Parisian prostitution, as against the evolution of its images, is also of interest. Its first stage was in the renown of the Palais Royal, which was not only the birthplace of the French Revolution owing to the speech that Camille Desmoulins made there on July 12, 1789, but also, until 1820, the locus classicus of a new type of Parisian prostitution, with brochures advertising what was available and how much it cost. Benabou refers to this as the stage of "organized publicity."[17] One might also mention an 1815 painting by an anonymous artist who shrewdly called attention to the association of prostitution with the city's new arcades: the scene features courtesans, soldiers, and the offices of a money-changer. Clearer symbolism cannot be imagined. In a comic but related mode, Hortense Schneider, the Grand Duchess of Gerolstein and mistress of Napoleon III's half-brother the duc de Morny, was often called "la passage des princes," a reference to her dissolute ways (she was not wise—*pas sage*) and also a reference to the *passages* or arcades, which had become the symbol of commercial Paris).

The most salient point about nineteenth-century Parisian prostitution, however, was less in its reality than in the political and cultural burden it was made to bear. After 1830, for the anti-capitalist (and already communistic) Parisian left of the period, the exploited, mythologized, commercialized prostitute of the imperial feast (who was no longer the *fille de joie* or *fille de noces* of an earlier time) was the symbol of the inhumanity of a hyper-individualistic society in which people cared only for selfish profit and sensual self-indulgence. When work becomes prostitution, noted Walter Benjamin, prostitution becomes work. Parisian prostitution was now reconceptualized by the left as the place where the strong (rich men) encountered the weak (poor women). Which also meant, incidentally, that the reformist left took little interest in male prostitutes (*les alphonses,* as Jules de Goncourt called them).[18] Female prostitution was a social issue. Male prostitution was a moral vice and therefore beyond the reach, or beneath the notice, of political reformers.

In the socialist imagination, however, female prostitution was everywhere: bourgeois marriage itself was considered by some to be an elegant form of prostitution, as had been explained before 1800 by Mary Wollstonecraft, the English feminist, friend of the Girondins, and sometime Parisian (as well as the mother of Mary Shelley and therefore the grandmother of Frankenstein). For the left, in a curious inversion of normal purchases and sales, a bourgeois seemed to be a basically amoral man who bought a husband for his daughter by handing her over to a purchaser who also needed ready cash. In a store or a restaurant, one paid *after* being served, but one paid a prostitute *before* using her services, just as a bride's dowry and marriage contract were settled *before* the honeymoon.

Not surprisingly, the right stood this subversive reasoning on its head. For the bourgeois, anti-revolutionary right after 1830, the prostitute became the perfect symbol of the shadowy depths in which the laborious and dangerous classes voluntarily cohabited. For the left, prostitution was a kind of bourgeois vice. For the right, it symbolized the derangement of the lower orders. In the bourgeois imagination, the prostitute, as the complete antithesis of the respectable woman, was no longer seen (as before 1789) as a victim of society but rather as society's intimate enemy. Victor Hugo has a rebellious prostitute climb atop a barricade in 1848 to lift her skirts in a gesture of contempt for government troops. In response, the soldiers spontaneously fire a lethal fusillade.

Just as politics revolved around the violent struggle of right and left, so did social life now seem to revolve around two poles: on the one hand the "respectable woman" and on the other the "fallen woman," who inevitably ended up as a prostitute. Only suicide saves a corrupted Madame Bovary from what would otherwise have been her fate (and was probably to be the fate of her unfortunate daughter).

Think, too, of the many novels of Joséphine de Gaulle (1806–1886). The grandmother of Lille's most celebrated son had only one plot: a provincial girl falls into debauch and flees to Paris, the accursed capital. There she flirts with ultimate disaster only to come to her senses and realize in the end that her only hope lies in religion, family, and her native province, a thousand leagues from the capital.

Pre-revolutionary prostitution had been a general European and urban phenomenon. But under the July Monarchy prostitution became a moralized social fact and, in the imagination of the times, a primarily Parisian phenomenon. Hence it comes as no surprise to learn that between 1830 and 1880 the control of prostitution in the capital became an obsession whose most typical expression is to be found in Alexandre Parent-Duchâtelet's 1836 book, *De la prostitution dans la ville de Paris, considérée sous le rapport de l'hygiène publique, de la morale et de l'administration* (On Prostitution in the City of Paris, Considered out of Concern for Public Hygiene, Morality, and Urban Management). It is difficult to overstate the importance of this work. As Alain Corbin notes in his own book on prostitution in Paris during the late nineteenth century, "although [Parent-Duchâtelet's book] predates the period I have chosen to study by several decades, to neglect it would be to forgo any possibility of understanding the debate that unfolded over the course of the century's three final decades."[19] Parent-Duchâtelet's influence was immediate, and his book spawned any number of other works, including *Les Filles publiques de Paris, et la police qui les régit* (Public Women in Paris, and the Police Who Regulate Them; 1839), as well as books by Eugène Buret and H.-A. Frégier.

The private sexual behavior of legally married couples did not interest Parent-Duchâtelet, whom we think of as obsessed by sex and waste but who described himself as a "man of science . . . a free man with no official position . . . a man exempt from prejudice."[20] High-class courtesans and kept women did not interest him either. Unlike the sociological novelists of the later nineteenth century such as the Goncourts and Emile Zola, who were fascinated by what would later be called sexology, that is, the sexual behavior of *all* men and women, Parent-Duchâtelet was interested only in delinquency and crime. Only *les filles publiques* fell within his purview.

For him the Paris prostitute was the incarnation of absolute evil because of her fundamental place in the new sociability of the modern city: "In places where large numbers of people live together, prostitutes are as inevitable as sewers, dumps, and rubbish heaps." If there were no *filles publiques,* "the man who has desires would pervert your daughters and your servants; he would break up homes." (Note, by the way, that the association of impure women with Paris sewers proved to be a most durable theme. For example, Hitler, in a conversation just hours before his suicide, alluded to the idea that the lipstick worn by French women was made from grease obtained from the sewers of Paris.)[21]

In order to protect the pure and healthy from the impure and corrupt, it was therefore essential that prostitution be isolated and confined. Parent-Duchâtelet was obsessed above all by the idea that prostitutes might invade the city's better neighborhoods—"They are coming into society, they are all around us . . . They are invading our homes, coming inside our houses"—an especially pernicious turn of affairs because the prostitute, who had ostensibly chosen to live outside the law, still dreamed in her heart of hearts of worming her way back into a society that she had done everything in her power to destroy.[22] (In this description opera lovers will recognize the story of *La Traviata,* in which a courtesan with a heart of gold, prompted by her lover's father, voluntarily rejects a young bourgeois who is ready to introduce her into the family circle. One can also read in this plot a sense that family life in France—but especially in Paris—was unusually frail. As Balzac explained, when the French had decapitated Louis XVI they had also decapitated all fathers.)

Prostitution was hell; bourgeois respectability was paradise. So pervasive was this Manichaean mythology that not even the most intelligent people could help seeing the mingling of these two antithetical worlds as scandalous or at least piquant. Think once again of Flaubert's Frédéric Moreau, a guest of the Dambreuses, the rich, titled, cynical, and sinister couple who for Flaubert represented the essence of the July Monarchy. In their salon full of elegant women, Frédéric (but really Flaubert) observes:

> Sitting beside one another on backless seats. Their long skirts, puffed out around them, looked like waves above which their figures emerged, and their low-cut bodices revealed their bosoms to the eye. Almost every one carried a bunch of violets. The dead colour of their gloves intensified the

natural whiteness of their arms; ribbons and pearls hung down their shoulders; sometimes, when one shivered, her dress seemed about to fall. But the daring of their costumes was counterbalanced by the respectability of their faces; some wore an expression of almost ruined complacency, and this assemblage of half-naked women made him think of the inside of a harem; indeed, an even coarser comparison came into his mind.[23]

Edgar Degas would have been the perfect artist to illustrate this revealing passage.

FROM THE (SHAMELESS) mistresses of Louis XV to the (reputedly lesbian) wife of Louis XVI to the (overly intellectual) salonnières, we can follow the evolution of the negative myth of the Parisian woman. The city of Paris, now masculinized, progressed through the ages; but woman, often perceived as the incarnation of a perverted nature (an idea that obsessed Baudelaire) was seen as slowing or even reversing the march of civilization.

A negative myth then, and one that had some political effect, for example during the September massacres of 1792, when the Princesse de Lamballe had her head lopped off while hundreds of prostitutes also lost their lives; these common-law prisoners, most of whom were bludgeoned and stabbed to death, far outnumbered the political victims, the nobles and the priests who refused to swear loyalty to the revolutionary government.

Then there was the bloodbath that marked the repression of the Paris Commune in May 1871. Within a few days, roughly 20,000 Parisians were court-martialed and shot. In the long Franco-French war that began, tragically enough, with the euphoric unity of the Parisian Fête de la Fédération on July 14, 1790, nothing—from the 1793 Vendée massacres of (peasant) whites by (republican) blues and blues by whites to the tortures inflicted by the Vichy-fascist *milice* during the Second World War or the beating and killing of collaborators in 1944—can rival the vindictiveness that the soldiers of Versailles showed toward the city they recaptured in May 1871.

Having recently suffered defeat at German hands, the troops felt themselves to be in danger. Prostitutes may have been a threat to the social order, but only passively. In the minds of the soldiers, however, there was nothing passive about the (alleged) behavior of the so-called *pétroleuses* who were said to have set Paris afire. Twenty years later, in the 1890s, Daniel Halévy, the future biographer of Charles Péguy, was still struck by the aura of the Commune's Passionaria, Louise Michel, whose "powerful and ravaged ugliness had been transfigured by age . . . What she said seemed to me of little interest, but the speech itself, the organ, the piercing voice, had a strange effect."[24]

This repression was rooted in the supposed connection between political revolt and sexual immorality. For example, much of the celebrity of Raoul Rigault, the ex-bohemian who became chief of police during the Commune and who was one of the few terrorists on the Parisian side, stemmed from the belief that he had called for institutionalizing "the promiscuity of the two sexes." Concubinage, he defiantly asserted, was a "social dogma." The bourgeoisie took note.

The pétroleuses were real, but it matters more that they were very few: some women did indeed take part in the burning of the Tuileries, the Hôtel de Ville, and the Cour des Comptes (which stood at the time where the Musée d'Orsay is now), but the vast majority of the Communard incendiaries were men. Perceptions were quite independent of the facts of the matter, however. The pétroleuses can be seen as the incarnation of a myth whose origins go back to the celebrated *tricoteuses* of Year II: think of Mme Lafarge in Dickens's novel of the French Revolution, *A Tale of Two Cities*. This myth was reinforced by the ideology of the Communards and the disparity between the role women were allowed to play in the Commune and the bourgeois image of woman.[25]

Again, the myth was not made up out of whole cloth: many women had indeed been active in the Commune in many public ways. To be sure, women had been active in populist Parisian politics as far back as Year II: sansculotte women, reacting to higher food prices, had often egged their men on. And political participation in the Revolution had often involved couples as well as individual men and women. Think of Louise de Keralio and her husband, Pierre Robert, of Théophile Leclerc

Honoré Daumier, *Nadar Elevating Photography to the Height of Art*, 1862. Unfortunately, Boston rather than Paris appears to have been the first major city to be photographed from the air. Daumier's cartoon illustrates the Parisians' interest in the new medium of photography, but it also speaks to their sense—and ours—that their city possessed a particular character that could be made visible by the discerning observer, who might be a poet (Baudelaire), a novelist (Flaubert), a painter (Manet), or a photographer.

Léon Leymonnerie, *The Artists of the Opéra in Homage to the Queen of England, rue Lepelletier, August 1855*. Leymonnerie was a "topographer" in the employ of a French administrative service whose 2,000 drawings and watercolors are an unusual record of Parisian ceremonies in the 1840s and 1850s, and especially of their mise-en-scène by Haussmann. Queen Victoria and Albert visited Paris in August 1855 after Napoleon III and Eugénie had been to London in April, the two countries having been successful allies against the Russians in the Crimean War. A street in one of the most Haussmannized and renovated parts of Paris bears Victoria's name to this day.

Robert Delaunay, *The Eiffel Tower*, 1926. More than any other edifice, Eiffel's metallic tower today symbolizes Paris, a great irony given the mixed welcome it received when inaugurated in 1889. In this painting it still looks geometrical, faintly cubist, and quite commanding. But today it seems to most visitors quaint and somewhat antique: Paris, once the capital of myth and now the capital of world nostalgia.

Giuseppe Canella, *View of the City and the Pont-Neuf from the Bank of the Louvre,* 1832. Communication was a favored theme for both the painters and the photographers of Paris in the nineteenth century, as it was in real life for Haussmann: where the city had been picturesque and outmoded, the prefect would make it practical and efficacious. Known for his precise renditions of daily life, Canella presumably shows us the Pont-Neuf and the Ile de la Cité as they "really were." Traffic is dense. Pedestrians walk on both street and sidewalk. The river is still a center of life.

Adolphe Braun, *Pont-Neuf, Paris,* 1855. The feel of Braun's photograph is still that of Canella's canvas: Haussmann has yet to strike in earnest. But already the sixteenth-century Pont-Neuf, with its fetishistic statue of Henri IV, seems strangely old-fashioned. Whereas this bridge was once the heart of Parisian life, by now the center of the capital has moved to the grand boulevards, which in their Haussmannian form will become, especially on the Right Bank, the focus of Parisian modernity, both aesthetic and financial.

The Metropolitan Museum of Art, David McAlpin Fund, 1947. (47.149.27).

William Parrott, *The Quai Conti,* ca. 1843. Parrott's tranquil and romanticized rendition of this space seems particularly idyllic to those who experience it today as a (spectacularly beautiful) superhighway, car and bus infested. Parrott is also remembered for a set of twelve lithographs of the Thames and London, a match for another twelve lithographs of the Seine and Paris, a juxtaposition which reminds us that the history of Paris could also be imagined as one half of a tale of two capitals at once very similar and very different.

OPPOSITE: Thomas Shotter Boys, *Pavilion de Flore,* ca. 1839. This view of the Louvre and the Pavilion de Flore, probably done in the late 1830s, is to the right bank what Parrott's Quai Conti (almost directly across from it) was to the left bank. Partially burned down in 1871, the Pavilion de Flore was rebuilt by the architect Hector-Martin Lefuel, and in 1969, after negotiations that lasted forty years, it was handed over by the ministry of finance to the Louvre museum. In the early decades of the nineteenth century, architecture rather than wheeled traffic was Boys's favored subject; some of his renditions of this scene include isolated passersby, and some have none at all.

Thomas Shotter Boys, *Notre Dame, Paris, from the Quai St. Bernard,* ca. 1839. In this view of the banks of the Seine, with its washerwomen and its barrels of wine on their way to the neighboring Halle aux Vins, Paris looks a bit like Naples. Clearly, popular and medieval Paris seemed picturesque to Boys, but what charmed this English visitor (and his wealthy, foreign patrons) would soon repel Haussmann, who had little use for river traffic, despised run-down popular housing, and was determined to transform everything, including Notre Dame. Originally the cathedral had lorded it over the surrounding buildings, as it does here. But in Haussmann's Paris Notre Dame was monumentalized, restored, historicized, and even improved, but it was also "de-medievalized" and, like the banks of the Seine, "de-romanticized."

From *Picturesque Architecture in Paris, Ghent, Antwerp, Rouen, etc.* Typ 805.39.2315 PF, Department of Printing and Graphic Arts, Houghton Library, Harvard College Library.

Jacques-Henri Lartigue, *Avenue du Bois de Boulogne, January 1911*. After Delacroix's mythological Goddess of Liberty of 1830 and the politically correct woman of 1889 came the perversely elegant Parisienne of the Belle Epoque, whose spirit Lartigue catches in this photograph. Proust would have understood and perhaps admired this self-conscious lady with her pet dogs. The chauffeured automobile adds a touch of contemporaneity to the scene. Musée d'Orsay. © Ministère de la Culture—France / AAJHL.

and Pauline Léon, of Camille Desmoulins and his wife, of the two Rolands, and of the king and queen. In 1830, too, women had helped to build barricades and had joined their men in defending them. Nonetheless, in 1871 women were more deeply involved than ever. The women of the Commune formed their own political organizations and debated issues such as wages, rents, education, divorce, religion, and unemployment. They nursed the wounded and fed the troops. They organized the defense of their neighborhoods and in some cases fought and died on the barricades.

Of course, not everyone connected with the Commune held identical views about women: some disciples of Pierre-Joseph Proudhon shared the master's anti-feminist attitude. And women among the Communards sometimes disagreed among themselves. For example, Louise Michel held that the future of women depended more on the fate of the Commune than on what women might achieve with a revolution of their own. This view, by the way, was echoed by the Marxist parties in both Germany and France at the end of the nineteenth century: equality for women, claimed this orthodoxy, would come as a consequence of the victory of the working class as a whole. Not everyone agreed, either then or in 1871, when the Russian princess turned communist Elizabeth Dmitrieff and the Commune's only female journalist, André Léo, called for what has since come to be known as *parité,* or strict equality between men and women in all areas, including military service. Couldn't *les parisiennes* of the present accomplish feats as great as Jeanne Hachette's defense of Beauvais against Charles the Bold in 1472?

To the soldiers of Versailles, however, such differences were insignificant. In their eyes, all Communards, whether of the left or the extreme left, were potential pétroleuses, the heirs of the revolutionary vampires of 1793–94.

The pétroleuse had become for those on the right the incarnation of political evil, and from that myth a link was soon made between pétroleuse and prostitute. In the work of writers such as Léon Bloy, Alexandre Dumas *fils,* and Maxime Du Camp, certain pétroleuses leapt straight out of Paris slums like Little Poland and Greater Bohemia, or out of the Saint-Lazare hospital. (Dumas *fils* was so afraid of these revolutionary women that he became, oddly enough, a feminist. As he explained in a book published in 1880 and entitled *Les Femmes qui tuent et les femmes qui votent,* if these harpies had to be either murderers or voters, better the latter than the former.)

Prostitute, pétroleuse, and sometimes lesbian. Here was another myth of woman that had made its way in Paris. (It was around 1850, incidentally, that the word *lesbienne,* which had previously meant simply "woman of ill repute," took on its current meaning.) As early as 1824 an ordinance was issued prohibiting women residing in regulated brothels from sharing beds; and at about that time Parent-Duchâtelet denounced lesbian prostitution and the habits of prostitutes who began as hetero-sexuals but became lesbians either because they needed money or be-cause heterosexuality had become for them a purely commercial, and therefore distasteful, transaction. (In his defense, it must be said that he wrote of this with "une extreme réserve.")[26] Henri de Toulouse-Lautrec, who lived in brothels for several years, painted a number of canvases on this theme. We also have from Degas in 1879 some monotypes on this theme which are probably fragments of a series that has not survived.[27]

At the end of the nineteenth century the journalist Jean Lorrain, a professional student of decadence, went so far as to produce a detailed map of the new lesbian prostitution in Paris. This phenomenon cap-tured the attention not only of sociologists and painters but also of writ-ers. Paul Adam went so far as to offer his readers a prostitute who was a Jew as well as a lesbian. But it was Baudelaire who made the lesbian prostitute the very symbol of modern and therefore diabolical Paris. The title *Les Fleurs du mal* was not his first choice: for a while he had thought of entitling his poems *Les Lesbiennes.*

And since in Paris every myth has its counter-myth (if the basilica of Sacré Coeur was built to expiate the sins of the Commune, Monsieur Eiffel's ultra-modern tower was needed to restore the balance), so it was that in February 1874 a statue of Joan of Arc was placed on the rue des Pyramides, opposite the ruins of the Tuileries Palace alleged to have been burned to the ground by the pétroleuses. The statue has since be-come a kind of fetish. (In 1878 Monseigneur Dupanloup supposedly urged Catholic women to gather there to celebrate the hundredth anni-versary of Voltaire's death.)[28]

MYTHS ARE HARD; phantasmagorias are soft. In myth, a pre-sumed past is extended into a collective present which it simul-taneously explains and complicates. In phantasmagoria, by contrast, an artificial present is excused by a distortion of current reality that is justi-fied by simplification and embellishment of the past.

Paris 1900: La Belle Epoque. The Dreyfus Affair would soon be over. (President Loubet had just ordered the release of the Jewish officer.) The Republic had been triumphant for twenty years. Its future seemed serene. The economy was improving. (In 1913 the French were the second-wealthiest Europeans, trailing only their neighbor across the Channel.) A symbol for all this was soon found. As Louis Chevalier noted years ago, "The word *badaud* [gawker] had long since ceased to refer to a class or social type and now evokes a general characteristic of the [Parisian] population as a whole. Other types once seemed indelible as well, yet only one has survived: *La Parisienne.* Of all the myths of the capital, hers is probably the oldest, the most immutable, the most sacred. Myth? It ought to be called a dogma." Or better still, it should be called a phantasmagoria, known and admired by, among others, the 50 million visitors to the Universal Exposition of 1900 who gazed approvingly on Binet's statue.[29]

How can we describe this object of adulation, La Parisienne? As Monsieur de la Palice, that master of truism who was always stating the obvious, might have put it, she was first of all a woman—for if the Parisian spirit was perhaps masculine, the Parisianism of the Belle Epoque was above all feminine. Fanny Trollope, the novelist's mother, put it this way: "The dome of the Invalides, the towers of Notre Dame, the column of the Place Vendôme, the windmills of Montmartre, do not come home to the mind as more essentially belonging to Paris, and Paris only, than does the aspect which caps, bonnets, frills, shawls, aprons, belts, buckles, gloves—and above, though below, all things else—which shoes and stockings assume, when worn by Parisian women in the city of Paris."[30]

As Jean Favier rightly points out, *la* parisienne was the incarnation of a certain type of woman, as against *le* parisien, who was no more than a typical person residing in Paris, vain, somewhat superficial, and excitable. La Parisienne of the Belle Epoque was not necessarily venal, and even if she was, she retained her independence. Young Frenchwomen were raised far more strictly than young Englishwomen and, *a fortiori,* than young American women (as Tocqueville noted with surprise). But once grown up and married, the Frenchwoman, especially in Paris, was more independent, more her own person: "It is pretty," Jules de

Goncourt remarked in 1878, "to see a parisienne walking down the street, paying no heed to the crowd as she brushes past and smiling at her own thought."[31]

Jules Vallès made a similar observation. In London (a city in which Vallès lived for a long time and which he detested), a woman was only a quarter or a fifth of a man; in Paris, a woman was half of a couple: "She brings to the kitchen, to the teller's window, and to business as much practical sense as a London businessman." Not only was she more resourceful than her English counterpart, she was also more of a woman: "La Parisienne wins by dint of her grace and charm, her genius for grooming, her coquettish air, and the fragrance of sensuality that rises from her bosom and falls from her skirts . . . [This] native of the boulevard, who looks like the angel of vice, has more down-to-earth qualities than the Englishwoman, who seems possessed by the demon of virtue."[32]

Though individualistic, La Parisienne was also gregarious: it was impossible to imagine a Parisian woman who did not like to be seen. The guide to the Paris Exposition of 1867 notes:

> There are Parisian women who would die if they weren't able to stroll every day around the lake [in the Bois de Boulogne]. For them, this daily walk is no longer a habit but a need . . . For an hour or two these beautiful strollers thus circle the lake as squirrels circle their cages, but more slowly. They glance at one another, greet one another, and rip one another to shreds. They remark that Madame X . . . has been wearing the same green dress for a month and that, by contrast, Madame Z . . . has changed hats seven times in a week . . . In the evening this tittle-tattle is bandied about the best salons of the two faubourgs, and, like Titus of old, les parisiennes can say that they did not waste their day.[33]

This elegant Parisian woman was of course obliged to wear clothes designed by a famous couturier. For men, the center of fashion was London, where, in the novels of Maurice LeBlanc, the elegant burglar Arsène Lupin, a "gentleman cambrioleur," sent his shirts to be laundered and starched. But women's fashions were made and unmade in Paris.

There is general agreement, however, that the idea of fashion originated not in Paris (alas!) but in the Lombard plain and came to France only in the fifteenth century through the Burgundian court. Its influence in the Paris of the Grand Siècle and the Age of Enlightenment was rather diffuse: Mme de Pompadour, who took a keen interest in the arts, is shown wearing quite sumptuous dresses in François Boucher's portraits of her. But this was not fashion as such, because the function of these paintings was not to call attention to the up-to-the-minute elegance of this Parisian woman and friend of Voltaire but to accentuate her role as a patron of the arts, free-spending partner of the king, and protector of Parisian luxuries.

Rose Bertin, Marie Antoinette's dressmaker, may well have been the first artist-couturière to serve a truly international clientele, for her customers included both Russians and the Duchess of Devonshire. But this was only the timid beginning of Parisian *haute couture,* which did not come fully into its own until Parisian culture changed in about 1840 with the invention of the romantic woman-as-object, the ephemeral woman conceived as the companion of the masculinized genius, artist, banker, or celebrated military leader: "Ah, j'aime les militaires" was Hortense Schneider's best-known song. Maxime Du Camp, the author of a history of "concrete Paris," the Paris of sewers and gas pipes, wrote that "fashion is the always vain, often ridiculous, sometimes dangerous quest for an ideal superior beauty," and indeed, the crinolines and corsets of the 1860s were instruments of one of the most bizarre stylizations of the female body in the history of humanity, rivaled only by the Chinese custom of binding women's feet.[34]

Parisian fashions were blatantly artificial to the point of self-conscious silliness: as Victor Fournel observed in 1858: "In some of these splendid and charming get-ups . . . there is nothing that belongs to the woman herself: not the hair, which is dyed black and embellished with foreign braids; not the cheeks, which have been patiently manufactured out of lilies and roses; . . . [and] not the lips, cleverly colored, or the eyebrows, plucked with pincers; any more than the shoulders [or] hips . . . I shall stop here, having no wish to delve too deeply into these redoubtable mysteries." (Humorists attributed Haussmann's widening of the capital's boulevards to the need to accommodate women's more ample skirts.)[35]

The deeper explanations of the importance of fashion are complex; what can be said here as preface to that theme is that the identification of Paris with its women and fashions became so strong throughout the world that it is impossible to think of the French capital in the second half of the nineteenth century without it. In an 1867 text featuring a preface by Victor Hugo, Mme Emmeline Raymond went one step further: "It is difficult to think of Fashion without also thinking of La Parisienne. The two words are complementary, and the meaning of each would be shrunken without the other. One cannot study Paris without recognizing that the tastes and whims of its women have played an important role in establishing the supremacy that the city enjoys throughout the world. In Paris, half the female population lives off fashion, while the other half lives for fashion."[36]

Six months after the traumatizing fall of the Commune in 1871, Théophile Gautier was thinking on the same lines: "One shivers at the thought of the extravagant hats and ridiculous dresses and stupidly expensive jewels that the world would wear if Paris . . . no longer set the fashion, thereby bestowing its grace on the merest rag. Women would become ugly." Fashion now made of even the most respectable parisienne a kind of *flâneuse,* or idler, except for two things: as she was a determined buyer of merchandise, there was a certain amount of will in her idling, which will was antithetical to the true *flâneur;* and second, she did her idling not on the grand boulevards but in the grand department stores. Edmond de Goncourt wrote in 1883: "Princess Mathilde, during today's turn about her park, spoke eloquently and at length about how women's lives today are filled with questions of dress. She blamed the great department stores, where a Parisian woman now spends a few minutes of every day of her life."[37] Empress Eugénie's sartorial budget came to more than 100,000 gold francs per year.

The identification of Paris with fashion might be expanded into a series of equations: Paris = La Parisienne = fashion = actress. La Parisienne was an elegant, independent, not very sincere creature, and, perhaps for that very reason, infinitely seductive. It was often said of Réjane, for example, that she was the most parisienne of all parisiennes. Actresses, who had no choice but to make spectacles of themselves, were

necessarily spokeswomen for fashion, or rather fashions, since each actress had her own favorite couturier: for Réjane it was Jacques Doucet;
for Eve Lavallière, Parin; and for Eleonora Duse, Jean-Philippe Worth,
to whom Sarah Bernhardt once sent a desperate *petit bleu* (a message
transmitted through a system of pneumatic tubes) that read, "When
you do not help me, my roles lose their magic."[38]

For Balzac, dress was "the expression of society," but Baudelaire (to
whom we shall return) went even further, since for him artifice and disguise were the only hope for woman, that unhealthy, inferior, and hopelessly natural creature. Thus women's extravagant fashions reflected (albeit inversely) the very nature of woman, just as men's lugubrious
fashions expressed the nature of modern life. The black habit and frock
coat, he wrote, "not only have their political beauty, which is the expression of universal equality, but also their poetic beauty, which is the
expression of the public soul; an endless series of undertakers, political
undertakers, amorous undertakers, bourgeois undertakers. We are all
celebrating some burial." Not long afterward, in 1874, another poet,
Stéphane Mallarmé, published a "Gazette de la fashion" under the name
Mademoiselle Satin.[39]

From Charles Frederick Worth (an English expatriate) in 1860 to
Paul Poiret in the early 1900s, Paris fashion neutralized and fetishized
women, which brings us back once again to Walter Benjamin: every
generation, Benjamin wrote, seeks in the fashions of the immediately
preceding generation "the most radical anaphrodisiac imaginable . . .
Every fashion comprises an acerbic satire on love and contains in embryo
the most pitiless form of every perversion. Every fashion is in conflict
with organic life. Every fashion is a matchmaker that seeks to wed the
living body to the inorganic world. Fashion defends the rights of the ca-
daver over the living. The fetish . . . is its vital center."[40]

Rifâ at-Tahtâwi, a future Egyptian minister of education who was
probably the first Egyptian to write of his stay in the French capital, in a
work entitled *The Gold of Paris* (1831), was struck by the Parisian obsession with the ephemeral and unstable: "Among the traits of the French
we find curiosity, the passion for novelty, and love of change and transformation in all things, especially dress. Clothing is never constant in

France . . . This does not mean that they change their dress altogether, but they introduce variations. For example, they do not give up wearing hats in favor of turbans, but now they will wear one sort of hat, now another, different in shape and color from the first, and so on." This Muslim visitor was on the right track, but if he had looked at women as well as men, he would have emphasized the way fashions as a whole changed from year to year rather than concentrating on relatively trivial daily adjustments. Benjamin's judgment was harsher and closer to the mark: the more ephemeral a period is, "the more dependent on fashions . . . fashions are a collective medicine designed to compensate for the deadly effects of *l'oubli.*"[41]

FALLEN WOMAN, woman of luxury, vampire woman: La Parisienne was more surprising and seductive than she was amiable or sympathetic. "Ah, handsome hermit, handsome hermit!" a seductress whispers into the ear of Flaubert's poor Saint Anthony. "If you were to lay your finger on my shoulder, a train of fire would course through your veins. The possession of the least part of my body would fill you with a joy wilder than if you had conquered an empire. Bring your lips closer."

According to the myth, La Parisienne is devoured by this same selfishness and lust. Let us listen once more to that shrewd observer Mme Raymond: although it was true, she wrote in 1867, that "the selfishness of women is evident in places other than Paris . . . it will never attain the proportions it can reach in the soul of La Parisienne . . . La Parisienne does not just favor herself in every situation, she naturally sets herself up as a divinity. The only cult to which a parisienne truly devotes herself in the depths of her soul is the one in which she simultaneously plays the roles of idol and priest."[42]

Woman, parisienne, idol, goddess, egoist, vampire, unrivaled beauty. "Daughter of the God who is worshipped in Rome, fruit of the garden of Jesus," the Turkish commentator Fazil-Bey wrote around 1800 on the subject of French women, none of whom he had ever met, "you are blessed with an elegant beauty, as burnished as a bar of silver!"[43]

INDEED, but it is revealing that Roger Caillois, in his wonderful introduction to the study of the function of myth in general and myths of Paris in particular, also pondered the representations that different cultures have made of the praying mantis. For some, the mantis is diabolical: it has the evil eye. In Rome one said, "The mantis has looked at you." But for the Hottentots, the mantis was a deity that nourished its worshippers. Scientists, for their part, ask why the female mantis eats her mate: is it "out of physiological necessity or pure cruelty and sadism?"[44]

Like the praying mantis, women in Paris—and in particular La Parisienne, be she a prostitute, a pétroleuse, or an ordinary female resident of the capital—have had their mythology known the world over; but that fame has had its price. Many observers—including, curiously, many Parisian women, no doubt afflicted with "false consciousness"—have praised the supposed French pattern of sexual relations (nuanced negotiation and adaptation) and denigrated its supposed Anglo-American counterpart (brutal confrontation and exploitation). But the Parisian myths of woman as superficial and destructive—like the history of women in the capital in 1848 or 1871—do little to support this feeling of superiority.

6

Capital of Science

A MYTH THRIVES on the variety and complexity of the facts that it serves to explain. In 1830, for example, the new myth of Paris as the capital of revolution explained to Parisians the trajectory of their political destiny: in the "habitus" of Parisians, in the historical memory they distilled from their actual experiences, all residents of the capital—whether rich or poor, right or left—found the inspiration that enabled them to understand the monumentality of their city. Myth transforms and explains history, but mythical explanations are convincing only if they can be adapted to a diverse range of contexts, some concrete, others ideological—contexts with respect to which myth functions simultaneously as cause and effect.

And what was true of the political history of the capital was also true of its scientific renown: there can be no chrysalis without a cocoon, material and ideological. Later Parisian politics needed the memory of 1789 as a point of reference. The myth of Paris as the capital of world science from 1800 to 1840 needed a material base (its world-famous scientific institutions like the Muséum d'Histoire Naturelle, the Ecole Polytechnique, and the Faculté des Sciences of Paris). But just as critically, it also depended on the prestige that science enjoyed, both in the city itself and in the entire North Atlantic world.

This was a crucial conceptual frame. Alexis de Tocqueville believed that the politics of his own time, especially the protest politics of democrats and social democrats, was a kind of new religion; and, *mutatis mu-*

tandis, the same thing can be said of science in the nineteenth century: the ideologized and scientific aura of Paris, supported by its material and scientific institutions, also derived from a quasi-religious sentiment. Viewed from the standpoint of the history of science, the lives and ideas of the era's Parisian scientists were not merely a chapter within the history of Paris or even that of France; they also marked "a time and a place crucial to the history of science and Western humanity when science sought to make itself the possessor and master of men."[1]

HERE EVERYTHING was (as always) intertwined: like Paris itself, science stood at the heart of the Enlightenment idea of culture, so that it was almost inevitable that this city, already a political and cultural capital, would become a scientific capital as well. Before the Revolution of 1789, science, literature, and the arts in Paris were part of a unified whole, a single and unique culture: that of the enlightened *honnête homme.* Rousseau was an ardent botanist, and d'Alembert was not only a mathematician but an amateur musician and the author of a celebrated work entitled *Essay on the Liberty of Music* (1759), in which he sought to grant each musical genre its place in the sun. Voltaire prided himself on his ability to understand astronomy and explain Newton. (His friend Mme du Châtelet, Newton's translator, wrote a book entitled *The Institutions of Physics.*) Readers of Linnaeus did not distinguish between his style and his system but admired the confluence of his diverse talents as botanist, physician, and classifier, which made his work so much more convincing than the drier writing of his fellow botanist Antoine de Jussieu.

The myth of science, rationality, and mechanics, of a universe created by the Great Watchmaker and made comprehensible by the application of pure reason, enjoyed wide currency in the eighteenth century, and in every domain. Etienne de Condillac's eloquent title *L'Homme machine* (Man as a Machine) speaks volumes. When the First Consul asked the mathematician and astronomer Pierre-Simon de Laplace (born a marquis) what role God played in his system, Laplace replied that God was a hypothesis he did not need: the celestial machine functioned perfectly well without it.

It would be possible to multiply examples of this pan-European mechanistic mind-set: the *Kriegspiel* of Frederick the Great in Prussia sought to turn war into a scientific exercise, and what was Pierre Choderlos de Laclos's *Liaisons dangereuses* if not a Parisian and quasi-scientific manual of seduction, a compendium of mathematically infallible recipes for sexual success in the salons of the capital? To the Parisian way of thinking at the end of the Enlightenment, all lives, public or private, were data to be deciphered, hence potential objects of scientific (and soon sociological) knowledge. Emblematic of this way of thinking were various chess-playing machines, many of them of Swiss or Parisian manufacture (and on display today at the Musée National des Arts et Métiers), even if these devices were not machines at all but containers in which it was possible to conceal a child, a midget, or an amputee in such a way as to dupe credulous idolaters of rationality.

The Physiocrats, on the right end of the Enlightenment's cultural spectrum, believed that science, nature, economics, and politics together constituted a single whole, which they set out to delineate. Out of that effort came the modern field of statistics.

In the center, Condorcet, who was a marquis before becoming a Girondin deputy and then falling victim to the Terror, was also a scientist, a mathematician, an analyst, a mechanic, and even an astronomer. Among other things, he wrote about the inclination of the ecliptic and the three-body problem and "applied the calculus of probabilities to what we would call the social sciences."[2]

And on the far left, meanwhile, Jean-Nicolas Billaud-Varennes, a Montagnard with sansculotte leanings, explained politics to the Convention in terms of mechanics: "In government as in mechanics, anything that is not precisely assembled in terms of both number and extent will be hindered in its operation, leading to total disintegration."[3]

I N PARIS from 1750 to 1840, therefore, science, mechanics, universalism, and progress were terms whose meanings overlapped. The prestige of one carried over to the others. Parisians were convinced that cultural and social progress would inevitably involve scientific advances, of which Paris would—of necessity—be the primary site: to be sure,

Leonhard Euler, the mathematician from Basel who became a professor in Berlin, preferred Saint Petersburg, where, as Condorcet wrote of him in 1783, he simultaneously "ceased to calculate and to live." More typically, however, the astronomer and mathematician Joseph-Louis Lagrange, a native of Turin (and a relative of Descartes), went to Berlin for a time, where he succeeded Euler, but in the end chose to settle in Paris, where he was granted not only an official apartment in the Louvre but also an important position with the Académie des Sciences. Later he became a senator and finally, in 1808, a count of the Empire. An overlap of identity and principles, then, that would survive the Revolution and persist in Paris until roughly the Second World War: from 1789 until the relatively recent advent of ecological politics, the entire culture, but especially the left, not only in Paris but throughout Europe, would be resolutely scientistic.

For Marx, the scourge of utopian socialism and the inventor of scientific socialism, technological know-how set the pace of historical progress, of which Paris was the political laboratory. Although the author of *Das Kapital* did not actually use the word "technology," he nevertheless believed that the history and progress of mankind were triggered by "machinism" and applied science.

The democratic and republican left largely shared this view. Students of the Ecole Polytechnique defended Paris in 1814, welcomed Napoleon in 1815, and took part in the revolutions of 1830 and 1848. The engineer Gustave Eiffel dedicated his tower to science, and the names of scientists from many countries are engraved in gold letters around the periphery of its first platform, unfortunately in characters too small to be read from the ground. But Eiffel, technical man though he was, also invoked the Republic and even democracy: "I do not believe that I am being vain," he responded to Parisian critics of his work, "when I say that no project has ever been more popular. I have daily proof that there is no one in Paris, no matter how humble, who is not aware of and interested in it. Even abroad, when I travel, I am astonished by the stir it has aroused."[4]

In a similar vein, Georges Clemenceau and Jules Ferry, leaders of the Radicals and the Opportunists respectively, both wrote for the journal *Philosophie positive,* which was founded by Emile Littré and Grégoire

Wyrouboff in 1867. The political implication was obvious enough when in 1873 Littré approvingly quoted a text by the English historian Thomas Buckle to the effect that "in eighteenth-century Paris [that is, just before the French Revolution] enormous crowds attended scientific meetings; halls and amphitheaters were no longer large enough to hold the audience."[5] The parallel Littré had in mind was clear: Paris, already a scientific center in 1773, invented the Revolution shortly thereafter. Hence to anyone capable of reading history, Paris, hailed (optimistically) as a center of science in 1873, also heralded the coming triumph of republicanism in his own time. To no one's surprise, Jean Jaurès—the patron saint of applied socialism in France—proclaimed that "science is naturally republican"; and it was the Dreyfus Affair that brought together the group of physicists (Perrin, the Curies, Langevin) who dominated French scientific institutions of the final decades of the Third Republic.

One member of this group, Emile Borel, deputy director of the Ecole Normale Supérieure, was also a radical socialist deputy; in 1920 he created the Confédération des Travailleurs Intellectuels (Confederation of Intellectual Workers) to encourage progress "of the entire country toward a technological organization and a regenerated politics." In 1936 Jean Perrin, the official philosopher of the Popular Front and a man blessed, we are told, with "all the appropriate credentials," insisted that "liberation through Science . . . [is] a goal worthy of our Republic." In a report on plans to create a Palais de la Découverte (Palace of Discovery) in Paris in connection with the 1937 World's Fair, he wrote: "Over the centuries we see not only a parallelism in the specific research programs of the sciences, the arts, and even letters but also a concordance of anxieties, a superposition of simultaneous curiosities, a mutual assistance profitable to all." His Palais was built, and in a speech delivered at the Sorbonne to the Congrès du Palais de la Découverte, this representative scientist concluded on an enthusiastic note by welcoming to this Parisian palace of science his fellow "scientists of the world, on whom (as it is our duty to say without false modesty) the future and happiness of all mankind depend"—a statement that would have puzzled the inhabitants of Hiroshima in 1945.[6]

Indeed, in 1936 scientific imperialism seemed, to those on the left, so insignificant a threat that Perrin's colleague Michel Florisoone of the Direction des Beaux-Arts could recommend that the décor of the Palais de la Découverte be chosen to embody a "global aesthetic" whose purpose was to encourage "theoretical and practical exchanges" between science and the fine arts. Thus the visitors, after learning about the scientific theory of color (from the work of Eugène Chevreul, the inventor of organic chemistry, to that of James Clerk Maxwell), would be led to a series of paintings, mostly by Parisian artists (Monet, Seurat, Signac, Van Gogh, Picasso, Gris, Braque, Picabia, and Delaunay), which they would now be better equipped to understand. Similarly, sculpture by Herbin and Henri Laurens, complemented by models crafted by Gropius and Le Corbusier, would serve as "authentic sketches in geometry." And the playwright and essayist René Daumal (1908–1944) hoped to counter the irrationality of Nazism by "restoring science to the place of honor it deserves in a fundamental and real culture." All this, of course, was to be done in Paris, still the capital of the free world.[7]

Progressive Parisian science was therefore dominant, but, it must be added, not wholly hegemonic. In (futile) reaction to its domination, many nineteenth-century Parisian conservatives, especially religious conservatives, were suspicious of science and its leftist practitioners. Of course some brilliant scientists were politically on the right. In this connection it is customary to mention Augustin Cauchy (1789–1857), a legitimist baron born in Paris and celebrated as early as 1811 for his studies of regular polyhedra. Despite exceptions of this kind, however, most right-wing (or in any case extreme-right-wing) politicians were hostile to science and especially to the lessons that their progressive antagonists wished to draw from science.

The timing of anti-scientific reaction in Paris varied: for some conservatives and reactionaries, 1793 and 1794 were more than enough. Thus Antoine de Rivarol, in a 1799 pamphlet, was critical of the analytical obsessions of those heirs of the Enlightenment, the Idéologues, and of their destructive political program. At about the same time Jean-François La Harpe spoke in praise of the old scholasticism and Joseph de Maistre asserted that science cannot tell us what is truly important.[8] But other conservatives did not declare their opposition to science until

Darwinism and positivism reared their (simian?) heads: Ernest Renan's *L'Avenir de la science* (The Future of Science; 1848) was a bible for some, but it soon became a new quintessence of evil for others. So it was that Renan's contemporary Louis Veuillot in his *Odeurs de Paris* said he "always thought it was perfectly fine to ignore physics and chemistry. I have clearer ideas as a result, and I waste no time in changing systems."[9] After Hippolyte Taine and Renan died, Ferdinand Brunetière wrote three articles grouped under the title "La science et la religion," the first of which bore the programmatic subtitle "Après une visite au Vatican." "If free thought rested its hopes on the idea that science would become a religion," Brunetière intoned, "indeed the only religion, it is becoming clearer with each passing day that it will have to give them up." His primary target was his fellow Parisian Marcelin Berthelot, the "illustrious" Collège de France scientist who had said that "the universe holds no more mysteries."[10]

B UT THESE WERE VOICES in the wilderness, and in Paris from 1750 to 1950 science was a child of the Enlightenment successfully supported by the left, by the state, and by many rich Parisians: on the eve of the Revolution the city counted more than 200 private natural history collections, owned by persons as diverse as Cardinal Edouard de Rohan; the marquis de Marigny, Mme de Pompadour's brother who was superintendent of royal buildings; the atheist philosopher Paul-Henri d'Holbach; the comte d'Angiviller, who succeeded Marigny as superintendent of royal buildings; the financial minister Charles-Alexandre de Calonne; the actress Claire-Joseph Clairon; and the Prince de Conti.[11] Mention should also be made of the Athénée, or "Musée," created in 1781 by Jean-François Pilâtre de Rozier, who supervised the physics collection of Monsieur, the king's brother. Pilâtre was an intrepid aeronaut as well as a physicist; as history's first aviator, he flew, accompanied by the marquis d'Arlandes, at an altitude of 1,000 meters from the Château de la Muette to the Butte-aux-Cailles in a hot-air balloon—a balloon made in Paris on the rue de Montreuil, in the Réveillon wallpaper factory that was to become the scene of the first riot of the

Revolution in April 1789. Pilâtre soon thereafter crashed and died, a victim to his passion for flying, but the chemist Antoine Lavoisier reorganized his Musée, which was renamed "Lycée" in 1785, and before long there were three of them, and the Lycées became known as "antechambers to the academies."[12]

Science also had an important place in the capital's salons, where, for instance, Franz Anton Mesmer's experiments with animal magnetism and hypnosis became social events. On the eve of the Revolution, electricity was all the rage in the capital. Jacobins were not alone in believing that "the friction of ideas" could have beneficial consequences.

Some salons were in fact more scientific than literary. Lavoisier fell victim to the Revolution; but after 1800 his widow, remarried and now known as Mme de Rumford, presided over a salon that was probably the capital's leading scientific venue. Her contemporary Alexander von Humboldt (1769–1859), the author of *Cosmos* (which the Catholic nationalist Veuillot judged to be a "well-written book, at least in German"), also lived in Paris for several decades, where he was not only a powerful scientific personage but also a prominent socialite, adept at conversation in the Parisian style. "Sometimes he talked about science," wrote Jean-Baptiste Dumas, "and then astronomy and physics and the various branches of natural history would succeed one another in the dialogue, or, rather, monologue . . . delivered in a slow, somewhat monotonous voice." (Incidentally, Humboldt, a Parisian Prussian, also used his social influence to see to it that Jacques-Ignace Hittorf, a Parisian Rhinelander from Cologne, was awarded the commission to rebuild the Place de la Concorde.)[13]

And Dumas (no relation to the novelist), who eventually became the principal pillar of the "state scientific apparatus" in nineteenth-century

---

Phallic top hats were everywhere in mid-nineteenth-century Paris, in the paintings of Manet, for example, and in this scene from the Universal Exposition of 1878. Balloons were also prestigious. In 1870 it was in a balloon that Léon Gambetta escaped a besieged Paris to lead the resistance to the Prussian invaders. And this balloon of 1878 seems pleasingly complex, sturdy, and scientific. It is tethered to the earth in the Cour du Louvre, now the site of I. M. Pei's glass pyramid. The Burndy Library, Dibner Institute for the History of Science and Technology, Cambridge, Massachusetts.

L'EXPOSITION DE PARIS

JOURNAL HEBDOMADAIRE

Prix du numéro : 50 centimes

ABONNEMENTS. — PARIS : **14 FR.** — DÉPARTEMENTS : **16 FR.**

Rédacteur en chef : **Adolphe BITARD**

N° 23. — 7 SEPTEMBRE 1878

BUREAUX
7, RUE DU CROISSANT, PARIS

Prix du numéro : 50 centimes.

LA PUBLICATION SERA COMPLÈTE EN **30** NUMÉROS

Adresser les mandats à l'ordre de l'administrateur.

LE BALLON CAPTIF. — L'APPAREILLAGE DE LA NACELLE.

Paris, also moved in the upper strata of society. Isidore Salle, the author of *Histoire naturelle drolatique et philosophique des professeurs du Jardin des Plantes* (Natural, Recreational, and Philosophical History of Professors at the Jardin des Plantes; 1847), tells the story of Dumas's irresistible rise. Although ill at ease in public initially, the young provincial from Alès "worked with such perseverance that within a few years he became an excellent professor. His speech acquired elegance: he now spoke clearly and precisely and at last learned to profess properly, or nearly so."[14]

In this period, then, the propagation of scientific ideas in Paris took place in private as often as it did in public. Arcueil, for example, became an important quasi-official center of scientific research because the chemist Claude Berthollet decided to buy a house and set up his laboratory there in 1801. (Joseph-Louis Gay-Lussac would be his first assistant.) In 1806 Laplace also moved there, and in 1807 a Société d'Arcueil was established, a private but also public entity since Berthollet received a subsidy of 150,000 francs from Napoleon in 1807. (Berthollet was a senator as well as a scientist, and as such received an annual salary of 22,000 francs plus the use of the erstwhile episcopal palace of Narbonne.)

The Société d'Arcueil eventually boasted as many as fifteen members, nine of whom became correspondents of the London Royal Society. These Parisians published research reports in 1807, 1809, and 1817 and met every other week (except in December and January because of the harsh winter weather and the distance between this then-remote suburb and the capital) until the 1820s. The English scientists Humphry Davy and John Dalton met with their colleagues in Arcueil, whose Société exerted a substantial influence on the evolution of the Ecole Polytechnique.

I MPORTANT AS SUCH private or semi-private associations were, the direct support of Parisian science by the machinery of state (whether in the hands of the right or the left) was yet more crucial. One can conceivably imagine Delacroix painting *Liberty Leading the People* without the support of Louis Philippe or the approval of the salons, but it is difficult to imagine scientific research in Paris without the Muséum d'Histoire Naturelle or the Académie des Sciences or even the Sorbonne, and it is particularly revealing that the relations between science and the state were already close in the seventeenth century.

The ancien régime can be imagined as a deeply schizophrenic political system. To be sure, the regime's role in modernization was the less visible of its two faces. What one saw in Paris was primarily the ceremonial aspect: royal entries, the birthdays and weddings of princes of the blood, the court etiquette, and the close relationship of church and state. All of this constantly reminded the subjects of the Most Christian King that the ritual of monarchy was the embodiment of all the ancient traditions of the French nation and also that their monarch was descended from two saints, Charlemagne and Saint Louis.

Gradually, however, this medieval conception of shared sovereignty developed a new offshoot, which grew vigorously from the time of Richelieu: a second, far more important monarchy, administrative rather than ceremonial, efficient and rationalized in its operations, which involved dossiers and censuses and functionaries and intendants and councils, some of which still exist today. This (somewhat confused) vocation of modernity led in 1666 to the creation, by Jean-Baptiste Colbert, Louis XIV's finance minister, of the Académie Royale des Sciences, located in Paris. No other seventeenth-century scientific institution, including the Royal Society of London, a decade older than its French counterpart, received more consistent financial support, a fact that is especially striking because financially the final years of Louis XIV's reign were among the most difficult of the monarchy.

In return for this aid, the Académie dutifully served the state. Parisian academicians accepted the monarchy's imprimatur as well as its subsidies, and in 1699 were even granted a home in the royal apartments of the Louvre, though they had to share it with the skeleton of an elephant dissected by Claude Perrault. Academicians received a space, and the academicians in return allowed the Bourbon monarchy to present itself as a model of modernity and efficiency. In addition, the state looked to its scientists for certain kinds of practical assistance, especially after the marquis de Louvois replaced Colbert. As the Académie's charter indicated, these official scientists were not to occupy themselves exclusively with "curious researches" or "chemists' amusements"; they were expected to engage in useful research bearing some "relation to the service of the king and the State."[15] They could be cartographers, for instance, and offer advice on matters of relevance to a ubiquitous mercantilist state on subjects ranging from public health and epidemics to the architecture of royal palaces. Meetings of the Académie des Sciences, though closed to the general public, drew wide public attention, and Louis-Sébastien Mercier noted that "nowadays even the most insignificant of artisans comes with blessings from that illustrious body."[16]

The eighteenth century is sometimes thought of as a time of titanic struggle between an obscurantist state (Voltaire's *l'infâme*) and the forces of the future, of the Enlightenment, whose triumph would come at last in 1789. This reading relies too heavily on the judgment of the revolutionaries themselves, and it neglects the many ways in which the monarchic state was powerfully allied with the forces of Parisian modernity, not only in science, but also in the realm of letters. Speaking for his colleagues in the Académie Française a century before the Revolution, the playwright Jean Racine had gone so far as to say that "all the words of the language, all of its syllables, seem precious to us because we look upon them as instruments to serve the glory of our august protector."[17] Voltaire was a less dithyrambic but equally polished courtier, not only in Potsdam with Frederick the Great but also in France, where, as a protégé of Mme de Pompadour, he obtained the post of royal historiographer. And speaking of Voltaire, the Montagnard and model revolutionary Abbé Grégoire later called him the "toadying poet of the court and the reigning divinities."

The close relationship between the ancien régime and the academies, those handmaidens of the Enlightenment, ended only with the disappearance of both in the torments of the Revolution: before 1789, Lavoisier, a fermier général or tax farmer (who was guillotined in 1794), and the comte de Buffon, a man ennobled by Louis XV, were both great scientists and men who enjoyed great privileges.

Science and state-sponsored academies; science and educational institutions: the latter link was not as tight before 1789 as it became at the

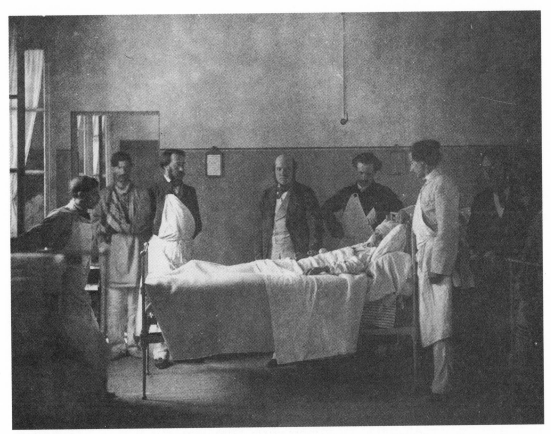

Charles Nègre, *Imperial Asylum at Vincennes; The Doctor's Visit,* 1860. In our age of digital reproduction, photographs of earlier times have become auratic. This rendition of a Paris hospital seems strangely poetic to us, at once stylized and true, artificial and unique. The solemn physician surely thought of himself as immensely learned. By 1860 many non-Parisian scientists were probably less convinced of this than he was. Philadelphia Museum of Art: Purchased: Smith, Kline, and French Foundation Fund, 1971.

end of the nineteenth century. Yet pre-revolutionary French higher education, in the nation at large and also in Paris, though largely controlled by the Church, was probably less hostile to science than people used to think. The twenty-two French universities included ten faculties of medicine, some of which were world famous. (It was to attend one of them that Laurence Sterne, the author of *Tristram Shandy,* lived for a time in Montpellier.) And in pre-revolutionary Paris anatomy was taught at the Jardin du Roi and at the Sorbonne (which, along with Montpellier, was the birthplace of French physiology). Physics also figured in the curriculum of most pre-revolutionary Parisian *collèges* (secondary schools), especially those run by the Oratorians. It was not until the middle decades of the nineteenth century that the Collège de France came into its own, yet even before the Revolution (which the institution weathered without undue difficulty) this jewel of Parisian academic life offered instruction in mathematics, physics, experimental physics, astronomy, chemistry, history, philosophy, rhetoric, poetry, French, Greek, Arabic, Persian, and Turkish.

FOR THESE MANY REASONS, the *esprit géométrique* did not await the Revolution to establish itself in Paris, and the Revolution in no way impeded its development. Indeed, the revolutionary spirit, even in its harshest Jacobin variants, was favorable to the development of science, despite the execution of Lavoisier, who died not as a scientist but as a former tax collector. Many Parisian scientists were prominent revolutionaries, such as the astronomer and historian of science Jean-Sylvain Bailly, who in 1789 belonged to three academies and became the first mayor of Paris; Joseph-Louis Lagrange; Laplace; Gaspard Monge; Joseph Fourier; the chemists Antoine Fourcroy and Claude Berthollet; Marat; Cabanis, Mirabeau's doctor; and finally Jean-Henri Hassenfratz, a hardcore Jacobin and scourge of the Girondins as well as an "incompetent professor."[18] In the political life of this so-called bourgeois and mercantile revolution, scientists and publicists were far more numerous and played a far more important role than did bankers, manufacturers, shipping magnates, or industrialists.

Also numerous and popular in revolutionary Paris were applications of new scientific discoveries. For François de Neufchâteau (who would later organize the first Parisian industrial fair), one of the goals of the Revolution was to ennoble the mechanical arts that ancien régime's academies had neglected. As he explained in Paris in 1798:

These arts, which the ancien régime thought to debase by calling them mechanical, and which had long been left to instinct and routine, are nevertheless amenable to deep study and unlimited progress . . . Diderot hoped that they would have their own academy, but despotism was a long way from understanding him! It saw in the arts only slaves of idle luxury, not instruments of social happiness . . . The commonest arts, seemingly the most simple, are illuminated by the light of science. Mathematics, physics, chemistry, and design applied to the arts and crafts ought to guide their methods, improve their machines, simplify their forms, and, by doubling their success, diminish the amount of labor they require.

One might be listening to a speech by an International Monetary Fund expert to some Third World country today.

So numerous were the practical applications of scientific knowledge that the Convention, responding to a proposal from Abbé Grégoire in October 1794, decided to create a Conservatoire des Arts et Métiers in Paris to serve as "a public repository of machines, models, tools, descriptions, and books of all the varieties of arts and crafts." (Note, by the way, that the full, and premonitory, title of Diderot's encyclopedia was *Encyclopédie ou dictionnaire raisonné des sciences, des arts, et des métiers par une société de gens de lettres* [Encyclopedia or Comprehensive Dictionary of the Sciences, the Arts, and the Trades, by a Society of Men of Letters].) In this, the world's first museum of science, citizen-demonstrators would explain to Parisian citizens how all these things worked, for "there is no citizen who is not interested in the progress of the arts and crafts," an admirable and revolutionary idea, even if its implementation had to await the arrival of Napoleon. By March 1806 a visitor could comment that the Conservatoire "has long been regarded by artists and amateurs as one of the most useful establishments in the French Empire . . . Since it has the advantage of being the only one of its kind in Europe, foreigners (and Frenchmen) are eager to admire and study the various models on display in its galleries."[19]

Nonetheless, the Revolution's chief contribution to the future of science in Paris was not ideological, nor did it have anything to do with the favorable attitude of the revolutionary authorities toward the mechanical arts. Rather, it involved the establishment, or encouragement, of an educational system based on a series of *grandes écoles,* about which opinion has been divided ever since. In the sciences, however, these schools were virtually without equal in Europe or North America for some five decades, until about 1850.

To be sure, the Revolution did not invent the *grandes écoles.* The Ecole des Ponts et Chaussées was founded in 1747 to train engineers under the direction of Daniel Trudaine, a Parisian, and Jean-Rodolphe Peronnet, a master bridge builder and creator of the sewer under the quai des Tuileries, which can be seen as a trial run for Haussmann's rebuilding of the city's drainage system. Somewhat later, in 1778, the Ecole des Mines was founded in Paris and initially housed in the new Hôtel des Monnaies (Mint), the first building anywhere in the world designed specifically to house those departments of the government devoted to currency, which had previously found space wherever they could in royal palaces and even private mansions.

The Revolution, then, did not initiate but did dramatically accelerate the development of higher education in Paris, with the founding of the Ecole Normale in 1794 and the Ecole Polytechnique in 1795. Monge, Laplace, Louis Daubenton, Constantin de Volney, and Jacques-Henri Bernardin de Saint-Pierre taught in these institutions. Symbolically, it was to the Ecole Polytechnique that Napoleon entrusted the most powerful electrical "pile" or battery available at the time so that its scientists could vie with Humphry Davy in England and Alessandro Volta in Italy.[20]

Parisian science and politics cohabited happily to 1800, and after that as well: Bonaparte's relations with the great writers of the time (Mme de Staël and Chateaubriand) were strained, but his dealings with the scientific establishment were relatively serene. As a student at the Académie Militaire of Paris, he had taken courses in 1785 from Louis Monge (less well known than his celebrated mathematical brother Gaspard) and from the marquis de Laplace, who was one of his examiners before the Revolution and would later serve briefly as his minister of the interior. It was not uncharacteristic that the young general should have searched in Italy for the mercury that the chemist Berthollet needed in Paris, or that Berthollet should have later followed Bonaparte to Egypt, where he joined Monge in directing the celebrated Institut d'Egypte. (There is today in Cairo, as there is in Paris, a rue Monge.) In 1797 Bonaparte himself was elected a member of the Institut National (which had been created in 1795 to take the place of the royal academies), in the section of mathematical and physical sciences, and in 1799 Laplace dedicated the first volume of his *Mécanique céleste* (Celestial Mechanics) to his young colleague. As president of the section, Bonaparte took care to establish a well-publicized prize for the study of "voltaic electricity."

As one might expect, the emperor's interest in science was not disinterested. He wanted something in return, and in his eyes the primary purpose of science was to serve the state, as is evident from his decision to militarize the Ecole Polytechnique in 1804—a decision against which, as it happens, Monge, Berthollet, and Fourcroy vainly protested. The emperor expected that, like the Université Impériale of 1808, Parisian scientific institutions would, if not pay their own way, then at least produce practical results as well as offer docile political support to his regime. In fact, many scientists, such as Jean-Antoine Chaptal, served in high-ranking positions in the imperial government. Like other authoritarian regimes in France, the Napoleonic regime appreciated the help of prestigious technocrats, who were in theory competent men unlikely to be troubled by pangs of conscience.

In brief, then, during the First Empire Parisian science had become, literally, an affair of state, and we see this in an unusual accord between France and Switzerland, which provided that "twenty young Helvetians shall be admitted to the Ecole Polytechnique of France after taking the examinations prescribed by the rules."[21]

SCIENCE WAS THE PROVINCE of the left. The Restoration situated itself on the right. Yet the emperor's fall had almost no effect on the development of science in Paris. And the period from 1815 to 1835 or so was, paradoxically, among the most brilliant in the history of Parisian science. This was the age of Jean-François Champollion and his study of hieroglyphics; Berthollet and chemistry; the Belgian-born Jacques Quételet and statistics; Jean-Baptiste Lamarck, Darwin's precursor; Etienne Geoffroy Saint-Hilaire and Georges Cuvier (both professors of biology at the Collège de France); Laplace, Lagrange, and Jean-Baptiste Fourier in mathematics. The number of people doing scientific research in Paris doubled between 1775 and 1825. Victor Hugo and Edgar Quinet, before finding their paths in life, dreamed of attending the Ecole Polytechnique, and Stendhal wrote in 1828 that he knew "only one place on earth where large numbers of young men, as they call themselves, are doing serious work. That is Paris, and the workers are youths who hope to make themselves famous by means of new discoveries in the natural sciences and thus win admission to the Académie des Sciences of Paris, the only good one."[22]

Parisian science, though potentially republican, could not be ignored by the political right; and it continued to thrive in schools, in academies, and, until the death of Geoffroy Saint-Hilaire in 1844, in the Muséum d'Histoire Naturelle, whose origins can be traced back to the old Jardin du Roi. (Founded in 1640 by Guy de la Brosse, a bold innovator in his day and a fierce critic—in French rather than Latin—of Aristotle, the institution had later been directed by Buffon, named to his post in 1739, at the age of thirty-nine. Jacques-Henri Bernardin de Saint-Pierre, the author of *Paul et Virginie,* had held the post in June 1794, when the Revolution transformed the royal garden into a genuine scientific institution.)

The Muséum d'Histoire Naturelle was "without rival anywhere in Europe."[23] Having become a research center, it began publishing its own periodical in 1802. Its library, open to the public, held approximately 15,000 volumes by 1822, and its collection of quadrupeds and birds, which numbered some 1,500 specimens in 1789, had grown to 40,000 by 1820. A chair of comparative physiology was set up there in 1837 for Frédéric Cuvier, the brother of the paleontologist Georges Cuvier. The museum's budget of 300,000 francs was considerable for the time: in 1825 the Académie de Médecine received only 196,000 francs and the Faculté des Sciences only 75,000. The museum's professors were paid 5,000 francs annually, an amount comparable to the (high) salaries paid to professors at the Collège de France. (Workers earned about 500 francs a year in those days.) Buffon's post-revolutionary emulators also lived in official apartments, and Adolphe Thiers, as first president of the Third Republic, offered them even higher pay. Many foreigners sought positions there as well, including Alexander von Humboldt and the Swiss Louis Agassiz, who ended up in the United States as a professor at Harvard University.

A stellar array of talent, which, once assembled, attracted still more talent. So it was, a bit later, that Jean-Baptiste Dumas, welcoming Joseph Bertrand into the Académie Française, congratulated his new colleague for understanding how much he owed to his predecessors, great men like Alexandre Brogniart, Dominique Arago, Laplace, Cuvier, Geoffroy Saint-Hilaire, André-Marie Ampère, and Louis-Jacques Thénard. And Dumas knew whereof he spoke: hardly had he been chosen to serve as Alexander von Humboldt's secretary when he "began to reflect on the fact that Paris was the only place where, under the auspices of teachers of physics and chemistry with whom I hoped soon to make my mark, I could find the advice and assistance I needed to carry out the work I had been meditating for some time. My mind was quickly made up: I must go to Paris." To Henri-Alphonse Esquiros, Paris was symbolically the book in which his life would be written, and he turned this exercise into a clever history of the capital that began with the Jardin des Plantes and proceeded from plants to animals and then to man and, finally, to the Parisian. Goethe had science in mind as much as literature in his 1827 encomium to Ampère, who had made "something of himself at twenty-four" in that "universal city, where every step onto a bridge or square recalls a grand past" and "where the finest minds of a great empire are gathered."[24]

THERE ARE OF COURSE many reasons for the flourishing of science in Paris in the 1820s and 1830s. One issue not yet mentioned was the city's vampiric relation to the rest of France: very simply, the scientific establishment of the capital thrived in no small part because it had far more and far better endowed scientific institutions than any other French city. Indeed, Auguste Comte, though a native of Montpellier, went so far as to suggest that the concentration of scientific endeavor in Paris was beneficial not only for the growth of institutions but also for the structure of scientific thought, because it encouraged the formation of an "instinct for contemplation and generality."[25]

Although the first signs of "Parisianization" began to appear during the ancien régime (when the Jesuits, for example, acquired the habit of training teachers in Paris), provincial scientists were still numerous before 1789, and provincial academies, especially the one in Caen, were still important centers. In this respect, as in so many others, the Revolution marks a break:[26] during both the Empire, which was centralist on principle, and the Restoration, which supposedly favored decentralization but did precious little on its behalf, the faculties of medicine in Strasbourg and Montpellier languished. J.-D. Gergonne established his *Annales de mathématiques* in Nîmes and Montpellier, but in 1836 the journal moved to Paris. In Lille Pasteur could draw no more than 250 people to his lectures, whereas at the Sorbonne Dumas taught as many as 1,000.

Provincial scientific institutions were neglected, and it was partly at their expense that the ones in Paris attained new heights. By exercising a "useful influence on [public] opinion," Laplace wrote, the Institut and the academies "dispel errors welcomed in our time with an enthusiasm which in another age would have perpetuated them."[27] Which was an elegant if convoluted way of saying that only the Parisian bourgeoisie, enlightened by its elites, was capable of reasoning scientifically. (The emphasis here must be on elites: when cholera struck in 1832, the residents of the rue Vaugirard stoned a man to death because they believed he had poisoned a fountain.)

T HE "STATE SCIENTIFIC APPARATUS," bolstered as it may have been ideologically, culturally, and institutionally by society at large, was not the only thing that encouraged the concentration of science in Paris in the early nineteenth century. Also crucial was another factor that is far more difficult to pin down precisely: the very nature of scientific thought at the time. The politicized place of science in Western culture was one critical factor in the prestige of scientific thought in Paris, but it was complemented by the way science was conceived by scientists, its practitioners.

Today it is obviously impossible for any one nation, let alone any one city, to be at the forefront of every scientific discipline. Indeed, this impossibility had already become apparent by 1850. And it is even more impossible to imagine that every discipline might somehow depend on a single principle and source of inspiration available in only one place on earth. But in Paris in 1820 people believed just that. The systematic unity of all sciences—which had seemed so foreign to Plato—was taken for granted after 1815 by the Aristotelian subjects of the restored Bourbon monarchs.

Two complementary factors were at work here: first, the diversity of Parisian scientific research, and second, the confidence of scientists that they could absorb it all. From 1750 to 1840 all the sciences were brilliantly represented in Paris: with, for example, Monge, Augustin Cauchy, and the ill-starred algebraic genius Evariste Galois (1811–1832), Paris had the reputation of being the world capital of mathematics. But Paris had also long been a prestigious center of physics, especially noted for work on the relation of physics to astronomy. Bernard le Bovier de Fontenelle (1657–1757), for instance, though no physicist, had preferred "the spirit of physics" ("clearer, simpler, more independent") to both the spirit of chemistry, which was all confusion, and the practice of medicine, which was also dubious. "We anatomists," he wrote in 1722, "are like the lockpickers of Paris, who know even the smallest, most out-of-the-way streets but have no idea what goes on inside the houses."[28]

The Parisian infatuation with physicists would last until the Revolution: in the 1780s Mesmer attracted vast audiences, but Benjamin Franklin was even more popular thanks to his experiments with lightning. Parisian women even began wearing tall hats that were called *chapeaux paratonnerres,* lightning-rod hats, in his honor. And at a more exalted level, Laplace represented the glory of physics at the Institut. It was in Paris, more than anywhere else, that physics became the science that could explain everything from "the clockwork to the boiler," from mechanical description to organic analysis, culminating in the work of Sadi Carnot, who was born in Paris in 1796 and died there of cholera in 1832 after discovering the Second Law of Thermodynamics.[29]

But with all due respect to Fontenelle and his successors, mathematics, physics, and even medicine were not the only important disciplines to thrive in Paris. Chemistry and physiology were also associated with the city, and in a way that greatly reinforced the prestige of the Parisian scientific establishment: if physiology and chemistry were, as many scientists began to think, the "mother sciences," and if Paris was the best place to study them, Paris would necessarily be the capital of Western scientific thought.

For Diderot, chemistry, as the most analytical of the sciences, had already seemed the most apt to serve as a link between philosophers and empirical workers (*manouvriers de l'expérience*). In 1783 Mercier praised "the modern miracles of chemistry." Alexander von Humboldt had gone further and made Lavoisier's work a necessary starting point: "It is the portico of the gate to the Temple: the other gates are only ways out." In a letter sent in 1822 to the young Jean-Baptiste Dumas, who, though born in Alès in 1800 lived in Geneva from 1819 until 1822, the Genevan Augustin-Pyrame de Candolle (1778–1841) went straight to the heart of the matter: "Your future is in Paris, [and] chemistry is your career. Botany does not offer you the necessary scope; physiology without chemistry is impossible. It is toward chemistry that you should direct all your strength. You can do chemistry seriously only in Paris." And Balzac, royalist and reactionary though he was, chose chemistry as the science to inspire his César Birotteau, a provincial perfumer on his way to a bankruptcy that would ruin his good name.[30]

On a par with chemistry in Paris was physiology, which at the time included what would today be fields as distinct as pathology, biology, and biochemistry.[31] The scientific writer Jean Sénebier explained all this in 1778 in his eulogy of Albrecht von Haller, the father of modern physiology: "Physiology is the basis of medicine; it presents to the medical practitioner the natural state of the machine he is to maintain . . . This science is a part of physics; it almost requires knowledge of all the others. One has to delve deeply into anatomy . . . One must acquire a solid knowledge of general physics, mechanics, hydrostatics, pneumatics, acoustics, and chemistry in order to understand various phenomena that would be incomprehensible if one were not in perfect possession of the principle of these sciences."[32] This ecumenism was surely overly optimistic, but it bears highlighting because this very sense of wholeness was what most clearly distinguished Parisian science from the way science was envisaged in England or Germany at that time.

As a new science, all but unknown to the general public in 1795, physiology was not entitled to its own section in the Institut National des Sciences, but this gap would soon be filled under the Directory. So well filled, in fact, that the new discipline became the backbone of scientific thinking in the capital during the three or four most illustrious decades of Parisian science, from 1800 to about 1840, with as its most prominent practitioner Xavier Bichat, the author of *Recherches physiologiques sur la vie et la mort* (Physiological Studies of Life and Death; 1800).

The development of physiology was also closely linked to the city's medical institutions. The Académie de Médecine was founded in Paris in 1770, followed by a veterinary school in Alfort in 1776 (which was reorganized in 1784). These pre-revolutionary institutions were reinforced after 1789 by the creation of the Ecoles de Santé in December 1794, along with a college of pharmacy. The institutional strength of Parisian physiology, then, grew rapidly, and all the more so because of the Parisian scientific zeitgeist of the time, with its notion that there existed a science of organic functions that was capable of subsuming all the other sciences from medicine and anatomy to chemistry and physics—a way of thinking that was typically French and that privileged theory over empirical observations.

To be sure, Parisian physicians did not scorn direct experimentation (especially after 1840), but they clearly preferred to work in the realm of medical theory and on the nature of life itself rather than on scientific experiments, and it was only after 1822, when François Magendie (1783–1855) discovered the complex sensorimotor function of the spinal nerve, that Parisian physiology began to move gradually toward sustained experimentation. But Magendie and, after him, Claude Bernard (1813–1878) never abandoned "the idea that organic phenomena have a specific character." In this we see the Parisian tendency toward unifying abstraction, and no more unrepentant apologist for that tendency could be found than Auguste Comte. For the father of modern sociology, the importance of abstraction, the superiority of "speculative genius" over "industrial genius," was beyond argument.

Comte's thinking in 1825 was typical of the unitary and abstract scientific mood that prevailed in Paris at the time. He railed against "the overly pragmatic spirit of the present century," which to his mind was an unfortunate consequence of the undue prestige accorded to the applied sciences. By contrast, it pleased him to observe that "the philosophical spirit as such was . . . more fully developed in France than anywhere else under the theological-metaphysical ancien régime, and much closer to a true rational positivism, exempt from both English empiricism and German mysticism." The English, "despite their real advantages," were, he believed, "less prepared today for such a solution [that is, less open to the new scientific spirit] than any other branch of the great Western family except Spain."[33]

But when Comte said France, what he really meant was Paris; and for that reason he called in 1832 for the Collège de France to establish a chair in the general history of the physical sciences and mathematics. Was it not essential, he wrote to François Guizot, the leading conservative politician of his day, to counter the narrow-mindedness and pinched taste of the great specialized technical institutions, especially the Ecole Polytechnique? "In this state of our intelligence," he continued, "human science in its positive aspect can be seen as one, and so therefore can its history." In 1846 Comte expanded his proposal to encompass a chair "in the general history of the positive sciences." No science, he believed, "can be known in a fully rational way unless one traces the historical filiation of its principal advances. Only this filiation can make unquestionably clear the ineluctable links with what precedes and what follows it in the natural course of our mental evolution." (Guizot, by the way, did not act on the proposal. He described Comte, whom he had met in 1833, as "a simple, honest man, deeply convinced, devoted to his ideas, modest in appearance although basically deeply proud, who sincerely believed that he had been called to inaugurate a new era in the history of the human spirit and human society." In 1848 Littré revived Comte's proposal, once again without success, and it was not until 1892 that Pierre Laffitte, "Comte's successor in positivist orthodoxy," was appointed to the Collège de France to teach this science. Wyrouboff, Littré's former colleague, succeeded him shortly thereafter.)[34]

Paris, world capital of science, incarnation of the Promethean myth of the constructed unity of the sciences in the service of
man: it was a state of mind that lasted only briefly, from about 1800 to
the 1840s. The end was sudden, and rather paradoxical, since the decline in the capital's scientific achievements after 1850 came at a time
when the prestige of science and of individual scientists was still on the
rise in Paris and when the benefits of science, or at any rate the benefits
that public opinion associated with the growth of scientific knowledge,
contributed to this rise.

For science, however theoretically conceived by its leading practitioners, did improve the standard of living in nineteenth-century Paris.
The best symbols of that improvement were, surely, gas and electric
light: the City of Light had not always been well lit, but by the time of
the Revolution the idea that it might be had become at least plausible.
Streetlights were introduced in 1745 and *falots,* or lanterns, began to be
carried about the streets at night by roving lantern-holders. In 1797
Philippe Lebon started his investigation of gas lighting, whose practi-
cality the English had demonstrated. After he was murdered in a nighttime assault, his widow demonstrated his "thermolamp" in 1811 in an
installation on the rue de Bercy as well as in the Galerie Montesquieu of
the Palais Royal. Later came the first experiments with electric lighting:
arc lights were used to light the Place de la Concorde in December
1840. Then, in 1889, the first residential consumer of electricity (at 18,
rue du Pont-Neuf) was hooked up to a generator at Les Halles, and the
first electrically lit advertisement appeared in 1912.[35]

But in the end all this activity, abstract or practical, was of no avail:
though both discoveries and scientific applications became ever more
numerous in the life of the capital, the earlier emphasis on the centrality
of Paris and the unity of scientific thought could not be sustained. In a
general way, the decline of scientific Paris in the second half of the nineteenth century can be described in terms of a reversal of the same factors
that led to its rise in the first part of the century.

Consider, first, the most complex of these, the structure of scientific knowledge itself. In 1830 it was still reasonable to think ab-
stractly about science as a whole: Auguste Comte, as we have seen,

prided himself on following the development of all the sciences of his time. Berthelot was far more modest in 1901, however: "It has become almost impossible for one man to follow the advance and progress of even a single science such as chemistry in its entirety. I am one of the last—I believe the last—who can say that he possesses an idea of the full extent of chemical science, and I can do so only because I arrived at a time when it was still possible to take in all the elements of the subject. From now on, this will not be feasible."[36] Laplace (1749–1827) had been the unchallenged master of the kingdom of Parisian science. Even before the end of the Restoration, Cuvier (1769–1832) had been unable to assume that role.

And just as the idea of the unity of science waned, so did the "apparatus" of Parisian science go into decline. By 1860 everyone in the capital was aware that France was not investing enough in science. Only five days after the end of the Franco-Prussian War, the Académie des Sciences met on March 6, 1871, so that its members, one by one, could denounce the ruinous state of science in France. Pasteur met with enormous difficulties when he tried to raise funds to create the institute that bears his name. When Pierre and Marie Curie began their research on radium, they had to pay out of their own pockets for the many tons of pitchblende that their experiments required.

Compounding the lack of funds was a lack of energy, illustrated by the decline of the Muséum d'Histoire Naturelle. Cuvier's conservatism injured the institution's prestige, and in 1886 the chemist Chevreul was still teaching there at the age of 100. In 1873 Maxime du Camp wrote that the Prussians had bombarded the Muséum in 1870 so that it "would no longer just vegetate but die."[37]

Parisian indifference to work done in other countries was also a problem. Darwin's ideas, which Littré claimed had been anticipated by "Lamarck, without any change to their essential features by Darwin," were only slowly assimilated in Paris because they were "too English."[38] Few scientists followed the Polish-born Marie Curie in her efforts to assemble an international team of collaborators.

In short, Parisian science, though republican in principle, became in the second half of the nineteenth century nationalist, masculinist, dependent on patronage, and often unoriginal. Pasteur advertised himself, and was accepted, as a solitary genius. Few people knew at the time, and many still do not know today, that he did his best to conceal the contributions of some of the young colleagues who worked with him in developing an anthrax vaccine.

By 1850 scientific initiative had passed from Paris to Germany, where Justus Liebig (1803–1873), a chemist trained by Gay-Lussac and Humboldt, led the establishment of new research institutes in the universities (an example that Dumas would have liked to follow at the Ecole Polytechnique). England and the United States then also set up laboratories that had no equivalent in Paris—which, when Marie Curie arrived, had only one chair in theoretical physics and no laboratory comparable to the one that Henry Cavendish had established in 1870 at Cambridge specifically to compete with Germany's new institutions.

THUS PARIS, which had been the uncontested world capital of science in 1820 and 1840, no longer held that title by 1900, although at the end of the nineteenth century the city did find a new scientific mission that still gives us food for thought today. As Anne Rasmussen has eloquently demonstrated, the distinctive contribution of fin-de-siècle Paris was to serve as a setting for a new mode of scientific sociability: "Virtually unheard of before 1850, the 'international congress' form crossed a quantitative threshold after 1875 when it was extended to a great variety of disciplines, and its growth from then until 1914 was exponential." To cite just one of many possible examples, a Congress of Physics was held in Paris in 1900, bringing physicists from around the world together for the first time in an "international physics community." (In 1900, 87 percent of "world congresses" were held in Paris.) The Curies, Antoine-Henri Becquerel, Jean Perrin, and Paul Langevin participated, of course, but so did Max Planck, Ernst Mach, J. J. Thomson, William Thomson, and Alexander Graham Bell. In the laboratory the scientist worked alone, but at congresses, as Rasmussen notes, "the priority of oral communication tended to re-create . . . the old rituals of the Republic of Letters, which celebrated the majesty of science."[39]

Myth and fantasy: the categories can be applied to the history of science in Paris as well as to the history of politics and literature. But the evolution of scientific research toward greater international collaboration at the end of the nineteenth century may also be taken as a harbinger of a new direction, one that Paris might follow today. For if the French capital can no longer hope to be the world capital of science that it was from 1800 to 1840, it can still, as the most European of the world's great international cities, be a meeting ground, a place for exchange and discussion, a site of noble, cosmopolitan, and continuing exchange.

7

Reading the Parisian Myths

MYTH PROVIDES STRUCTURE to the quotidian, helps us make sense of our everyday lives. To do this, however, it requires a material incarnation. Take, for instance, the anointing of the French king. Originally this was a ceremony (performed in the cathedral at Rheims) that turned the king into a religious personage and a miracle worker—a creature of myth. It established a bridge from the present to the past and the future, and it bound the king's subjects to God. But this mystical statement had to be given material substance as well, and it was Versailles that became royalty's magical envelope, giving tangible embodiment to the myth of the absolute Christian monarch. Without the ritual coronation at Rheims there could have been no divine-right monarchy, but without the unrivaled material prestige of Versailles the politico-religious myth of the French kings would not have prospered as it did.

In this same register, during the nineteenth century the myth of Paris (as capital of La Grande Nation or as world capital of modernity) was made monumentally "real" in a manner that still makes sense to us today. One can live in Paris without reading Baudelaire or looking at Manet's paintings or attending lectures at the Collège de France. But it is difficult to live in the city without constantly looking at, and "reading," such historicized symbols as the basilica of Sacré Coeur, an emblem of Catholicity; or the Eiffel Tower, an audacious symbol of modernity; or the Montparnasse Tower, a symbol of something that with luck may never come to pass, namely Chicago-sur-Seine.

Some cities one never visits for the first time. Can one imagine a visitor arriving in Paris knowing nothing about it, unable to identify a single monument? Hugo believed that "this will kill that"—that the book would put an end to concrete facts and memory-laden monuments—and this may indeed be true of Paris in the (narrow) sense that many of us first come to the city by way of books (or films or television); it may well be through what we have seen of the monuments of Paris in books, in films, or on the Internet that our understanding, our reading, of Paris begins. For some time now Paris has been a continuous show, a spectacle. The positive dimension of this "virtuality" is that Paris has become more familiar and, in some ways at least, easier to decipher than, say, London, Moscow, or Berlin.

I T IS IMPORTANT, however, to understand that the idea of the city as a made-up and legible "spectacle" is relatively recent, dating from roughly the beginning of the nineteenth century. The issue is complex, as it hinges on the nature of much larger cultural transformations. More particularly, as Jürgen Habermas has taught us, it depends on the creation in Paris, in France, and in Europe of new divisions between the traditional and the new, between a new private and a new public, between signs that had been inherited and signs that had to be invented.

No doubt medieval cities—medieval Paris included—were also legible in the sense that their social and professional stratifications were both manifest and public. Many people, most shops, and every trade had a special emblem, publicly displayed, that even the illiterate could decipher. And a medieval monarch was both a private and a public person: he would step outside his private condition from time to time to affirm and display in parades, tourneys, and "entrances" his sovereignty as well as that of the state he led, even while he remained first and foremost a private individual *(primus inter pares)*, obliged, at least in theory, to *parlementer* (speak and negotiate) with his peers for funds.

Indeed, one could even say that in the Middle Ages each person's social condition was constantly externalized, and to a far greater extent than is the case today. Our clothing, for instance, often serves more than one social purpose; in style, form, and function, it can "migrate" from one country to another, from one social class to another, and even from one sex to another. By contrast, in 1400 the Parisian bourgeois dressed as a bourgeois, the noble as a noble, the pilgrim as a pilgrim, the Jew as a Jew, the nun as a nun, and so on. No two costumes were interchangeable. Even Ivanhoe, the unknown Desdichado, wore an escutcheon that no one dared ignore. In the government and courts of England and the Anglo-Norman isles one still finds vestimentary survivals of such medieval practices, mostly of French origin.

And yet this medieval social mapping by dress, this early theater of social and urban stratification, was very different in spirit from the ostensibly voluntary and public character of modern dress. After 1800, in the confusion of a newly constituted and modern society, where ancient feudal survivals coexisted with a new and worrisome proletarianization of the poor, a need was now felt (and perhaps in Paris more than elsewhere) to impose, on both individuals and cities, signs that marked an altogether new kind of comforting public legibility. It was with some discernment that Flaubert's friend Maxime Du Camp, also a writer as well as a photographer and an experienced traveler, noted that the Paris of 1880 was "registered, catalogued, numbered, surveyed, illuminated, cleaned, disciplined, groomed, administered, regulated, judged, imprisoned, buried."[1]

In this post-feudal period, a more structured legibility was needed that would be based neither on personal preference (as ours often is) nor on birth or status (as in previous arrangements). New and ever more stringent signs would have to be invented to serve the need of a newly dominant but still uncertain bourgeoisie.

In the Middle Ages signs had carried an inherited, unreflected, and self-evident meaning. Private and public had been conflated. In nineteenth-century Paris, convulsed by revolution, private and public were separated: it could no longer be assumed that a wealthy person would also hold public office. In consequence, if he did hold office, he would now have to dress in a way that would make that political fact plain. The rebellious dandy of Balzac's and Baudelaire's imagination, like the egotistical if not frankly solipsistic *flâneur* described by Walter Benjamin, was a world unto himself; but these arrogant figures also sought (sometimes desperately) to express themselves through dress that was not just personal but also public. Bohemian clothing expressed the alienated poet's relation to bourgeois-dominated public life. It marked his threatened refusal to conform to the prevailing moral code, and in a way that was designed to *épater le bourgeois,* just as—in an inverse manner—the uniform of the prefect of police was designed to impress and reassure.

By 1850, then, the signs in Paris of the new and collective modes of stratification were as universal as they had been in the Middle Ages, but now simultaneously individuated and compulsory (as was social conformity generally in individuated bourgeois life). Style of dress was still imposed in part by custom, but was also imposed by the state, which required some people to wear uniforms, or by the internalized fashions and cultural habits of the triumphant bourgeoisie, or, in some cases, by all three powers combined: state, fashion, and vestigial, nostalgic "tradition." All Parisians now felt obliged, or better yet wanted, to appear in the proper costume, appropriate not to their birth but to their social and public situation or expectations. Writing of the Salon of 1840, the art critic A. Tabarant reported:

> The staircase was crowded with people, affording a unique opportunity to break out the new suit and show off the new shawl. The silk top-hat was in. The blue redingote bourgeoisie fraternized with the dashing hazel topcoats. The sales clerk in his twenty-nine-sous yellow gloves is utterly amazed to be rubbing elbows with the fashion-plate of the boulevard, who sports a sleek, glossy, regal coiffure and struts about in an overcoat by Human made of navy cloth. The latest fetching styles for shopgirls feature velvet and percaline. Cashmere elegance from Gagelin looks radiant under light-colored bonnets adorned with neck-ruffles and tied with English lace.[2]

Balzac could not have put it better.

In this new context, changing fashion made *la parisienne;* and standardized sartorial norms made *le parisien,* especially the Parisian statesman. In pre-revolutionary portraiture, military and police uniforms were largely unknown. During the ancien régime the monarch, even

when depicted in armor, wore court clothing beneath the vaguely utilitarian breastplate, whose function was in fact purely decorative. By the
nineteenth century, however, times had changed, and the English king
was now portrayed, tellingly, as a uniformed admiral; the Prussian sovereign, convincingly, as a uniformed officer of the general staff. In Budapest, Belgrade, Bucharest, Moscow, and Athens, monarchs likewise appeared in uniform, but here designed as regional garb of a fantastic
kind. In a sarcastic comment on a drawing by Constantin Guys representing the German-born king of Greece, Baudelaire wrote: "King Otto
and his queen, standing on a podium, are dressed in traditional costume, which they wear with marvelous assurance, as if to give evidence
of the sincerity of their adoption [of "Greekness"] and of the most refined Hellenic patriotism . . . His skirt is flared with all the exaggeration
of the national dandyism."[3]

In Paris the uniforms (of soldiers, firemen, policemen, national
guardsmen, postmen, priests, lawyers, academicians, street sweepers,
bus drivers, kings, emperors, and, for a while, even deputies) became
easily comprehensible visual tokens of a historicized and newly created
public life, expressions of a new cultural unity fashioned by reference to
the nation's (largely imagined) history. French soldiers at Yorktown in
1781 had fought under the personal insignia of the monarch. In 1873,
by contrast, the political future of France hinged on the choice of a national flag: would it be the tricolor, the symbol par excellence of post-
revolutionary France, or the white banner with fleurs-de-lis favored by
the backward-looking comte de Chambord, who, in his Austrian exile,
was no longer able to understand the nation, or the society, over which
he wished to reign.

And it is important to remember—once more—that this conceptual
evolution toward self-conscious public sign and spectacle was not just
very deeply felt (even if Chambord did not understand it) but, in 1850,
quite new as well. The historian Pierre Nora, in order to explain this
point, goes back to the Middle Ages, when "every gesture, down to the
most routine, [was] experienced as the religious repetition of what had
always been done in a carnal identification of act and meaning." In order
for modern history (and modern signs) truly to exist, he continues, one

had to wait for the "moment when it was no longer a matter of living life but rather of representing it . . . Memory is rooted in the concrete . . . History fastens exclusively on temporal continuities, evolutionary processes, and relations."[4]

INDEED, and in the history of Paris the evolutionary moment when passive memory yielded to modern—and modernly legible—history was the age of the Enlightenment, when representation, history, and myth became the means of explaining the present (in Paris as elsewhere), of cataloguing it, of writing it, of making it legible, accessible, and authoritative to all. In the French capital, it was toward the end of the eighteenth century that a whole range of previously private activities became newly public through the press, advertising, criers, and posters, as well as through the renown of the many virtuosos who came to Paris to show off their talents and whose celebrity drew steadily growing crowds.

Before the Revolution, a king's entry into the capital had indeed been a major event, but one for which Parisians by and large organized spontaneously. Students turned out en masse without being officially ordered to do so. By contrast, the festivals of the Revolution, after some initial hesitation, quickly became quite stylized, as were the military parades of the day. (The militarized ceremonies in Paris of July 14, Bastille Day, are a surviving echo of this republican antecedent.) And it is perhaps worth mentioning that in our own postmodern age, when social lines are far more blurred than they used to be, Paris has been treated to yet another type of public spectacle, such as the one organized in 1989 by Jean-Paul Goude for the bicentennial of the Revolution, a celebratory spectacle that was entirely fantastic and calculatedly tendentious. (A similar development occurred in the rather depressing evolution of the Parisian carnival, which in 1830 was still spontaneous and orgiastic, but which by the eve of the First World War had become entirely commercialized.)

Historians and sociologists will obviously have different views on an issue as complicated as the transition from medieval to modern "spectacularity"; but what is clear, again, is the extent to which the new ways of perceiving affected the appearance of the French capital. With the Revolution and its sequels, public celebration in the city reached a new level of spectacularity, as did any number of great public virtuosos and internationally known performers such as Paganini, the greatest violinist of his day, Fernando Sor, the greatest guitarist of his day, and Franz Liszt, the greatest pianist of all time. ("Le piano, c'est moi," Liszt exclaimed half ironically.)

To be sure, Paris had always had its share of talented oddities, like a young woman named Margot who in 1429 became the tennis champion of her day, "devant main, derriere main, très puissament, très malicieusement, très habillement, comme pouvait faire homme" (forehand and backhand, mightily, cleverly, skillfully, and just like a man).[5] But such exceptions, which had formerly seemed freakish, now became supremely normative, and Parisians paid high prices to see world-famous artists.[6] And not just artists but virtuosos of all kinds: at the Café de la Régence, for example, Philidor (François-André Danican), who spent several months of each year in London, transformed the status of the Parisian chess player. His successor, Louis-Charles Mahé de La Bourdonnais, made chess a professional and public sport, publicized by the first magazine devoted to the game, *Palamède* (1836), whose editors expressed the view that La Bourdonnais's victory over the English chess master Alexander MacDonnell was tantamount to "Napoleon's revenge."

It was also around 1789 that the first great Parisian restaurants opened their doors. What had been a private rite confined to the dining halls of great nobles now became a public ritual celebrated in the great restaurants of Paris, which dazzled by virtue of their sumptuous decor and public display of fine cooking.

So, for example, the specialty of Marie-Antoine Carême, the chef of chefs and the chef to kings (especially Louis XVIII, who reigned, on and off, from 1814 to 1824), was the *pièce montée,* or sculpted ornamental display. In the time of Louis XIV (born in 1638), everything that was placed on the king's table was edible; but for Carême, the architect-chef, the spectacle mattered more than the taste. Abandoning his ovens, this ambitious artist boasted of having put together some of his concoctions not with the edible pastes of an earlier era but with a "mastic," which, though inedible, was also indestructible, so that he could put his noble creations "on display" day after day not only in Paris but also in Vienna, London, and Saint Petersburg. For Balzac, this was "gourmandise of the school of Louis XVIII," which allied sumptuousness of two kinds, "that of the container and that of the content."[7]

This was also the time when museums—those legible mirrors of the world—sprang up all over Europe, but especially in Paris: the Louvre was inaugurated as a museum on August 10, 1793. Works of art, once collected by princes, then by wealthy private individuals, now became public spectacles as well. Note, too, that the painter Jacques-Louis David (good Jacobin though he was) charged a hefty price to people who wished to visit his studio. Likewise, Théodore Géricault, after being criticized in Paris, made up for it by paying to have his painting *The Raft of the Medusa* shown in London. Indeed, the Revolution itself, with its Parisian journées and its festivals (on the Champs de Mars, and at the Pantheon when Voltaire was reinterred, for example), can be seen as having been a permanent spectacle, a precocious aestheticization of politics, which totalitarianism would develop to the full. As one wag put it at the time:

> Il ne fallait au fier Romain
> Que des spectacles et du pain;
> Mais au Français plus que Romain
> Le spectacle suffit sans pain.
> (The proud Roman required
> only bread and circuses;
> but for the Frenchman, greater even than the Roman,
> the spectacle without bread is enough.)[8]

And the revolutionary guillotine, the "national razor" as it was sometimes called, was likewise a spectacle of a sort, the star in a drama whose plot varied little but of which some people never tired.

For Shelley, in principle a revolutionary optimist but more often than not a melancholic poet afflicted by the eternal wretchedness of all things, the essential metaphysical significance of every monument was to call attention to the helplessness of man. He cited the legend inscribed on the pedestal of a gigantic statue in Thebes (now Luxor), which became ironic when the statue collapsed in ruin and the pedestal was smashed (it has since been reconstituted):

> My name is Ozymandias, king of kings:
> Look upon my work, ye Mighty, and despair!

But when the elders of nineteenth-century Paris contemplated their existence and that of their predecessors, they did not think of these ruins. Throughout that century and the next, but especially under the Third Republic, any number of statues were erected in the capital to honor and commemorate the great men of the past: there were 9 in 1870, 100 in 1914, 300 in 1940. Since then their number, it is true, has steadily diminished: 75 were melted down during the Occupation, and in 1964 André Malraux, in his capacity as minister of cultural affairs, banished others.[9] Léon Gambetta lost his statue in the Tuileries in 1942; its pedestal went in 1964. Still other monuments fell victim to traffic, such as the statue of Alfred de Musset at the corner adjacent to the Théâtre Français, which also was removed in 1964.

The monuments of Paris can be seen as part of this same organized spectacularity: they too are texts, whose essential purpose today is to ensure the legibility of the city. Some *lieux de mémoires,* or "sites of memory," as Pierre Nora calls them, acquired their status by accident, but others were conceived as such. Indeed, it is no exaggeration to say that the capital's various monuments form a coherent whole, a monumental grammar, in which each site is expressive not only in itself but also as a function of others like it, or for that matter antithetical to it.[10]

Claude Lévi-Strauss's explanation of myth as a way of reconciling in the realm of morality what cannot be reconciled in the realm of the concrete applies elegantly to the varieties of these modern Parisian spectacles. In terms of division and reconciliation, "Parisianness," that indefinable (and mythical) hybrid quality, enables us to understand why a right-wing parade down the Champs-Elysées must—inevitably—be answered by a left-wing parade from the Bastille to the Place de la Nation, above which looms Jules Dalou's statue *The Triumph of the Republic,* itself a riposte to the statues of Saint Louis and Philip Augustus placed on Claude-Nicolas Ledoux's fluted columns by orders of Louis Philippe, king of all the French.[11] Monumental Paris seems at first glance to be schizophrenic, but it is nonetheless easy to conjugate: the Musée d'Orsay, Paris was; the Grande Arche and the new Bibliothèque Mitterrand, Paris is; and the Pompidou Center and the Musée des Sciences, Paris will be.

It is also important to note that the vast majority of the French capital's highly legible monuments refer not just to the city itself but to both Paris and something grander, such as humanity (the mini–Statue of Liberty, for example) or the nation: in order to be fully Parisian, a monument in the capital of France must also be national or international. Consider here the case of Etienne Marcel, whom the historian Alfred Fierro has called "a man nostalgic for the past." For us, Marcel is not an altogether appealing figure: this medieval mayor of Paris was hardly a democrat.[12] What is more, this friend of Charles the Bad and enemy of the wise Charles V was, objectively speaking, an ally of the English, the all but hereditary enemies of a martyred France. In other words, Marcel was not enough of a national hero to become a true Parisian hero. The city did eventually honor him with a statue—it had to—but it was done rather discreetly, almost cozily, one might say, in the protective shadow of the Hôtel de Ville. By contrast, Joan of Arc, that heroic provincial, was quickly fetishized, and her statue, erected in 1874, is to this day a fetishistic and gilded object.

The monuments of Rome are primarily religious, while those of London are monarchical (the Tower), political (the Houses of Parliament), or frankly imperial (above all in the statuary). The monuments of Munich and Barcelona, Hamburg and Venice, suffer from being chiefly municipal or regional. A Parisian monument is expected to propose a broader message, one that is simultaneously civic and universal and therefore more apt to express the readable and representative myths that the capital incarnates.

Some Paris monuments must therefore be counted as relative failures because they are too intimately intertwined with a particular ideology rather than associated with the more general identity of the nation and its metropolis. Some memorials are too closely linked to the right, such as Sacré Coeur or, even more, the expiatory chapel built in memory of Louis XVI. (The Commune planned to destroy this edifice, which was saved only by the intervention of a Parisian royalist who successfully posed as an American tourist interested in purchasing it; even then everyone knew that American tourists are always looking for a good buy.)

Similarly, the former Sainte-Geneviève church, which became the Pantheon, is "an impossible monument," because the great men to whom (according to the inscription on the building) the *patrie* owes a debt of gratitude are essentially men of the left: symbolically, on November 11, 1920, the Chamber of Deputies simultaneously voted to place the heart of Gambetta (a republican politician) in the Pantheon and to inter the remains of the unknown soldier under the Arc de Triomphe, a less politicized and more national structure, which, one might add, is now thought of by Parisians as their own war memorial, a kind of mega-municipal Monument aux Morts. It was no doubt to short-circuit such anxieties that Edgar Quinet in 1867 proposed turning the Pantheon into an apolitical or even anti-political monument, a monument devoted not to the nation but to thought. It is also worth noting that this building is seldom mentioned in the literature of Paris: André Breton wrote a poem about it, but it was the Place du Panthéon rather than the Pantheon itself that the Surrealists loved.

The Wall of the Fédérés in the Père-Lachaise cemetery also suffers from an excess of partisan legibility and particularism. Its memory of the repression carried out there in 1871 by Versailles troops began to develop in the 1880s and was subsequently taken over by the Communist Party. In 1883 the first red flags went up, and in May 1888 socialists and anarchists scuffled at the site. In 1936 the socialist Léon Blum and the communist Maurice Thorez turned up there together along with their political friends Jules Moch and Marcel Gitton (Gitton had been a police agent since 1935 and would be executed during the war by those he had deceived). Even today the cemetery's "section 97" is a solemn pilgrimage destination for many Parisians. The historian Madeleine Rebérioux points out that "it has never been possible for the Wall to be co-opted by the right or the extreme right."[13] But that is the problem, because this very impermeability accounts for both the strength and the weakness of this memory site, where undocumented and marginal foreign workers ill-advisedly chose to end a demonstration in 1997.

Other Parisian monuments followed the lead of many of the Third Republic's politicians and made a more widely acceptable switch from the left to the right or at any rate to the center of the political spectrum. The Eiffel Tower, for example, was initially the target of vehement attack: Charles Garnier, Georges Clemenceau, Alexandre Dumas *fils,* and Guy de Maupassant called for tearing down this representation of modernizing technocracy. Not for long, however. Given its nature as a symbol of republican modernity, and as the only monument of its type in the *beaux quartiers,* the chic neighborhoods, of Paris, the tower would seem to have had no chance of garnering support from those who worship the past. Yet it soon did, and it quickly became "the belfry of the city of Paris," symbolizing France itself as well as its capital in the work of Utrillo, Delaunay, Dufy, and Chagall. The tower, in brief, had moved rightward, a displacement for which the precondition was the construction of the even more revolutionary skyscrapers of New York, whose effect was to "demodernize" Eiffel's masterpiece.

To be successful, then, a monument in Paris must be simultaneously Parisian, ecumenical, national, and international. No doubt that is why, of all the royal palaces, the Louvre, as a prime repository of world culture (which it already was to a certain extent before the fall of the ancien régime), has been the most successful. Fontainebleau still evokes memories of the Valois, Versailles of the Bourbons, Compiègne of the Bonapartes; but the Louvre, though not really republican, is no longer in any sense a royal palace.

L EGIBILITY OF CLOTHING, legibility of monuments, and also legibility of the city as a whole. As one might expect, the question of what Paris signified was of little concern before the seventeenth century. Paris existed, and that was enough. Palaces rubbed shoulders with hov-

Jean-Paul Moreau-Vauthier, *The Wall of Victims of Revolutions,* 1909. In this work near the Père-Lachaise cemetery, the last site of fighting in 1871, the spectator grieves for the fallen, whose Parisian deaths were not in vain. Their struggle goes on, carried forward to the "grand Soir" or *Götterdämmerung* of proletarian revolution. Photo: F. Vizzavona. Réunion des Musées Nationaux / Art Resource, NY.

els. Streets ran every which way, but no one was scandalized. People inhabited not a city but neighborhoods, a habit that would survive for some time: in 1864 a German visitor could still write:

> A few steps from the Place de la Bastille, people still say "I'm going to Paris." This faubourg has its own ways and its own customs and even its own language . . . The municipality set out to number the streets as in all the other parts of the capital, but when you ask a resident of this faubourg, he'll always give you the name of his house: "Au roi de Siam" or "Etoile d'or" or "Cour des deux soeurs" or "Nom de Jésus" or "Panier Fleuri" or "Saint-Esprit" or "Bel air" or "La Muette" or "La bonne graine."[14]

A person born in a particular neighborhood was likely to marry and die there as well: during the Century of Enlightenment, 17 percent of the bakers in Paris married girls who lived not just in the same neighborhood but on the same street.[15]

Parisians, then, were used to the city just as it was. They made do. The notion of a rational order that might be underlying all this chaos came as something of a surprise to those who stumbled on it, as a royal official named Lamarte did in 1705. After collecting all royal decrees concerning Paris in a single volume, he reported: "I discovered in these regulations, which I was obliged to peruse, so much wisdom, such profound order, and such perfect harmony among the various elements of policy that I thought I might, by going back to first principles, reduce this science to art or practice."[16]

So much for the past. But after 1650 the regulatory absolutist state, which in France was the orchestrator of a new modernity, began to see things differently. Where the ramparts of Charles V and the fortified enclosure of Louis XIII had stood, it established the elements and signs of a new, regularized urban legibility: new boulevards covered with sand and lined by four rows of trees. (The etymology of the term *boulevard,* from the Dutch *bolwerk,* or rampart, reminds us of its military and governmental origin.)

The highly readable message of the absolutist monarchy of the Bourbons to the capital of the kingdom spoke of two things: urbanism and political domination. Louis XIV did not cut deeply into the living flesh of the capital, but his destruction of the old defensive walls nevertheless weakened the capital militarily vis-à-vis the monarch. And while the city was thus symbolically encircled, it was simultaneously attacked here and there from within through the construction of the new *places royales* (Place des Vosges, Place Vendôme, Place des Victoires, and Place Louis XV), each embellished by an equestrian statue representing a triumphant monarch symbolizing the new absolutist royal power: in order for the Republic to live in January 1793, Louis XVI not only had to die but had to die on the largest of the former *places royales,* then renamed the Place de la Révolution.

Even the nomenclature of Parisian streets respected this switch from a self-evident to a more personalized and at times state-sponsored and better-ordered monumentalism. In the past, street names had been chosen randomly or in relation to the site's topography, flora and fauna, or social use: witness the rues de la Contrescarpe, de la Butte-aux-Cailles, des Peupliers, des Ursulines, and des Bernardins. Henceforth, however, streets would bear names of provinces, and after that of local entrepreneurs. The Pont Marie has nothing to do with the Holy Virgin: Marie was a real estate promoter (and a seventeenth-century French precursor of the Levitt who built Levittown, Pennsylvania, in the 1950s) who built and sold new houses laid out on a rectangular grid on the Ile Saint-Louis. And toward the end of the eighteenth century, when everything was being individualized, streets began to be named after all kinds of people, from actors and writers to generals and statesmen. As Louis-Sébastien Mercier ironically put it in his *Tableau de Paris,* "A bourgeois achieves the height of glory when he becomes an alderman. He has had his fill of honors when he sees a street named after him."[17] (Paris streets bore their new names literally as well as figuratively: the first street sign indicating the name of a Paris street went up on the rue Saint-Dominique in 1643. In 1728 the city began using plaques of painted tin, which proved insufficiently durable. Next, street names were engraved right into the stone of buildings. The current blue plaques with white lettering date from 1847.)

In 1779 a new system of street numbering was introduced, but in a manner that did not please everyone: Augustin Saint-Aubain, in his *Tableau général* of Paris in 1799, deplored the numbers' lack of legibility: "It is impossible to calculate the amount of time wasted, the number of mistakes made, and the embarrassment caused by this confusion." On the rue Saint-Honoré, for example, number 394 stood opposite number 395, and number 1 stood opposite number 729 at the corner of the rue de la Ferronerie. The numbers "were white on a red background on streets parallel to the river" and white on a black background on streets perpendicular to the river.[18] Napoleon, in a Tocquevillian manner, perfected this administrative innovation of the ancien régime; in 1805, at the behest of the prefect Nicolas Frochot, a new arrangement was instituted, with rising even and uneven numbering on opposite sides of the street, the lower numbers being closest to the Seine.

MORE ORDERED STREETS, then, or at least more ordered in their nomenclature. And what held for the parts held for the larger whole as well: in 1650 the inconsistency, irregularity, and impenetrability of medieval Paris had still seemed tolerable, but the rationalist sensibility of the Enlightenment found the city's defects less and less acceptable. As early as 1753 the architect Marc-Antoine Laugier condemned the Paris of his day as an unhealthy place and, above all, as one that made no sense:

> Our cities are still what they have always been, a bunch of old houses piled one on top of the other without system, economy, or plan. Nowhere is this disorder more acute or more shocking than in Paris. The center of the capital has remained all but unchanged for three hundred years. There one still finds the same number of narrow, winding little streets, which stink of filth and garbage and which are constantly clogged by carriages that block one another's passage . . . On the whole, Paris is anything but a beautiful city. Its avenues are wretched, its streets poorly laid out and overly narrow, its houses . . . coarsely built, its squares too few, . . . its palaces badly situated.[19]

Continuing this eloquent critique was a book by Pierre Patte entitled *Monuments érigés à la gloire de Louis XV* (Monuments Erected to the Glory of Louis XV; 1765). Here, for the first time, Paris became an object of scientific study. Patte deplored the "nonorganic nature" of the capital, which was not so much a city as a collection of inward-looking neighborhoods. He proposed a "total plan," one sufficiently detailed to incorporate "all local circumstances." "There are entire neighborhoods," he explained, "which have almost no communication with other neighborhoods. One sees only narrow streets . . . where encounters between carriages are constantly endangering the lives of citizens and clogging traffic." Particularly deplorable in Patte's opinion was the fact that the city's water supply was far inferior to what the Romans could have achieved; equally scandalous was the location, right in the center of the city, of the Hôtel Dieu, a hospital full of patients with "contagious diseases [which infect] part of the river water [and] exhale air of the most corrupt and unhealthy sort." Patte—the Corbusier of the Enlightenment—was particularly interested in the renovation of the Ile de la Cité, and his idée fixe was to build a new cathedral on the Place Dauphine.[20]

The case of Claude-Nicolas Ledoux (1736–1806) is even more eloquent. Paris obviously has mixed memories of this prolific architect, who gave the city not only a dozen *hôtels particuliers* or private mansions, only one of which (the Hôtel d'Hallwyl of 1766) survives today, but also, in 1785, the customs wall of the tax farmers with its forty-seven pavilions, some of which still exist (in La Villette, for example, and at Denfert-Rochereau). But Ledoux, a visionary, was also a proponent of *architecture parlante* or speaking architecture, in which the shape of a building evoked its function in a way accessible to all, literate and illiterate alike. Communication, function, and legibility in architecture: these were the grand passions of this architect/engineer. For communication he designed theaters so that each spectator should have an unobstructed view of the entire stage, and for function he designed each row of seats to be occupied by a specific social group, ranging from prostitutes to nobles and notables (as in the Wagner Theater in Bayreuth, there were no boxes or balconies).

Communication and rationalization, yes, but also, some would say, surveillance and authoritarianism: it is a pity that Theodor Adorno was unfamiliar with Ledoux's masterpiece, not in Paris but in the saltworks at Arc-et-Senans, where the central building, the residence of the all-powerful administrator, was surrounded by other residences and factory buildings arranged in a semicircle. This was to be a place where order, calm, luxury, and sensuality were ubiquitous, under the watchful eye of an overseer.

Laugier, Patte, and Ledoux are not especially well known as urbanists. It might seem, therefore, that their interest in spectacle and legibility was merely the preoccupation of a small elite. Nothing could be further from the truth: there is every reason to think that their concern for global wholeness was ever more widely shared, especially after 1820. Take, for example, during the middle decades of the century, the strange obsession with panoramas, those great circular tableaux that were hung in rotundas with conical roofs and lit from above, placed in such a way that spectators had the illusion of viewing a scene stretching all the way to a genuine horizon.

Alas, the all-encompassing panorama was not a Parisian invention. The first one seems to have been staged by Robert Barker in London in 1799. Perhaps that explains why the first Parisian panoramas were produced in February 1800 by two Americans who had spent time in the English capital: Robert Fulton, the inventor (or reinventor) of the steamboat, and his colleague James Thayer. Their canvases were displayed near the boulevard Montmartre, at the entrance to what would come to be called the passage des Panoramas, which still exists in the Second Arrondissement. There for an entrance fee of 1 franc 50 one could admire "The Evacuation of Toulon by the English," a rather blatant homage to the newly enthroned First Consul. And rather successful it was: Napoleon was drawn to representations of this kind, which were useful as propaganda, and gave thought to ordering a dozen such to commemorate his greatest victories. In *Napoléon Bonaparte ou trente ans de l'histoire de France* (Napoleon Bonaparte, or Thirty Years in the History of France), a play written in 1831, Alexandre Dumas gives us a tout who tries to entice a crowd of curious Parisians into a Napoleonic panorama: "Come in, come in, Citizens! You don't have to pay a thing until you've seen it, and if you're not satisfied, you pay nothing, absolutely nothing, nothing at all. Come in, come in, Citizens!" Mercier wrote of the one he had seen that "painting never provided a more complete illusion."[21]

Other panoramas offered Parisians an inclusive and eminently read-able view of their city from the top of the Tuileries, and this aroused en-thusiasm even in the painter David, who took his students to see it: "Truly, gentlemen," he told them, "this is where you should come to study nature." Chateaubriand visited a third panorama in 1821, this one featuring Jerusalem. "The illusion was complete," he wrote. "At a glance I recognized all the monuments, all the sites, and even the little courtyard adjoining the room I lived in at the Convent of the Holy Sav-ior. Never was a traveler put to so rude a test. I had no way of knowing that they were going to bring Jerusalem and Athens to Paris in order to convict me of lying or telling the truth . . . Fragments of my *Itinéraire* were used as programs and explanations of the tableaux." (It is amusing to contrast this self-indulgent traveler's naive opinion with another view much closer to our own, that of Baudelaire, an inveterate Parisian and lover of artifice: "I want to be taken to dioramas whose brutal and egre-gious magic is capable of placing me under the spell of a useful illusion. I prefer to contemplate certain kinds of theatrical scenery, in which I find my most cherished dreams artistically expressed and tragically con-centrated. Such things, because they are false, are infinitely closer to the truth.") In 1828 Victor Hugo reflected on the importance of panoramas, and in 1834 Balzac wrote in *Père Goriot,* whose action is set in 1819, of "the recent invention of the Diorama"—an anachronism, since it was ac-tually invented later—"which carried optical illusion to a higher de-gree of perfection than in the Panoramas." Balzac has Vautrin joke about an incredible "froitorama" (it is winter, and the weather is *froid,* cold). Other habitués of the Pension Vauquer speak of "Gorioramas" and "Rastignacoramas."[22]

As the nineteenth century went on, the global pictorial legibility of Paris (or of Jerusalem in Paris, which in a broad cultural way comes to the same thing since these foreign scenes were all geared to pleasing Pa-risians) was steadily enhanced. At stake here, for example, was the di-orama, an ingeniously illuminated, constantly changing, and therefore even more realistic type of panorama, invented in 1823 by Daguerre, the father of photography, who got his start in a partnership with the painter Charles-Marie Bouton. (There were also the "neoramas" of the painter Pierre Alaux, who received no fewer than sixty commissions from a parsimonious Louis Philippe: the Citizen-King opined, it is said, that "Alaux paints and draws well; he is not expensive, and he is a colorist.")[23]

This Parisian vogue lasted quite some time, culminating in the Exposition of 1889 and its seven panoramas, including one depicting the history of the nineteenth century, which allowed the spectator to shift easily from legibility in space to legibility in time. Technically speaking, the "beau idéal" of the genre was probably an 1892 panorama on the Champs-Elysées depicting the 1794 battle of the ship *Vengeur,* whose sailors were said to have sung the "Marseillaise" as the ship went down. The panorama featured a moving platform that gave visitors the illusion of standing on the deck of a ship and taking part in the battle.

Clearly, the special effects in today's films are less revolutionary than one might think. And there was indeed a connection between panorama and cinema, because it was the vogue for cinema that finally killed off panoramas, the last examples of which date from the Exposition of 1900: ironically, it was the Lumière brothers' invention that soon destroyed what their fellow photographic innovator Daguerre had created. The Shah of Persia was charmed on a visit to Paris by a panorama of Madagascar ("you have to have seen it with your own eyes to understand its quality"), but he was especially taken with a "Cinématographe."[24] If the "Maréorama" of the same exposition marked the end of an era, the "Cinéorama" with its ten projectors showing ten segments of a horizon in rapid succession was a prophetic instrument. We can also note here that the number of movie theaters in Paris rose rapidly in these years: from 2 in 1907 to 160 in 1913.

W HAT WERE THE UNDERLYING REASONS for the popularity of panoramas, which Alfred Fierro, in his excellent dictionary of Paris, rightly calls a "colossal success"? One explanation, typically British perhaps, was based on the savings the new invention made possible. As *Blackwood's Magazine* asked in 1824, why travel to Naples to see Vesuvius? "Panoramas are among the happiest contrivances for saving time and expense . . . What cost a couple of hundred pounds a half year ago, now costs a shilling and a quarter of an hour."[25] (This may have been the world's first paean to virtual tourism.)

But a nobler, more Parisian explanation would focus, once again, on the nineteenth century's concern with the legibility of public life and its orderly classification. The panorama and its avatars, from the diorama to the Musée de l'Univers, were part of a broader cultural and positivist phenomenon, as were in different ways realistic novels and statistics. Here was a city where idlers on the boulevard des Capucines and, in 1844, on the Champs-Elysées as well, could view not just paintings of Paris but also celestial globes.[26] And also bear in mind the vogue for historical painting, ranging from Guy-Nicolas Brenet's *La Mort de Du Guesclin* (1777) to the Napoleonic canvases of Ernest Meissonier (1815–1891): the need to understand Paris and its past as a living, visible, and ordered organism was ubiquitous. Think also of Nadar (Félix Tournachon), the aeronaut-photographer, who gave us one of the nineteenth century's first aerial photographs of a city, taken from a balloon over Paris: the subject was the boulevards radiating out from the Arc de Triomphe. Daumier scornfully entitled a lithograph *Nadar Elevating Photography to the Level of Art.*

Balzac's words are quite eloquent as Rastignac stands after Goriot's funeral on the heights of Père-Lachaise, from which it was possible at the time to look down on all of Paris:

> Eugene, now alone, walked a few steps to the topmost part of the graveyard. He saw Paris, spread windingly along the two banks of the Seine. Lights were beginning to twinkle. His gaze fixed itself almost avidly on the space between the column in the Place Vendôme and the cupola of Les Invalides. There lived the world into which he had wished to penetrate. He fastened on the murmurous hive a look that seemed already to be sucking the honey from it, and uttered these words: "Now I'm ready for you!"[27]

Rastignac's eroticized, penetrating gaze on the city that is the object of his desire is evocative: to read and comprehend something is also to possess it. Paris made legible and "real" becomes an object.

Bᴜᴛ ɪᴛ ᴡᴀs Georges Haussmann, a Parisian by birth and a graduate of the Lycée Henri IV and the Paris Faculty of Law, who finally gave perfect form to the Enlightenment's idealized urban project: rationality, regularity, clarity, comprehension, transparency, legibility. Haussmann did not invent the idea of urban readability as the standardization of urban spectacles. Indeed, Françoise Choay, in her lucid and enlightening book *La Règle et le modèle* (Rules and Models), traces this normative concept back to Sir Thomas More. For her, Haussmann was not really a systematic thinker, and his modernizing discourse was coherent in appearance only (Choay speaks of a "surface logic"). The real coherence of Haussmann's ideas, she argues convincingly, lay in their relation to urbanist traditions stemming from the Renaissance, which he merely amplified. Recall the verdict of Haussmann's closest collaborator, Adolphe Alphand, that "Haussmann had an amazing faculty for assimilation and 'often took as his own, with the greatest good faith, the ideas he had once adopted' from others."[28]

And yet Haussmann did have genius, perhaps not in the conception, but in the realization of plans that others before him had elaborated in piecemeal fashion at best. He did not invent urban modernity or legibility, but he had no peer when it came to achieving these goals through planning.

One can, if one wishes, give a materialist or naively political explanation of what Haussmann was up to. In the 1850s, Bonapartism was after all what the people wanted (or what the notables responsible for interpreting the will of the masses wanted), but it was also what the police and especially the army wanted—an army that was hyper-politicized and, in consequence, militarily weak, as was soon to become apparent, unfortunately, at Sedan during the Franco-Prussian War.

At times Walter Benjamin espoused this militarized view of Haussmann's purpose, and for once he was on the wrong track:

> The true purpose of Haussmann's work was to secure the city against civil war. He wanted to make the erection of barricades in Paris impossible for all time. With such intent Louis Philippe had already introduced wooden paving. Yet the barricades played a part in the February Revolution. Engels studies the technique of barricade fighting. Haussmann

seeks to prevent barricades in two ways. The breadth of the streets is intended to make their erection impossible, and new thoroughfares are
to open the shortest route between the barracks and the working-class
districts. Contemporaries christen the enterprise "strategic embellishment."[29]

It is of course true that the Célestins barracks near the Bastille (today a Republican Guard headquarters), like the barracks on the Place
Monge not far from the rue Mouffetard (the most thoroughly barricaded
street in Paris in June 1848), was hardly an ephemeral structure. And
yet by 1860 the military uselessness of barricades was well known,
and Gustave-Paul Cluseret, a military leader of the Paris Commune,
would soon urge the Communards to confront Versailles's troops in
their homes and in burned-out public buildings precisely because barricades were of little use. And what this soldier of the Commune knew,
Haussmann, who had had an opportunity to admire the new Krupp can-
non at the Exposition of 1867, surely also knew. Benjamin might have
noticed this as well, had he not been so influenced by the disdain for
Haussmann's Paris that was so common in the 1930s, especially among
the Surrealists.

It is therefore reasonably safe to assume that military concerns were
only a secondary consideration in the reconstruction of Paris. We can
conjecture that Haussmann may even have used such concerns as a subtle tactic to sell his plans for modernization to the more hidebound conservatives. As he noted in a report of a conversation he had with Napoleon III, "although the population of Paris was as a whole sympathetic
to the plans for the transformation, or, as it was then called, 'embellishment' [of the city], the greater part of the bourgeoisie and almost all of
the aristocracy were hostile."[30]

The force of the Haussmannian boulevard lay far more in its political
legibility—as proof of the creative power of the bourgeoisie—than in its
resistance to barricades. Winding, narrow streets, symbolic in a different way, enforced their own kind of law, with consequences that were
not always foreseeable. Circulation there was slow and difficult. Hidden
within their warrens, the people felt themselves to be strong; the police
felt weak and conspicuous. In the eighteenth century, engravers of street

names had had to work at night to avoid the insults and blows of the *petit peuple,* who knew that knowledge of the neighborhood would benefit the police they had previously been able to elude.

The new boulevard, by contrast, allowed the visual as well as the military penetration of the city. The straight streets attested to the power of their creator and the principles that guided his activity: in one sense this was a war of symbols in which everyone knew the stakes were high. The historian Maurice Agulhon has made us aware of the rivalry that existed in every nineteenth-century French village between the town hall and the church, the statue of the Virgin and the bust of Marianne, each representing a different myth. The Communards understood such rivalries as well. At the painter Gustave Courbet's behest, they did topple the Colonne Vendôme (with the intention of replacing it with a statue of Liberty), but—and this is more interesting—they also felt the need to build superb, boulevard-obstructing barricades, militarily useless but visually imposing, such as the one on the rue Saint-Florentin adjacent to the Place de la Concorde, a crucial symbolic site for Frenchmen of every political stripe. We even know the name of the architect in command: Napoléon-Louis Gaillard, a shoemaker honored in Paris as the inventor of the rubber overshoe, who proudly posed for photographers in front of his masterpiece, the Château Gaillard, named after the mighty fortress the medieval kings of England had built to protect their Normandy provinces from the Capetian kings.

Visibility is the key: Haussmann's long perspectives made it possible to take in an entire avenue at a glance, to decipher and organize the city's space. Not even the Internet is quicker. Moreover, the city became legible by night as well as by day: "Now that gas has reached the little streets of the big city," the author of *Paris au gaz* explained in 1861, "night truly is no more, because darkness has been banished."[31]

Communication and legibility now became such obsessions that the relation between the street and the monument was reversed. In the religious, monarchical Paris of churches and royal squares, monuments were primary and the streets leading to them secondary (on the Ile de la Cité, the section of Paris most completely redesigned by Haussmann, there were no important streets, only monuments). This relationship—

the monument immanent, the street in a supporting role—is illustrated perfectly by the Esplanade des Invalides, which exists (or at any rate existed originally) only to set off the edifice that dominates it.

By contrast, the new boulevard was typically a straight and legible line of communication offering a view of a public monument, at times built to order, whose sole purpose was to lend nobility to an urban traffic corridor. For instance, the primary function of the église de Saint-Augustin was to beautify the boulevard Malesherbes, which was an end unto itself. (Note also that since 1833, when Claude-Philibert Rambuteau was prefect, Paris boulevards had been equipped with benches, which allowed the members of the bourgeoisie to settle in as if they owned the streets.) Similarly, the only purpose of the église de la Trinité was to beautify the Chaussée d'Antin. And what would the Opéra be without the avenue de l'Opéra, which was originally to be called the avenue Napoléon? The Pantheon offers a rather curious example of this newly aestheticized relationship between monument and avenue. From up close, it unambiguously dominates the rather short rue Soufflot, and that was its primary function in the eighteenth century. Today, however, we are more likely to catch sight of the monument while driving northward along the avenue des Gobelins, even though that avenue stops at the foot of the Montagne Sainte-Geneviève on which the Pantheon stands because Napoleon III was disappointed in his desire to extend the avenue up to the Pantheon. In Hegelian jargon, though intended by the ancien régime as a monument in itself, the Pantheon today serves merely as a distant and useless embellishment to the (ironically incomplete) access route leading from the A7 superhighway into central Paris. Haussmann, one might add, regretted not having shifted the north-south axis of Paris slightly eastward, a shift that would have wreaked havoc in the city, but that would have allowed him to create an axis running from the Gare de l'Est to the Sorbonne and the cupola of its elegant chapel.

Walter Benjamin was struck by the perspectives opened up by the long series of these streets: "This corresponds to the inclination, noticeable again and again in the nineteenth century, to ennoble technical necessities by artistic aims. The institutions of the secular and clerical dominance of the bourgeoisie were to find their apotheosis in a framework of streets."[32]

Visibility, communication: these were Haussmann's hobbyhorses—and when it came to traffic flow, the prefect was even more imperialistic than the emperor. Napoleon III, a former artilleryman and apprentice engineer, had ideas of his own. For example, he would have liked to see the bridge linking the Place de la Bastille to the Left Bank built in the classical manner, perpendicular to the river but offset with respect to the boulevard Henri IV. For Haussmann, meanwhile, it was important that the axis of the Pont Sully run diagonal to the river in order to facilitate traffic flow, but above all so as not to spoil the view from the Place de la Bastille in the northeast to the Pantheon in the southwest. (Haussmann's preference, incidentally, was shared by the Third Republic architects who completed his work as he wished it to be.)

This concern with visibility and legibility often became downright theatrical, as Haussmann himself must have realized: witness a description of the inauguration of the boulevard de Sébastopol: "At 2:30, as the [imperial] procession approached the boulevard Saint-Denis, the vast curtain that masked the end of the boulevard de Sébastopol was drawn aside. The curtain had been stretched between two Moorish columns, the pedestals of which were adorned with figures representing the Arts, the Sciences, Industry, and Commerce."[33]

One cannot help admiring this image of the boulevard de Sébastopol, which is rather seedy today, as a theater of modernity and bourgeois respectability. In the 1850s Léon Leymonnerie immortalized such "ephemeral triumphs" in an agreeable series of watercolors, commemorating not only the return of the Army of the Orient in 1855 but also the inaugurations of various urban projects, such as the opening of the avenue Victoria in 1856 and of the boulevard du Prince Eugène (now the boulevard Voltaire) in 1862. (It is not hard to understand why Benjamin thought that, in Paris, it was "as if streets went through the entire city where houses seemed to be there not to be lived in, but as a corridor through which one moves along.")[34]

The ambition of the Haussmannian modernizers was to make Paris theatrically legible, and, determined as they were in that purpose, they were not satisfied with simply improving what lay on the surface: underground Paris had to be done over as well. Nadar shot aerial photographs from a balloon, but he also photographed the city's sewers. For the first time in history, photography made it possible to "read" an underground realm, with models dressed as sewer workers to lend realism to the scene (models were necessary because in those days it took eighteen minutes to expose a photographic plate).

"Adieu, vile sewer, vile Paris," is a not very affable comment from Eugène Sue, author of the celebrated *Mystères de Paris.* Balzac, resorting to similar rhetoric, once compared the Chaussée d'Antin to a "moral sewer of Paris." After 1820 the idea of Paris as sewer, as disgusting cloaca, filthy quagmire, quickly became commonplace. Pierre Citron has found twenty poetic texts from the period 1830–1848 that touch on the theme, and six more from the period 1848–1862. For Alexandre Parent-Duchâtelet, the sewer, along with the sexual organ of the prostitute, was the quintessential symbol of the filth that needed to be scoured out of the city at all costs. Victor Hugo agreed. For Hugo, the sewer was the best way to read the history of the capital: "The history of man is reflected in the history of SOMETHING . . . the sewers of Paris were a formidable thing. It was a sepulchre and a refuge. Crime, intelligence, social protest, freedom of conscience, thought, rape, everything that human laws punish or punished was hidden in that hole."[35]

All that would now change, and Haussmann's cleanup of Paris necessarily extended to a total renovation of this foul and decrepit part of the city. Thanks to the prefect and his engineer, Eugène Belgrand (for whom, as for his superior and colleague Alphand, a street was named), new sewers were dug beneath the vast majority of Paris streets during the Second Empire. By 1870 the underground network was four times as extensive as it had been twenty years earlier. Eleven collectors received sewage from the entire city. The olfactory tyranny of foul-smelling waste (of which Parent-Duchâtelet had identified six types) gave way to the reign of cleanliness and order.[36] Many people who came to Paris for the Exposition of 1867 visited the new sewer system, which quickly became a tourist attraction and *lieu de mémoire,* the perfect symbol of the myth of Paris, virilized capital of modernity.

Louis Veuillot (1813–1883), an intransigent Catholic, saw clearly what was happening. In his book appropriately entitled *Les Odeurs de Paris,* this friend of old Paris stood the rhetoric of the sewer builders on its head in order to criticize modernity, which for him was nothing but a new form of paganism. Haussmann's boulevards, he wrote, were sewers awash with modernity: "Paris is a flood that has submerged French civilization."[37]

B Y 1870 PARIS had become, for the partisans of modernity, the wholly legible city—a view in which they were joined, albeit in a somewhat ambiguous fashion, by the Impressionists, who in this respect were precursors of a new "modernist" modernity. The Impressionists too understood the legibility of the new modern city, but, critically, they saw it as a much colder city than the one it had replaced. Manet's *Rue Mosnier,* Caillebotte's *Pont de l'Europe,* and Pissarro's *Boulevard de l'Opéra* all express a new anxiety.

An anxiety that Haussmann himself, of course, did not feel. What mattered for him was that he had made the city the showcase of the nineteenth century. And taken on his terms, his enterprise was extraordinarily successful, as we can still sense today if we compare his Paris, now more than a century old, with the vast new cities of the Third World, because it is still the Paris of 1860, rather than these newer cities or the older cities of the Renaissance, that strikes us as the normative, rational, desirable, and necessary model of a perfect modern city.

8

The Urban Machine

IN THE NINETEENTH CENTURY, when machines were a source of wonder, a fascination with order, physics, and mechanics gave rise to the myth of the city imagined as a perfectly regulated instrument, as a place free of traffic jams or slums, the kind of ideal place, perfectly planned and conceived, that had been proposed by Claude-Nicolas Ledoux, the architect of the royal saltworks at Arc-et-Senans.

In this rejuvenated frame, the incomprehensible city of the Middle Ages would be supplanted by a new, completely legible vision of the city stemming from the Enlightenment—a cosmogonic and therefore mythical vision. Here was the city taken to be the centerpiece of a new moral order, as represented today by the Masonic symbolism on the American dollar bill, with a pyramid on one side standing for eternity and on the other side a portrait of the man who in 1789 was president of the new and luminous American republic, the firstborn child of modern Europe.

The primary concern of the great urbanists of the 1850s and 1860s was thus to improve the mechanics of city life, to regulate both its positive energy (by improving the flow of traffic) and its negative energy (by limiting prostitution, reducing crime, and restricting the movements of the lowlifes of the slums and the not much less disreputable denizens of the rooming houses). A Sisyphean task if ever there was one, for the pertinent boundaries were, as Françoise Choay has said, "fluctuating [and] impossible to pin down."[1]

Movement, then, but of what kind? In urbanism as in politics and literature there is an important distinction between the regulation and the mere negation of movement. Balzac's royalist and reactionary dream city would have been static, perfectly organized, changeless, and made corporate once again with guilds and estates. Nineteenth-century Paris fascinated the novelist precisely because it stood as the perfect antithesis of this neo-Catholic utopia. Balzac, as we shall see, was horrified by the capital's frenetic pace, by its cruelty and dynamism, as a result of which everyone in the city, rich and poor, male and female, noble and bourgeois, lived in constant torment, endlessly ascending and descending the degrees of unhappiness and misfortune: think of Grandet growing steadily richer but loved less and less; or Goriot growing steadily poorer but also less and less loved.

And Balzac was not alone. Until the dark years of the Vichy regime, one whole wing of French culture, and even of Parisian culture, shared his nostalgic sensibility. With the Great Revolution of 1789 converted into myth in 1830, and then with the expansion of "machinism" and the railroads, French society divided between proponents of what people at the time called "resistance," on the right (the constitutional monarchists behind Casimir-Périer, flanked by Berryer's traditionalist legitimists), and, on the left, advocates of "movement," whether it be the dynastic, constitutional left with Tocqueville or the republican and democratic left with Ledru-Rollin. It was the past pitted against the future, a rivalry that we find cropping up again and again in this period: for instance, in the opposition between Georges Cuvier's static model of nature and the more evolutionary theories of Etienne Geoffroy Saint-Hilaire and other heirs of Lamarck. (Michel Foucault has stressed the important influence of scientific discipline on Parisian political and cultural thought: in his view, the shift from description to analysis in the natural sciences allowed a parallel evolution in other realms.)

In Balzacian and post-Balzacian mythology, and also in Baudelaire's thinking, movement in the city was as ubiquitous as evil itself. Haussmann shared their view, but with a major difference, because this tough-minded prefect believed unequivocally that the dark side of modernity could be subjugated: once Paris was finally modernized, he thought, nefarious drives would be transformed into productive, creative rationality. The central idea of Haussmann's project may even have been to facilitate movement, and by regulating it, to make it more productive, the diametrical opposite of the chaotic movement that Balzac saw so clearly whenever he thought about Paris. The writer and the prefect were practically contemporaries: only a decade separated them. Both were aware of the menace inherent in the laborious/dangerous classes, but their responses to that menace could not have been more different.

Haussmann's schemes of the 1850s were of course not without precedent: mention has been made of eighteenth-century urbanists; and during the Revolution there was an "artists' plan" for renovating the capital. The authors of this proposal justified their recommendations by citing the need to create "outlets to facilitate the flow of traffic" and to "eliminate narrow, winding streets where the air barely circulates, thereby fostering corruption and creating unhealthy conditions." By Haussmann's time, however, this was a distant memory, and so, too, perhaps, given the pace of historical change in his day, was the barricading of narrow streets in 1848, which many have seen—erroneously it seems to me—as a determining cause of his work. These memories and antecedents had relatively little influence on the visionary prefect, who saw himself as an "artist of demolition," pragmatic, Protestant, modern, efficient, and unconcerned with ideology or history, whether past or present.

If Haussmann had little use for the past, the future was always on his mind. In this respect he was a faithful exponent of the *pensée unique,* at once liberal and conservative, of the Second Empire bourgeoisie, which was perhaps motivated by the memory of crime and civil war, but especially seduced by the allure of healing progress. Parisians in 1830 shared this concern with the future, in relation not only to city planning but to the social and political fate of the Western world in general. (This was the preoccupation not only of Comte and Marx but also of Alexis, comte de Tocqueville, an aristocrat by birth, the son of a prefect of Charles X, and a reluctant admirer of American modernity. Indeed, many people who clung to the past would accuse Haussmann of trying to "Americanize" Paris.)

By 1850, then, many people in Paris believed that the city and its political system would have to be democratized or at least modernized along with everything else. But if modernization was inevitable, what would it be like? What needed to be changed? Had Haussmann been asked that question, he would no doubt have answered, "Everything," from the means of communication to the system of water supply (in Paris in 1850 only one house in five had running water). Gardens would have to be done over and cesspits drained (most of Paris did not yet have sewers). It was no longer enough to work piecemeal, improving the Place Saint-Sulpice or extending the rue de Rivoli, as had been done under Napoleon I; or to dig a reservoir at La Villette, as 1,500 Russian and Austrian prisoners had been forced to do between 1806 and 1809; or to build the odd bridge across the Seine, as Louis Philippe had done, or to clear the way for a few new streets, as another prefect, the timid innovator Claude Rambuteau, had done under the Citizen-King. Haussmann planned to tear up the entire city, including the cemeteries: death (that is, the past) would have to make way for life. And, not surprisingly, Haussmann would have liked to move (to Méry-sur-Oise) the most celebrated Paris cemetery, Père-Lachaise, a bucolic necropolis with 12,000 trees that had been created in 1804 on the site of a *folie,* or retreat, that had once belonged to the Jesuits. "With Haussmann," Pierre Véron wrote in 1867, "Paris has no time for the past." Robert Herbert has written that Manet "forced open a gap with history, which could no longer be held up to the present as an intact world. It would not be imitated or emulated, only quoted, and the quotation marks would be visible." Indeed, and it is no surprise that Manet was perhaps, of all the Impressionists, the most sympathetic to, and the most accurate chronicler of, Haussmann's Paris.[2]

Indomitable administrator that he was, Haussmann even managed within a very short period to shift the location of the city's center. It had moved before, to be sure, but slowly: from the Pont Neuf in 1713 ("the busiest place, with the heaviest traffic, in the entire city") to the Palais Royal on the eve of the Revolution, when that enclosed space was the capital of the capital. Then, year by year, the heart of the city moved from boulevard to boulevard, as described by Balzac: "From the rue du Faubourg du Temple to the rue Charlot, where all Paris gathered, the life [of the city] shifted in 1815 to the boulevard des Panoramas. In 1820 it settled on the so-called boulevard de Gand [now the boulevard des Italiens] . . . And now, it is showing signs of moving again, toward La Madeleine." After Balzac's death, the center of Paris moved still more rapidly from the rue de la Paix in 1860 toward the Place de la Concorde and the new elegance of what Proust would call "the dolorous quarter of the Champs-Elysées." (One can hardly refrain from asking where the essence of Paris is today: in the television studios on the quai Kennedy? Or perhaps on the Internet?)[3]

Reinforcing the sense that social and political change was inevitable was a feeling that the time had come to eliminate unhealthy conditions that had previously seemed immutable. Perhaps the most important catalyst of this side of the new spirit was the memory not of barricades or political events but of two cholera epidemics: the first, in 1832, afflicted 40,000 people and killed 20,000, including the prime minister, Casimir-Périer; and the second, in 1849, claimed 19,000 victims, including Marshal Bugeaud, who had become famous for his victories in North Africa.[4] For the Parisian modernizers, cholera was the AIDS of the day, "an Asiatic demon," according to Alexandre Dumas *père,* a medieval survival of foreign origin, an alien, barbaric menace that had made its way from China and India through Eastern Europe, Poland, and Russia and was sometimes listed as one of the traits of the wandering Jew.

The determination to rid France of these "alien miasmas" was intensified by the misinterpretation of the nature of the epidemics in the light of prevailing scientific fantasies. For the "anti-contagionists" (whose explanations would soon be shown to be invalid and who knew nothing about *Vibrio cholerae,* yet to be discovered), the disease resulted from a lack of air and light and from the deficiencies of the capital's system of food and water supply. In other words, cholera was the result of precisely those public hygiene problems that Haussmann had set out to fix forever. The problems were indeed numerous: in 1880, out of a Parisian population of roughly 2 million, there were 15,000 deaths per year from tuberculosis, 2,000 from diphtheria, and 1,500 from typhoid fever; 1,000 women died every year in childbirth. (Pasteur, who as a young man wrote that Paris was a sordid and repulsive city, lost three of his children to typhoid fever.) In 1885 a republican functionary could still deplore the persistence of epidemics in the capital, related as these were to "prejudices that are difficult to eliminate, all the more so in that they date back as far as the Middle Ages."[5]

Memories of disease mattered, and so did the practicalities of the situation: with or without epidemics, the very size of the capital's population made some sort of reform imperative. There had been only 300,000 Parisians in 1600, 400,000 under Louis XIV, and perhaps 550,000–600,000 in 1800. At that point, however, growth accelerated, and the population passed 700,000 in 1830, a million in 1846, 1.2 million in 1856, 1.8 million in 1872, and 2.5 million in 1896. Something had to be done for these new Parisians and their 100,000 horses, like it or not, just as today, like it or not, the city's leaders cannot forget about the new and diverse suburbs that surround their city.

ANDRÉ SIEGFRIED, a founder of modern French sociology, who knew the Third Republic and its ways of thinking so intimately, was amused by the prevalence of the word *petit* in the average person's conversation before the First World War: at the Café du Commerce, he remarked, the provincial readers of *Le Petit Parisien* were always saying *petite femme, petits plats, petits pois, petit journal, petite maison, petits métiers,* and so on. In Haussmann's Paris, by contrast, everything was *grand: Grand Hôtel, grands boulevards, grands magasins, grands couturiers.* François Loyer, one of the leading specialists in Haussmannian urbanism, is right to call attention to the idea of a *grande composition.*

Haussmann's Paris was a truly democratic enterprise in the—not insignificant—sense that everyone, rich or poor, would enjoy the health benefits of his public works projects. First there was the improvement of the water supply: the system put in place by the hydrological engineer Eugène Belgrand brought water to the city from 253 kilometers away, with 17 bridges, 6 kilometers of aqueduct, 7 kilometers of siphons, and 28 kilometers of underground channels. The system for the evacuation of human waste (as has been seen) was greatly improved as well. There is no doubt that public health in the capital rapidly improved, as is evident from the virtual disappearance of cholera (although there was a mini-epidemic in 1884 and a brief resurgence of the disease in July 1892).

And then too, the emperor (who was, in his own way, a democrat and even claimed to be a socialist) went so far as to subsidize the construction of a number of model residences for workers. One of these was the Cité Napoléon at 58, rue Rochechouart, with 86 apartments renting for 100–300 francs a year for a bedroom with fireplace, a well-lit sitting room, and a small kitchen, with toilets and drains for waste water located "at the extremities of the building." A similar inspiration led to the development of the Bois de Vincennes, which became to the humbler sections of eastern Paris what the Bois de Boulogne already was to the west end.[6]

In the main, however, Haussmann's Paris—though renovated from top to bottom for all to enjoy—was nonetheless strictly stratified by wealth, as was the new bourgeois society that expected to see its image in the renovation of this ancient city. As Françoise Choay points out, "The twofold nature of Haussmann's writings, dictated on the surface by universal rationality and at a deeper level by an occult logic, . . . anticipates . . . the duplicity of present-day administrative texts."[7] Haussmann was always concerned with financial hierarchies and often with social hierarchies as well. Indeed, as François Loyer notes, we find in Haussmann's work a "hierarchy of urban elements" embedded in the very materials out of which the new city was built and therefore plainly legible to anyone with eyes to see. The wealthiest Parisians lived in ostentatious buildings of dressed stone with or without ornamental sculpture. A notch lower on the scale were buildings whose nobler portions were of this type but which also included more modest areas where any ornament was of industrial ceramic. Still lower on the scale were buildings with metal frames and ever-thinner brick walls (the presence or absence of brick is crucial to the classification of real estate in Paris). And at the bottom, more recently, we have added houses of stuccoed cinderblock, ideal for building detached suburban homes. According to Paul Leroy-Beaulieu, this hierarchy of building types corresponded to a hierarchy of rents, which ranged from 4,000–25,000 francs for the opulent class to 2,000–4,000 francs for the wealthy bourgeoisie to less than 400 francs for more than 70 percent of Parisian dwellings.

This hierarchy went hand in hand with a new specialization of neighborhoods and urban functions, a reorganization of the geography of the city that undoubtedly was dictated by real estate costs but also deliberately carried out quite apart from any financial motivation. Evidence for this assertion can be seen in the high density of certain provincial cities, which were built in imitation of the Parisian model despite much lower land costs.[8]

Just as there was a hierarchy of building materials, so too would there henceforth be a hierarchy of urban geography. To be sure, a certain specialization of Paris neighborhoods was already evident well before 1800. Jean Favier notes that it was between the time of Louis XIII and the personal reign of Louis XIV that the bourgeoisie developed "a notion of fashionable neighborhoods, which had previously been confined to the aristocracy."[9] In 1800 some Paris neighborhoods, such as the Place des Vosges, the Marais, and the Faubourg Saint-Germain, were decidedly more aristocratic than others. Others, such as the Faubourg Saint-Marcel, were infinitely less so (there were virtually no noble families living there in 1789).

What struck observers at the time, however, was the mixing rather than the separation of people of different conditions: "Unique city," Louis-Sébastien Mercier exclaimed in his *Tableau de Paris,* "in which a simple dividing wall finds a pious choir of devout and austere Carmelites living on one side and wild and libertine scenes of a joyous seraglio on the other; in which, in the same house, one person dreams of investing a million while another dreams of borrowing an écu!" Until 1840 it was common for rich and poor to live together: social stratification was vertical, by floor, rather than horizontal, by neighborhood. For instance, Zola's Gervaise rises story by story as her social decline accelerates. As a ruined alcoholic, Zola tells us, she dreams of "seeing herself in person downstairs under the porch near the concierge's lodge, her nose in the air, examining the house for the first time." And listen to Pierre-

Joseph Proudhon: "I sorely needed civilizing. But shall I admit it? What little I got disgusted me. I hate houses with more than one floor, which stand the social hierarchy on its head, with the poor confined above and the rich established close to the ground."[10]

Haussmann's housecleaning changed all this, not least because his urban renewal policies received an unexpected boost from a new technology, the elevator, which dates from approximately 1867 and was first used in the city's new and grand hotels. (In 1896 the architect Charles Girault opined that the elevator shaft should be given pride of place. Motifs "inspired by eighteenth-century art" were, he thought, particularly suitable as decorations for the elevator's interior.) And in truth, who nowadays would not choose a sunny seventh-floor apartment with elevator and view over the former *étage noble,* which may have been noble but was also dark? Representations of Paris from the first half of the nineteenth century invariably insist on the variegated social life of the average Paris apartment house, but that arrangement became a victim of progress.

So it was that, in the newly efficient post-Haussmannian Paris, hierarchy and social specialization came together and then also fused with functional specialization. True, out of concerns for "liberalism," Haussmann's discourse still made no mention of zoning restrictions.[11] And yet specialization there was: the university remained on the Montagne Sainte-Geneviève, an area familiar to Haussmann, who as a young Parisian student had often made the trek from the Chaussée d'Antin to his school on the Place du Panthéon. Prostitution was henceforth centered in Montmartre and around the Place de Clichy. Businessmen gathered around the Bourse; and wholesale suppliers congregated in the area of Les Halles. Exotic animals went to the Jardin des Plantes, fish to an aquarium created in 1859, and other beasts to the abattoir of La Villette, which was erected in 1863–1867. The ease of communication made everything function more efficiently.

Here we touch on the core of Haussmann's idea of urbanism: for him the modern city was a place for exchange, for movement from one specialized area to another, and for the mechanical meshing of movements and exchange. In Paris he therefore built 200 kilometers of new streets, lined by 34,000 new buildings containing 215,000 new apartments. Perreymond, a Fourierist urbanist of the 1840s, had also dreamed of modernizing Parisian transportation, but his idea was to improve the link between river traffic and the new rail traffic. In Haussmann's circulation plans, by contrast, the Seine was of relatively minor importance. The two critical elements were horse-drawn traffic and rail traffic.

Today the steam locomotive is a picturesque symbol of tamed industrialism. Here and there, on a Sunday during the summer, a locomotive is taken out of storage and demonstrated for curious crowds of onlookers. In the nineteenth century, however, the steam locomotive was the mythical symbol of a new modernity, a machine that had definitively triumphed and was often given as the emblem of a new Paris: "Four locomotives guarded the entry to the machinery annex," Edmond and Jules de Goncourt wrote of the Universal Exposition of 1867, "like the great bulls of Nineveh or the great Egyptian sphinxes that stood outside temples . . . All four were in motion." One is not surprised to learn that Euloge Schneider, the president of the ironworks at Le Creusot as well as of the Corps Législatif or lower house of the legislature, interrupted the debates of that august assembly in 1867 to announce to his colleagues that a locomotive "made in France" had just been sold to England, the birthplace of the new technology. (In this connection, it is worth noting that in 1848 the city of Paris "imported" 5,763 metric tons of steel rail; in 1854, 11,000 tons; and in 1867, 62,000 tons.) "Just think," wrote Théophile Gautier. "Somebody came up with a contredanse called *le chemin de fer* (the railroad). It begins with an imitation of those horrible whistle blasts that announce the departure of a train. The rattle of the machinery, the crunch of the bumpers, and the clank of iron are all imitated to perfection." Berlioz composed a Saint-Simonian *Chant des chemins de fer.* Similarly, the first act of Offenbach's *Gaieté Parisienne* is set in a railroad station.[12]

Haussmann, then, did not neglect (public) railroad stations or trains, but his first obsession was with boulevards, which improved travel by (private) carriage. In the reign of Francis I, it is said, there were only three authentic carriages in Paris, but from that time their number increased steadily, to 300 in 1660 and to 14,000 in 1722.[13] (In 1674 the Prince de Condé imported the first carriage with glass windows from Brussels.) In the 1860s some 12,000 horse-drawn carriages drove past the Gare de l'Est each day, and 18,000 crossed the Pont-Neuf. (For comparison, note that in 1950, almost a century later, some 79,000 automobiles crossed the Place de l'Alma daily, and 62,000 crossed the Place Saint-Augustin.) As early as 1866, Louis Veuillot, an unbending enemy of progress, remarked that "the wider [the street], the more difficult the travel. Carriages clog the broad avenues, and pedestrians clog the wide sidewalks."[14] We can add here that Parisian traffic was first made to flow in a circle and counterclockwise at the Arc de Triomphe in 1909; the first attempt to regulate traffic flow by stationing policemen with red and white disks at major intersections came in 1912; the first traffic lights, modeled on lights in Berlin, arrived in 1922; and the first network of one-way streets was established in 1950. And to go on with this automotive line, the first motor vehicle to drive across Paris was a Panhard automobile, which made the trip in 1891 (Panhards continued to be produced in France until 1967). There were 25,000 automobiles in Paris in 1914 and 300,000 in 1930, when one of every three French cars was Parisian. By 1980 the number had increased to 850,000.

The history of the tramway also proceeded in stages. Streetcars were first tried in 1854 but did not become common until 1875 and all but disappeared by 1937, having been supplanted by cars and buses (of which there were 1,733 in 1930 and 4,067 in 1937).

Haussmann's keen interest in traffic flow was perhaps the most durable of his legacies to the Parisians of today. How else to explain their atavistic indulgence of the automobile and its many attendant nuisances: pollution, disfiguration of the banks of the Seine, traffic accidents, congestion, and the proliferation of parking garages? No doubt the capital's residents, and Georges Pompidou in particular, internalized an updated version of Haussmann's noxious equation: big city = traffic = automobiles. It is to be hoped—I suppose—that those Parisians who are still too fond of driving about their city today are aware of and grateful for his efforts.[15]

COMMUNICATION AND, as a corollary, straight lines were the essential principles of the Haussmannian urban machine. In Edmond About's *L'Homme à l'oreille cassée* (The Man with a Broken Ear; 1862), we meet a Colonel Fougas, who, it seems, was frozen while in Russia with Napoleon and has only recently been thawed out. When Napoleon III asks what he would like to see in Paris, the colonel replies: "Above all, you need to straighten out the course of the Seine. There's something shocking about its irregular curve. A straight line is the shortest path . . . for rivers as well as boulevards." And of necessity that selfsame rectilinearity offended the aristocratically minded Goncourts: "I am a stranger to what is yet to come and to what is, as I am also a stranger to these new boulevards without curves, without adventures or prospects, which are implacably straight and no longer redolent of the world of Balzac, [and] which make you think of some Babylon of the future."[16]

The history of the Place de la Concorde is revealing in this respect. Fortunately, it is no longer used as a parking lot, as it was for twenty or thirty years now happily forgotten, but today one might say that it has become the world's most beautiful highway interchange. (More than any other place in Paris, this is where the city's north-south and east-west axes cross: the Châtelet, the Rond-Point de l'Etoile, the Alma, and the Place de l'Opéra all serve a similar function but in a less obvious way.) This was not the first function of this marvelous space, however: in the minds of the Parisian notables who proposed it to the king, the Place Louis XV, like the Esplanade des Invalides, was to have no useful purpose. At the time there was ordinarily little traffic on this jewel of Bourbon absolutism. Moats (since filled in) made it impossible. Indeed, the Pont de la Concorde, which "utilitarianized" the place, so to speak,

---

Widening the Pont de la Concorde, 1930–1932. Urban traffic was Haussmann's prophetic obsession, and today it is hard for us to imagine his boulevards without the flow of motor vehicles. The Place de la Concorde was created in 1763. During the French Revolution more than a thousand people were executed there, and the bridge leading to it was built at that time, in part with stones from the Bastille. The expansion of the bridge in 1930–1932 made it harder to defend during the "pre-fascist" riots of February 1934. Copyright: Harlingue—Viollet.

was not inaugurated until 1791, or nearly half a century after the inauguration of the Place de la Concorde itself. Several engravings from the period show us the site looking much as the Terreiro do Paço in Lisbon looks today, sitting alongside the river and leading nowhere (in the "Paris as a seaport" genre). Remember, too, that the Pont de la Concorde was not widened until 1932 (a project that, incidentally, helped spur on the rioters of February 1934, who were now less easily contained). In 1853 the architect Jacques-Ignace Hittorf, a failed poet no doubt and therefore indifferent to the needs of circulation, hoped that the Place de l'Etoile would be rebuilt as a decorative and triumphal forum in the image of a shining (mythical) sun facing Paris and set off by monumental gates, all combined with a vast and spectacular racetrack for horses on what is now the avenue MacMahon. Haussmann rejected this impractical proposal out of hand.[17]

There were, it is true, some lacunae in Haussmann's obsession with communication. He did not hesitate, for example, to eviscerate the Ile de la Cité, but mention should be made of some exceptions to his destructive rules. Haussmann was pitiless with clerical survivals, but he also knew when it was necessary to tiptoe around the sensibilities of the rich and powerful, especially in aristocratic neighborhoods such as the Marais and the Faubourg Saint-Germain. Many of the streets that should have been cut in these parts of the capital to improve the operation of the Paris machine never went beyond the planning stage.

To be fair, one should add in Haussmann's defense that other Parisian planners have also been far too deferential to certain prominent Parisians. For instance, there was no logical reason why the number four Métro line linking the Porte d'Orléans and the Gare Montparnasse to the Porte de Clignancourt had to hook around as it does through the Place Saint-Michel in order to reach the Châtelet intersection, which for its part should have been located farther to the north and west. But the plans were drawn as they were so as not to vex the members of the Académie Française, who wanted no part of a subway line passing beneath the Palais Mazarin: the vibrations of the trains might have disturbed their sage deliberations. It is fortunate for the prestige of French high culture that the millions of travelers condemned each day to interminable underground promenades in the Châtelet station are not better versed in the history of their own city!

It is also curious that Haussmann did not more fully ponder the example of London in his day. Its subway system (today's "Tube"), begun in 1863 as the Metropolitan Railway linking Paddington and Farringdon, was quickly successful: within six months, 26,500 Londoners traveled this way every day, perhaps encouraged by assurances from the Metropolitan that steam and coal smoke were good for the lungs, especially for those with tuberculosis. By contrast, the Paris Métropolitain did not begin operation until the Universal Exposition of 1900, even though Michel Chevalier, a man of Saint-Simonian leanings as well as the negotiator (with Richard Cobden) of the British-French free trade agreement of 1860, pointed out the importance of an underground railway for the growth of Paris as early as 1864. Such a railroad, Chevalier proposed, "would decrease congestion, which is already intolerable at times and cannot but increase on the magisterial avenues of this great city." But Haussmann was not moved.[18]

Haussmann also displayed a certain poverty of imagination about the possibilities inherent in the fortifications that surrounded the capital. These had been rebuilt after 1840 and were by the standards of the time quite vast: 450 meters in width and 39 kilometers in length, with behind them, after 1861, the circumventing "boulevards des Maréchaux," which surround the city to this day. An impressive achievement, then, but of dubious military value, as was pointed out at the time by political enemies of Adolphe Thiers, who was the new wall's first sponsor (ironically, as it happened, since Thiers was to head the Versaillais government whose troops easily stormed that selfsame wall in May 1871). What a pity, therefore, that Haussmann failed to see the opportunity to use this space to improve road and rail communications in the city. The railroad known as the Petite Ceinture, designed in 1851 to connect all the gates of Paris, might have served as a starting point, if not for one fatal drawback: it did not connect to the center of the metropolis. Over many years, from *les fortifs* of old to the *périph* (peripheral highway) of today, this gap was never really filled. Gustave Péreire considered this shortcoming in his tracts on the future subway in 1897, and again in

1901 in his *Notes sur l'utilisation des terrains des fortifications* (Notes on the Use of Space of the Fortifications), but the debate on the "Cornudet law" of 1919, which was to govern the urbanization of the capital in the interwar years, dealt only with the aesthetic improvement of this land and took little account of questions of housing or communication.[19]

On the whole, then, we have to conclude that Haussmann took little interest in *public* transportation, a thought that brings us back to the nature of Haussmannian planning, which, as Françoise Choay has noted, was too liberal and insufficiently collective. Paris omnibuses, or horse-drawn public carriages, did exist, often with picturesque names: Les Dames Blanches, Les Tricycles, Les Favorites, Les Citadines, Les Ecossaises, Les Béarnaises, Les Batignollaises, Les Gazelles, Les Sylphides, Les Excellentes, to name a few. But although subject to official sanction since 1828, and eventually integrated into a single company, these public conveyances remained privately controlled, and it is hard not to conclude that Haussmann's basic premise was that his precious boulevards should serve those who could afford to ride in a privately owned horse-and-buggy or a fiacre. (The word *fiacre,* incidentally, was first applied to the hackney carriages offered to the public around 1650 by Sieur Nicolas Sauvage, who did business under the motto "A l'image de Saint-Fiacre." Some 11,000 of these fiacres crisscrossed the city in 1900; the last horse-drawn fiacres disappeared from the capital in 1933.)[20]

I F HAUSSMANN'S communicative schemes were too individualized, they were also too abstract and ideologized. Even in the privileged realm of communication, his myth often outstripped the reality it encompassed, and Napoleon III, much more down-to-earth than his subordinate, often reproached the prefect for emphasizing the aesthetics of communication over the means of communication.

Underlying this divergence was a difference of opinion concerning crossroads and roundabouts. Among the Haussmannian interchanges that we might wish had been designed differently are the intersection of the grand boulevards with the avenue de l'Opéra and of the boulevard Saint-Germain with the boulevard Saint-Michel, as well as the famous

Rond-Point Charles-de-Gaulle-Etoile (the traffic circle around the Arc de Triomphe): seen from the air, that circle is pleasantly laid out, but it is seldom seen from that flattering vantage point.

To be sure, Haussmann cannot be held directly responsible for today's traffic jams and accidents. Such problems existed long before his time. Arlette Farge has recently discovered a police account of a previously unknown exploit of the marquis de Sade: caught in a tie-up of carriages on the Place de la Concorde, the "divine marquis" plunged his sword into a horse hitched to a carriage that happened to be blocking his route. Writing in 1790, the Russian N. M. Karamzin likewise reported that "the illustrious Tournefort, who had safely traveled almost around the world, returned to Paris only to be crushed by a fiacre because during his voyage he had unlearned the art of leaping about the streets like a gazelle, a talent indispensable for all who live here." And what of the sad fate that befell Henri IV in 1610, when his heavy carriage with its poor suspension and leather curtains and its six white horses was stalled at the intersection of the rue Saint-Denis and the rue de la Ferronnerie? Baudelaire, terrified as he so often was, described in *Le Spleen de Paris* the dynamic chaos of horses and carriages "in which death comes at a gallop from all sides at once."[21]

Clearly, then, traffic jams were old problems, but often Haussmann, in trying to solve them, instead helped to render them insoluble. Why plan the imperial rue de Rennes if it was only to end in a virtual cul-de-sac at the église Saint-Germain and the rue Bonaparte?[22] Haussmann can also be blamed for making traffic flow everywhere, even in streets devoted to commerce. There seems to have been some confusion in the prefect's mind about the true function of the rue de Rivoli and the boulevard de Sébastopol. Were they arteries of communication or commercial centers? The two functions did not mesh easily. Much the same thing could be said about the approaches to the Gare Saint-Lazare.

Paris was now intended to be an urban machine: both a machine for circulation and, simultaneously, a machine for more efficient consumption. In the Haussmannian narrative of what a truly modern city might be, the most characteristic sentence might be parsed as follows: [*subject*] pedestrian consumer (preferably female) [*verb*] carries [*object*] purchases through the streets. The boulevards ran from railway station to railway station, but the passengers, remember, were also consumers.

Unlike London, that vast seaport and entrepôt, Paris was never a center of international trade. New York and Berlin were essentially industrial cities, particularly in the second half of the nineteenth century, but Paris never really became an industrial city, and certainly not in Haussmann's time. To be sure, Parisian goods were known the world over, and the *Paris Guide* prepared for the Exposition of 1867 proudly noted that the "great American Union . . . buys 80 million francs worth of merchandise in Paris, followed by England (35 million) and Switzerland (14 million)." Paris, Alphonse de Lamartine proclaimed to the Chamber of Deputies in 1841, "is a vast workshop. Europe comes here, admires, buys, and exports our products everywhere." True enough, but the artisans employed in that vast workshop were not industrial workers but artists proud of their talent who were used to working in small groups and often for customers they knew: only 14 percent of the furniture and 17 percent of the clothing manufactured in Paris in 1860 was shipped outside the city's walls.

If Paris was not an industrial powerhouse, it was a more serious contender as a modern financial center thanks to its banks and its Bourse, which faced the apartment occupied by the anti-Semitic journalist Edouard Drumont of *La Libre parole,* who shook his fist at it every morning. Since money attracts money, moreover, much of the wealth of France flowed toward the capital: in 1914, 7 percent of Parisians owned property worth at least 50,000 francs, compared with just 3 percent of the French generally. The capital was also home to two-thirds of all Frenchmen worth at least five million francs.[23] Still, the Parisian bourgeoisie, even in the era of the audacious Haussmann, was not yet economically audacious. As Adeline Daumard, who, along with François Furet, studied the history of the Paris bourgeoisie, observed: "Wealthy Parisians, the bourgeois aristocracy, avoided extravagance. In the nineteenth century . . . the desire to amass wealth was general [in Paris], but it was limited by a concern with maintaining established positions."[24]

In most economic respects, Paris was not yet a truly modern city. Despite the Péreire brothers' creation of the Crédit Mobilier (an investment bank much more deeply involved in industrial development than was the bank of the Péreires' coreligionists and long-time rivals the Rothschilds), the French capital's great contribution to nineteenth-century economic development was not really in banking. Indeed, the creation of the Bank of England, in which some Huguenot refugees participated, preceded that of the Banque de France by roughly a century.

The true economic originality of the city was not in the realm of production, industrial or financial, but in consumption. Its economic history featured the creation and development of arcades and the modern department store.

"Paris is not, never has been, and never will be a commercial city." This statement by the Revolution's great orator Mirabeau is more than a little perplexing. Paris, though not industrial, had long been a fully developed regional and national commercial center. Even before the end of the ancien régime, the city's shops sold their goods at fixed prices, which is one of the most basic characteristics of commercial modernity (or, rather, was—the Internet may have changed this). Some stores not only offered fixed prices but also made available new products, such as cashmere shawls and exotic colonial goods: the first establishment of this sort, Le Tapis Rouge, opened its doors in 1784. Although such "novelty shops" were not yet "department stores" in the modern sense, their numbers increased steadily after the Revolution. During the Restoration we find such shops as Le Diable Boiteux, Les Deux Magots, Le Petit Matelot, Pygmalion, La Belle Jardinière, Aux Trois Quartiers, and Le Petit Saint-Thomas. In his *César Birotteau,* Balzac explained how these new temples of Parisian commerce worked.

Equally important in both symbolic and practical terms were the new arcades, the illustrious forebears of the great department stores and precursors of today's global commerce—whose inventor was none other than Philippe d'Orléans, later Philippe-Egalité, Louis XVI's cousin and the father of the Citizen-King, Louis Philippe. In 1786 he opened the Galeries du Palais Royal to the public. This was not a permanent structure but a series of wooden stalls that earned the sobriquet "Le Camp des

Tartares." Louis XVI, who had about as much of a head for business as he did for politics, teased his royal relative: "So, cousin, you're going to open a shop? No doubt we'll see you only on Sundays in the future."[25]

As commercial machines, however, before the Revolution these early galleries were not yet complete because they were located within pre-existing structures. By contrast, in a great step forward, the passage Feydeau (1790–1791) was designed from the ground up. It was followed by the passage du Prado (1795); the passage du Caire (1799), which initially specialized in lithography; the passage des Panoramas (1800); and, from 1822 to 1829, fourteen other, similar "shopping malls." By the end of the 1840s there were more than a hundred. Built of glass and metal, the arcades embodied the latest ideas in industrial design. The first public space in Paris to be illuminated by gas, in 1816, was none other than the passage des Panoramas. (As for streets, the Carrousel and a portion of the rue de Rivoli would not be illuminated until 1829, and the grand boulevards not until 1837.) Among the arcades that have survived the passage of time, the most picturesque are the passage Vivienne of 1823 and the passage Véro-Dodat of 1826, the latter named for two wealthy butchers, MM. Véro and Dodat, who formed a partnership to finance its construction. "No expense was spared to make this gallery magnificent," a contemporary observed. Its mirrors, capitals, and coffered ceilings all drew admiring comment: "The sidewalk consists of slabs of marble, and the ceilings of the uncovered parts of the windows are painted to depict landscapes and other subjects framed by gilt molding."[26] In this gallery the actress Rachel lived for a time in the late 1830s,[27] and the poet Nerval, we are told, liked to walk his lobster on a leash.

Today, for lovers of old Paris, these arcades are among the few places in the capital where nostalgia is still what it used to be. Maurice Bedel was right that "there is a poetry of the Parisian arcades: it is the poetry of a greenhouse ornamented not by orchids, gloxinia, and cineraria, but by children's toys, musical instruments, and all sorts of shiny objects ranging from glossy, textured postcards to vividly colored series of colonial stamps." But even if commerce in the arcades now seems strangely obsolete, as if preserved in a museum, from 1810 to 1850 these same galleries were among the world's most audacious commercial sites: in the passage Véro-Dodat alone there were fashionable shops, novelty shops, and shops selling frivolities. Money-changers and high-class prostitutes also congregated here. Mme Lapostolle, the most fashionable of Paris milliners, held court, as did the chocolate manufacturer Marquis; Susse, the seller of fine stationery; and Farina, the maker of cologne. This was where, in a prefiguration of our own modernity, Parisians went to buy things they did not need, along with curious novelties of whose existence they had previously been unaware. "In Paris," the *Véritable conducteur parisien* explained in 1828, "the word arcade is applied to covered passages restricted to pedestrians by which one passes in front of any number of shops while proceeding from one street to the next . . . They are generally illuminated by gas . . . The shops are splendid and well-endowed but rather expensive." Walter Benjamin, who made large department stores a central element in his cultural analysis of Haussmannian capitalism, is right to frame that question by asking "Which of the novelty shops were located in the arcades?"[28]

All the ones that mattered, we are tempted to reply; and structurally speaking the arcades were to the first half of the nineteenth century what the Parisian *hypermarché* and the American shopping mall are to the present day. It is therefore no surprise that they profoundly affected opinion. Indeed, the galleries were especially appealing to the utopian theorist Charles Fourier, who liked to think of them as a way of bringing architectural technology to bear on the future of his society of "phalansteries": "The gallery-streets," he wrote of his forthcoming utopia, "are a method of internal communication, which in itself sets civilization's palaces and most beautiful cities in the shade. [They] are one of the most precious charms of the Palace of Harmony . . . The phalange has no external street or avenue exposed to the insults of the atmosphere. All the quarters of the nominal edifice can be explored via a broad gallery, which dominates the second floor of each structure."[29]

In 1869 Tony Molin offered a similar observation in a book entitled *Paris en l'an 2000:* "After the socialist government became the legal owner of all the houses of Paris," he wrote during the reign of Napoleon III, "it turned them over to the architects with orders . . . to create gallery-streets . . . Once Parisians had experienced the new galleries, they no longer felt any desire to set foot in the old streets, which, they said, were no longer good for anything but dogs." In 1886 Léo Claretie published a book about Paris from its beginnings until the year 3000 in which he described the building, in 1987, of a glass roof over the entire city to protect it from rain. With prophetic vision, he thus removed Paris from the realm of nature to that of virtuality.[30]

But the commercial history of Paris did not stop there: after the novelty shops and the arcades of the 1820s and 1830s, brilliant insights led further toward the synthesis of all previous commercial concepts, namely to the Paris department store. For Adorno, the department store was an alienating instrument of exploitation; for Walter Benjamin, a "dream machine" that made it possible to imagine a society in which material goods, now made plentiful and cheap, would be equally available to all. In this view, the department store was to the articles used in daily life what the camera was becoming for heretofore auratic works of art: photography had made canonical art available to all. For the moment, only the middle and upper classes could frequent the *grands magasins,* but thanks to inexpensive photographs it was already possible to learn about (a now demystified) Leonardo da Vinci without a costly trip to the Louvre. Like photographs of great art and like museums, department stores, for Benjamin, enabled the bourgeois customer to think beyond his times: "The realization of dream elements, in the course of waking up, is the paradigm of dialectical thinking. Thus, dialectical thinking is the organ of historical awakening. Every epoch, in fact, not only dreams the one to follow but, in dreaming, precipitates its awaken-

---

Jacques Lambert, *The Avenue of High-Rises: An Extraordinary Project to Resolve the Question of Housing in the Paris Region,* 1922. Skyscrapers have been the classic expression of urban modernity since the Equitable Building in New York of 1868–1870, which was seven and a half stories high. To be modern—or so many people reasoned—Paris would have to have them too. Blessedly, this vision has by and large not been realized, despite Auguste Perret, Le Corbusier, and the Tour Montparnasse. This illustration shows the extent of the urban catastrophe that might have been if Haussmann's Paris—so despised by the Surrealists of the 1920s—had been overwhelmed in turn, as it had overwhelmed medieval Paris half a century earlier. Published in *L'Illustration,* August 12, 1922. The President and Fellows of Harvard College.

ing. It bears its end within itself and unfolds it—as Hegel already noticed—with cunning. With the destabilizing of the market economy, we begin to recognize the monuments of the bourgeoisie as ruins even before they have crumbled."[31]

The first of these Parisian "ruins," so to speak, was the Bon Marché, of which Zola, in a work of fiction more vivid than the reality, has left an excellent portrait in *Au Bonheur des Dames*. The actual store on the rue de Babylone was managed jointly by Aristide and Marguerite Boucicaut. It did 500,000 francs' worth of business in 1852, 5 million in 1860, 27 million in 1869, and 72 million in 1877. The figures for the Grands Magasins du Louvre followed a similar pattern, increasing from 5 million in 1855 to 13 million in 1865 and 41 million in 1875. In 1887 Pasteur burst into tears at the sight of the check for 250,000 francs that Mme Boucicaut gave him for his institute. (The emperor of Brazil was also included in the list of donors, but his contribution was only 1,000 francs.)

The 1830s and 1840s were the golden age of arcades. The Belle Epoque of the Third Republic, 1880–1914, was the heyday of the department stores, whose business was expanded by the work of another genius of commerce, Georges Dufayel (1855–1916), the inventor, or at any rate the popularizer, of catalog sales and installment purchasing. He began by selling photographs on credit. By 1900 this Napoleon of the installment plan had expanded his clientele to 2.4 million; by 1904 the figure had reached 3.5 million. At that point he employed 800 investigators, who checked up on the solvency of his clients by such means as bribing concierges for information. The ingenious Dufayel sold not only merchandise but also coupons that his clients could redeem in more than 400 establishments, including the Samaritaine, which Ernest Cognacq founded in 1870. Dufayel's cut came to 18 percent on each transaction.

New activities bring new men to the fore, and we learn a great deal about the modernity of the great department stores from the fact that most of them were created by men and women who began with nothing. This was true of both Aristide Boucicaut and Ernest Cognacq. Cognacq began with 500 francs in savings, with which he bought a small store on the site of what is now the Samaritaine. In 1872 he married Louise Jay, the assistant manager of the Bon Marché's dress department, who had contrived to put aside a nest egg of 20,000 francs. By relying on their own savings, the Cognacq-Jay couple never had to borrow. Likewise, Alfred Chauchard, who founded the Magasin du Louvre, began as a salesman in a shop aptly named Le Pauvre Diable. Paternalistic and highly authoritarian, the new department store magnates were ingenious entrepreneurs who were careful to share their profits with their managers. They looked on their work as a vocation: the Cognacq-Jays had no children (their residence is now a museum).

And along with the new forms of Parisian commerce came new forms of advertising. Here again, the modern history of Paris is one half of a tale of two cities, since London was perhaps more advanced in this realm than Paris. But the French capital was not far behind. By multiplying classified advertisements, Emile de Girardin was able in 1836 to reduce the price of a subscription to his newspaper, *La Presse*, from eighty to forty francs. (Girardin's innovations in advertising were soon copied by other Parisian entrepreneurs, such as the owners of the newspaper *Le Siècle*, and in 1845 by Charles Duveyrier with his Société Générale des Annonces.)

"Among the passions of democracy," wrote the royalist and reactionary Louis Veuillot in *Les Odeurs de Paris*, "none is more insistent or widespread than the need to be seen, the most vulgar expressions of which are also the most successful . . . pompous signs, advertisements, grotesque and brazen deceptions, theater—are all of a piece . . . a democratic nation is a nation of second-rate actors." And there was of course a great deal of truth to his complaint. In the corporatist Paris of guilds and of the ancien régime, advertising had been pointless and even unseemly because it implied unfair competition between journeymen who had in theory resolved to work (and to exclude) in concert. But in the new Parisian order of sign and commerce, advertising was essential. Balzac, like Zola, possessed remarkable insight into the new way of doing business, and with the "illustrious Gaudissart" gave us the very type of the traveling salesman who became in the Human Comedy "the Napoleon of publicity." And recall that Balzac's Birotteau, inventor of perfumes and Parisian merchant, bore the imperial first name "César"; his bankruptcy, Balzac explains, was to his family what the crossing of the Berezina had been to Napoleon's army. In Paris, advertising and commerce had become epic battlefields.

In Benjaminian terms, advertising served a practical purpose: it alerted customers to the existence of goods they might use. But it did far more than that: the end of medieval life, with the ensuing separation of the public and the private, had removed the production of things from the private and familial sphere of the corporatized master and his artisans; but advertising, by making of banal objects the building blocks of fantasized dream worlds (as did the display cases of the department stores), enabled (illusorily, for Benjamin) the bourgeois customer to integrate his private desires with the new capitalist modes of production. By tailoring public norms to private taste, the *grands couturiers* for some, the *petites couturières* for others, and the alterations experts in the department stores for their less fortunate customers, all worked to individuate production so as to give private substance to the public and publicized fantasies of pleasures that advertisement deployed. Even the very poor benefited from this trend: in pre-revolutionary Paris the destitute and artisans alike had often worn (ill-assorted) clothing discarded by the rich, but now that they could afford new clothes, it mattered that the garments should be fitted to their needs. Consumerism here advanced on a very broad front: the first stores selling ready-to-wear apparel opened for business in 1825; and in 1830 Coutard on the rue des Petits-Champs offered ready-made suits to men on a budget, a shift that marked a revolution in taste and attitudes. The firm prospered and by 1867 employed forty workers, male and female.[32] Selling this new type of apparel was one of the specialties of La Belle Jardinière, which in 1866 moved to a superb building near the Pont-Neuf.

Commercialization, advertising, big department stores—along with all these, inevitably, came the commodification of sexuality. By 1900 all these features, which we take to be characteristic of big-city modernity, had existed in symbiotic interrelationship in Paris for nearly half a century. Listen, for example, to what Zola has to say about the fictional department store he called Le Bonheur des Dames: "In a calculated way, mirrors on both sides of the window . . . reflected the models and multi-plied them ad infinitum, filling the street with beautiful women for sale, with prices where their heads should have been." And about Nana: "She loved the passage des Panoramas. From her youth she retained a passion for showy Parisian goods, fake jewels, gold-plated tin, . . . card-board passing for leather. When she passed a display, she could not tear her eyes away, any more than when she was a child with her eyes glued to the sweets in the window of a chocolate shop . . . She was especially taken by the gaudiness of the cheap trinkets . . . sacks full of toothpicks or Vendôme columns and obelisks holding up thermometers."[33]

What we see, then, in this specific place, Paris, and at this specific time, between 1850 and 1870, is the convergence of at least two great myths: the political myth, culminating in the liberation of humanity (this was the Communard myth of Paris as capital of revolution, which Marx incorporated into his blueprint for scientific socialism); and, ironi-cally, the Haussmannian myth of the modern city based entirely on communication, commerce, and material development. Indeed, we can presume that, paradoxically, many Parisians were caught up in both of these contradictory "machines," so as to be almost simultaneously con-sumers at the Bon Marché and Communards manning the barricades, just as Parisians who had been churchgoers before 1789 became sans-culottes afterward. The Communard writer Jules Vallès observed with some astonishment that the Café de Madrid "made as much money [during the Commune] as in the heyday of the Empire."[34] It would be interesting to know more about the history of Parisian commerce dur-ing the Paris Commune.

THE MYTH OF THE CITY as machine, ordered and rationalized, has long since faded from our minds. The First World War completed the modernist rebellion against the mechanical by coupling modern-ism—at least in its leftist varieties—to a hatred of the deadly machinery of war. Machines now lost their mystique: Zazie, the eponymous heroine of Raymond Queneau's novel *Zazie dans le Métro,* adored the subway sys-tem that Haussmann should have built, but its employees were often out on strike. In her eyes, Paris's underground railway network was not only strange and beautiful but also deceptive and ill-conceived.

And yet it is difficult for us to imagine Paris except the way Haussmann imagined it, if only because the authoritarian prefect was also a visionary who instinctively sought to fit reality into preexisting myth. It is thanks to him that, consciously or not, every twenty-first-century Parisian must daily negotiate the distance between the reality of contemporary Paris and its underlying myth born in the middle decades of the nineteenth century. In a way, because of Haussmann, anyone who lives in Paris has to be a historian.

9

Capital of Alienation

IN 1859, from the island of Jersey, Victor Hugo wrote to Charles Baudelaire about *Les Fleurs du mal*: "I fully understand your philosophy (for, like all poets, you have a philosophy). I more than understand it, I accept it, but I shall cling to my own. I never said, Art for Art's sake; I always said, Art for progress. At bottom, this comes to the same thing, and your mind is too penetrating not to realize this. Forward! is the slogan of progress. It is always the cry of Art."

Was ever a literary judgment more bizarre than this one? Progress! And to speak of such a thing in a letter to Baudelaire, who believed that "the great industrial folly" had ruined "the pleasure of dreaming" and that "the great chimera of modern times" was "the inflatable monster of perfectibility and progress"; who called the belief in progress "a lazy man's doctrine, a doctrine for *Belgians*"; and who wrote to Manet in June 1865 that he didn't "give a fig about the human race" and to his mother that he hoped "to set the entire human race against me . . . that would give me pleasure enough to console me for everything else." Three years earlier, moreover, in August 1862, he had described Hugo's *Les Misérables* as "a vile and inept book" and added: "About this subject I've demonstrated that I know how to lie."[1]

The vaguely social-democratic idea of modernity on which Hugo prided himself was antithetical to Baudelaire's idea of Parisian modernity and, in a roundabout way, rather similar to Haussmann's. For Haussmann, modernity meant the apotheosis of standardized, homogenized urbanism, or, to put it another way, the victory of a scientific moral order. To be sure, Hugo's modernity was far milder than Haussmann's, but between these two worldviews there was a clear family resemblance. Neither, moreover, shared the sense of dispossession and alienation that made its first appearance in the work of the Parisian Baudelaire long before Vienna, Prague, or Berlin had even heard of modernism.

With Baudelaire, then, we come to a third episode in the history of the mythical definition of the self, of the cosmogonic Parisian interpretation of eighteenth- and nineteenth-century European individualism. What is an individual? Do individuals express themselves through civil society or against it? Who are we? Where do we come from? Where are we going? Perhaps as early as 1750, and certainly by 1830, mythified Paris was offering a variety of responses to these vexing questions.

To restate the sequence, in the years leading up to the Revolution, in the Enlightenment Paris of salons and salonnières, in the capital of the Republic of Letters, individualism and the public good were initially seen as complementary values. The Jacobins of 1789 preserved that unifying civic ideal, which remains to this day, though in a much attenuated form, the touchstone of French political culture, just as the pluralistic, multicultural, yet still republican Madisonian interpretation of the U.S. Constitution of 1787 (also in a much attenuated form) remains the touchstone of American political culture.

Then, in the first half of the nineteenth century, Paris witnessed the emergence of a new form of individualism, an individualism charged with the energy needed to build a new world—call it Promethean individualism. This was the Paris of the triumphant bourgeoisie, a Paris that had broken with its medieval past. It was this Paris that found prostitution so threatening: indeed, it was precisely because prostitution symbolized the terrifying survival of the rejected past that Alexandre Parent-Duchâtelet combated it so strenuously.

Before 1848 this second individualism found relatively tepid political expression in the July Monarchy, which took tentative steps to reorganize the French economy on the basis of individuated economics—

or capitalism, if you will. And after 1848 a far more potent form of this same individualism was incorporated into the Haussmannian ideal. Haussmann's railway stations and arrow-straight boulevards symbolized the expansion of individual capabilities and the rationalized deployment of individual energies. The ultimate expression of this new ideal was the Universal Exposition of 1889, which made the Eiffel Tower the very symbol of Paris. The reign of the stock exchange also began around this time, as the "cash nexus" began to influence all aspects of urban life: in 1863 art lovers, consumers of commercialized sexual favors as well as consumers of commercialized art, could gape at Manet's *Olympia,* which depicted a woman who perhaps could not be bought but who certainly could be rented by the hour.

This same self-assured individualism gave literary Paris young Rastignac's celebrated (and endlessly cited) apostrophe to the heartless, multifarious capitalistic capital of Balzac's *Père Goriot* (1834) as he looks down on the city from the heights of Père-Lachaise. Below, he sees the Faubourg Saint-Germain and its antithesis, the Montagne Sainte-Geneviève—the one fabulously noble, the other unspeakably wretched, yet each in its own way a monument to self-interest. (Indeed, one could see the Pension Vauquer on today's rue Tournefort as a salon of sorts, whose habitués were prepared to do whatever it took to get ahead.)

Parisian individualism had transformed Rastignac, the innocent young provincial; and the prestige of Paris in the early decades of the nineteenth century hinged in no small measure on its supposed ability to transform ordinary men (and women, such as George Sand or the socialist writer Flora Tristan) into world-historical artists and visionaries. With his "whiff of grapeshot" on the steps of the church of Saint Roche in 1795, Bonaparte started to become Napoleon; just as his self-appointed intellectual nemesis, Chateaubriand, on his return to Paris from the banks of the Mississippi, chose to become René, the embodiment par excellence of the "mal du siècle." When the painter Ingres declared that his role model, Raphael, had been of divine and Christlike essence, he was also making a statement about his own place in the world and about the amplifying power of Parisian spectacle.

EVERY TRIUMPHAL MYTH engenders opposition, and the triumphal myth of Parisian individualism was no exception. It engendered a third (and Baudelairean) phase in the history of Parisian individualism: the phase of self-alienation as a reaction to the commodity fetishism of a city whose bourgeois modernity left the poet feeling stripped of his humanity. (And by "poet" I mean what Baudelaire meant, namely, any human being who shared the pain of his *semblables et frères,* of all humanity.)

Baudelaire, but also Flaubert. Baudelaire, the artist-*flâneur* who wrote *Les Fleurs du mal* (Flowers of Evil), remained in spite of everything Parisian to the core, and was intimately tied to the new Paris, which, however much he detested it, he could not do without. By contrast, Frédéric Moreau, the hero of Flaubert's *L'Education sentimentale* (1869), eventually became bored with everything, including Paris. A native of Nogent-sur-Marne (that is, of nowhere), Frédéric ultimately returns there to while away his last years in ennui after spending ten equally tedious years in the capital. It is noteworthy, moreover, that the (anti)hero of this greatest of French novels makes his first appearance as he is about to leave the city. For Flaubert, absence marks the experience (or non-experience) of love, politics, and the city. It is not in Paris but in the forest of Fontainebleau that Frédéric and his mistress Rosanette experience the *journées* of June 1848.

The advent of alienation thus marks a third era in the mechanism of Parisian myth. This theme of alienation, of denaturing, was coupled with praise for marginal individuals of many kinds: not only the *poète maudit,* Baudelaire's "swan," but anyone unable to feel at home in modernity. Indeed, this myth of alienated man had wide import for the history of nineteenth-century Paris: it figures as the last-born of the great Parisian myths. It is a myth that still touches us today, and perhaps more so than any other aspect of the Parisian culture of that time, because it survives in two distinct forms: in our existential fear of boredom and our anxieties; but also, and more subtly, in the curious way it has been adapted by the indestructible, all-encompassing entrepreneurial capitalism of our time. The ideal twenty-first-century "manager" no longer resembles the acquisitive Rastignac. Today's young urban professional is more likely to rent property than to own it; the modern-day

Frédéric Moreau is reconciled to his fate. He is adaptable, active, and easy-going. He is "plugged in" to many different "networks" and prefers to avoid obstacles rather than to confront them. He adjusts his economic strategy in response to unpredictable events, and his fluid personality is also a work in progress, forever shifting to suit the changing needs of the moment. In short, a sensibility that emerged in Paris in the 1850s and that was seen in the 1890s as a pathology of modernism has been transformed by the "regenerated" capitalism of the new millennium into a civic virtue.[2]

In another context, the mid-nineteenth-century myth of alienation can be viewed as occupying the middle ground between two distinct eras in the long history of Paris—the era of ambient myth (from 1750 onward) and the subsequent era of phantasmagoria (after the 1890s). The advent of an insuperable sense of self marked a first turning point in the history of the capital: from 1750 on, every great Parisian myth had led inexorably to another—from Paris, capital of the modern self and of the Republic of Letters, to Paris, capital of revolution, to the Paris of Haussmannian modernity, crime, women, and fashion. By contrast, the new myth of Paris, capital of alienation and self-doubt, though it did occasion various responses (modern managerialism being ironically one of them), did not engender any counter-*myth* as its predecessors had done. Baudelaire railed against his times, but he did not hold out the prospect of a new or better world. (I shall come back to this point.) He simply pointed out that Hugo was in some ways a fool: a fool of genius, perhaps, and of national significance; no doubt an incomparable technician, but still a fool. Furthermore, it was of little concern to Baudelaire whether or not anyone agreed with him about this.

This set of attitudes is of general significance for Western culture, but it can also be seen as marking an important step in the demythification of Haussmannian Paris, the Paris of the bourgeoisie. It takes us toward the Paris of the 1920s and 1930s, which the Surrealists at once devalued and overvalued. And more mundanely, it also takes us toward the politically demythified Paris of the 1950s and 1960s, when leading Paris intellectuals turned their backs on the city—no longer the carrier of a world-message—and focused instead on the Third World, to the detriment, as it happens, of both the Third World and the capital of France. Abandoned by those who should have wished to defend it, this great city was delivered into the hands of indifferent politicians and avid speculators, whose great collective achievement was the brutalization of the city, with the banks of the Seine transformed into expressways and the skyline defaced by high-rise office towers at the Gare Montparnasse and the Porte d'Italie. We may hope, incidentally, that this sad phase in Parisian history has finally come to an end with the completion of the regrettable, soulless, and depressing Bibliothèque Nationale de France– François Mitterrand.

ALIENATION AND DENATURING: the sense of living a life that is not one's own. Louis XIV's Bishop Bossuet also used the word "alienation," which strikes us as so apt for capturing the state of mind of certain Parisians during the Second Empire, but in a quite different sense: "O, mortal body, with which I can be neither at war nor at peace, for I must forever be coming to terms with it and forever spurning those terms! O, inconceivable union, and no less surprising alienation!" At issue here is the classic religious, and later Cartesian, distinction between soul and body.

The word "alienation" can also be found in Emile Littré's dictionary of the 1860s, but again the definition is not useful. "Alienation," Littré tells us, can refer to the alienation of a piece of property (as in Rousseau's *Social Contract,* book 1, chapter 4) or to a separation, in the sense of an aversion that one feels, not from one's true nature, but, classically, from others.

Despite this gap in the lexicon, in 1850 alienation as we understand it today was not an entirely new theme in Paris. In the eighteenth century, Jean-Jacques Rousseau and many others had felt isolated in the capital. Recall from Chapter 2 that in 1788 Vittorio Alfieri compared Paris to a "fetid sewer," and that in 1790 the city made N. M. Karamzin feel like "but a grain of sand in a dizzying torrent or whirlwind."[3] For these men, however, the situation they deplored was more sociological than metaphysical. Outside of Paris skittish poets still hoped to return to a state of grace by taking solitary walks during which they would achieve harmony with daffodils (why not?) and perhaps with humanity as well.

The experience of alienation in nineteenth-century Paris was far more profound. Alfred de Musset, in a sonnet published in 1829, was perhaps the first writer to exhibit a modern and Parisian sense of alienation, to which he gave voice by describing the Paris of his dreams, a more personal, individualized Paris radically different from the vast, troubling, overwhelming, unnatural city that the capital had become.[4] Within twenty years such anxieties had become commonplace, as Théophile Gautier, the fine craftsman of art for art's sake, noted in 1847 in an essay on the Bals de l'Opéra, the lavish dances that Manet would later portray in a famous painting:

> At the opera, one must give up all claim to individuality, all privacy. You are but an atom in a whirlwind. You may be handsome or hideous, stupid or witty, clad in rags or in satin; you may dance like a bear or like Carlotta Grisi in *La Favorite*. It's all the same. Stay, go: your presence or absence makes no difference. Even if your lungs were made of brass, your voice would be lost in the general tumult. Though you were Hercules, you could not struggle against the current. You must surrender and stay in line. Therein lies the beauty of the Bals de l'Opéra as well as the drawback: there are so many people around that no one is really there.

Twenty years later the Goncourts recorded the view of a boulevardier named Lavoix: "In Paris one is really only a third of oneself. So many impressions, ideas, thoughts, and things come to you from other people that I go to Brittany to replenish my personality and become entirely myself again."[5]

Writers were quick to exploit this latest existential deficiency in a variety of ways. For Jules Michelet, the Paris crowd had been an ambiguous source of riches: the alert Parisian could learn something by observing it, but from a distance. "In order to judge movement," he wrote, "you have to be both in it and not in it. You have to be both *solitary* and *informed*. You have to see the crowd without becoming caught up in its whirl and made dizzy by it . . . In the midst of Paris there are populous solitudes. There you can experience great impressions."[6]

Charles de Sainte-Beuve's character Joseph Delorme also experienced the crowds, but in a different way: "Soon, in the unfamiliar crowd, [he] would drown his sorrow." But even this, Victor Hugo's friend and enemy Sainte-Beuve was quick to add, would offer only momentary relief. What came next? Only the sound of singing, loud voices, drunken brawls,

> Ou qu'amours en plein air, et baisers sans vergogne,
> Et publiques faveurs.
> Je rentre: sur ma route on se presse, on se rue;
> Toute la nuit j'entends se traîner dans ma rue
> Et hurler les buveurs.
> (Or outdoor lovemaking, shameless kisses,
> and public favors.
> I head home: on my way people gather in crowds or hasten along.
> All night long I hear drinkers loitering in my street
> and screaming.)[7]

Pretty

And from the crowd as enemy of the self it was but a short step to the theme of urban solitude, the Dickensian paradox of loneliness in a crowded city—loneliness of an unprecedented kind and therefore all the more painful, loneliness henceforth characteristic of the bruised sensibilities of a speeded-up Paris (ironically) organized by Haussmann in such a way as to promote more rapid transit.

great

Balzac, for his part, often interpreted this isolation in terms of Catholic "familyism": it was foreordained, for example, in the Human Comedy that women could find fulfillment only in the bosom of the family. Spinsters were essentially incomplete semi-humans. Solitude, Balzac believed, caused a woman's character to deteriorate steadily, and lonely women inevitably became cantankerous or even wicked. In rather coarse terms, Joris Karl Huysmans (1848–1907) lamented the fate of the unmarried man, but in a somewhat unusual context. His Parisian bachelor is having dinner in a restaurant when he suddenly recalls a young woman he might have married ten years earlier: "He sees himself married to her, eating a nice, solid piece of meat and drinking a good, clean Burgundy . . . Those deceptive slices of roast beef and illusory oven-cooked legs of lamb that you find in restaurants fill the embittered souls of old bachelors with airy thoughts of former mistresses."[8]

We should note that this literary trope of Parisian isolation and of the capital's hostility to marriage, and hence to happiness, was not without material foundation. As it happens, in real life as well as in literature, many Parisians were indeed reluctant to have large families or even to  marry. "The bourgeois of Paris," wrote the political commentator A. Bazin in 1833, "has two [children], no more: a son and a daughter was what he wanted, and after that, he says, 'I called it quits.' He repeats this phrase so often that his wife has finally gotten used to it."[9] Statistically, abstention from procreation was more common in Paris than in any other city of Western Europe or North America. In 1885, 323 of 1,000 Parisian couples were childless.[10] In this connection, it is enlightening to compare Edgar Degas's glacial depictions of family life with his representations of the warm if sordid intimacy of the capital's bordellos.

Parisian solitude led to sterility and also, for observers of sensibility, to Parisian boredom, as an ironic Flaubert explained in his *Dictionnaire des idées reçues* (Dictionary of Accepted Ideas): in Paris, ennui was the mark of a distinguished sensibility and an elevated mind. Despite—or perhaps because of—the multitude of distractions available, the capital of the imperial feast was also a city in which the idle liked to think of themselves as being bored to death. One commentator on Parisian ways, Mme Ancelot, invoked boredom to explain the deeper meaning of the Parisian salon: it was more pleasant to be bored in company than to be bored alone. Alphonse Daudet referred to Sunday as that "dreadful day"; many Parisians, he believed, suffered from a "fear of Sundays." Other Parisians at the time were also afraid of the alienating boredom of routinized labor. As early as 1840 Michelet was denouncing "the infernal boredom" of textile work in particular. "Again, again, again: that is the word that rumbles in our ears from the machinery that makes the floor vibrate beneath our feet. You never get used to it." Alphonse de Lamartine's France also knew boredom: middle-of-the-road politics, thought this Romantic poet, could not satisfy the French.

Roger Caillois theorized this point nicely. "Romanticism," he argued, "pointed toward a theory of boredom [by acknowledging] man's growing awareness of a series of instincts that society has a powerful interest in repressing; but in large part, romanticism . . . reflected the abandonment of the struggle . . . The romantic writer went in for a poetry of refuge and escape." But what Balzac and Baudelaire attempted was exactly the reverse, he continues, since they now "tended to integrate into life yearnings that the Romantics resigned themselves to satisfying solely in the realm of art. Their project was therefore closely related to myth, which always signifies an increase in the role of the imagination in life."[11]

This is a brilliant insight, which is tantamount to saying that Parisian boredom, first contemplated as a distant ideological or social phenomenon, soon became an existential one. In this same frame, the fear of boredom, that is to say, the sense that one is living someone else's life, led inexorably to escapist solutions, as exemplified by the many substitutes with which Baudelaire attempted to take his mind off the capital's hateful but unavoidable modernity: paid sex, hashish, idleness, cruelty (in the parable of the wicked glazier), and perhaps homosexuality as well, all of which could be seen by a moralist as modern incarnations of Pascal's hated *divertissement*. Boredom is also the central theme of a whole section of Walter Benjamin's *Passagenwerk,* a self-styled Marxist work that contains this remark: "It may be important to find out what the dialectical opposite of boredom is." To which question the proper Marxist response would surely be that boredom is a form of bourgeois false consciousness. To be bored, for the Marxist, must be the fate in this world of those alienated souls who are lucid enough to understand the emptiness of the society of spectacle but are unable to embrace the only true remedy, namely a dialectical conception of revolution, politics, and community.

Pᴀʀɪsɪᴀɴ ᴇɴɴᴜɪ and idleness were all the more painful because they were linked, paradoxically, to the deceptive agitation of the city's social life. For Edmond About, writing in the *Paris guide* in 1867, "big cities, in the current state of civilization, are nothing but concentrations of people in a hurry." In a less sociological, more direct way, the Goncourts, Huysmans, and Henri Rochefort also pondered the idea that in Paris the excitement of modernity had somehow gone wrong. To theorize this sensibility, Marx, more critically and also more grandly, wrote of "the agitation of modern life," as Nietzsche did of its "overexcited worldliness." Benjamin, in his description of the period, took a more sociological approach, distinguishing between superficial *Erlebnis* (typical of this age) and the more profound *Erfahrung:* mere experience was unable to bring comprehension. Only Marxist-inspired rumination—or for that matter, dialectical dreaming—could point to a way out.[12]

Historians who have studied the myth of alienation as it took shape in Paris around 1860 have also dwelt on various themes, such as that of the flâneur—or that of the collector (described in Chapter 3), who was in this domain a critical archetype, observing life carefully but from outside, without really participating in it. The hallmark of the collector is that this lover of objects is quite incapable of producing anything. The collector buys, but as La Rochefoucauld pointed out in the seventeenth century, it is easier to buy than to sell, and his purchases do no more than create an illusion of existing. The collector, Benjamin wrote, "dreams that he is in a better world . . . in which things are exempt from the chore of being useful . . . He transfigures objects in order to make them his own. His task is Sisyphean."[13] In the disillusioned 1930s Jean Renoir, in his film *La Règle du jeu* (The Rules of the Game), used the collector as a symbol for the Parisian upper class as a whole: the charming marquis de La Chesnaye is an elegant and philandering banker who collects automata and watches—that is, things that are artificially alive—and whose artificiality reflects his own human disabilities.

Collectors then, but especially flâneurs. In *Paris, ou le livre des cent-et-un* (Paris, or the Book of 101), we are told that "the flâneur can be born anywhere, but he knows how to live only in Paris." A certain type of flâneur was already a familiar figure in Paris in the First Empire. In 1806, for example, he had made an appearance in the title of a thirty-page pamphlet: *Le Flâneur au salon ou M. Bon-Homme: Examen joyeux des tableaux mêlé de Vaudevilles* (The Flâneur in Mr. Everyman's Salon: A Joyful Look at Sketches and Vaudevilles). But this precocious flâneur wore a "Jansenist" hat and a brown suit. At bottom he was merely an idle bourgeois. This was not enough to establish him as a permanent fixture of modern alienated life; and it was not until the era of the "physiologies" that the flâneur really became a familiar figure. Balzac's *Physiologie du mariage* (1826) awarded him his Parisian patents of nobility: his habit was to stroll about the capital observing the lives of other people, who took little notice of his presence. He "cultivated the science of the sensual" and indulged in "visual gastronomy." Other Balzacian flâneurs appear in *La Fille aux yeux d'or* (The Girl with the Golden Eyes) and *Ferragus.*

The typical Balzac character succumbs to the temptations of the world or to his own passions, each reinforcing the other. By contrast, what is distinctive about the flâneur in Balzac's works is that he has no passion: he lives a life of retirement, as an observer, a failure. Some of Balzac's flâneurs freely choose to live this way. Others, like the artist Wenceslas Steinbock in *La Cousine Bette* (1846), slip into *flânerie* out of indolence or inadequacy: in the Human Comedy, the flâneur is the antithesis of the artist, who is heroic, creative, and Promethean. Despite certain affinities of sensibility, these two types are completely different because the flâneur is totally unfit for the work as well as for the suffering that Balzac believed indispensable to the creation of art. By contrast, the Balzacian artists, such as Daniel d'Arthez and the painter Joseph Bridau, though they do stop work from time to time, do so only in order to do better work later on. Balzacian *flânerie* was quite the opposite of an ascetic existence.

This was an incomplete view, but far in advance of the celebrated and yet banal contemporary description of the flâneur by Louis Huart. In his *Physiologie du flâneur* (1842), Huart drew a series of distinctions between the flâneur and other figures of the Paris streets (*le badaud,* or gawker, *le musard,* or dawdler, and *le batteur de pavé,* or pavement pounder). But Huart's categorization was a mere typology of Parisian indolence, in which the flâneur was nothing more than a "mobile spirit" who sniffed about the streets in search of city life but without really understanding what it was all about, and the pavement pounder was really just a beggar in disguise, waiting for a handout that would never come. For Huart, in the end, flâneurs were a "happy, spineless species" whose members were "the only truly happy people in Paris, savoring its moving poetry at all hours."

Louis Huart, illustration from *Physiologie du flâneur*, 1841. Huart's flâneur is more elegant
and far less desperate than that of Baudelaire and Walter Benjamin. Indeed, this aristocra-
tized observer is more above society than beside it. He is still an idler, as flâneurs have
always been, but his self-distancing idleness has taken on a quasi-metaphysical dimension.
Reproduced by permission of the Rare Book and Manuscript Library, Columbia University.

With Ferdinand Gall, in *Les Parisiens* (1845), we move forward again. The flâneur, he tells us, "is always in full possession of his individuality. That of the gawker, on the contrary, disappears, absorbed by the outside world."[14]

But it was Flaubert and Baudelaire, as one might expect, whose analyses of the flâneur's aberrant individuality crystallized this Parisian social type. In their work the flâneur finally became the incarnation of the alienated self, hence a more important but also more somber figure.

Strictly speaking, Frédéric Moreau is not a flâneur. In any case, Flaubert never applies that term directly to the hero of *L'Education sentimentale,* which is largely set during the revolution of 1848. But he is an indolent youth, sensitive as well as ineffectual, and thus has all the characteristics of the flâneur. What is more, much of the action of the novel unfolds as Frédéric moves aimlessly about the city. The young provincial's pointless Parisian peregrinations are doubly revealing, because they have nothing in common with the precise and invariably instructive promenades that took Balzac's young Rastignac in the 1830s from the Montagne Sainte-Geneviève and Mme Vauquer's sordid pension to the heavenly *hôtels particuliers* of that promised land, the Faubourg Saint-Germain. For Balzac, the Left Bank and the Right Bank were very distinct places, as were the capital's various *quartiers:* some stood for the nobility and the past, others for capitalism and the future, and still others for poverty. By contrast, Frédéric Moreau wanders from one anonymous place to another, often without knowing precisely what street or neighborhood he is in: "In the air he heard what sounded vaguely like the refrains of dance tunes. His swaying as he walked left him feeling slightly giddy. He found himself on the Pont de la Concorde."[15]

As a flâneur, Frédéric is also keenly sensitive to fashion, an essentially feminine preoccupation which Flaubert's hero internalized completely: in a world shaped by "commodity fetishism," women who had nothing to do and who needed a dowry and trousseau in order to marry, had instinctively gravitated toward the department stores and the world of fashion (in the literature of the period at any rate). Revealingly, Frédéric likewise dresses very carefully and decorates his apartments with refined, delicate taste. The German sociologist Georg Simmel, a contemporary of Thorstein Veblen, explained Frédéric to us at the turn of the twentieth century, even though he had probably never heard of the young Parisian. Fashion, Simmel wrote, exerts a powerful fascination on rootless modern men and women because they are more susceptible to "life's transitory and vacillating elements."[16]

THE FLÂNEUR was bourgeois and in some cases quite wealthy. Frédéric Moreau certainly was. Vaguely ill at ease in modernity, the bourgeois spectator could easily recognize himself in this cultural type, in whom his own anxieties were magnified out of all proportion. But the theme of alienation also took a more material form, translating the apprehensions of the bourgeoisie to the other extreme of the social spectrum. Out of this came a new fascination with the social outcasts of the capital: tramps, homeless people, and street people. The flâneur was close to the dandy ("as a downwardly aristocratic and gentry figure"), but conceptually he was also close to the bohemian and the plainly marginal; and, inevitably, these social types now came into their own as well.[17]

There had always been outcasts in Paris, but the excluded now took on a mythical image as the new incarnation of "the other," so different from, but also so similar to, the bourgeois observer, who feared that he too might one day be excluded by modernity. This was truly new. The Parisian outcasts of the thirteenth to fifteenth centuries whom Bronislaw Geremek describes in his beautiful book *The Margins of Society in Late Medieval Paris* were simply poor. But with Baudelaire, Manet, and their contemporaries, outcasts came to share many of the characteristics of flâneurs: they too were spectators, maladapted individuals who took social failure to be a moral victory. In pre-revolutionary Paris outcasts were people who, born poor, had grown even poorer. The new outcasts were in their own way visionaries, not unlike the jesters and fools who both entertained and troubled the princes of the Renaissance by their insights into human nature as it had been defined by their times.

From the marginal flâneur to the marginalized outcast was then but a short step. Champfleury (Jules Husson), for example, the author of *La*

Mascarade de la vie parisienne, assumed that one could not understand the all-important "masquerade" of what we might call "premodernist" Parisian life without also understanding its underside. "There," wrote Alexandre Privat d'Anglemont, "far away, in a remote corner of an impossible faubourg . . . in a neighborhood that no one has ever visited, there exists something terrifying and strange and charming, appalling and admirable . . . It is a city within a city, a people lost in the midst of another people."[18] These were not workers, declared enemies of society, or even criminals, but creatures of another sort entirely, who presented no concrete danger but whose existence was nonetheless troubling.

In the work of the anthropologist and mythographer Mary Douglas, the great modern city is defined not by what it produces but by what it rejects, by its refuse. This was also the theme of Privat and Champfleury, and one also finds it at about the same time in Dickens's novel *Our Mutual Friend,* where London is explained not so much by what Londoners want or by what they buy—the positive aspects of their existence—as by what they throw away as garbage.

Parisians now renewed their interest in the wretched of the earth, in marginal street performers, jugglers, acrobats, and the like. From Champfleury we know that many of these remarkable but sad social outcasts lived in the vicinity of the Gobelins. In 1845 Privat d'Anglemont honored them with a sonnet, "A une jeune saltimbanque" (To a Young Street Performer). Later came Baudelaire's prose poem "Le Vieux Saltimbanque," about a man who is described as friendless, homeless, childless, and penniless, degraded by misery and public ingratitude, "whose hovel an oblivious world disdains to enter."

A whole literature grew up around the existence in Paris of these strange people and occupations, curious—and curiously symbolic—exceptions to the bourgeois order of social life. Jules Janin described them in 1839: porters, scrapers, messengers, coconut sellers, public writers, professional rhymesters, and usurers, to name a few. "Paris," Janin tells us, "is full of workers who belong exclusively to the big city, whose work makes no sense outside the walls. They work in the industries of the sewer and the street corner, the attic and the gutter. Or in the industry of chance, which has its apprentices and masters and central headquarters. Or in the industry of rags, old nails, and broken glasses, of epic poems and vaudevilles." Frédéric Soulié began the fifth volume of his *Nouveau tableau de Paris* with an article on the capital's "problematic existences." Included under this heading were pimps, front men, and "professional corrupters." In an essay entitled "Le Festin des Titans" (1848), Théodore de Banville told the story of a wealthy English lord who allegedly offered a prize of 10,000 francs to the person with the most unusual occupation. Among the contestants was the "syringe man," who was employed by cheap restaurants to sprinkle oil on vegetable soup to make it look like beef bouillon; the "polisher of turkey claws," whose job was to make the birds look fresher than they were; and the "indoor goatherd," who raised goats in his sixth-floor apartment. The prize, however, went to a "lyric poet [who lived] by his writing," an exceptional accomplishment for any poet but especially for a lyric poet. This one earned his keep by writing verse for weddings and baptisms.[19]

Street performers, poets, and above all—among what Victor Fournel called "the *infiniment petits* of Parisian industry . . . who come to sit at, or rather under, the Parisian table wherever they can so as to fight over the crumbs that fall"—the ragpickers.[20] Ragpickers too were by no means newcomers to the Paris scene: as early as 1698 there had been an ordinance regulating their movements. Still, we may assume that the royal officials who issued that early legislation did not see the fate of these broken people as a cautionary tale that had a bearing on their own monarchic status.

Parisians of the 1850s were fascinated by the lives of these ragpickers, by the cafés they frequented (in the Place Maubert and the Place de la Contrescarpe) and the dishes they ate (veal bouillon at one sou per liter). As Pierre Citron reminds us, the ragpicker was an "important personage for all [Paris] *noctambules,* or night people, in the middle of the [nineteenth] century."[21] Jean Pons Viennet was among the first to recognize their existence in his *Epître aux chiffonniers sur les crimes de la presse* (Epistle to Ragpickers on the Crimes of the Press; 1827). Baudelaire soon followed suit with his *Vin des chiffonniers* (The Ragpickers' Wine). Between 1848 and 1852 one might have noticed the existence of a so-called Villa des Chiffonniers, and a whole body of folklore (or anxieties) grew up around this social category.

Félix Pyat, who did more than anyone else to make Marianne the symbol of republicanism and who later became a Communard deputy, wrote a play in 1869 called *Le Chiffonnier de Paris*. It was an enormous success, with Frédéric Lemaître in the role of Father Jean, a sort of philosophical ragpicker and latter-day Diogenes. In it, Pyat seemed almost astonished by what he had only recently discovered: "It isn't much, Paris as seen in a ragpicker's basket . . . Just think, I've got all Paris there in that basket."[22] The lithographer Gavarni (Sulpice Guillaume Chevalier) had made the same point metaphorically in a frontispiece he did in 1844 for an edition of *Le Diable à Paris* (one of the many collections of essays on life in Paris that appeared after 1840): the Devil is shown trampling on a map of Paris and peering through opera glasses at the city's invisible inhabitants. He is clearly modeled on the publisher Jules Hetzel, known for his editions of Victor Hugo's *Notre-Dame de Paris.* In his left hand this literary devil holds the kind of stick that was used by garbage pickers. He is also holding a magic lantern of the sort used to create illusions. His ragpicker's basket is overflowing with books, no doubt infallible guides for understanding what had become of sociability in the harsh and calculating city.

Elaborate typologies of ragpickers became commonplace: first, we are told, were nighttime ragpickers and *chiffonniers gadouilleurs,* or sewage rakers. Also of consequence were the *chiffonniers coureurs, chiffonniers du tombereau, ouvriers chiffonniers,* and *chiffonniers placiers,* who paid concierges for the privilege of examining garbage before it was put out on the street. In 1854 Alexandre Dumas *fils* wrote in *Les Mohicans de Paris* about a "*chiffonnier ravageur* . . . so called because of the nature of his business, which was not to pick through the usual rubbish heaps but to

Eugène Atget, *The Ragpicker's Hut, Paris,* ca. 1910–1914. Flâneurs, street performers, and below them in the bourgeois social scheme the *chiffonniers* or ragpickers, who live in the geographically androgynous area beyond the city's limits, actual or metaphorical. Fascinated by the unusual, Atget repeatedly photographed these people, and his work appealed to the anti-Haussmannian Surrealists. Musée d'Orsay. Photo: Gérard Blot. Réunion des Musées Nationaux / Art Resource, NY.

stick the point of his hook into the gaps between the paving stones of the gutter." This class of worker had disappeared "some eight to ten years earlier, partly because they had been banned by the police but above all because sidewalks had replaced the old avenues." There were also *chiffonniers trieurs,* whose job was to sort through what others gathered, as well as *chiffonniers chineurs, picqueurs,* and *sacquiers,* all belonging to the Orders of the Ogres, those master ragpickers who, according to the *Petit journal,* in some cases were so rich that they could afford carriages and boxes at the Opéra. L.-A. Berthaud, in the third volume of *Les Français peints par eux-mêmes* (The French Painted by Themselves; 1841), described one master ragpicker named Bertrand as a "chiffonnier héroïque," "among the bravest of his fellows," and reported that his fellows had named him General Bertrand, "like the austere companion of our great Emperor Napoleon."[23]

Eugène Poubelle was the prefect who required that all refuse be placed in trash cans before being put out on the street for collection, an order that ensured his immortality, since his name, *poubelle,* has since come to mean "trash can" in French. But he also complicated the work of the ragpickers, especially after another regulation was issued stipulating that the cans were not to be placed on the street more than fifteen minutes before the arrival of the trash collectors. With the tacit consent of the public, however, this quarter of an hour quickly stretched to an hour or more. Ultimately, the bureaucrats even made it lawful to empty the contents of trash cans briefly onto pieces of canvas. In fact, the 1,800 Parisian ragpickers at work in 1832 do seem to have constituted a fairly structured society. Their number had increased to 12,000 by 1870, and in 1903 there were still as many as 5,000–6,000 when Etienne Atget photographed them at the base of the city's fortifications in the area known as "the zone," which was in some ways close to Paris proper, but in other ways quite remote.

SINCE PLATO, indeed since the Chosen People of Israel wandered the desert in tribes, a central tenet of Western culture has been the assumption that for man, by nature divine but fallen, the visible reality of this world is merely the representation of another reality that is remote and abstract and more difficult to interpret. This other reality is for some eternal and divine, for others secular, cultural, and/or political. For all, our true being is not of this world as it now exists. To live in the world is to feel estranged from another kind of nature that is more distant but also truer than the nature we know.

In the Paris of the 1860s, the myth of alienation drew on this classic theme. In this respect there was nothing very remarkable about it. But there was something new about the Parisian variant of the eternal myth of Job on his bed of straw. Now what mattered was not the metaphysics of the case but, more (or less?) simply, the commercial modernity of nineteenth-century capitalism. One was no longer dealing with the incomprehensible mystery of things or the just wrath of the gods. Baudelaire may have been a Christian poet in disguise, but he was certainly a poet of modernity. In his work, which was of such crucial importance for Walter Benjamin, the prostitute, as a commodity, symbolizes not only the nature of things but also the essence of the new era, the same new era that the propertied flâneur, at the other end of the social spectrum, also rejected. The new society was a society of the marketplace, and in Paris its traces were everywhere. The Parisian prostitute, wrote Benjamin, was "saleswoman and wares in one."

IN A LETTER to Maurice Schlésinger, Flaubert, who was nothing if not facetious, had something to say about the relationship between the new spirit of Paris and Haussmann's transformations: "I expect to find Paris probably as stupid as I left it, if not stupider. Platitude is making headway with the widening of the streets; cretinism is rising to the level of the embellishments."[24] This amusing observation reminds us that no reductive, materialist explanation of sensibility can ever fully satisfy us. Of course, social surroundings, as Roger Caillois points out, are merely "the external components of myth." Still, it is impossible not to assume that there was a relation of some kind between the new sensibility and the contemporary commercialization of Parisian life, a material transformation symbolized by the proliferation of arcades and big department stores and, as we have seen, by the flourishing of a new, different, and more commercial press.

225

In an operetta by Offenbach, commoners invited to a masked ball purchase the right to be addressed as "Monsieur le Comte" or "Madame la Baronne" for the night. As well they might: in the Paris of the imperial feast, everything was for sale, and journalists were no exception. Their representativeness might hinge on that ironic fact alone. But more to the point in the history of the capital's anxieties and alienation is not just the corruption of the press but the *kind* of newspapers and newspaper stories that were now being published in Paris. Indeed, the evolution of the press in this respect illustrates better than anything else the transition from one phase of Parisian culture to another: newspapers had been the voice of public opinion in the capital for nearly a century; now they also became the voice of new anxieties. In the Paris of the 1860s, the bourgeois was (in theory) very much a bourgeois, just as the ragpicker was (in theory) very much a ragpicker. But in an age of capitalism and social individuation, when all fortunes were both changing and uncertain, the Parisian public yearned for a press that spoke to its new worries even if it could not cure them.

The Paris press dates back to Théophraste Renaudot in 1631, and as early as 1749 Marc-Pierre Voyer de Paulmy d'Argenson attributed the effervescence of the mind of the man in the street—that is, the Parisian in the street—to the newspapers. The importance of journalism during the Revolution is now quite widely acknowledged (500 newspapers appeared in Paris between 1789 and 1799). The leading Jacobins and sansculottes were often journalists of one stripe or another: Mirabeau, Carra, Brissot, Desmoulins, Robespierre, Hébert, Marat, Roux, Babeuf.

Balzac, too, in *Les Illusions perdues* (Lost Illusions) had a great deal to say about the new association between the press of his day and the worlds of politics and money, both of which exerted an influence on artists and their renown. But it was not until Emile de Girardin (1806–1881) that the Paris press became a mass phenomenon and a money-making machine. Girardin was an illegitimate child but of the most stylish sort: Greuze would paint a portrait of his mother, Mme Dupuy, and Ingres one of his adoptive mother, Mme de Sessonnes. At the age of 23 he plunged into a journalistic career. His fashion newspaper, *La Mode,* soon grew to a circulation of 130,000. Gavarni, an artist admired by the Goncourts, did illustrations for it from time to time.

It was not in the world of fashion that Girardin would make his mark, however. His great invention, which he promoted with the flair of a shrewd impresario and which he perfected with the touch of a supreme artist of the genre, was the tabloid newspaper—whose rise was both a cause and an effect of the new state of mind.

Tabloid journalism dates back to about 1850. In Paris it reached a zenith of sorts in 1869 and 1870 in connection with the trial and execution of a man named Troppman, who was convicted of murdering a pregnant woman and her five children—a man vicious enough to bite the hand of the executioner as he was being lashed to the guillotine. The emperor himself followed the investigation minute by minute, and Girardin saw to it that this essentially private matter was transformed into a veritable affair of state. Turgenev also attended the trial of the famous criminal.

The new journalism eschewed the *canards,* or hoaxes, that earlier journalists had invented to entertain their readers (or perhaps themselves). The news reported by the tabloids was supposed to be true; in some cases it actually was. It was apolitical, focusing primarily on private matters, a change that was in keeping with the individualization of moral norms. It therefore reflected the triumph of the subject and of bourgeois modernity, which made the individual and the vagaries of individual existence the center of social life. Proust said that Paris was like "one huge scandal that has been brought to light."[25]

Even when publicized, the earlier scandals of Balzacian times were not perceived as "universalizable" events. To the contrary, they were like indiscreet peeks into the private lives of the rich and famous. By contrast, Girardin's newer tabloids transformed these earlier representations of public life and now made of them a series of bizarre episodes and strange incidents that were nonetheless familiar. Here were events that might have happened to anyone, but that were also random and unpredictable, and as such were troubling signs—like the ragpickers' existence—of the hazardous nature of modern social life.

Here then was a new view of social existence that made Parisian sense, and that became ubiquitous. Take, for example, Manet's strikingly revealing *Execution of Maximilian* (1867), in which the painter has transformed a historical event into a kind of random political happening. The soldiers in the firing squad mechanically aim their weapons at the deposed "emperor" of Mexico. Without emotion of any kind, their commander, who might be at a horse race, raises his arm to give the signal for the execution. (Manet later used the same formula to represent the bloody executions of May 1871.) "The news," Benjamin wrote of this new mode of reportage, "is the yeast that causes the big-city masses to rise into the realm of Baudelairean fantasy."[26] The disparate content of the press, he goes on, with its oddly juxtaposed headlines, unconsciously reflects the incoherence and discontinuity of modern life.

Unsurprisingly, then, the new tabloid press met with instant success. At one point, the circulation of *Le Petit Parisien* was larger than that of any other newspaper in the world. In their efforts to attract new readers, the papers proved to be highly imaginative and technically innovative. They often published interviews with witnesses to crimes and, if possible, with the victims as well. The interview was then a new genre, invented by James Gordon Bennett, the editor of the *New York Herald Tribune,* in 1836. (The first interview explored for the public the feelings of a mother whose daughter had just been murdered.) Along with sensational journalism, the tabloids also went in for abundant illustration. Photographs added a further dimension of (ostensible) realism to the reporting. By the 1890s both *Le Petit Journal* and *Le Petit Parisien* were publishing color supplements. *Le Journal illustré* began publishing in 1864. And from 1840 to 1860 Constantin Guys, whom Baudelaire admired greatly, was the Paris correspondent of the *Illustrated London News.*

Alienation, commercialization, tabloids: how can we physically map these transformations of Parisian cultural life? Today, the Right Bank is (with the business district of La Défense) the center of business, bureaucracy, and politics; while the Left Bank is supposedly livelier, more futuristic, and farther to the left politically. And so it was in the 1840s. Balzac's dream life was sited in the Faubourg Saint-Germain, but Haussmannian modernity, which included among other things the modernity of the Impressionists, especially after 1870, was centered on the Right Bank more than on the Latin Quarter or Montparnasse. Think of Gustave Caillebotte and the Place de l'Europe; Pissarro and the avenue de l'Opéra; Manet and the rue Montorgueil; Monet and the Gare Saint-

Lazare. "Unlike civilization, which proceeds from East to West," Dumas *fils* explained in 1854, "Paris, the capital of the civilized world, proceeds from south to north; Montrouge invades Montmartre."[27]

IN THE 1950s Marxist critics reproached Parisian premodernists, especially Baudelaire and Manet, for their failure to assume their place in history. Had they really sought to reject the Haussmannian model for Paris, or so it was then suggested, these authors and artists of the mid to late nineteenth century should have followed or even surpassed the example of Gustave Courbet, that self-consciously proletarian artist. In Marxist terms, to embrace society's outcasts as individuals, as Baudelaire did, was, "objectively speaking," to betray the interests of the poor taken as a group. To ignore the working class as a class was to renounce the people's cause and therefore to condemn oneself to impotence and failure. Jean-Paul Sartre made a similar point: because the Parisian intelligentsia had been in the service of the bourgeoisie since 1789, it had been unable, he thought, to transcend and transform the powerless contempt it felt for its masters. In their state of confusion, irate but non-Marxist intellectuals could ultimately do no more than to marginalize themselves. Flaubert's Frédéric Moreau had indeed witnessed the uprising of 1848, but as a powerless spectator. For Baudelaire, the advent of Napoleon III had been a genuine scandal, but he had experienced the Revolution of 1848 as nothing more than "a moment of intoxication."[28]

In the not-so-distant past when every progressive thinker in Paris believed in the fiction that the working class was the bearer of a universalist message, that rather naive Marxist view may have seemed plausible. It seems much less so today. For us, the presence of social outcasts in the literary and artistic imagination of Paris in the second half of the nineteenth century is one of the most powerful signs of the Parisian myth of alienation. We see this not as a mark of abandonment of the working class but rather as a token of the extraordinary ability of Parisian artists living in the time of Baudelaire and Manet to grasp the meaning not only of their alienated modernity but also of our own travails.

10

Paris in the World

IN 1867, the year 11 million people attended the Universal Exposition in Paris, a humorist wrote: "Italy, Spain, Denmark, and Russia will be incorporated by decree into the Parisian municipality. Three days later, the city's limits will be pushed back all the way to New Zealand and the Land of the Papuans. Paris will be the world, and the universe will be Paris . . . Paris will sit upon the clouds, will scale the heights of heaven, will make planets and stars of its suburbs."[1]

Indeed, by 1860 it was commonplace to assume that history had singled out Paris as the permanent seat of modernity, science, urbanism, and the arts. At a less exalted level, Paris was also the chosen city in fashion, food, and for that matter philology: it was clear, for example, to Victor Cousin, proud of his role in creating a chair of Slavic studies at the Collège de France whose first occupant was to be the Polish poet Adam Mickiewicz, that Paris—and not Berlin, Warsaw, or Saint Petersburg—was now the most important center in the world for the study of Eastern European literature.

As one of the authors of the *Paris guide* put it in 1867:

The influence of Paris has now reached the inhospitable valleys of Montenegro, the impregnable asylum of Serbian patriots . . . After abolishing the theocratic regime [and] restoring the former national government, the energetic Danilo I Petrovich, successor to Peter II, sought inspiration in Paris [which he visited in 1857], and his experience greatly influenced everything he did thereafter. The code of laws he promulgated, the reforms he initiated, and everything about his policies proved that his goal was to persuade an intrepid nation to love the civilization whose advantages had commanded his admiration. His wish was for his nephew, who succeeded him under the name Nikitza I Petrovich after he himself succumbed to an assassin's attack, to be educated at the Lycée Louis-le-Grand . . . Princess Darinka, . . . who made the trip to Paris with him, has been as zealous as the prince in introducing Tsernagora to the benefits of civilization.[2]

By 1860 Parisians and foreigners were singing the same tune: Paris was the capital of the world. The only difference was that foreigners were even more likely than Parisians to think of the city as an almost magical place. "Yet there is a feeling," Alexander Herzen wrote, "with which Parisian natives, having experienced everything to the point of fatigue, are unfamiliar, namely, that which we [foreigners] feel upon arriving in Paris for the first time. Ever since childhood, Paris has been our Jerusalem, the great city of the Revolution, the land of the Tennis Court, of '89, of '93."[3] In other words, as Pierre Citron notes, Paris had become "the epitome of the universe, the asylum of liberty, the center of sensual pleasure and the arts, a world, a university, a whole country unto itself."

But what was distinctive about the Paris of this epoch? What was it, specifically, that set off the City of Light from other European or North American cities? Or, conversely, what did this unique city share with other capitals? Conceptually, two kinds of explanation are possible. We can look at how the shape of Paris changed over time, at the memories and monuments it accumulated over the course of history: if Paris was a mythical city in 1860, it had not yet been such a place in 1660 and had still not been much of one in 1760. But it is also possible to think in terms of space, not time, by comparing Paris with other great nineteenth-century cities such as London and New York, which were gigantic, or Vienna and Budapest, which were not quite so imposing.

If there was a Paris-sur-Seine, there was also a Paris-in-Europe and a Paris-in-France. True, Paris was much like other great cities with which its inhabitants were in constant touch. But Paris was also quite different: the place of Paris in the national imagination of France was not the same as the place of the capital in the national imagination of other countries. There are no doubt a thousand ways to underscore that situation, but I will dwell, later in this chapter, on only one of them— the importance of opera, the national musical genre par excellence of both Paris and Central Europe.

I T IS BEST to begin modestly: Paris, the capital of the nineteenth century, was indeed unique, but it also resembled other cities in many respects. Paris, after all, has never existed in hermetic isolation, except perhaps from 1940 to 1944, when it would no doubt have preferred still greater isolation than it actually endured.

Why was Paris not cut off from the rest of the world? Among the many reasons, the simplest was surely the constant presence of foreigners. (In 1789 the number of foreign residents was about 5,000, or one percent of the city's total population.) Then, too, Parisians, though supposedly fond of staying at home, did travel a little nevertheless. Before the Revolution, Louis-Sébastien Mercier gently mocked his neighbors who, upon returning to Paris after a Sunday barge trip to Saint-Cloud, were as happy as Ulysses to be home at last after such a long voyage. The painter Jean-Baptiste-Siméon Chardin is said to have left Paris, the city of his birth and death, only twice in his life, once to be presented to Louis XV at Versailles and again to restore some paintings in the neighboring palace of Fontainebleau.

Still, there were some Parisians who did travel farther than Saint-Cloud, even farther than Versailles. A number of them became famous for their accounts of journeys outside France: in the early nineteenth century alone there were Chateaubriand, Michel Chevalier, and Alexis de Tocqueville for the United States (as well as Talleyrand and Louis Philippe, but less voluntarily); the Marquis de Custine for Russia; Stendhal for Italy; Balzac for the Ukraine; Baudelaire for India (perhaps!) and the islands of the Indian Ocean and also for Belgium (which he despised); Alexandre Dumas *père* for Switzerland; Gérard de Nerval for Germany; Edouard Manet and Prosper Mérimée for Spain. In 1900

Edgar Degas poked fun at Paul Gauguin, whose paintings he nevertheless admired: "Can't one paint as well on the rue des Batignolles as in Tahiti?" But the master was of course only joking.[4]

If some Parisians made proper journeys, others restricted themselves to "armchair travels." Danton, Marat, and Louis XVI (all Parisians more or less) could read English easily. In 1800 Giovanni Antonio Galignani, an Englishman of Italian origin, opened a bookstore that bore his name (and which still exists under that name on the rue de Rivoli, although the original location was on the rue Vivienne). By 1850 the store boasted a stock of some 30,000 volumes in English, German, Italian, and Spanish. Subscriptions could be had for ten sous per day or six francs per month. Galignani's *Messenger,* the ancestor of today's *International Herald Tribune,* was the first English-language newspaper in Paris. And between 1819 and 1894 Galignani's guides to France and its capital, particularly appreciated by American tourists, went through many editions. The English novelist William Makepeace Thackeray gently mocked his compatriots who huddled together at the Meurice hotel and seldom left it: "It is, as you will perceive, an admirable way to see Paris, especially if you spend your days reading the English papers at Galignani's as many of our foreign tourists do."[5]

And so, through travel and the exchange of ideas, through music and plays (think of Berlioz and Shakespeare, Baudelaire and Wagner), Paris, like all the great cities of the Western world, or at any rate of Europe and North America, was in constant contact with its neighbors, allies and rivals alike. Indeed—and on reflection, unsurprisingly—this international exchange involved not only people and ideas but also poetic tropes. As Citron points out, the same metaphors and images that Byron used to describe London in *Don Juan* (1822) were applied to mythified Paris after 1830: the bustle, light, and sound of the river in Victor Hugo; the volcano and furnace in Alfred de Vigny; the fog and smoke in Alcide de Beauchesne, Gustave Drouineau, and Hugo.

It was not until the end of the nineteenth century that art and ideas became arenas of international competition as the new and exclusive identities of nation, culture, and metropolis took hold. Yet even in that sadly chauvinistic era, Paris (along with Vienna) stood out in contrast to London, Moscow, and Berlin for its (relative) insistence on universality, especially in science.

Paris in the world, then, was comparable to many other great cities in that much of its mythical prestige in the late eighteenth and nineteenth centuries depended on how the entire Western world understood not just the City of Light but capital cities in general, urban centers whose collective triumph around 1800 came at the expense of both the countryside and the princely residence, as can be seen by comparing London with Hampton Court, Madrid with the Escorial, Berlin with Potsdam, or Saint Petersburg with Tsarskoe Selo. The second half of the eighteenth century was a key period in bringing about this change.

In an earlier phase, Physiocracy, the economic doctrine championed by the elder Mirabeau, who died in 1789, and Dr. François Quesnay, to whom Adam Smith would have dedicated *The Wealth of Nations* (1776) had the good doctor not passed away in 1774, attached primary importance to agricultural productivity. Robespierre, who had started out as a lawyer in Arras, sang the praises of the republican farmer. Thomas Jefferson, a slave-owning planter, an amateur of French wines, and an American correspondent of a number of Parisians including the Abbé Grégoire and Dr. Pierre-Jean-Georges Cabanis, also idealized the "yeoman farmer," perhaps because he didn't know any.

Between 1820 and 1830, however, a dramatic shift became evident not just in France but everywhere in Europe. Great novelists such as Balzac, Dickens, and Dostoevsky preferred cities—Paris, London, Saint Petersburg—to the countryside. Life was in the metropolis, and visitors from the city were often pictured as intruders who disturbed the torpor of tranquil rural towns: witness, for example, Eugénie Grandet's Parisian cousin Charles in Saumur, or Pushkin's Eugene Onegin. Marx made fun of the "idiocy of rural life." As he saw it, Louis Napoleon, whom he called "Crapulinski," came to power in 1848 as the choice of the army and the bureaucracy but above of all of the peasants. History became an urban phenomenon: "In the city, time becomes visible," as Lewis Mumford remarked. But this was a truth whose full import could not have been recognized before the nineteenth century, and even then it was recognized in Paris more than anywhere else.

B UT IF PARIS became a great city as other great cities also flowered, its trajectory in the end was quite distinctive. For one thing, it was more "multifunctional" than its peers. Some cities, such as Rome, Florence, and Venice, are art and history incarnate. Others, such as New York, London, and Berlin, are embodiments of modern finance and government. Only Paris was in the truest sense all these things at once. Paris was simultaneously a capital of the arts, politics, religion, finance, administration, and science (especially medicine and physiology).

Complementing the city's functional diversity was its aesthetic diversity, a product of its longevity that is still evident today. Is there any architectural style, from the Roman of antiquity to the minimalism of recent memory, that is not represented in Paris? Upon returning from a trip to Soviet Russia, still mired in tradition, and to the much younger United States, the poet Blaise Cendrars wrote that only in Paris had modernity been successfully blended with the memory of the Middle Ages.

Historically speaking, Paris thus presents a perfect contrast with New York. For Walt Whitman (born in 1819), New York stood for the same thing as Paris did for Baudelaire (born in 1821), namely, the incarnation of a newly emerged modernity—but Whitman's modernity, unlike Baudelaire's, was hardly tinged with anxiety. Whitman's New World modernity was full of hope, democracy, energy, and creativity that was as much moral as material:

A million people—manners free and superb—open voices—hospitality—
the most courageous and friendly young men,
City of hurried and sparkling waters! city of spires and masts!
City nested in bays! my city![6]

For the Surrealists and their fellow traveler Djuna Barnes, Paris in the 1920s and 1930s was a place of "neo-medieval" mysteries, surprising culs-de-sac, and bizarre sights that lurked hidden within the old city. In

New York, however, Barnes saw only modern streets laid out in a predictable grid: to her the American city was rational, efficient, productive, and supremely legible.

It is also easy to forget about New York's industrial past. Yet as recently as 1950 a million New Yorkers, or 30 percent of the working population, were still employed in some 60,000 factories. Unlike Paris and London, New York is a city whose population is still increasing, because once-industrial neighborhoods such as Soho, Noho, and Tribeca are being surreptitiously repopulated in defiance of obsolete building codes, whose enforcement in any case is lax.

FAR MORE COMPLEX than the relationship between Paris and New York was the one between Paris and London, if only because the cultural history of the Western world, especially in the nineteenth century, was, to borrow from Dickens, a tale of two cities. This was so in part because the modernization of the two capitals often involved a kind of symbiosis. In many ways Louis Napoleon and Haussmann, for example, looked upon London as an urban model. John Nash's Regent Street anticipated the great boulevards of Paris; Hyde Park was a model for the Bois de Boulogne; Edwin Chadwick's sewers antedated Eugène Belgrand's.[7] After Eugène Sue published his *Mystères de Paris* in 1842 and 1843, another novelist, Paul Féval, thought it a good idea to produce in 1844 his *Mystères de Londres,* despite the fact that he had never set foot in that city. For Baudelaire, both London and Paris were home to "life's vast gallery." "When God is feeling bored in Heaven," Heinrich Heine wrote in 1832, "he opens the window and takes in the boulevards of Paris." For Heine, only Paris was of central importance. But his compatriot Theodor Fontane, the author of *Effi Briest,* though of French Huguenot descent, said much the same thing about London in 1844: for Fontane, London (which he did not much like) was the world "in miniature," the "quintessence of the entire globe."[8] Paris was no doubt the capital of the world, but London was also "a unique city" (to borrow the title of Steen Eiler Rasmussen's classic history of the British capital).

How to compare these two capitals?

As might be expected, the chronology of their rise to world fame is roughly contemporaneous though not identical: if the history of Paris as a great city began in 1750 and that of New York in 1840, the modern history of London began with the great fire of 1666. But the saga of London, like that of New York but unlike that of Paris, was at first commercial and industrial. (For Mercier in 1788, London was a point of commercial reference, and when he wished to suggest that the Palais Royal had become the vital commercial center of Paris, he wrote that the decrepit Pont-Neuf was to the newer and more vital center "what Vienna is to London.") In 1824 Thomas Carlyle wrote to his brother that "Paris scarcely occupies a quarter of the ground [of London], and does not seem to have the twentieth part of the business."[9] Symptomatically, Paris until 1870 was fueled by raftloads of wood from the Nivernais region (with the perverse consequence that when the weather turned cold enough for the Seine to freeze, the city ran short of fuel), whereas London had converted to coal by 1750: well before the Revolution, the English capital was already famous throughout Europe for its smoke. Diderot argued that the resulting bad climate, along with a heavy diet marked by a surfeit of beer and beef, was the key to the English proclivity for suicide, known on the Continent in his time as "the English disease." In Romantic poetry, the smoke of Paris was likened to that of a volcano, the smoke of London to that of a factory. Shelley went one step further in 1819:

> Hell is a city much like London—
> A populous and smoky city;
> There are all sorts of people undone,
> And there is little or no fun done;
> Small justice shown, and still less pity.[10]

The demographic statistics for the two cities are likewise at once alike and different: in 1700 Paris and London were roughly equal in population, with 400,000–450,000 inhabitants each. But after this London, driven by the fast pace of commerce and industry, grew much more rapidly than Paris, which remained primarily an administrative and cultural capital. London tripled in size in the seventeenth century, then doubled again in the eighteenth, until by 1800 it was the first city in the world to reach a population of a million. During the nineteenth century that number increased fourfold. By 1940 the population of greater London was almost 9 million, and not until the 1940s did the percentage of industrial jobs in the capital drop below the average for England as a whole, largely because the Board of Trade refused to issue industrial building permits.

Time and again, then, in a comparison of the two cities, the cup of similitude is half full or half empty, depending on one's point of view. Dostoevsky, the bard of the tormented Slavic soul, visited London and Paris and has left us a sarcastic account of his impressions. As one might expect, he was contemptuous of both, but in different ways that speak to the similarities and differences between the two Western metropolises: Parisians struck him as arrogant and superficial, whereas Londoners were materialistic, money-grubbing, and unfeeling.

In many ways, London and Paris were as different as New York and Paris. But then again, not quite as different as all that: there was much that was similar in the cultural evolution of the two European capitals. With respect to high culture, Paris was much closer to London than to the American megalopolis. To Dr. Johnson, who was born in Lichfield in 1709 but died in London in 1784, as well as to his indefatigable Scottish acolyte James Boswell (who had, while in France, seduced Thérèse, Rousseau's companion), London was an extraordinary encyclopedia. Johnson is famous for the aphorism "When a man is tired of London, he is tired of life." Like Paris, London was in its way a capital of the Republic of Letters, a spectacular and always exciting city. The theme of the young provincial who goes to the capital to make his fortune was by no means exclusively Parisian. In addition to Rastignac and Julien Sorel, one has only to think of Becky Sharp in Thackeray's *Vanity Fair* or of Dickens's *David Copperfield*. And London, like Paris, knew alienation, that extreme form of solitude which is paradoxically the fate of the modern city dweller. Indeed, symptoms of alienation may have appeared earlier, and may have been more pronounced, in London than in Paris. For the great English Romantics, including both those who fled London such as Wordsworth and those who remained such as Blake, the English capital was not so much an encyclopedia as a nightmare. From a coach on Westminster Bridge, Wordsworth did admire the formidable power of the still slumbering city:

> Earth has not anything to show more fair . . .
> Ne'er saw I, never felt, a calm so deep! . . .
> Dear God! the very houses seem asleep;
> And all that mighty heart is lying still!

And yet the fact remains that the poet was singing London's praises only as he was leaving it. Blake was less harsh than Wordsworth on the subject of urban anonymity, but he made up for this by being more intransigent—and more perspicacious—on the new and troubling nature of London's modernity:

> [I] mark in every face I meet
> Marks of weakness, marks of woe.
> In every cry of every man
> In every Infant's cry of fear,
> In every voice, in every ban,
> The mind-forg'd manacles I hear.

The place of London in the work of Charles Dickens (who has a street in Paris named after him and whose dates, 1812–1870, are within a decade of Flaubert's and Baudelaire's) was also typically ambiguous, and in a way that, typically, has many Parisian analogues. More than any other author, Dickens has been identified with London, much as Victor Hugo and Jules Michelet are identified with Paris. It is particularly suggestive, then, that his thinking about the English capital grew darker as the years passed: after the exuberant *Sketches*, published under the pen name Boz in 1836 and 1837, came the far less optimistic *Nicholas Nickleby* (1838–1839) and *Dombey and Son* (1846–1848). The London of *Bleak House* (1852–1853) is frankly repulsive, a city of filth and smoke and, like all big cities, a "void" in which millions of people tied to one another by invisible bonds nevertheless live in isolation, inactivity, secrecy, and solitude.

Undeniably, then, the two metropolises elicited cultural responses at once comparable and dissimilar: after Balzac and Hugo as the counterparts of Dickens, Thomas Carlyle, in turn, echoed much of Baudelaire's sensibility. For the dyspeptic Scottish author of *Sartor Resartus,* "Weissnichtwo" (I know not where), a thinly disguised reference to the English capital, was a place of unprecedented moral squalor, whose inhabitants were crowded together like sardines—or like vipers in an Egyptian bottle. And after this, George Gissing can be imagined as an English Zola, though more pessimistic about London than Zola was about Paris. And last but not least, T. S. Eliot employed a Baudelairean vocabulary in writing about London in *The Waste Land.*

So it would be difficult to write the history of one of these two cities without also discussing the history of the other; and it may even be that we should discuss the two capitals as if they were warring sisters, each of whom presented the other with a cruelly distorted image of herself in the sense that each saw in the other an exaggeration of the ills she feared for herself.

Well before the French Revolution, British patriotism was already thriving on Gallophobic and anti-Parisian sentiment, with Protestantism and parliamentarianism its other chief staples, or so in any case thought the ex-Communard Jules Vallès, who wrote from his London exile: "Make no mistake: the Englishman feels a blind, instinctive hatred for everything French. Every habit of the Parisian pains him greatly, and he either dismisses it, or is rankled by it, or takes a different way to work." There was much truth to this judgment; and as moderate and traveled a man as Dickens, who knew Paris quite well, commented upon the death of the courtesan Marie Duplessis, later to be immortalized as La Traviata, that "Paris is corrupt to the core . . . You would have thought it was a question of the death of a hero or a Joan of Arc."[11]

Though the two cities were in many ways comparable, then, many Londoners did not like Paris, and many Parisians, it must be said, did not much like London either: Léon Faucher asked himself if he could live in London, only to answer that to do so would be "fatal to the vigor of the body and to the purity of morals."[12] For Flora Tristan, London was a "monstrous city." And for Vallès, the English capital's countless offenses were essential parts of its being: it shared the faults of Paris (the

gap between rich and poor and the narrow self-interest of the bourgeoisie), but in London these took on an even more sinister aspect because of
English Protestantism, which served as a justification for commercial-
ism and drained the gaiety from life. London was "gray, dirty, and malodorous. Adultery is impossible here. Religion is virtually compulsory
and highly disagreeable. The English God is ugly, unsympathetic, and
yellow with age . . . Catholic ecstasies pose a danger to the chastity of
women. The reformed religion is therefore not something blondes are
likely to go wild over." It is odd to see a Communard like Vallès extol-
ling the Catholic faith (even for fostering adultery), but the idea that
Protestantism had done much harm was a commonplace of the period in France, and on this point Théophile Gautier, a notorious anti-
Communard, agreed with his political enemy, writing in 1842: "The
English are wealthy, energetic, and industrious . . . but the art of speaking well will always elude them . . . They are nothing but burnished
barbarians . . . What is more, the English are not Catholics: Protestantism is as inimical to the arts as Islam, perhaps more so. Artists can only
be pagans or Catholics."[13]

Which of these two cities, then, really was the Capital of the Nineteenth Century? Much could be said on both sides; but it may be relevant that although Paris and London were both cities of refuge, foreigners, especially artists, journalists, and men of letters, felt more relegated
to the fringes of social life in London than in Paris. In the French
capital, foreigners (such as Frédéric Chopin and Adam Mickiewicz,
Gioacchino Rossini and Gabriele D'Annunzio, John Singer Sargent the
Anglo-American painter and Mihály Munkácsy the Magyar artist) often
found themselves at the center of society in a city that prided itself on
its universality. Gautier, delighted to be eating a risotto prepared by the
Italian contralto Ernesta Grisi, exclaimed that in Paris "you can travel
around the world without an interpreter!"[14] "London," G. K. Chesterton
wrote in *All Things Considered* (1908), "is a riddle. Paris is an explanation." And indeed, where else but in Paris, the mythical capital of Europe, would one be likely to run into not only the republican enemies of
Dom Pedro II, the emperor of Brazil, but also the former emperor himself after he was deposed in 1889?

Paris, London, and New York: all have defined themselves, at times, in relation to one another. But they have also imagined themselves in their differing relations to the nations whose values they do (or do not) express. As a wag once said, the United States is the only country in the world without a consulate in New York: many Americans feel uncomfortable in the city, as if visiting a foreign country. New York City was only briefly the capital of the new republic, and today it is not even the capital of New York State. In 1643 the 500 inhabitants of New Amsterdam already spoke 18 languages. Between 1820 and 1920, 33 million immigrants passed through the port of New York, 16 million in just over 30 years (1892–1924). In 1870 there were some 24,000 Jews living in Paris; by 1881 the influx of Jews from Alsace had increased that figure to roughly 40,000. In New York, where Jews were present as early as 1654 (as refugees from Brazil), they numbered 50,000 in 1850 and more than a million in 1910. In 1890, 71 percent of the population of the New York boroughs consisted of immigrants or the children of immigrants. If there is such a thing as the capital of the twenty-first century, New York has to be it, but until 1910 it was staunchly "a-national" though not, for all that, cosmopolitan or universal. This city of immigrants may once have been an adequate mirror of a society that was also new, but in the nineteenth century the gap grew wide between the ever ebullient, perpetually changing city and a country whose social and ethnic composition was much less varied, and much less brutally present, than that of its largest city.

The relationship of Paris to France has been much closer. Paris was never the capital of world capitalism, as London and New York are today, but it has indubitably been the capital of modern France. And much of its distinction and prestige, of its myth, has been magnified by the will of the French bureaucracy as well as that of the French people. Americans will remember the headline that ran in one New York paper after President Gerald Ford announced his unwillingness to provide the city with financial aid: "Ford to City: Drop Dead." In France such an attitude toward Paris is unimaginable. In 1871 many fervent republicans (such as Georges Clemenceau) looked upon the Paris Commune as a mistake because it seemed as unthinkable to them as France without Paris.

Is London the capital of England or of the British Empire? Can it claim to be the capital of the Welsh and the Scots? Perhaps. Is it the capital of Northern Ireland? To be sure, the British state has always had a presence in London, but it was more of an imperial presence than a strictly national one, and, as Roy Porter rightly remarks in his social history of London, "the key to the capital is the British Empire."[15] Indeed, British national feeling itself is, or rather was, a product of empire, since it was created in the eighteenth century as a means of holding the new empire together.

By contrast, Paris, if we leave aside the brief episode of the Colonial Exposition of 1931, was never really the capital of an empire. And in any event Paris has never much cared about France's empire; but by contrast it has always borne the mark of the state, be it royal, imperial, or republican, from the Louvre palace created by Charles V to the so-called *grands projets,* the ambitious public building efforts of recent years, of which the next scheduled for completion is to be a museum housing what used to be called "primitive art."

In this respect, Paris once again differs dramatically from London, for, as the Danish architect Steen Eiler Rasmussen so convincingly showed more than half a century ago in *London: The Unique City,* the genius of London lies in what is private, whereas for centuries the public life of Paris has been administered by the state. A critical difference, and one whose most obvious urban and physical sign is the disparity between London's squares and Paris's *places royales,* even if Inigo Jones's Covent Garden of 1630 was originally inspired by Louis XIII's Place Royale, today the Place des Vosges. Haussmann's genius lay in the grand boulevards; that of the ancien régime, or rather of Bourbon absolutism, lay in the *places royales,* from the Place des Vosges to the Place de la Concorde; but all of these were quite different in function and origin from London's famous squares, and the difference here speaks to the dramatic role of the French state in making Paris what it was and still is, the capital of France.

First among the English squares was Soho Square in 1731, followed by Grosvenor Square in 1737, which was to be the archetype of all later imitations, owing not only to its vast size (more than seven acres) but also to the fact that it was created not by the state or even by the city of

London but by a private individual, Richard Grosvenor, on land that had been his mother's dowry when she married in 1677 at the age of 12. Also worthy of special mention is Bedford Square, built in 1776 and closed to the public until 1893.

In the 1930s a humorist by the name of Ferdinand Lope, echoing the playwright Alphonse Allais, advocated clearing the air of Paris by rebuilding Paris in the country. Oddly enough, something very like this was the ambition of the early modern English urban reformers who sought, on behalf of the great landowners who employed them (and with no regard for the English state), to remake London in the eighteenth and nineteenth centuries. The motto inscribed on the facade of Buckingham House (which George III bought in 1762 and made into a royal residence and his son George IV had rebuilt as Buckingham Palace) said it all: "Rus in Urbe" (the country in the city). There was a time, back in 1771, when sheep grazed on the grass in Cavendish Square, irritating an observer who made fun of city squares disguised to look like country fields: "They are parks, they are sheep walks, in short, they are everything except what they should be. The *rus in urbe* is a preposterous idea at best." When Michelet visited London in 1834, he was astonished, almost shocked: "The West End, which is home to high society and the aristocracy, produces little and consumes a great deal. Meadows cover much of this section. Sheep graze in the shadow of Whitehall and Westminster . . . The subtlety is charming, but it cannot endure much longer." Overstated, perhaps: Michelet was no admirer of English life. Still, it is a shame that Marie Antoinette was not queen of England. Had she built her "hamlet" on Pall Mall rather than at Versailles, she would no doubt have become immensely popular.[16]

Heinrich Heine never commented on London squares and Parisian *places,* but he was not entirely wrong to think in 1831 that France was but an extended suburb of its imposing capital: "France is like a garden from which one has cut the finest flowers to make a bouquet, and that bouquet is called Paris." In March 1848 George Sand wrote about the capital on her return to the provinces: "What a dream Paris is, what enthusiasm there is there, and yet what decorum and order! I've just come from the city: I flew there and saw the people in their grandeur, sublime, naive, and generous, the French people gathered in the heart of France, in the heart of the world, the most admirable people in the universe. I went many nights without sleep, many days without sitting down. People are mad, they're intoxicated, they're happy to sleep in the gutters and congregate in the heavens." No one in Britain has written about London in this way.[17]

AND HOW TO APPROACH the question of the relationship of Paris to the nation whose purpose and existence it expresses? The monumentality of Paris is probably still the most visible and substantial evidence of the close links that existed between Paris, France, and history, especially in the early part of the nineteenth century. Parisians, for example, instinctively look upon the Arc de Triomphe at L'Etoile with its eternal flame in honor of the unknown soldier as their own war memorial, even though it is officially a national monument.

But monumentality is only one of the many links that tie Paris to its nation. Much the same connection appears, as it happens, in an altogether different context: music, especially opera. And this context is all the more revealing for its eccentricity. Paris, Vienna, Budapest: in all three, music enjoyed considerable prestige, but of different kinds. For nearly a century Paris was the opera capital of the world, as well it might have been, because opera was a history-laden genre and Paris was also the capital of a historic nation—the most historic of all nations, as people in Central Europe liked to say. In Paris, then, historicized opera; and to the east, in striking contrast, the anti-historicism of the operetta in the two capitals of an empire, Austria-Hungary, that was threatened by history and, on the eve of the First World War, also threatened by the irresistible rise of national and ethnic demands.

THANKS TO THE former minister of cultural affairs Jack Lang, France today is the home of an annual, nationwide, and—France being what it is—subsidized music festival. In a state where culture is a key to prestige, the impoverishment of the French musical imagination was considered nothing less than an affair of state. As long ago as the nineteenth century, there was already general agreement that the French were somehow musically deficient. In 1848 Hector Berlioz wrote that "only a person blindfolded with a tricolor flag could fail to see" that French music was dead.[18] A half-century later Romain Rolland quipped that all the great French composers were foreigners. That was perhaps a bit too harsh, but the fact remains that some of the finest moments in French musical history were provided by visiting foreign composers rather than by native-born musicians. Mozart visited Paris twice, in 1763 and 1778; though unhappy and bewildered in the French capital, he wrote there two symphonies, five piano sonatas, and the music for a ballet. Christoph Willibald Gluck, or Monsieur le Chevalier de Gluck as he was then known, visited Paris five times between 1773 and 1779 as a protégé of Marie Antoinette. François-Joseph Gossec, a Belgian and a protégé of Jean-Philippe Rameau, lived there from 1751 to 1829. Other noteworthy foreign composers included Rossini; Cherubini, a Florentine by birth and a director of the Conservatoire de Paris; Chopin, who died on the Place Vendôme; Meyerbeer; Liszt; Verdi; Offenbach; and of course Wagner, who, by virtue of his marriage to Cosima Liszt, was not only Liszt's son-in-law but also the brother-in-law of the French prime minister Emile Ollivier. (Wagner, by the way, hated the French capital, which had ridiculed him and fêted the equally hated Meyerbeer. In 1870 he urged Bismarck to shell the besieged city.)

Some musical facts speak for themselves. During the Second Empire there were only fifty teachers of music in Paris schools. Still, Paris was by no means a musical wasteland. Franz Liszt mused in 1837 that despite the Parisian public's fondness for frivolities, "Paris nonetheless contains a considerable number of men who are seriously devoted to Art and who work conscientiously at their musical education." L.-G. Bocquillon, for example, created a Parisian choral society during the July Monarchy. And there were many glee clubs, such as the Carolingiens and the Athéniens de Montmartre, who became the Montagnards in 1848 and then, after the Republic collapsed in 1852, the more anodyne Tyroliens. Incidentally, most Parisian singers were industrial, clerical, or shop workers, whereas in the provinces it was common for the upper classes to take part in municipal musical festivals.[19]

The Société des Concerts du Conservatoire, created by Luigi Cherubini and François-Antoine Habeneck, was a worthy successor to the
Concerts des Amateurs, which had been organized by Gossec in 1769
but had gone bankrupt in 1781. The Société's audience was perhaps
even larger than that of its predecessor as well as more bourgeois.[20] Its
concerts introduced Parisians to the music of Beethoven. In March
1828, a year after the master's death, Cherubini proposed that the new
society's first concert should start with one of his own works followed by
the Seventh Symphony of the "genius of Bonn." Two weeks later came
another concert "dedicated to the memory of L. V. Beethoven" and featuring a program of his works, in particular the *Eroica,* which was "universally requested." These performances were praised by Liszt and even
Wagner, and became renowned throughout the world. The concert series organized by Jules Pasdeloup in 1861 at the Cirque d'Hiver du
Boulevard des Filles du Calvaire also did much to expand the audience
for great music in Paris. There, every Sunday, one could listen to the
music of the masters: Beethoven, Mozart, Haydn, Weber, Meyerbeer.
Wagner was therefore quite unjust when he wrote that the audience for
serious music in Paris, unlike the allegedly more varied and communal
audiences to be found in Germany, comprised "a class of wealthy individuals and idle aristocrats."[21]

Indeed, the place of Paris in the musical life of nineteenth-century
Europe must have been quite impressive, especially if we remember that
the great Parisian musical genre of the nineteenth century was neither
orchestral nor chamber music but opera. This was so for political and social reasons, as we shall see, but also because of opera's nature as an all-
encompassing aesthetic genre. (Recall here the Parisian scientists' view
of the nature of scientific knowledge.) For Gautier, who, like Baudelaire,
denigrated nature, the opera house was the last refuge of poetry and fantasy. Crude reality was not allowed. Nothing topical or true was permitted. One entered an enchanted world. The opera house was "the temple
of modern civilization . . . the culmination of art, luxury, elegance, and
all the refinements of the high life." French composers of the period
were under no illusion about this: Charles Gounod asserted in his auto-
biography that if one wished to become truly renowned as a musician in
France, opera was the only way. Indeed, in the first half of the century

conservatory training focused primarily on vocal music, and candidates for the Prix de Rome were required to compose a cantata.[22]

The supposed centrality of opera to culture was not a uniquely Parisian idea. The key role of these "music dramas" was universally acknowledged: Louis Huart, in 1840, depicted opera as "the central point of civilization."[23] Friedrich Nietzsche, who admired Wagner, later broke with the composer but not with opera as a musical genre. Late in Nietzsche's life, *Carmen* (the Spanish national opera, composed in 1875 by a Parisian to a Parisian libretto) elicited as much enthusiasm from him as *Tannhäuser* had earlier. For Nietzsche, in this respect a faithful disciple of Wagner, opera was the only true *Gesamtkunstwerk,* what the symphony had been for Schopenhauer: a *rerum concordia discors,* an epitome of man's complementary and contradictory passions. Berlioz called Meyerbeer's *Les Huguenots* a "dramatic opera" and a "musical encyclopedia," an artistic melding that mirrored the nation's political melding of its citizens, and Meyerbeer's *Robert le diable* determinedly combined lyric drama with the most modern staging and scenic effects.

A diorama of 1877 offered a striking example of this will to incorporation: it presented a circular view of Paris, not of the city's buildings but rather of great Parisians of the day assembled in concentric circles around the new Opéra. Included were artists, society people, politicians, and industrialists—"An astonishing parade," Bruno Latour remarks, "which used the new Opéra as a pivot around which the beau monde revolved."[24] Instinctively, the Opéra's architect, Charles Garnier, had built his palais as a temple to all the arts: a warm-hearted Parisian, he was also careful to dispense commissions to the painters, architects, and sculptors who had always been his friends, such as Paul Baudry, Gustave Boulanger, Eugène Guillaume, and Jean-Baptiste Carpeaux.

The prestige of opera in the nineteenth century, then, was due to its place in the aesthetic preferences of the European—and Parisian—intelligentsia. Also of some relevance were the intimate habits of Parisian high society (dancers from the Opéra were often the mistresses of fashionable members of the Jockey Club, who made their acquaintance in the celebrated lobby of the opera house). But the political dimension was even more important.

By 1860 opera had long been associated with prestige in France, and in particular with the prestige of the French state: "To go to Paris without seeing the Opéra," wrote the young Russian Nicolai Karamzin in 1790, "is like someone who has been to Rome and has not seen the pope." Politics was the civic property of the nation, and attending the opera was the cultural right of every Parisian bourgeois. Where does the wigmaker go on Sunday? Mercier wondered. "To the Opéra, to see Mademoiselle Guimard dance and to sing her praises. He finds himself sitting next to the person whose wig he fitted that morning. Now he can rub shoulders with his neighbors without fear and be buffeted by the ecstatic crowd. He's no longer a gawker. Now he's a judge of music." Indeed, in the eighteenth and nineteenth centuries opera was the most popular and democratic of all the forms of high culture, and especially of Romantic high culture.[25]

Opera was a Parisian passion, and for the French nation a costly passion, because it fell to the monarch to subsidize the art (with funds derived ultimately from the royal household or the king's civil list), to the delight of his courtiers since it was common practice for the king to provide his favorites with free tickets. (It was not until the July Monarchy that subsidies were taken not from the monarch's private funds but from the public funds of the ministry of the interior.) From Louis XIV to François Mitterrand, relations between the state and the opera certainly varied, but they were invariably costly. In 1828 the Paris Opéra cost the state more than a million francs, a subsidy that accounted for 60 percent of the Opéra's budget. Although small by today's standards, such a sum was colossal for the time. During the Second Empire, the director of the Paris Opéra was paid roughly 100,000 francs per year, or more than 100 times the annual wage of a skilled worker. Emilio Naudin, the greatest tenor of his day, received 110,000 francs for his role in Meyerbeer's L'Africaine (1865).

Perhaps the ratio of the supply of talent to the demand explained these enormous fees, but if so it was only because the state artificially stimulated demand. Theodore Zeldin reminds us just how ambitious the programming of opera in Paris was in the nineteenth century. In 1866, for example, Parisians could have heard two versions of Don Juan, one at the Théâtre Lyrique, the other at the Opéra; as well as *Giselle, Robert le diable,* Gounod's *La Colombe,* operas by Verdi and Donizetti, Halévy's *La Juive,* and various works that are no longer performed, such as Victor Massé's *La Fior d'Italia* and *Massa Pepita.* (Although some of the names on this list are unfamiliar, they are far less obscure than would be the names of composers whose works were performed in Paris during the Restoration, because it was only as the nineteenth century progressed that a normative French musical repertoire was constituted, a repertoire that still largely coincides with our own.)

Money, then, coupled with aesthetic prestige, and with all of that, politics: opera thrived in Paris because the French state, and the various regimes that directed it, viewed the vicissitudes of Parisian opera as a barometer of their own success. So it was, for example, that even an authoritarian, militaristic regime like the Second Empire found its ideal expression and architectural culmination in a Palais de l'Opéra rather than in a simple palais or, better yet, in a system of military defenses, an important colony, or a new seaport. To be sure, precedents for concern abounded: many eighteenth-century architects (both monarchists and republicans) had long since thought about designing a spectacular new opera house for Paris. For example, Germain Boffrand (1667–1754) dreamed of creating a vast monumental ensemble including a new opera house, a new *place royale,* and a Palais National des Arts in what had been the Louvre. But it was not until 1860 that the Paris-born Garnier, who had grown up on the rue Mouffetard, was definitively entrusted with this task. He had a ready answer for Empress Eugénie when she asked him to describe the style of his soon-to-be-constructed opera house. Without missing a beat—or so goes the legend—Garnier re-

---

Jean-Baptiste-Edouard Detaille, *Inauguration of the Paris Opéra, January 5, 1875: Arrival of the Lord Mayor of London (with entourage), greeted by Charles Garnier.* Garnier's Opéra house was the aesthetic masterpiece of the Second Empire, although the Empire died on September 4, 1870, while the building was not finished until a few years later. On that occasion, and on the Grand Staircase of this decidedly grand building, French and Parisian dignitaries in modest republican and bourgeois garb greet their gorgeously dressed counterparts from monarchic London. Châteaux de Versailles et de Trianon. Photo: Gérard Blot. Réunion des Musées Nationaux / Art Resource, NY.

sponded that it would be neither Renaissance nor classical but "pure Napoleon III." One could say that Napoleon the Great had his Arc de Triomphe at L'Etoile while Napoleon the Small would have only the Opéra Garnier; but peace is better than war.

To speak of politics and the state in nineteenth-century Europe is of course to speak of nationalism and national passions. And here again was a challenge that opera easily surmounted, especially in Paris: no theatrical or musical genre was more politicized, nationalistic, and historicist than opera: Meyerbeer, as Charles Rosen notes, "gave extraordinary vitality to historical melodrama,"[26] to which one might add that the history in question was the history of nations, an obsession that produced *Aida* and *Semiramis* on the history of ancient Egypt; Saint-Saëns's *Samson et Dalila* on ancient Israel; César Franck's *Ghiselle* for the Dark Ages, with Donizetti's *Ugo, conte di Parigi* for 987; Rossini's *William Tell* and Halévy's *La Juive* for medieval Switzerland, Meyerbeer's *Robert le diable* for medieval France, and Verdi's *Sicilian Vespers* for medieval Italy; followed by, for early modern times, Verdi's *Don Carlos,* Saint-Saëns's *Henry VIII,* Meyerbeer's *Les Huguenots,* Moussorgsky's *Boris Godunov,* and François Boieldieu's *La Dame blanche.* (Adapted in 1825 from Walter Scott's novels, *La Dame blanche* was performed 1,500 times in Paris by 1874.) And for the Revolution, Giordano's *Andrea Chénier* and Puccini's *Tosca.*

Emile Zola, who wrote librettos for several operas, remarked that French lyric drama could be seen, without regard to purely musical effects, as an expression of the "lively clarity of the genius of our race." (Wagner of course would develop this last obsession to the utmost degree, and Hitler, who was perhaps even more devoted to national aestheticism than to national socialism, saw this clearly and on several occasions went to Bayreuth with members of his family to visit Winnifred Wagner, the composer's daughter-in-law.) Heinrich Heine, who admired Louis Philippe, also located the opera of his day in a political frame, though quite gently, as in his warmly satirical explanation of *Robert le diable,* which was performed at the Paris Opéra 758 times from 1831 to 1893. (The Robert of the title is the son of a thirteenth-century Duchess of Normandy.) Robert, Heine wrote in 1831, hesitates as to whether to follow the example of his father or that of his mother. His father was a demon as depraved as Philippe-Egalité, but his mother was a princess as pious as the daughter of the duc de Penthièvre. Robert's atavisms drive him toward wickedness and revolution, but the memory of his mother recalls him to the path of righteousness, that is, to the ancien régime: "These two innate natures combat each other in his soul. He floats between two principles . . . [Robert] is *juste-milieu*."[27]

Opera in Paris was closely related to both monarchy and nation, and republicans too inevitably had to concern themselves with this musical genre. In a book entitled *French Grand Opera as Politics and Politicized Art,* Jane Fulcher quotes at length from an unfortunately anonymous 1848 text devoted to the question of what republican opera ought to be. To close the opera house would sow panic: the "sinister news" would upset the public. More than that, the anonymous commentator opines, "Opera is still . . . one of the glories of Paris. It is the theater of the grandest artistic magnificence. The Republic, in its advent, cannot repudiate the superb heritage of luxury, of elegance, and of poetry that [has] been bequeathed to it." What should be done, then? For the author of this text, the only solution was to create a new opera house in order to remove opera from the realm of

> private speculation, and to make it a public establishment, belonging to the state, administered under its direction and under its control . . . [with] periodic performances at reduced prices that would put this rich spectacle at the disposal of the popular classes . . . It is a beautiful tribune that Republican propaganda should reserve for itself alone; it is here, by the triple attractions that lure, seduce, and transport the soul, the eyes and ears, it is by this that [the Republic] should act on the population.[28]

This, when you think about it, just about sums up Jack Lang's program for the Opéra Bastille.

Indeed, the communitarian and nationalist purpose of Parisian opera was so marked that composers had to adjust the aesthetic conventions of the genre to suit the spirit of the capital. Thus Rossini, in his *William Tell* of 1829, "systematically excised all the passages where the chorus was to have merely repeated the words of soloists [who had come to the end of an arioso or an ensemble], and instead wrote new larger, self-contained numbers that were wholly choral." Conversely, Verdi's *Un ballo in maschera* (A Masked Ball), as performed in 1859, is considered by some to have been the beginning of the end of Paris grand opera because in that work "the responsibility for the destruction of human lives and dreams of a better existence does not lie with the unfathomable otherness of the crowd, but with all individuals, because they can no longer resist being absorbed by the all embracing mass of a society that has become anonymous." Rephrased, this is to say that opera, which had once reflected Parisian national passion, had now come to reflect the rise of the *faits divers* instead.[29]

Opera, that paragon of politicized national art, was bound to occupy a special place in the life of a capital which, especially during the Second Empire, was also the capital of History. How could such a national, indeed nationalistic, regime have failed to interest itself in opera, a Parisian obsession? It interested itself, one might venture to say, out of necessity, and in a way appropriate to its own hybrid nature: the imperial repertoire would of course be "national," that is, French; but in political terms Napoleon III's opera had to be simultaneously on the left and on the right, just as the Empire itself was simultaneously conservative in Brittany and red in the southwest, nationalist at Solferino in 1859 yet ultramontane in Mentana in 1867.

We can reflect further on what the Second Empire expected from this musical genre if we draw an analogy between opera (an oppositional historical genre) and the historical novel as described by the Hungarian Marxist critic Georg Lukács. Reduced to essentials, Lukács's argument is quite simple: the historical novel (like nineteenth-century opera) was primarily a bourgeois and national genre. Hence it naturally flourished in this period, because the bourgeoisie also flourished as monarchies and aristocracies declined.

For the bourgeois reader in the period 1770–1840, any historical reference was necessarily positive: even if Quentin Durward does not assassinate the tyrannical Louis XI, and even if d'Artagnan (though the lover of a young and innocent bourgeoise, Mme Bonacieux) remains the faithful servant of an all too Christian and absolute monarch, the bourgeois

Honoré Daumier, *The Saltimbanques Changing Place*, ca. 1865.
Daumier's *Saltimbanques* roughly coincides in time with Baudelaire's
prose poem on this theme. The flâneur chooses to become marginal.
He chooses to disdain alienating, fetishistic bourgeois life. These
street performers have no such choice. Their child, to be sure, is still
defiant, but his broken parents understand that there is no way out.

Nouveau Paris monumental. Haussmann was a ruthless modernizer, hostile to those who would carry an active memory of the past into the world of today and tomorrow. But he was not hostile to the past itself, provided that it had been made safely monumental. Indeed, Haussmann provided for the restoration of many Parisian sites, including Notre Dame. Palaces and churches had their place in his new capital, but as framed jewels that would give distinction to his work.

Physionomie de l'habitat parisien, 1967. This map, color-coded by age and type of structure, reveals at a glance the vast extent of Haussmann's rebuilding of the capital. Private buildings of the Renaissance and of early modern Paris (let alone of the Middle Ages) are very few. Haussmann's stamp, by contrast, is everywhere present; the city's reality, and especially its image, are still as he made them. Ironically, it is onto this once ultra-modern and (for many Impressionists and Surrealists) alienating vision of the city that we have grafted our image of Paris as the capital of a golden past for which we yearn.

From Jacqueline Beaujeu-Garnier, *Atlas de Paris et de la région parisienne* (Paris: Berger-Levrault Editions, 1967). Courtesy Harvard Map Collection, Harvard College Library. Reproduced by permission of Berger-Levrault Editions, Paris.

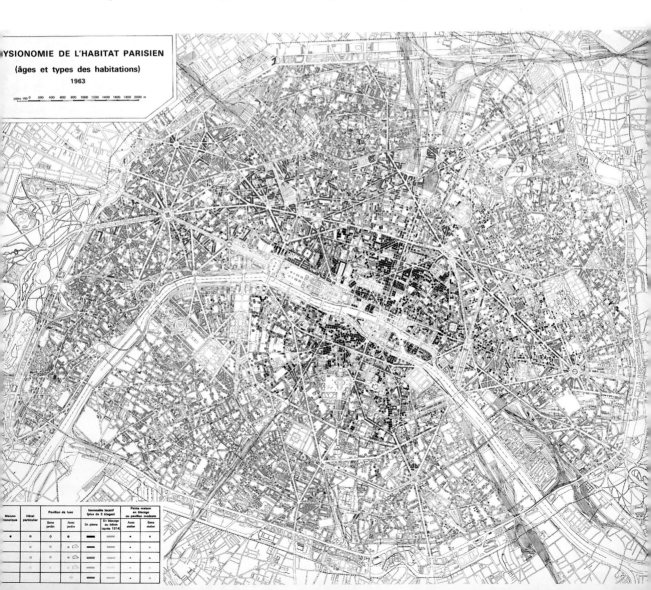

Hilaire-Germain-Edgar Degas, *The Ballet from "Robert le Diable,"* 1872. It is often through the eye of Degas that we see the Parisian women of his day: elegant women at the races, laundresses, milliners, performers, prostitutes, and, as in this painting of a scene from Giacomo Meyerbeer's opera, dancing nuns.

The Metropolitan Museum of Art, H. O. Havemeyer Collection, Bequest of Mrs. H. O. Havemeyer, 1929. (29.100.552) Photograph © 1992 The Metropolitan Museum of Art.

Thomas Shotter Boys, *St. Etienne du Mont, with the Pantheon,* ca. 1839. The Baudelairean and alienated spirit of Charles Meryon's *The Pont-Neuf in 1853* (see p.273) is highlighted by this contrasting romantic scene, done in a style that Victor Hugo might well have liked. The Gothic elements of the church (gargoyles, buttresses) and the Renaissance windows are emphasized to the detriment of the cold and neoclassical eighteenth-century Pantheon in the background.

Samuel F. B. Morse, *Gallery of the Louvre,* 1831–1833. Morse is less well known today for his canvases than for his invention of the telegraph. This painting of the Louvre, with its accumulated treasures and its diligent copyists (some of them, no doubt, American apprentices), illustrates the way artists of the New World like Morse related to the masters of French and European art.

Oil on canvas, 73 3/4 x 108 in. Terra Foundation for the Arts, Daniel J. Terra Collection, 1992.51; Photography courtesy of Terra Foundation for the Arts, Chicago.

Henry Ossawa Tanner, *The Arch,* 1914. Tanner, perhaps the first African-American painter to settle in Paris permanently, painted Napoleon's Arch of Triumph (completed in 1836) at a time when it was soon to become the site of the tomb of the unknown soldier and, unofficially, the Parisians' own municipal war memorial. Another of Tanner's canvases hangs today in the Musée d'Orsay.

Oil on canvas, 39 1/4 x 38 3/8 in. Brooklyn Museum of Art, Gift of Alfred W. Jenkins, 32.10.

Faith Ringgold, *Dinner at Gertrude Stein's,* 1991. Paris in the 1920s was an important place for American letters, both for the white writers of the "lost generation" and for African-American writers. But the two groups did not have much to do with each other, except perhaps in the pictorial imagination of Faith Ringgold, whose "French Collection" of the 1980s and 1990s memorably celebrates some of the high points—and lost opportunities—in the lives of these Americans in Paris.

Acrylic on canvas, tie-dyed, pieced fabric border, 79 x 84 in.; from the Series "The French Collection #9." Faith Ringgold © 1991, Private Collection.

reader of these texts knew that beyond all the vicissitudes of these novels' complex plots lay a happy ending—namely 1789, the fall of the ancien régime, and after that the universal triumph of the Revolution's
principles in Europe and the yet-to-be-colonized world at large.

And, broadly speaking, the same vision of history sustained the repertoire of the Paris opera. As it did many other aspects of Parisian life,
such as Delacroix's painting of the Revolution of 1830, with the medieval towers of Notre Dame in the background while, in the foreground,
as required by History, a goddess of Liberty wearing a Phrygian cap
leads the people of Paris to ultimate victory in this city and the world.

But, Lukács continues, in 1848 everything changed. Suddenly the
bourgeoisie noticed that History was moving much too far and much
too fast in the direction of socialism and communism. Consequently,
Lukacs argues, the tone of the historical novel changed entirely. In 1819
Walter Scott's *Ivanhoe* had portrayed a foreign, exploitative, and aristocratic race (the Normans) and a triumphant hero of Saxon descent,
Ivanhoe. By contrast, Flaubert's *Salammbô* (1862) compensated for its
ideological vacuousness by adding a surfeit of rather tiresome pseudo-
historical detail, much of it salacious. Whether Salammbô wins or loses
may (or may not) interest the reader, but her fate has nothing to do with
the march of History.

During the Second Empire, opera in Paris followed a similar defeatist
trajectory, exemplified by typical changes in the staging of *La Muette de
Portici* (The Mute Girl of Portici). This opera by Daniel Auber, which
inspired the revolutions of 1830 in Paris and 1831 in Brussels and
which Wagner described as having lifted the spirit *(Geist)* of Paris to its
loftiest height, premiered in 1828. In it Alfonso, the son of the Spanish
duke who rules Naples as viceroy, seduces Fenella, a mute girl living in
Portici. Miraculously, Fenella's brother Masaniello, whom the people
have chosen as their leader, overthrows the Spanish-backed regime. (The
very literate Karl Marx remarked in his history of 1848 that Louis Napoleon was a second Masaniello.)[30] But Masaniello becomes a tyrant in
his own right and is poisoned by his former friend Pietro, a Neapolitan
fisherman. Masaniello dies, the Spaniards return, and Fenella hurls herself into the crater of the erupting Mount Vesuvius.

In 1828 this hyperpoliticized work about an oppressed people marked a turning point in the history of Parisian opera. Masaniello appeared literally as a standard-bearer, dressed in blue, white, and red and wearing a Phrygian cap, to the horror of the royal censor. At the Opéra Comique, the censor reported, "the revolution of Naples was presented in all its crudity . . . The sovereign people and above all Masaniello spoke too much of insurrection, of liberty, of country . . . and the coloring of the work was generally sad and funereal."[31]

Restaged immediately after the Revolution of 1830, Auber's work quickly became symbolic once again. Underscoring its topical message, Adolphe Nourrit, who had played the part of Masaniello in 1828, ended the opera with an enthusiastic rendition of "La Parisienne" (by Casimir Delavigne and Auber), the song that was virtually the French national anthem during the July Monarchy:

> Peuple français, peuple de braves
> La Liberté rouvre ses bras.
> On nous disait: Soyons esclaves!
> Nous avons dit: Soyons soldats!
> (French people, courageous people
> Liberty again opens her arms.
> They told us, Be slaves!
> We said, Be soldiers!)

In 1860, more than a decade after the June Days and the defeat of the Paris workers, *La Muette de Portici* was still in the repertoire (as it continued to be during the Commune). It was no longer the same, however. To be sure, Napoleon III stood for modernity, the people, 1789, and the tricolor flag. The Empire in its own way was still History, and its officials could not afford to ban a historicizing opera that was still quite popular in Paris. What was needed, they concluded, was a new staging, suitably bowdlerized. The 1828 presentation had emphasized the historical topicality of the work. By contrast, the 1860 presentation sought to emphasize the Neapolitan locale and the temporal remoteness of the action. The lush sets and the expanded cast compensated for the political emasculation of the drama: after Ivanhoe, Salammbô. This was not an iso-

lated strategy: embarrassing passages were similarly eliminated from
Meyerbeer's *Les Huguenots,* in whose fourth act the chorus of conspirators
with its echoes of "La Marseillaise" was replaced by what were called
"divertissements."

In a related aesthetic realm, the new home of the Paris Opéra, the
Palais Garnier—to go back to that building whose construction the
emperor is said to have followed quite closely—was also a historicizing amalgam, a fundamentally pseudo-historical intermixture of quite
different styles (Byzantine, Venetian, Genoan, and Versaillais), which,
along with its size and extravagance, made it the perfect expression of
the aesthetic-political phantasmagorias of the day. Listen to Théophile
Gautier, speaking for the prevailing taste of his time: "A singular thing,
defying any idea of proportion, this jumble of columns, capitals, bas-
reliefs, enamels, and mosaics, this hodgepodge of Greek, Roman, Byzantine, Arab, and Gothic style, produces the most harmonious ensemble
. . . This temple . . . made of contradictory bits and pieces, enchants and
caresses the eye better than the most correct and symmetrical architecture is able to do: its unity is a consequence of its multiplicity." As it
happens, Gautier was describing Saint Mark's Cathedral in Venice. But
a comparable eclecticism was also the goal of Charles Garnier, a talented
pasticheur. Having set itself at odds with History, the Second Empire instinctively sought to fabricate false historical references wherever possible, and Garnier made sure that the facade of his opera house included
both the double columns of the Louvre's colonnade and the arches of
its courtyard, since both motifs were considered fixtures of the French
architectural repertoire.

In the 1850s and 1860s Paris, opera, state, and empire were closely
associated; and it was in a presumably involuntary homage to this
politico-cultural conjunction that the luckless conspirator Felice Orsini
chose to hurl his bomb at Napoleon III in 1858 as the monarch traveled
from the Tuileries to the Opéra. But it is important to see that opera,
which in Paris had once been mythical and revolutionary, was by the
time of the Second Empire, politically and even aesthetically, an art of
illusion, a falsely democratic phantasmagoria.

And speaking of false democracy, it is worth mentioning that of all the monuments and buildings in Paris, Garnier's Opéra was the only one other than the Invalides that Hitler found truly interesting. During his lightning tour of Paris in June 1940 in the company of the architect Albert Speer and Arno Breker, an erstwhile student of Rodin who had become a sculptor of Aryan bodies, the Führer did not fail to visit the Opéra, and the questions he asked showed that he was thoroughly familiar with its design. Legend has it that the French watchman on duty at the Opéra refused the tip that the German visitors offered him—a noteworthy detail.

WHEREAS IN PARIS state, nation, and opera were closely linked in the public mind, this was not the case, to put it mildly, in the great cities of Central Europe. Hence the remarkable fact that no grand opera was composed in either Budapest or Vienna between Beethoven's *Fidelio* (1805) and Richard Strauss's *Salome* (1905).[32] The key to this hiatus is that the two halves of the Austro-Hungarian Empire, unlike France, were multicultural political entities, without deep national roots or particular affinity for their respective capitals.

True enough, Vienna and Budapest were musical capitals—not of opera but of operetta, a musical genre that was despised in Paris for its supposedly corrosive social effect. In his satirical work of 1869, *The Brigands,* Jacques Offenbach did rather pointedly suggest that thieves should steal in a manner commensurate with their social rank. But leftist writers of the time were as a rule not amused: Zola considered Offenbach an offensive creature who ought to be "strangled like a dangerous animal behind the prompter's box . . . I cannot refrain from barking whenever M. Offenbach's sour music strikes my ears . . . Never has stupid farce displayed itself with such impudence."[33] And during the Exposition of 1867 the republican politician Camille Pelletan, speaking to the Corps Législatif, criticized "the inferior art of the operetta." And if the inception of the Third Republic in 1870 meant a loss of prestige for the Paris Opéra, which now lost much of its political function, there was no compensatory increase in the prestige of Parisian operetta. To be sure, one could cite Charles Lecocq's reactionary work of 1872, *La Fille de*

Mme Angot, but this was an exception to the general rule of disdain. There is no French equivalent to Gilbert and Sullivan.

In Vienna and Budapest, by contrast to Paris, operetta was *the* musical genre of the nineteenth century. In Paris, where everyone believed in the unity of the nation (including those on the left, such as the Communards, and those on the right, such as the Maurrasians, who wanted— each in their own way—to turn the nation into a federation), opera was understood to be a national historical epic, at once musical drama and national celebration. But no such understanding exited in Budapest or in Vienna, where even the (often anti-Semitic) ethnic Germans were reluctant to identify with the polyglot and philo-Semitic Hapsburg Empire. At the end of the century many German-speaking Austrians, including the bohemian artist Adolf Hitler, dreamed instead of a Greater German Reich whose capital would be not Vienna but Berlin. Although the action of Franz Lehár's *The Merry Widow* is set in Paris, Lehár (a descendant of Germanized and Magyarized Slavic peasants whose brother became a general in the Hungarian branch of the Imperial Army) gives us in this work a cast of characters of indeterminate nationality, no doubt natives of a "Ruritania" of some sort.

Central European operetta was a composite not only in its dramatic situations but also in its musical antecedents, which included the Italian *opera buffa* as well as the Austro-German *Singspiel.* Take, for example, *Der Zigeunerbaron* (The Gypsy Baron), which tells the story of a Hungarian landowner who is pardoned and ennobled by Empress Maria Theresa. This operetta includes a number of Viennese waltzes by Johann Strauss, a libretto written by the great Hungarian novelist Mór Jokai, a German military band, and a series of Gypsy tunes. Franz Jauner, the director of the Vienna Theater, called the work "a victory for democracy."[34]

In Vienna and Budapest, to be a student of history (that is, to accept opera) was to anticipate the tottering empire's ultimate collapse. By contrast, to identify with and appreciate operetta was to believe that what already existed could go on existing for quite some time. "So lang er lebt" (as long as he lives), people said in 1900 of old Franz Josef, who had led the "Empire of the Center" since 1848 and would continue to do so until 1916. The Austro-Hungarian operetta was therefore bi-national and socially neutral. Its plots were fantasies, tinged with mild social criticism. Its audience came not so much from the ruling class as from the middle class and the petite bourgeoisie. Hence, as the Hungarian historian Péter Hanák has noted, operetta, which in Paris was seen as an impoverished art form, was in Budapest a means of upward cultural mobility.[35]

MORE THAN ANY OTHER national capital, Paris—the "central city of the globe," as the Jacobins of the Year II called it—was the place with which its entire nation identified, and if Paris was the capital of myth in the nineteenth century, it was in part because the French government and the French people wanted it that way.

One myth can hide another, but myths can also sustain one another. Sustained by the French national myth, the myth of Paris helped the French understand their place in history and helped foreigners, both in France and abroad, understand what La Grande Nation could be. When we reflect on what Paris might yet become in a Europe at last united, the long history of France's relation to its capital city gives us much food for thought—and perhaps also for optimism, if Paris should become for Europe what it has been for France.

11

Three Literary Visions

P ARIS, capital of modernity. In the history of the capital during
the nineteenth century, this is surely the myth of origin, the Ur-
mythos, the cosmogonic myth par excellence: the narrative that, more
than any other, shaped the worldview of Parisians, be they intellectuals
(as they would not be called until the Dreyfus Affair) or ordinary bourgeois. It was this modernity that was proclaimed as much by the new
department stores as by the tower of Gustave Eiffel, a republican and a
Freemason, or by the steel frames of the Bibliothèque Nationale and the
Saint-Lazare railway station designed by Eugène Flachat (1802–1873).
And as we have seen, this very modernity also gave rise to potent antitheses, such as the myth of old Paris and the far more important myth of
alienation, of the "lonely crowd," of "the eternal misery of everything,"
to quote Flaubert.[1] Fear now cohabited with hope: in Balzac's work, the
social modernity of Paris inspired terror. In Baudelaire's, the city became the stage on which a new kind of moral squalor revealed itself. For
Zola, in the last decades of the century, the city seemed to regress, reduced as it was to something far more modest: a focal point for material
rather than moral modernity.

it was a change-unknown

By then, however, the era of Parisian myth was drawing to a close.
The age of disenchanted phantasmagoria was about to begin.

❧

FOR BALZAC, an amateur political scientist and sociologist of sorts, Paris was a city ripe for investigation. It was in this city that the heroes of modernity could best define themselves by nurturing their cults of the self and of individual energy. From this came young Rastignac's apostrophe to Paris: "A nous deux maintenant!" (Now I'm ready for you!)

We gain access to the inner life of the Balzacian hero through his social context. Each character in the Human Comedy is *sui generis,* but all Balzac's creations also draw upon a vast social taxonomy that is in turn based on a single fundamental principle: the struggle of all against all, and within that frame, the struggle of each class against every other class. Thus we have the incessant war between the young and the old, between the honest and the dishonest, between the rich and the less rich and the poor, between the provinces and Paris, between men and women, and so on. For Balzac, "marriage is all-out war, prior to which the prospective husband and wife ask the Almighty for His blessing, because there is no undertaking more brazen than the promise of a man and a woman to love each other till death do them part. Soon the battle begins, and victory, which is to say freedom, goes to the more adroit."[2]

Few and precious were the exceptions that confirmed Balzac's rule. For each untouchable provincial lady, such as the revealingly named Mme de Mortsauf (literally: Dead-safe) in *Le Lys dans la vallée* (The Lily in the Valley), how many examples do we find, especially in Paris, of unbridled passion, greed, and malevolence?

All of which seemed so depressing, in fact, that Balzac, though an intellectual opportunist and a commoner to the core, transformed himself into a Catholic noble who believed in a remedially organic conception of society. His naively reactionary cynicism still astonishes us: "Catholicism has the authority of facts in its favor. The most beautiful philosophical doctrines are powerless to discourage theft (and debates about free will may even encourage it), yet the sight of a cross, of Christ and the Virgin—sublime images of the devotion that societies require if they are to continue to exist—are enough to keep whole nations in line, constrained to suffer in misfortune and indigence."[3] Bonaparte, who played the Messiah to the Jews of Italy in 1796 and then seized subsequent opportunities to play at being a Muslim in Cairo in 1798 and a Catholic in Paris in 1802, could not have said it better.

But there was more to it than base calculation. Balzac also sincerely believed that only the Christian spirit of charity could stop the crimes of liberalism, of Parisian individualism run amok. In the past, he wrote in *Le Médecin de campagne* (The Country Doctor), "I considered the Catholic religion to be a hodgepodge of shrewdly exploited prejudices and superstitions, which an intelligent civilization ought to do its best to expunge. Here, though, I've come to recognize the [political and moral need for religion.] I've come to understand its power from the very word itself: religion means bond, and there can be no doubt that without the cult, that is, the outward form in which religion manifests itself, society cannot endure." What a pity, therefore, that "nowadays, as far as the general state of society is concerned, there is less faith among the upper classes than among the people, whom God promises to reward one day with heaven in compensation for their willingness to endure their woes without complaint." Equally pitiful was the mediocre intellectual condition of the French aristocracy, with its hostility to scientists, artists, and of course novelists, even the best of whom (himself?) it never dreamed of rewarding. "Far from adopting the redemptive policy of seeking power where God bestowed it, these petty nobles despised any strength not coming from themselves."[4]

On the whole, then, Balzac found modernity repulsive, and more so in Paris than anywhere else. Which judgment the progressive writers of the day forgave out of respect for his incomparable method. Victor Hugo, for example, the most politically correct and libidinous author of his century, especially recalled Balzac's acerbic critique of the upper classes: "This great man had the brain and the heart of a democrat. The only thing monarchical about him was his imagination. Before long, he too would have come to accept the beautiful dogmas of democracy." Friedrich Engels went even further. In 1888, five years after the death of Marx, Engels wrote that he had "learned more [from Balzac] than from all the works of all the professional historians, economists, and statisticians of the time. In politics Balzac was no doubt a legitimist. His great work is a perpetual elegy deploring the irretrievable breakdown of high society. His sympathies lie with the class that is condemned to die. Yet in spite of all that, his satire is never more biting, his irony never more bitter, than when he sets those aristocrats in action, those men and women for whom he felt such deep sympathy."[5]

Paris was central to Balzac's view of the world, and the city never ceased to fascinate him as the incarnation of both good and evil, but especially of modern evil: it was in the Balzacian order of things that Mme de Mortsauf should fear that no good could come of "that dreadful Paris" for the young and childlike Félix de Vandenesse. In Paris, Vautrin explains to young Rastignac in *Père Goriot,* one makes one's way "by the brilliance of genius or by corruption." Nor did the beauty of the city impress Balzac. Paris always struck him as ugly, filthy, and foul:

> If the air of the houses in which most bourgeois live is rank, if the atmosphere of the streets hides the cruel vapors lurking in back rooms where the air grows thin, you must also know that, beyond that pestilence, the 40,000 houses of this great city bathe their feet in filth that the government has thus far refused to make any real effort to confine within concrete walls, which alone might prevent the fetid muck from filtering its way through the soil and poisoning the wells, in a subterranean way thereby bestowing upon Lutèce its celebrated name, which in Celtic means "nauseating swamp."[6]

From the beginning of Balzac's literary career in the 1820s, Paris was a constant presence in his work. The central character in *Ferragus,* the work that marked his transition from youth to maturity, from *Le Code des honnêtes gens* (The Code of Upright Folks) to *Père Goriot,* was Paris. A note in *Ferragus* addresses the reader: "If the author has succeeded in painting Paris in some of its aspects while exploring it from top to bottom and from one end to the other—from the Faubourg Saint-Germain to the Marais, from the street to the boudoir, from the stately house to the garret, from the prostitute to the face of a woman who invested her love in marriage, from the bustle of life to the repose of death—perhaps he will have the courage to carry on with this enterprise."[7]

He did indeed muster up the requisite courage, and in *La Fille aux yeux d'or* (The Girl with the Golden Eyes; 1834) he went on to set forth the basic rules of Parisian life. Paris is a battlefield, a field of death across which scurry figures whose faces are merely "masks," where one must kill or be killed, cheat or die. "You have to plunge into this mass of people like a cannonball or else worm your way in by sly corruption." The city is a "vast pleasure factory," a "chamber of horrors." "Here everything smokes, everything glows, everything burns, everything boils, everything ignites, evaporates, dims, rekindles, sparkles, crackles, and is consumed."[8] Paris is the capital of desire, a city in which everyone is caught up in a rush toward gold and pleasure—in other words, a scene of relentless social struggle.

change in pace, what was once socially unacceptable is the norm.

Beyond this general view of the city, Balzac had a precise idea of what he took to be the capital's social composition. The entire social structure rested, he believed, on "the man who has nothing, the worker, the proletarian." Society "is an instrument (dare I say a machine) in the service of people of property, who shamelessly exploit the proletarian and who also deceive him with promises of mountains of gold, for Paris from top to bottom is consumed by the monster of speculation."

fan of AG?

The common people of Paris were not pleasant to look at, eaten away as they were by toil and vice and above all by alcoholism, whose political consequences were considerable: "Without the taverns, wouldn't the government be overthrown every Tuesday?" These Parisians constituted "an ugly and powerful nation, sublime in its mechanical intelligence, patient when it feels like being patient yet terrifying one day every century, as inflammable as gunpowder, and primed by brandy for revolutionary conflagration."[9]

Of all the common people in Paris, however, only servants really interested him. Balzac never delved very deeply into the life of the working poor, nor was he much interested in the new world of industry, which is surprising in view of his fascination with scientists, who enjoyed tremendous prestige at the time. (Perhaps the reason that Balzac's Parisian workers do not toil in factories is that the Parisian workers he knew were artisans dispersed among countless minuscule ateliers, whereas the new industries tended to concentrate in larger plants on the city's outskirts, to which he seldom went. As Parisian rents increased, the new working class of the Restoration and the July Monarchy inevitably gravitated toward the suburbs, where employers found that they could both offer lower wages to their workers and pay lower rents. Balzac, though unaware of these facts, may have instinctively sensed their consequences.)

One step above artisans and servants in Balzac's Parisian world are the petits bourgeois, gluttons for toil and creatures at once tiny and gargantuan. Their "desires run dry," lashed as they are by "the whip of self-interest . . . the scourge of ambition." For Balzac, this segment of society was the most Parisian of all, along with the journalists, who formed a distinctive milieu of their own. Above them reigns the bourgeoisie proper, the world of affairs, "the belly of Paris . . . For them there are no mysteries: they see the underside of society, for they are its confessors, and they hold it in contempt." Imprisoned within their specialties, they inevitably lack breadth of spirit: "Vanity epitomizes all their passions." This middle and upper bourgeoisie envies, imitates, and detests the aristocracy. Yet Balzac's Parisian bourgeois have one great dream: to marry into this social class which they secretly abominate.[10]

At odds with this rich and calculating new bourgeoisie are the painters and men of letters. Their lot is no more enviable than that of their enemies: "Worn out by the need to produce, unable to keep up with their costly fantasies, fatigued by a consuming genius, starved for pleasure, the artists of Paris all charge excessive prices in the hope of filling pockets emptied by sloth . . . [They] seek in vain to reconcile society with glory, money with art."[11]

And above them all, the aristocracy of the capital is scarcely any happier: vanity is even more rampant here than among the bourgeoisie. Anticipating Baudelaire's idea of Parisian life, Balzac's aristocrats live in a world they find increasingly tiresome. Existentially, the noble-born Parisian is a nonperson of sorts. He does not really exist. In *La Peau de chagrin* (The Wild Ass's Skin) and *La Fille aux yeux d'or,* Balzac drew a depressing portrait of "this empty life, this perpetual wait for a pleasure that will never arrive, this permanent boredom, this inanity of spirit, heart, and mind, this lassitude of the great Parisian ragout, [which] is reproduced in the premature wrinkles of the rich man's face, distorted by helplessness, illuminated by the glitter of gold, and devoid of intelligence."[12]

One must add in passing that Balzac's powerful taxonomy of Parisian society—at once stylized and very detailed—reminds us in both structure and content of the Parisian texts written by one of his most devoted readers, Karl Marx, in the last days of the July Monarchy and during the rise of Napoleon the Small, or Crapulinski, as Marx dubbed the lesser Bonaparte. In *The Eighteenth Brumaire of Louis Bonaparte,* Marx categorically states that there are and can be only two genuine social classes: the working class and the triumphant bourgeoisie. Rural society, though a preponderant presence, was of no conceptual interest. Only urban, indeed Parisian, realities mattered: it was in the capital that the tormented, steadily dwindling class of property owners confronted the miserable, steadily growing, ever more impoverished class of proletarians, according to the iron law governing the relation between mechanization and pauperization.

And yet, within this rather crude narrative, Marx the historian and witness to his time offered, like Balzac, a marvelously nuanced account. Marx very carefully distinguished between Legitimists and Orleanists, and, within the Orleanist camp, between banking and finance, between Thiers the centrist and Guizot the rightist, between the disreputable Louis Napoleon and the very respectable party of order. The political autonomy of the peasantry and bureaucracy did not escape his notice either. Nowadays we have little to learn from Marx the economist, but Marx the historian-philosopher of Paris in 1848 still commands our full attention, and Balzac is his fellow traveler.

For Baudelaire, Balzac was a "novelist and scholar, an inventor and observer, a naturalist familiar with the laws governing the generation of living things as well as ideas. He was a great man in the fullest sense of the word, a creator with a method and the only one whose method is worth studying."[13] How true! for if Balzac had limited himself to reproducing literary types within the framework of a materialist social analysis, his work would have been a deadly bore: take, for example, César Birotteau, the royalist perfume dealer and hero of *La Grandeur et décadence de César Birotteau* (The Grandeur and Decadence of César Birotteau), who is at once a literary type and a portrait from life. To describe Birotteau one could easily apply a series of clichés taken from standard descriptions of Parisian life: father, Christian, unlucky entrepreneur, ignorant petit bourgeois. But Balzac's Birotteau is more than that. He is, as one might expect, a victim of the wickedness of others, but he is also a victim of his own simplicity and passionate extravagance, his naïveté and his craftiness.

In his descriptions of Paris, Balzac liked to move from one stylized type to another, but each of them is individuated, often miraculously so. In his work, every stylized house and room has its own unique character. The Pension Vauquer, where Père Goriot lives on the street known today as the rue Tournefort, is both typical and unmistakable, characterized as it is by its wallpaper and by the bathrobe that Mme Vauquer wears.

We move in Balzac's world from house to house, all of them alike, but all of them also different, from the Faubourg Saint-Marcel, where social failures gather, to the Faubourg Saint-Germain, reserved for a sterile and benighted nobility. And neither is at all like the rue Lafitte, with its not very scrupulous bankers. It was there, incidentally, that Balzac situated the world of money, which he described as bounded "by the Faubourg Montmartre and the rue de la Chaussée d'Antin, between the heights of the rue de Navarin and the line of the boulevards."[14] He might have been describing the location of a fortress on a topographical map.

Class conflict was everywhere in Balzacian Paris; but for all that, the city was hardly the site of any class solidarity as one traveled from class to class. Tensions separated all classes from one another, but hatred also thrived within each social group, each stratum, and each profession, where every individual was also at odds with every family: "He dishonored us all," says old Marshal Hulot of his dissolute and corrupt brother in *La Cousine Bette,* "he robbed the state. He made my name odious to me. He made me want to die. He killed me." Père Grandet, who becomes Monsieur Grandet thanks to the Revolution and speculation in real estate, is a tyrant to his wife and daughter. His bankrupt Parisian brother commits suicide. Père Goriot, who speculated on grain during the Revolution, is tyrannized and martyred by his social-climbing daughters, for whose corrupt morals he himself is responsible. When young Rastignac takes his first steps into the world of high society, he has two guides. One, Vautrin, is a former convict, a criminal, and a ho-

Seems to be a constant struggle

mosexual, an outcast even among outcasts. The other, Mme Bauséant, is among the noblest luminaries of the Faubourg Saint-Germain, but she, too, has been humiliated and betrayed. *Homo parisianus homini lupus est* (The Parisian man is a wolf to his kin).

Hence it will come as no surprise to discover that, for Balzac, the anthropological model that most fully captured the reality of the Parisian social hell—the war of all against all—was that of the North American Indians, which he learned about from the novels of James Fenimore Cooper (who, by the way, lived in Paris for many years). Indeed, for some disapproving readers, Balzac's characters were "Mohicans in monkey suits" or "Iroquois in topcoats." As Walter Benjamin, who was close to the Surrealists, explains, it was from Cooper's work that Balzac (as well as the Surrealists) learned how important it was to portray "a tree trunk or a beaver dam or a rock or a buffalo hide or a motionless canoe or a leaf floating on the surface of the water . . . The poetry of terror, which the stratagems of the warring tribes spread throughout the forests of America and from which Cooper profited so greatly, [fastened upon] the most minute details of Parisian existence. Pedestrians, shops, carriages, a person standing in a crosswalk . . ." All were clues that anyone who wished to understand Paris would have to learn to interpret.[15]

In a related vein, Balzac's Paris is dotted with funereal spaces, from the Père-Lachaise cemetery (a miniature city of the dead) to the cemetery of Montparnasse (inaugurated in 1824) and including the Palais Royal, a magnet for suicides.[16] In Balzac one finds people who have triumphed in Paris but, more often, people who have succumbed: Rastignac among the former, Colonel Chabert among the latter—a fallen, Baudelairean personage, a tragic flâneur, a man who has lost everything, including his social identity. Of this war hero who returns home to a society that no longer wants anything to do with him, Balzac says in *Colonel Chabert:* "Perhaps, like a stone hurled into a pit, he went cascading down lower and lower until he ended up among that ragtag sediment with which Paris abounds." To the wife who has repudiated him Chabert writes: "Live in peace. I renounce forever the name to whose renown I may have contributed my share."

And yet Balzac's Paris was not just a hell; it was also a city of invigo-

[handwritten margin note: seems changes in Paris brought conflicting feelings]

rating contrasts, a city of intellect and powerful emotions: "Although true feelings are rare here, one does find, as one might find anywhere, examples of noble friendship and boundless devotion." The usurers Gobseck and du Tillet are not more Parisian than Horace Bianchon, the self-sacrificing doctor in the Human Comedy, or Mme de Bauséant, Rastignac's cousin, who eventually becomes a nun. Paris, as Balzac explains,

> is the head of the globe, a brain bursting with genius and guide to human civilization, a great man, an inexhaustibly creative artist, a clairvoyant politician who inevitably has a furrowed brow, the vices of a great man, the fantasies of an artist, and the jadedness of the political operator. His physiognomy belies the germination of good and evil . . . This city cannot be more moral or more tonic or cleaner than the boiler of one of those magnificent pyroscaphes that you admire as they knife through the waves. Isn't Paris a sublime vessel laden with intelligence?[17]

[handwritten margin note: Sums it up pretty much]

Bernard Guyon is quite right to conclude that Balzac "adores Paris as much as he abhors it." For the author of *La Fille aux yeux d'or,* Paris was "the most delicious of monsters." It was also an old acquaintance: many commentators have remarked that Balzac's Parisian characters are constantly moving about their city, and it is through the writer's descriptions of their lonely promenades that we know Balzacian Paris in such minute detail, far better than we know, say, the Paris of Flaubert. As already mentioned, we can, for instance, precisely trace the route that Rastignac took from the Montagne Sainte-Geneviève to visit his distant, noble, but saintly and amiable cousin in the Faubourg Saint-Germain. These detailed accounts of Paris strolls were but a literary transposition of reality, for Balzac himself liked to walk in the capital. He counted himself among the few who "savor their Paris," for whom "Paris is a creature," and a dearly beloved creature at that. In the "women's novels" of Mme de Staël, Mme de Souza, and Mme de Genlis, Paris, when not entirely absent, was at best a vague presence. By contrast, Balzac's Paris—and the Paris of realist fiction in general—was precise and concrete.[18]

O^{F ALL THE GREAT} French poets, as Pierre Citron notes, Baudelaire is "the one whose life was most permanently riveted to Paris." How revealing that this poet should have thought of walking in Paris as a way of understanding himself, as had also been true for Louis-Sébastien Mercier in 1780, for Nicolas-Edme Restif de la Bretonne and his *Nuits de Paris* (Paris Nights) of 1788–1793, and for the Surrealists in the 1930s, and as is true for the modern flâneur and commentator Jacques Réda today. "On the Ile Saint-Louis," Louis Thomas, the author of *Curiosités sur Baudelaire,* wrote in 1912, "Baudelaire thought of himself as being at home everywhere. Whether on the streets or on the quays, he was as comfortable as if he had been in his own room. Wherever he walked on the island, it was as if he was still on his own property, so that one might run into him in slippers, hatless, wearing the smock that was his working clothes." Baudelaire lived at no fewer than forty-three different Paris addresses, mostly on the Left Bank when he was young (he was born there) but later, after 1845, on the Right Bank (where he died). His forty-fourth residence (in this world, at any rate), as Claude Pichois wryly notes, was the cemetery of Montparnasse, where he has resided since September 2, 1867.[19]

As a young man Baudelaire already adored Paris. His brief stay in Lyons was a painful exile, and Paris, for better or (mostly) for worse, was his irreplaceable home, even though he cursed it constantly: "Paris horrifies me," he wrote in 1858, "as does the bitter life I've led here for the past sixteen years." Often it was too hot: "Paris is frying," he complained to Théophile Gautier in 1859. "Every day Phoebus Apollo pours a couple of pots of molten lead on anyone unfortunate enough to be out and about on the boulevards." In 1865, however, it was too cold: "In this season? . . . A deluge of water, filth, and snow! With its marvelous gardens, Paris is beautiful only when the sun is out." "This monstrous pile of men and stones" exasperated him. Paris was "an accursed city," "an infamous city," a "city of filth," a "disgusting city," a "horrible city . . . infatuated with pleasure to an atrocious degree," a city "where the sun sheds its light on the depraved animal's furtive pleasures."[20]

Despite these feelings, or more likely because of them, Paris is omni-

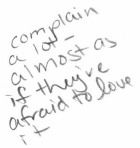

complain a lot – almost as if they've afraid to love it

present in Baudelaire's work, whether it be the *Paysages parisiens* (Parisian Landscapes) of 1857, the *Fantômes parisiens* (Parisian Phantoms) of 1860 (later collected in *Tableaux parisiens*), or the *Petits poèmes en prose* of 1861 and 1862, which also take Paris as their subject or, at least, as their backdrop. A noted French cleric declared during the Second World War, "Pétain c'est la France, et la France c'est Pétain"—and one might parodically suggest that though Paris is not Baudelaire, Baudelaire is, in some real sense, Paris. But the Paris that is ubiquitous in his poems is not a concrete, physical city. Baudelaire's Paris has none of the palpable relief, the accumulation of minute details, of the Paris of his contemporaries Balzac and Jules Michelet. As Citron points out, the mountain from which the poet symbolically contemplates the city in *Le Spleen de Paris,* whether it be the Buttes-Chaumont or Montmartre, was not actually in Paris in Baudelaire's day but outside the city limits. Walter Benjamin explains all this: "There is not the slightest hint of a description of Paris in *Les Fleurs du mal.* This alone would suffice to distinguish these poems from the 'big-city lyricism' that was to follow. Baudelaire raised his voice amid the din of Paris as one might speak above the ocean's roar. His words . . . remain entangled with that din, which helps them to carry farther and imbues them with an obscure meaning."[21]

"Obscure" is the right word: the politics of the day are central to *L'Education sentimentale,* but in Baudelaire's Paris, in Citron's words, "Napoleon III exists . . . only insofar as Constantin Guys drew a picture of him in his capital."[22] The birds that are so common in Gérard de Nerval's Paris do not exist in Baudelaire's, which contains only silent, sinister cats. Nor are there any statues of famous personages. Only one *place* is mentioned, the Place du Carrousel, and then only to evoke the memory of wretched outcasts in all times and all places: "Andromaque, je pense à vous" (Andromache, I think of you).

Baudelaire's Paris is entirely abstract, or, rather, entirely imagined. Paris exists for Baudelaire exclusively as a state of mind, as the psychological theater of human misery par excellence.[23] Through what the poet calls "correspondences," Paris thus becomes an allegory for all humanity, past and present, but above all an allegory in which (because Baudelaire was in his own way a Jansenist poet) humanity's wretched condition has

Charles Meryon, *The Pont-Neuf in 1853.* Meryon was, with Manet and (inexplicably) Constantin Guys, one of Baudelaire's favorite artists. This is the Pont-Neuf as Piranese might have seen it: mysterious, threatening, prisonlike; in a word, medieval. It is also the Paris that Haussmann hired a photographer to record for posterity even as Haussmann himself was doing his best to destroy it. Musée Carnavalet. © Photothèque des musées de la ville de Paris / 90 CAR 0200: Habouzit.

been made even more wretched by Haussmannian modernity. It was in Paris more than anywhere else that

> Et nous alimentons nos aimables remords,
> Comme les mendiants nourrissent leur vermine.
> (And like a pet we feed our tame remorse
> As beggars take to nourishing their lice.)[24]

It was in Paris that evil and self-destruction, alluring specters that have always haunted humankind, were more visible and more irresistible than anywhere else:

> Imbécile! . . .
> Si nos efforts te délivraient
> Tes baisers ressuciteraient
> Le cadavre de ton vampire.
> (You fool! . . .
> If our efforts delivered you forth
> Your kisses would waken again
> Your vampire lover's corpse!)[25]

Pierre Emmanuel was not wrong to argue that Baudelaire was a lapsed Christian poet for whom man was alienated from himself because alienated from God: "Sin," wrote this critic, "struggle, mortifying lucidity, redemptive pain, flagellation of the spirit . . . these are obviously Christian themes, exercises in the Christian tradition. From them, by way of neo-Platonism, comes the 'Christian' accent in Baudelaire." "Here below, it is the devil who pulls the strings that move us," and "from the irreducible distance between the outside and the inside, and from their connection and their struggle," as Sabine Melchior-Bonnet puts it, "Baudelaire creates the condition of self-consciousness itself: "To live and sleep before a mirror." Baudelairean man feels both hunger for good and desire for evil, and for Paris he feels both love and hate.[26]

What, for Baudelaire, was newly distinctive about Paris? Perhaps the fact that in 1860 it was in this city that the ancient, even eternal, noxiousness of humankind was most clearly displayed, intensified by the new Haussmannian modernity and by the modernity of the democratized masses that Baudelaire detested. Also at stake in the Paris of his

modernity
what detested
gov influence
Napoleon

day was the cult (which he also despised) of progress and universal suf-
frage and *chosisme,* "thingism," to borrow a word that Baudelaire used in
commenting on the Universal Expositions, for which he felt supreme
contempt. *Chosisme,* to be equated with "Americanism," was a novel
phenomenon that destroyed man's last remaining faculties. "Pitiful man
[that is, the average Frenchman] is so Americanized by zoocratic and industrial philosophers," Baudelaire observed in 1855, "that he has lost
any notion of the differences that characterize the phenomena of the
physical and rural world." In 1859 he wrote to Victor Hugo that "a day
in our sad, in our boring Paris, in our Paris–New York, would be
enough to effect a radical cure in you."[27]

So Paris was an unprecedented hell, but a hell that he could not do *addiction*
without: "Parisian life is, in spite of everything, fertile in marvelous poetic subjects . . . It surrounds us like the air we breathe but do not see."[28]
In Baudelaire's words, "the painter, the true painter, would be someone
able to make us see and understand how great and poetic we are in our
cravats and polished boots." The "true painter," then, is the Parisian
flâneur, the self-marginalized individual who rejects modernity yet understands it so well that he is able to perceive the distance that separates
him from the daily experience of the masses, whom he simultaneously
loves and despises. Though misanthropic, the flâneur is nevertheless
gregarious. The Baudelairean crowd stifles the man of sensibility, but it
also protects his delicate feelings, since it is composed of people just as
marginalized as he is: "The pleasure of being in a crowd is a mysterious
expression of the joy of multiplication."[29] This is also the theme of one
of the most famous poems in *Les Fleurs du mal,* the sonnet "A une
passante," to a woman glimpsed briefly in the crowd:

> Ne te verrais-je plus que dans l'éternité?
> Ailleurs, bien loin d'ici! trop tard! jamais peut-être!
> Car j'ignore où tu fuis, tu ne sais où je vais,
> O toi que j'eusse aimée, ô toi qui le savais!
> (Will we not meet again this side of death?
> Far from this place! too late! never, perhaps!
> Neither one knowing when the other goes
> O you I might have loved, as well you know!)[30]

For Walter Benjamin, Victor Hugo's work was a milestone because he "was the first to give collective titles to his works: *Les Misérables, Les Travailleurs de la mer.*" Baudelaire apprehended this insight, and in spite of himself, as it were, admired Hugo's democratic and instinctive feeling for the new, detestable, but also inevitable crowd. One of the three poems in *Tableaux parisiens* that Baudelaire dedicates to Hugo ("Les Septs Vieillards") begins with "an invocation to the populous city, the 'teeming city, city full of dreams.'" "For the perfect flâneur," Baudelaire wrote in *Le Peintre de la vie moderne* (The Painter of Modern Life), for the passionate observer, "it is an immense pleasure to settle among the numerous, the fluctuating, the seething, fleeting, and boundless."[31]

Thanks to the (Parisian) crowd, the Baudelairean flâneur (read: the disembodied Parisian intellect) was at home everywhere (and nowhere). As Citron puts it: "Like a wandering soul seeking a body, [the flâneur] can take on any persona. For him alone, all is vacant . . . What men call love is petty, limited, and feeble compared with the holy prostitution of the soul that gives all of itself, poetry and charity, to the unexpected visitor or unknown passerby."[32]

The Baudelairean *promeneur* was thus diametrically opposed to Rousseau's solitary dreamer.[33] Jean-Jacques was a wounded, misunderstood person but entirely present and even vindictively self-righteous. By contrast, the Baudelairean personage exists only in remorse and universal contempt, for himself and for others. It is revealing in this respect that the two kinds of Parisian space that truly interested Baudelaire were the ephemeral lodging in which the flâneur sought refuge (even poets have to live somewhere) and the anonymous street where other marginalized individuals, the poet's simultaneously loved and reviled *semblables et frères,* also wandered: ragpickers, aged beggars, ragamuffins, lonely old ladies, ugly prostitutes, and, as Citron lists them, "the blind and the sick, isolated by their suffering; the dying, already weaned from life; thieves, crooks, and street performers."[34]

The flâneur was protected not only by his isolation but also by his cult of the artificial. For Baudelaire, to be sure, this artificiality was only a palliative that would eventually prove useless, and yet it was preferable to the corporeal and, above all, to the feminine, woman being an entirely corporeal creature. "A woman does not know how to distinguish between soul and body. She is simplistic, like the animals. A satirist would say that this is because she has only a body."[35]

Indeed, nature in all its forms was horrifying, whether the second sex, the gardens of Paris, the Belgians, or the sea at Honfleur. To the poet, only facticity was acceptable, and of all forms of artifice, Parisian life no doubt struck him as the most stylized, the most studied, and therefore the most desirable. An elegant Parisian woman was an object of fascination to Baudelaire precisely because of her unrivaled artificiality. She was bound to be inaccessible and hard. In *Fusées* (Rockets) Baudelaire offers a short list of "airs" that "rescue a woman [read: a Parisienne] from her natural vulgarity and transform her into an enchanting creature":[36]

The blasé air
The air of boredom
The featherbrained air
The impudent air
The cold air
The air of inwardness
The air of domination
The air of willfulness
The naughty air
The air of illness
The feline air combined with the airs of childishness, nonchalance,
    and malice.[37]

In the same vein, note that Baudelaire was intensely interested in fashion, of which Paris was already the world center. This was because fashion, particularly for women, was quintessentially artifice, disguise, and stylization. But Baudelaire was interested in other kinds of Paris fashion as well, particularly in dandies, those "Narcissuses of imbecility." There is a prototype of the dandy in "La Fanfarlo": a "great idler," a "sad man of ambition, a disappointed somebody," who, in the words of Melchior-Bonnet, "cannot even miss a crumb of himself as a spectacle; when a tear comes to his eye, he runs to the mirror to watch himself cry." The dandy's "immoderate concern with grooming and physical elegance," according to Claude Mouchard, ". . . is merely a symbol of the superiority of his mind . . . The only thing that matters is to be a great man and a saint in his own eyes." "A woman is the opposite of a dandy," Baudelaire said in *Mon cœur mis à nu* (My Heart Laid Bare), by which he meant an unfashionable, non-Parisian, "natural" woman.[38]

And from the flâneur's obsession with marginality, impotence, and the cult of the artificial it was but a short step to an obsession with death. Here one can contrast Baudelaire, who had a marvelous understanding of the Paris of his time, with his fellow poet Théophile Gautier, who was no more than an observer. The relation of both to Manet, with his representation of the city's commercialized spirit, will serve to situate them.

As a young Romantic, Gautier had worn a scandalous red vest to the premiere of Hugo's play *Hernani* in 1830. By 1863 he had calmed down considerably and, what is more, had become a "Haussmannist." Whereas Baudelaire detested his epoch, Gautier had now made his peace with much of it. Predictably, he found Manet's *Olympia* detestable: "Here, I'm sorry to say, there is nothing but a determination to attract attention whatever the cost." Gautier thus joined the boulevardier Paul de Saint-Victor, who had this to say in 1863: "People crowd around Monsieur Manet's rank *Olympia* as around a corpse in a morgue. When art descends to such depths, it is beneath criticism." (According to Georges Bataille, Manet's *Olympia* was "the first masterpiece . . . to be loudly jeered by the mob.")[39]

Gautier, then, despised this most revealing of portraits in an age of alienation; and it is very striking that Baudelaire, who truly understood the Paris of his time, also understood Manet, if on his own terms: "Vous êtes le premier," he wrote to Manet, "dans la décréptitude de votre art" (You hold the first rank, but in a decrepit field.) Baudelaire and Manet: as Paul Valéry observed, the two men were linked by an affinity of anxieties, and both of them, in consequence, were preoccupied by the same Parisian themes: death and prostitution.[40]

Of course these two themes have a lengthy history in the art and literature of Paris, from Villon in the late Middle Ages to Hubert Robert and his paintings of a future and utterly ruined wing of the Louvre (in which, as it happens, he lived from 1779 to 1806). Constantin de

Volney and Mercier likewise allude in their descriptions of Paris to van-ished capitals of yesteryear such as Babylon, Thebes, and Carthage.[41] In Haussmannian Paris, however, the theme of death—closely related to that of alienation—was one of more topical urgency, which comes up re-peatedly in Baudelaire's work ("L'Embarquement pour Cythère," "Le Voyage") as well as in Manet's, in such images as a dead toreador, a sui-cide laid out on a bed, or a powerful Union battleship, the USS *Kearsage,* lying in wait for the Confederate corsair *Alabama,* doomed to destruc-tion as soon as it ventures out of the port of Cherbourg, as sooner or later it must. (Trainloads of Parisians hastened to the coast to watch the ship's sinking.)

Baudelaire's verdicts on the morbidity of Parisian modernity have been variously interpreted. One appealing—and thoroughly Parisian—interpretation has it that Baudelaire was in fact the great forebear of the modernist worldview that would dominate the culture of Europe from 1890 to 1930 or beyond, a worldview that went far beyond the bour-geois modernity of Haussmann's Paris. In 1930, for example, for T. S. Eliot, the Anglo-American poet (and a great admirer of the anti-Semitic Charles Maurras, the leader of the Action Française), Baudelaire even more than Rimbaud was the "greatest archetype for all poets of modern times in all countries."[42] For Eliot Baudelaire was a brilliant forerunner of modernism, that is, of the rediscovery of the unconscious and of un-certainty as to the profound nature of the self, along with, as a side ef-fect, the discovery of travel and of the value of non-Western cultures.

Marxist-inspired interpreters have taken a different view. Bertolt Brecht, for example, contrasted Baudelaire with the imprisoned insur-rectionary Louis-Auguste Blanqui: "The defeat of Blanqui was the tri-umph of Baudelaire—of the petite bourgeoisie. Blanqui succumbed, while Baudelaire met with [posthumous] success." For Brecht, Blanqui was a tragic figure and Baudelaire almost a comic one, "like the cock whose triumphant song heralds the hour of betrayal."[43] The dialectical reasoning of the Marxist Brecht is easy to understand: Baudelaire, the most Parisian of poets, understood modernity (in his own way, to be sure), but only to reject it, whereas Blanqui, even in prison, persisted in his dream of revolution.

Walter Benjamin's thinking, also Marxist-inspired, went one step further and was a good deal more complex. Baudelaire, he wrote, was an isolated figure who wanted to explain the phenomenon of commodification as "allegorical experience." This attempt, thought Benjamin, was a hopeless task, but it did expose the brutality of the reality that Baudelaire was yearning to explain. The poet's view of bourgeois life, and especially of women within that context, seems sadistic today, and this, thought Benjamin, was because Baudelaire misdescribed reality, but only, as it were, "by a hair."

One can elucidate this interesting analysis by interpreting "the commodification of experience" in simpler terms: what Benjamin means is that in Baudelaire's Paris, men and (especially) women had become negotiable objects. Being neither corporatized subjects of the king nor empowered citizens of a republic, Parisians were now reduced to being mere producers and/or consumers. (Which takes us back to Manet's Olympia, who rents her body to sex-consumers.)

What Benjamin meant by "allegorical experience" is more difficult to grasp. To do so, we must pause for a moment to consider Benjamin's analysis of the seventeenth-century German Trauerspiel, a theatrical genre that developed in a country devastated by squabbling princes and the Thirty Years' War. Benjamin had examined the development of this genre closely in his rejected doctoral thesis. In the Trauerspiel of this tormented epoch, he explained, the traditional defense of Christian values like charity and love had lost all credibility. It followed that the allegories on which these plays depended also seemed false. They were therefore incapable of conveying a credible message and could do no more than establish a "style." This type of theater consequently had a paradoxical effect on its spectators, contrary to the wishes of playwrights supported by princely patronage. Because the times had made these traditional Christian allegories seem contrived and unbelievable, their hidden but profound effect was to undermine the traditional values upheld by the religious authorities and princes who claimed to be the "fathers" of their people and were consecrated as such by the established churches.

In other words, the failure of baroque allegory served to point up the fact that reality had become the opposite of what allegory claimed it to be. And Benjamin's argument is that the same was true of Baudelaire, where this poet was yet another allegorical writer who refused to understand the deeper meaning of the industrial and proletarian reality of his age. Or, to put the same theme in another way, Baudelaire yearned to wipe out the present by establishing "correspondences" between present and past sensation, a perennial wish since it would enable him to overcome his "spleen" and horror of modern life, but this attempted elision was bound to fail.

Hence, for Benjamin, and somewhat paradoxically, the "irreplaceability" of Baudelaire's *Les Fleurs du mal* lies precisely in the poet's *inability* to deny the destructive nature of modern, commodified life by invoking allegorical links to a premodern, pre-Parisian past; and it is indeed remarkable that Baudelaire, though every inch a Parisian, did not know or care to know the material, financial, and industrial causes of a new sensibility whose effects he understood better than anyone else in Paris.

From Benjamin's perspective, then, it was natural that Baudelaire the failed allegorist should have made of the Parisian prostitute the quintessential symbol of the material reality he detested. But by doing so he had failed to understand, according to Benjamin, that in the new capitalist society of commodity fetishism and spectacles, this moralistic, neo-Christian, allegorical representation of sin no longer carried conviction. More plainly yet: it was absurd in the Paris of the 1860s to think of the prostitute as nothing more than a fallen, immoral woman who could serve as a credible symbol of what Haussmannian Paris had become. Indeed, Benjamin, pondering the lot of such women in the Paris of the Second Empire, added that prostitution "can claim to be considered as a form of 'labor.'" The prostitute of 1860 was a proletarian, the most wretched proletarian of all.

For Benjamin the whores of Paris were ahead of their time in their refusal to disguise themselves as women in love. They were "sex workers" who demanded payment for the time their customers spent with them: they asked for "wages." Olympia is under no illusions as to what she

[handwritten margin note: would like to learn more about]

[handwritten margin mark]

is, and she does not seek to deceive anyone else. A passage from the Goncourt brothers' journal offers a humorous illustration of this Marxist argument regarding commercial sex: the story is about Adèle Courtois, an actress and much-sought-after courtesan: "One evening, a gentleman proposed to escort her home. She said, 'Yes.' Then another, to whom she said, 'Maybe.' And yet another, to whom she was forced to say, 'Impossible.' And finally a fourth, who so exhausted her patience that she finally could not help blurting out, 'What a disgusting business, you can't even hire girls to do the work!'"[44]

By refusing to see (or failing to understand) what the prostitute had become in Haussmannian Paris and reserving his venom for women who had become marketable commodities, Baudelaire chose a "target" for his work (to borrow Benjamin's term) that may seem, to those who understand what Baudelaire failed to grasp, sadistic or even pathological. Baudelaire would have liked to make of Haussmannian modernity a new version of an eternal misery. For the more or less Marxist Benjamin, by contrast, it was important to recognize that Haussmannian modernity was something unprecedented in human history.

Benjamin's criticism of Baudelaire is very apt, and harsh as it may be, it applies just as well to the details of the work as to the oeuvre as a whole: it is both strange and revealing, for example, that Baudelaire, who took such a keen interest in dandies and flâneurs (that is, in de-individualized individuals who refused to take their place in a society they despised), did not really ponder the meaning of "the locus classicus of *la flânerie,* the arcade," despite its importance in the economic and cultural history of his time.[45]

We can go one step further: it is because Baudelaire positively did not wish to understand the economics of his time that he proved unable to understand its politics. Consider his notes on his "intoxication" during the Revolution of 1848 in *Mon coeur mis à nu:* "1848 was charming only because it was so utterly ridiculous . . . The horrors of June. Insanity of the people and insanity of the bourgeoisie. Natural love of crime."[46] What Baudelaire ought to have seen (according to Benjamin) as a tragic class struggle became instead yet another absurd manifestation of man's ahistorical bestiality.

Paris: mythical capital of social modernity for Balzac and of moral modernity—human or inhuman—for Baudelaire. And, strangely enough, of a more circumscribed, materialistic modernity for Emile Zola, their successor in time, who saw himself as a simple "soldier of truth."[47]

Zola was young when he went to Paris, where his first few years were very hard indeed. Like young Rastignac, the writer from Aix found his way first to the Faubourg Saint-Marcel, the neighborhood that Balzac associated with social failure. In this depressed period of his life, Zola lived at 4, rue Rollin: "I deliberately chose a new garret, the one where [Jacques-Henri] Bernardin de Saint-Pierre wrote most of his works. A real gem." In fact, it was a cheap furnished room without a fireplace, where Zola's equally penniless friend Paul Cézanne came to visit.[48]

Zola, Pierre Citron notes, outdid all other writers in his determination to "paint the panorama of Paris."[49] Ten of his novels are set in the capital. In 1884, looking back on his youth, he wrote that he had "dreamed of writing a novel in which Paris, with its ocean of roofs, would be a character, something like a Greek chorus." En route to a brief exile in London after the publication of "J'accuse" in 1898, he thought it particularly unjust that "after a lifetime of labor [I should] be obliged to leave my magnificent Paris in this way, the Paris that I have so enthusiastically adored and celebrated." Indeed, Zola did truly cherish the capital ("I am in love with the great city's horizons"), as did Pierre, the central character of the novel he entitled *Paris:* Pierre "believed in France's mission of initiation. He believed in Paris, the brains of today's world and tomorrow's, the fount of all knowledge and justice. Years ago the idea of liberty and equality was launched here upon the great winds of revolution, and ultimately the city's genius and valor will complete the task of man's emancipation."[50]

The dream of ultimate emancipation took a variety of fictional forms: for example, the admiring Pierre, the former priest who has embraced the cause of revolution, eventually contemplates blowing up Montmartre's Sacré Coeur. (Zola did not much like the new church, which had been built in expiation of the supposed and innumerable sins of post-revolutionary France: "It is hard to imagine a stupider piece of

Writing a way to communicate politics

nonsense. Paris, our magnificent Paris, crowned—dominated—by this temple to the glory of the absurd. After centuries of learning, isn't such an affront to plain common sense simply unacceptable—such an insolent need to trumpet victory upon the heights in broad daylight?")[51]

Zola's Paris novels are not notable, however, for the subtlety of their psychological or moral analysis of the capital's inhabitants and monuments. Nor, for that matter, for the subtlety of their social analysis: Balzac and Marx offer far more nuanced social portraits. For all their bluntness and metaphysical abstraction, those two geniuses were more delicate in their perceptions than Zola. Jules Lemaître was not far from the mark when he said of Zola's Nana in 1884 that she was "woman reduced to her simplest and crudest expression." Like so many other writers, Zola relied on the well-known standard "physiologies," mythologized, or at any rate stereotyped, representations of nineteenth-century Parisian society. In his hands, however, these images often became caricatures. Take, for instance, Muffat, the wealthy old man who tries to please Nana by obeying her order to remove his court uniform: "When his clothes were on the floor . . . she screamed at him to jump, and he jumped. She screamed at him to spit, and he spat. She screamed at him to trample on the gold, the eagles, the decorations, and he did." This scene calls to mind not Paris but Berlin in the Age of Expressionism after the First World War: Marlene Dietrich in *The Blue Angel*.[52]

didn't he give away information regarding war

It was not, however, so much the details as the whole of Parisian life that fascinated Zola. In his work Paris is sometimes a gigantic thing, an ocean of roofs, just as it is for Balzac and Hugo: "Everything about the city, including its constant roar, reminded him of a rising tide pounding a rocky cliff." And sometimes it is an inanimate contraption, a machine: "To Denise at that moment it felt like a high-pressure steam engine, whose vibration made even the shop windows rumble. No longer were they the cold windows of that morning. Now, trembling from within, they seemed warm and vibrant." Zola's Paris is a locomotive: the stock exchange "is the vibration, the roar [of a] machine with a full head of steam." A firm called the Universal Investment Company reminds him of "an engine crammed full of coal and launched down the tracks on a diabolical course until, in one final crash, it was smashed to smithereens and blown sky high." The employees of Le Bonheur des Dames, the department store in the novel of that title, are "swept along by the momentum of the machine, abdicating all individuality and simply pooling their strength in the common cause."[53]

Zola's deepest understanding of Paris as a minor capital of capitalism was revealed in *Le Ventre de Paris* (The Belly of Paris) and *Au Bonheur des Dames*. In the latter novel one finds the classic description of the great Paris department store, a veritable "selling machine" featuring everything under the sun and then some—for in Paris lying, hypocrisy, and especially artificiality could be highly profitable. As Zola put it in *La Curée* (The Entrails of the Beast), the Bois de Boulogne was like a "freshly painted prop" with "an adorable air of fakery about it." (Interestingly, Proust would later make this theme his own: for the author of *Swann's Way*, it was the "complexity" of the Bois de Boulogne that made it "an artificial place" and, "in the zoological or mythological sense, a Garden.")[54]

Zola's fictional department store (a representation of the Bon Marché or La Samaritaine) stands for a Darwinian Paris, where individuals and businesses thrive at each other's expense: "It was as if this colossus, having expanded several times, had become ashamed of the dingy neighborhood from which it sprang, and in disgust had first strangled it and then finally turned its back on it, leaving behind the filth of those narrow streets and setting its newly prosperous face toward the bright raucousness of the new Paris." Symbolically, Octave Mouret, the manager of Le Bonheur des Dames, marries Denise, the niece of one of the small shop owners condemned to death—literally as well as figuratively—by the shape of modern commerce. Those who struggle live; those who are inert die; and not surprisingly, Denise, despite her family ties and rather to her own dismay, feels quite at home in the teeming new city: "She sensed that it was good, that this wretched dungheap was necessary to the health of tomorrow's Paris . . . True, blood would flow, every revolution makes martyrs, there is no way forward but to tread upon the corpses of the dead. Her fear of being a wicked soul, of having conspired in the murder of the people she loved, now dissolved in distress at the sight of these irremediable woes, the pangs that attend the birth of each new generation."[55]

Zola's portrait of Paris lacks both the psychological acuity of Baudelaire and the sociological originality of Balzac. And yet, more than any other writer, Zola succeeds in giving us an idea of the city's physical power and influence, of the impact that late nineteenth-century Paris had on everyone who came anywhere near it, and of its transformation as it moved from the mythical to the phantasmagorical: "Paris lay stretched out below," concludes *Au Bonheur des Dames,* "but it was a diminished Paris, consumed by this monster. The houses, as humble as country cottages, disappeared in a welter of indistinguishable chimneys. Even the monuments seemed to melt away: on the left were two dashes for Notre Dame, on the right a circumflex for the Invalides, and off in the distance the Pantheon, ashamed and abandoned and not even as big as a bean. The horizon crumbled into dust, nothing more than a neglected frame, all the way to the heights of Châtillon and the vast countryside beyond, a blue blur in the distance signifying slavery."[56] Zola's uncanny intuition leads him to picture a Paris in which even the monuments, the monumental grammar in terms of which the city could read its history, had been reduced to insignificance.

THREE VERY DIFFERENT visions of Paris, then, ranging from the lugubrious (Baudelaire) to the relatively optimistic (Zola), yet all three historicized and therefore mythical: in the work of these Parisian writers (Parisian by birth or adoption, that is), the city has its place in an imagined journey through the vastness of nineteenth-century time.

Among the countless definitions of myth, the one best suited to the history of Paris—or so it has been suggested here—is surely the one that sees myth as a form of becoming, a tale of inception that explains the present in terms of the past and the future: the Communard of 1871 is willing to die because he understands 1789 and his own life as stages en route to a better world. But—as has also been remarked—other definitions of myth need to be considered too, such as the structuralist version of Claude Lévi-Strauss, for whom a myth serves to explain what could not be explained in any other way. In this symbolic context, a myth is an ideal structure, a notion that takes us back to Benjamin's idea of Paris as the capital of the nineteenth century as well as to the very different images of Paris conceived by Balzac, Baudelaire, and Zola.

It would be difficult to find three more divergent interpretations of Paris than the ones put forward by these three writers, the youngest of whom was born in 1840 and the oldest of whom died in 1850. Yet all three portraits of the city strike us as true. "Paris, capital of the nineteenth century": Benjamin's marvelous formula is profoundly true because it was in that "enormous city" (to borrow a phrase from Baudelaire's *Le Spleen de Paris*), far more than in London or New York, that the nineteenth century managed to express its essential meaning as well as all its many contradictions.

12

Capital of Pleasure

PARIS: mythical capital of the Republic of Letters since 1750 and, later, of Haussmannian modernity. And also of other passions: Heinrich Heine, for example, wrote in 1831 that French politics had become a new religion (Alexis de Tocqueville, as mentioned earlier, more or less came to share this view), with Paris as its new Jerusalem and a model for modern political action (an opinion that the author of *Democracy in America* most definitely did not share).

Forty years later, in October 1871—a few months after the demise of the Commune he abhorred—Théophile Gautier also pondered Paris's place in the world. But his thinking now ran counter to that of Heine, the self-exiled German Jew. To be sure, Gautier also believed that Paris was unique, but for its intelligence and chic rather than its metaphysics or libertarianism. "If Paris were to be extinguished," he wrote, "night would descend upon the world, as if the sun had vanished never to return. The thousands of stars in the firmament could never replace this unique source of light, without which the day does not exist. Darkness would reign in the best of minds." How fortunate it was, he went on, that the other nations of the world would not permit France to do away with Paris even if she wanted to: foreigners "need [Paris] too much; they know and accept this. The czarevich himself says that Paris keeps the world from becoming stupid." The czarevich (none other than the future and reactionary Alexander III) to the rescue of Paris! We are already a long way from the revolutionary or modernizing dreams of Proudhon the anarchist and the still more pitiless imaginings of Haussmann the prefect.[1]

Before 1870 boredom and existential fatigue were mortal Parisian en-emies for the likes of Flaubert, Manet, and Baudelaire—that is, for any-one who had fully comprehended the new myths of the capital, which Baudelaire called "this dreadful Paris, which I instinctively feared, and whose dark and dazzling ghost looming on the horizon of my dreams pained my poor heart, the heart of a prospective bride." By 1900, how-ever, for the more practical "phantasmagorics" of the Belle Epoque, it had become impossible for clever people to feel bored in Paris, the cap-ital of bourgeois pleasure. "Ennui is the enemy," wrote a prescient com-mentator in 1867, "and I confess that I cannot understand how anyone can feel bored in Paris. It seems to me that you have to work hard to concoct a share of boredom for yourself, because there's none to be had on the market." Henry James shared that view, at least regarding the pleasures the city offered to visitors: this extraordinary Paris, he wrote in 1899, was "the biggest temple ever built to material joys and the lust of the eyes . . . It is a strange great phenomenon—with a (great) deal of beauty still in its great expansive symmetries and perspectives—and *such* a beauty of light."[2]

Thus was a volcanic city, whose task it had been to illumine the fu-ture of humankind, now transformed into the artificial capital of plea-sure and worldly sophistication. The old myth had come into being spontaneously, naturally, and not as a source of profit for anyone; but now people everywhere began to think of the new, demythified Paris as a machine for manufacturing luxury and entertainment for the privileged. The austere, universalizing myths of old now gave way to refined plea-sures available only to connoisseurs and initiates. In an article pub-lished in the *Paris guide* of 1867, a writer who identified himself only as "X" waxed ecstatic about the things to be seen on the avenue de l'Impératrice (today the avenue Foch): "The woods! The lake! Authentic barouches, hired coupés, smiles everywhere, people dressed to the nines . . . But what elegance, too, and what splendors! Dowries to be had for the asking, and love bobbing on the tide. All the world's seductiveness is here, hard at work, armed for battle."[3] *La Vie parisienne,* a magazine that commenced publication in 1863 and did not cease until 1949, bore the subtitle *La Vie élégante.*

Light, elegance, and of course plenty of savoir faire in the choice of

always something to do

pleasures: "People," Gautier tells us, "accuse the noble city of Paris of lacking in ideals, of doubting the existence of the soul, of believing in nothing, of despising virtue and plunging headlong after material pleasures. How mistaken they are, or how slanderous." In the eyes of this talented poet and novelist but mediocre philosopher, the pleasures of Parisian life transcended mere pleasure: in Paris, luxury was a sort of ideal. The Parisian gourmet "looks for refined little dishes," Gautier explained:

> His vice is to become slightly inebriated on the wines of Champagne . . . His naughtiness, which is fundamentally not very sensual, consists in amusing himself by crumpling a bit of lace or a ribbon or a corsage, engaging in amorous banter, and reeling off a list of paradoxical emotions. In a pretty mouth he prefers a sharp tongue to a voluptuous kiss. By virtue of his taste he has, as it were, spiritualized matter, dissipated its weight and given it wings . . . What did he have for dinner? Oftentimes he cannot say. But what sauces, what condiments, what skill in presentation and service!

Precisely, for as Baudelaire prophetically observed in 1860, "Phantasmagoria has been extracted from nature. All the material substance with which memory is burdened has been classified, organized, harmonized, and subjected to a forced idealization that is the result of a childish perception, which is to say, a perception that by dint of being ingenuous is acute and magical."[4]

The deodorization of Paris, whose history Alain Corbin so brilliantly traced in *The Foul and the Fragrant,* can be considered in the same context, as creating the environment necessary for a new sensibility to emerge.[5] After burdensome myth comes pleasurable and refined artifice. The new and easily understandable sophistication of material life, the "forced idealization" of nature, makes irrelevant the memory of days that were grander but also more painful.

OF COURSE the pleasures of Paris were not invented out of whole cloth during the Second Empire: in the 1720s the fictional Manon Lescaut was already hungry for them, and Nicolas-Edme Restif de la Bretonne has left us interesting accounts of what they were like in the middle decades of the eighteenth century. For Alfred de Musset, writing well before Gautier, Paris, and especially the area around Tortoni and the Café de Paris, was already "one of the places on earth where pleasure is concentrated."

Until the final decades of the nineteenth century, however, the idea of Parisian pleasure was only peripheral to the city's image. It was then that it became firmly ensconced, as suggested by the title of Alfred Delvau's book *Les Plaisirs de Paris* (1867), and it has remained so ever since. "Nowhere other than Paris . . . have people more fully savored the pleasures of a naive yet still quite sensible insouciant way of living. There, this way of life received splendid encouragement from the beauty of the surroundings, the mildness of the climate, the wealth and tradition." Stefan Zweig, soon to be an Austro-German Jewish exile, wrote these words in 1932, little more than a decade after the First World War, one year before Hitler, and just two years before the fascist-tinged riots in Paris of February 1934.[6]

Paris was neutral to WWII

The French capital thus became a city of new, more expensive, and more bourgeois pleasures. For these, the physical backdrop had been shaped by Haussmann's modernizing zeal, which had by this point completed its work, and the moral backdrop was the diminution of "popular" Paris and of its libertarian instincts as well. In 1860 Théophile Gautier offered this emotional description of the Parisian theaters of his youth:

> Theatergoers, who were less demanding back then, were happy if they could see and hear approximately what was going on. They put up with bad weather in all seasons, often waiting patiently in line for many hours. They sat crushed together in small boxes with narrow aisles and endured the elastic pressure of the pit. The air was stuffy with exhalations of every variety and warmed by gaslights, but this did not seem to bother them very much. Theaters built in this way were in harmony with the winding streets deprived of air and light and the dark houses with low ceilings and airshafts as deep as wells that filled much of the city.[7]

By 1871 all of this was gone, and Gautier was glad of it. What he does not say is that Haussmann's wrecking crews destroyed much of Parisian popular culture along with these old and authentically Parisian theaters (such as the Théâtre de Porte-Saint-Martin, the Théâtre de l'Ambigu, and the Théâtre des Folies-Dramatiques). Where now was "Bobino, ton Bobino, le Bobino de tes vingt-ans," the vaudeville theater whose passing Charles Monselet lamented in his *Petit Paris* of 1879: "It goes without saying that there is no lawyer, doctor, or judge anywhere in France today who didn't visit the theater of Bobino as a student . . . No student could avoid Bobino, just as no veteran could avoid the Vendôme Column. Bobino complemented the Law School, the Medical School, and the Collège de France."[8] But no more.

The theaters—and repertoires—that replaced these popular and student venues were a very different kettle of fish. At first the classic theaters offered crowd-pleasing attractions by artists such as Eugène Labiche and Jacques Offenbach, tailor-made for the new bourgeoisie of the imperial feast. Then, after 1880, came a new form of pseudo-popular entertainment of the most phantasmagoric sort imaginable, which was often associated with the name of Aristide Bruant, a cabaret singer and shrewd entrepreneur: this was the *café-concert,* of which there were more than sixty in Paris.[9] These featured so-called street singers, a social development chronicled by Edgar Degas, who was always cruel because always on the lookout for signs of a modernity that he could well have done without. Among the *chanteuses de caf'conc'* he painted were Emma Valadon (1837–1913) and Thérésa, better known as "La peau du chien" (The Dog Skin), who liked to sing:

> Ah, qu'il est crevant,
> Mon p'tit Ferdinand
> On voit sa petit' jambe
> Toujours en avant.
> (Oh, he's priceless,
> my little Ferdinand
> with his little leg
> always sticking out.)

These performers were quite well paid: Yvette Gilbert made as much as a thousand francs a night. But not everyone liked the new forms of commercialized popular entertainment. After returning home from a

pretty

Interior of a Café-Concert, ca. 1860. Paris, capital of sin and pleasure. In the eighteenth century Venice had been the European capital of disguise, surprise, spying, and prostitution; after 1840 Paris inherited many of these distinctions, especially as far as sex and entertainment were concerned. By our own standards of nudity and sensual self-indulgence, this French cancan in a *caf'conc'* is very mild—but to many of Henry James's American compatriots a scene of this kind seemed quite wild. Copyright: Collection Viollet.

Paris: Capital of sin & pleasure

café-concert, Edmond de Goncourt wrote that he had "seen a comic in a black costume. He sang several incoherent songs punctuated by clucking and the sounds of farm animals in heat and the gesticulations of an epileptic—the Saint Vitus' dance of an imbecile. The audience went wild . . . I don't know, but it seems to me that we're on the verge of a revolution."[10] And a revolution it was, though not of the kind that Goncourt imagined.

[handwritten margin note: how "romantic" were prostitutes' lives]

C ULINARY—or, more precisely, gastronomic—history offers yet another example of the evolution from myth to commercialized pleasure. Parisian gastronomy, thank heaven, is neither merely a phantasmagoria nor a recent fad. Alfred Fierro, the author of the invaluable *Histoire et dictionnaire de Paris,* tells us that Parisian cuisine began with a late fourteenth-century text, *Le Viandier,* by Guillaume Tirel, chef to Charles V. In 1577 a Venetian ambassador with an ear for the latest news reported to the rulers of the Most Serene Republic that "the French spend their money on nothing so willingly as on food and what they call good cooking." In the century of absolutism, these national and urban traditions were taken up by the monarchy and further refined: "The art of eating well was part of [Parisian] conversation," Fierro notes. "The potager, the ancestor of the stove [used for making soups], . . . was replacing the fireplace in Parisian homes."[11]

This gustatory amelioration can be illuminated by a comparison of French with English cuisine: in Great Britain, where the neo-absolutist Stuart dynasty was overthrown first in 1641 and then definitively in 1688, the "gentry," or lesser rural nobility—with its penchant for modernization and its fondness for land, substantial wealth, and robust ways—imposed its culinary tastes on the nation, so England ate roast beef, Yorkshire pudding, and steak-and-kidney pie—nourishing food, to be sure, but not very sophisticated.[12] By contrast, in Paris, where the nobility, brought to heel by the absolute monarchs Louis XIV and Louis XV, had found a role for itself in serving the state and imitating the court, the culinary impetus came not from the countryside but from Versailles, as Norbert Elias demonstrated. The title of François

Massialot's *Le Cuisinier royal et bourgeois* (The Royal and Bourgeois Cook; 1691, translated into English in 1702) was programmatic, as was that of its new edition of 1748, *Le Nouveau Cuisinier royal et bourgeois, ou cuisine moderne* (The New Royal and Bourgeois Cook, or Modern Cooking). Indeed, one could generalize this pattern: after the famed cabinetmaker André-Charles Boulle created a new style of furniture for the king in Versailles, the cabinetmakers of the Faubourg Saint-Antoine went to work reproducing it for the nobles and notables of Paris.[13] Cuisine and furniture followed more or less the same absolutist course.

So much for the "gustatory" aspect of the question. The social history of the Paris restaurant is also worth a look. The eighteenth-century *table d'hôte* was hard on tourists and foreigners. Those in the know always sat as close as possible to the center of the table, where the food was served. "Woe unto him who is slow to chew his morsels," wrote a German visitor in 1718. "No matter how much he begs the waiters, the table will be empty before he can fill his plate."[14]

Thus the invention, in 1765, of the Paris restaurant, where diners were served at individual tables, marked a major advance, as did the à la carte menu, which first appeared around 1770 but did not become popular until Antoine Beauvilliers, the former chef of the comte de Provence, adopted this innovation at the Taverne Anglaise, the restaurant he opened near the Palais Royal in 1786.[15] By 1789 Paris could boast of fifty or more such restaurants. A number of the new restaurateurs set up shop—instinctively, one might say—in the Palais Royal, near the very spot where Camille Desmoulins addressed the crowd on July 13, 1789, and where the duc d'Orléans had created his galleries, the forerunners of the arcades and department stores. The story goes that the Constitution of Year II was drafted in the restaurant run by Méot, the former chef of the Prince de Condé. It was also in one of the new Palais Royal restaurants that the Montagnard *conventionnel* Michel Lepelletier de Saint-Fargeau was assassinated in January 1793. (Lepelletier, though a wealthy noble, had voted for the execution of the king, and might therefore be described as the great ancestor of what is known today as *la gauche caviar,* the Parisian equivalent of the Limousine Left or Radical Chic.)

Jacobins, Mme de Genlis tells us, did not like good manners, good behavior, or good food. But after their political demise, the rise in the early 1800s of Bonapartist rule—and even more, the fall of the Empire in 1815—led to a new flourishing of restaurants in Paris: by 1825 there were, it is said, more than a thousand in operation. They came in many varieties, from "greasy spoons" on up. The Bouillons Duval, founded in 1855 and recommended by the Baedeker Guide, were the McDonald's of the time: fast, simple, and inexpensive. In 1860 there were even two English restaurants in Paris, one on the boulevard des Capucines, the other on the rue Richelieu, but according to Theodore Zeldin, a British historian with a connoisseur's knowledge of French ways, they enjoyed only modest success.[16]

Other restaurants were veritable pleasure domes: Balzac in *Le Cousin Pons* portrays the Paris restaurant as a hotbed of lust and debauchery,[17] and Roland Barthes rightly observed that one of the most eloquent forms of Parisian pleasure (or at any rate of fantasized masculine pleasure) has been to converse with a beautiful, young, and intelligent woman in a famous and luxurious restaurant in Paris—three different forms of orality, if you will.

During the Restoration, the Rocher de Cancale on the rue Mandar, near the rue Montorgueil, was the most fashionable place for this sort of feast. Balzac sang its praises. Under Louis Philippe the great restaurants migrated to the grand boulevards. Elegant contemporaries of Manet and General de Gallifet (who was minister of war during the second Dreyfus trial) now gathered at the Café de Paris, Tortoni, the Café Riche, and the Café Anglais. There, Babette of *Babette's Feast* prepared their meals, Père Goriot ordered dinner for his beloved daughter, and Rosanette dined with her lover, Frédéric Moreau. Françoise, who cooks for Marcel's family in Proust's great novel, went to the Café Anglais to improve her cooking technique: to her it was "the kind of place that looks as if it serves good old home cooking . . . How hard they work! But you know, they're really raking it in over there." It was a sign of good taste to know something about food, and in "La Fanfarlo" (1847) young Baudelaire, who was something of a poseur, took pleasure in singing the praises of the truffle, "that secret and mysterious vegetation of Cybele's, savory malady that she hid in her entrails longer than precious metal, exquisite matter that defies the science of the agronomist as gold defies that of Paracelsus and his ilk; the truffle, which distinguishes the ancient world from the modern, and which, before a glass of Chio, has the same effect as adding a string of zeroes after a number."[18]

By 1848 restaurants where one could eat such fanciful fare represented major investments. One sold for 320,000 francs. Maxim's was launched with financial backing from the Lebaudy sugar firm. And the chef at the Café Anglais earned 25,000 francs per year, at that time roughly the equivalent of a subprefect's salary. This master of his craft became so well known that he was even chosen to serve on the Conseil Général of his département: "This will give you some sense of the depth of Parisian follies," the Goncourts observed. The pastrymaker Germain-Charles Chevet and his son became world famous. By 1869 a Chevet of the fourth generation was exporting pastries to places as far away as New York and Saint Petersburg. Major American hotels began hiring their first Parisian chefs around 1850.[19] And it was in a restaurant that Offenbach would situate the final scene of his operetta *La Gaieté parisienne*.

THE THEORY of the Paris restaurant, like its social history, followed a curve that went from craftsmanship and fine cooking ("Let us praise the French," wrote Heine, "they are concerned with mankind's two greatest needs, good food and civic equality") to mythologized cuisine and from there to the "phantasmagorized" and ruinously expensive cuisine of La Belle Epoque.[20] *food to incredible*

The theorization of Parisian *digestion* gastronomy began with Alexandre-Balthazar Grimod de la Reynière (1758–1838), a wealthy financier's spendthrift son, who was a philosopher before being a gourmet. Renowned for his "philosophical and nutritious lunches," he wrote that food "considered from a moral and philosophical standpoint is a vein that writers have yet to explore." Paris was where he liked to be, because it was "without a doubt the city with the best food in the world and the only one in a position to furnish all civilized nations with excellent chefs." In

Paris, moreover, good food went hand in hand with good conversation and good manners, as was reflected in his guest list, which included liberal commentators and dissident publicists like Louis-Sébastien Mercier and Restif de la Bretonne. For Grimod, great cooking was an art, and there was "as much distance between [a lark] and a quail [as between] . . . the Great Racine and a certain tragic playwright of the present day, whose name will go unmentioned since I do not wish to humiliate anyone." Recipes and aphorisms, cuisine and literature, were like two sides of the same coin, and so were cuisine and politics: "As for le potage à la Necker," Grimod remarked about a soup named after the not-very-successful minister of finance, "it is no doubt called that by derision or antithesis, since it is excellent."[21]

Like most of the philosophes and their immediate successors (Beaumarchais, the Abbé Raynal, Barthélémy, Bailly, Rivarol, Chamfort), Grimod rejected the Jacobin ideal: to his way of thinking, the Year II was a disaster not only politically but also economically and socially. It dismayed him that philosophical lunches had been replaced by "fraternal meals staged in the gutters of every street, where the prevailing tone, as signs on every building proclaimed, was one of 'fraternity'— presumably that of Cain and Abel, since there was never less liberty or equality in France than when signs on every wall proclaimed those virtues as well."[22]

If Grimod granted Parisian cuisine its patents of nobility, his contemporary Jean-Anthelme Brillat-Savarin, the author of *La Physiologie du goût* (The Physiology of Taste; 1825), revolutionized its very principles. For this theorist of "fine dining" who liked to call himself an "amateur physician," the evolution of cooking was a social phenomenon. As "prolegomena to his work and eternal basis of all science," Brillat was a prolific author of aphorisms and philosophical judgments: "The universe is nothing without life, and everything that lives eats." "Gastronomy is the rational understanding of everything that relates to man insofar as he nourishes himself." "Gastronomy is related to natural history . . . physics . . . chemistry . . . commerce . . . and . . . political economy." For Brillat, to put it in a nutshell, "The destiny of nations turns on how they feed themselves."

Brillat was a fertile thinker, then, and his mode of thought was carried further in 1846 by Eugène Briffault, who in his *Paris à table* placed even stronger emphasis on the important role of gastronomy in the history of Paris and in its image as the "universal city." For Briffault, all great cities were wonders to behold, but "If a city is noteworthy not only for its magnificence and size but also for its vitality, for the momentum and energy that it imparts to civilization . . . [and] if that city is called Paris, everything about it is magnified." Indeed: "When Paris sits down to dine, the whole earth trembles with excitement. From all parts of the known universe things arrive: created things, products of every realm, things that grow on the surface of the earth or that lie enfolded in its bosom or that are hidden in and nourished by the sea or that fill the air—all these things hasten to Paris and jostle and vie for the favor of a glance, a caress, or a bite. For France, dinner in Paris is the great national affair."[23]

As this theorized view of the matter gradually took hold in Paris, cooking achieved nothing less than the dignity of art. In 1850 Eugène Delacroix wrote in his journal: "As I looked at my composition . . . which did not please me until yesterday after I made changes in the sky with pastel, I said to myself that a good painting is exactly like a good dish, made up of the same elements as a bad one. The artist does it all."[24]

For Grimod, gastronomy went hand in hand with philosophy. For Briffault, it was an integral part of the myth of Paris, capital of the nineteenth century. But now, in the second half of that century, Parisian gastronomic discourse, like crime reporting and the penny press, suddenly went commercial.

As early as the July Monarchy, the Paris press began to take an interest in haute cuisine. *La Gastronomie,* a culinary periodical, commenced publication in 1839. Baron Brisse (1813–1876) became the first food columnist to write for a Paris newspaper. He was followed by Charles Monselet, another food writer who enjoyed such renown in Paris that the newspaper magnate Emile de Girardin (whose place in the history of fashion, publicity, and crime reporting was remarked on earlier) set him to work editing Chateaubriand's *Mémoires d'outre-tombe* (Memoirs from beyond the Grave).[25] Monselet in turn was followed by Curnonsky

(1862–1956), whose real name was Maurice Sailland and whose contribution was to lend a more bourgeois and in some ways more democratic tone to the new Parisian gastronomy. In 1907 Curnonsky came up with the idea of Bibendum, the symbol of the Michelin Guides, who today, in a slimmed-down, politically correct form, still appears in advertisements for Michelin tires (or tyres) in the United States and Great Britain. Curnonsky was also the founder of the Académie des Gastronomes, whose members included a prime minister, André Tardieu, and a poet, Maurice Maeterlinck.[26]

Roland Barthes took a keen interest in these images of French gastronomy (in his book *Mythologies,* but recall from the Introduction that what Barthes calls "mythology" I call "phantasmagoria"). In 1957 Barthes wrote that there existed a "cuisine of dissimulation" or even "decorative cuisine." According to Barthes, in the cooking column of the magazine *Elle*—a "real treasure trove"—"the dominant substantial category is the table . . . *Elle*'s cuisine is purely visual. It makes no bones about being a cuisine of fantasy, as is proved by the magazine's photographs, which capture dishes only from above, as objects close to hand yet inaccessible, which can be completely consumed at a glance. It is in the fullest sense of the word publicity disguised as food, totally magic, especially when one remembers that the magazine is widely read in low-income homes." It would be difficult to give a better description of the phenomenon, except that a more historical analysis would begin not with the 1950s but with the end of the nineteenth century.[27]

T HE IDEOLOGICAL CRIMES of gastronomy as consumerist spectacle will seem more serious to some people than to others. The phantasmagoric element in Paris, the pleasure capital of the Belle Epoque, is equally apparent, and certainly more somber, in the realm of sexuality or, to put it more precisely, the sex industry.

Some Parisians prided themselves on their city's reputation as the "capital of sex." (It was around 1865, incidentally, that the word *gauloiserie,* or ribaldry, entered the vocabulary of modern French.) "Is there any place on earth unfamiliar with the reputation of the Jardin

Mabille?" asked a contributor to the *Paris guide* of 1867. "What savage, be he a native of Papua or a son of the Ojibwa tribe, has not heard of the daughters of Eve one encounters there? It is the rather noisy asylum of youth in its hour of dawn, of curious provincials, of seamstresses with heads full of fantasies, of students bent on folly, and even, on occasion, but secretly, of high-society ladies out for a lark."[28]

It is possible, however, to look at all this with a different eye. Once again, as in the account of Parisian prostitution in Chapter 5, the origins of the commercialization of sex can be traced back to the late eighteenth century and to that temple of modernity, the Palais Royal, where during the Revolution a spectacle was staged featuring "a putative savage who copulated in public with a woman of his species." Spectators were charged "twenty-four sols apiece" to watch. Because of shows like this, Paris became ever more closely associated with sexual transgression in the minds of Europe and of Protestant America. Jules Vallès remarked on this in his own characteristic fashion: "If Paris is eager to aid and abet a charming intrigue, London, by contrast, seems to have taken it upon itself to discourage the impetuous and passionate. Where can one go to make love there? . . . One is hounded into virtue by London's architects."[29] Less amused, the Goncourts noted in their diary for 1863 that Paris had become "the foreigner's bordello . . . These days, not a single woman is kept by a Frenchman. They all belong to Hanoverians, Brazilians, Prussians, and Dutchmen. As far as the phallus is concerned, the year is 1815." And that was not all: "The realm of lovemaking has lately been invaded by old fogies. I have no idea what savage morals have come into this country with the millions from the Ural, Brazil, and Moldavia, to say nothing of the priapism and spinal-cord diseases of the American apes and Siberian Cossacks. Paris is turning into something like the Palais Royal, where money, like Blücher, bluntly demands a whore. Within a few years, pleasure in Paris will no longer be French." Theaters, especially, struck them as sexual supermarkets:

> The boxes are like beds in which prostitution flourishes. A theater is a fine thing, a veritable circle of debauchery! From stage to audience, from wings to stage, from audience to performers, and among members of the audience themselves: dancers' legs, actresses' smiles, people peering

through opera glasses—all of this going on at once creates everywhere a picture of Pleasure, Orgy, Intrigue. Nowhere else can you find so many stimuli to the appetite and inducements to copulation in such a small space. It's like a nocturnal exchange whose stock in trade is women.[30]

Less of a moralist and more of a theoretician, the Italian writer Riciotto Canudo, who was close to the Surrealists and was the first to call the cinema "the seventh art," said of Paris in the 1920s that it had become "the brains and gonads of the modern world . . . [It] influences the world sexually with the powerful seductiveness of a female and the fertile seed of a male. Paris acts on the world sexually with the omnipotence of the great Babylon . . . Paris is the modern world's vast melting pot, analogous to what Babylon and Nineveh, Memphis and Crete, Athens and Rome were long ago. Paris the city is the very visage of the world today."[31]

Reality conformed rather closely to these theoretical expositions. In the 1890s there were some thirty-odd burlesque shows in the capital and at least as many licensed brothels and brasseries of the sort that Alphonse Daudet, the author of *Le Petit Chose,* particularly liked because they were places where he could satisfy certain unusual desires of which his lawful companion wanted no part. In 1893, when students at the Bal des Quatz Arts "coaxed a ravishing Mona Lisa to divest herself of her clothing piece by piece until she was as naked as Eve," the prefect of police took a dim view of the matter, leading to a riot, arrests, and a death.[32] In 1919, however, a woman appeared in the nude at the Folies Bergères without incurring retribution of any kind. In 1923 the Folies collected receipts of 10 million francs, less than the Opéra's 12 million, to be sure, but more than the take of the Comédie Française or the Opéra Comique. In fact, commodified sex figured one way or another in most forms of Parisian entertainment: Jean Lorrain described the café-concert as "a meat rack, a depressing, sexual meat rack . . . In the harsh-

Georges Scott, *Looping the Loop at the Olympia,* 1903. This drawing celebrates the Parisian exploits of an American cyclist named Vanderwoort, also known as Diavolo, whose loop propelled him at a speed of up to fifty miles per hour. Paris, the capital of pleasure for the moneyed rich, was also the capital of mass entertainment. Published in *L'Illustration,* March 14, 1903. The President and Fellows of Harvard College.

ness of daylight one sees the hideousness of this hideous thing, which is disguised at night by the shadowy surroundings and clever lighting."[33]

One might look at this from the standpoint of sexual emancipation for women as well as men, liberated at last from the "sexual misery" that any number of novelists and historians have described as characteristic of the life of the unmarried at the end of the nineteenth century—a misery that was even worse for those who also belonged to the proletariat. Colette, for example, does not seem to have been unduly mortified by her participation in "unclothed intermezzi of 'Parisian beauties'" at Bataclan in 1912. But Walter Benjamin, whose lead I will follow here, saw the matter in a different light: "In the form that prostitution took in big cities," he wrote, obviously with Paris in mind, "women were seen not only as commodities but also as articles of mass consumption in the strict sense of the word. The use of makeup to disguise individual expression beneath professional expression was one allusion to this. Later, the girls in uniform who appeared in music-hall reviews reinforced the same point."[34]

GASTRONOMY, SEXUALITY: late nineteenth-century Paris also offered other pleasures. There were horse races and pari-mutuel betting (invented by Joseph Oller in 1867); sports (rugby and soccer, both recent imports); the music hall (the Moulin Rouge in 1899 and the Olympia in 1893); the bars and cafés of Paris (the first of these was established in the Saint-Germain quarter in 1672 by an Armenian visitor named Pascall, and by 1900 there were some 27,000 in the capital, roughly one for every hundred Parisians). Much was also made of the roofs of Paris (which under the ancien régime were usually slate or tile, with the first zinc roofs appearing only around 1840). Taken together, all of these realities, principles, institutions, and innovations pointed directly toward a unifying and presumably redemptive theme: Paris, capital of charm. All figured as themes in the promotion of Paris, both formal and informal, toward the end of the nineteenth century (if not well before). Charles-Augustin Sainte-Beuve (1804–1869) was already quite fond of the used booksellers on the quays of the Seine and the Ile Saint-

Louis. Gautier praised the Jardin du Luxembourg and the Jardin des Plantes. Alfred de Musset (1810–1857) sighed that he loved "ce temps gris, ces passants, et la Seine / Sous ses mille falots, assise et souveraine" (the gray weather, the passersby, and the Seine / Beneath its thousand lanterns, poised and sovereign).[35] Anatole France likewise wrote nostalgically, in his autobiographical novel *Pierre Nozière* (1899), of the city of his birth:

> If ever I savored the remarkable delight of having been born in the city of generous thoughts, it was while walking on the quays, where, from the Palais Bourbon to Notre Dame, the stones themselves tell the story of one of the greatest of all human adventures, the history of ancient France and modern France. There one sees the Louvre, cut like a gem; the Pont-Neuf, whose robust back, once dreadfully hunched, for three centuries and more bore the weight of Parisians loitering among the jugglers on their way home from work . . . One sees the Place Dauphine with its houses of brick. One sees the old Palais de Justice, the restored steeple of the Sainte-Chapelle, the Hôtel de Ville and the towers of Notre Dame. There, more than anywhere else, one is aware of the toil of generations, the progress of time, the continuity of a nation, the sanctity of the work done by our forebears, to whom we are indebted for our freedom and studious leisure.

In 1844 George Sand published a very harsh criticism of the city in *Le Diable à Paris* (The Devil in Paris). She did not mince words: "I hate Paris so much that, if forced to spend time there, I shut my eyes and ears the whole time so that I don't have to see or hear the comments that this cheerful capital's charm and preciousness elicit from wealthy foreigners. My aversion has reached the point of monomania." Two decades later, however, she too had succumbed to the newly advertised charms of Paris, now become a capital of pleasure, to the point where she was able to write an article on walking in the city for the *Paris guide* of the 1867 Exposition. "The truth is," she maintained in the article, "that I know of no other city in the world where ambulatory daydreaming is more agreeable than in Paris . . . In the fine weather of spring and autumn, [the pedestrian] . . . who knows how happy he is [is] a privileged mortal." Perhaps, she added, Haussmann's new streets were "too straight for the artistic eye," but they were "eminently safe . . . [and] allow us to walk with our hands in our pockets without getting lost." Parisians, she conceded, were usually hurried now that it was as common "in Paris as in America to say that 'time is money.'" Still, in the capital there was now life everywhere, and if fake English gardens like the Parc Monceau struck her as ridiculous, the city's "decorative gardens" were truly marvelous. She found everything about the city enchanting, even the memory of its makeover on the day when Parisians were stunned to discover that hundred-year-old trees had arrived from the provinces to line the new boulevards and "from one day to the next spread their seigneurial shadows over the new gardens."[36]

Capital of many things

PARIS, capital of pleasure. Many Parisians now gravitated toward more distant playgrounds—the Alps, the Côte d'Azur—and to nearby resorts. Trouville, explained its city fathers in 1868, "is the boulevard des Italiens of Norman beaches. If the flâneur of city pavement, dozing on a divan at the Café Richelieu while digesting his succulent dinner, were suddenly transported by the rug of the Thousand and One Nights to the casino in Trouville, he would not believe that he had left Paris when he awakened there."[37] Others, less fortunate, took in the city's suburbs instead.

By the 1860s there were three sets of these. The first set (Grenelle, Vaugirard, Belleville, Ménilmontant) had more or less ceased to exist as suburbs after being incorporated into Paris proper by Haussmann. A second group comprised the depressing suburbs south, east, and above all north of the city (for example, Saint-Denis and Aubervilliers). These places became crowded with the lower classes that Haussmann had evicted from the center of the city. In the 1850s Félix and Louis Lazare, though "generally benevolent observers of the imperial oeuvre," called these new suburbs "veritable Siberias with winding, unpaved streets, no lighting, no markets, no water—in a word, with nothing." As the politician and sometime historian Philippe Séguin has noted, it is unfortunate indeed that the emperor's wish to "complete Paris by adding the rest of the département de la Seine, or eight additional arrondissements," was not heeded: presumably more attention would have been paid to them if they had been formally included within the city's perimeter.[38]

The third group of suburbs, by contrast, seemed to exist as a playground for Parisians. These were mainly to the west of the capital: Asnières, Argenteuil, Versailles, Sèvres, Bougival, and Saint-Germain. "I asked myself," Gérard de Nerval mused in 1854, "why I didn't move to Versailles or Saint-Germain . . . Honestly, what's half an hour on the train every morning and evening? You have the resources of a city, and you're practically in the country."[39]

Others made identical calculations about Le Vésinet and Le Pecq, whose growth was directly linked to the new railroads connecting them to the capital. The presiding spirit of the second of these two paradises was one Alphonse Pallu, a friend of the emperor's half-brother, the duc de Morny. A development company was founded in 1856, and when several hundred acres divided into small lots were offered for sale in 1858, 924 parcels of land were quickly sold. Miraculously, in 1862, a state-subsidized railroad arrived to serve the new town. What is more, rail transportation would remain free until 1875 for anyone who owned property there. In 1866 this successful project was capped by the construction of a horse track, and as recently as 1966 a prominent citizen of Le Vésinet could observe that the "community buildings" there "were distributed in such a way that they still do not detract from the city's elegance."[40]

Asnières also took its place in world history at this point. Its population increased from 1,300 in 1856 to 15,200 in 1886.[41] Among the recreational activities available there were sailing, swimming, and rowing. People also shot pigeons, rode horses, walked, attended concerts, and shopped in the marketplace. In 1867 Asnières, like other resort towns west of Paris, imitated the capital by organizing its own mini-exposition: in a novel by the Goncourts published that year, Manette Salomon liked to unwind there along with other "actresses from Grenelle" and "unemployed lorettes." And they were not alone: every Sunday during the summer 6,000 Parisians made the round trip. Gustave Doré satirized them in a drawing depicting their joy upon arriving and sadness at the end of the day when their newfound paradise was temporarily lost until the next weekend. In 1873 Monet painted the Seine at Asnières, and Renoir did the same in 1879.

A MYTH often best endures if it serves to explain some concrete survival from the past. The myth of the permanent revolution—that is, the consecration in 1830 of the Revolution of 1789—would hardly have survived as it did had it not been legitimated in turn by the barricades of the Commune. And phantasmagorias, which were morally impoverished by comparison, required an even more obvious underpinning to appear truthful: in the last decades of the nineteenth century, this support was provided by the irresistible force of domestic comfort.

It comes as no surprise, then, that the era of Parisian phantasmagoria was also the era of elevators, electricity (which Haussmann had neglected), "gas on every floor," bathrooms, improved hygiene—in short, of comfort and a kind of bourgeois elegance. Here the Henri II style was considered appropriate for the dining room, which bridged the gap between familial intimacy and the public performance of the dinner party.[42] (The idea of setting aside a large part of a living space solely for the purpose of dining was a statement in itself.) For the bedroom of the lady of the house, however, a more intimate, more personal, gentler—and also more phantasmagorical—style was required: that of Louis XVI. Women living in the newer Paris apartments no longer had the boudoirs to which their mothers had been accustomed, but in compensation they were allowed to feminize the entire residence.

Praise for the new bourgeois interior could be rather extravagant: César Daly, who had once been a socialist but was now the author of a magisterial nine-volume study entitled *L'Architecture privée au XIXe siècle sous Napoléon III* (1864–1877), became its apostle. For him, the Paris apartment was to be the perfect domestic machine and a complete antithesis of the boulevard. In this perspective, public life was less to be inflected than to be ignored. This general dictum applied to every detail of domestic architecture: Daly now believed that the semi-public reception rooms of an apartment should be totally different in design from the rooms in which the family actually lived. Eugène Viollet-le-Duc took a similar line in his *Habitations modernes* (1875): in an artificially enchanted world, the personal was emphatically not to be political. Instead it was to be a refuge—a refuge that can be read as the domestic expression of Paris, world capital of pleasure.

P HANTASMAGORIAS, then, but ones that were not universally accessible. Louis XVI furniture and mantelpieces decorated with period clocks and vases were not, after all, within reach of ordinary mortals. And here, perhaps, is yet another distinction between the phantasmagorized Paris of 1900 and the mythified Paris of 1840. The Paris myths of revolution and modernity were systems of inclusion; Paris, the capital of the nineteenth century, was the capital of the entire century, taken as a whole with its contradictions and its revolutions. In perfect antithesis to this, phantasmagoria was an ideological mechanism of exclusion. Not everyone could dine at the Tour d'Argent. Everyone knows Freud's joke about this: A wealthy Viennese gentleman, no doubt a friend of Franz Josef himself, gives money to a beggar and then runs into him a few hours later in one of Vienna's great restaurants. He takes the man to task, but the beggar is indignant: "What do you mean, I shouldn't be in here? When I have no money, I can't afford to eat here, and if I'm still not allowed in when I do have money, when will I ever get to eat my fill?"

And in any case, of those who might by some stretch of the imagination have been able to afford to eat in a great Parisian restaurant, how many would have felt comfortable doing so? In the nineteenth century, every one of the countless glasses, knives, forks, and plates perfectly arranged on the dinner table had its specific use, which only initiates knew: even table manners were a mechanism of exclusion, as Pierre Bourdieu has explained in detail in his book *La Distinction*.

Fin-de-siècle Paris did not invent inequality, but this phantasmagorical city did give it a new dimension all its own: by turning cuisine, fashion, and comfort into minor art forms, it bestowed legitimacy on fabulously expensive forms of pleasure. Under the ancien régime, the rich man ate better because he was rich. A century later, a man dined at the Café Anglais because he was a connoisseur, an artist, a dandy, a boulevardier, a *flâneur de luxe,* and, above all, a Parisian.

EXCLUSION OUTSIDE as well as inside the city: to say that Paris was the city of pleasure, a place of incomparable charm, and the capital of the Belle Epoque was to imply that the provinces were the exact opposite, emblems of boredom, torpor, and failure. Once Paris became the capital of pleasure, it became necessary to look at both foreign countries and the French provinces in a new light.

During the Revolution, some thought was given to dividing France into rectangular départements (something like the states of the western United States or the provinces of western Canada). Each département was to have a capital with a boulevard de la Liberté running from the Place de la Révolution to the Place de la Justice, all arranged so that Jacobin strollers, as they traversed identical itineraries in each town, could orient themselves not only geographically but also politically. In 1801 Jean-Baptiste Pujoulx, the author of *Paris à la fin du XVIIIe siècle,* proposed a curious variation on this theme of pedestrian pedagogy. To him, the medieval nomenclature of Paris streets seemed obsolete and incoherent, and he therefore suggested that the streets of the capital be named after provincial cities, with the names of large cities applied to large streets and the names of small cities to small ones. The longest streets were to be named for the various rivers of France. Every Parisian promenade would thus become a lesson in the nation's geography.

This identification of France with its capital was crucial to the propagation of the myth of Paris as having a purpose beyond itself. For Jules Michelet, Paris was the "true center of the world." The city, he wrote in 1838, "represents the world. The influence that Paris worked on our provinces now works on the whole of Europe . . . The city is the crossroads where roads from all nations meet." Paris was a microcosm of both France and the world. The Right Bank, with its boulevards, Michelet believed, belonged metaphorically to "the northern part of France, industry and commerce," while the Left Bank expressed "the French Midi:

education in the Latin Quarter and aristocracy in the Faubourg Saint-Germain." For Michelet, "the spirit that has animated Parisians in all ages and, it must be added, has made them so odious at times to the provinces, that spirit created the unity of Paris . . . starting with Paris." A noble interpretation, and one that was echoed by Paul Valéry as recently as 1937: "Paris reflects the essential complexity of the French nation. A collection of provinces, populations, customs, and tongues so dissimilar had no choice but to create an organic center of their relationship, an agent of and monument to their mutual comprehension. In reality, that is the great, inherent, and glorious function of Paris."[43]

And in actual fact and earlier decades, this mythologizing appreciation had at times seemed reasonable. Throughout the nineteenth century, something akin to a "nationalization" of the Parisian population did in fact take place. In 1867 nearly two out of three residents of Paris had been born in the provinces. Or, to cite a less noble statistic, in 1765, 78 percent of Paris prostitutes were natives of the region north of the celebrated Saint-Malo–Geneva line, which divided the France of the future in the industrial north and east from the France of the rural past in the south and the west.[44] Alexandre Parent-Duchâtelet made a similar observation about the recruitment of Paris prostitutes in the period 1816–1821. But by the end of the nineteenth century this was no longer the case: sex workers in the Paris of the Belle Epoque came from all over, not only from all of France but from the rest of the world as well.

In the last decades of the nineteenth century, however, and regardless of demographics, bourgeois Parisians of the Second Empire and, even more, of the Third Republic no longer shared Michelet's dream of representativeness and inclusiveness. No doubt the Revolution of 1848 and its sequels were at stake here, with the anti-Bonapartist city's rejection in 1871 of a conservative and sometime Bonapartist and obviously provincial peasantry. But also critical was the "phantasmagorization" of Paris, capital of pleasure.

Now the gap between Paris and the (boring) provinces steadily expanded. From the lycée in Tournon, Stéphane Mallarmé, who hoped to be able to go to Paris soon, wrote to his best friend, also desperate at not being in the capital: "In the first place, not every place is called Tournon. And then, it is inevitable that one day you'll get to Paris, whether through the university or through the name you'll have won by your lonely labors." A few months later he added: "I need people, Parisian girlfriends, paintings, music. I'm hungry for poets." Henceforth, Paris, to quote the novelist Alexis Ponson du Terrail, would be "the homeland of all who have a glimmer of genius in their brain." The novelist Théodore Muret put that idea into the mind of Gustave, a young poet from Besançon: "There was one name that buzzed in Gustave's ear like a superhuman voice, a name full of emotion and prestige: Paris! Paris! . . . Paris the great capital, which sober and timorous parents describe to their sons as a place fraught with peril, an impure Babylon."[45]

This widening gap would henceforth separate the capital from the rest of France. The Goncourts—friends of the emperor's cousin Princess Mathilde but also anti-Bonapartists—attributed this gap, in 1861, to the effects of the Revolution and the First Empire: "the great social effect of '89 [was] the centralization in Paris: Paris became, as one says in the argot of the railroads, the 'end of the line' for every provincial fortune. In twenty years, not a single son of anybody who's struck it rich will remain in the provinces." A year earlier they had written: "We can assume that the provinces are dead. The Revolution summoned all men of talent to Paris. Everything comes to Paris eventually, be it brains or fruits. It's going to be a colossal city that soaks everything up: a polyp of a city, like Rome in the time of Aurelian."[46]

Moreover, although proud of the noble "de" in their name and of their provincial roots, the Goncourts were convinced that genuine thought was impossible in the provinces, where ennui was such that even the rain was "a kind of entertainment." In the minds of these two Parisian writers, provincials were hopelessly gullible and thought that "anything which is printed is an authority. They believe in the books they have in their libraries and in the newspapers they read. That is one side of the provincial: the absence of criticism, the faith in the printed word."[47] Flaubert, though less vehement, shared this view: "To stop loving Paris is a sign of decadence. Not to be able to live without it is a sign of stupidity." All of which no doubt explains why Mme Bovary, who devours Parisian novels (which she reads at the dinner table while her husband is talking to her), also pores over guidebooks to the capital and traces with her finger elegant itineraries from boulevard to boulevard.

In a related mode, much has recently been made of the sharp degradation of the image of the Breton in Paris. At first, in the early nineteenth century, Brittany was seen as a charmingly old-fashioned place to which one could finally travel thanks to the railroads, but it soon became fashionable to look down on the region and to make fun of its inhabitants, especially if they came from a place called Concarneau. The mere mention of that city was enough to set off gales of Parisian laughter. Paris now was everything, the provinces were nothing. "Mailings in the city and abroad," one can still read on the front of the Tour d'Argent restaurant: outside those two destinations, no salvation was possible.

Rarely did anyone achieve the status of provincial and Parisian at the same time. It did happen, though: writing about the poet and publicist Charles Péguy, Daniel Halévy said that he was "too provincial to become a true Parisian, yet too French to disdain to be one. To anyone who might have disparaged Paris or slandered it in his presence, he might well have borrowed the response of Montaigne, another provincial who claimed to love Paris, warts and all."[48] Montaigne and Péguy! Those were not easy examples to live up to.

Contempt for the provinces extended to all aspects of life, including restaurants. If nations were defined by the dishes they liked, so were the provinces of France. As Auguste Luchet explained in 1867:

> The Russian is easy. He has confidence. Of all foreigners, he is the one who eats the most and drinks the best, always the finest things. The Englishman, by contrast, knows nothing about food and always thinks he is being deceived. The American spends a lot, wastes, eats copiously without drinking, and drinks endlessly afterward . . . The Italian has dislikes and manias, prejudices and recipes. You can satisfy him by giving in to them. The Frenchman from the provinces wants sophisticated, complicated, difficult dishes, and only mediocre wines agree with him. Perhaps only the Parisian truly appreciates what you serve him. And if he seldom complains, it is not because he is unaware. There is pleasure to be had in treating him very well.[49]

In the Parisian clash of theses and antitheses, the provinces, though excluded, no doubt benefited indirectly from the phantasmagorical and

313

exclusive conception of the capital: to see Paris as the capital of pleasure was also to imply that the provinces were a more chaste, more sober, more honest, and—for some—more Christian place: "How touched I am by your conversion, accomplished by Grace during a hike in the pure mountain air!" the Catholic poet Francis Jammes wrote to a friend in 1915. "How you pleased me when, tired of wandering in the filth of Paris and wearying your eyes with too much light, you returned home [to southwestern France] to breathe the air in [Father] Michel's chapel . . . and to rest your eyes in the dim light of the altar."[50] And Proust, on a visit to Méséglise, had this to say about that village's Saint-André-des-Champs: "How French that church was!" Would he have said the same thing about a church built in the same style but located on the rue Saint-André-des-Arts in Paris? In 1928, when the Third Republic was on the verge of coming apart, Charles Brun, a regionalist writer, concluded in his contribution to a work entitled *Psychologie de la table* that "it is only in the provinces that people really eat."

Similarly, for some provincials, as well as for some Parisians (of Jansenist disposition, no doubt), Paris was not only the noxious capital of excessive pleasure, artifice, and decadence but also of homosexuality, which they reviled. In this respect, Robert de Montesquiou in the salons, the comte de Charlus in *A la recherche du temps perdu,* and Jean Cocteau after the First World War—these were no doubt the most Parisian of Parisians. Liane de Pougy, Mathilde de Morny, Elisabeth de Grammont, the duchesse de Clermont-Tonnerre, and the American Natalie Barney are still celebrated today.

The evolution of attitudes in this domain was rapid. The Parisian homosexuality of Jean-Jacques de Cambacérès, who served as Second Consul of the Republic from late 1799 to May 1804, and of the novelist Joseph Fiévée and the travel writer Astolphe de Custine in the 1820s and 1830s was widely known but seldom discussed. In Balzac's *Père Goriot,* Vautrin's homosexuality is alluded to but not elaborated upon. In 1881, however, Maupassant was quite explicit in a story entitled "La Femme de Paul," in which a young man is driven to suicide when his mistress proves to be more attracted to other women than to him. And by 1900 themes of this sort had become common in Paris. What is more, not just male homosexuality but male homosexual prostitution was a subject of concern: in 1867 a prefect, François Carlier, discussed it in his book *Les Deux Prostitutions: Etude de pathologie sociale* (The Two Prostitutions: A Study of Social Pathology), and during the Exposition of 1900 it was estimated that 4,500 men lived in Paris on what they earned from prostitution. The Symbolist writer Jean Lorrain, who later fought a duel with Marcel Proust (like himself, a homosexual), was the first to offer to the public a description of homosexuality among the Parisian elite, as well as the first to treat male homosexual prostitution as a subject for poetry.

Though questioned, then, the exclusiveness and superiority of Paris at the end of the nineteenth century were still overwhelming: the provinces were excluded *en masse*—and the gap between them and the capital had become unbridgeable. Moreover, many Parisians were also ignored. Indeed, much of the city's own bourgeoisie was banished from the magic circle of the phantasmagorical capital of pleasure: not all Parisians shared in the prerogatives of "Parisianism." In this regard it is revealing that many late nineteenth-century Parisian plays (one thinks of Georges Courteline's comedies of the 1890s, for example) turned on the common sense of a typical petit bourgeois Parisian mocking the pretentiousness of a neighbor or friend who had succeeded only too well in entering high society.

E XCLUSION and humiliation. Where, then, were the blessed elect, those excluded from the exclusion (to parody Hegelian jargon) that characterized phantasmagorias generally? They constituted the "Tout Paris," the upper crust, a confraternity, as Frédéric Hoffet put it, "more durable than any regime, which has remained unchanged through all our revolutions." If the phrase "Tout Paris" was unknown to Balzac, Edmond de Goncourt used it in 1868, albeit sarcastically: "Tonight, illustrious Tout Paris gathered at the Italiens for a private performance. Well, the reflection to which this gathering gives rise is the following: French aristocratic high society is dead. There is nobody left nowadays but financiers and tarts, or women who look like tarts. What is supremely defunct, for example, is the type that used to be known as the

Parisian woman of the world." By the end of the First World War, how-ever, "Tout Paris" came to have its current meaning: chic, well-bred Paris society. We can also note in passing that the first edition of the *Bottin mondain,* the French Social Register, dates to 1904.[51]

Like the so-called Grandes Ecoles, whose essential characteristic is that they are *petites* rather than *grandes,* the point of Tout Paris was that, contrary to the literal meaning of the words, it included only a small proportion of the capital's population. (In 1887 Alphonse Daudet's wife, speaking of the roughly 500 people who traded invitations and also attended the meetings of the Académie Française, called those meet-ings "almost a family reunion.")[52] Where then were the real Parisians in the new phantasmagorical system of seeing the capital? Who were the Parisians whom no one would dream of excluding? Were they in the Académie? At the Institut? In the salons of the Faubourg Saint-Germain, perhaps? At the Jockey Club? Among the "200 families" said to control the Banque de France? Or perhaps at the Collège de France? In modern and phantasmagoric Paris, this unanswerable question was—and still is—on everyone's mind. But who had thought of asking it when Parisian change was still structured by its myths?

13

The American Imagination

THE GREAT MOMENT in the life of General Porfirio Díaz (1828–1916) was his victory over Emperor Maximilian's French allies at Puebla in 1867; and yet, when forced into exile in 1911, the fallen Mexican dictator chose Paris as his new home. There, incidentally, as far as we can tell, he never met Mexico's greatest painter, Diego Rivera, who also lived in the city, off and on, from 1911 to 1920. Díaz had a favorite saying: "Poor Mexico, so far from God and so close to the United States." By contrast, Mexico, though a long way from Paris in miles, was nonetheless quite close to Paris in spirit. If one wants to talk about "Americans" in Paris, one should therefore talk about the prestige the city has enjoyed in Latin America as the capital of a Latin nation—the "eldest daughter of the Church"—that was nonetheless ultramodern and anticlerical. Indeed, the emotional bond between South America and the City of Light has proved surprisingly durable, and its history can be traced from Francisco Miranda (a Venezuelan general who served the First Republic in 1792) and Simon Bolívar (who lived in exile in Paris) to Alejo Carpentier, Fidel Castro's unhappy ambassador to France and the author of the most interesting of all the novels about the French Revolution, *El siglo de las luces* (The Century of Enlightenment).

North America, after it achieved independence from Great Britain, remained culturally close to the mother country. By contrast, the former colonies of Spain and Portugal turned their backs on their home countries soon after achieving independence. And in that reaction they turned their attention elsewhere: to London and New York, or, more broadly, to England and the United States—countries simultaneously admired for their modernity and detested for their economic and political power—and to Paris. Listen to the Argentine literary critic Juan Pablo Echague writing in his Paris journal in May 1911: "France is for us the great nation of instruction; it is from her that we borrow our ideas, our tastes, our civilization; it is thanks to her that we hope one day to be worthy inheritors of the Latin tradition."[1] In 1888 the French capital also became home to Eça de Queiroz, the author of the Portuguese national novel *The Maias.*

All these threads could be bound together: countless Spanish- and Portuguese-speaking writers and other visitors from South America were drawn to Paris. The city plays an eminently symbolic role, for example, in the work of Carlos Fuentes, who served in the 1970s as Mexico's ambassador to France. In his novel *Terra nostra* (1975), Paris is the *ultima ciudad,* the city in which an informed observer is most likely to detect the premonitory signs of imminent apocalypse.[2] And perhaps it is worth noting that at one time Paris was even the world capital of the tango. True, its preeminence in this field lasted only from 1910 to 1911, ending when the archbishop of Paris, Léon-Adolphe Amette, no doubt concerned in his own way about apocalypse now, condemned that graceful dance as lascivious, as Pope Pius X would soon also do—a sequence of blame that had complicated effects, since it was after its Parisian success and scandal that the tango was taken up by the elite of Buenos Aires, who had previously disdained it. Too bad that Carlos Gardel, the renowned singer of tango music, was born in Toulouse rather than Paris!

The myth of Paris in Latin America is a rich theme well worth exploring, but we must leave it for now: Latin America and Anglophone America are very different. And so for that matter are the two great Anglophone traditions, the British and the American. It would be quite interesting to trace the history of the place that Paris has occupied in the English imagination. American Francophobia, generally inconsequential, is usually tinged with a certain sympathy; but British Francophobia is a more important and more strident phenomenon whose adepts are far less repentant than their American counterparts. As Linda Colley, the leading historian of eighteenth-century Britain, has ably shown, the fear of Papist, absolutist France—a fear compounded by contempt—has been a basic ingredient of British national feeling since the seventeenth century. An amusing and Oxonian variation of Lord Acton's well-known dictum concerning absolute power holds that "culture corrupts, but French culture corrupts absolutely."

But, as with Latin America, studying the place of Paris in the self-understanding of England (and of London) would take us too far from the place of Paris in the imagination of the United States. In the late eighteenth century both Horace Walpole and Thomas Jefferson lived in Paris, Walpole as a friend of Mme du Deffand and Jefferson as America's minister plenipotentiary. Both were or had been subjects of King George III, and both were also habitués of Parisian salons. But one was a republican, the other not, and they imagined Paris in quite different ways.

F OR NEARLY two centuries, from 1780 to 1960 or so, Paris occupied an important place in the North American imagination. Liberty, beloved liberty: political libertarianism was central to the myth of Paris in the United States, from Jefferson the freedom-loving and slave-owning planter to James Baldwin, the leading African-American writer of the twentieth century. For many Americans, a trip to Paris was a journey of initiation and liberation (as it clearly was for Henry James and—if less clearly—for James Baldwin). To go to Paris (or to dream while still at home about a "virtual Paris") was to move in search of a freedom to live and think as one pleased, and also in search of opportunities for spiritual and cultural growth.

Then too, for thousands of Americans from the American Revolution until at least the 1960s, and perhaps to our own time, Paris has been a Mecca of high culture. In the first days of the American republic, Jefferson frequented the philosophes, enjoyed French theater, and is on record as having attended Racine's *Les Plaideurs,* Molière's *Amphytrion,* and Beaumarchais's *Le Mariage de Figaro.* (During his stay he also patronized the young John Trumbull, then honing his skills in Paris as a historical painter, and still had time to grow Indian corn in his garden on the Champs-Elysées, "for the use of my own table, to eat green in our manner.") Two decades later, in 1805, Washington Irving, the premier American *littérateur* of his day, likewise thrived in the French capital's bookshops and theaters, where he befriended the famous actor François-Joseph Talma, though, he said, "I do not admire the french [*sic*] style of acting."[3]

For the American feminist Margaret Fuller, Paris in the 1840s was an extraordinary school in which ignorance ceased to be burdensome because, there, it could be remedied. Of all the schools she had known, Fuller added, Paris was the only one in which teachers really were more gifted and learned than their students. Her opinion was shared by James Fenimore Cooper, the author of *The Last of the Mohicans,* who lived in Europe, and mostly in Paris, from 1826 to 1833. A friend of General Lafayette, Cooper was ostensibly engaged in a comparative study of the public expenditures of republics and monarchies. Paris, he wrote, was the center of Europe, and living there was a learning experience that every American ought to have before visiting the rest of the continent.[4]

The cultural prestige of Paris was unrivaled in America at that time, and some Yankees found clever ways to capitalize on this. In 1840 a syndicate of American speculators organized a tour across the United States for a painting, *Adam and Eve,* by the painter Claude Dubuffe (1790–1864), an artist esteemed above all others by one of Balzac's characters and labeled by that author as a consummate ignoramus, and, in a word, as "the Grocer."[5] The syndicate made no less than $100,000. The successful entrepreneur-aesthetes went back to Paris and commissioned Jean-Baptiste Isabey, Eugène Lami, and two of their friends to paint four scenes from the American Revolution for 40,000 francs (approximately $8,000).

On a less exalted level, Paris was also a destination for American sexual tourism. The French capital, by its very size and location, offered many Americans not just the anonymity of a big city but novel customs and pleasures. Paris was a city where people could do pretty much as they pleased provided they had the means: to put it bluntly, for many Americans Paris was a city of sex, alcohol, and drugs. For Hemingway

and most of his friends Paris was one long binge, all the more delightful
because it was so inexpensive. For these visitors Paris was a high-class
prostitute. The poet e. e. cummings called Paris "the putain [whore]
with the ivory throat," to which he added, in French, "bon dos, bon cul
de Paris" (Paris: nice back, nice ass).[6] And Henry Miller, a sex enthusi-
ast, wrote advertisements for Le Sphinx, which in those days was the
most popular and fashionable brothel in Montparnasse—it was even air-
conditioned, a first for such an establishment in Paris. More nobly, for
Gore Vidal, the author of *The Judgment of Paris* (1952), a stay in the
French capital was also a step toward public acknowledgment of homo-
social inclinations.

This sexualized American appreciation of the charms of Paris existed
even before the Revolution of 1789. For John Adams—a diplomat in
Paris in 1783, before he succeeded George Washington as president of
the United States—the immorality of the high French aristocracy, both
in Paris and in Versailles, was a matter of public knowledge. As it was
also, but in a different way, for Benjamin Franklin, who at the age of 74
was still quite avid for the companionship of women.

Franklin, who fled Boston, where he had been born poor, for Philadelphia, where he was soon rich, tried hard to be a model bourgeois in the
Quaker city. After making a fortune there, he engaged in civic and scientific pursuits in a manner befitting a British gentleman of the period.
(From these activities came his celebrated lightning rod.) But in Paris
Franklin was a very different man. Since the French thought of him as a
noble savage of a kind, Franklin amicably played the role: he not only
rejected wigs but sported a beaver cap that would have delighted Jean-
Jacques Rousseau but astonished Franklin's contemporaries in Philadelphia. Ever eager to please, Franklin also adopted the amorous ways of
French high society, if rather innocently, and courted the widow of
Claude-Adrien Helvétius, the philosophe and tax farmer, but in the end
she turned down his proposal of marriage. The company of Parisiennes
charmed him immensely. As he told one of his nieces, young Frenchwomen had taken to being kissed on the neck; to kiss them on the
mouth would be too audacious, and to kiss them on the cheek would
mar their makeup.

Paris, capital of sex: along with Paris, capital of liberty, this was an *idée fixe* that thrived in the Puritan imagination of America from the time of the city's early myths to the time of its phantasmagorias. The first striking thing about Paris, Henry Miller noted in the 1930s, was the nature of sexuality. According to Miller, there was more promiscuity in America, but American sex was oppressive and unexpressive.[7] Paris was more free, and, especially, more fun.

FROM BEFORE 1789, then, Paris was a place for Americans to develop their individuality in its various forms. First and foremost, however, even before the end of the ancien régime, Paris was for many Americans the world capital of political liberty.

Among the philosophers of freedom who were at once Parisian and American, the best known is no doubt, once more, Thomas Jefferson. This eminent Virginian traveled widely in France. For example, he admired the Maison Carrée in Nîmes and used it as the model for a public building in Richmond, Virginia. He was also interested in the classification of Bordeaux wines. (The system used in his day resembled the one that would be formalized during the Second Empire, which was essentially the same as the one we use today.) And he tried (albeit unsuccessfully) to introduce vineyards and olive groves to his home state like those he had seen in the south of France.

Still, for Jefferson France meant neither the Nord nor the Midi, neither the provinces nor Versailles, but Paris. Every man has two homelands, he declared, his own and France—but by "France" he meant Paris, that is, the Paris of the Enlightenment and the salons, of Lafayette, and of the liberal aristocracy of the Ségurs, the La Rochefoucaulds, and the Clermont-Tonnerres. (It is worth noting that many talented and libertarian Parisians inverted this pattern of migration and settled in the United States in Jefferson's own times. To take just the field of architecture, one could cite Major L'Enfant, the Paris-born planner of Washington, D.C., and the less well known Joseph Ramée, who was in a sense the creator of the American college campus, since he designed one of its first incarnations for Union College in Schenectady, New York.[8] The

Duponts—or Duponts de Nemours, as they called themselves—would become the most famous of these eighteenth-century French immigrants.)

True, when the Revolution veered into excess, first with the Terror and then with the rise of Bonapartism, Paris's reputation as the capital of liberty suffered in America, but it was not entirely destroyed. Indeed, all the Parisian socialist utopias of the nineteenth century had their American imitators: the Transcendentalists' Brook Farm, for example, was a Fourierist community established in the country outside of Boston. And the American socialist Albert Brisbane, who lived in Paris in the 1830s and 1840s, was an indefatigable apologist for the Parisian view of the world that Fourier's disciple Victor Considérant tried to transplant to America, and to Texas in particular, by founding socialist communities such as La Réunion (which attracted the Parisian architect César Daly, but which foundered when the French and Belgian colonists had a falling out).[9]

Paris was thus the land of liberty for Americans in the nineteenth century; and in the twentieth, for the novelist John Steinbeck (who, during the Vietnam war, moved from the extreme left to the extreme right, or close to it), the French capital was still the great site not just of political liberty but also of the very conception of the rights and duties of humankind.[10] When Jessye Norman appeared at the celebration of the Bicentennial of the French Revolution draped in a tricolor flag and singing "La Marseillaise," her African ancestry was perhaps as significant as her nationality, but her presence in Paris symbolized at least the memory—and perhaps even the extension—of the myth of two sister republics, each pursuing her own "civilizing mission" and therefore perpetually the rival as well as the ally of the other. (In this manner optimists could reason that Franco-American relations are fundamentally always good because they seriously deteriorate only when things in general are going rather well.)

At the same time, we should bear in mind that the political and social judgments of Americans by the French and of the French—especially Parisians—by Americans have often been quite negative. In 1789 Jefferson imagined that it would be relatively easy for French and Parisian society to embrace the new principles of liberty and equality already proclaimed by his compatriots, and he was no doubt pleased that the French Declaration of the Rights of Man of August 1789 was partly inspired by Virginia's Bill of Rights. (Jefferson left France only a few weeks after the assault on the Bastille.) But John Adams and especially Gouverneur Morris, who succeeded Jefferson as American minister in Paris, were far more critical, and wondered how the morally demanding principles of liberty and republicanism could be grafted onto a society steeped in absolutism, religious intolerance, and the aristocratic ethos of hierarchy and exclusion. Indeed, long after the Revolution of 1789 many Americans in France (such as Henry James) continued to be struck by the countless survivals of aristocratic customs in French and particularly Parisian society. (The same theme provides the background for Diane Johnson's late twentieth-century bestseller, *Le Divorce*.)

And in the opposite direction, even Alexis de Tocqueville's perception of American life—like that of many of his French and Parisian peers—was not always positive. For that melancholy nobleman, America mattered because American society had succeeded politically where the French Revolution had dismally failed: only the Americans had successfully combined the advent of political democracy with the expansion of individual liberty, a fragile value whose origins could be traced to the chivalry of the Middle Ages but which French nobles had been unable to defend against the absolutism of the Valois and their successors. (England was also of some interest to Tocqueville, because the English aristocracy, especially the country gentry, had managed to preserve liberty in a country much like his own. Nevertheless, for him Great Britain was no more than an image of what France might have been, whereas America offered an image of what he wished France might be in the future.)

But it is also true that Tocqueville displayed little enthusiasm for what America represented socially, and that he never returned to the United States after his 1831 excursion. This Norman aristocrat (who was born in the suburbs of Paris and spent most of his adult life there as well) was dismayed by the brutality of American slavery, the tyranny of mediocre majorities, the rise of a new aristocracy (of lawyers), and the neglect of the Indians, whose failure to adapt to modern society (as he may have viewed their situation) was reminiscent of the similar failure of the French nobility, which was also warlike, backward looking, and inefficient. In brief, French—or Parisian—doubt about social freedom in America was one side of a coin whose other side was American anxiety about the French conception of freedom.

At times the French may admire America's political system or economy, yet they remain suspicious or even contemptuous of the social values that America represents: the limits that an immanent civil society imposes on the state seem quite admirable from a Parisian standpoint, but American society (which the French see as characterized by Disneyland, McDonald's, the death penalty, and "multi-culti" values) ordinarily elicits little enthusiasm in the City of Light. Curiosity and proximity do not always engender friendship or sympathy.

PUBLIC LIBERTY, private liberty, high culture, and untrammeled sexuality: these are the components of the myth of Paris in the American imagination. Before tracing the consequences of this state of mind in the work of a number of famous Americans, we would do well to review a few basic facts and figures about the American presence in the French capital.

What is distinctive about Americans in Paris is that while these visitors seek to acculturate themselves—often quite energetically—to the local scene, they rarely do so completely by becoming French citizens and turning their backs on their homeland. (Reciprocally, the number of French immigrants to the United States has also been quite minimal. In the nineteenth century more people emigrated to America from Norway than from France, even though Norway's population was not even one-tenth that of France, which was then the most populous country in Western Europe.) Many substantial French and Parisian families can trace their roots to the British Isles. (The Hennessy family, from which the cognac takes its name, and the ancestor of Patrice MacMahon, an early president of the French Republic, came from Ireland; the forebears of William Henry Waddington, a French politician and prime minister, as well as President Jules Grévy's crooked son-in-law Daniel Wilson, came from England.) Other than the writer Julien Green, however, is there in the history of Paris a single preeminent public figure of American origin?[11]

This lack is all the more striking because from 1780 to the present (leaving aside of course the years of the Occupation, 1940–1944) Paris has always been home to hundreds if not thousands of Americans, some of whom achieved a certain prominence. In an earlier chapter we encountered Robert Fulton and his panoramas. Going back to revolutionary times, we also find Benjamin Thompson, Count Rumford, a native of New Hampshire who was ennobled by the king of Bavaria and who, like the illustrious Antoine-Auguste Parmentier, did much to popularize the potato in France. And then came Joel Barlow, a revolutionary poet in Paris in 1792 and an honorary French citizen who ran for, but failed to win, a seat in the French Convention, where he would have sat next to Tom Paine: in 1812 Barlow returned to France as the U.S. envoy to the emperor's court, and he died in Poland while trying to join Napoleon and the Grande Armée. (Barlow, Fulton, and Barlow's wife, Ruth, had lived together for some years in a Parisian ménage à trois.)

During the nineteenth century hundreds of Americans flocked to Paris, the world capital of the arts and sciences, to study. As early as 1830 there were some fifty Americans studying or practicing medicine in the capital. In 1839 Levin Smith Joynes, a young medical student in Virginia, after attending a lecture about his surgery professor's European tour, wrote to his father that he wished to go and see for himself: "The interesting statement which he gave of the decided superiority of Paris greatly increased my desire to enjoy its advantages."[12] And it may be noted that the first woman to practice medicine in Paris was an American, Elizabeth Blackwell (1821–1910). The dentist who treated the Orléans family was also American, as was the dentist who attended to

---

Delivery of the Statue of Liberty, by M. Bartholdi, to M. Morton, Minister of the United States, 1884. American symbols in Paris: this drawing celebrates the official handing over to American authorities of Bartholdi's statue (and of Eiffel's frame for it), which would be officially inaugurated in New York Harbor on July 4, 1886. A small-scale replica of the statue stands in Paris today on an island in the Seine near the Grenelle bridge. Published in *L'Illustration,* July 12, 1884. The President and Fellows of Harvard College.

Empress Eugénie and who, on September 4, 1870, helped her flee Paris and make her way to England.

In 1867, of the approximately 119,000 foreigners living in Paris, 34,000 were German, 9,000 English, and 4,400 American, among whom were a number of political refugees who had fled the former Confederacy following its defeat in 1865. A drawing by the caricaturist Cham (Amédée de Noë) shows a pitiless Yankee exchanging fire with a fierce Rebel on the horse-drawn Clichy-to-Odéon omnibus in Paris as frightened Parisians look on in horror. In 1927 the Chamber of Commerce estimated that there were 15,000 Americans living in Paris. The police proposed an even higher figure: 35,000.

Parisians were often fascinated by these American visitors, be they of European, African, or Native American descent. Buffalo Bill's visit to Paris in connection with the Exposition of 1889 is well known, but the Indian art show at the Louvre in 1845, which included paintings by George Catlin and performances by his hired troupe of Native Americans, was probably even more picturesque. It was a gala affair. Victor Hugo attended, as did Alexander von Humboldt, the great German scholar and explorer, and George Sand (always on the lookout, apparently, for naturalist and regionalist material, however exotic). The "Peaux-Rouges" (redskins), as Parisians called them, took a bus to the Tuileries, and there were presented to the citizen-king by the American ambassador. Catlin described their appearance: "Every article of dress and ornament had been put in readiness; and, as the hour approached, each one came out from his toilet, in a full blaze of color of various tints, all with their wampum and medals on, with their necklaces of grizzly bear claws, their shields and bows and quivers, their lances, and war clubs, and tomahawks, and scalping knives." The occasion was captured in a painting by Karl Girardet that hangs today in the Museum of Versailles. (One of Catlin's paintings of Native Americans would be shown at the Salon of 1846 and was praised by Baudelaire, the translator of Edgar Allan Poe.) The "show" was a great success, though apparently not for the Native American performers: several contracted tuberculosis, and the ones who survived all opted to return to the United States.[13]

In these mid-century decades, American tourists also visited Paris in ever greater numbers, many of them to shop in newly specialized establishments where young Parisian saleswomen, or so wrote one tourist in 1838, "have an irresistible way of recommending their wares, charming you by their ineffable sweetness and apparent naïveté, while they draw as liberally on your purse."[14] Before the Civil War, rich southern ladies were especially fond of the city's seamstresses (one irate southern planter warned, however, that "they are a great set of rascals and must be watched"); and after the Civil War and the Paris Commune, many of these same southerners were quick to draw analogies between their own sad situation and that of elegant and besieged Parisians: to one "French nobleman" who had opined that the Communards were "worse than the niggers," Mrs. F. J. Willard responded that they were "a great deal worse . . . I think it quite a disgrace to the negroes that such a comparison should be made, for negroes were faithful to their masters."[15] It became a commonplace in the reconstructed South to draw analogies between the Union authorities and the Paris Commune.

Paris, mythical capital of liberty and culture and sexuality and, later, phantasmagorical capital of pleasure. Many Americans understood this shift from myth to phantasmagoria, perhaps most notably Henry James. It is in the nature of things, however, that we usually miss the great moments in our own times, and this was quite true of the Parisian experience of the most American of American authors, Mark Twain. Twain was obsessed by the myths of America that were prevalent in his day, and he was also moved by the tragic experience of black Americans, symbols of his nation's original sin. But in Paris, where he lived for a number of years, he saw virtually nothing and understood even less. In fact, one wonders why he chose to live there at all, since everything about the capital displeased him, including the climate: France, he noted in 1879, was cold, damp, and rainy. Its capital was "Paris the damnable."[16]

André Maurois wrote that reading the works of the author of *Huckleberry Finn* was what first aroused his sympathy for the United States. But his sympathy was misplaced in that Twain is a shining example of a fairly common and rather exasperating type: the American Francophobe (or, more precisely, Parisophobe, since Twain knew scarcely anything about France outside of Paris) who nevertheless gravitates to Paris, apparently because he must constantly feed his desire to criticize the city. Like Baudelaire, who both loved and hated Paris, Twain was a visitor who more than anything else loved to hate it.

It was in New Orleans that Samuel Clemens, then a Mississippi river boat pilot and not yet Mark Twain, discovered a certain kind of pleasurable Frenchness along with Creole cooking—although his negative impressions of Paris would eventually supplant his positive experience of New France. What little French Twain knew he learned in Louisiana. In notes written in 1882 he sang the praises of the Gallic tongue: "How beautiful that language is."[17] More often, however, he spoke disparagingly about it. After *La Revue des deux mondes* published one of his stories, Twain amused himself by making a burlesque English translation of the text.

Some aspects of French life did please him: he admired Emile Zola for defending Dreyfus and praised Joan of Arc, about whom he wrote a book he mistakenly believed to be excellent. Zola and Joan: a curious juxtaposition, yet one that is easily explained. Zola's courage (for Twain he was "the manliest man in France") and Joan's chastity had one thing in common: neither resembled in any way what Twain thought he had observed during his sojourn in France from 1890 to 1895.

The eclecticism and incoherence of his reading in French literature are still astonishing. He read Mme de Sévigné, was interested in her letters, but despised their author. He disliked Flaubert's *Salammbô*. Rabelais and Paul Bourget were also not to his taste. He appreciated Saint-Simon and Anatole France but was not interested in Balzac, Baudelaire, or Paul Valéry. He knew the history of the Revolution of 1789 only from the work of Thomas Carlyle and Hippolyte Taine, one of whom treated the event as a sick struggle between two clans of godless Mediterraneans and the other as a fatal moment in the history of a morbid, rotten country that had fallen into the hands of the dregs of the populace.

Huckleberry Finn (1885), for all its faults, was a memorable event in the history of American literature. In this novel, for the first time, a former slave was made to be the bearer of an American message of humanity and dignity. Similarly, in an article entitled "Concerning the Jews" (1889), Twain declared himself a universalist. But what rule has no exceptions? And for Twain, the French in general and Parisians in particular—especially in his unpublished notes—constituted a race apart. French nationalism, perhaps even the very idea of the French nation, exasperated him. The French, he believed, were the most bellicose of peoples. They were a savage nation: the "French are the connecting link between man and the monkey." Question: What is virtue for a Frenchwoman? Answer: "A woman who has only one lover and don't steal." A Frenchwoman on her deathbed blessed her husband, her children, and their nine fathers. "A Frenchman's home is where another man's wife is." The French "have bestialities which are unknown in civilized lands."[18] France was governed by prostitutes. It was not the Prussians but the French who burned Saint-Cloud in 1870. No Frenchman had the breadth of spirit to admire Germany and German culture. Twain had no sympathy for Americans who settled in Paris: he reproached them for being unnatural as well as denaturalized and for aping their hosts. One of Twain's compatriots, Thomas Appleton, the brother-in-law of Henry Wadsworth Longfellow, had uttered an aphorism that became famous: "Good Americans, when they die, go to Paris." Twain's version, written in his notebooks during a European tour in 1879, was: "Trivial Americans go to Paris when they die."

Not all Parisians like America, and not all Americans like Paris, and for all his blindness Twain is a useful if disagreeable antidote not only to the sentimentalism that sometimes colors descriptions of Franco-American relations but also to the overly abstract idea that the myth of Paris was somehow irresistible. Paris was indeed the capital of the nineteenth century, but not everyone grasped or accepted that fact.

I̶T IS WITH genuine relief that we leave Mark Twain and turn our attention to the supremely subtle and delicate novels of Henry James, who, like Twain, lived extensively in Paris, but not at all in the same way. Born in New York in 1843 and raised in London, Paris, and

Geneva, James lived in the French capital in 1875 and during that year sent a series of perceptive articles to the *New York Tribune.* Unlike Twain, James spoke excellent French, as the Gallicisms sometimes embedded in his carefully nuanced English prose attest. In a collection of essays entitled *Portraits of Places,* James wrote half-mockingly that the two or three square miles between the rue Scribe and the rue de Rivoli, which were very popular with American tourists at the time, constituted a promised land whose "most sacred spot" was the intersection of the avenue de l'Opéra and the boulevard des Capucines.

As an American who settled in England and, during the Great War, became a British subject to express solidarity with his adopted country, James was a great European generally. Yet France (though perhaps he loved Italy more) was for him the foreign country par excellence, the place where the alert American could learn most about understanding what he called, in French, *l'entente de la vie*—that is, in the vocabulary of myth, the meaning and end of history. For James, life in Paris was more agreeable than life elsewhere because it was conceived more intelligently. Charming, gay, picturesque, and clever—these are words that occur frequently in his descriptions of the city. He liked everything about Paris, even if the "boulevard theater" was sometimes "too clever" and some Parisian painters were "odiously clever." Paris was a "vast, bright Babylon," but a very agreeable Babylon as well, "the most interesting of great cities."[19]

Conversation in Paris sharpened one's wits:

There were opinions at Woollett, but only on three or four [subjects]. The differences were there to match; if they were doubtless deep, though few, they were quiet—they were, as might be said, almost as shy as if people had been ashamed of them. People showed little diffidence about such things, on the other hand, in the Boulevard Malesherbes, and were so far from being ashamed of them—or indeed of anything else—that they often seemed to have invented them to avert those agreements that destroy the taste of talk.[20]

To be sure, in Paris salons it was customary at times, perhaps most of the time, to say the opposite of what one actually thought. This could be shocking. (Being American, James, although very elegant, was nonetheless, of necessity, a democrat.) Yet he believed that such verbal deceit, which offended Rousseau, was tolerable because Parisians used it not to win arguments or to hide what they truly believed but to enhance the pleasure of talking and listening. Admittedly, the statues and gardens of Versailles struck him as too well "administré," as did many other things in France (James used the untranslatable French word in his *Parisian Sketches*).[21] But all of this was part of the French décor, and James did not complain about it overmuch.

James understood the Paris of his time very well both in the large and in the small. For example, he treats the commercialization of art (a phenomenon that perplexed the Goncourts) intelligently and at length in his letters to the *Tribune* of 1875 and 1876. Unfortunately, in those letters James does not discuss the Impressionists, but it is clear that he had little sympathy for the highly official and "finished" or *léché* painting of the period; and what he says about a painting by Ernest Meissonier is reminiscent of what Baudelaire thought about the work of Horace Vernet, whose precision in representing uniforms, gaiters, and buttons could not make up for the mediocrity and meretriciousness of his inspiration. In his article on the Meissonier, James dwells on the $76,000 that a rich American paid to own the work, a sum so fabulous that although the painting at first struck him as mediocre, James ironically remarks, it was actually enhanced by the amount of money that someone was willing to pay for it. In Paris, he concluded, the presentation of art by dealers was in itself an art.

James's lengthiest explanation of what Paris could represent is at the heart of one of his finest novels, *The Ambassadors* (1903). The outline of the work is familiar: Mrs. Newsome, an invalid and a patron of the arts, is the widow of an industrialist from Woollett, Massachusetts (the name today sounds faintly ridiculous, and it did so in James's time as well, even before the invention of Woolite). She delegates her fiancé, Lewis Lambert Strether, a character in many ways reminiscent of the author of the novel, to bring her son Chad, who has ensconced himself in Paris for far too long, back to Massachusetts, where business is business.

Her messenger, or ambassador, Strether (who speaks for James and whose name pays homage to Balzac, the author of a novel named *Louis*

Lambert), knows France and its culture well and is especially familiar with its capital, where he has lived for a time. He expects to find Chad spoiled by a more or less dissolute bohemian life inspired by his reading of Henri Murger's *Scènes de la vie bohème* (1848; a work revived for James by the premiere of Puccini's *La Bohème* in 1896).

As it happens, however, Chad, the Parisianized young American, is a much improved human being, more sensitive to art and to *l'entente de la vie.* His Parisian companion, Mme de Vionnet, who is ten years older than he (and who is in fact his mistress, as Strether eventually understands in a belated moment of revelation), is a perfect woman, a flawless Parisian Diotima whose charm and dignity bring out by antithesis the chaste and rather vulgar superficiality of Mrs. Newsome, also a great lady, but in the manner of Woollett rather than of Paris. In the end things turn out rather badly. Strether, made infinitely more lucid by Paris, understands that he has wasted his life. His engagement to Mrs. Newsome is broken off. Chad appears likely to abandon Mme de Vionnet to return to the United States, where he will no doubt amass a huge fortune.

This novel, marvelously complex and difficult to read, will elicit an enthusiastic response from anyone interested in the history of Paris, not only because it is there that the plot unfolds but also because the text, which examines the moral transformation of two Americans in Paris, one young, the other old, subtly evokes the transformation of a Haussmannian and mythical Paris into Paris, capital of pleasure. James shows us Paris as a capital of world culture in which a young American can find his way, but we also discover in his pages a Paris in which a sensitive person can learn to avoid a modernity that has become a troubling phantasmagoria. Like Haussmann's Paris, Chad, who is fundamentally not very sensitive and not worthy of his French companion, has been "improved." But his renewal, like Haussmann's urban renewal, is in some respects troubling. His behavior has become theatrical and superficial. The young man wears a mask: "It's like the new edition of an old book that one has been fond of—revised and amended, brought up to date, but not quite the thing one knew and loved." Like Haussmann's Paris, in other words.

That James, an aesthete who was well aware of, and in certain ways anxious about, the capital's evolution from myth to phantasmagoria, should also have sensed the burden of Parisian alienation that we find in the mythifying work of Manet—and above all in that of Baudelaire—will come as no surprise. It is easy, moreover, to find any number of specifically Parisian and Baudelairean themes in James's writings, including the crucial theme of the flâneur, which occurs in one of his first novels, *Roderick Hudson* (1875). (There we learn, for example, that the first talent of the experienced flâneur is "the simple, sensuous, confident relish of pleasure"—a definition that Baudelaire would have understood although he would undoubtedly have wanted to modify it somewhat, since the flâneur in *Les Fleurs du mal* savors his pleasure but is powerless to satisfy his desires.)[22]

Two Parisian themes, then, that of the flâneur and that of the art market—which are conjoined in *The Ambassadors* with a third theme, that of the collector. In neo-Marxist literature (as has been described), the flâneur is an alienated character who cares deeply about his private setting, which for him is a refuge. The Benjaminian flâneur-collector is a superior if frustrated intellect who sets himself apart from a modernity at once despised and unavoidable. He strives to collect objects whose number and proximity give them a higher value than that attributed to them by the market, whose mechanisms he finds both contemptible and irresistible.

James understood this Parisian theme and developed it at some length. What a contrast we find, accordingly, between the apartment of an ill-informed modernizing transatlantic collector, Miss Gostrey, and that of Chad's Parisian friend, Mme de Vionnet, an aristocratic and discreet, not to say secretive, incarnation of history, who sets herself outside the new world, outside the new "society of the spectacle," and outside the present. Strether, when he calls on Mme de Vionnet, finds her surrounded by cherished objects that she has inherited, and whose elegance immediately sets her salon apart from Miss Gostrey's mediocre little museum as well as from young Chad's quarters, pleasant though they had seemed at first sight: "[Strether] recognized it as founded much more on old accumulations that had possibly from time to time shrunken than on any contemporary method of acquisition or form of curiosity. Chad and Miss Gostrey had rummaged and purchased and picked up and exchanged, sifting, selecting, comparing; whereas the mistress of the scene before him, beautifully passive under the spell of transmission—transmission from her father's line, he quite made up his mind—had only received, accepted, and been quiet."[23]

A disciple in some respects of the Goncourts, James believed that novels could be fictionalized but still scientific and historical narratives, and James the novelist had a full grasp of the history of Paris as it made its way from modernity to modernism: Haussmann, speaking in the name of progress and the future, had proposed a mythified, antiseptic Paris that was to be the incarnation of progress. Then, after his grand boulevards of the 1860s, came the resurgence of the myth of Paris, capital of revolution, with the Commune of 1871. And James in 1903 was keenly aware of all this history: Strether, leaning on the windowsill of an apartment in the Faubourg Saint-Germain, listens to the sounds that envelop him:

> The windows were all open, their redundant hangings swaying a little, and he heard once more, from the empty court, the small plash of the fountain. From beyond this, and as from a great distance—beyond the court, beyond the corps de logis forming the front—came, as if excited and exciting, the vague voice of Paris. Strether had all along been subject to sudden gusts of fancy in connexion with such matters as these—odd starts of the historic sense, suppositions and divinations with no warrant but their intensity. Thus and so, on the eve of the great recorded dates, the days and nights of revolution, the sounds had come in, the omens, the beginnings broken out. They were the smell of revolution, the smell of the public temper—or perhaps simply the smell of blood.[24]

Though often sharp-tongued on the subject of the French bourgeoisie ("the men do not look like gentlemen as so many Englishmen do"), James admired Parisian workers, whom he found more expressive, more intelligent, and above all more human than their English or American counterparts: "The Paris *ouvrier*, with his democratic blouse, his expressive, demonstrative, agreeable eye, his meagre limbs, his irregular, pointed features, his sallow complexion, his face at once fatigued and animated, his light, nervous organisation, is a figure that I always encounter again with pleasure. In some cases he looks depraved and perverted, but at his worst he looks refined, he is full of vivacity, of perception, of something that one can appeal to."[25]

Young and naive, Sally Pocock, Chad's sister, thinks she has understood Paris, its seductions and its mechanism—that is, the facile and legible Paris of Haussmann. But Strether, more profound and more modernist, is disoriented by what he sees, not only by the city's energy but also by the new complications of its daily life. The light of Paris blinds him, and throughout the novel James uses the city's light as a symbol to explain Strether's (and James's own) descent into himself, his groping toward greater complexity and greater doubt. Paris has changed Chad's life; and that life has also changed Strether: "It was dragging him, at strange hours, up the staircases of the rich: it was keeping him out of bed at the end of long hot days; it was transforming beyond recognition the simple, subtle, conveniently uniform thing that had anciently passed with him for a life of his own."

In attending to Paris and its history, Strether, in this respect a typical American, comes to understand himself better and also comes to understand the importance of love affairs in his life as well as the lives of Parisians. Here the more human myth of the French capital displaces the more severe myth of Puritan America, at least as it was experienced in Woollett.

Strether is already fifty-five when we first meet him. A widower, he has been left sad and even overwhelmed by the death first of his wife and then, a few years later, of his only child. On his arrival in Paris he compares himself to a museum-goer who moves from one canvas that is beyond his ken to another. Paris—even Paris—that "most interesting of great cities," cannot do much to compensate for this deep failure. But thanks to Paris, and to a Parisian woman, Mme de Vionnet, Strether becomes more clearsighted and honest with himself, as well as freer and more independent. He breaks off his engagement, and his career as an editor is probably ruined. (Mrs. Newsome is not one to tolerate insubordination.) Yet his failure brings him a strange satisfaction. He is diminished, resigned, and abandoned, but purified as well.

For AMERICANS in Paris, however, the great hour was not that of Twain, James, or Edith Wharton but that of the celebrated and rather sizable Lost Generation, the term generally applied to Ernest Hemingway and his many friends. Robert McAlmon, who had the happy idea of marrying Winnifred Ellerman, a wealthy lesbian who took little interest in his doings but gave him the means to discover American Paris in the Roaring Twenties, claimed to have been acquainted with some 250 American painters and writers living on both banks of the Seine.

What is most striking about this cohort of writers and artists is the superficial nature of their relation to the capital. The Paris that they treasured was a Paris that had never existed, a Paris found only in tourist brochures. Henry James studied Paris life closely: in the 1870s, when he was still young, he showed considerable interest in French politics, and, for example, he was among the first to understand, along with Léon Gambetta, that the future of the Republic was also the future of provincial as well as urban France. But one finds nothing of this sort in the Lost Generation. Would anyone reading the work of these writers come away with the slightest notion of what France had suffered in the First World War, of how bitter the aftermath of that war was, of how deep were the country's economic difficulties, or of how fascism first began to make its presence known? Was there nothing to be found in André Breton? Surrealism? Fauvism? Matisse? Picasso? or the Jewish and Russian painters of the Paris School?

The Lost Generation kept to itself. Its writers preferred to read their own works and the works of their disciples, and Paris at the time could boast of as many as five publishing houses specializing in the work of English-language authors as well as several English-language literary magazines, the most important of which, Eugène Jolas's *Transition,* was read by perhaps 4,000 subscribers between 1927 and 1936.

What then attracted the Lost Generation to Paris? For some, it was the low cost of living made possible by postwar rates of exchange. (The franc fell from 5.45 to the dollar in January 1919 to 50 to the dollar in July 1926.) F. Scott Fitzgerald and his wife had only $7,000 to their name. In New York this wouldn't have amounted to much, but, they asked themselves, might it not be enough to live rather well in Paris? Indeed, it is worth noting how often Hemingway and his friends commented in their work about the avarice of Parisians. This is not difficult to understand: since these writers' only relation to Paris was based on money and sex (the two often being inextricably intertwined), it is hardly surprising that the intellectual and moral qualities of the French men and women with whom they came in contact might have escaped them. One of Hemingway's characters, Jake Barnes, while seated in a café, calls a prostitute over to his table to talk and is dismayed, even shocked, by the young woman's inability to engage in conversation. But it is difficult to sympathize with his plight.

THE PARISIAN TRAJECTORY of African Americans in Paris, both in the period between the two world wars and after the Second World War, is of greater interest. Literary tourists like Hemingway and Fitzgerald were, in the main, consumers of an ersatz Paris, but their black compatriots were more involved in the city, and as sellers rather than buyers. In a phantasmagorical society of cultural consumption, this was a mark of originality and even of a certain grandeur.

To be sure, both black and white Americans traveled to Paris in search of a freedom in life and work that was unavailable to them in America at the time. But they looked for that freedom in different ways: whites in a phantasmagoria within reach of their empty wallets; and blacks for the most part in the survival of the myth of Paris as a home of liberty, in work, and in the ordinary joys and pleasures of Parisian daily life. It is therefore worth pausing a moment to delve into the history of the African-American presence in Paris, which is less well known but more appealing than the history of Hemingway and Gertrude Stein, whom an unfriendly Parisian critic has labeled a "pet-de-nonne gonflée de vanité méprisante" (a swollen, sugary soufflé filled with vain disdain).[26]

The first African Americans to arrive in Paris from the United States were probably the slaves of Thomas Jefferson, one of whom later became the mother of at least one of his children (as confirmed recently by DNA analysis). In the middle of the nineteenth century, free blacks from Louisiana also found their way to Paris. They spoke French, and some of them even owned slaves. But the modern history of African Americans in Paris began in earnest in 1886, when the actor Ira Aldridge appeared to much acclaim in the role of Othello. Alexandre Dumas, the grandson of General Dumas, whose mother had been a Haitian slave, welcomed the American actor with open arms: "My dear brother, I too am a Negro." After that, the number of black visitors to Paris increased rapidly. In 1894 W. E. B. Du Bois, who held a Harvard doctorate, often visited the Louvre and attended plays in Paris, especially those in which Sarah Bernhardt appeared.

An important milestone was reached in 1891 when Henry Ossawa Tanner (1859–1937), the son of a minister in the African Methodist Episcopal church, continued his study of fine arts by moving from Philadelphia to Paris, a city that for him was a haven of tranquillity. There he achieved genuine success: several of his paintings were featured in Salons from 1894 to 1899. Made a Chevalier of the Legion of Honor in 1923, Tanner became the patron and teacher of a whole generation of black artists in Paris. One of his paintings now hangs in the Musée d'Orsay.

Another African-American artist who thrived in Paris was a young female protégée of Rodin's named Meta Vaux Warrick Fuller (1877–1968), one of the first sculptors to portray blacks. Later, other black Americans, such as Lois Mailou Jones (born in 1905), enrolled in the Académie Julian, where Pierre Bonnard and Maurice Denis were also students.

Ideologically, as Du Bois's periodical *The Crisis* explained, the Great War raised a troubling question of conscience for black Americans. How could they not fight for democracy? But why fight for a white democracy that marginalized blacks? The warm welcome that black American soldiers received in France, the mythical fatherland of human rights, to some extent resolved this dilemma. About 160,000 African Americans served in France in 1917 and 1918, most of them fighting under the American flag, although some joined French units. (The American "brass" did not allow black American soldiers to march in the victory parade on July 14, 1919.) Conflicts between white and black American servicemen were numerous, and after one such incident at Saint-Nazaire, where many African-American soldiers worked unloading supplies, two members of the French Chamber of Deputies demanded that the government take steps to stop "the harassment, attacks, and crimes perpetrated on colored French citizens and subjects" (one was from Martinique) by American soldiers and M.P.'s.[27]

Jazz made its Paris debut with a black military band. Legend has it that at one early jazz concert President Raymond Poincaré, a man of very serious mien, forgot himself to the extent of keeping time with his foot. The clarinet and saxophone virtuoso Sidney Bechet arrived in Paris in 1919, and Josephine Baker's *Revue nègre,* carefully Africanized and staged by Parisian directors, opened in October 1925. Louis Armstrong came to Paris in 1933, and Duke Ellington took his music from Harlem's Cotton Club to the Salle Pleyel in 1934 and the Moulin Rouge in 1937.

The vast majority of black Americans in Paris led quiet lives, had daily contact with Parisians, and were not particularly close to their white compatriots, who in turn took little notice of them. "Everyone," we are told, came to Gertrude Stein's apartment on the rue de Fleurus: foreigners, tourists, and artists. But not everyone received the same welcome. Gwendolyn Bennett, a black poet and painter, was invited once for tea, but that was as far as things went.[28]

For African Americans, Paris was an enriching place. On the whole, Parisians welcomed them enthusiastically, especially the renowned musicians and restaurateurs among them. Josephine Baker's success is legendary, and the performer and club owner Ada Louise "Bricktop" Smith was not far behind.

The Paris Surrealists took a particular interest in these visitors and looked upon their presence (bourgeois though it was) as a premonitory sign of the impending collapse of canonical Western culture. And at the same time, some of the black Americans who went to Paris to discover France were quite astonished to discover Africa there as well. The Harlem Renaissance, though an authentic native product, owes more to Paris than is generally recognized. Langston Hughes (who as a young man had worked briefly as a busboy at Bricktop's restaurant in Montmartre), traveled to the French capital several times, as did his fellow poet Countee Cullen, who first visited the city with Alain Locke. For these writers, and for the Trinidadian Claude McKay, the Afro-French concept of *négritude* developed by Léopold Senghor and Aimé Césaire was an important influence.[29] Harlem gave an audience to black culture, but, as Abiola Irele has rightly pointed out, it was Paris that nurtured it, because it was in Paris that three important trends first intersected: first, the presence of a new African-American elite; second, modernist and realist currents in Parisian thought; and finally, a modernist Haitian and Afro-French literature that emphasized "Africanness," intuition, and spontaneity.[30]

Alas, most of this came to an end with the Depression, the Second World War, and the German occupation, but the African-American presence revived in 1945. In fact the 1950s marked a high point in exchanges between Parisians and black Americans. Thousands of black GIs settled in the capital, including Leroy Haynes, a former artist whose soul-food restaurant on the rue Clauzel enjoyed considerable success. Martin Luther King Jr.—for whom Paris does not seem to have been of great interest—went to Haynes's restaurant to unwind.[31]

In the 1920s most African Americans in Paris lived in Montmartre, which Léon Daudet of the ultra-right-wing Action Française called "a neighborhood of loathsome debauchery reserved for foreigners, mainly Americans." An American columnist, Joel Rogers, wrote: "The boulevard de Clichy is the 42nd and Broadway of Paris. Most of the nightlife of Paris centers around it, and most of the colored folks from the States, too. If you hear that some friend from the States is in Paris, just circulate around this boulevard from the Moulin Rouge down the rue Pigalle as far as the Flea Pit, and it's a hundred to one shot you'll encounter him or her, at least twice during the night." After the Second World War, however, most African Americans in Paris migrated to Montparnasse and its environs, where some 3,000 of them were still living in 1960.[32]

Of all the postwar African-American Parisians, the most celebrated was no doubt Richard Wright, the author of *Native Son* and *Black Boy*. A former Communist, Wright had been blacklisted by the U.S. Department of State, and it was only at the insistence of French authorities that he was issued the passport that allowed him to go to Paris in 1946. Wright and his family became permanent expatriates. Jean-Paul Sartre and Simone de Beauvoir introduced him to the capital's intellectuals. In September 1956, with Alioune Diop, one of the founders of *Présence africaine,* a journal of négritude, Wright organized a Congress of Negro Artists and Writers in Paris. W. E. B. Du Bois sent a telegram of congratulations.

Paris for these African Americans was still a capital of public freedom, as it was for others in a more private way. Chester Himes, whose detective stories were published in French before they appeared in English, went there in 1953 to find not just peace of mind but also sexual partners. Many white American men in the nineteenth century had done the same, but whereas they had sought to escape from puritanical repression, many black American men in the Paris of the 1950s sought in relationships with white women the affirmation of their right to be themselves regardless of their race. As Himes was to put it: "All of the American blacks whom I knew had white women . . . Richard Wright had his white wife, Oliver Harrington was a great favorite of all the foreign white women in the Latin Quarter . . . I never met an American black man at that time in Paris who wasn't living with one or more white women or married to one."[33]

For many black Americans, Paris in the Roaring Twenties meant jazz and Josephine Baker with her ephemeral suit of bananas, but for African-American writers, Paris in these same years meant modernism and an interest in things African rather than in Parisian politics, which during the 1920s and 1930s were dominated by conservative or even fascistic writers and politicians. But in the late 1940s and the 1950s, when the Parisian literary scene was dominated by communists and fellow travelers, life in the French capital for many African Americans was a lesson in implicitly or (as it was for Angela Davis) explicitly radical politics. Their experience was probably one of the last echoes of the great nineteenth-century myth of Paris as capital of liberty, and in retrospect this last hurrah was clearly more serious and more consequential for the future of America than the ephemeral events of 1968 were for France.

James Baldwin's stay in Paris, where he arrived on November 11, 1948, marks another threshold: with the author of *The Fire Next Time*, the heroic—or, if you prefer, mythical—story of African Americans in Paris came to an end. Black artists who travel from the United States to Paris today have no particular destination in mind. As Baldwin might have said, he didn't come to Paris; he left New York.

It was the American civil rights movement in the 1960s that transformed the meaning of Paris for African Americans. Before 1960, and even more before 1939, going to Paris meant choosing the freedom to be oneself. But after 1960 staying in Paris meant, at least in some measure, turning one's back on the fight for freedom at home. However at ease they may have been in Paris (and as David Leeming notes, Baldwin's *Giovanni's Room* is "the most Parisian of all African-American novels"), black Americans kept in close touch with events at home. To put it in a Parisian context, they had found themselves and had no further need of the French capital. Revealingly, Baldwin now said, in a comparison of his own book to James's *The Ambassadors*, that *Giovanni's Room* was like Strether's revealing journey: it was "about what happens to you if you don't tell the truth to yourself . . . about the failure of innocence." Paris had been, as it were, a learning experience that had come to an end.[34]

In Paris in December 1963 the painter Beauford Delaney, a close friend of Baldwin's, received a letter from Knoxville, Tennessee: "We have all been saddened by the death of our Beloved President," his brother wrote, "a dedicated man and loved by so many millions of people . . . the future looks dark." Whatever the complications of life in America, for black Americans like Delaney, after the assassinations of Martin Luther King Jr. and the Kennedys, staying in Paris no longer seemed the option it had been. In a 1961 film version of *Paris Blues*, Harold Flender's novel about black musicians in Paris, a black high school teacher visiting from Chicago admonishes a "Parisianized" black friend who has turned his back on America: "Things are much better than they were five years ago and they're gonna be still better next year. And not because Negroes come to Paris, but because Negroes stay at home." Of course Parisian African Americans were by no means passive in these matters: when in August 1963 James Baldwin and the actor William Marshall called on Americans in Paris to express their solidarity with King's March on Washington, about fifty people showed up, black and white. But gestures of this kind, which might have sufficed in earlier decades, no longer seemed enough.[35]

And perhaps there is a positive aspect to this change: perhaps the freedom that Americans once sought in Paris can now be found at home. "We go to Europe to be Americanized,"[36] wrote Emerson, but today that need has lapsed, and may even have been reversed. It is by visiting New York (or London) that many Parisians today come to understand the unique historical specificity of their own city.

IN 1890 the American Impressionist painter Childe Hassam took an interest only in those aspects of New York life that reminded him of Europe. After 1900, however, his paintings show us a "New-Yorkish" New York. The same is true of Thomas Eakins. And in a reversed motion, Parisian avant-garde painters such as Francis Picabia, Marcel Duchamp, and Albert Gleizes now crossed the Atlantic in order to grasp the spirit of modernism: the forms of New York soon found their way into Cubist painting. Picabia evoked the modernity of New York. The city overwhelmed these artists, as it did many other European Dadaists or constructivists like George Grosz and Bertolt Brecht, who had fled the millenarianism of the Third Reich and said of New York that the city seemed indestructible: built on rock, it would last a thousand years.[37]

Paris, capital of the nineteenth century; New York, capital of the twentieth century. Paris and ancient mythologies? New York and a New Age? In these two frames, we can at any rate begin to imagine the alpha and omega of our recent modernity and cultural history.

14

From Myth to Phantasmagoria

IN AUGUST 1855, upon returning from a performance of fifteen tableaux by Théodore Barrière and Paul de Kock entitled *The History of Paris* (Barrière had written a hundred pieces in the same genre), Théophile Gautier noted in his diary: "Paris is à la mode . . . It has been celebrating itself in the Dorian and Lydian modes."

Gautier was on the right track: for more than a century, from 1830 to 1940 or thereabouts, Parisians were indeed quite fond of adoring themselves. Indeed, a penchant for self-adoration may have been their *péché mignon,* their chief and not-so-secret weakness. But the real self-celebration of Paris took place less in the theater than in a century and a half of international expositions, most notably those of 1867 and 1889. For Walter Benjamin, expositions "took the place of museums" from 1850 to 1890. "Compare the ideological underpinnings of the two phenomena," he advised.[1] This is an excellent idea, because the international expositions that were staged in Paris were indeed museums of culture and of the imagination—not just figuratively but also literally, since they included displays of hundreds of paintings. For nearly a century the Paris exposition was a sort of general celebration of the myth of Paris, a city that in 1867 was still capital of the world but by 1931 had been whittled down to merely the capital of the French colonial empire.

Here, then, we have a recapitulation of the general evolution that led from the Republic of Letters in 1750 to the myths of 1830 and the phantasmagorias of Belle Epoque Paris, but generalized to the utmost degree. Fyodor Dostoevsky, a Slavophile of sorts, criticized Western-oriented Saint Petersburg—that creation of Peter the Great—as "the most abstract and intentional city in the whole world." But nineteenth-century Paris, mythified as it had become, was far more "abstract" and "intentional" than Saint Petersburg. Moreover, this dimension of the city's life was apprehended not by a mere handful of intellectuals (like Dostoevsky, his few friends, and his many enemies) but by vast numbers of ordinary people. Few of the Revolution's politicians had been welcomed into pre-revolutionary Parisian salons; the number of militant sansculottes was under 6,000; and Baudelaire sold only 3,000 copies of his works during his lifetime. These are paltry numbers. By contrast, millions of Parisians visited the expositions.[2]

THE FIRST GREAT international exposition, and perhaps still the most celebrated today, was the Crystal Palace Exposition held in London in 1851, which drew more than 6 million visitors (108,000 of them from France).[3] By way of comparison, the Paris Exposition of 1855, the French imperial riposte to the London event, drew only 5 million visitors. (The use of a new invention, the metal turnstile, to count the visitors presumably means that this figure is fairly reliable.) By 1867, however, those 5 million had grown to 11 million, and thereafter attendance figures continued to increase: to 16 million in 1878, 32 million in 1889, and nearly 51 million in 1900 (a figure not surpassed until the Osaka World's Fair of 1970).

The number of exhibitors followed a similar pattern: from 14,000 in London in 1851 it rose to 24,000 in Paris in 1855 to 52,000 in 1867 to 62,000 in 1889 and 83,000 in 1900. The Exposition of 1937 marked a precipitous decline in every department: it attracted only 34 million visitors and 11,000 exhibitors. It also lost a shocking amount of money. If we were to measure the success of these expositions and plot the results on a graph, the curve would rise steadily until 1900 and then fall off—at times sharply—until the eve of the Second World War.

THE NINETEENTH CENTURY was the great era of Parisian myth, but these republican and bourgeois myths had earlier roots: the idea of Paris as capital of the Republic of Letters, for example, goes back to 1750. It is no surprise, therefore, to discover that expositions, even expositions of industrial products, were likewise not a nineteenth-century invention, even if we generally associate them with that era.

In the Victorian age, exhibitions associated industrial prowess with capitalist performance. But the first Parisian exhibitions were differently oriented. For one thing, crafts were a pivotal concern. So, for example, the ancien régime organized exhibitions of artisanal handiwork in mini-expositions that could be seen as echoes of medieval fairs. The first of these was held in the halls of the Louvre in 1719. But with the Revolution, the theme of expositions moved forward, not yet to capitalism, but away from crafts and toward politics and their celebration. The Jacobins, seeking to reconcile the divergent principles of their ideology (individualism as embodied in the Le Chapelier Law, which banned workers' and employers' coalitions or unions, and communitarianism as embodied in a republic of virtue), outdid themselves in the invention of ecumenical ceremonies. Among the values they celebrated were social harmony, fraternity, and integration, symbolized by the harmony of soloists and choir, men and women, the elderly and the young. Besides the political-religious Festival of the Supreme Being there were political-social Maratist festivals of woe, as well as many commemorative *fêtes:* such was the variety of ways in which the Jacobins of Paris and the provinces strove to remind themselves (or to convince themselves?) of the underlying unity of their political doctrine.

From such universalizing concerns it was but a short step to the elaboration of a festival of industry, provided that industry, as in Diderot's *Encyclopedia,* could be cited and displayed to celebrate the ingenuity of the entire human race. Robespierre and Jacques-Louis David were well situated in 1792–1794 to understand the need for a festival of arts and crafts, but, though interested, they had little time to devote to such a project. By general agreement, then, the first great Parisian industrial festival or exposition opened on the Champs de Mars on September 22, 1798, six years to the day after the birth of the First Republic—and on that day of the year when the length of the night is precisely and symbolically equal to the length of the day.[4] The 110 exhibits featured already well known products such as tapestries from Les Gobelins and La Savonnerie, glass from Saint-Gobain, wallpaper, and clothing, but there were also some genuine innovations, including steam engines, industrial metalwork, and chemicals. The architect of the whole venture was the minister of the interior, Nicolas-Louis François (or François de Neufchâteau, as he styled himself; 1750–1828). The exposition meshed nicely with the neo-republican policies of the Directory, whose orientation remained Jacobin though only in a watered-down sense. The new imperative was to promote not the virtue of the republican farmer but increased production and trade—in other words, the market economy.[5]

Fittingly, therefore, the center of the 1798 exposition was the Temple of Industry, and visitors were explicitly invited "to pay homage to the tutelary deity [of industry] whose statue stood in the middle of the Temple."[6] In the minds of contemporaries, the ancien régime had been a time of indolence, inefficiency, luxury, fireworks, and ephemeral events. The Directory sought to invert these values by celebrating industry, emulation, and competition. Prizes were awarded to the best of the exhibitors, most of them Parisians, including the watchmaker Bréguet, the printer Pierre Firmin-Didot, and the textile works in the Gros-Caillou quarter.

The political novelty of this episode bears emphasizing. The Directory, which viewed the exposition as an important event, was socially conservative (as is clear from the speeches of François de Neufchâteau) but at the same time it was on the left, not only because it harshly condemned the ancien régime but also because it kept faith with the great principles of Year II even as it modified them. One sees this in the rhetorical trappings of the event: the Directors arrived in Roman garb, followed by republican processions with figures symbolizing the "Republic, one and indivisible"; and the day ended with a victory parade featuring Roman-style chariots decked with flags symbolizing the sovereignty of the people. Beyond republicanism, however, meritocracy was also recognized in its varied forms: Citizen Pierre Oriot, a 33-year-old butcher who lived on the rue de la Grande Truanderie, was acclaimed as the winner of the strong-man contest, and although the painter Carle Vernet failed to win the horse race, his was understood to be a noble effort nonetheless.

With encouragement from the scientist and minister of the interior Jean-Antoine Chaptal, Napoleon authorized a continuation of the effort to synthesize politics with industry (an amalgam that would matter a great deal to the Second Empire). In 1801 another exposition of the arts and industry was held in the court of the Louvre and sited once again on the Champs de Mars. This event was less republican but more appealing. It included an exhibition of painting and sculpture, where—or so we can assume—the art was meant to make up for the regime's "democratic deficit." The artists balked, however, at showing their work under the same roof as the craftsmen, and two halls had to be constructed, one for handicrafts, the other for fine art.

The Restoration also staged expositions in Paris, and the one held in 1819 was particularly successful. But the liberal industrialists of the time turned up their noses at these events, which were organized by a regime that they basically disliked. As a result, the Paris expositions held in this period were more crafts fairs than truly innovative industrial displays.

The advent of the July Monarchy turned things around a bit: industrialists played a prominent role in the Parisian expositions of 1834 and 1839. In 1844 the tenth Exposition de l'Industrie, held in the Carré Marigny, drew nearly 4,000 exhibitors, and the "hall of machinery" was much admired.

Matters became even more serious with the Revolution of 1848. In 1849, after a year of turmoil and insurrection, the exposition of that year with its 5,494 exhibits signaled a return to political normality. It was organized by Michel Chevalier, who, like many exposition organizers in this period, was first a leftist Saint-Simonian and then an apostle of liberalism. It is also interesting to note, in this context of changing politics, that the spate of expositions gave Eugène Labiche the idea for a vaudeville entitled "Expositions of Products of the Republic" in which an English—and therefore politically naive—visitor is seen contemplat-

Gino Severini, *Nord-Sud*, 1913. Modernism was a European current, but one in which Paris mattered a great deal; think of Proust, Picasso, Stravinsky, and Apollinaire. Here the new Nord-Sud subway (which dates from 1910 and would later merge with the Métropolitain) seems to rush through the city. Much to his credit, Severini was of all the Italian futurists the only one the fascist regime did not like.

Photo: Ernani Orcorte. GAM, Galleria Civica d'arte Moderna e Contemporanea di Torino.

Celestial Globe and Eiffel Tower, Universal Exposition of 1900. Globalization is not new. Economically, it reaches back to the Portuguese expansion of the late Middle Ages, and perhaps, for that matter, to the spread of agriculture in the neolithic age. Culturally, for Paris, globalization was born in the 1750s and reached its apogee during the 1840s and 1850s. In 1889 Paris was still, with London and New York, a capital of modernity. By 1900—despite this "celestial globe"—the tide had turned perceptibly.

Porte Monumentale, Universal Exposition of 1900. The Exposition of 1900 has left us many traces, but its most spectacular edifice, this impressive gateway, is unfortunately no longer with us. And yet it spoke for an age, as did its crowning statue of "la Parisienne"—chic, emancipated, willful, and faintly perverse, an odd mix of Sarah Bernhardt and Delacroix's Goddess of Liberty.

Galerie des Machines, Universal Exposition of 1889. The Exposition of 1889 was one of the great moments in the history of Paris, capital of the nineteenth century, and the crux of the fair was the Galerie des Machines, with, among myriad exhibits, 493 inventions by Thomas Edison. Paris, having become, thanks to Haussmann's rebuilding, an urban machine, seemed the ideal site to celebrate that mechanization of life which, thirty years before, had so horrified Baudelaire.

Photographic Archives, National Gallery of Art, Washington, DC, Gramstorff 11397.

Universal Exposition, 1900, shown inside "Ombres Chinoises" Toy Theater, ca. 1900. Pleasure crafts and gondolas float by in this "faux naïf" rendition of the new Alexander III bridge and the fireworks of the Universal Exposition. Music, fireworks, boat rides: a good time is being had by all. International expositions were about capitalism's adoration of itself, but they were also prefigurations of our own "theme parks," rather like the re-creation of "Gay Paree" in Las Vegas today.

Mauclair-Dacier, Paris, publisher. The Metropolitan Museum of Art, Gift of Lincoln Kirstein, 1970. (1970.565.508)
Photograph © 2000 The Metropolitan Museum of Art.

Giorgio de Chirico, *Gare Montparnasse (The Melancholy of Departure)*, 1914. Parisian Surrealism (the sequel to the Modernism of the 1900s and 1910s) was a truly international and even intercultural phenomenon. Surrealists were fascinated by non-Western myths and cultures, African, Asian, Native American, Mexican. Many of them came to Paris from abroad, such as Tzara, Dali, Magritte, Max Ernst, Meret Oppenheim, Man Ray, and Chirico. Surprisingly, although Paris mattered so much to Surrealist writers, it figures very seldom in the work of Surrealist painters, and Chirico's exceptional *Gare Montparnasse* owes much to an Italian tradition of cityscapes that was not shared by his new friends.

Gustave Caillebotte, *Paris Street; Rainy Day,* 1877. Paris is in our imagination as Haussmann rebuilt it, but we see his work through the eyes of the Impressionists, who painted it, by and large, after his fall from power. Often these renditions are amicable or admiring, as in the work of Manet, Degas, Monet, Morisot, Pissarro, and especially Renoir. They are more precisely and geometrically presented in the cerebral work of Caillebotte. This painting was displayed in the Impressionist exhibit of 1877, which Caillebotte organized.

Oil on canvas, 212.2 x 276.2 cm. The Art Institute of Chicago, Charles H. and Mary F. S. Worcester Collection, 1964.336.
Photograph © 2002, The Art Institute of Chicago, All Rights Reserved.

Gustave Caillebotte, *The Pont de l'Europe, Paris,* 1876. This painting speaks to many themes. Its first subject is the metallic modernity of Haussmann's Paris, with this view of a railway line and a bridge. But it also speaks to the individuation and solitude of life in Haussmann's Paris: the leaning worker pays no attention to the strolling bourgeois couple, whose elegant costumes (like the buildings in the background) have little to do with the architecture of the bridge. Even the dog's solitary promenade seems symbolic. Central to the aesthetic fame of "Paris, capital of world art" were the efforts of Parisian artists to capture the changing spirit of the nineteenth century, sequentially romantic, realist, and impressionist.

Oil on canvas, 125 x 180 cm. Petit Palais, Musée d'Art Moderne, Geneva. Erich Lessing/Art Resource, NY.

Henri Gervex, *A Session of the Painting Jury at the Salon des Artistes Français,* 1855. This academic canvas speaks for itself, but it gives us no clue to Gervex's breadth of spirit. We think of one school or type of painting as distinct and even hostile to other ways of seeing, but Gervex contributed to the state's purchase of Manet's *Olympia* and was a lifelong friend of Renoir and Degas. He also illustrated Balzac's *La Fille aux yeux d'or.*

Oil on canvas, 299 x 419 cm. Musée d'Orsay, Paris. Réunion des Musées Nationaux /Art Resource, NY.

ing one of the hundred or so liberty trees planted in Paris in the heady days of 1848. He is surprised to find that the tree is now stunted. The chorus sings: "Might it be the Paris air?"[7]

It was, however, not until 1855 that the first of the nineteenth century's twenty-six great *expositions mondiales,* or world's fairs, was held in Paris, one of six to take place in the French capital. As Alfred Fierro notes, "Only a country as proud of itself as France and a government as spendthrift as the French under Napoleon III and the Third Republic [were] prepared to bear the burden of the enormous deficit that events of this type could generate."[8] And indeed, from 1855 to 1889 the terms "Paris," "modernity," and "exposition" became synonymous in the minds of all who saw themselves as heirs of the Enlightenment.

There were several reasons for holding the Exposition of 1855. The regime of Napoleon the Small, as Victor Hugo labeled Napoleon III, was new. Its prestige needed bolstering by expeditions to the Crimea, Italy, China, Indochina, Senegal, and Mexico, to be sure; but it also needed to be enhanced in Paris. It was an affair of state that the Paris exposition be at least as impressive as the one at the Crystal Palace in London in 1851. The rivalry between the two cities was never far from the surface in this matter, even when it came to describing the weather: was it not obvious, Claude Vigier asked in an advertisement for the event, "that Paris, the metropolis of taste and leisure, offers its visitors a milder, purer atmosphere and a more cheerful and attractive spirit than the eternally fogbound city of London could afford?"[9]

Prince Napoleon, the emperor's cousin, known as "Plon-Plon" to his intimates, was named chairman of the affair. In his inaugural address, Plon-Plon presented expositions as a French invention (and an imperial one): he did not mention the Directory's republican expositions, suggesting instead that the Exposition of 1855 would consecrate the first years of the new regime "in accordance with the traditions of the first emperor." He did not, however, invoke this imperial past to explain why the imperial government had also decided that it would pay a private firm (the Compagnie du Palais de l'Industrie) to erect a building to house the exposition on land provided by the emperor. (The painter

Eugène Delacroix, displeased with this decision, commented that if this Americanization of business ethics continued in Paris, the Jardin des Tuileries would probably soon be up for sale as well.)

That the emperor would endorse his cousin's point of view was very much to be expected: politically, the Second Empire, a post-revolutionary regime that initially neither the left nor the right wanted, had to make do with whatever material was at hand, including international fairs. Napoleon III tried, as has been said, to please both the anticlerical nationalists (by defending Italy against the papacy) and also the Church (by defending Rome against Garibaldi). Likewise, Napoleon III needed to reassure the new industrialists, whose success would redound to the credit of his regime, while at the same time attempting to combat unemployment, the great fear of the working class. This was at least part of his reason for undertaking the reconstruction of Paris. (In view of some of the rather unorthodox methods used to finance that reconstruction, as well as the emperor's prior extra-legal and conspiratorial associations, critical humorists who had earlier said that the confiscation of the property of the Orléans family was *le premier vol de l'aigle,* a pun on the double meaning of *vol*—either "the eagle's first flight" or "the eagle's first theft"—now made fun of the emperor, a former Carbonaro, by saying that he had been sentenced to life at hard labor in Paris.)

The regime, in short, sought support on every side. For the Exposition of 1855, approval was expected from the Church whose blessing was invoked, from the bourgeoisie whose wares were displayed, from the workers (who would, at least in theory, now be able to buy things at relatively reasonable prices), and also from artists whose creations, handsomely remunerated, would ennoble the exposition, marking a high point in the age-old relationship between Parisian painters and the state. In this last instance the regime may have been more generous than it had to be: of the 5 million people who visited the exposition, fewer than a quarter would visit the fine arts section. But subsidizing the arts was doubly useful: countless French churches would eventually receive as gifts from the state religious paintings for which the government had paid an emperor's ransom, thereby pleasing both the churchgoing pub-

lic and the artists, whose attendance at Mass was often less than assiduous.

Beyond politics, the novelty of the Exposition of 1855 was no doubt
the cult of mechanization and the idea that the key to the future of humankind lay in industrialization, in a universal technological modernization of which Paris would be the beacon. The Goncourt brothers went
to view the exposition with Théophile Gautier: "We wandered around
that great, thing-filled monster known as the Exposition . . . A fantastic
Pantheon . . . A Babel of industry . . . A Coliseum for the Chamber of
Commerce, a Villa of Hadrian containing a compendium of the world's
monuments as reconstructed by . . . the Ecole Polytechnique, a Babylon
of the future, the Paris of the twentieth century."[10]

The two organizers of the exposition were both technocratic graduates of the Ecole Polytechnique: Michel Chevalier (once again), now
a convinced proponent of free trade, and Frédéric Le Play, a socially
minded Catholic. The daughter of one would soon marry the son of the
other. For them, the exposition was supposed to be a vision of the future.
The writer Eugène de Mirecourt grasped this idea perfectly in his *Paris
la nuit* (1855), which sketched a vision of what Paris would look like in
a hundred years, on the basis of what he had just seen of the exposition:
"A multitude of electric suns cast their rays upon the city from atop a
hundred immense light towers. They take the place of God's sun."
Night no longer exists. Stores are open around the clock. A gigantic
crystal palace built for the fictional Exposition of 1955 will celebrate the
splendors of this "infinite Jerusalem." Arsène Houssaye was no less lyri-
cal in *Paris et les Parisiens au XIXe siècle:* in the year 2855 the Champs-
Elysées would be "paved with iron pipes and covered with a crystal roof
[about which] the bees and hornets of finance [will buzz] . . . Capitalists
in Ursa Major will talk things over with arbitrageurs on Mercury! Why,
just today, shares were issued on the debris of Venus, half consumed by
her own flames."[11]

The cult of technology was here made both abstract and practical, because what especially aroused the enthusiasm of the Parisian crowd in
1855 were the innumerable objects—or, to speak more plainly, the

things—that industry had at last brought within everyone's reach: central heating, Singer sewing machines, metal furniture, cashmere and cotton fabrics that cost twenty francs rather than the four hundred that Mme Bovary had been obliged to pay (or rather had failed to pay) to the merchants of Rouen. The Coignard brothers staged a successful show that revolved around the supposed invention of a new machine that consumed entire sheep and turned out both lamb chops and wool coats at affordable prices.[12]

The exposition with its 5,000 exhibits was a great success. Somewhat carried away, no doubt, Abdelkader, a captured Algerian rebel, called it "the palace of intelligence animated by the breath of God." More down to earth, Ernest Renan remarked that "Europe [had] turned out to see the merchandise."[13]

The promises of 1855 were consciously developed in 1867. Once again the exposition had a political aspect and was part of the celebration of the Empire, whose luster had already begun to fade. Visits by the czar of Russia, the sultan of Turkey, and the Prince of Wales helped to refurbish it somewhat, however, as did Bismarck's next-to-last trip to France in the company of his friend General von Moltke and his master, Wilhelm, at that time still only king of Prussia but soon to become, after Germany's victory at Sedan in 1870, the first emperor of the Second German Reich, which would be proclaimed at Versailles. (When the two sovereigns met, Napoleon III gave Wilhelm a copy of the general plan of the soon-to-be-completed new Paris, which is invaluable to historians because the original was lost when the Hôtel de Ville burned in 1871.)

Diplomacy was only a sideshow, however. Now more than ever, the primary purpose of the exposition was to celebrate the progress of an entire civilization and to remind the world that Paris was the epicenter of that progress. Obviously, the Exposition of 1867 had to surpass the Exposition of 1855 in size; and its central building was surrounded by no fewer than 101 smaller pavilions housing exhibitions from Japan, Bavaria, and many other distant places. More industrial than its predecessor, the Exposition of 1867 was also better organized. Le Play, who again served as general chairman, changed the overall conception of the event.

In 1855 industries specializing in the manufacture of luxury goods had been placed at the center of a building whose metal frame was chastely hidden beneath a veneer of stone and plaster. In 1867, by contrast, Le Play proposed a vast oval gallery in which visitors would first view heavy machinery and other large objects like the artillery pieces manufactured by the German firm Krupp (with which the Franco-Prussian War was soon to make Parisians all too familiar) and then, as they moved toward the center, encounter displays of more refined objects, including works of art. The canvases of Jean-François Millet were particularly admired. As in a game of chutes and ladders, the center was special: it held a complete assortment of currency in circulation around the world, symbolizing progress, universality, and the social context in which globalizing progress must thenceforth be situated.

Not only was the new exposition larger in scale and more industrial than the previous one, but it was also more geographically comprehensive, including mosques, Russian dachas, Swiss chalets, Turkish kiosks, Swedish farms, English lighthouses, and even Egyptian palaces with stables of camels (the Suez canal was being built at the time). Special passes entitled certain lucky visitors to take in a mini-Egypt: the Champs de Mars contained not only a reproduction of the Temple of Philae but also a "collection of mummies." In these various edifices, Maxime Du Camp reported, young Parisian women, "décolletée, made up, impudent and provocative, dressed as Styrians . . . [or] Spaniards [or] Dutch, poured out drinks for passersby." An "International Publication Authorized by the Imperial Commission" explained: "The exhibition hall is round, like the globe, and to take a turn around it is literally to travel around the world. Every nation is represented: enemies live in peace, side by side. Just as the divine spirit in the beginning hovered over the face of the waters, so too does it hover now over this globe of iron."[14]

Clearly mythical in its conception, the exposition aspired to universality not just in space but also in time. Exhibits depicting the history of labor allowed visitors to survey the various stages through which European society had progressed on the way to its present superior stage of civilization. Equally noteworthy was the fact that exposition marked a turning point in the history of French education: seven hundred provincial schoolteachers were invited to Paris by the emperor.[15] One much-talked-about section of the exposition featured a display of textbooks. It was at about this time that the *leçons de choses* (primers in elementary science) made their first appearance; the Third Republic would later demonstrate a particular enthusiasm for this educational innovation.

In order to allow everyone to participate in the event, a number of new tramway lines were established to bring crowds from the capital to this open-air mass. Today's *bateaux-mouches,* the tourist boats that ply the Seine, first entered into service at this time as well: the *bateaux-mouches* of 1867 were small, fast-moving steam-powered vessels (*mouche* means "fly"), modeled on similar boats that had already seen extensive use in London. The enterprising Thomas Cook promoted the exposition as a pilgrimage site for tourists: under his auspices, some 12,000 English visitors made the round trip from London to Paris for an all-inclusive price of one pound, sixteen shillings:[16] the French, it seems, knew all about the economic and touristic importance of "theme parks" long before Disney. Indeed, the Goncourts, as one might expect, saw all this as proof of France's cultural degradation: "The Universal Exposition [represents] the Americanization of France. Industry takes precedence over art, steam-powered threshing machines consume space that might otherwise be devoted to painting, and there is nothing to see but covered chambered pots and outdoor sculpture—in short, the Federation of Matter."[17] Maxime Du Camp would later look back on this extravaganza as a harbinger of the terrible things to come in 1871.

The Exposition of 1878 was the least Parisian, least universal, and most nationalistic of the great nineteenth-century world's fairs. Its purpose was not to glorify Paris or modernity but simply to celebrate the rebirth of France after the wrenching and humiliating tragedies of 1871, defeat and civil war. On June 30, 1878, there was a Festival of Peace, complete with electrical illumination. The historian Gabriel Hanotaux said it was a "festival of the people [and] a veritable baptism of the Republic."[18] During the first week alone, some 200,000 people visited the exposition. They admired a pile driver manufactured by Le Creusot, a machine soon to be made famous by a celebrated children's book entitled *Le Tour de France par deux enfants* (Two Children's Tour of

France). A balloon known as Le Grand Captif and capable of lifting fifty people was also greatly admired.

By contrast, the Exposition of 1889 really did mark the apotheosis of Paris, capital of the nineteenth century. Inevitably, it was also a kind of fair. (The conservative writer Maurice Barrès once said that expositions mixed lemonade with prostitution.) Children enjoyed the Cirque Fernando and the opportunity to explore inside a blue statue of an elephant. So great was the overflow that Buffalo Bill was relegated to Neuilly along with his cowboys, cowgirls, and "redskins"—a cast of some 200 in all, plus 20 buffalo and 150 horses.[19]

All things considered, however, the Exposition of 1889 was more than a "show." It was also a significant and quite serious cultural "machine." Once again, the magnitude of the undertaking (958,752 square meters, 60,000 exhibitors) gives us an idea of the importance attached to it. The Exposition of 1878 lost money, but that of 1889 made a profit. Assisted by Adolphe Alphand (formerly Haussmann's assistant in the reconstruction of Paris), Lucien Dautresme, the minister of public works, oversaw the entire enterprise. A fixture in a changing world, this rather drab politician retained his portfolio through three successive governments: his project was obviously too important to be yet another victim of political instability.

The exposition, along with the new Eiffel Tower that was a part of it, filled several cultural needs. In the first place, it was clearly politicized (far more so than the Exposition of 1878, which had been only inadvertently republican). The inaugural date was carefully chosen: May 5, 1889, one hundred years to the day after the fateful meeting of the Estates General in Versailles that marked the beginning of the Revolution. Another reminder of that event came during the exposition itself, with the dedication of a plaster model of Jules Dalou's statue representing the triumph of the republic. Victor Hugo, the republican poet who had been buried in a grandiose Parisian funeral in 1885, was present not only in spirit but also in a historical panorama that showed him admiring an allegorical monument representing France flanked by other allegories of national defense, the fatherland, and work. A replica of the Bastille with the rue Saint-Antoine turned into a fairground with a balloon ride, a jousting arena, and a festival of Bacchus was widely acclaimed.

The exposition was not only staunchly republican but also—matters being as they were at the time—almost openly anticlerical. One of Gustave Eiffel's collaborators, Frantz Jourdain, who would later design department stores, spoke in praise of the exposition and its "bravely variegated architectonic palette, [which] delights the eye, reflects the sun, and exalts the triumph of the French spirit, of Gallic gaiety, and of rationalism," all in contrast to "a dreary and prehistoric scholasticism." The comparison was not calculated to please the Church, and Jourdain compounded the offense by contrasting the Gallic gaiety of the Eiffel Tower (one wonders exactly what he had in mind) to the ineffable sadness of the Sacré Coeur basilica, intended to expiate French sins, that had recently been built atop the hill of Montmartre—a position that inevitably made it the rival of the "300-meter-high tower." Catholic polemicists answered in kind: in a not very ecumenical spirit, *La Semaine religieuse de Rennes* opined that the "brand new Eiffel Tower is a Tower of Babel, a hideous, horrible, phallic skeleton that stands in stark contrast to the white of Sacré Coeur."[20]

The exposition was not only republican but also patriotic, with Danton's statue near the Odéon and two statues of France, one at the Palais des Industries in which France is shown distributing wreaths to other nations and the other, atop a fountain, depicting France bringing light to the rest of the world. It also displayed a social conscience: at the insistence of the Protestant politician and government minister Jules Siegfried, there was a building devoted to "the social economy" and workers' housing.

Most significant of all, the entire exposition was placed under the sign of triumphant science. Paris, which Haussmann had turned into the mythical capital of urban modernity, now became (in theory at least) the capital of progress, technology, science, and rationality—in short, of the ideology of "enlightenment" in the literal as well as the figurative sense, as it was illuminated by 1,150 arc lamps and 10,000 incandescent bulbs. The myth of Paris was made concrete and linked to the great ideas of the century, symbolized by the sculptor Jules Coutan's *Fountain of Progress,* in which progress was represented by a ship "on whose deck France stood in a Phrygian cap."[21]

The Gallery of Machinery was also much admired. It was built of modern materials, glass and steel, and stood 45 meters high, 400 meters in length, and 110 meters in width. As Albert de Lapparent rightly noted in his *Le Siècle de fer* (The Century of Iron; 1890), the exposition had "been celebrated, above all, to the glory of iron."[22]

The gallery, with its 16,000 machines, astonished people, but the tower built by the engineer Gustave Eiffel elicited real enthusiasm. True, there were nay-sayers. For Alexandre Dumas, William Bouguereau, Guy de Maupassant, and Ernest Meissonier, the tower was nothing but a vile smokestack, a horror "that even commercial America would want no part of, . . . a stain on the honor of Paris."[23] Most people admired it, however, and some even adulated it. It was not only marvelously light (it weighed only 7,300 tons, complete with its 2 million rivets) but, when it was built, at any rate, purposeful without purpose. (Later it was used for radio broadcasting and military observation.) What is more, there had been only one serious accident during its construction. From the first, the tower stood as a symbol both of Paris and of French patriotism: Eiffel himself climbed the 1,710 steps to the top and there unfurled a tricolor, the flag of France. "This," he proclaimed, "is the only flag to fly on a staff three hundred meters long." *L'Illustration,* a fairly progressive magazine at the time, published the unreservedly enthusiastic reaction of Frantz Jourdain: the tower, he said, "is mathematically implacable, like fate, and its proud head, above which the tricolor waves, seems almost worthy of divinity to the peoples of the world who for months have been repeating the name of the new deity with almost religious devotion." Agénor Fenouillard, a cartoon character, put it somewhat more provocatively: "This monument," he explained to his admiring daughters, comically named Artemisa and Cunegunda, is "a crown of glory thrown down as a challenge to other nations!"[24]

The Exposition of 1900 was even vaster than its predecessor and no less successful or widely renowned. In retrospect, however, it represented a clear ideological retreat: the festival of 1889 was intended to be a mythical event, the culmination of a series of political and scientific triumphs; that of 1900 was far more phantasmagorical.

To be sure, the 1900 exposition had its positive aspects. For example, it marked the inauguration of the first line of the Paris Metro, which ran from the Porte de Vincennes in the east to the Porte Maillot in the west. The new electric lighting on the Place de la Concorde also made it easier for the steadily growing crowds to find their way to the exposition by night. A moving sidewalk was likewise much admired. Last but not least, the Exposition of 1900 marked a moment of national and international pride. (As it happens, we have a precise measure of these sentiments in the record of ticket receipts from the various panoramas: the one representing the battle of Austerlitz brought in 42,127 francs; another of the Revolution earned 16,385 francs; but a third, representing the Crucifixion, took in only 5,139 francs.)

Czar Nicholas II came to lay the first stone for a bridge dedicated to his father: the Pont Alexandre III. Germany, absent from previous expositions, was much in evidence at this one: exhibitors from the German side of the Rhine took 2,000 prizes and honorable mentions, and there were more German visitors than English and Russian combined. Coming as it did after the pardon of Captain Dreyfus, the exposition also marked a moment of national reconciliation: 20,277 mayors were invited to Paris for one of the largest banquets ever held there. Each participant was entitled to two bottles of wine, and one might look upon this repast as a metaphor for the Third Republic: a Jacobin regime but of a very mild sort, run from Paris by provincial (and basically conservative) radical socialists of whom it was mischievously said that they were like radishes, "red on the outside, white on the inside, and never far from the butter dish."

Considerable effort was invested in attracting visitors, and it paid off handsomely. Eager to record their visit, 17 percent of them came with cameras (the first Kodak had been introduced in 1888). Many came to see and to ride the Big Wheel, a copy of the wheel designed by George Washington Ferris and featured at Columbian Exposition in Chicago in 1893, which could hold sixteen hundred people at a time. Some of the amusements were rather bizarre, not to say grotesque, such as "the upside-down manor house," a small, Gothic-style house that was built with its foundation up in the air and its chimney planted in the ground. Others were more successful: at the Exposition of 1867, Edmond de Goncourt had admired a "small, rustic Japanese house . . . with its bamboo fence, its gate with big sculpted flowers, and its tiny trees resembling flourishes of handwriting"; in 1900 the exotic element was magnified many times over, with huge panoramas that allowed Parisians to make virtual tours of the globe and to visit places such as India, China, and Portugal. In a disturbing prefiguration of the Colonial Exposition of 1931, some exhibits featured real, flesh-and-blood people. (Indeed, Tuaregs had already been displayed in Paris after the fall of Timbuktu in 1894.)[25]

Ideologically, however, what distinguished the Exposition of 1900 from that of 1889 was its relation to technology on the one hand and to contemporary art on the other—in other words, combining both themes, its relation to modernity. The Exposition of 1889 took place in an era when Art Nouveau formed part of a vast array of "public technologies" and social experiments. By contrast, the Exposition of 1900 presented Art Nouveau as little more than a style appropriate to small, "feminized" domestic objects having no relation to any broader historical trends. The modernizing rationalism of the Eiffel Tower gave way to a more modernist sensibility that was excessively private, not to say privatized, as represented at the exposition most notably by the Maison de l'Art Nouveau designed by Siegfried Bing. As Walter Benjamin explained, the real significance of the "modern style" lay not so much in its expression of personality abstracted from its social context: "[Modern style] mobilizes all the resources of interiorization . . . It represents the ultimate response of art besieged in its ivory tower by [industrial] technique."[26]

Another sign of this shift in modernizing—or anti-modernizing—sensibility can be seen, incidentally, in the simultaneous flourishing in Paris of a neo-Baroque style, which had become a critical aspect of the officially sanctioned art of the Third Republic, with the pseudo–Louis XIII style of lecture halls at the New Sorbonne and of the reading room in the old Bibliothèque Nationale on the rue de Richelieu, a defeatist, anti-modern shift that is also reflected in the contrast between Parisian Art Nouveau, which was often backward-looking and even reactionary, and the Jugendstil of Vienna, which eschewed all fake historicizing and was truly forward-looking.[27]

In this new and reactionary climate, the use of steel as an aesthetic element in architecture was also deemphasized at the Exposition of 1900. Although the Grand Palais and the Petit Palais had steel frames, these were now made invisible. The formal entrance to the exposition, the Porte Binet, was also made of steel, but what attracted the most comment was not the gate itself but the statue that crowned it, *La Parisienne,* a sixteen-foot-high effigy of an elegantly dressed Parisian woman based on a model provided by the couturier Paquin of the rue de la Paix. Ominously, while French exhibitors were rewarded for good taste, it was the Germans who took the prizes for scientific innovation.

The Exposition of 1889 had stood for Paris, the mythical capital of the nineteenth century. The Exposition of 1900 showed the world the aestheticized capital of a bourgeois ethic that was no longer supreme in science or master of its fate. Lenin was not wrong to think that the Exposition of 1900 revealed the gap between the bourgeoisie's dreams (he might have said phantasmagorias) and the realities of industrialism, realities that would display their unimaginably brutal and bloody side in the Great War of 1914–1918.

THE BACKGROUND of the Colonial Exposition of 1931 was even more troubling: here, the signs spoke of a worldwide economic depression, fascism on the rise in Germany, and, in France, a hidebound political regime in its death throes. Paris, once the capital of revolutionary freedom and later the capital of bourgeois modernity, had pulled in its horns by 1931: "The genius of Paris," wrote Paul Morand in 1930, "is precisely that of a meticulous peasant."[28] Paris was now the capital of a nervous nation and of a vast colonial empire. Yet that empire, despite its vastness, would collapse within a scant thirty years.

Because of the rapid evolution of a historical and postmodern sensibility, today even Stalin's communist empire already seems a relic of the distant past, as does the obsession of Parisian intellectuals with communism in the late 1940s and throughout the 1950s. And so does the Colonial Exposition of 1931. Yet in actual time it is not all that remote from us, as appears from a photograph of Marshal Lyautey attending the fair with a foreign dignitary, namely the Duchess of York, who would later be the Queen of England and later still the "Queen Mum," the mother of Queen Elizabeth II, who at this writing is still very much in possession of the British throne.

Like every other fair, the Colonial Exposition of 1931 was not without its immediate Parisian precursors and sequels. Looking forward, one might mention the Salon d'Outre-Mer held in Paris in 1933; an exposition marking the tricentennial of the French presence in the West Indies in 1935; and, also in 1935, a celebration of the fortieth anniversary of the conquest of Madagascar. New colonial pavilions were likewise to be erected in a compound on the Ile des Cygnes for the international exposition in 1937. And later still, the Vichy government, which until 1942 prided itself on its fleet and its empire, two remaining jewels in the crown of its otherwise precarious sovereignty, held celebrations in Paris honoring "colonial pioneers and explorers" and "a hundred and fifty years of colonial literature." Still, the Colonial Exposition of 1931, held in the Bois de Vincennes rather than in the center of Paris, was the chef d'oeuvre of this genre.

And looking backward, the exposition had had many precursors, reaching back to the Exposition of 1855, which included a colonial section. Colonial concerns were also present in the 1867 exhibit, which is not surprising given the military efforts of the Second Empire in Asia, in Africa, and (none too successfully) in Mexico as well. Nothing remains of the colonial buildings that were constructed on the Champs de Mars, but in the Parc de Montsouris a small-scale replica of the Bardo Palace in Tunis has survived to this day as an observatory. The Exposition of 1878 also had a colonial wing, but its extent was limited: a single building housed replicas of an Algerian mosque, a Tunisian bazaar, and a Moroccan shop.

Colonialism was more of a presence in 1889, the final year of a decade that witnessed a spectacular expansion of the European presence in Africa. The exposition of that year featured not only items from the colonies but also miniature replicas of African and Asian cities. The exoticism was rather third-rate and often of questionable taste. In a mockup of a Cairo street, for instance, visitors could admire the charms of the Algerian belly dancers in a place known as La Belle Fatma, a sight that apparently shocked the puritanical prime minister Jules Ferry, an earnest educator and colonialist. Semioticians will be interested to learn that the colonial section was placed opposite a mock fortress erected by the ministry of war and an exhibit devoted to "the social economy."[29] This conjunction of the colonial, the military, and the economic says a great deal about the motives underlying the colonialist ventures of the time.

The Exposition of 1900 marked another step forward (or backward!), but again the emphasis was on the picturesque side of the French colonial empire. Some of the organizers, including Eugène Etienne, a leader of the colonial lobby, would have preferred that prominence be given to the educational, commercial, and strategic goals of empire. The choice, however, was to put the lives of non-Europeans on stage, as it were: no one gave a second thought to the wisdom of exhibiting "the citizens of our colonies, soldiers and civilians alike, artisans plying their trades in the public eye."[30]

The imperial idea never had the importance for Paris that it had for London, capital of the British Empire, but it continued to make steady progress nonetheless. Thus, in 1913, in the course of planning a still larger exposition to be held at some date in the imminent future, Louis Brunet explained what was at stake: "Our overseas empire has grown. Its organization has been improved. Its wondrous resources have increased. The time has come to assess what has been achieved, to tabulate the vital results, and to acquaint the public with the facts and accomplishments. This is a job for an exposition." It was decided that this should be held in Marseilles in 1916, and that it should be followed by a new international exposition in Paris.

The First World War interrupted these plans. But on November 13, 1918, two days after the armistice, the municipal council of Marseilles revived the issue. Its zeal in doing so would bring disappointment: the

aims of the colonial exposition had become so grandiose that its planners no longer considered Marseilles a suitable venue. As a consolation
prize the city was granted a national-colonial mini-exposition, but the
great International Colonial Exposition that had been in the works for
ten years was now destined for Paris, with 1925 as the target date.

The magnitude of the project led to postponements, but in 1927 the
city agreed to site the exposition at Vincennes, with its picturesque lake,
and Marshal Lyautey agreed to serve as its general chairman. The presence of this fearless and incorruptible proconsul, who for years had been
an outspoken proponent of a social role for the army and had been able
to institutionalize his ideas as the de facto ruler of Morocco for more
than a decade, guaranteed that the project would be taken seriously. In
some respects Lyautey was irretrievably attached to the past. He was insistent, for example, on preserving the authority—or at least the appearance of authority—of the sultan in Morocco. Yet this Catholic army officer was also a bold modernizer. Casablanca was intended to be an
efficient, modern city, as Paul Rabinow has shown so well in his aptly titled book *French Modern.*[31] Lyautey's brand of colonialism aimed to lead
the vast segment of humankind still living in underdeveloped countries
into the modern world under the aegis of Europe and the United States.

The conceptual failure of the exposition was therefore commensurate
with the ambition of Lyautey's plan, if only because the Exposition of
1931 was at first intended as an international rather than a merely national—or Parisian—event. Originally the goal was not to celebrate the
power of France alone (and certainly not to glorify Paris) but rather to
portray French colonizing efforts as contributing to a great leap forward
for all humanity. In the event, this internationalist hope would be disappointed. Although Lyautey traveled to London twice (in 1928 and
1929) to try to enlist the participation of the British, they declined, as
did Germany and Spain. The United States was represented, but just
barely, with a replica of Mount Vernon, George Washington's colonial
plantation. Belgium, the Netherlands, and Portugal also participated,
however, as did, significantly, Mussolini's Italy. In his inaugural address,
the Italian minister of colonies, Prince Lanza di Saclea, thanked France
for her hospitality and expatiated on "the Homeric Odyssey of the white

race, which, having now reached every corner of the globe, has transformed, or is in the process of transforming, barbaric continents into civilized regions."[32]

And because the international aspect of the exposition turned out as it did, a different justification had to be proposed. Prominence was in consequence given to three themes: colonization as technological and moral modernity, which resonated with ideas of which Lyautey had long been the champion; colonization as an encounter between different but equally noble moral traditions, that of France and those of the colonized peoples, who were never portrayed simply as exotics but always as people with an undeniable dignity of their own; and colonization as a material advantage for France in the struggle for superiority among nations.

Propaganda for the exposition heavily stressed both the strategic and the financial advantages of the empire for all the French: "Mr. Frenchman, your colonies buy 14 billion francs' worth of goods from you every year and provide you with 8 billion francs' worth of raw materials. All this for what it costs to keep 165,000 colonial soldiers, an outlay of about 2 billion francs." In other words, 22 billion francs' worth of business for an expenditure of 2 billion. "How many of your investments earn that good a return?"[33]

Lyautey said much the same thing, though more elegantly, when he laid the first stone for the permanent Musée des Colonies in November 1928: the exposition would be "essentially economic and practical in character." It would serve as a point of departure for various "permanent institutions," including a Maison des Colonies and a Colonial Office, which would gather under one roof bits and pieces of the colonial administration that had previously been scattered throughout Paris. Symbolically, Lyautey therefore insisted that two welcome booths (he called them "loges de concierges") be placed at the entrance to the exposition as a service to French and foreign businessmen and industrialists looking for information about business opportunities in the colonies.[34]

The exposition also gave prominence to the role of the colonies as a potential source of military assistance for the defense of the mother country. France, short of native sons, had been obliged to call on the colonies in the past and might need to do so again in the future. A million colonials had fought or labored more or less forcibly under the French flag in the First World War, and perhaps as many as 250,000 of them had died for their adoptive and not very grateful fatherland. Now the idea was that the colonies constituted a "greater France," *la plus grande France,* as mentioned in the title of a book published in 1928 by Léon Archambault, a radical socialist deputy who served as secretary of the National Assembly's budget committee for the colonies.

For all the emphasis on practical themes, however, the Colonial Exposition was more than anything else a mystical celebration. France's colonial effort (a latter-day "gesta dei per Francos"; gesture of God through the Franks) was presented as an important chapter of the national epic. The magazine *La Vie* asked whether "the colonial campaigns are not in reality our tenth and eleventh crusades."[35] And were not the great colonizers (such as Pierre Savorgnan de Brazza), who had often led lives of pain and sacrifice, the true successors to the knights of old?

Mystical and practical, but nonetheless apolitical: one would have searched in vain around Daumesnil Lake for an explanation of the various types of government that the Republic had deemed it useful or prudent to establish in its various colonies: Algeria was treated as a département of France; Morocco was a colony administered through a local regime; colonies in French Equatorial Africa and French West Africa were administered directly. In some places colonials were integrated with their French administrators to one degree or another (this was true of certain Algerian and Senegalese veterans), while in other places such as Indochina local elites were systematically excluded from positions of power. None of this was made clear at the exposition.

Nor was there any sign of the early political rumblings of what, after the Second World War, would become a successful colonial liberation movement. The war in the Rif mountains of Morocco (which had eventually led to Lyautey's removal from Morocco), the bombardment of Syria, and the first glimmerings of communist rebellion in Indochina went unmentioned.

In 1920 a radical socialist minister, Albert Sarrault, had laid down as a fundamental principle that any colonial exposition should be a "living apotheosis of France's foreign expansion under the Third Republic." In

367

1930, however, a book published with the backing of François Pietri, the Bonapartist minister of the colonies, made no allusion to the Republic.[36] Republican political references were just as rare in ceremonies connected with the exposition. Léon Gambetta's name was never mentioned, nor was that of his disciple Eugène Etienne. There was a ceremony honoring Jules Ferry, but in his native Saint Dié rather than in Paris.

The exposition, which was silent on the theme of colonial politics and had little to say about the Republic, was by contrast quite eloquent on the subject of the colonizers' *mission civilisatrice.* The work of both Protestant and Catholic religious missionaries was abundantly discussed (at Lyautey's insistence). The Alliance Israélite, a Jewish and francophone charitable and educational organization, was not mentioned, although it was one of the sponsors of the Jewish Palestinian pavilion, whose chair hailed both Judeo-Arabic friendship and the "civilizing task" of France and Great Britain.[37] The League for the Instruction of the Illiterate was asked to set up a branch of its "French School for Natives" at the exposition site.

The theme of France's civilizing mission was also justified by antithesis: in the Dahomey pavilion, for example, visitors and participants could view a "Tower of Sacrifices" consisting of skulls mounted on long stakes, the skulls (according to the Exposition Guide) being all that remained of slaves executed by the Dahomeyan chieftain Behazin, who had once sought help from the German Empire.

Lyautey's top deputy in planning the exposition, Marcel Ollivier, later gave a lengthy explanation of what had been meant by the choice of "cultural progress" as a theme:

> In 1910 it was natural to focus on exoticism, which was then brand new. The idea was to recapture, but with new luster and greater sincerity, the picturesque, albeit false and at times outrageous, ambiance that had been responsible for the success of the colonial sections in the Expositions of 1878, 1889, and 1900 . . . [But] another thought . . . animated . . . the initiators of the impending exposition . . . Therefore, as the importance of the colonial experience became clear to everyone, the initial conception of an Exposition of Exoticism was expanded and enriched and di-

rected toward nobler ends. The idea was no longer to use architectural pastiches and crowds of actors to reconstruct an exotic ambiance artificially but rather to allow visitors to see an impressive compendium of the results, present realities, and future of colonization.[38]

The argument was a subtle one. On the one hand it was essential to show that these far-off lands were making progress toward civilization thanks to colonialism. But it was also necessary to underscore the intrinsic nobility of non-European cultures. The contrast was interesting, in some ways reminiscent of the exposition's zoo, in which animals were allowed to roam "in apparent freedom."[39]

A proposal by the Fédération Française des Anciens Coloniaux (FFAC) to display male and female Pygmies was therefore dismissed out of hand. The organizers let it be known in no uncertain terms that there would be no place at this exposition for humiliating exhibits of indigenous eccentricities. Excluded from Vincennes, the FFAC nevertheless imported a Melanesian village, which they set up in what had been a zoo in the Bois de Boulogne at the opposite end of Paris. There, in a hut devoted to the subject of cannibalism, Alain Laubreaux, a journalist of the extreme right who would later play a minor role at Vichy, ran into a former Melanesian student of his, a man named Prosper. As a child in New Caledonia, Prosper "had attended the mission school every day. In those days, he, like all children of France, knew that his country was once called Gaul and that the Gauls were his ancestors . . . And now I find him twelve years later, a cannibal in Paris."[40]

The aesthetics of the exposition, traces of which remain today at the Porte de Vincennes as well as in plaster models at the Musée Guimet, captured rather well the various inspirations of its organizers. One salon, named for Marshal Lyautey, was particularly eloquent in this regard. Behind an armchair conceived "on patriotic and republican themes"[41] (featuring a rooster flanked by symbols of the Republic) were murals by André-Hubert and Ivanna Lemaître "evoking Asia's contribution to France by way of the Vedic myths," Indian myths in Sanskrit said to derive from a revelation of Brahma. Another salon was named for Paul Reynaud, minister of colonies at the time, and it featured a symbolic evocation of "the spiritual contribution of the Maghreb." Here visitors could see an imam who bore a remarkable resemblance to traditional paintings of Christ; a woman wearing a veil and holding a sacred text open in her hands; and a mounted lancer, a sort of Muslim Saint George attacking a winged dragon. Other frescoes portrayed the French nation as handmaiden to the goddesses of justice and liberty.

All the buildings were very carefully designed, perhaps too carefully according to Charles-Robert Ageron, who noted that this was "an art show . . . [in which] architectural beauty and color at times outweighed the strict requirements of realism." For instance, the Cameroon pavilion, which was supposed to be a plausible reproduction of a "Bamoom hut," may have been too successful. André Maurois admired its "red, white, and black friezes, like the decorative bands on an ancient Greek vase." Similarly, a replica of the Temple of Angkor Wat resembled a cathedral with an Asian accent and was obviously meant to portray colonialism as the convergence of the spirituality of the West with that of the colonized East. Maurois made the analogy explicit: viewed from the Tonkin pavilion, the Cambodian temple reminded him of Notre-Dame viewed from the Ile Saint-Louis.[42]

The use of electricity—the "sound-and-light show" aspect of the exposition—also struck many visitors. Was it meant to draw in tourists? Of course. But the lighting of Angkor Wat and of the much-admired Fountain of Totems also had a symbolic value. The floodlights aimed at the temple expressed Lyautey's idea of what the work of the colonizer should be: the light was to the temple what France was to her colonies.[43]

The Surrealists and the Communists were critical of the exposition, indeed quite vehemently so: "Respond to the impressive speeches and construction by demanding the immediate evacuation of the colonies and indictment of the generals and officials responsible for the massacres in Annam, Lebanon, Morocco, and Central Africa."[44] A counter-exposition was organized: the poets Louis Aragon and Paul Eluard supplied some fine pieces of primitive art from their private collections, which they displayed next to some rather dismal religious statuettes. The former were labeled "black fetishes," the latter, "white fetishes." For Lyautey, the exposition, while recognizing the nobility of non-Europeans, was also supposed to underscore the gap between the technical prowess of the West and the primitive state of the colonies. For the Surrealists the gap was just as vast, but in their minds it was the gap between the fertile mysteries of primitive art and the sterility of a mechanical, indeed hypermechanized, society, of a Haussmannian Paris they despised. In a more satirical but milder vein, *Le Canard enchaîné* claimed that Josephine Baker had been anointed "Queen of the Colonies." After the eminent deputy Auguste Sabatier delivered a welcoming speech, according to the paper, Baker allegedly replied: "Me much pleased with Missi Sabati. Me teach him belly dance and roly-poly and hanky-panky and all that . . . Big brain Missi Sabati. Ooh, yes!"[45]

Despite such satire, the counter-exposition drew only 5,000 visitors, while the exposition could boast of more than 33 million visits by 8 million people, including 4 million Parisians. Several thousand students arrived in "scholastic caravans." André Tardieu (a future prime minister who at the time was nicknamed "Tardieu l'Américain") was not altogether wrong to declare the exposition an enormous success, "a triumph, a lesson, a hope." Lyautey (who, before agreeing to serve as chair, had taken the precaution of insisting on the extension of the Number 8 Métro line to bring in crowds of visitors) commented in November 1931 that the exposition had scored an "unhoped-for success." For Lucien Romier, a friend of Marshal Pétain and a future minister of Vichy, the enthusiasm of the crowds fulfilled the expectations of the organizers: "The Colonial Exposition restored the nobility of Europe."[46]

"With thoughts of patriotic solidarity and fraternal union," predicted Jean de Castellane, president of the Conseil Général de la Seine, at the inaugural ceremonies, "peoples will come to Paris to examine, appreciate, and admire, against the cheerful backdrop of this verdant wood, the veritable image of integral France, the France of the five continents."[47] No doubt. But that was not how the Parisians of 1871, whether friends or enemies of the prefect Haussmann, had conceived of their city. Revealingly, a great fad for regionalist (that is, anti-modern) novels swept France in the 1930s, and one might say that, for Parisians, the discovery of their colonial vocation was a sad analog of that backward-looking view of the world.

THE EXPOSITION OF 1937 also marked a step backward, but in a different way. For Jean Favier, this exposition as a whole had "no particular purpose." But there were two pavilions that everyone remembers. They stood opposite each other, each symbolizing the advent of a new civilization: the one communist, from the USSR; the other fascist, from Nazi Germany. Paul Valéry wrote a long article in which he invoked the memory of Descartes: "Because of its date, which is the three-hundredth anniversary of the *Discourse on Method,* the whole exposition points toward . . . a melding of history, philosophy, and poetry." For the Republican heirs of Descartes, however, the exposition marked a resounding ideological and pragmatic failure, even if it did provide a number of republicans in charge of "major [Paris] media outlets" with an opportunity to reinforce their "apparatus."[48]

The Exposition of 1937 demonstrated a retreat not only on the political but also on the architectural front. The Exposition of 1889 had marked the year of steel, the year of Paris triumphant, capital of modernity. If the Exposition of 1900 had already been a step backward, it nevertheless had sought to establish a link between tradition—the sinuosities of yesterday's baroque—and the contemporary modernist or so-called *nouille* (spaghetti) style. Seemingly the intention in 1937 was again to emphasize the modern, because its point, ostensibly, as noted by André Laveillé (who was, with Jean Perrin, influential in the design and style of the Palace of the Exposition), was to break with the past: "All the tangles of women with ample bosoms and over-elaborate displays of foliage have disappeared to make way for a sober and solid architecture in which strongly accentuated verticals mark the impulse toward progress and clearly delineated horizontals indicate the eternity of committed work." In fact, however, the architecture of 1937 was backward looking in that it yearned to mark a return to the classical monumentality of monarchical France. The modernist style of the German and American Bauhaus had no place in this Parisian display. Similarly, Edmond Labbé, one of the leading organizers of the exposition, explained that one of its aims was to entertain and thus to win back the attention of "our sons and daughters who today, in order to shake off their boredom, look to American Negro tunes—which are to be sure surpris-

ingly vigorous—or to rhythms dear to Parisian gangsters" (the celebrated Apaches).[49]

Another sign of this turning backward was an exhibition of 1,300
works of art, including 430 paintings, mounted at the behest of the
painter Robert Delaunay and authorized by the prime minister, Léon
Blum. The idea was to legitimize Impressionism and Modernism, but
what it did instead was to emphasize the long-term continuity of metropolitan French and Parisian culture. Virtually no machines were exhibited in the French pavilion, but the display of French traditionalism was
impressive.

PARIS, capital of the French Empire, may have seemed important in
1931, but compared with Paris, capital of the nineteenth century, it
really did not amount to much. Myth and phantasmagoria, alas. Paris,
once the capital of modernity, had not yet become the capital of world
nostalgia, but it was nonetheless far removed from what it had been half
a century before. In the shrinking of its ambitions, we have to see the in-
timations of coming catastrophe. The road was to be very short—far
shorter than even the most pessimistic had imagined possible—from
the cultural failures of 1937 to the military disasters of 1940 and the occupation once again of Paris by a victorious German army.

15

The Surrealists' Quest

WHAT IS THE DEEP NATURE of the self? What are the innermost structures of the psyche? These were the great questions of the Surrealists.

Of their various methods for revealing the recesses of the unconscious and reestablishing contact with our primitive and primary nature, the most celebrated was no doubt automatic writing. This, they believed (at least for a time), was the best way to reveal humankind's mysterious drives: the horrors of the Great War had in a sense left everyone speechless, and in that context composition by intuition was an acceptable solution.[1] In the First Surrealist Manifesto, André Breton offered this definition: "Surrealism: masculine noun. Psychic automatism by means of which it is proposed to examine either orally or in writing or in any other way the real operation of thought."

Another favored method was *not,* as one might expect, drugs, even if there were true drug addicts among the Surrealists, such as René Crevel, Antonin Artaud, and Jacques Vaché, the last of whom died of an overdose and had obtained drugs "from the bathroom attendants at Le Dôme and La Jungle." Rather, it was what they called "objective chance."[2] By this they meant chance encounters and random occurrences: by juxtaposing words and images chosen at random, they believed, they should be able—collectively—to come up with otherwise impossible images and marvelously suggestive new sentences. The classic example, for which we are indebted to the Surrealist phalanstery on the rue du

Château, is still "The exquisite corpse will drink the new wine." Similarly, for Max Ernst, Surrealist painting began with ostensibly aimless rubbing. (Breton described this *frottage* as "the true equivalent of automatic writing.") Paper covered with graphite was set down at random on a parquet floor, and then, "through a series of spontaneous suggestions and transmutations, similar to hypnagogic visions, the images obtained in this way will gradually shed the characteristics of the interrogated matter [the wood] and emerge with unexpected clarity, very likely in such a way as to reveal the primary cause of the obsession or to produce a likeness of that cause."[3]

Their oneiric connections were therefore of all kinds, but for many Surrealists the dreams and fantasies stimulated by the oddities and wonders of life in the French capital were the best of all. Back in the days of Napoleon III, people had read Emile de Girardin's anecdotal Parisian reportage with a certain anxiety: Girardin's innovative journalism appealed because it reminded them that in a decorporatized society revitalized and destabilized by capitalism and industrialism—that is to say, in the Paris of their day—anything could happen to anyone at any time and sometimes did. By the 1920s, however, what had worried the unenlightened petit-bourgeois readers of the popular press in the 1860s now delighted the clever and "disenlightened" Surrealists. "Paris," Breton wrote, "your monstrous reserves of beauty, youth, and vigor—how I would love to extract from your brief nocturnal hours all that exceeds the contents of the polar night! How I wish that everyone were capable of deep meditation on the eternal, unconscious powers you harbor within, warnings to all against the dangers of forbearance and retreat!"

As inexplicable as they were unpredictable, the same random Parisian events that had caused anxiety in the nineteenth century were now elevated by the Surrealists—in an age of modernism—to the status of "objective chance" and turned into objects of delight. Breton dwelt on this theme at length in his novel *Nadja*: "The human heart, a lovely seismograph. Realm of silence . . . It will always be enough if the morning paper brings me news of myself." This was followed by an account in telegraphic style of an airplane lost over the ocean, a story having nothing (or everything?) to do with the story of Nadja. For Louis Aragon in the

375

Passage de l'Opéra, for Philippe Soupault on the Chaussée d'Antin, and for Breton on the rue Lafayette, a walk in Paris was a way of looking at the city from this skewed angle, "as it crosses one's path."[4] Breton explained the principle in *La Clé des champs*:

> The steps that for years and years take us back, for no compelling reason, to the same places in a city attest to our growing sensitivity to certain aspects of the place, which for obscure reasons strike us as favorable or hostile. A walk down even a single street, provided it is long and varied enough, such as the rue Richelieu, can, if we pay close enough attention, take us, within an interval that we could specify precisely, through alternating zones of well-being and malaise. A map of great significance, perhaps, could be drawn up for each person by indicating in white the places he frequents and in black the places he avoids, with a range of grays in between marking lesser degrees of attraction and repulsion.[5]

The Surrealists' Paris was thus the focal point of an inward quest for mystery, surprise, and astonishment. In this city everything was a matter of allegory, of fortuitous encounter, of objective chance and convulsive beauty—once again, the exquisite corpse. As Aragon explained in his early, pre-Stalinist style, "There are relations other than the real that the mind can grasp, and which are just as primary, such as chance, illusion, the fantastic, the dream. These various species are brought together and reconciled in a genus called Surreality." The alert observer was more likely to find these quasi-magical objects in Paris than in any other city; they were "locks that do a poor job of sealing off the Infinite," and by fiddling with them more or less spontaneously a person could gain access to his innermost self. The classicist Academician Paul Valéry wrote that he would "infinitely prefer to write . . . something poor in full consciousness than to bring into the world by way of a trance . . . the most beautiful of masterpieces." But for the Italian Surrealist painter Giorgio de Chirico in 1924, the allure of Paris lay in the fact that in that city "ogni muro tapezzato di réclames è une sorpresa metafisica; e il putto gigante del sapone Cadum, e il rosso puledro cioccolato Poulain sorgono con la solennità inquietante di divinità dei miti antichi" (every wall covered with advertisements is a metaphysical surprise; the gigantic putto for Cadum soap and the red foal for Poulain chocolate rise with the troubling solemnity of ancient myths).[6]

In Paris, for Aragon and many of his friends, "the strangeness of certain neighborhoods [is] like their second face; the face that seems more accessible is only the most superficial aspect." For the Surrealists, the map of Paris was like a map of their own psyches, mysterious for the time being but perhaps decipherable before long. "Pluck out my heart," exclaims Aragon's Paysan de Paris (Paris Peasant—the title of one of Aragon's books), "and in it you will see Paris." At the sight of one or another of the capital's landscapes, this shrewdly naive (hence his "peasant" status) native of the city experiences a malaise of which Paris is at once the cause and the perfect expression: "Before me stretches a vast, deserted space, a sort of restful meadow. My word, it's the Restaurant Saulnier . . . the avenue Secrétan was deserted at that hour, wholly surrendered to the void." For Breton, as Marie-Claire Bancquart observes in her excellent book on the Surrealists' Paris, this "city is modeled on the poet's unconscious, lends itself to his way of doing things, and either reinforces his certainty or creates it."[7]

In the Jungian theory of the collective unconscious, Paris might well prove to be, of all the cities of the world, the one most apt to facilitate the encounter—crucial for artists—between conscious reasoning and the contents of the unconscious mind. In the random occurrences of the capital's streets, the self-psychoanalyzed flâneur hoped to find the event or object that would suddenly and unexpectedly reveal the depths of his being, hitherto unsuspected aspects of his psychic existence. "I love people," Breton wrote, "who allow themselves to be locked up in a museum at night so that they can contemplate at their leisure, after hours, the portrait of a woman illuminated by a veiled lamp. Clearly, they need to know more about this woman than we do." Similarly, by shutting themselves up in Paris, by opening themselves up to Paris, the Surrealists believed they could achieve a higher level of consciousness about their city and themselves. For Walter Benjamin, Breton's explanation was tantamount to "an inward metamorphosis of the museum."[8]

But whatever one thought of museums, for the Surrealists the best museum was Paris itself. For them the capital was like a collective unconscious, a diffuse collective memory in which anyone could find sudden inspiration by walking around intelligently. Paris represented "an overdetermination, a mistress of poetry," and dreamed "its own existence, because a dream is a release of energy." Paris was at once the most mysterious and mystical of places, a place that destroyed the familiar relations among objects by inciting the dreamer to dream more ambitious dreams. "On the boulevard de la Madeleine they've just knocked down a big chunk of realism," Aragon wrote in 1924, "and through the breach you can see a little of the landscape that continues in the work going on at the Moulin-Rouge, around Cité Véron, in the demolition of the city's fortifications, in the sculpture gardens of the Tuileries, at Les Gobelins illuminated at night by the phosphorescent letters of the word Pardon, and in the vaults of the Metro where Poulain Chocolate's golden horses gallop."[9]

Eugène Sue wrote *Les Mystères de Paris* for readers fascinated by what remained of the criminality of a bygone era—a remnant that had no place in the legible, rationalized, Cartesianized Paris soon to be created by Haussmann. The Surrealists did the opposite. For Breton, Aragon, René Magritte, Max Ernst, and Man Ray, the modernized, planned, bourgeois, mechanized Paris of the Second Empire was necessarily a fraud, an unhealthy illusion, an inversion of life: Haussmannian facades were as depressing as the doorless, windowless streets in the paintings of their friend Giorgio de Chirico. Only mysterious Paris was truly worth anyone's attention.

Paris from 1750 to 1830 or 1840 witnessed the rise of myth; 1890 marked the descent into phantasmagoria of Paris, capital of pleasure. And a third phase began with Dada's arrival in Paris in 1920, followed by the Surrealist Manifesto of 1924 (Surrealism began as a dissident movement within Dada). Breton, Aragon, and Soupault ushered in the

---

Man Ray, *289 boulevard Raspail,* 1928. Since visual Paris did not interest the Surrealists as much as the unexpected thoughts that the city's unexpected sights might trigger, some Surrealist artists made of the city's monuments what Dali called "objects of symbolic function," as Man Ray did with this bizarrely incomplete building on the boulevard Raspail. Photo provided by Telimage, Paris. © 2002 Man Ray Trust / Artists Rights Society (ARS), NY / ADAGP, Paris.

end of an era with their willful destruction of the great Parisian myths of the nineteenth century. It was the end of a long journey, which began in the rationally legible Paris of the 1860s and ended in the mysteriously (il)legible Paris of the Surrealists, which was also mythical, perhaps, but in a different and ultimately idle way.

IN ORDER TO set the Surrealists' ideological voyage in relief, let us cast another brief glance at the cultural history of the capital. We begin with the 1850s, during the middle phase in the evolution from one myth of Paris to another from 1750 to 1900, where the simplest definition of myth is that it represents "different functions of the psyche, and their relation to one another reflects the psychic life of man, divided between opposing tendencies toward sublimation and perversion." Here Zeus represents the mind; Apollo, the harmony of desires; Hades, repression; and so on. Alternatively, Claude Lévi-Strauss puts it this way: "Identity is a sort of virtual center to which we cannot help referring in order to explain certain things, even if it never truly exists." Which is to say that our reality, and our own selves, is made up of bits and pieces of images more or less clearly defined, ideologized entities that we cobble together in order to understand ourselves and the world.[10]

In the nineteenth century any number of Parisian publishers and writers produced "typologies" that clearly filled the same need, as ingredients of a new, larger, and, alas, unstable whole (social classes, nations, genders, races). Thus in Balzac's *Père Goriot,* Vautrin, identified by the police, was imagined by his author less as a man than as "the prototype of an entire nation of degenerates, a savage and logical people." Some of these typologies functioned horizontally, in space (any informed Parisian could find in them convincing descriptions of both his friends and his enemies), and others, vertically, in time (every era, and especially contemporary Paris, could also be recognized, identified, and pinpointed by means of these socio-psychological schemes, which explained the present in terms of the past). As they were widely circulated, these typologies can also be looked at as the popular equivalent in space of the great historical and allegorical canvases in time, canvases that were prized by both the conventional painters of the period and their bourgeois spectators. In these representations, and in realist literature as well, particular cases and individuals mattered only if they were representative, and as such symbols of a vast social metaphysics. Madame Bovary was no exception. "Madame Bovary, c'est moi," said Flaubert.

This was a new principle of literary creation, and one that did not please everyone: in 1824 the critic Aimé Laurent complained about it bitterly. Discussing an essay by Victor Hugo about Lord Byron, he wrote: "This pretension to express a society—for in order to answer these gentlemen, one has to speak their language—is but one more bizarre aspect of a poetry that works exclusively in terms of abstractions and is perpetually propelling itself into an ideal and fantastic world."[11]

But the century did not share Laurent's ill-tempered view. For nineteenth-century Parisians, the related types and typologies of Sir Walter Scott, Hugo, and countless other writers, painters, and historians formed a unified whole, a mythology, if you will, which seemed to them to express the whole of modern life. After Ivanhoe and Rebecca (because the historical novel was the predecessor of realistic fiction and art), the indefatigable writers and painters of Paris would offer their audience a vast—and, to their way of thinking, realistic—array of grisettes, lorettes, demi-mondaines, prostitutes with hearts of gold, heartless Parisian bankers (many of them Jews), and so on. In Théodore Géricault's monumental painting *The Raft of the Medusa,* each portrait, each detail, pointed the Parisian spectator toward the grand overarching view that obsessed the painter, that of a society and a nation in distress. Honoré Daumier's talent lay precisely in his ability to portray his anecdotal characters as actors in a great and continuing drama, namely the daily life of the ordinary Parisian men and women of his time.

Balzac's work can strike us in the same way. (Samuel Beckett would later call Balzac's characters "mechanical cabbages.") And, strangely enough, Théophile Gautier went so far as to write that Baudelaire's sources of inspiration for *Les Fleurs du mal* were types rather than individuals, a viewpoint that Baudelaire could accept since he saw himself not as a "naturalist" (by which he meant what we would call a realistic novelist) but as a "supernaturalist." "In art," Baudelaire wrote, "I do not think that the artist can find all his types in nature; the most remarkable ones are revealed to him in his soul, as the symbol of innate ideas, and in the same instant." For George Sand, the great appeal of Flaubert's *L'Education sentimentale* was that it was an "animated, changing representation in which each type acts within a group of accomplices and dupes."[12]

All realist and naturalist literature was subject to these dictates. Thus the (grotesque) ins and outs of the social and professional odyssey of Bouvard and Pécuchet, the protagonists of Flaubert's unfinished novel of that title, interested their author and still interest us because we can instantaneously situate these characters in a vast and consequential universe: that of the Parisian bourgeoisie of the 1860s, or even of bourgeois types since the Middle Ages and especially since 1789. Similarly, what made the engravings of Gavarni (Sulpice Chevalier) interesting to the Goncourt brothers was precisely what makes the work of that realistic artist seem so banal to us today. (Gavarni's works typically bore generic titles such as *Hommes et femmes de plume, Bourgeois, Artistes, Petits Commerces, Philosophes.*) The (reactionary and anti-Semitic) Goncourts were the inventors of naturalism and friends of Flaubert and Zola, and for them the imaginary universe of types and typologies created by their friend Gavarni was truer and more present—in a word, more real—than the isolated or idiopathic individual.[13]

These literary types were twinned to the extraordinary vogue for "physiologies" that swept Paris from about 1820 to 1870. Examples include Jean-Anthelme Brillat-Savarin's *La Physiologie du goût* (1825), which we encountered in Chapter 12 in the discussion of Parisian gastronomy; Louis Huart's *Physiologie de l'étudiant* (1841); and above all, *Le Diable à Paris* and *Paris et les parisiens,* the phenomenal bestsellers that Jules Hetzel, whom we met in Chapter 9 in the guise of a demoniacal ragpicker, published in 1845 and 1846. Balzac offered readers his own *Physiologie du mariage* in 1829, a *Physiologie de l'employé* in 1841, and an "Histoire et physiologie des boulevards de Paris" in Hetzel's collection *Le Diable à Paris.* It has been estimated that half a million of these physiologies were sold in Paris in the 1840s alone. It is worth noting that Hetzel did not employ just anyone: his writers included George Sand, Charles Nodier, Théophile Gautier, Gérard de Nerval, Balzac, Arsène Houssaye, and Alfred de Musset.

This enthusiasm coincided with a rage for a whole gamut of related genres: the Parisian age of physiologies was also the heyday of Parisian caricature, that is to say, of typology in the form of drawing. The four decades between 1830 and 1870, between the July Revolution and the invention of photogravure, witnessed simultaneous golden ages of Parisian myth, melodrama, bourgeois comedy, and caricature, with Charles Philipon—whose journal *Caricature* first appeared in 1831 and quickly made famous a rendition of Louis Philippe's self-satisfied features which, in a series of sketches, gradually turned into a pear, at once rotund and triangular—and with Grandville (Jean-Ignace-Isidore Gérard), Henri Monnier, and Daumier. Baudelaire called Gavarni and Daumier "complements of the Human Comedy." One might also mention the surprising popularity of pantomime and of the two Debureaus (Jean-Baptiste and Jean-Charles), Pierrots made famous forever by Jacques Prévert and Jean-Louis Barrault in their 1943 film *Les Enfants du Paradis.* "The pantomime," wrote Gautier, "is the real human comedy, and though it doesn't employ 2,000 characters like Balzac, it is not less complete: with just four or five types it manages everything."[14]

These literary and cultural creations were a large part of what made it feasible to imagine Haussmannian Paris as a mechanism, a machine that could be assembled and disassembled at will—comprehensible, efficient, and legible. This concept appeared, for example, as early as 1832 in the work of Philipon, who used a text by Pierre-Numa Bassaget about the twelve arrondissements of Paris (as they had been defined in 1795 and as they would remain until 1860, when Haussmann increased their number to twenty) as the basis for a drawing in which each district of the city was symbolized by a woman conceived as a type whose appearance corresponded to a precisely defined habitat.

T HE SURREALISTS of the 1920s and 1930s turned this orderly view of life—and of Paris—upside down. It is difficult to imagine a more complete or more dramatic contrast between two eras so close to each other in time: 1896 was the year of both Edmond de Goncourt's death and André Breton's birth. We often complain about the acceleration of history, but more years have elapsed since Breton reigned as the pope of Surrealism (more than half a century ago) than separated Breton from Zola (a scant twenty years). It was in a very brief period that the image of Paris traveled from one myth (Haussmann's view of Paris as the capital of modernity) to another (the Surrealists' view of Paris as the antithesis of bourgeois modernity).

From one Parisian myth to the next, then; and in this context we must remember that Surrealists were very taken with the idea of myth. Their myth-making was extensive and involved: any number of Surrealist painters (including Dali, Ernst, and André Masson) took Oedipus, Echo, Narcissus, and Theseus as subjects. A posthumously published text of Breton's bears the title *On the Survival of Certain Myths and On Certain Nascent or Growing Myths*. The Surrealists, Breton wrote in another work, "in no way intend to court absurdity and ridicule by seeking to promote a new myth of their own." But, he added, they nevertheless wished "to give substance to a certain number of haloed creatures or objects." Indeed, as the Surrealist Philippe Audouin explained, with the Second World War the Surrealists' call to construct new myths "grew more urgent and was radicalized. Myth [was] then considered not as the fabulous expression of a certain social state but as a possible means of action."[15]

One could no doubt go further and argue that it was the Surrealists' fascination with myth that led some of them not just to praise Paris to the skies but also to commit political errors of the worst kind, especially in their later phase during and after the Second World War: politically naive as they were, and obsessed with the publicity value of symbolic gestures, the Surrealists were radically mistaken about the significance of the myths invoked by authoritarian systems. On the right, Pierre Drieu la Rochelle (initially a fellow traveler of the Dadaists and the Surrealists who became an active collaborator with the Germans in 1940–1944) paid with his life in 1945 for his enthusiasm for fascism—a thing "immense and red," as he put it. And on the left, an equally disastrous trajectory carried Aragon first toward the Resistance and then toward Stalinism, as was also true of his comrade Paul Eluard.

"The time has come," Eluard proclaimed in 1927, "when all poets have the right and duty to maintain that they are deeply involved in the lives of other men, in the common life"; and his subsequent commitment to Stalinism was as total as Aragon's. In 1950 Breton publicly urged him to intercede with the Stalinists in Prague, who had condemned to death the Czech Surrealist (and friend of both Breton and Eluard) Zavis Kalandra. (Kalandra's confession was hardly Surrealist in its language: he admitted to having contributed "to the stiffening of the discriminatory blockade imposed on Czechoslovakia by the Western imperialists in order to undermine its economic prosperity and force it to accept Marshallization.") But Eluard, sacrificing friendship to his political loyalty, responded that he was "too busy with innocent people who proclaim their innocence to bother with guilty people who proclaim their guilt."[16]

In any case, the Surrealists of the 1920s and 1930s, as they sought historical and universal sanction for their doctrine, emphasized what Surrealism had in common with all eternal myths, and did so all the more because they had to contend with the mythical universalism of communist and fascist ideology. Hence they, and Breton in particular, tried to show that their way of looking at things and at the nature of man could also claim universal significance. "It is time to elaborate a dialectic of our own," wrote André Masson, ". . . [one] that will place us morally . . . above the Bolshevism of Lenin and Trotsky."[17]

To achieve that general significance, the apprehension of myth was precisely what was needed: the myth of the Surrealist revolution needed to enlist as an essential ally the myth of the authentic political revolution. Didn't the Surrealist poets of Paris and the proletarians of the banlieues have a common enemy? A revolution could be internal as well as external. Of the two avenues of assault, which would prove the more effective: the attack of the armed proletariat in the streets, or the Surrealist writers' attack on the mind, intended to undermine the values of bourgeois culture? For Masson, the mythical and subversive nature of the Surrealist artist was obvious: "The only justification of a work of art, a poem, or a discovery in biology or psychoanalysis is to help open man up to the transmutation of all values, to the denunciation of social, moral, and religious hypocrisy, and thus to the denunciation of the ruling class." And in a mirrored expression of that same concern, Aragon fascinated Walter Benjamin, that Marxist dreamer whose guiding intuition was to pay close attention to the theme of the flâneur, the lucid observer marginalized and alienated by Haussmann's bourgeois Paris.[18]

Driven by contempt for Cartesianism and for the moribund civilization of the West, the Surrealists were especially enthusiastic about the cultures and myths of what was not yet called the Third World. As early as the third issue of *La Révolution surréaliste,* for instance, they invoked the blessings of the Dalai Lama: "O great Lama! we are thy most faithful servants. Give us, send us thy enlightenment in a language that our contaminated European minds can understand."[19]

For Breton, hundreds of places might be found around the world where new sensations, many of them visual, could stimulate "latent feelings and [trigger] something like an intellectual revolution."[20] In New York, where Breton lived during the Second World War, there was the sight of the aurora borealis, for example; in Canada the Gaspé Peninsula; and in Arizona the Grand Canyon. But the myth of a newly exoticized Paris was the Surrealists' greatest passion: as Roger Caillois, the Surrealist theorist, explained in 1937, the power of the City of Light was manifestly implied by the kinds of works that were being published at the time:

> New works are constantly appearing in which an essential if diffuse role is played by the city, and the fact that the name "Paris" figures in almost all their titles is proof enough that the public likes it that way. Under such conditions, how can the reader fail to develop the intimate conviction, which we still see today, that the Paris he knows is not the only one, not the true one, but only a brilliantly illuminated if all too normal backdrop, which the mechanics will never discover and which hides another Paris, the real Paris, the elusive, nocturnal, phantom Paris?[21]

Paris, it seemed, had been fated to become the mythologized and mysterious capital of Surrealism, the integral city, in a sense—just as the integral man, with his dreams and fears, was central to Surrealist literary preoccupations. To be sure, Breton's Paris was not exactly the same as the Paris of the grand bourgeois Soupault or the sentimental *banlieusard*

Eluard. But all these figures were in one way or another Parisians. Having embarked on a great journey to the end of the world, some did indeed quit Paris—but got no farther than Orléans. Breton in America stubbornly refused to learn English. Their literary references were almost exclusively French and even Parisian: Nerval, the comte de Lautréamont (Isidore Ducasse), Arthur Rimbaud, Baudelaire. So were their enemies: Anatole France, Maurice Barrès, and, eventually, Paul Valéry. Their literary magazines were published in Paris and their paintings were shown there also. The First International Exposition of Surrealism was held in the capital in 1934; it would be followed by a series of others, in 1947, 1959, 1965, and 1974. Aragon never went to Mesopotamia, he maintained, because all he had to do to understand that country was to take a walk in the direction of Les Buttes-Chaumont. Paris appealed to the Surrealists through its countless mysteries and, strangely enough, through its innocence, as Breton noted in *Les Vases communicants*:

> You have to climb to the top of the hill of Sacré-Coeur early in the morning to see Paris slowly emerging from her splendid veils before stretching out her arms. A vast crowd, dispersed, frozen, detached, unfeverish, at last cuts like a ship into the great night, which makes no distinction between trash and miracle . . . At that hour beauty attains its highest level; it is confounded with innocence; it is the perfect mirror in which everything that was or is destined to be bathes adorably in what is about to be this time.[22]

It was a confirmation and not a denial of the ancient city's mythological potential that the new and all too legible sections of Paris held little interest for Breton and his comrades. It is difficult, for instance, to imagine them wandering around Neuilly or dreaming on the sidewalks of the elegant avenue Foch or avenue Henri Martin. Philippe Soupault remembered his childhood thus: "I played in the Parc Monceau: the Parc Monceau, that depressing square, that pantheon of false glories!" (He might have been less stringent had he known that hundreds of Communards had been buried in that elegant park in 1871 after being shot by firing squads.) But other Paris parks struck him as entirely propitious to mystery and myth because, unlike the Parc Monceau, they wedded "nature to men's dreams." Some of them he compared to "women of the spirit," with man in the role of rake, shovel, or pebble.[23] For Aragon, Paris parks were like fortune-tellers.

And equally propitious were the arcades. For Walter Benjamin, these shopping galleries expressed the underlying nature of commercial capitalism in Paris; later they became for him the quintessential symbol of alienation, the territory of choice of the *flâneur:* Nerval, as mentioned earlier, strolled through them with a lobster on a leash. And the Surrealists soon made them their favorite stomping ground as well. As early as April 14, 1921, the proponents of Dadaism, the precursor of Surrealism, had tired of Montparnasse and found a new home in the Café Certa located in the Passage de l'Opéra. Shortly thereafter, Aragon wrote warmly about the same arcade in *The Peasant of Paris.* Slated as it was for destruction, the passage symbolized for him the fragility of the concrete and the ephemeral nature of everyday reality. The arcade was, he thought, a mysterious place, a "human aquarium . . . concealing any number of modern myths," and a rampart against the worst enemy of Paris, namely "the great American instinct, imported into the capital by a Second Empire prefect, who tried to redraw the map of Paris along perfectly straight lines."[24]

Haussmann's Paris had been all too solid, but for the Surrealists the threatened Paris arcades (once new but now made essentially useless) were fluid sites of transitory sociability, sexual assignations, and brothels reminiscent of the aquatic, unstable nature of human existence. There, explained Aragon, one could "offer oneself a special treat," and that "treat" was "life's most substantial fabric."[25] For the Surrealists, the Passage de l'Opéra, near the Opéra Comique, was, in a sonorous play on words, the "Passage de l'Opéra Onirique" (Arcade of the Opera of Dreams). No wonder then that Breton took a keen interest in the uncertainty principle of the German physicist Werner Heisenberg, who was awarded the Nobel Prize in physics for showing that it is impossible to have precise knowledge of both the momentum and position of a particle because the act of observation alters the thing observed.

Haussmann, to be sure, had also been interested in the capital's sew-

ers and water supply but, in a sense, only to dry them up, or at any
rate to clean them up—so much so that we tend to associate his name
with such eminently solid and stable things as boulevards and building
codes. (Curiously, on this one issue Baudelaire, who despised all things
natural, agreed with the forceful prefect whom he otherwise disdained.
For even though Baudelaire admired the "ever-changing [Paris skies]
that laugh and cry according to the wind," he detested water when it
was unfettered: "I like it to be a prisoner, in restraints, confined by the
geometric walls of a quay.") For the Surrealists, by contrast, all of Paris
resembled the restless, troubling sea: in *The Peasant of Paris,* "no simile
is more common than that one." Paris shared "the vastness, nourishing
liquidity, healthy agitation, and ubiquity" of the ocean. "I waved my
handkerchief at your flower beds like an emigrant on the deck of a ship,"
wrote Aragon. "And already the boat is vanishing into the distance. On
the sandstone in the garden . . . the simplest desires, the colors of the
night, dry along with my shirt. The sun leaves us a pot of geraniums in
its will."[26]

For Soupault in *Westwego,*

> Toutes les rues sont des affluents
> Quand on aime ce fleuve où coule tout le sang de Paris
> Et qui est sale comme une sale putain
> Mais qui est aussi la Seine simplement
> A qui on parle comme à sa maman.
> (All streets are tributaries
> when you love this river in which all the blood of Paris flows,
> and which is filthy, like a filthy whore,
> but which is also simply the Seine,
> to which you speak as you would speak to your mama.)[27]

Likewise, when on March 12, 1933, the editors of *Le Surréalisme au
service de la Révolution* (a highly programmatic title) asked readers to describe what the site of the Porte Saint-Denis had looked like in the year
409, Roger Caillois suggested "a pool of mercury" and André Breton "a
very beautiful pool of petroleum with dappled automatic swans passing
overhead." Such fluid Parisian images were common in the work of
Breton, who wrote in *Poisson soluble* (Soluble Fish): "There is a large wa-

tering hole on the Montagne Sainte-Geneviève where, when night falls, all the troubling beasts and carnivorous plants that still inhabit Paris come to drink . . . What precious blood continues to flow at that spot." And in *Chants magnétiques* (Magnetic Songs; 1919) he saunters off in the direction of the Seine, which is at once the sea (la mer) and the mother (la mère) of Paris:

> je descends lentement le boulevard Saint-Michel
> je ne pense à rien
> je compte les réverbères que je connais si bien
> en m'approchant de la Seine
> près des Ponts de Paris
> je parle tout haut
> toutes les rues sont des affluents.
> (Slowly I descend the Boulevard Saint-Michel
> I'm not thinking about anything
> I count the streetlights that I know so well
> as I approach the Seine
> Near the Bridges of Paris
> I talk out loud
> all the streets are tributaries.)

Indeed, "the pivotal plane of Paris" was located, for Breton, on the quays, near Saint-Germain-l'Auxerrois.[28]

The Surrealists' Parisian promenades were not just subtly soluble: they were also agitated. As many commentators have observed, the mysterious Paris of the Surrealists was a place of shifting sands. In Aragon's work, places in Paris were "acts, movements always in progress: doors, gardens, fountains, storefronts." And for Caillois, subway entrances were insatiable urban orifices. The streets of Paris elicited from the Surrealists a whole vocabulary of their own: "to open up, to relax, to slide, to flow, to snow, to take flight, to capsize, to rove, to dissolve, to decompose, to unravel."[29]

Fluidity, coupled with movement and feminization. Listen once more to Aragon: "The whole sea in the Passage de l'Opéra. Reeds sway back and forth as gently as seaweed. I had not yet gotten over my enchantment when I noticed a shape swimming among the various displays in the shop window. It was a little smaller than the normal size of a woman . . . The apparition was swimming just behind the glass." For Breton, the Place Dauphine was "unmistakably the genitalia of Paris"—female genitalia, necessarily, as indicated by "the triangular shape" of the place, "slightly curvilinear, and the slit that bisects it into two wooded areas."[30]

For the Surrealists, walking in Paris was supposed to illuminate the psyche and make the mysterious familiar. This was especially true because they often walked at night, and the Parisian night made even familiar things seem unfamiliar. For Aragon, nighttime is "the great, dark illusion," and thanks to it his narrator is able to delve more deeply into himself "than his strength would otherwise allow . . . I delve into myself and I touch the concrete sense of existence, which is entirely shrouded by death . . . Darkness or confusion, it's all the same: the night does not give up its ships."[31] Brassaï drew attention in 1933 with a collection of sixty-two black-and-white photographs entitled *Paris de nuit* (Paris by Night).

In a way, as the Surrealists fully understood, their Parisian walks were alternatives to Freudian psychoanalysis. Indeed, as early as 1919 automatic writing was described as yet another unconscious mechanism (like Freud's dreams) capable of revealing "the real operation of thought," which was also unconscious and deterministic.[32] The Surrealists were early admirers of psychoanalysis, and Breton went to Vienna to see Freud in 1921. But they had certain reservations: Freud's ideas about infantile sexuality did not particularly interest them. Moreover, for Breton an artist was not the same thing as a doctor, especially a Surrealist artist; and by the same token, a doctor was never an artist. "It would be paying undue homage to [psychoanalysis]," Breton wrote, "to claim that it exhausted the problem of dreams." As for psychiatrists more generally, in the name of science they were often nefarious people: "They locked up Sade. They locked up Nietzsche. They locked up Baudelaire." And Freud, a poet who nonetheless saw himself as a physician and a scientist, returned the compliment, stating that he was "tempted to regard the Surrealists, who have apparently chosen me as their patron saint, as pure madmen, or at any rate ninety-five percent pure, like alcohol."[33]

The difference between the Viennese doctor and his Parisian admirers was basically this: Freud looked upon the analysis of dreams as a step toward a possible cure, whereas the Surrealists looked upon it as an end in itself. For Freud, not all psychic drives were positive, but all Surrealists were bound to admire all of the dreams of the sleeping poet who had posted a sign on his bedroom door saying "Poet at work." Unlike the psychotherapist, the Surrealist welcomed all forms of spontaneity, including those inspired either by neurotic dreams or by Paris walks.[34] Surrealism, to quote Breton, hoped to "redeem all the powers of the psyche." And in *Nadja* Breton wrote that "the well-known absence of any boundary between non-madness and madness does not make me apt to grant any difference in value to the perceptions and ideas produced by the one as opposed to the other."

The contemporary experience of Paris was therefore important to the Surrealists, even more important than psychoanalysis. It is worth noting, however, that by contrast to lived Parisian life, the city's *past* seems to have held no real interest for Breton and his friends, and their view of Paris was "stripped of the incidents of its history." How many people lived in Paris in the year 409? Caillois answered with disarming insouciance, "409," because in those days "years were counted by the number of people who lived in Paris." The history of Paris in the narrow sense, especially the political history of Paris, interested the Surrealists only insofar as that history represented a rejection, and therefore a justification, of their own cultural rebellion. "Today I am learning to respect people who refused to commit treason," Soupault wrote, and "it is from reading forgotten old books about the Commune that I am beginning to understand what respect means and what greatness is like. Nothing seems more beautiful to me than the indictment of the Commune . . . From now on, these are my models." But to take an interest in the history of Paris in this selective way was not really to take an interest in it at all.[35]

The same inattention can be found in a Surrealist survey concerning changes to be made to Paris monuments, whose grammar and immutability were—and still are—the most telling expressions of the city's history. "How might Paris be rearranged," the Surrealists asked, and their not very respectful suggestions included bending the towers of Notre Dame to resemble a cruet; arranging for the obelisk on the Place de la Concorde to be held by a woman's hand; and skewering the Lion of Belfort at the Place Denfert-Rochereau. For others, it seemed more important to surround the Tour Saint-Jacques "by a circular virgin forest" to restore its mystery, while others preferred that it be "delicately inserted into the steeple of the Sainte Chapelle."[36] The Place du Panthéon interested them more than the Panthéon itself, and Zazie (the heroine of Raymond Queneau's *Zazie dans le Métro*) regularly confused the latter with other city monuments.

Everything in the Surrealists' Paris was worth keeping, but on condition that it be deformed, "dehistoricized," and recomposed—as in the paintings of Magritte, who liked to paint faces or objects in a realistic, indeed highly finished, style but truncated or oddly juxtaposed so as to suggest, sometimes overtly, the opposite of what they seemed to indicate: "This is not a pipe." So, for example, the slaughterhouses of Paris attracted the eye of the painter André Masson, but as a contemporary version of the temples of antiquity in which Greeks and Romans sacrificed animals to the gods, and Marie-Claire Bancquart is quite right to conclude that, in the Paris of the Surrealists, "places are waypoints and never described in a comprehensive way but simply named . . . scenes of events so surprising that they disorient the reader and inhibit a comfortable sense of identification." It is also revealing that Paris seldom (indeed almost never) appears in Surrealist painting, and it is pertinent to note, in the words of Susan Sontag, that the (literary) Paris of the Surrealists was like an accumulation of "urban debris," an amalgam of virtual *objets trouvés*. The Surrealists found the streets of Paris evocative, to be sure, but because of the associations and fantasies they provoked rather than in themselves.[37]

In this realm of secret correspondences, moreover, at the Surrealist Exposition of 1938, the representations of some of the high points of Surrealist Paris (such as the rue Vivienne and the rue Nicolas Flamel and the Passage des Panoramas) were linked not to specific historical memories but to female mannequins, and the exhibit's chilliness was intended to recall that of another show whose theme had been not "Paris as it is," but "Paris, theater of secret passions." Masson's work for this occasion was deemed particularly successful, wedding as it did "symbolism and allusion, poetic reverie and Freudian illustration": the base of one of his mannequins was strewn "with coarse salt, from which small red pimentos, prisoners caught in a trap, rose like so many miniature erections toward the mannequin's genitalia."[38]

For better or for worse, Surrealism saw itself as a new form of myth and therefore as having affinities with other new forms of myth, be they political or religious. But should we conclude that Surrealism marked the end or the renewal of myths of Paris? In 1935 Breton asked—perspicaciously—if Surrealism would not disappear along with the bourgeoisie that it despised. The question was indeed a good one. The two were closely linked, and although Marcel Duchamp was not wrong to write, after Breton's death, that Breton had loved "as a heart beats" and had been "a lover of love in a world that believes in prostitution," it is also true that Salvador Dali, the most famous of the Surrealist painters, became the darling of New York's wealthy elite in the 1930s and 1940s, to the extent that his erstwhile friends began to refer to him as Avida Dollars. Of this reverence for cash, Jean-Paul Crespelle rightly remarks that it was "the darkest stain on Surrealism. The most indelible."[39]

Parisian Surrealism was also phantasmagorical by dint of its preciosity. André Breton claimed to share in the popular pleasures of Luna Park, and Sonia Delaunay in those of Bullier, a popular dance hall. But we should be suspicious of this professed love of popular Paris. Brassai and André Kertész claimed to share it, yet their photographs today often strike us as sentimental or even condescending. Breton detested the Métro at rush hour: "How can these people be interesting if they tolerate work with or without all the other miseries? How can work raise them up if the rebellious instinct in them is not more powerful?" Bancquart reminds us that the mythical Paris of the Surrealists "remains highly individual . . . and no indication is given of the method that might induce everyone to have visions comparable to those of Aragon."

There is something to Julien Gracq's idea that Breton would have liked to turn Surrealism into a private club or even a secret society: the approval of the public, the master wrote, "is to be shunned above all. The public must be kept out entirely if confusion is to be avoided. I hasten to add that it must be kept waiting at the door, exasperated by a system of challenges and provocations."[40]

In theory, the Surrealists were universalists without borders, but in all too many respects they were as Parisian as can be, in the particularistic and therefore negative sense of the word. If Robert Desnos sought a wider public, Breton by contrast preferred "profound occultation." Their universalism was peculiar, if not downright dubious. True, Breton's attitude toward colonialism and the Nazi persecution of the Jews was irreproachable, but the Surrealists' feminism was ambiguous in the extreme.

Breton and his friends were fascinated by the feminine, and their myth of the primordial unity of creation was couched in terms of fusion of the male and female principles. Their views of Paris and of the Place Dauphine, as has been seen, were of a feminized city. Imagination would save humanity, and it existed primarily in the feminine: "The nude woman of the Electric Palace inspires a sense of the sacred rather than erotic feelings." When Breton kisses Nadja, he thinks of the consecrated Communion wafer. The colors of Paris (red and blue) were not only the colors of the Tarot but also symbols of complementary principles: the blue stood for the feminine, aquatic, and nocturnal, while the red represented the masculine, igneous, and luminous.[41]

In their lives and writings, however, the women who fascinated the Surrealists were often mechanical or associated with the mechanical (think of the celebrated Man Ray photograph, for example, in which the artist Meret Oppenheim appears nude, lashed to the huge wheel of a machine). In *The Peasant of Paris,* women's hair is referred to as *cheveux-vapeurs,* "steam hair," or hair that embodies the power of modern machinery.[42] And women were not only machines; they were also, at times, objects, children, or fairies.

The Surrealist woman was a goddess, often remote and abstract, a "convulsive beauty" composed of disarticulated parts. "We wander the streets [of Paris]," Breton says of Nadja, "next to each other but quite separate." "The surrealist woman," Bancquart tells us, "is more the mediator of sexual pleasure and poetic imagery than a person who experiences pleasure or creativity in her own right." "Who am I?" Nadja asks. "Who is alive? Is it me alone? Is it myself?" Revealingly, women were more important in the diaspora of Surrealism than in its original Parisian incarnations.[43]

The principle of Surrealism aimed to be universal. It wished to free all minds. But the practical reality of the Surrealist movement was of unceasing calumny and exclusion, in the literal as well as the figurative sense: the pattern was set as early as May 18, 1926, when Aragon and Breton harangued the audience at the Théâtre Sarah Bernhardt at the premiere of Prokofiev's ballet *Romeo and Juliet.* The two writers urged the crowd to lambaste their former comrades Max Ernst and Joan Miró for having agreed to paint scenery for the production, a dishonorable act, in Aragon's view, because ballet was an inferior artistic genre.[44] (Francis Picabia's interest in the Swedish Ballet, which was quite popular in Paris at the time, earned him a similar rebuke.)

From then on, exclusion was one of Surrealism's most ritualized gestures: Tristan Tzara and Dadaism were excluded in 1922; and Artaud and Roger Vitrac were expelled for rejecting communism in 1927; Aragon and Georges Sadoul were excluded for *accepting* communism in 1932; Eluard was excluded for being too far to the left in 1938; Dali, for being too far to the right in 1939.[45]

Was Surrealism, then, truly a mythical and modernizing ideology? Selectively, perhaps, especially in its relation to cinema and photography. (Interestingly, women among the Surrealists were noted more as painters and photographers than as writers. Meret Oppenheim, whose name we encountered earlier, worked in both genres.)

Ultimately, however, Surrealism has to be seen as an amusing form of rejection rather than a genuine project or a genuine myth, and perhaps as phantasmagorical in its very essence. What Breton and his friends were looking for in Paris was not a new Paris but an insubstantial ghost, a pre-Haussmannian Paris that no longer existed and—more important—had never existed at all. "It is fashionable," a contemptuous

Haussmann wrote of his overly literate, overly learned antagonists in the 1860s, "to admire an old Paris that they know only from books." What would he have thought of their successors?

Though fascinated by myth, Surrealism, once the moment of its inception was past, was far less myth than phantasmagoria, artifice, and joke. Is it possible to imagine a Surrealist without excluded, flabbergasted spectators? By contrast, is it possible to imagine a myth that does not transform the passive spectator into an active participant?

It may well be, in the end, that Surrealism—which wanted to be a creative revolution and ended up as a bourgeois amusement—is of interest primarily as a reminder of the lamentable state in which Europe and its first capital found themselves after the slaughter of 1914–1918. This insight in turn leads us to think more generally about Paris and its myths in relation to other, broader contexts. To quote Metternich again, when France sneezed, Europe caught pneumonia. Reciprocally, when Europe nearly died in 1914–1918, so did the myth of Paris decline and then atrophy.

As for the Surrealists, this is to say that their Parisian sensibility did not constitute a permanent milestone in the life of the capital. It was instead an exasperated reflection of the modernist crisis of European consciousness that had been developing since 1890, a crisis radically amplified by the suicidal massacres of the First World War. The Surrealists, like the Romantics and realists of the nineteenth century, sought to merge everyday life and art. But they did so very much on their own terms, by trying to connect the eccentricities of Parisian life to the highly personal vagaries of their imaginations. And in doing so, paradoxically, they proved in the end to be much further from Paris and its citizenry than had been Haussmann, whom they despised but whose rebuilding of the French capital was not just a great achievement but, in its own way, a genuinely oneiric tour de force.

16

Capital of Art

"WHERE DO WE come from? Who are we? Where are we going?" reads the legend on a canvas that Gauguin (who was born in Paris in 1848) painted in Tahiti in 1897. Mythical and metahistorical questions, to be sure, and ones that could no longer be answered by the phantasmagorias of Belle Epoque Paris, capital of luxury and pleasure, in a society that had reached a new phase of industrial development. Nor for that matter are we much better off today: our commercialized fantasies and virtual phantasmagorias dull our existential anxieties without resolving them.

How wide the gap, then, between our own times—in Paris or elsewhere—and the Paris of the nineteenth century when, in an age of myth, ever more direct answers jostled ceaselessly at History's gate, each seeking to encompass all the others, literary or scientific, and all of them intertwined. "In the most vital phase of intellectual research," Paul Valéry asserted, "there is a merely verbal difference between the inner activity of an artist or poet and that of a scholar."[1] In the period 1800–1830, especially in Paris, some believed that it was primarily science, of which their city was the capital, that would usher in the radiant future of humankind. Later, others sought salvation in the related political promise of a Parisian and climactic night of ultimate struggle in 1848 or in the Commune of 1871. And still others dreamed of a perfect Haussmannian city of easy and efficient communication, while Baudelaire, Walter Benjamin, and others rejected, on equally mythical grounds, the same idea of rationalized urban life.

Different and powerful ideas, all of them interwoven, and each of them viewed by its votaries as a key to the scriptures. But of the many Parisian myths, the most durable of all, and the most influential throughout the world, was that of Paris as the capital of art, and especially of painting. Despite Fantômas and Arsène Lupin, Paris was only briefly the world capital of crime—from about 1830 to about 1850. In many other domains, as in science, the prestige of the capital was even more ephemeral. And in music, as we saw in Chapter 10, Vienna, or even London (which gave Haydn his European renown in the late 1790s), always had a better claim to being the world center for both creation and performance (except for opera): of the first forty conductors of the New York Philharmonic (founded in 1842), nearly all were foreigners, but there were ten Germans for every Frenchman.[2] Musically, the Germanic world mattered more than France; as did Vienna, Berlin, and even Munich more than Paris.

For more than a century and a half, however, Paris was the undisputed capital of Western painting and, to a lesser degree, sculpture. Generations of artists and aesthetes settled there not only in the hope of understanding the sources from which Greek and Roman art had sprung but also in order to grasp the deeper nature of their time and to divine what the art of the future would be.

And, strangely enough, the birth and death dates of this mythic prestige are for once precise. It all began on August 20, 1785, when Jacques-Louis David showed his *Oath of the Horatii,* an extraordinary prefiguration of the revolutionary public spirit: united by the promise of a communal sacrifice, these universalist citizen-brothers—who, incidentally, are self-reflectively aware of their heroism—swear to conquer or die. (On the right side of the canvas, their particularist wives, overcome by emotion, weep over the misfortune of their clan.) Goethe gave this canvas the accolade it deserved; with this painting, he said, Paris had usurped the place that Rome had occupied for several centuries.

So much for the date of birth. And as for the death of Parisian predominance, that came on June 14, 1940, when Hitler's troops entered Paris: on that fateful day the center of the art world fled to New York along with Peggy Guggenheim and her canvases. And there it remains to this day, or so New Yorkers like to think.

To be sure, the end was not absolute for either Rome in the 1780s or Paris in 1940: the Parisian painting of the 1950s and 1960s seems more consequential today than it did thirty or forty years ago. Contemporary Paris is still an important artistic center. Its galleries and auction houses—not to speak of its innumerable museums—are world famous. In this domain of decline, exceptions to the rules have always been numerous: if painting in Munich, for example, enjoyed a certain reputation in Paris and the world in the 1820s, it was largely because those French artists who had persisted in going to Rome, which was then still a vital center of art, had mingled there with Bavarian painters of the so-called Nazarene school. Thus the eclipse of the Italian capital around 1800 was like that of Paris after 1940, neither all that sudden nor total: Jean-Auguste-Dominique Ingres, chagrined by the cool reception that one of his portraits of Napoleon met in Paris, lived in Rome from 1806 to 1820 and again after 1835. Not until Eugène Delacroix (1798–1863) do we find a French artist of the first rank who could have gone to Rome but chose not to do so.

Still, between the ascendancy of Rome in the seventeenth and eighteenth centuries and the heyday of New York after the Second World War, Paris was the primary home of a series of schools of painting (Neoclassical, Romantic, Realist, Impressionist, Symbolist, and then Modernist in its various forms—Cubist, Orphic, Fauve, Surrealist) that define the mainstream of the art history of the West in the past two centuries.

NOWADAYS art is our religion: it is by way of aesthetic experience that many of us hope to pass from the immanent to the transcendent; and we say of certain artists that they are (or were) the chosen prophets of this religion. (We prefer the dead to the living.) As children, some of us dreamed of being kings. As adults, we dream of having known Delacroix, Vermeer, or Velázquez; and it would be convenient to be able to think of the extraordinary artistic presence of Paris in terms of such exceptional individuals, of genius pure and simple. Then we could simply say that Manet, Degas, and van Gogh were men of matchless talent; and that would be enough to explain the rise of Paris as the capital of art. We can, after all, admire Shakespeare without knowing much about Elizabethan England: this playwright suffices unto himself. We may likewise be interested in the social and political context of the work of Goya, Pushkin, or Turner, but such interest does not usually enlist our passions.

Instinctively, however, we sense that it would be a mistake to personalize the myth of art in Paris. Indeed, in the history of Paris taken as a whole it is not at all unusual for events to have transcended individual volition: "Men make their history," wrote Marx in a book on Parisian politics, "but they do not make it as they please." How true! In Paris in 1793 Sieyès, Danton, Robespierre, Saint-Just, and Marat were powerful personalities; but we sense there too that a circumstantial, anecdotal, personalized explanation of the Revolution will not do. On this point, if on few others, historians as diverse as Lamartine and Michelet, Albert Soboul and François Furet could all have agreed. And, *mutatis mutandis,* Paris, capital of art, is arguably a similar sort of phenomenon. Take away Ingres, Courbet, Renoir, or any number of others and the edifice still stands. The talent of these artists was all-important, but we now know that their enormous abilities were propelled and even amplified by a great machine whose parts and workings demand our full attention. As the painter Eugène-Louis Boudin observed, the perfection of art in Paris was a collective accomplishment.[3]

Some ingredients of that achievement are concrete and easy to identify: state aid; the role of critics, salons, and art dealers; the importance of studios, prizes, medals; and so on. But others are far more elusive and more distinctively Parisian, such as the capital's "atmosphere," with its public, its buyers, and its critics. How can this spirit of the city be defined? Perhaps the answer is to be found in a maxim favored by Honoré Daumier, who advised his young emulators "to be of their time": Paris was the capital of the nineteenth century first and foremost because it was in Paris that people most fully understood the modernity of the age. Painters, too, followed that elusive dream, and it was to Paris—inevitably, one would like to say—that the artists who most fully expressed the values and anxieties of their own societies gravitated. In Barcelona Pablo

Picasso was merely an extraordinarily talented young man; in Paris he quickly became one of the leading lights of the early twentieth century.

The history of art in Paris must be seen in this wider context of complex cultural exchange, that is to say, in the interplay of the different definitions of what was modern and what was "real," a theme to which we will return in a moment. What can be said right away, however, is that it is in relation to modernity that art thrived in the French capital. Therein lies the essence of the city's aesthetic rise, and, alas, of its fall as well. Even before the First World War, New York, having become even more modern than Paris, was beginning to pose as a rival to the French capital: the Armory Show, which featured such modern painters as Duchamp, Picasso, and Matisse (and which scandalized some American art lovers), took place in 1913. When the Germans occupied Paris during the Second World War, the City of Light went into eclipse, but its star had been waning for some time. And by 1944 modernity was solidly ensconced in New York, as was money. Inevitably, art and artists soon congregated there too, as they had done in Paris, capital of the nineteenth century.

CONTEMPORARY CRITICS of "the cultural state" have been severe in their judgment of the supposedly excessive and even wasteful assistance that the French state offers artists, including allegedly incompetent amateurs. Billboards, these critics are shocked to see, proclaim that "the Regional Council [of Provence] is revitalizing the plastic arts." And in years past other critics—then of the left rather than the right—lambasted the grants that conservative and self-righteous politicians awarded to artists whose support they hoped to enlist. In the rather peremptory judgment of Romain Rolland, who won the Nobel Prize for literature in 1919, "everything the state touches, it kills." Fifty years earlier, the painter Gustave Courbet had been just as blunt: "The state is incompetent when it comes to art . . . Its intervention is entirely demoralizing and deleterious to art, which it confines to what is officially approved and condemns to . . . the most sterile mediocrity."[4]

Mark Tansey, *Triumph of the New York School,* 1984. Tansey's painting, at once autumnal and hilarious, chronicles the end of Paris as the capital of myth and modernity. In a manner reminiscent of Velazquez's *Surrender of Breda,* Tansey shows us André Breton, in a First World War uniform, signing the surrender document, to the shocked amazement of the fur-coated Picasso. At the right, relaxed and invincible, are Americans with their armored vehicle, for which the French cavalrymen are no match. Clement Greenberg and Jackson Pollock observe this ritual with feigned amusement and indifference. Whitney Museum of American Art, New York; Promised gift of Robert M. Kaye, P.84.5. Photo © 2000: Whitney Museum of American Art, New York.

In reality, however, notwithstanding the past and present criticism, one of the constants in Paris, capital of art, for more than three centuries has been precisely the fact that the French state, whether monarchical or republican, has always favored Parisian artists with commissions and on occasion with inspiration; at times it has even organized them. Art in Paris has received its staunchest support from the rich (that is, from the goodwill of the elite of civil society) and from state commissions. How could it have been otherwise? And where would artists in Paris be today if they refused to deal with the media or galleries and rejected all state aid?

THE STORY of modern Parisian art begins in the age of Louis XIV. Like all forms of activity in seventeenth-century Paris, as we saw in our survey of pre-revolutionary Parisian social forms, painting was at that time a corporatized profession. Painters were more like artisans than like artists, and they worked more or less as they willed: although the monarchy kept a close eye on painters as it did on all guilds in the capital (Paris was a "hyper-corporatized" city), the profession was relatively independent and capable of managing its own affairs.

Under the new Ludovician absolutism, however, this ancient autonomy inevitably came under suspicion. As early as 1655 the painter Charles Lebrun (1619–1690) attempted, with encouragement from Cardinal Mazarin, to trim the privileges of the old corporatized Académie de Saint-Luc for the benefit of a new, state-sponsored Académie Royale des Arts, founded in 1648 (and thus more or less contemporaneous with the Académie Française, 1635, and the Académie des Sciences, 1666, also products of an absolutist inspiration that was simultaneously authoritarian and modern). The intervention of Louis XIV's finance minister Jean-Baptiste Colbert in everything to do with painting and architecture in Paris—most notably in the episode of the colonnade of the Louvre, the eminent Italian architect Giovanni Bernini (who was basically dismissed because his Italianate design wasn't French enough), and Claude Perrault (who won the commission in the end)—is well known. The first Salons, or exhibitions of painting (and thus quite different from the private salons of the salonnières), were also organized under the protection of the state around that time. To be sure, it was not until 1737 that the Salons really came into their own in a process that culminated in the final decades of the nineteenth century, but an important milestone was passed much earlier when Louis XIV's architect Jules Hardouin-Mansart organized an exhibition at the Louvre in 1699.

Patronage for the arts, then, came from a state concerned with its efficiency and modernity as well as with its reputation in the Republic of Letters, and it was by instinct that Parisian painters turned to the state for support. That is, however, just one half of the picture; the other half is the relative autonomy of Parisian public opinion vis-à-vis the French state. One could summarize this paradoxical division between the capital of the nation and the capital of the monarchy by saying that Parisian painters of the eighteenth century were required to please both enlightened opinion in Paris and also, at Versailles, the absolutist monarch and his servants, who were themselves increasingly swayed by what the Parisian public wanted.

A CONVENIENT starting point for these shifts in taste and sponsorship might be, as in many other domains, the death of Louis XIV in 1715. At about that time the financier Antoine Crozat offered support and encouragement to a circle of amateurs and artists that is perhaps the earliest example of new trends. Members included the painter Antoine Watteau (1684–1721) and the Abbé Dubos, a theorist of art. Later, toward the middle of the century, the work of Jean-Baptiste Greuze (1725–1805) marked a second stage. His sentimental anecdotal style (*The Paternal Curse, The Village Betrothal*) offends our modern sensibility, but it was a precursor of the self-styled "realist" Salon painting of the following century. With Greuze, bourgeois (and therefore modern) life became an acceptable subject for high art. The rise of neoclassicism completed this cycle of Parisian innovation.

Of course monarchically supported baroque art, or rococo, as its French variant was known, did not disappear from Paris overnight. With an annual salary of nearly 40,000 livres at a time when a professor at the Sorbonne earned about one twentieth of that sum, the rococo master François Boucher (1703–1770) was probably one of the best-paid artists of his time. And Jacques-Louis David (1748–1825), who would become a central figure of neoclassicism, began his career as a follower of Boucher's student Jean-Honoré Fragonard (1732–1806).

Soon, however, the new and modernizing Parisian public issued increasingly forthright verdicts, which, importantly, the monarchic state eventually endorsed: baroque art, which in the 1710s had benefited from being at odds with the absolutist classicism of Versailles, was increasingly seen in Paris as old-fashioned, superficial, amoral, and ultimately immoral. By 1747 La Font de Saint-Yenne, said by some to have invented the literary genre of art criticism, was tirelessly advising his enlightened readers of the urgent need to create new art forms that would be more classical, more sober, more exemplary, and, one would like to say, more republican. Diderot praised Greuze for his ability to "touch, instruct, correct, and exhort to virtue."[5] Paris spoke loudly in these matters.

Versailles, meanwhile, was falling mute, and it seems fair to say that by 1750 the elements of a new artistic system were in place. These included the painters of the Académie, the state bureaucracy headed by the superintendent of the king's buildings, the press, and the public that attended the Salons.[6]

Writing in the 1780s, Louis-Sébastien Mercier deplored the haphazard display and crowded conditions of the Salons: given a choice between the judgment of the refined connoisseur and that of the uninformed general public, his preference seemed inevitable. And yet in the end Mercier, an adept of the Enlightenment and a partisan of progress in all things, could not ignore the judgment of the public, which he believed to be a force for independence and political virtue. Likewise, it was Paris, far more than Versailles, that encouraged the new vogue for history painting, which of course dealt not with actual, contemporary, monarchical history but with mythology, with ancient history, with the Rome of tribunes rather than of emperors—with the history, to put it in a nutshell, of ancient liberty. In 1779 Louis de Carmontelle, a draftsman and writer, spoke for his age when he declared that because "servitude is not the natural condition of man," the freedom-loving admirer of the fine arts, even if he lived under a monarchy, was bound to develop a sensibility that was neither that of the savage, indifferent to the arts, nor that of the hypercivilized man, indifferent to the welfare of all.[7]

At the same time, although modern bourgeois or neoclassical painting now answered to a newborn Parisian public opinion, at this juncture neither painting nor public opinion had yet wholly turned against the monarchy. It is important to stress once again—the point is crucial—that the French monarchy of the ancien régime was not just a feudal relic. The monarchy, as Alexis de Tocqueville remarked (and as the late historian François Furet eloquently reminded us), tried hard in its own clumsy way to respond to the demands of enlightened modernity: the

ministers Machault, Terray, Maupeou, Turgot, Necker, and Calonne
all attempted to reform the monarchy's decaying administration and
finances. The monarchy's ties to the world of finance and banking and
to large-scale colonial and international trade were far closer than
would soon be the highly ambiguous ties between Jacobinism and capitalism.

And the relation between the Bourbon state and the new aesthetic
tendencies that had triumphed on the Parisian scene was also close.
Officials serving Louis le Bien-aimé and his grandson Louis XVI did almost nothing to counter the modernizing and aesthetic tendencies of
the Parisian public, whether bourgeois or neo-republican. On the contrary: Greuze was protected and encouraged by the marquis de Marigny,
superintendent of buildings and brother of Louis XV's mistress and
confidante Mme de Pompadour (*née* Antoinette Poisson); and Quentin
de La Tour was paid 48,000 livres for his portrait of the king's companion.

Even more revealing were the choices of Marigny's successor, the
comte d'Angiviller, who also encouraged history painting, but of the nation's history, preferably showing the monarchy as the nation's constant
benefactor—as, for instance, in François-Guillaume Ménageot's 1781
painting of Leonardo da Vinci dying at Amboise in the arms of Francis I.
The same Angiviller accorded David his "constant interest and protection."[8] In fact, David hoped to sell his *Belisarius Begging for Alms* to the
royal government. The painting's eponymous hero, the Roman philoso-
pher-soldier Belisarius, was the subject of a 1767 novel by Jean-François
Marmontel, a writer condemned by the Sorbonne but also protected by
Angiviller. It would be possible to mention any number of similar cases.
And note, for a later period, that David, a regicide who supported Napoleon during the Hundred Days, was duly exiled to Brussels, but his
Oath of the Horatii, which during his lifetime had been placed in the
Musée du Luxembourg by order of the emperor, and was transferred in
1826, in the reign of Charles X, to the Musée du Louvre. Had he wished
to do so, David could no doubt have persuaded the ultra-royalist monarch to allow him to leave Belgium and return to Paris to live out
his days.

S O MUCH FOR the pre-revolutionary age. And as for Parisian art after 1789, it too functioned within a tightly woven and state-regulated net. The ancien régime's close association with the modernizing artistic tendencies of the Enlightenment may seem surprising today. By contrast, there is nothing surprising about the nature of the tie between Jacobin art and public opinion during the Revolution. The Jacobin Abbé and later Bishop Grégoire, a fundamentally honest man, thought he was merely stating a self-evident truth when he explained that, France having undergone regeneration, "painting, engraving, poetry, and music will regain their original dignity among us. Among us as among the ancients, they will be instruments in the hands of the government."[9] This view was shared by David, who by now was a member of the Committee of General Security, an admirer of Robespierre, the painter of the celebrated portrait of Marat in his bathtub, and the orchestrator of revolutionary festivals. And while Claude-Nicolas Ledoux was incarcerated and barely escaped the guillotine, many architects, like Etienne-Louis Boullée, had proto-revolutionary tendencies. In 1793 the revolutionary government more or less commissioned an "Artists' Plan," which though it was never realized, was in many ways a precursor of Haussmannian urbanization.

The revolutionary state, then, rewarded individual artists, but one might say it rewarded the idea of Art as well, because the decade of revolution also witnessed the invention in Paris of the modern museum, which can be seen as having been yet another link between the state, the artist, and the enlightened public. For half a century before the Revolution, some private Parisian collectors (including the art collector and patron Crozat) allowed interested individuals to visit their collections. In 1750 an authentic museum was created in the Palais du Luxembourg. (In London, by the way, the British Museum was established in 1753.) The museum was open to the public two days a week for about three hours each day. Shortly thereafter, in 1776, Angiviller proposed to collect the king's paintings in the Louvre. This was to be a patriotic museum, largely devoted to displaying the glories of the French nation.

But this monarchic project met the same fate that had befallen the economic reforms of Angiviller's patron Turgot in 1776. In 1789, to quote an associate of Alexandre Lenoir, soon to be the enemy of vandal-ism and the founder of the Musée des Monuments Français, "Paris [still] had neither museums nor public collections. Out of pride, masters hid the masterpieces of great painters from their pupils, set themselves up as sole models, and turned their pupils into slaves obliged to wear the liv-ery of their betters."[10]

The Revolution, however, revolutionized the exhibition of art as it did so many things; and a new national museum was opened in the Lou-vre on August 10, 1793, the first anniversary of the fall of the monarchy, whose collapse had made possible the "cultural regeneration" of the erst-while royal palace, now at last a national monument. In November 1793 visitors were permitted to stroll about the gallery at their leisure for three days of every *décade* (the Revolution's rationalized ten-day re-placement for the seven-day week), while the museum was reserved for artists one day out of five. In 1803, however, the Louvre, renamed the Musée Napoléon, became what it still is today—and what it was no doubt destined to be, according to Siegfried Giedion, a Marxist-inspired German writer of the 1920s whom Walter Benjamin admired—namely, a mirror of its times. "It seems," wrote Giedion, "that almost every era, owing to its internal makeup, concentrates most intently on a specific architectural problem: for the Gothic era, it was the cathedral; for the Baroque, the castle; and for the early nineteenth century, which had a tendency to look backward and steep itself in the past, the museum." How true, and from that day forward, a visit to the Louvre has served more or less the same purpose as had a visit to Rome in earlier times.

The Directory (1795–1799)—still republican but far milder than the Republic of Year II, was also more solicitous of the well-being of artists, provided that they were equally solicitous of it: "Artists," proclaimed François de Neufchâteau, minister of the interior and mastermind be-hind the raids of artworks carried out by French troops in Belgium and Italy, "honor a nation that honors you!" It was also part of the politi-cal strategy of the Thermidorians, who took power with the fall of Robespierre, to associate the terror presided over by the ousted and re-viled Jacobins with the deleterious effects of revolutionary, ideologically driven destruction of works of art (even though the word for this destruction, "vandalism," had in fact been coined by the Abbé Grégoire, a sincere Jacobin). In order to distinguish itself from the previous regime, it was therefore logical for the Directory to promote the opposite of vandalism, namely art. Among "a free people," Neufchâteau declared on 9 Thermidor, Year VI, "the fine arts . . . are the primary instruments of social happiness as well as an auxiliary trumpet in the hands of philosophy, which promotes the good of the human race." If the political effects of the Roman civic spirit had proved difficult to live with, the example of Athens might yet inspire the artists of a more sober republic, as the art critic Pierre Chaussard explained in 1798: "Do not concern yourselves with national subjects . . . Give us the great monuments of Antiquity adapted to our customs, our climate, and our genius . . . Wed us to ideal beauty, to faithful imitation of expressive Nature. Out of these principles came the miracles of Greek art."[11]

Napoleon inflected but did not reverse such opportunistic concerns, and once again the case of Jacques-Louis David and his fawning, Bonapartist, and propagandistic art illustrates to perfection the close relationship between the French state and the arts in Paris under the First Empire. After being crowned emperor, Napoleon took an interest not only in the welfare of scientific researchers but also in the prestige of artists of every stripe whose support he had enlisted. Many were decorated, and a number were called to noble status. And those artists, without notable exception, came through when he needed them: the Salon of 1808 alone featured twenty-seven portraits of the emperor. This marked, incidentally, a significant accentuation of the cult of personality, since only forty portraits of Louis XV had appeared in Salons during the last thirty-eight years of his reign and only fifteen had been exhibited of his successor.[12]

Imperial favor thus contributed mightily to the flourishing of painting in Paris, but an even more significant factor was the administrative centralization achieved by the Revolution. After a brief federalist, decentralizing phase (which lasted from 1789 to 1792), the Jacobins, the Directory, and the Empire all contributed in one way or another to the centralization of French artistic life in Paris, just as they contributed to the centralization of the country's political, administrative, and financial structures.

Many great provincial centers had earlier enjoyed a vigorous artistic life. From 1751 on, regular exhibitions of painting had been organized in Toulouse. Marseilles had followed suit in 1756. Poitiers and Abbeville had mounted occasional exhibitions. Many provincial cities, such as Dijon, prided themselves on their local academies and drawing schools.

After the passage of the Le Chapelier Law, however, these provincial academies, associated as they were with the reviled values of corporatism and particularism, no longer had a place in the Jacobin *Weltanschauung,* which imperiously rejected intermediate bodies of any kind as obstacles that separated the citizen from the national community. They were therefore abolished, as was the Paris academy, which David vengefully disliked. Yet when the neo-Jacobin Thermidorians revived the Institut de France in 1795, the effect was simply to confirm the preeminence of the capital. Hence, as the art historian Raymonde Moulin rightly points out, the dominant phenomenon in the production of art in nineteenth-century France was "the standardization of provincial artistic production in accordance with canons laid down by the Académie in Paris. Artists born in the provinces had their work recognized in Paris."[13]

Despite a few exceptions (including thirty-four provincial museums and fifty-five art schools, as well as a number of provincial Salons, including one in Nantes in 1839, at which Corot, Delacroix, Théodore Rousseau, and Paul Flandrin all showed paintings), art in the provinces declined steadily. An 1831 report expressed regret that cities such as Nancy and Strasbourg remained outside the artistic movement of the time, which they failed to follow "even by way of prints." On this point, figures speak with eloquence. The review *L'Artiste* estimated that in all of France in 1835 there were some 300 provincial painters living on the proceeds of their work (mainly portraits), which was far fewer than the number of painters living in Paris. (According to other estimates, there were 354 painters and sculptors in France in 1789; 509 in 1810; 1,375 in 1830; 2,159 in 1838; and 4,000–5,000 in 1862.) It was not until the second half of the century (or later) that provincial artists began to reorganize themselves through local art associations. The Second Republic did little to improve this situation: "If despotic states have encouraged the development of art," the republican Charles Blanc (half-brother of

the socialist Louis Blanc) wrote in 1848, "it is simply because in governments of that kind one man can control a vast concentration of capital.
Nothing prevents a similar concentration from existing in a democracy,
except that then the patron is everybody." True enough, but "everybody" was now not only republican but also Parisian.[14]

P ARIS, capital of art in the nineteenth century: we will never fully
understand the manifold causes of this extraordinary flourishing.
Obviously the immense talent of the men and women involved had
much to do with it. But nothing like this could have happened had
there not also been hundreds and probably thousands of more or less
unknown drawing teachers, painting restorers, bronze casters, studio
assistants, and talented artisans of many kinds in Paris. Parisian standards were exacting, and the academician Ernest Meissonier was no
doubt perfectly sincere when he denounced Monet's paintings as detestable scribbling because—he thought—Impressionists could neither
draw nor paint. In those days, anyone with talent, artists and artisans
alike, trained in Paris. Autodidacts of any kind who emerged from the
void beyond the capital were rare indeed. Monet, Renoir, Alfred Sisley,
and Frédéric Bazille all trained under the painter Charles Gleyre, who
took over the studio of Paul Delaroche. Manet owed a great deal to
Thomas Couture. John Singer Sargent was on the friendliest of terms
with his teacher, Emile-Auguste Carolus-Durand.

Painting was a highly organized profession in nineteenth-century
Paris, and apprentices learned the trade in prestigious studios (Antoine-
Jean Gros had more than 400 students), or at drawing schools and academies (the Académie Julian, created by a former wrestler, enjoyed a particularly good reputation among women and Americans), but above all
at the Ecole des Beaux-Arts. Founded in 1795, this school was the heart
of the Parisian system, the breeding ground of new talent. To have been
a student there was a virtual guarantee of professional success. More
than two-thirds of the graduates of Beaux-Arts received some kind of
medal in the Salons. To be sure, the school produced countless conventional painters, known in French as *Pompiers* (the adjective is said to

derive from a painting of Leonidas by David, in which the helmet of
this Greek hero reminded wags of the headgear worn by contemporary
French *pompiers,* or firemen); but it also turned out the Impressionists
Pissarro and Sisley.

At the Ecole des Beaux-Arts, students learned to paint under the
aegis and protection of the state (whether of the right or left), and this
same French state never failed to reward its better pupils. The protection that the Bourbon monarchy had afforded to budding artists did not
diminish after the convulsions of revolution and empire but, on the contrary, steadily increased: as has been said, the state sponsorship of art was
one of the few things about which everyone agreed during a century
when France knew two empires, two monarchies, and three republics,
to say nothing of communitarian or communist-inspired insurrections.
Each regime, regardless of its political coloration, saw protection of the
arts as part of its political vocation. Thus for Balzac it was self-evident
that an aristocratic-monarchical regime was supposed to find and nurture elite thinkers. For democrats, conversely, art was supposed to inspire the people. And under the Second Empire a member of the Corps
Législatif—a Bonapartist deputy with well-timed pre-totalitarian instincts—expressed the view that "in this country, where the division of
fortunes tends to level conditions and spread prosperity, the state must
take the place of private individuals." And note one important detail:
Salons and exhibitions were usually held in national palaces. "Anywhere
but in the Louvre," Louis Peisse explained in 1843, "there would be no
Salon, there would be only painting boutiques."[15]

The French state trained and rewarded artists. It also commissioned
paintings, on quite generous terms. A good example of this can be seen
in the politically impervious career of the painter François Gérard, a pu-
pil and, during the Revolution, a friend of David's: Gérard was commissioned by the emperor to decorate Malmaison, and later was ennobled
by the restored monarchy though in his earlier days he had been a
member of the revolutionary tribunal. The state-sponsored career of
Meissonier is equally instructive, if in another register: born in 1813,
the painter received a third-class medal at the Salon of 1840, a second-
class medal in 1841, and a first-class medal in 1843. Named Chevalier

of the Légion d'Honneur in 1846, he was promoted to Officier in 1855, Commandeur in 1867, and Grand Officier in 1880. In 1861, moreover, Meissonier became a member of the Institut, of which he was ultimately elected president in 1876.

But the main means of bestowing official, not to say sacred, status on art after 1815 was through the Salons, which were organized by either the Institut or the Académie des Beaux-Arts and sanctioned and paid for by the government. To be sure, there were any number of other major art exhibitions in Paris, especially during the expositions (although the expositions of 1867 and 1878 had no special sections set aside for the fine arts). In 1834, moreover, an exhibition of "works of painting and sculpture" was organized "in the galleries of the Chambre des Pairs for the benefit of those wounded on July 27, 28, and 29, 1830."[16]

Yet almost all Parisian painters gravitated toward the Salons—which were biennial until 1833 and annual thereafter. The stakes were complex. Certain paintings were singled out for special attention by the way they were hung. One year, for example, the focus was on female painters: the work of Adélaide Labille-Guiard, who would later paint a portrait of Robespierre, was hung next to that of Elizabeth Vigée-Lebrun, who had done a portrait of Marie Antoinette. David's portraits, which were relegated to the fourth rank in 1787, were, after the Revolution, among the featured works in 1791. (The choice location, we might add, was at middle height: when hung too high on the wall, paintings could not be seen; but viewers likewise could not judge canvases that were too low and too close to them.) To refuse to participate in the Salons was to commit an act of cultural or even political insubordination. Napoleon, speaking through his minister Jean-Antoine Chaptal, insisted that all top-ranking artists exhibit their works in the official Salon, and he did so in the most effective way possible by announcing that he would buy only paintings that he had seen there. Kings came to the Salons to congratulate the artists. During the Restoration, in 1825, Charles X went to the Salon on his name day to hand out awards and medals. The prince-president, Louis Napoleon, did the same in 1849. Marshal Vaillant, Chief of the Imperial Household, represented him in later years. To use today's jargon, the Paris Salons were media events with political impact.

The Salons were huge, costly machines. It is estimated that between 1791 and 1860 some 7,000–8,000 painters exhibited 68,238 paintings, or approximately 9 per painter. The numbers rose steadily: there were 1,000 paintings in 1810, and 5,184 exhibitors in 1880—and those were among the blessed, for in that year some 3,000–4,000 applicants were rejected. The number of visitors was also notable: 520,000 people attended in 1876, and in 1904 there were 10,000 visitors on just the first day of the show (although that figure is less impressive when compared with the 40,000 visitors who crowded in for the inauguration of the Salon de l'Automobile that same year).

This Parisian art system thus had two poles: the rejected artists, or *refusés;* and the jury, usually dominated by members of the fine arts section of the Institut. Some juries were quite harsh, particularly during the authoritarian Empire, when the Ecole des Beaux-Arts was the fiefdom of the comte Alfred de Nieuwerkerke, a friend of the emperor's cousin Princess Mathilde who became superintendent of fine arts. By contrast, other Salons were more democratic, as in 1849, when 800 painters were asked to elect the 12 members of the jury, and 6 of the 12 elected nevertheless turned out to be members of the Académie de Peinture.

Caricaturists ridiculed the juries endlessly—and rather unjustly: although dominated by academicians, and even by *Pompiers* painters, the juries never succeeded in systematically banning heterodox painters from the Salons, nor did they ever really try to do so. All the Impressionists—including, in 1882, the most untamed of all, Cézanne—showed their work at the Salons. The Salon des Refusés of 1863 proved a crushing failure for the exhibitors, of whom 90 percent in any case had nothing to do with nascent Impressionism.

Rejected by the Salon! Daumier immortalized the despair of the artists dealt this cruel blow by fate. Zola said of his novel *L'Oeuvre,* whose hero is a painter: "The question of acceptance by the Salon takes up my entire book." "You have to be a painter and to have suffered the ordeal of the exhibition to understand," observed Alfred Leroy. And in 1866 Léon Legat added: "Some, completely discouraged, will abandon their careers . . . Others, unable to bear what they believe to be an indelible stain on their reputation, will kill themselves." Some rejections had political or even diplomatic implications, not surprisingly since, as Gustave Larroumet put it in 1895, "Every artist, Parisian or provincial, has an official protector in the form of his deputy or senator or even both." In 1834 a first-class medal was awarded to the Russian painter Karl Brulov after the Russian ambassador spoke to Louis Forbin, the director of the royal museums.[17]

Few painters were powerful enough to refuse to submit to this ordeal, as Ingres did: from 1834 to the Exposition of 1855, stung by criticism of his *Martyrdom of Saint Symphorien,* he did not submit any of his work to the approval of any jury. After becoming famous, Courbet likewise refused to participate in the Salons and even tried to organize counter-exhibitions. Earlier, however, he had been far more conformist: "A month wasted!" he wrote to his friend Champfleury (Jules Husson) in 1854 on the eve of the opening of the Salon. "When I've never had a day to waste."[18]

L IKE IT OR NOT, we are all now disciples of Michel Foucault, keenly aware of the ways in which cultural power is exercised in the theory and practice of cultural life and also in relations between the sexes. Male chauvinism was the rule in the Parisian art world in the nineteenth century, when authority was invariably exercised downward from the top of the social ladder and by men over women. Female artists were tolerated in the Salons, but just barely. In 1835, for example, there were only 235 women among the 1,500 artists whose work was on display. The proportion of women did increase slightly over the course of the century, from 10 percent at the beginning to 20 percent at the end. Women were not accepted as students at the Ecole des Beaux-Arts until 1892, and both before and after that date they were expected to restrict their activity to certain types of art. From an article published in *L'Artiste* in 1839, for instance, we learn that "the female artist rarely tries her hand at history painting. She prefers pastel or pencil to oil . . . She is very skilled at composing portraits, genre paintings, watercolor landscapes, lilies, violets, and roses; she excels in miniature," preferences that were of course imposed, if only because women were not allowed to work from male nude models. Rosa Bonheur (1822–1899) did paint more virile subjects, such as animal fairs with dashing horses, but she was the exception that confirmed the rule. (The ambiguities of her case are revealing: though a lesbian, she took care not to offend, complied with the police order that required women to seek a permit for cross-dressing, and was eventually awarded the Legion of Honor.)[19]

By contrast to women, foreigners were much in evidence at the Salons, both as artists and as buyers. What is more, their presence in Paris reminded anyone who may have wished to forget it in other art centers such as London and Munich that Paris was the city to which painters from all over the world went in search of recognition.

In 1867 the historian Hippolyte Taine asked himself a question: Who comes to the Salons? The general public, he answered, the intelligentsia to some degree, and of course collectors and art dealers. But also, he added, "Frenchmen who have struck it rich: bankers and speculators [who] want to embellish their châteaux and town houses. They know that painted murals set a home apart from the run of the mill, and so, like headwaiters or entrepreneurs, they order . . . allegories and mythologies for their ceilings." Art ennobled wealth, especially wealth dubiously acquired. This was true, of course, not only of French wealth but also of foreign wealth: "The Brazilian, Moldavian, or American who has made a fortune or who feels bored among his slaves and peasants comes to Paris to enjoy life . . . He buys a carriage . . . wears a diamond tie pin . . . orders several Venuses from some artist . . . and the artist gives him what he wants." A few years earlier Alphonse de Lamartine had formulated the same idea in gentler, nobler terms: "To have been painted in Paris is for an *objet d'art* a mark of value, a certificate of taste, a proof of illustrious provenance."[20]

For art lovers, Paris was Mecca, and foreigners who could not visit the capital themselves followed what went on there in the press. Celebrated writers gave them things to dream about: Henry James was in Paris as an art critic for the *New York Herald,* and, through Turgenev, Zola became art critic for the *Messager de l'Europe de Saint-Pétersbourg.* James had ironic words for his compatriots, who paid for paintings the equivalent of their weight in gold. And it took nothing less than a patriotic gesture by Alfred Chauchard, the owner of a large department store in Paris, to bring Millet's *Angélus* back from the United States for the staggering sum of 800,000 gold francs.

Some foreigners came to buy, but others came to paint. Among those who lived in Paris for extended periods were Sargent from the United States, Mihály Munkácsy from Hungary (the best-known Hungarian painter of his day), and Alphonse Mucha from Czechoslovakia (who became famous overnight thanks to a poster he painted for Sarah Bernhardt in 1894). For some foreign painters, Parisian residence even ran in the family, so to speak: the Spaniard José de Madrazo worked in David's studio; his son Federico came to Paris in 1833; and two subsequent generations of Madrazos also resided in the capital. When a French ambassador suggested to the German painter Alfred Rethel (1816–1859) that he show his work in Paris, Rethel replied: "To have my painting accepted in Paris would be the height of success and would mean the world to me. If it happens, you'll soon know about it. What more could I want? Am I not the happiest of men?"[21] More than a hundred American painters showed works in Paris Salons in the nineteenth century, the first of them being John Vanderlyn, who showed his work in the Salon of 1800 as a student of François-André Vincent. The romance of Paris persisted for American artists until quite recently. In the aftermath of the Second World War, there were still 250 American artists living in the capital thanks to the G.I. Bill, and the hero of the film *An American in Paris* is of course a painter. Some Parisian painters made a sort of specialty of acting as mentors to foreign artists: for example, Camille Pissarro, a native of the island of Saint Thomas in the Caribbean, prided himself on serving as guide to a fair number of young painters from Central America.

If the nineteenth-century Parisian art system, then, was a machine for manufacturing and exhibiting paintings, it was also—dare I say above all?—a machine for *selling* works of art at prices that ranged from nearly nothing to the plainly ruinous. Money mattered a great deal. Some artists lived in poverty. Others scraped by with help from their families: initially this was true of the Impressionists, most of whom, other than Renoir, came from bourgeois backgrounds. But many others were authentic luminaries, decorated, respected, and fabulously well paid. In

1822 Horace Vernet sold his *Battle of Montmirail* for no less than 10,000 francs; and Ingres sold his *Odalisque de Pourtalès* for 12,000 francs with an additional 24,000 francs for the reproduction rights. In 1849 Horace Vernet sold a painting to the czar for 99,000 francs. In 1878 Meissonier received 250,000 francs for his *Cuirassiers de 1805.* According to Raymonde Moulin, painters came to Paris looking not so much for a pure doctrine or the great tradition as for "a way to establish themselves in the public eye and, in particular, in the eyes of potential buyers." "I will try to explain to you why I'm sending my work to the Salon," Renoir wrote to the dealer Paul Durand-Ruel in March 1881. "There are 80,000 people who wouldn't buy a thing if a painter was not in the Salon. That is why I send two portraits every year, as little as that may be . . . My shipment to the Salon is entirely commercial." The Salon could take a painter a very long way indeed. Once his work was accepted and perhaps even awarded a medal, he could sell to private buyers and possibly even to the state. The ideal was to have a painting in the Musée de l'Art Contemporain, which until 1937 was located in the Palais du Luxembourg. He might even hope to earn a thousand francs or, on occasion, far more: in 1855 Auguste Vinchon won 20,000 francs for his *Départ des volontaires.*[22]

If the Salon and the state were the twin teats that nursed Parisian painting in the nineteenth century, additional nourishment came from art dealers, who were to artists as publishers had become to musicians, namely a critical link between the artists and the public. Although Jean-Antoine Watteau's *Gersaint's Shopsign,* painted for the art dealer Gersaint in 1720, is well known, it was not until about 1830 that this aspect of the Parisian art system really got off the ground. Adolphe Goupil's arrival in 1845 marked a turning point, and by 1861 more than a thousand dealers had set up shop in the capital, mostly in the vicinity of the grand boulevards and the rue Lafitte, the heart of the art business.[23] Durand-Ruel (1831–1922) opened his doors in 1862, not far from Goupil's shop on the boulevard Montmartre. For Théophile Gautier, the rue Lafitte was like a permanent Salon, where paintings could be viewed even at night thanks to carefully illuminated shop windows.

The role of these art dealers was crucial, as the case of Durand-Ruel makes clear. With aid from the banker Feder and the Banque de l'Union Catholique (which went under in 1882), Durand-Ruel bought quantities of art, more or less monopolizing the output of certain artists: in 1866 he bought seventy paintings by Théodore Rousseau, and in 1872 he paid 35,000 francs for twenty-three paintings by Manet. What is more, Goupil, Durand-Ruel, and many other Paris dealers were quick to open branches in New York (Goupil did so in 1846). "Works of art are very strange," wrote the Goncourts in 1860—and for once the brothers were naive: "You never set your own price. The price is not absolute, even in your own eyes. It is not your price. It is almost always the price set by someone else."[24]

Relations between the Salons, which were controlled by the Académie, and the dealers, who were of course subject to the influences of the art market, were supposedly strained, to judge by the accounts of the interested parties. But in reality the entire machine operated as a well-coordinated system. Some art dealers took a fairly broad view, moreover, and tried to link their own fate to the fate of artists, as Louis Martinet did in 1863 with his Société Nationale des Beaux-Arts, which exhibited works by Delacroix, Courbet, Narcisse Diaz, Gustave Doré, Millet, and Constant Troyon. Count Walewski, the minister of foreign affairs, and Théophile Gautier were associated with this venture for a time, and Gautier served as art critic in the journal *Fantaisies parisiennes, courrier artistique,* whose goal was to help young painters who had not yet managed to gain entry to the Salons.[25] Van Gogh's brother Theo was an art dealer (and for a time an employee of Goupil) who supported the painter with a monthly stipend of 150 francs.

These dealer-operated galleries also served as sales offices, as did certain artists' ateliers. For instance, Narcisse Diaz, a member of the Barbizon School, organized ten sales of his works between 1848 and his death in 1876. (When his 1849 sale proved not very successful, his paintings fetching only 740–1,000 francs apiece, the new republican government paid him 4,000 francs for a painting that he never finished.)[26] Motivated by a similar desire for financial independence, many Parisian artists (such as Delacroix) tried to organize artists' associations. The best known of these were sponsored by an English patron of the arts by the name of Baron Isidore Taylor, who organized a "society for the mutual support of dramatic artists," and, in 1844, a second group with a similar goal for painters, sculptors, architects, and engravers. In 1879, moreover, the artist Edouard Detaille organized a Société des Aquarellistes Français (Association of French Watercolorists). Along these lines, it is worth noting that the motives of the artists who participated in the celebrated Salon des Refusés were probably more pecuniary than aesthetic. As were those of the buyers who organized exhibits, such as the one staged in the 1860s by the Cercle du Beau Paris.

Money was very important for the prestige of the Salons, for the future of the artists, and also for their choice of subjects. "As for the Parisian bourgeois," the writer Victor Fournel observed puckishly in 1858, "unless he has been decorated or is a member of one of the academies, he does not yet dare to commission a full-size statue of himself while he is still alive and confines himself to a bust or a medallion. Most of all he confines himself to the portrait." In 1873 the critic Marius Chaumelin blamed vanity and money for the disappearance of "great painting." In visiting one Salon he "counted 320 portraits in oil and 203 in pencil, or one-fifth of the works displayed." The Goncourts noted: "Religious painting is a thing of the past . . . Painters of the nineteenth century are left with genre painting . . . as a practical means of earning a living." We associate Impressionism with painting in the open air, but in fact Manet, Renoir, and Degas were also assiduous portraitists: in the rivalry between "gourmet painting" (which might have been called "paying-the-rent painting") and "ideal painting," the question of how the painters themselves were supposed to eat was not without importance.[27]

Salons, state subsidies, art dealers, and the artistic press (such as *La Gazette des beaux-arts*): these were the key elements in the production of art in Paris, the capital of the nineteenth century. Completing the system was a personage of great influence: the art critic. In the 1750s La Font de Saint-Yenne—decidedly a key figure—saw himself as a moral guide to the Parisian public, and his nineteenth-century successors (such as Duranty, Astruc, Burty, and Woolf) were no less ambitious. Not all of them were pernicious, and some promoted new talent, as Tedesco did for the young Delacroix. The systematization of their role was impressive, as were their numbers: no fewer than a hundred critics plied their trade under Napoleon III. Some, as Theodore Zeldin explains, came to art criticism from the worlds of journalism, academia, literature, and public service, while others had been painters with insufficient talent to succeed at it.[28] Together they became the architects of a varied and ever-changing discourse on the nature of art, so that every artist in Paris could immediately situate himself in relation to the reigning orthodoxies and aesthetic discourses.

P ARIS, capital of (the system of) the arts, up to a point in the eighteenth century, and with a vengeance in subsequent decades: it is relatively easy to understand the importance and the nature of this mechanism of interconnected cogs and wheels. Yet the strength of this system from David and Ingres to Picasso and Chagall, from 1780 to 1940, depended not just on the formal institutions—though they were very important indeed—but also on another essential ingredient, one that was informal and intangible yet critical, what we might call the air or atmosphere of Paris. In Paris, capital of the nineteenth century, painters were simultaneously causes and effects of Parisian modernity, and even today our visual imagination of the nineteenth century is largely dependent on their work (as some of the illustrations in this book demonstrate). The power of Paris, as well as the inspiration of its painters, lay for once precisely in the embarrassment of its riches, in the conjunction of its various myths (capital of revolution, of urbanization, of fashion, of alienation, of science, and so on).

Of course, Paris was the capital of art partly because it was home to a vast art machine maintained by public as well as private resources, but even more because nineteenth-century painters instinctively understood their era in terms of what people in Paris thought about it: so it was, for example, that Paris in the 1880s became the world capital of *Japonisme* not only because Europeans there imitated Japanese motifs but because many Japanese artists went there to study. Indeed, it is because those artists were able to insert their work into the various definitions of Parisian modernity that their canvases still seem modern to us today. On returning from the Impressionist show of 1877, the art critic for *L'Homme libre* offered a judgment in line with that of many others: that the show "demonstrates that painting is not strictly an archaeological art and can accommodate modernity effortlessly." When Cézanne was asked to comment on Renoir's work, his answer was succinct: "He painted the woman of Paris."[29]

Thus the great moments in Parisian painting coincided—necessarily, one would like to say—with the great moments of Paris as capital of modernity: its genesis (David and the Revolution) and its blossoming (the Impressionists and the Haussmannization of Paris). With, at the other extreme, the turning inward of Paris with the Colonial Exposition of 1931 and the Occupation of 1940–1944, which coincided with the end of the city's reign as capital of the arts and the rise of New York.

In the end, what made the art of nineteenth-century Paris so powerful was that it gave us representations of modernity in paintings that seem to us to have been the most truthful images of that time, just as the art of New York in the period 1940–1960 (the age of Jackson Pollock, Franz Kline, and Piet Mondrian) is powerful because it gave us the new forms that have helped us understand our own age. And when Paris gradually ceased to be the capital of change, innovation, and modernity, art migrated across the Atlantic. No doubt New York, in turn, will cease to be the world capital of art when modernity establishes itself somewhere else—or everywhere.

All of which means, for the history of Parisian art, that it behooves us to dwell on the various kinds of ties—cultural, ideological, and aesthetic—that bound artists to Paris. Here, a first point might be, on the most banal level, that artists took part in the daily and ordinary life of the city. We like to think of painters and poets as revelers, habitués of brothels, and absinthe drinkers. And a fair number of them probably were: Rimbaud, who aimed to blur life and language as well as the one and the other (*I* is an *other*), and Verlaine, a symbolist whose lyric verse radiates musicality, were not just great poets but also disreputable lovers, one of whom shot and wounded the other. Balzac, for his part, distinguished the decent misery of the doctor without patients, and the gay misery of the office worker, from the poetic but sad misery of the artist and the student. Thackeray likewise told his English audience that the life of the young Parisian artist "is the easiest, merriest, dirtiest existence possible. He comes to Paris, probably at sixteen, from his province; his parents settle forty pounds a year on him, and pay his master; he establishes himself in the Pays Latin," and there leads a life of reckless pleasure. These were seductive fictions (they still are), and artists themselves were seduced by them (they still are). "What attracted me," Pierre Bonnard wrote, "was not so much the art as the life of the artist, which I imagined to be full of fantasy and freedom to do as one pleased. Of course I had long been attracted to painting and drawing, but the passion was not irresistible, whereas I wanted at all cost to escape from a life of monotony."[30]

Clearly, some Parisian artists lived more freely than others. And no one would deny that artists shared certain distinctive and characteristic ways of living and thinking. Some painters lived in the city's cafés, or, in the case of Courbet—the future scourge of the Colonne Vendôme— in the Brasserie Andler. Even Delacroix, whom Baudelaire called "un parfait gentleman" and who was said to be the illegitimate son of Talleyrand—bishop, prince, and minister—sometimes felt ill at ease in society. "Dined with M. Thiers," he wrote in his journal in 1847. "I don't know what to say to the people I meet at his house, and they don't know what to say to me."[31]

Nevertheless, the vast majority of nineteenth-century Parisian artists lived entirely bourgeois and quite unrevolutionary lives. Monet's estate at Giverny was no garret. Most painters shared the tastes and vanities of their time and moved into the better neighborhoods as soon as they could afford to do so. The Impressionists and their successors were notoriously of bourgeois or even noble origin (as was the case with Degas to a degree and Toulouse-Lautrec certainly). If one had to name a typical Parisian artist in this respect, it would not be Courbet in his brasserie or Gauguin in Tahiti but Matisse, who, when interviewed by the *New York Times,* asked the reporter to assure American readers that he was the soul of good behavior: "Above all, tell the Americans that I am a normal man, a devoted husband and father, that I have three beautiful children, that I go to the theater, that I ride horses, that I have a comfortable house and a beautiful garden that I love, flowers, and so on, just like anyone else."[32]

If Parisian artists were men of their era in their daily lives, most were also men of their time in their political opinions. Some were on the right: Degas was a zealous anti-Dreyfusard and Cézanne a convinced Catholic. Some on the left, such as Courbet, Manet, and even Pissarro, were ultimately more inclined to democracy than to socialism, and not very different in this respect from the majority of the Parisian middle class in the second half of the nineteenth century. To be sure, the lapsed painter Claude Lantier in Zola's *L'Oeuvre* "saw the revolution in a carrot," but such an aptitude was the norm more in literature than in life, and in any case it was the portrayal of the painter in this novel that put an end to Zola's long friendship with Cézanne, his old schoolmate from Aix.

Broadly speaking, then, the opinions of Parisian painters of this first period did little to mark them out as a political or cultural avant-garde. To be sure, from Théodore Géricault's *Raft of the Medusa* (illustrating a shipwrecked France in distress, wounded by the Bourbon restoration) to Picasso's *Guérnica* from the time of the Spanish Civil War, art was usually—though mildly—on the left, as was science, but scarcely more than was the Parisian middle class. The work of Emile Gallé, who in 1892 was commissioned by a group of young intellectuals to "crystallize" the thought of Pasteur (which he did by creating a transparent crystal filled with microbes), has symbolic value: bourgeois painting and science joined together in the service of humankind.[33]

Integrated into the middle or upper middle class, and mildly progressive in their political views, nineteenth-century Parisian artists, especially those who saw themselves as politically audacious, dreamed not of laying down a challenge with their art but, on the contrary, of merging their art into the mainstream of the moment, of turning it into "a powerful means of infusing morality into the masses," as David d'Angers wrote in 1843.[34] This attitude toward art is obviously open to devastating criticism, and Flaubert bitingly satirized it in *L'Education sentimentale,* a novel featuring a painter by the name of Pellerin, a democrat and *quarante-huitard,* who never finishes his masterpiece depicting Christ at the controls of the locomotive of progress (an interesting foretaste, incidentally, of Soviet-style socialist realism).

One could list any number of other affinities—cultural, scientific, and moral—linking nineteenth-century art to its Parisian substrate. It is unreasonable, for example, to insist on the importance of the innovative packaging of paint in tubes (in London in 1824) for the flourishing of open-air painting; but it is clear, by contrast, that the Parisian trajectories of technology, science, and the arts, so divergent today, were very close during the nineteenth century. For example, the color theories of the physicist Michel-Eugène Chevreul were of keen interest to his contemporaries. And the invention of lithography (in 1796, with improvements by the printer Godefroy Engelmann in 1837) was a scientific innovation that played an important role in the birth of realist painting: by heightening "the sense of the instantaneous," lithography was more flexible and "presented no obstacle to the artist's freedom and control, as etching or engraving does."[35] The invention of the daguerreotype in 1838 (Jules Janin explained the technique in that same year to readers of *L'Artiste*, as François Arago did to the Académie des Sciences in August 1839) had a similar effect. Some artists, most notably Degas, took an active interest in the evolution of photography.

Social background, political views, interest in natural science—these were strong connections. And yet, in the end, they were merely indices of the modernizing sensibility that allowed Parisian artists to externalize "the real," that is, the essence of Parisian modernity. Parisian artists were invariably concerned with this issue: all of them could have agreed with Champfleury, who wrote of "a distinguished woman" who had rightly proposed to her Parisian colleagues in 1850 that they "seek the causes and methods that give the appearance of reality to works of art." (Baudelaire, in his notes on Champfleury, sought to set himself apart from that "perverse child" by asserting that poetry was most real when it considered "what is true only in *another world*.") That art should in some sense be "real" and in any case should be aware of modernity, he certainly did not deny.[36]

And how did Parisian artists hope to conceive and create verisimilitude? Their opinions varied widely, as do our own efforts to understand them. Some commentators today emphasize the relation of these artists to the opinions of their times. Others hold that the successful creators of the "real" were those who best set their work in an "intertextual" rela-

tionship with other texts and situations. And still other critics stress the
reliance of nineteenth-century artists on the production of quasi-photo-
graphic detail: the Goncourts noted with disappointment that "Balzac
is perhaps not so much a great physiological anatomist as a great painter
of interiors. It sometimes seems that he observes furniture more closely
than characters." Their disciple Zola, however, would pride himself on
emulating the author of *Père Goriot:* "I suffer from hypertrophy of true
detail, leaping into the empyrean from a springboard of precise observation."[37]

Indeed, it is difficult for us today to understand or even to define the
categories of the realism that seemed self-evident to Parisian artists: it
seems obvious to us that we should distinguish between Pompiers artists and Romantics, between Romantics, Realists, Naturalists, and Impressionists; but these distinctions were far less clear in Paris at the
time, because in one way or another every Parisian artist saw himself as a
realist or at least as some kind of "verisimilist." As the art historian
Gérald Schurr remarked some time ago, "between the Pompiers and the
Avant-garde of the day, there were many painters who never asked
themselves which camp they belonged to and who never opted either for
the academicians or against the revolutionaries." Take, for instance, the
strange case of Dominique Papety, who, in painting *Le Rêve de bonheur* (A
Dream of Happiness) in 1843, decided one day to replace a steamboat
with a Greek temple. Such a change strikes us as grotesque, but we may
assume that this artist believed he was being faithful to truthful realism
because, for him, either image could express what he took to be the ideal
representation of happiness. Robert Herbert has rightly underscored
the continuities that ran from Naturalism and caricature to Impressionism.[38]

The works of Thomas Couture in the 1840s and of Pierre Puvis de
Chavannes after 1870 illustrate the complexity of any taxonomy, especially one that would transcend the boundaries between different forms
of artistic work: to some listeners, Wagner was a "realist" compared with
the Italian "illusionists." Indeed, François-Joseph Fétis called Wagner
"the Courbet of music," which did not keep Champfleury from calling
him a "hyper-romantic." (Baudelaire, who admired Wagner but wished

to distance himself from the realism of Courbet, wrote that Fétis's "indigestible and abominable" pamphlet was nothing but a "distressing diatribe" and "the irritation [of an] old dilettante.") The critic Théophile Thoré, who had mocked painters given to flattering contemporary taste—the "fashionable" school, he called them—was enthusiastic about the work of "Monsieur Delacroix" because that painter in his view had derived "his revolutionary value from a marvelous sense of modern ideality." Whether "real" *(The Massacre of Scio)* or obviously fictitious *(The Death of Sardanapalus)*, Delacroix's subjects were, in the eyes of a connoisseur like Thoré, "alive" and therefore, in some deeper sense, real. The centuries, the critic continued, "do not count for him, any more than distance counts . . . [He] is their contemporary, he lives among them." *The Raft of the Medusa* was by no means a topical work in the narrow sense, yet to Géricault this carefully composed painting was meant to be a faithful representation of the state of mind of a France badly led by a backward and in its own way "unreal" social class, the restoration nobility.[39]

B UT EVEN if we find it difficult to distinguish and analyze successive schools of Parisian painting, we can see that Parisian artists drew much of their "realistic" strength (whatever that might have been) from their supposed ability to "read" the legibilities of Parisian life. And we can also see that Parisians in turn justified their place as the foremost artistic public of the age by endorsing the successive images of themselves that the various schools of Parisian painting produced.

For Meissonier and Jean-Léon Gérôme, who were immensely popular and "state-praised," this meant *léché* painting, that is, painting that was precise and perfectly smooth, intended to be "photographically" realistic with virtually no trace of brushwork. In such painting the artist insisted on "the painting as an open window or an illusion"[40] of grasping the real without interposing a screen of any kind between the art lover and the subject. In 1860 this principle was still generally accepted in Paris. By 1900, however, in part because of the dissemination of photographic equipment (but for many other reasons as well), it had lost this acceptance.

For the Impressionists, by contrast, verisimilitude arose from other sources, such as their choice of subject (a Paris street, a group of laundresses, the new *cafés-concerts,* the suburbs where Parisians went to enjoy themselves). Also at stake, and to an even greater degree, was the newly defined intersection of the eye of the informal observer with the abstracted subject placed before it by the painter. Courbet painted what he saw, including the celebrated *L'Origine du monde* (The Origin of the World), but Manet's indifference to the specifics of landscape was notorious.

Change here was very swift, and, crucially for the place of Paris in world art, the Paris public was able to follow this modernizing shift quite quickly. In the early 1860s Boudin was receiving between 100 and 250 francs for each painting he placed with Durand-Ruel. Georges Seurat, as André Breton recounted with amazement, "calculated the price of his masterpieces at the rate of seven francs per day of work (with a reduction allowed out of respect for the identity of the buyer)."[41] In 1869 Monet was on the edge of poverty; Durand-Ruel paid him only 300 francs apiece for his paintings in 1871. By the end of the second Impressionist exhibition of 1876, however, Monet's price had risen to 2,000 francs per painting. At the Universal Exposition of 1889 van Gogh's brother Theo sold one of Monet's canvases to an American for 9,000 francs. In 1899 each of his "Water Lilies" went for 5,000–7,000 francs. Earlier, in 1890, the painter had become prosperous enough to buy his house in Giverny.

And so it was that Paris at the end of the nineteenth century negotiated a major cultural and pictorial shift in its continuing quest for what was truly real, that is, for what was truly modern. It had greater difficulty, however, with a subsequent shift toward an even more modernist and less representational style.

A Parisian harbinger of this further change came as early as the 1860s in the form of a flattening of perspective in some paintings by Manet (most notably *The Bar at the Folies Bergères*). Cézanne, who of all the Impressionists was the most estranged from the Salons as well as the boldest and most "modern" in style, made a prophetic specialty of this decomposition of forms. Shortly thereafter, Picasso became famous for giving these new principles of painting a frankly modernist direction: in

1905–1906 he was still in his "blue" and "pink" periods, but by 1906–1907, with the *Demoiselles d'Avignon,* the rupture with the past was complete.

But here the Parisian public balked: it proved much slower to warm to the Cubists and Surrealists, whose acceptance was never to be as wide as that of the Impressionists. Berthe Morisot's paintings of motherhood, Eugène Boudin's beaches, and Monet's landscapes quickly constituted a universally recognized and cross-class vocabulary that is still current today, but recognition of the work of their successors was far less certain. Hence, also in the final decades of the nineteenth century, there arose in Paris a so-called avant-garde, made up of those art lovers who were capable of appreciating what the general public could no longer understand as realistic in the new and deeper sense of the word.

The expression "avant-garde" originated in Paris, as it had to. We owe it to a Fourierist by the name of Gabriel Désiré Laverdant, who coined it in a book entitled *De la Mission de l'art et le rôle des artistes.* But he used it in a sense entirely different from ours: for him it meant that the true artist, in order to paint correctly, had to place himself at the head of the segment of humanity that was en route to a better world, as that better world was imagined in Paris in 1845.

To a sarcastic Baudelaire, the term had a military ring, and "avant-garde" for him referred to left-wing Parisian literati, to social democrats who subordinated art to politics. It was not until the Modernist and Post-Impressionist period that the term was taken to apply to whatever "astounds the bourgeois," a broad rubric that included any number of Parisian farces ranging from Alfred Jarry's play *Ubu roi* to the extravagances of the Surrealists: elaborate practical jokes that once seemed hilarious but that strike us today as largely puerile, since we no longer share the aesthetic teleologies of the avant-gardes of the past.

Indeed, it seemed at the time that the existence of an avant-garde was a critical aspect of the vitality of Parisian aesthetic culture. But in retrospect the reverse seems more true. When Paris was the capital of the nineteenth century, thousands understood the works of the city's artists: "Can there be a more pleasing walk in the whole world," asked Thackeray, "than to stroll through the Gallery of the Louvre on a fête-day; not to look so much at the pictures as at the lookers-on? Thousands of the poorer classes are there: mechanics in their Sunday clothes, smiling grisettes, smart dapper soldiers of the line, with bronzed wondering faces, marching together in little companies of six or seven, and stopping every now and then at Napoleon or Leonidas as they appear in proper vulgar heroics in the pictures of David and Gros."[42] But when Paris became the capital of a politically progressive but nevertheless elitist and excluding avant-garde, the city's glory days were numbered.

IT MUST BE emphasized again that the shift of artistic modernity from Paris to New York, like the shift from Rome to Paris in the 1790s, was gradual. Paris was still the world capital of art in the 1920s and 1930s, and on certain days in Montparnasse one could easily have run into "foreigners such as Brancusi, Soutine, Severini, Kupka, Chirico, Van Dongen, Fujita, Diego Rivera, Pascin, Naum Gabo and his brother Antoine Pevsner, Mondrian, Lipchitz, Chagall, Zadkin, Calder, and Alberto Giacometti" along with such "natives" as Villon, Derain, Dufy, Vuillard, Signac, Marquet, and Laurens.[43]

It is also important that in the years between the two world wars Paris had not yet lost its vocation as the financial center of the world art market. The methods of the art dealer D. Kahnweiler were strangely reminiscent of those of Durand-Ruel: Kahnweiler bought paintings of Juan Gris and Picasso not by the pound but by the square inch, and what mattered was not their quality but their size. The state also continued to buy art: in 1935 various Paris museums bought works by Wassily Kandinsky, Yves Tanguy, and Robert Delaunay.

Yet in spite of all this, in the 1930s the myth of Paris, capital of art, was already waning. Critically, the Parisian public, even the left-wing public, could no longer keep up. Rightist opinions were not necessarily signs of aesthetic troglodytism: Léon Daudet, for example, though a royalist who had been thrilled to be asked by a young American woman if he really was, as she had heard, "the most reactionary man in the world," also believed that Picasso was a great artist. Similarly, in these years leftist opinions were no guarantee of aesthetic discernment, as became clear when Aragon, after abandoning Surrealism for communism, went on to sing the praises of Soviet Realism.

In general, Parisian art critics did not respond to the new modernism of art as metaphor and pure form. The selection of works to be displayed at the Universal Exposition of 1937 was not as audacious as that of the New York Armory Show of 1913. Delaunay, Picasso, and Miró were invited to participate, but Kandinsky, Duchamp, and Constantin Brancusi were left out.[44] A statue by Jacques Lipchitz on the Champs-Elysées drew angry criticism from the right and was dismantled and destroyed shortly thereafter. Many recent paintings made their way to the United States, just as Matisse's work had earlier made its way to pre-revolutionary Russia. It was also a sign of the times in the 1920s that the Parisian public during these "years of illusion" was more interested in exotic spectacles (ranging from the Ballet Russe and the Swedish Ballet to Josephine Baker) than in avant-garde art.

So it was that after the Parisian century came New York's turn in the sun. Most French artists had paid little attention to the Armory Show of 1913; and yet we now see that exhibition as a milestone in the history of art and in the history of New York as a center of art.[45]

Various factors account for the rise of New York in this field: they range from the end of the Great Depression to America's triumphal role in the Second World War and the postwar economic boom. American museums also played an important role. Even before the First World War the Metropolitan Museum of New York had bought a Cézanne, *Paupers' Hill* (for $6,700, a bargain compared to the asking price of $8,000). In 1936 Alfred Barr of the Museum of Modern Art (founded with Rockefeller assistance in 1929) organized a show of "Cubism and Abstract Art," which was followed by another show of "Fantastic Art, Dada, Surrealism." Then came a retrospective devoted to Matisse in 1931 and another in 1935 devoted to Fernand Léger, who had trained many American artists in Paris in the 1920s.

Adding to this orchestrated enthusiasm was the enthusiasm of wealthy private individuals. Whereas Mary Cassatt had left America to live in Paris, Peggy Guggenheim, when she moved back to New York from Europe during the Second World War, brought in her train some of the most illustrious stars of the Paris art world such as Max Ernst, Salvador Dali, Breton, Tanguy, and André Masson.

Nineteenth-century Paris had been an "art machine," and twentieth-century New York soon became one. The first focused on the representational, the second on metaphor and abstraction. New York museums and patrons of the arts gradually established relationships with local artists, including former Stalinists and Trotskyites whose political views had moderated considerably by the mid-1940s. The art critic Clement Greenberg (New York's Baudelaire) proved that the future of art lay in New York because American artists were not slaves to outmoded "taste" and to the obsolete French and Parisian insistence on "quality."[46]

All these elements now rapidly fell into place, and Paris art dealers were quick to respond to this transatlantic call, not least because any number of them had long since established branches in New York: Durand-Ruel had opened a New York office in 1886, Nathan Wildenstein in 1902. At one point Wildenstein's American holdings numbered some 2,000 paintings, including 8 Rembrandts, 79 Fragonards, 20 Renoirs, and 250 Picassos.[47]

In 1880 Edouard Manet was the very type of the Parisian artist: an elegant dandy unfortunately afflicted with syphilis. In New York in 1950 his equivalent was Jackson Pollock, an impeccable nativist and an alcoholic who reproached Willem de Kooning for being a "French painter" and who was to die like the fabled James Dean in an automobile accident with sexual overtones. These two artists and their two fates—the one in Paris and the other in New York—epitomize a much larger evolution.

In 1952 the Sidney Janis Gallery in New York organized a show entitled "American Art for Paris." Georges Bataille found it interesting, drawn as he was to the work of Kline, Robert Motherwell, and de Kooning. But the critic Jean-Pierre, writing in *Les Lettres françaises,* spoke of "disconcerting puerilities and alarming smears,"[48] and his was the more typical—and revealing—judgment. Aesthetic modernity had moved from one side of the Atlantic to the other, and Paris, no longer the capital of art, was now for artists what Rome had been for David.

17

A Universal City

Paris was not the capital of the twentieth century, and it will not be the capital of the twenty-first century. Indeed, the very idea of a world capital has probably ceased to make much sense: with the internationalization and globalization of culture and economics, centers and peripheries are shifting and blending together across national and urban boundaries.

Still, as Humphrey Bogart says to Ingrid Bergman in *Casablanca*, "We'll always have Paris"; and, as in Goethe's judgment, Paris will always be a universal city, perhaps the most universal and most distinctive of all. Paris is no longer what it was a century and a half ago: the mythological focal point of the present and the capital of the future. But even if it can no longer herald what is soon to come, contemporary Paris, more than any other city in the world, can serve to explain the course of Western culture. Its primary distinction today is to focus humankind's nostalgia for a golden past, and this is of consequence.

Moreover, to recall a theme with which we began, Paris is not just a city that happens to be incomparably rich in history: it remains one of the most vibrant and dynamic centers of contemporary urban life, less vibrant than New York perhaps, less dynamic than London perhaps, but better managed than the one, more humane than the other, and incomparably beautiful still. Is Paris merely a vast museum? To a certain extent, yes, and perhaps the most beautiful museum of all; but, unlike Venice or Florence, Paris is not *just* a museum. Paris may no longer be the capital of science, but scientific research of the first order is still carried on there, as recent work on the origin of AIDS has shown. Paris is no longer the capital of art, but artists of significance are still working there. And much the same can be said of technology, architecture, fashion, public transportation, the presence of immigrants, and the Internet. Paris no longer innovates in many of these domains. But it keeps up: every fact and every myth has left some productive trace.

Paris in Europe. But what is a European? A person who resides in the region that stretches from the Urals to the Iberian islands of the South Atlantic? From the steppes of central Asia to the "petite île" Saint Helena where Napoleon was exiled at the farthest corner of the globe? Up to a point, of course; but geopolitical definitions of this kind, though they are still of interest, are of little use in answering the kinds of questions that concern us today. Like nostalgia—to borrow once again from Simone Signoret's celebrated phrase—the territoriality of states is not what it used to be. Nor is the idea of Europe as no more than a shared—and excluding—sphere of prosperity likely to elicit a new and durable civic sense of public responsibility.

Other answers seem more relevant intellectually. Perhaps what it means to be a European today is to be the heir to a common and fratricidal history. Even if "Europe" is no longer an institution whose primary function is to make another war between France and Germany impossible, it was for that reason that the European Community was first conceived.

One might also agree with the German philosopher Jürgen Habermas that Europe is a collection of men and women sharing certain values, some of which are already understood and stated, while others will arise only after the creation of a Europe-wide constitution. Here law is the generator of myth. In this context of what Habermas calls *Verfassungspatriotismus,* Europeans are—or will be—people who share certain emotional ties and are willing to accept certain political responsibilities vis-à-vis their fellow citizens, some of whom may be neighbors in some nearby province while others may live farther away in another country: the Europeans of tomorrow will be people who agree to assist one another in various ways, just as today the citizens of, say, France agree to

435

grant certain inalienable social and civil rights to those whom they regard as French citizens,[1] whether they live in Burgundy or Touraine, or
for that matter in Corsica or the Basque country.

All of these ways of thinking intersect at various points. But there is
another definition of what it means to be a European that may have particular relevance to this urban biography: a European is a person for
whom Paris is not the capital of Europe—to make such a claim would
be excessive and grandiloquent—but for whom Paris remains *the* European city par excellence, a magical and once mythical place, the capital
of a multinational memory, a city even now alive with memories of German cabinetmakers, Spanish artists, Russian grand dukes and taxi drivers, Portuguese maids and novelists, English tourists and industrialists,
Swiss guards and bankers, Italian poets and conspirators, African migrants and North African refugees. In that definition, a European is anyone for whom Paris might now or in the future hold a key to some form
of self-understanding.

Paris in myth and modern history: Paris was once the mythical capital of a divided continent, and today, though "demythified," the city is
still unique, universally admired and loved, a capital of the civilizing
spirit. It can work to maintain that spirit by reaching out beyond its
closest borders first to the Paris region, which it has too often ignored,
and then to Europe and the world, whose auratic, monumental, and aesthetic urban conscience it now is and—or so we can fervently hope—
will remain for centuries to come.

Notes ❧ Acknowledgments ❧ Index

Notes

I. A CITY OF MYTHS

1. Nietzsche cited by Roger Caillois in *Le Mythe et l'homme* (Paris: Gallimard, 1938), 25.
2. Anne Alter and Philippe Testard-Vaillant, *Guide du Paris savant* (Paris: Belin, 1997), 609.
3. Walter Benjamin, *Reflections* (New York: Harcourt Brace, 1978), 155.
4. Pierre Citron, *La Poésie de Paris dans la littérature française de Rousseau à Baudelaire* (Paris: Minuit, 1961).
5. Michelet cited by Citron, ibid., vol. 2, 252. Caillois, *Le Mythe et l'homme*, 13.
6. David Pinkney, *Napoleon III and the Rebuilding of Paris* (Princeton: Princeton University Press, 1958), 45, citing Alphand, "Introduction," in *Mémoires du Baron Haussmann* (Paris, 1979).
7. Caillois, *Le Mythe et l'homme,* 22.
8. In *La Complainte de Fantômas,* with music by Kurt Weill, in 1933.
9. Thomas Carlyle, *The French Revolution* (New York: Modern Library, n.d.), 47.

2. CAPITAL OF THE MODERN SELF

1. In his introduction to *Paris et ses environs* in the Blue Guide series, George Lenôtre estimated that the number of "monographs," that is, books and articles, dealing with the capital numbered "certainly 200,000 and this could possibly be tripled, if we added, as we should, the gazettes, the journals of fashion or art, the memoirs, the studies of deaths, the biographies, the journals of sport and of theater, indispensable to all Parisian bibliographies." Cited in Louis Bergeron, ed., *Paris: Genèse d'un paysage* (Paris: Picard, 1989), preface.
2. See Peter Beilharz, *Postmodern Socialism: Romanticism, City, and State* (Carlton, Victoria: Melbourne University Press, 1994), 14.

3. Pierre Citron, *La Poésie de Paris dans la littérature française de Rousseau à Baudelaire* (Paris: Minuit, 1961), vol. 1, 9.

4. Alice Kaplan, *The Collaborator* (Chicago: University of Chicago Press, 2000), 69.

5. See Anne Lombard-Jourdan, "De la protohistoire à la mort de Philippe Auguste," in Bergeron, ed., *Paris: Genèse d'un paysage.*

6. Citron, *La Poésie,* vol. 1, 21; vol. 2, 33.

7. Ibid., vol. 1, 52. Ludovico Ariosto, *Orlando Furioso,* trans. Barbara Reynolds (London: Penguin, 1973), song 16, verse 38.

8. See Gilles Chabaud, "Images de la ville et pratiques du livre: Le Genre des guides de Paris (XVIIe–XVIIIe siècles)," *Revue d'histoire moderne et contemporaine,* April–June 1998, 340.

9. Jacques Hillairet, *Dictionnaire historique des rues de Paris* (Paris: Minuit, 1963), 375.

10. Jean de la Bruyère, *Caractères,* 21, VII.

11. Mercier, *Le Tableau de Paris,* cited by Louis Ducros in *La Société française au dix-huitième siècle* (Paris: Hatier, 1922).

12. Restif de la Bretonne, *Contemporaines* (1780), cited by Citron in *La Poésie,* vol. 1, 114.

13. David Hume, "My Own Life," in Hume, *Essays: Moral, Political, and Literary* (Indianapolis: LibertyClassics, 1987), xxxix. Paul Gerbod, "Visiteurs et résidents britanniques dans le Paris révolutionnaire de 1789 à 1799," in Michel Vovelle, ed., *Paris pendant la Révolution* (Paris: Sorbonne, 1989), 335–347. See also Harvey Levenstein, *Seductive Journey: American Tourists in France from Jefferson to the Jazz Age* (Chicago: University of Chicago Press, 1998), 22.

14. Frank Kafker, "L'Entreprise encyclopédique," in Vovelle, ed., *Paris pendant la Révolution,* 204. Malesherbes cited by Jean Chagniot in *Paris au XVIIIe siècle* (Paris: Hachette, 1988), 427.

15. Mercier cited by Antoine de Baecque in *Lumières et liberté* (Paris: Seuil, 1998), 44.

16. See Marguerite Glotz, *Les Salons du XVIIIe siècle* (Paris: Hachette, 1988), 57.

17. Chateaubriand cited by Pierre Bessand-Massenet in *Air et manières de Paris au fil d'un siècle* (Paris: Grasset, 1937), 59.

18. Theodor Herzl, *Le Palais Bourbon,* cited by Christophe Charle in *Paris fin de siècle: Culture et politique* (Paris: Seuil, 1998), 48n37.

19. See Lloyd Kramer, *Threshold of a New World: Intellectuals and the Exile Experience in Paris, 1830–1848* (Ithaca: Cornell University Press, 1988), 42.

20. Ticknor cited by Philip Mansel in *Paris between Empires* (London: John Murray, 2000), 127.

21. Théophile Gautier, *Paris et les parisiens* (Paris: Boîte à Documents, 1996), 19.

22. Norbert Elias, *The Court Society,* trans. Edmund Jephcott (New York: Pantheon, 1983), 52.

23. Robespierre, Nov. 5, 1792, Archives parlementaires, vol. 53, 159.

24. Glotz, *Les Salons,* 29.

25. Peysonnel cited by Chagniot in *Paris au XVIIIe siècle,* 430.

26. Marivaux cited by Citron in *La Poésie*, vol. 1, 92–93. Voltaire cited by Pierre Pinon in "A travers révolutions architecturales et politiques: 1715–1848," in Bergeron, ed., *Paris: Genèse d'un paysage*.

27. Rousseau cited by Citron in *La Poésie*, vol. 1, 100.

28. Rousseau cited ibid., 100–102.

29. Chateaubriand cited by Gérard Gengembre in "Le Paris révolutionnaire des mémoires d'outre tombe," in Vovelle, ed., *Paris pendant la Révolution*, 377. Alfieri, *Vita di Vittorio Alfieri scritta da esso*, cited by Gianni Oliva in "Voyageurs italiens," ibid., 355. Karamzin cited by Albert Babeau in *Paris en 1789* (Paris: Firmin-Didot, 1889), 29.

30. Mercier, *Le Tableau de Paris* (Paris: Maspéro, 1979), 38. Daniel Roche, *Le Peuple de Paris: Essai sur la culture populaire au XVIIIe siècle* (Paris: Aubier, 1981), 51. Guillaumot cited in Bertrand Lemoine et al., eds., *Paris d'ingénieurs* (Paris: Arsenal, 1995), 67.

31. I am grateful to Margaret Cohen for this insight.

32. Balzac, *Massimilla Doni*, cited by Françoise Escal in *Contrepoints: Musique et littérature* (Paris: Méridiens-Klinksieck, 1990), 41. Gautier cited by Roger Caillois in *Le Mythe et l'homme* (Paris: Gallimard, 1938), 163.

33. Jules and Edmond de Goncourt, July 20, 1857, *Journal* (Paris: Laffont, 1989), vol. 1, 285.

34. Caillois, *Le Mythe et l'homme*, 154.

3. CAPITAL OF REVOLUTION

1. See Albert Babeau, *Paris en 1789* (Paris: Firmin-Didot, 1889), 12.

2. Tocqueville, *Souvenirs*, in *Oeuvres complètes*, vol. 12 (Paris: Gallimard, 1964), 121.

3. Daniel Roche, *Le Peuple de Paris: Essai sur la culture populaire au XVIIIe siècle* (Paris: Aubier, 1981), 53–54.

4. These antecedents were admirably traced by Jean Favier in *Paris: 2000 ans d'histoire* (Paris: Fayard, 1997).

5. According to Rositza Tacheva in Michel Vovelle, ed., *Paris pendant la Révolution* (Paris: Sorbonne, 1989), 136.

6. "Anti-Parisian" customs barriers annually collected 30 million francs, 5 percent of the state's budget, a proportion that gives an idea of the economic weight of Paris in the French economy on the eve of the Revolution.

7. Richard Cobb, *The Police and the People: French Popular Protest, 1789–1820* (Oxford: Clarendon, 1970), 171, 206.

8. Marcel Reinhard, *Nouvelle histoire de Paris: La Révolution 1789–99* (Paris: Hachette, 1971), 164.

9. Borel cited by Pierre Citron in *La Poésie de Paris dans la littérature française de Rousseau à Baudelaire* (Paris: Minuit, 1961), vol. 1, 242. Melville, *Moby-Dick* (London: Penguin, 1994), 158.

10. Hugo and Heine cited by Citron in *La Poésie*, vol. 1, 287, 284.

11. Iskander (Alexander Herzen), "La Colonie Russe," in *Paris guide, 1867, par les principaux écrivains et artistes de la France* (Paris: Librairie internationale, 1867), 1099.

12. Hugo cited by Pierre Bessand-Massenet in *Air et manières de Paris au fil d'un siècle* (Paris: Grasset, 1937), 106. Ajasson de Grandsagne and M. Plant, *Révolutions de Paris,* cited by Walter Benjamin in *Paris: Capitale du XIXe siècle* (Paris: Cerf, 1993), 162.

13. Citron, *La Poésie,* vol. 1, 433.

14. Roulier cited by Jacques Rougerie in *Paris insurgée: La Commune de Paris* (Paris: Gallimard, 1995), 134.

15. Fournier, *Chroniques et légendes des rues de Paris* (1864), cited by Benjamin in *Paris: Capitale,* 163.

16. Tocqueville, *Souvenirs,* 51.

17. Ibid., 151. Karl Marx, *The Eighteenth Brumaire of Louis Bonaparte,* in *The Marx-Engels Reader,* ed. R. C. Tucker (New York: Norton, 1972), 443.

18. Tocqueville, *Souvenirs,* 117.

19. We can only regret that Marx—whose two history books both dealt with Parisian revolutionary history—did not write, as he wished to in 1844, a history of the Convention during the Revolution.

20. Lloyd Kramer, *Threshold of a New World: Intellectuals and the Exile Experience in Paris, 1830–1848* (Ithaca: Cornell University Press, 1988), 130–131, 145n73.

21. As explained by Kramer, ibid., 151.

22. Robert Service, *Lenin* (Cambridge, Mass.: Harvard University Press, 2000), 189.

23. Delescluze cited by Henri D'Alméras in *La Vie parisienne pendant le siège et sous la Commune* (Paris: Albin Michel, 1927), 121. Rougerie, *Paris insurgé,* 19.

24. Delescluze cited by Theodore Zeldin in *France, 1848–1945* (Oxford: Oxford University Press, 1973–1977), vol. 1, 739. The practical tasks of the Commune were made easier by the massive exodus of bourgeois families from the capital to the countryside after the end of the Prussian siege of the city. This ephemeral proletarianization of Paris would occur twice more, once in 1914 with the departure of approximately 700,000 people when the French government left for Bordeaux, and again in June 1940. Hence, in part, General Weygand's fear that the city might be taken over by the communists under the benevolent eye of the victorious Nazis, who had signed a nonaggression pact with the Soviets in 1939.

25. Rougerie, *Paris insurgé,* 65.

26. Benjamin, *Paris: Capitale,* 222.

4. MYSTERIOUS CAPITAL OF CRIME

1. Roger Caillois, *Le Mythe et l'homme* (Paris: Gallimard, 1938), 20.

2. See Daniel Roche, *Le Peuple de Paris: Essai sur la culture populaire au XVIIIe siècle* (Paris: Aubier, 1981), 52.

3. *Journal des débats* cited by Louis Chevalier in *Classes laborieuses et classes*

dangereuses à Paris pendant la première moitié du XIXe siècle (Paris: Plon, 1958), 354. Perreymond, *Le Bilan de la France, ou la misère et le travail* (Paris: Librairie phalanstérienne, 1849), 106.

4. Destigny cited by Pierre Citron in *La Poésie de Paris dans la littérature française de Rousseau à Baudelaire* (Paris: Minuit, 1961), vol. 2, 100.

5. Sue cited by Christopher Prendergast in *Paris and the Nineteenth Century* (Cambridge, Mass.: Blackwell, 1992), 87. Buret cited by Chevalier in *Classes laborieuses,* 595. Victor Fournel, *Ce qu'on voit dans les rues de Paris* (Paris: Delahays, 1858), 327.

6. Peter Brooks, *The Melodramatic Imagination: Balzac, Henry James, Melodrama, and the Mode of Excess* (New Haven: Yale University Press, 1995), 607.

7. Lachaise cited by Chevalier in *Classes laborieuses,* 370.

8. Gay cited by Nicolas Green in *The Spectacle of Nature: Landscape and Bourgeois Culture in Nineteenth-Century France* (Manchester: Manchester University Press, 1990), 42.

9. M. C. Barillaud, J. Bièque, and P. Dahlet, *Le Fait divers: Aspects théoriques, pédagogiques, documentaires* (Paris, 1986), cited by Eric Charlson in "The Fait Divers," manuscript, Harvard University, 31.

10. Baudelaire cited by Walter Benjamin in *Paris: Capitale du XIXe siècle* (Paris: Cerf, 1993), 298.

11. Théodore Rousseau cited by Claude Roger-Marx in *Maîtres du XIXe siècle et du XXe* (Geneva: Cailler, 1954), 44.

12. Roche, *Le Peuple de Paris,* 35.

13. Louis Chevalier, *Les Parisiens* (Paris: Hachette, 1967), 195.

14. Théophile Gautier, *Paris et les parisiens* (Paris: Boîte à Documents, 1996), 185. Gautier, writing in 1855, cited by Prendergast in *Paris and the Nineteenth Century,* 131.

15. Mercier cited by Citron in *La Poésie,* vol. 1, 128.

16. Vacquerie cited by Benjamin in *Paris: Capitale,* 758.

17. See Citron, *La Poésie,* vol. 2, 267.

18. Dumas cited ibid., vol. 1, 393.

19. Adolf Stahr, *Nach fünf Jahren, I, Oldenbourge* (1857), cited by Benjamin in *Paris: Capitale,* 146. Valette cited by Citron in *La Poésie,* vol. 1, 335.

20. Benjamin, *Paris: Capitale,* 122.

21. Privat d'Anglemont, *Paris anecdote* (1854), cited by Citron in *La Poésie,* vol. 1, 13.

22. Fournel cited by Benjamin in *Paris: Capitale,* 169.

23. Emile Souvestre, *Un Philosophe sous les toits: Journal d'un homme heureux* (Paris: Nelson, n.d.), 85.

24. Soulié cited by Citron in *La Poésie,* vol. 2, 331. Delon, *Notre capitale Paris* (1885), cited by T. J. Clark in *The Painting of Modern Life* (Princeton: Princeton University Press, 1984), 208.

25. Balzac, *Béatrix,* in *Oeuvres* (Paris: Pléiade, 1951), vol. 2, 320.

26. Louis Veuillot, *Les Odeurs de Paris* (Paris: Crès, n.d.), 4–5.

⚜

5. NEGATIVE MYTHS OF LA PARISIENNE

1. Bronislaw Geremek, *The Margins of Society in Late Medieval Paris* (Cambridge: Cambridge University Press, 1987), 219.

2. Erica-Marie Benabou, *La Prostitution et la police des moeurs au XVIIIe siècle* (Paris: Perrin, 1987), 407, 391, 235.

3. Mercier cited by Marcel Reinhard in *Nouvelle histoire de Paris: La Révolution 1789–99* (Paris: Hachette, 1971), 95.

4. Fougeret de Montbron cited by Benabou in *La Prostitution,* 466.

5. Benabou, *La Prostitution,* 498.

6. Ibid., 457.

7. Ibid., 459.

8. The Goncourt brothers, May 3, 1863: "What a difference between this Haussmannian promenade and the Palais Royal that their mothers used to frequent." *Journal,* vol. 1 (Paris: Laffont, 1956), 962.

9. Pierre Citron, *La Poésie de Paris dans la littérature française de Rousseau à Baudelaire* (Paris: Minuit, 1961), vol. 1, 380.

10. Theodore Zeldin, *France, 1848–1945* (Oxford: Clarendon, 1973–1977), vol. 1, 308. According to Zeldin, in Paris between 1871 and 1903 at least 900,000 women practiced prostitution at one time or another.

11. Hugo cited by Citron in *La Poésie,* vol. 2, 11.

12. Chevalier cited ibid.

13. Louis Chevalier, *Les Parisiens* (Paris: Hachette, 1967), 12.

14. Valéry cited by Georges Bataille in *Manet* (Geneva: SKIRA, 1983), 62.

15. The Goncourts cited by Christopher Prendergast in *Paris and the Nineteenth Century* (Cambridge, Mass.: Blackwell, 1992), 144.

16. See Charles Bernheimer, *Figures of Ill Repute: Representing Prostitution in Nineteenth-Century France* (Cambridge, Mass.: Harvard University Press, 1989), 134.

17. Benabou, *La Prostitution,* 505.

18. See, e.g., Goncourts, Sept. 2, 1882, *Journal,* vol. 2 (Paris: Laffont, 1989), 953.

19. Corbin, *Les Filles de noces: Misère sexuelle et prostitution* (Paris: Aubier, 1978), 13.

20. Parent-Duchâtelet, *De la prostitution dans la ville de Paris,* cited by Bernheimer in *Figures of Ill Repute,* 17.

21. Alexandra Richie, *Faust's Metropolis* (New York: Carroll and Graf, 1998), 599.

22. Parent-Duchâtelet cited by Corbin in *Les Filles de noces,* 16.

23. Flaubert, *L'Education sentimentale* (Paris: Garnier, 1961), 160.

24. Daniel Halévy, *Pays parisiens* (Paris: Grasset, 1932), 164–165.

25. This passage draws on the work of Daniel Sussner, "Methexis: The Politics of Female Allegory and the 1871 Paris Commune" (undergraduate thesis, Harvard University, 2000).

26. Alexandre Parent-Duchâtelet, *La Prostitution à Paris au XIXe siècle,* ed. Alain Corbin (Paris: Seuil, 1981), 113.

27. Sketches which according to the Surrealist photographer Brassai, who made notes on the "secrets of Paris," were probably made at 14, rue de Provence, not far from the grand boulevards and their art dealers.

28. Albert Boime, *Art and the French Commune: Imagining Paris after War and Revolution* (Princeton: Princeton University Press, 1995), 65.

29. Chevalier, *Les Parisiens,* 10. Jean Favier, *Paris: 2000 ans d'histoire* (Paris: Fayard, 1997), 545.

30. Fanny Trollope, *Paris and the Parisians* (New York: Hippocrene, 1985), 269.

31. Favier, *Paris,* 33. Goncourts, Oct. 21, 1878, *Journal,* vol. 2, 801.

32. Jules Vallès, *Le Tableau de Paris,* ed. Marie-Claude Bancquart (Paris: Messidor, 1989), 398.

33. "Paris la vie," in *Paris guide, 1867, par les principaux écrivains et artistes de la France* (Paris: Librairie internationale, 1867), 1242.

34. Pierre de Nouvion and Emile Liez, *Un Ministre des modes sous Louis XVI: Mademoiselle Bertin, marchande de modes de la reine 1747–1813* (Paris: H. Leclerc, 1911). Du Camp, *Paris,* cited by Walter Benjamin in *Paris: Capitale du XIXe siècle* (Paris: Cerf, 1993), 92.

35. Victor Fournel, *Ce qu'on voit dans les rues de Paris* (Paris: Delahays, 1858), 405. Benjamin, *Paris: Capitale,* 157.

36. Emmeline Raymond, "La Mode et la parisienne," *Paris guide,* 923.

37. Théophile Gautier, *Paris et les parisiens* (Paris: Boîte à Documents, 1996), 643. Goncourts, Sept. 27, 1883, *Journal,* vol. 2, 1023.

38. Bernhardt cited by Valerie Steele in *Paris Fashion: A Cultural History* (Oxford: Oxford University Press, 1988), 154. On Duse see G. Pontiero, *Eleonora Duse in Life and Art* (Frankfurt: Peter Lang, 1986), 201.

39. Balzac, *Traité de la vie élégante* (1830), cited by Steele in *Paris Fashion,* 59. Baudelaire cited by Benjamin in *Paris: Capitale,* 299.

40. Benjamin, *Paris: Capitale,* 104.

41. Rifâ'a al-Tahtâwi, *L'Or de Paris: Relation de voyage 1826–1831,* trans. Anouar Louca (Paris: Sindbad, 1988), 119. Benjamin, *Paris: Capitale,* 105.

42. Raymond, "La Mode et la parisienne," 923, 926.

43. Fazil-Bey, *Le Livre des femmes,* trans. J. A. Decourdemanche (Paris: Leroux, 1879), III.

44. Roger Caillois, *Le Mythe et l'homme* (Paris: Gallimard, 1938), 59.

6. CAPITAL OF SCIENCE

1. Michel Serres, "Paris 1800," in *Eléments d'histoire des sciences* (Paris: Bordas, 1997), 343.

2. Ibid., 339.

3. Parliamentary Archives, LXXIX (Paris, 1911), 453.

4. Bertrand Lemoine, *La Tour de Monsieur Eiffel* (Paris: Gallimard, 1997), 68, 102.

5. Emile Littré, *La Science au point de vue philosophique* (1873; Paris: Fayard, 1997), 528.

6. Perrin cited by Pascal Ory in "Une Cathédrale pour les temps nouveaux?" in Régine Robin, ed., *Masses et culture de masse dans les années trente* (Paris: Editions ouvrières, 1991), 183, 184, 201. Paul Vaillant-Couturier, during the same epoch, celebrated "the union of science and work."

7. Ibid., 193–194, 182.

8. See Louis Bergeron, *France under Napoleon* (Princeton: Princeton University Press, 1981), 199.

9. Louis Veuillot, *Les Odeurs de Paris* (Paris: Crès, n.d.), 295.

10. According to the eulogy by Aristide Briand after Berthelot's induction into the Pantheon in March 1907.

11. Yves Laissus, "Les Cabinets d'histoire naturelle," in René Taton, ed., *Enseignement et diffusions des sciences en France au XVIIIe siècle* (Paris: Hermann, 1964), 665.

12. H. Guenot cited by Dominique Poulot in "La Naissance du Musée," in Philippe Bordes and Régis Michel, eds., *Aux armes et aux arts* (Paris: Biro, 1988), 205.

13. Veuillot, *Odeurs*, 294. Marcel Chaigneau, *Jean-Baptiste Dumas: Sa vie, son oeuvre, 1800–1884* (Paris: Guy le Prat, 1984), 50–51.

14. Salle cited by Chaigneau in *Jean-Baptiste Dumas*, 61.

15. See Alice Stroup, *Royal Funding of the Parisian Académie Royale des Sciences during the 1690s* (Philadelphia: American Philosophical Society, 1987).

16. Mercier cited by Nicole and Jean Dhombres in *Naissance d'un pouvoir: Sciences et savants en France, 1793–1824* (Paris: Payot, 1989), 13.

17. Racine, "Discours prononcé à la réception de M. l'abbé Colbert," in *Oeuvres complètes* (Paris: Pléiade, 1966), vol. 2, 344.

18. Robert Fox, *The Culture of Science in France, 1700–1900* (Aldershot: Variorum, 1992), 447.

19. Alain Mercier, *Un Conservatoire pour les arts et métiers* (Paris: Gallimard, 1994), 39–40.

20. Fox, *Culture of Science*, 446. The Athénée, which survived until 1849, was equally revivified: Fourcroy, Chaptal, Monge, Vauquelin, Cuvier, Biot, Ampère, Say, Fresnel, and Geoffroy Saint-Hilaire taught there.

21. Cited by Dhombres in *Naissance d'un pouvoir*, 218.

22. Stendhal, *Promenades dans Rome* (Paris: Pléiade, 1973), 899–900.

23. Claude Schnitter, "Le Développement du Muséum national d'histoire naturelle de Paris au cours de la seconde moitié du XIXe siècle: 'Se transformer ou périr,'" *Revue d'histoire des sciences*, 49, no. 1 (1996), 54.

24. Dumas cited by Chaigneau in *Jean-Baptiste Dumas*, 52. Pierre Citron, *La Poésie de Paris dans la littérature française de Rousseau à Baudelaire* (Paris: Minuit, 1961), vol. 1, 65–66. Goethe, *Conversations avec Eckermann* (Paris, 1863), cited by Christophe Charle in *Paris fin de siècle* (Paris: Seuil, 1998), 22.

25. Annie Petit, "L'Esprit de la science anglaise et les Français au XIXème siècle," *British Journal for the History of Science* 17 (1984), 277.

26. Dhombres, *Naissance d'un pouvoir,* 217.

27. Laplace cited ibid., 216.

28. Anne Alter and Philippe Testard-Vaillant, *Guide du Paris savant* (Paris: Belin, 1997), 601. They also note that "the number of theorems discovered per resident is the highest in the world." Fontenelle cited by G. Canguilhem in "Physiologie," *Encyclopedia Universalis* (Paris, 1990–1993), 245.

29. Serres, "Paris 1800," 347.

30. Mercier, *Tableau de Paris,* ed. Jean-Claude Bonnet (Paris: Mercure, 1994), 330. Humboldt and Candolle cited by Chaigneau in *Jean-Baptiste Dumas,* 51, 52–53.

31. See J. V. Pickstone, "Locating Dutrochet," *British Journal of the History of Science* 11, no. 37 (1978), 53.

32. Sénebier cited by Canguilhem in "Physiologie," 244.

33. Comte, *Cours de philosophie,* 57th lesson, cited by Petit in "L'Esprit de la science anglaise," 279. Renan shared this suspicion of English science: "I don't know of a single English person—Byron perhaps is an exception—who has profoundly understood the philosophy of things." Ibid., 282.

34. Annie Petit, "L'Héritage du positivisme," *Revue d'histoire des sciences* 48, no. 4 (1995), 521–556, 530, 521.

35. Alter and Testard-Vaillant, *Guide du Paris savant,* 251.

36. Berthelot cited by Anne Rasmussen in "A la recherche d'une langue scientifique internationale, 1880–1914," in Roger Chartier and Pietro Corsi, eds., *Sciences et langues en Europe* (Paris: CNRS, 1996), 144.

37. Du Camp cited by Schnitter in "Le Développement," 86.

38. Petit, "L'Esprit de la science anglaise," 287.

39. Anne Rasmussen, "Science et sociabilité: Un 'tout petit monde' au tournant du siècle," *Bulletin de la société d'histoire moderne et contemporaine* 3–4 (1997), 49–50, 51n7, 77, 53.

7. READING THE PARISIAN MYTHS

1. Maxime Du Camp, *Paris: Ses organes, ses fonctions, et sa vie* (Paris: Hachette, 1873), vol. 1, 6.

2. Tabarant, *La Vie artistique au temps de Baudelaire,* cited by Andrée Sfeir-Semler in *Die Maler am Pariser Salon, 1791–1880* (Frankfurt: Campus Verlag, 1992), 49.

3. Baudelaire, *Le Peintre de la vie moderne,* in *Oeuvres* (Paris: Pléiade, 1961), 1173–74.

4. Pierre Nora, ed., *Les Lieux de mémoire,* vol. 1: *La République* (Paris: Gallimard, 1984), xix.

5. René Héron de Villefosse, *Bourgeois de Paris* (Paris: Bernard Grasset, 1941), 185.

6. Paul Metzner, *The Crescendo of the Virtuoso* (Berkeley: University of California Press, 1998).

7. Balzac, *Père Goriot* (Paris: Pléiade, 1951), 947.

8. Cited by Metzner in *Crescendo*, 213.

9. Jacques Lethève, *Daily Life of French Artists in the Nineteenth Century*, trans. H. Paddon (London: Allen and Unwin, 1968), 135.

10. For Françoise Choay, the meaning of public sites and buildings also has to do with a "relation syntagmatique" that connects all public edifices to their environment and opposes them as a public system to the system of private buildings. See Choay, *L'Allégorie du patrimoine* (Paris: Seuil, 1992), 149.

11. Georges Poisson, "Philippe Auguste et Saint-Louis," in Geneviève Bresc-Bautier and Xavier Dectot, eds., *Art ou politique? Arcs, statues, et colonnes de Paris* (Paris: Action artistique de la ville de Paris, 1999).

12. Alfred Fierro, *Histoire et dictionnaire de Paris* (Paris: Laffont, 1996), 41.

13. Rebérioux in Nora, ed., *Lieux de mémoire*, vol. 1, 643.

14. Cited by Walter Benjamin in *Paris: Capitale du XIXe siècle* (Paris: Cerf, 1993), 538.

15. Steven L. Kaplan, *Le Meilleur Pain du monde: Les Boulangers de Paris au XVIIIe siècle* (Paris: Fayard, 1996), 337.

16. Lamarte cited by Françoise Choay in *La Règle et le modèle* (Paris: Seuil, 1980), 44n2.

17. Mercier, *Tableau de Paris*, ed. Jean-Claude Bonnet (Paris: Mercure, 1994), 281.

18. See Benjamin, *Paris: Capitale*, 537.

19. Laugier cited by Choay in *La Règle et le modèle*, 269n1.

20. Patte cited ibid., 274–275, 276, 268–269n6.

21. Alexandre Dumas, *Napoléon Bonaparte ou trente ans de l'histoire de France* (Paris: Calmann Lévy, 1894), 55. Mercier cited in *Le Nouveau Paris*, ed. Jean-Claude Bonnet (Paris: Mercure, 1994), vol. 3, 1245.

22. Chateaubriand cited by Patrice de Montcan in *Guide littéraire des passages de Paris* (Paris: Hermé, 1996), 147–148. Baudelaire, "Le Paysage," *Salon de 1859*, cited by Benjamin in *Paris: Capitale*, 551. On Hugo see Pierre Citron, *La Poésie de Paris dans la littérature française de Rousseau à Baudelaire* (Paris: Minuit, 1961), vol. 2, 266.

23. Léon Rosenthal, *Du romantisme au réalisme* (Paris: Laurens, 1914), 12.

24. Muzaffar al-Din Shah, *Safarnameh* (Teheran, 1900), cited by Naghmeh Sohrabi in "Tamashakanah" (manuscript).

25. Cited by Vanessa Schwartz in *Spectacular Realities: Early Mass Culture in Fin-de-siècle Paris* (Berkeley: University of California Press, 1998), 151.

26. Jean Favier, *Paris: 2000 ans d'histoire* (Paris: Fayard, 1997), 757.

27. Balzac, *Père Goriot* (New York: Penguin, 1962), 275.

28. Choay, *La Règle et le modèle*, 213. David Pinkney, *Napoleon III and the Rebuilding of Paris* (Princeton: Princeton University Press, 1958), 45, citing Alphand, "Introduction," in *Mémoires du Baron Haussmann* (Paris, 1979).

29. Walter Benjamin, "Paris: Capital of the Nineteenth Century," in *Reflections* (New York: Harcourt Brace, 1978), 56–57.

30. Haussmann cited by Walter Benjamin in *The Arcades Project* (Cambridge, Mass.: Harvard University Press, 1999), 127.

31. Cited by Hervé Maneglier in *Paris impérial: La Vie quotidienne sous le Second Empire* (Paris: Armand Colin, 1990), 127.

32. Benjamin, "Paris: Capital of the Nineteenth Century," 159.

33. Emile de Labédollière, *Histoire du nouveau Paris,* cited by Benjamin in *Paris: Capitale,* 151.

34. Benjamin cited by François Loyer in *Paris XIXe siècle: L'Immeuble et la rue* (Paris: Hazan, 1987), 8.

35. Balzac, Nov. 1834, cited by Citron in *La Poésie,* vol. 2, 227; ibid., vol. 2, 97; Hugo, *Les Misérables,* cited by Christopher Prendergast in *Paris and the Nineteenth Century* (Cambridge, Mass.: Blackwell, 1992), 89.

36. Donald Reid, *Paris Sewers and Sewermen: Realities and Representations* (Cambridge, Mass.: Harvard University Press, 1991), 179.

37. Louis Veuillot, *Les Odeurs de Paris* (Paris: Crès, n.d.), 2.

8. THE URBAN MACHINE

1. Françoise Choay, *La Règle et le modèle* (Paris: Seuil, 1980), 295.

2. Véron in *Paris guide, 1867, par les principaux écrivains et artistes de la France* (Paris: Librairie internationale, 1867), 1696. Robert Herbert, *Impressionism* (New Haven: Yale University Press, 1988), 174.

3. Germain Brice, *Description de la ville de Paris* (1713), vol. 3, 240. Balzac cited by Louis Chevalier in *Les Parisiens* (Paris: Hachette, 1967), 305–306. Marcel Proust, *A la recherche du temps perdu* (Paris: Pléiade, 1962), 143.

4. David Pinkney, *Napoleon III and the Rebuilding of Paris* (Princeton: Princeton University Press, 1958), 23.

5. Patrice Debré, *Louis Pasteur* (Baltimore: Johns Hopkins University Press, 1998), 21. Auguste Ollivier, *Rapport sur la rougeole à Paris, ses progrès incessants, sa mortalité et la nécessité de mesures prophylactiques* (Paris: Chaix, 1885), 4.

6. Paul Chemetov and Bernard Marrey, *Architectures de Paris, 1848–1914* (Paris: Dunod, 1980), 32. Françoise Choay, "Haussmann et le système des espaces verts parisiens," *Revue de l'Art,* no. 29 (1975), 87.

7. Choay, *La Règle et le modèle,* 46.

8. Anthony Sutcliffe, *Paris and Architectural History,* cited by Bernard Marchand in *Paris: Histoire d'une ville (XIXe–XXe siècle)* (Paris: Seuil, 1993), 95.

9. Jean Favier, *Paris: 2000 ans d'histoire* (Paris: Fayard, 1997), 155.

10. Mercier cited by Pierre Bessand-Massenet in *Air et manières de Paris au fil d'un siècle* (Paris: Grasset, 1937), 24. Zola, *L'Assommoir,* cited by Nathan Kranowski in *Paris dans les romans d'Emile Zola* (Paris: PUF, 1968), 68. Proudhon quoted by Armand Cuvillier in *Marx et Proudhon* (Paris, 1937), cited by Walter Benjamin in *Paris: Capitale du XIXe siècle* (Paris: Cerf, 1993), 85.

11. See Marcel Roncayolo, "La Croissance de la ville: Les Schémas, les étapes," in Louis Bergeron, ed., *Paris: Genèse d'un paysage* (Paris: Picard, 1989).

12. Emile Levasseur, *Histoire des classes ouvrières et de l'industrie en France de 1789 à*

1870 (Paris, 1903–1904), cited by Benjamin in *Paris: Capitale,* 174. Théophile Gautier, *Paris et les parisiens* (Paris: Boîte à Documents, 1996), 203. David Cairns, *Berlioz: The Making of an Artist* (Los Angeles: University of California Press, 2000), 506. For Offenbach see Benjamin, *Paris: Capitale,* 175.

13. Alfred Fierro, *Histoire et dictionnaire de Paris* (Paris: Laffont, 1996), 752.

14. Veuillot cited by Bessand-Massenet in *Air et manières,* 251.

15. Serge Rodriguez and Marion Thuriot, *Le Roller à Paris* (Paris: Parigramme, 1999).

16. Edmond About, *L'Homme à l'oreille cassée,* cited by Pierre Citron in *La Poésie de Paris dans la littérature française de Rousseau à Baudelaire* (Paris: Minuit, 1961), vol. 2, 125. Goncourts, Nov. 18, 1860, cited by Philippe Seguin in *Louis Napoléon le Grand* (Paris: Grasset, 1990), 326.

17. Uwe Westfehling, "La Place de l'Etoile," in *Hittorf, 1792–1867* (Paris: Musée Carnavalet, 1986), 210.

18. Roy Porter, *London: A Social History* (Cambridge, Mass.: Harvard University Press, 1995), 313. Bertrand Lemoine et al., eds., *Paris d'ingénieurs* (Paris: Arsenal, 1995), 56.

19. Fierro, *Histoire et dictionnaire,* 480. Jean-Louis Cohen, *Des fortifs au périf: Paris, les seuils de la ville* (Paris: Picard, 1991), 80. Marchand, *Paris: Histoire,* 233.

20. Pinkney, *Napoleon III,* 18, citing Alfred Martin, *Etudes historiques et statistiques sur les moyens de transport dans Paris* (1894).

21. Karamzin cited by Arlette Farge in *Vivre dans la rue à Paris au XVIIIe siècle* (Paris: Gallimard, 1979), 18. Baudelaire, *Le Spleen de Paris,* "Perte d'Auréole," in *Oeuvres complètes* (Paris: Pléiade, 1961), 299.

22. Marchand, *Paris: Histoire,* 182.

23. Adeline Daumard, "La Bourgeoisie," in Fernand Braudel and Ernest Labrousse, *Histoire économique et sociale de la France* (Paris: PUF, 1980), vol. 6, 103–106.

24. Adeline Daumard, *La Bourgeoisie parisienne de 1815 à 1848* (Paris: Mouton, 1973), 273.

25. Louis XVI cited by Patrice Montcan and Christian Mahout in *Les Passages de Paris: Guide pratique, historique, et littéraire* (Paris: Sesam, 1991), 14.

26. Cited ibid., 124.

27. See J. A. Dulaure, *Histoire physique, civile, et morale de Paris depuis 1821* (Paris, 1835), vol. 2, 34.

28. Bedel cited by Fierro in *Histoire et dictionnaire,* 1053. *Véritable conducteur parisien* cited by Montcan and Mahout in *Les Passages,* 9. Benjamin, *Paris: Capitale,* 68.

29. Cited by Benjamin in *Paris: Capitale,* 75.

30. Molin, *Paris en l'an 2000* (Paris, 1869), cited ibid., 80–81. Claretie cited ibid., 134.

31. Walter Benjamin, *The Arcades Project* (Cambridge, Mass.: Harvard University Press, 1999), 13.

32. Theodore Zeldin, *France, 1848–1945* (Oxford: Clarendon, 1973), vol. 1, 433.

33. Zola, *Au Bonheur des Dames* (Paris: Fasquelle, 1953), 258. Zola, *Nana,* cited by Montcan and Mahout in *Les Passages,* 9.

34. Vallès, *Le Tableau de Paris* (Paris: Le Delphes, 1964), 42.

1. Baudelaire cited by Georges Bataille in *Manet* (Geneva: SKIRA, 1983), 29. Baudelaire, Aug. 10, 1862, in *Correspondance,* ed. Claude Pichois (Paris: Gallimard, 1973), vol. 2, 254.

2. See Luc Boltanski and Eve Chiapello, *Le Nouvel Esprit du capitalisme* (Paris: Gallimard, 1999).

3. Vittorio Alfieri, *Vita di Vittorio Alfieri scritta da esso* (Milan, 1803), cited by Gianni Oliva in "Voyageurs italiens," in Michel Vovelle, ed., *Paris pendant la Révolution* (Paris: Sorbonne, 1989), 355. Karamzin cited by Albert Babeau in *Paris en 1789* (Paris: Firmin-Didot, 1889), 29.

4. Pierre Citron, *La Poésie de Paris dans la littérature française de Rousseau à Baudelaire* (Paris: Minuit, 1961), vol. 1, 212.

5. Théophile Gautier, *Paris et les parisiens* (Paris: Boîte à Documents, 1996), 206. Edmond and Jules de Goncourt, Oct. 12, 1866, *Journal* (Paris: Laffont, 1989), 42.

6. Michelet cited by Citron in *La Poésie,* vol. 2, 246.

7. Sainte-Beuve cited ibid., 211.

8. J. K. Huysmans, *Croquis parisiens: A vau-l'eau, un dilemme* (Paris: Plon, 1908), 114–115.

9. A. Bazin, *L'Epoque sans nom: Esquisses de Paris, 1830–1833* (Paris: Mesnier, 1833), 40.

10. Robert Herbert, *Impressionism* (New Haven: Yale University Press, 1988), 59.

11. Roger Caillois, "Paris: Mythe moderne," cited by Walter Benjamin in *Paris: Capitale du XIXe siècle* (Paris: Cerf, 1993), 135.

12. Christopher Prendergast, *Paris and the Nineteenth Century* (Cambridge, Mass.: Blackwell, 1992), 5.

13. Walter Benjamin, *L'Homme, le langage, et la culture,* cited by Jeannine Guichardet in *Balzac: Archéologue de Paris* (Paris: SEDES, 1986), 361.

14. Victor Fournel, in 1858, reproduced this definition almost word for word: "[The dandy] is always in full possession of his individuality. That of the gawker, on the contrary, disappears, absorbed by the outside world, which ravishes it to drunkenness and ecstasy." Fournel, *Ce qu'on voit dans les rues de Paris* (Paris: Delahays, 1858), 263.

15. Flaubert, *L'Education sentimentale* (Paris: Garnier, 1961), 77.

16. Simmel cited by Herbert in *Impressionism,* 178.

17. David Frisby, "The Flaneur in Social Theory," in Keith Tester, ed., *The Flaneur* (New York: Routledge, 1994), 86.

18. Privat cited by Citron in *La Poésie,* vol. 2, 317.

19. Janin cited ibid., 312–313. On Parisian eccentrics see Georges Grison, *Paris horrible et Paris original* (1882; Paris: Ramsay, 2001).

20. Fournel, *Ce qu'on voit,* 304.

21. Ibid., 327. Citron, *La Poésie,* vol. 2, 373.

22. Maurice Agulhon, *Marianne into Battle* (Cambridge: Cambridge University Press, 1981), 127. Pyat cited by Benjamin in *Paris: Capitale,* 398.

23. Dumas, *Les Mohicans de Paris* (Paris: Gallimard, 1998), 34–35. Berthaud cited in Karlheinz Stierle, *Der Mythos von Paris* (Munich, 1993), 749.

24. Flaubert cited by Citron in *La Poésie,* vol. 1, 342.

25. Marcel Proust, "A l'ombre des jeunes filles en fleurs," in *A la recherche du temps perdu* (Paris: Pléiade, 1962), 533.

26. Walter Benjamin, *Charles Baudelaire,* trans. Jean Lacoste (Paris: Payot, 1979), 233.

27. Dumas, *Les Mohicans de Paris,* 9.

28. Baudelaire, "Mon coeur mis à nu," in *Oeuvres complètes* (Paris: Pléiade, 1961), 1274.

10. PARIS IN THE WORLD

1. Paul-Ernest de Rattier, *Paris n'existe pas,* cited by Walter Benjamin in *Paris: Capitale du XIXe siècle* (Paris: Cerf, 1993), 160–161.

2. *Paris guide, par les principaux écrivains et artistes de la France* (Paris: Librairie internationale, 1867), 1105.

3. Alexander Herzen, "La Colonie Russe," ibid., 1099. Herzen seems to have forgotten that the Tennis Court Oath took place in Versailles, not in Paris.

4. Degas cited by Jean-Paul Crespelle in *La Vie quotidienne à Montparnasse, 1905–1930* (Paris: Hachette, 1976), 21.

5. Harvey Levenstein, *Seductive Journey: American Tourists in France from Jefferson to the Jazz Age* (Chicago: University of Chicago Press, 1998), 32. Thackeray, *The Paris Sketch Book* (London: Smith, Elder, 1888), 25.

6. *The Poetry of Walt Whitman,* ed. Louis Untermeyer (New York: Simon and Schuster, 1949), 426.

7. Bernard Marchand, *Paris: Histoire d'une ville (XIXe–XXe siècle)* (Paris: Seuil, 1993), 156.

8. Baudelaire, *Le Peintre de la vie moderne,* in *Oeuvres complètes* (Paris: Pléiade, 1961), 1188. Heine, "De la France," in *Collected Works* (Berlin: Akademie-Verlag, 1977), 41–42. Fontane cited by Marion Villman-Doebeling in *Théodor Fontane im Gegenlicht* (Würzburg: Könighausen, 2000), 61.

9. Louis-Sébastien Mercier, *Tableau de Paris* (Paris, 1990), 74. Carlyle cited by Roy Porter in *London: A Social History* (Cambridge, Mass.: Harvard University Press, 1995), 257.

10. "Peter Bell the Third," *The Poems of Shelley* (Oxford: Oxford University Press, 1960), 350.

11. Vallès cited by Jacques Gury in *Le Voyage outre-manche: Anthologie de voyageurs français de Voltaire à Mac Orlan* (Paris: Laffont, 1999), 1071. Dickens cited by William G. Atwood in *The Parisian Worlds of Frédéric Chopin* (New Haven: Yale University Press, 1999), 242.

12. Faucher cited by Andrew Lees in *Cities Perceived: Urban Society in European*

and American Thought, 1820–1940 (Manchester: Manchester University Press, 1985), 62.

13. Vallès, *Le Tableau de Paris* (Paris: Le Delphes, 1964), 404. Gautier cited by Léon Rosenthal in *Du romantisme au réalisme* (Paris: Laurens, 1914), 101–102.

14. Gautier cited by Paul Jarry in *Cénacles et vieux logis parisiens* (Paris: Tallandier, 1929), 17.

15. Porter, *London*, 2.

16. Ibid., 113. *Critical Observations on the Buildings and Improvements of London* (1771), cited ibid., 114. Michelet cited by Gury in *Le Voyage outre-manche*, 197.

17. Heine cited by Lloyd Kramer in *Threshold of a New World* (Ithaca: Cornell University Press, 1988), 63. George Sand, letter to Charles Poncy, March 8, 1848, in *Correspondance*, ed. Georges Ludin (Paris: Garnier, 1971), vol. 8, 330.

18. Berlioz cited by Guy de Pourtelès in *Berlioz et l'Europe romantique* (Paris: Gallimard, 1939), 257–258.

19. Franz Liszt, *Correspondence*, trans. and ed. Adrian Williams (Oxford: Clarendon, 1998), 72. Theodore Zeldin, *France, 1848–1945* (Oxford: Clarendon, 1973–1977), vol. 2, 484.

20. Michel Brenet, *Les Concerts en France sous l'ancien régime* (Paris: Fischbacher, 1900), 356.

21. Esteban Buch, *La Neuvième de Beethoven: Une Histoire politique* (Paris: Gallimard, 1999), 141, 185.

22. Gautier cited by Charles Coligny in "Paris nouveau: L'Art polychrome et le nouvel Opéra," in *L'Artiste: Revue du XIXe siècle,* May 1868; see also Nora Morrison, "Grand Opera: Chicagoan and Parisian Interpretations of the Totalizing Art, 1860–1895" (thesis, Harvard University, 2000). Gounod cited by Jeffrey Cooper in *The Rise of Instrumental Music and Concert Series in Paris, 1828–1871* (Ann Arbor: UMI Research Press, 1983), 4.

23. Huart cited by Atwood in *The Parisian Worlds of Chopin*, 187.

24. Bruno Latour, *Paris: Ville invisible* (Paris: Institut Synthélaboé, 1998), 125.

25. Karamzin, *Letters of a Russian Traveler, 1789–1790* (New York: Columbia University Press, 1957), 197. Mercier cited by Pierre Bessand-Massenet in *Air et manières de Paris au fil d'un siècle* (Paris: Grasset, 1937), 14.

26. Charles Rosen, *The Romantic Generation* (Cambridge, Mass.: Harvard University Press, 1995), 645.

27. Zola cited in *Dictionnaire d'Emile Zola*, ed. Colette Becker (Paris: Laffont, 1993), 277. Heine cited by Jane Fulcher in *French Grand Opera as Politics and Politicized Art* (Cambridge: Cambridge University Press, 1987), 77–78.

28. Fulcher, *French Grand Opera*, 127–128.

29. Anselm Gerhard, *The Urbanization of Opera: Music Theater in Paris in the Nineteenth Century* (Chicago: University of Chicago Press, 1998), 89, 453.

30. Karl Marx, *The Eighteenth Brumaire of Louis Bonaparte* (New York: International Publishers, 1963), 114.

31. Fulcher, *French Grand Opera*, 26.

32. Péter Hanák, *The Garden and the Workshop: Essays on the Cultural Identity of Vienna and Budapest* (Princeton: Princeton University Press, 1998), xvi.
33. Zola cited by Siegfried Kracauer in *Orpheus in Paris: Offenbach and the Paris of His Time* (New York: Knopf, 1983), 349. See also *Dictionnaire d'Emile Zola*, 300.
34. Hanák, *The Garden and the Workshop*, 139.
35. Ibid., xx.

II. THREE LITERARY VISIONS

1. Flaubert, *L'Education sentimentale* (Paris: Garnier, 1961), pt. 3, ch. 1, 323.
2. Balzac cited by Bernard Guyon in *La Pensée politique et sociale de Balzac* (Paris: Armand Colin, 1947), 279–280.
3. Ibid., 527.
4. Ibid., 646, 662, 623.
5. Hugo cited by Jean Lemer in *Balzac: Sa vie, son oeuvre* (Paris: Sauvaître, 1892). Engels, letter to Miss Harkness, April 1888, cited by Guyon in *La Pensée*, 796.
6. *Le Père Goriot*, in *Oeuvres* (Paris: Pléiade, 1951), 936. Balzac, *La Fille aux yeux d'or*, cited by Michel Butor in *Paris à vol d'archange: Improvisations sur Balzac II* (Paris: Editions de la Différence, 1998), 48.
7. *Ferragus* cited by Guyon in *La Pensée politique et sociale*, 562.
8. *La Fille aux yeux d'or* cited ibid., 564.
9. Balzac, *La Fille aux yeux d'or* (Paris: Gallimard, 1952), 258, 257.
10. Ibid., 260–261, 264.
11. *La Fille aux yeux d'or* cited by Guyon in *La Pensée politique et sociale*, 565–566.
12. *La Fille aux yeux d'or*, 267.
13. Baudelaire, "Les Contes de Champfleury," in *Oeuvres complètes* (Paris: Pléiade, 1961), 601.
14. Balzac, *Un Homme d'affaires*, cited by Jeannine Guichardet in *Balzac: Archéologue de Paris* (Paris: SEDES, 1986), 124.
15. Walter Benjamin, commenting on André Le Breton, *Balzac: L'Homme et l'oeuvre* (1905), in Benjamin, *Charles Baudelaire*, trans. Jean Lacoste (Paris: Payot, 1979), 65.
16. Guichardet, *Balzac*, 401.
17. *La Fille aux yeux d'or*, 269, 267.
18. I am grateful to Margaret Cohen for this insight.
19. Pierre Citron, *La Poésie de Paris dans la littérature française de Rousseau à Baudelaire* (Paris: Minuit, 1961), vol. 2, 332. Louis Thomas, *Curiosités sur Baudelaire* (1912), cited by Walter Benjamin in *Paris: Capitale du XIXe siècle* (Paris: Cerf, 1993), 259. Claude Pichois, *Baudelaire et Paris* (Paris: Paris Musées, 1993).
20. Baudelaire cited by Citron in *La Poésie*, vol. 2, 335, 341, 383.
21. Benjamin, *Charles Baudelaire*, 233.
22. Citron, *La Poésie*, vol. 2, 358.

23. Ibid., 370.

24. Baudelaire, *The Flowers of Evil,* trans. James McGowan (Oxford: Oxford University Press, 1998), 4–5n26.

25. Ibid., 64–65.

26. Pierre Emmanuel, *Baudelaire: La Femme et Dieu* (Paris: Seuil, 1982), 154. Sabine Melchior-Bonnet, *The Mirror: A History* (New York: Routledge, 2001), 179–180, quoting Baudelaire, *Mon coeur mis à nu.*

27. Baudelaire cited by Pascal Ory in *Les Expositions universelles de Paris* (Paris: Ramsay, 1982), 50. Baudelaire, letter of Sept. 1859, in *Correspondance,* ed. Claude Pichois (Paris: Gallimard, 1973), 599.

28. Baudelaire, *Salon de 1846,* ch. 18, "De l'héroïsme de la vie moderne," in *Oeuvres complètes,* 952.

29. Baudelaire, *Mon coeur mis à nu,* cited by Benjamin in *Charles Baudelaire,* 87.

30. Baudelaire, *Flowers of Evil,* 189.

31. Benjamin, *Charles Baudelaire,* 97. Baudelaire, *Le Peintre de la vie moderne,* in *Oeuvres complètes,* 1160.

32. Citron, *La Poésie,* vol. 2, 380.

33. See Christopher Prendergast, *Paris and the Nineteenth Century* (Cambridge, Mass.: Blackwell, 1992), 140.

34. Citron, *La Poésie,* vol. 2, 373.

35. *Mon coeur mis à nu,* in *Oeuvres complètes,* 1288.

36. Gérald Froidenaux, *Baudelaire et la représentation de la modernité* (Paris: Jose Corti, 1989), 92.

37. *Fusées,* XI, in *Oeuvres complètes,* 1256.

38. Baudelaire, "La Fanfarlo," in *Oeuvres complètes,* 485. Melchior-Bonnet, *The Mirror,* 180. Claude Mouchard, *Un Grand Désert d'hommes* (Paris: Hatier, 1991), 160. Baudelaire, *Mon coeur mis à nu,* in *Oeuvres complètes,* 1272.

39. Gautier and Saint-Victor cited by Georges Bataille in *Manet* (Geneva: SKIRA, 1983), 57. Ibid., 16.

40. Baudelaire cited ibid., 42. Valéry cited ibid., 62.

41. Citron, *La Poésie,* vol. 1, 201.

42. Eliot cited by Emmanuel in *Baudelaire,* 19.

43. Brecht cited by Benjamin in *Paris: Capitale,* 392.

44. Ibid., 362–363. Jules and Edmond de Goncourt, June 5, 1858, *Journal* (Paris: Laffont, 1989), vol. 1, 363.

45. Benjamin, *Paris: Capitale,* 398.

46. *Mon coeur mis à nu,* in *Oeuvres complètes,* 1274.

47. Zola, *Correspondance,* May 27, 1879 (Paris: François Bernouard, 1928), 528.

48. *Dictionnaire d'Emile Zola,* ed. Colette Becker (Paris: Laffont, 1993), 307.

49. Pierre Citron, "Quelques aspects romantiques de Paris de Zola" (1963), cited by Nathan Kranowski in *Paris dans les romans d'Emile Zola* (Paris: PUF, 1968), 48.

50. Zola, *Paris,* cited ibid., 10.

51. Ibid., 516.

52. Lemaître cited ibid., 117. Zola, *Nana,* cited ibid., 109.

53. Zola, *Au Bonheur des Dames* (Paris: Flammarion, 1971), 53, 164. Zola, *L'Argent,* cited by Kranowski in *Paris dans les romans,* 126, 127.

54. Marcel Proust, *A la recherche du temps perdu* (Paris: Pléiade, 1962), 421.

55. Zola, *Au Bonheur des Dames,* 390.

56. Zola, *Au Bonheur des Dames,* ed. Colette Becker (Paris: Garnier, 1971), 405.

12. CAPITAL OF PLEASURE

1. Théophile Gautier, *Paris et les parisiens* (Paris: Boîte à Documents, 1996), 642.

2. Baudelaire, "La Fanfarlo," in *Oeuvres complètes* (Paris: Pléiade, 1961), 497. "La Vie," *Paris guide, 1867, par les principaux écrivains et artistes de la France* (Paris: Librairie internationale, 1867), 1002. James, letter to Edmund Warren, cited in Leon Edel, *The Life of Henry James* (New York: Penguin, 1977), vol. 2, 306.

3. *Paris guide,* 912.

4. Gautier, *Paris et les parisiens,* 644. Baudelaire, *Le Peintre de la vie moderne,* in *Oeuvres complètes,* 1162.

5. Alain Corbin, *The Foul and the Fragrant* (Cambridge, Mass.: Harvard University Press, 1986).

6. Zweig cited by Bernard Marchand in *Paris: Histoire d'une ville* (Paris: Seuil, 1993), 206.

7. Gautier, *Paris et les parisiens,* 231.

8. Monselet cited by Pierre Bessand-Massenet in *Air et manières de Paris au fil d'un siècle* (Paris: Grasset, 1937), 188.

9. According to Siegfried Kracauer, in 1869 the 63 café-concerts of the capital attracted 3,000–4,000 people each night. Cited by Jeffrey Cooper in *The Rise of Instrumental Music and Concert Series in Paris, 1828–1871* (Ann Harbor: UMI Research Press, 1983), 94.

10. Goncourt cited by André Sallée and Philippe Chauveau in *Music hall et café concert* (Paris: Bordas, 1985), 144.

11. Alfred Fierro, *Histoire et dictionnaire de Paris* (Paris: Laffont, 1996), 901, 902.

12. See Pascal Ory, *Le Discours gastronomique français* (Paris: Gallimard, Archives, 1998), 40.

13. On the history of Parisian furniture making see Leora Auslander, *Taste and Power* (Berkeley: University of California Press, 1996).

14. Fierro, *Histoire et dictionnaire,* 1137.

15. See Rebecca L. Spang, *The Invention of the Restaurant: Paris and Modern Gastronomic Culture* (Cambridge, Mass.: Harvard University Press, 2000), 76.

16. Mme de Genlis cited by Theodore Zeldin in *France, 1848–1945* (Oxford: Clarendon, 1973–1977), vol. 2, 739. Harvey Levenstein, *Seductive Journey: American Tourists in France from Jefferson to the Jazz Age* (Chicago: University of Chicago Press, 1998), 172.

17. Christopher Prendergast, *Paris and the Nineteenth Century* (Cambridge, Mass.: Blackwell, 1992), 20.

18. Proust, "A l'ombre des jeunes filles en fleurs," in *A la recherche du temps perdu* (Paris: Pléiade, 1962), vol. 1, 487. Baudelaire, "La Fanfarlo," in *Oeuvres complètes,* 507.

19. Goncourts cited by Bessand-Massenet in *Air et manières,* 164. Levenstein, *Seductive Journey,* 51.

20. Heine cited by Jacques Revel in *Aufklärung und Skepsis,* ed. Joseph Kruse (Stuttgart: Metzler, 1999), 931.

21. Grimod de la Reynière, *Ecrits gastronomiques,* ed. Jean-Claude Bonnet (Paris: Union Générale d'Editions, 1978), 29–30, 60, 74.

22. Ibid., 85.

23. Briffault cited by Ory in *Le Discours gastronomique,* 96, 100.

24. Delacroix, *Journal 1822–1863* (Paris: Plon, 1981), 241.

25. Ory, *Le Discours gastronomique,* 102.

26. Zeldin, *France, 1848–1945,* vol. 2, 748.

27. Roland Barthes, *Mythologies* (Paris: Seuil, 1957), 120, 121.

28. *Paris guide,* 1249.

29. Louis-Sébastien Mercier, *Le Tableau de Paris* (Paris: Maspéro, 1979), 114. Vallès cited by Louis Chevalier in *Les Parisiens* (Paris: Hachette, 1967), 344.

30. Edmond and Jules de Goncourt, *Journal* (Paris: Laffont, 1956), vol. 1, 952, 942, 777.

31. Canudo, *Mon âme propre: Roman de la forêt et du fleuve* (1918), cited by Giovanni Dotoli in *Paris ville, visage du monde: Canudo et l'avant garde italienne* (Fasano: Schena, 1984), 13.

32. Sallée and Chauveau, *Music hall et café concert,* 27.

33. Lorrain cited ibid., 12.

34. Ibid., 27. Walter Benjamin, *Paris: Capitale du XIXe siècle* (Paris: Cerf, 1993), 361.

35. Musset cited by Pierre Citron in *La Poésie de Paris dans la littérature française de Rousseau à Baudelaire* (Paris: Minuit, 1961), vol. 1, 212.

36. Sand, 1844, cited ibid., vol. 2, 67. *Paris guide,* 1195, 1206.

37. Cited by Robert Herbert in *Impressionism* (New Haven: Yale University Press, 1988), 294.

38. The Lazares cited by Pierre Lavedan in *Nouvelle histoire de Paris: Histoire de l'urbanisme à Paris* (Paris: Hachette, 1993). Philippe Seguin, *Louis Napoléon le Grand* (Paris: Grasset, 1990), 326.

39. Nerval cited by Claude Pichois and Jean Paul Avice in *Gérard de Nerval: Paris, la vie errante* (Paris: BHVP, 1997), 53.

40. Pierre Michet de la Baume, *Petites et grandes heures du Vésinet* (Saint-Germain: Diguet-Deny, 1966), 20.

41. From 1851 to 1872 the population of Saint Cloud grew from 3,800 to 9,000; that of Versailles from 35,000 to 61,000; and that of Boulogne from 7,600 to 19,000.

42. Monique Eleb treats this theme with elegance and discernment in *Urbanité, sociabilité et intimité* (Paris: Editions de l'Epure, 1997).

43. Michelet cited by Citron in *La Poésie,* vol. 2, 247, 249. Paul Valéry, *Oeuvres* (Paris: Pléiade, 1960), vol. 2, 1015.

44. Erica-Marie Benhabou, *La Prostitution et la police des moeurs au XVIIIe siècle* (Paris: Perrin, 1987), 273.

45. Mallarmé cited by Paul Mouchard in *Un Grand Désert d'hommes 1855–1885* (Paris: Hatier, 1991), 42. Ponson du Terrail cited by Marchand in *Paris: Histoire,* 65. Muret cited by Citron in *La Poésie,* vol. 2, 141.

46. Goncourts, *Journal,* vol. 1, 713, 554.

47. Ibid., vol. 2, 568, 573.

48. Daniel Halévy, *Pays parisiens* (Paris: Grasset, 1932), 209.

49. *Paris guide,* 1542.

50. Jammes cited by Frédéric Gugelot in *La Conversion des intellectuels au catholicisme en France, 1885–1935* (Paris: CNRS, 1998), 487.

51. Frédéric Hoffet, *Psychanalyse de Paris* (Paris: Grasset, 1953), 20. Goncourts, Nov. 27, 1883, *Journal,* vol. 2, 1030. Chevalier, *Les Parisiens,* 91.

52. Goncourts, *Journal,* March 31, 1887, vol. 3, 26.

13. THE AMERICAN IMAGINATION

1. Echague cited by Matt K. Matsuda in *The Memory of the Modern* (Oxford: Oxford University Press, 1996), 195.

2. Peter-Eckhard Knabe, "Paris comme métaphore et vision chez Cortazar et Fuentes," in *Paris et le phénomène des capitales littéraires* (Paris: Sorbonne, 1984), 592.

3. Irving cited by Brian N. Morton in *Americans in Paris: An Anecdotal Street Guide* (Ann Arbor: Olivia and Hill Press, 1984), 21.

4. Harvey Levenstein, *Seductive Journey: American Tourists in France from Jefferson to the Jazz Age* (Chicago: University of Chicago Press, 1998), 58.

5. Balzac, "L'Epicier," cited by Léon Rosenthal in *Du romantisme au réalisme* (1914; Paris: Macula, 1987), 33.

6. e.e. cummings, "little ladies more," cited by Sheri Benstock in *Women of the Left Bank* (Austin: University of Texas Press, 1986), 447. ("Avoir bon dos" also means to be quite pliable. But did cummings know this?)

7. Miller cited by Louis Chevalier in *Les Parisiens* (Paris: Hachette, 1967), 343.

8. See Paul Venable Turner, *Joseph Ramée: International Architect of the Revolutionary Era* (Cambridge: Cambridge University Press, 1996).

9. Jonathan Beecher, *Victor Considérant and the Rise and Fall of French Romantic Socialism* (Berkeley: University of California Press, 2001), 337.

10. See Chevalier, *Les Parisiens,* 20.

11. Solange Petit-Skinner, *Les Américains de Paris* (La Haye: Mouton, 1975), 15.

12. Joynes cited by John Harley Warner in *Against the System: The French Impulse in Nineteenth-Century American Medicine* (Princeton: Princeton University Press, 1998), 44.

13. Stephen Longstreet, *We All Went to Paris: Americans in the City of Light* (New York: Macmillan, 1972), 102. Catlin cited by Morton in *Americans in Paris,* 92.

14. George Putnam cited by Levenstein in *Seductive Journey,* 118.

15. Mrs. F. J. Willard, in *Pictures from Paris in War and Siege* (London, 1871), cited by Philip M. Katz in *From Appomattox to Montmartre: Americans and the Paris Commune* (Cambridge, Mass.: Harvard University Press, 1998), 46.

16. Twain, letter to General Lucius Fairchild, April 28, 1880, cited by Cyril Clemens in *Mark Twain the Letter Writer* (Boston: McAdor, 1932).

17. Twain, "Paris Notes," cited by George Feinstein in "Mark Twain's Literary Opinions" (Ph.D. diss., University of Iowa, 1945).

18. Twain cited by Levenstein in *Seductive Journey,* 199.

19. Henry James, *The Ambassadors* (Harmondsworth: Penguin, 1986), preface to the New York ed.

20. James, *Ambassadors,* 182.

21. James, *Parisian Sketches* (London: Rupert Hart-Davis, 1958), 26.

22. Henry James, *Roderick Hudson* (New York: Random House, Modern Library), 176.

23. James, *Ambassadors,* 236.

24. Ibid., 474–475.

25. Henry James, *Portraits of Places* (New York: Lear, 1948), 129, 126.

26. Jean-Paul Crespelle, *La Vie quotidienne à Montparnasse, 1905–1930* (Paris: Hachette, 1976), 169.

27. Levenstein, *Seductive Journey,* 232.

28. A number of incidents pitted black and white Americans against each other in Parisian cafés at the time. French opinion took note of these disputes, as it did of the segregation that was carefully enforced during the U.S.-sponsored visit to France of the white and black mothers of fallen American soldiers.

29. David Leeming, "The Negro in Paris: African-American Writers on the Left Bank" (paper presented at the Mercantile Library, New York City, April 21, 1999), 7–8.

30. In 1924 Langston Hughes had already met René Maran, a French African writer who introduced him to the Nadal sisters, the editors of the *Revue du monde noir.* Alain Locke, Claude McKay, and Hughes were in Paris at the time, as were Aimé Césaire, Léon Damas, and Léopold Senghor. See Lilyan Kesteloot, *Black Writers in French: A Literary History of Négritude,* trans. E. C. Kennedy (Philadelphia: Temple University Press, 1974).

31. Michel Fabre, "The Cultural Milieu of Postwar Paris," in *Explorations in the City of Light: African-American Artists in Paris, 1945–1965* (New York: Studio Museum in Harlem, 1996), 37.

32. Léon Daudet, "Paris vécu," in Daudet, *Souvenirs et polémiques* (Paris: Laffont, 1992), 264. Rogers cited by Petrine Archer-Straw in *Negrophilia: Avant-Garde Paris and Black Culture in the 1920s* (London: Thames and Hudson, 2000), 160.

33. Himes cited by Tyler Stovall in *Paris Noir: African Americans in the City of Light* (Boston: Houghton Mifflin, 1996), 210.

34. Leeming, "The Negro in Paris," 17. David Leeming, *James Baldwin: A Biography* (New York: Knopf, 1994), 255.

35. Delaney letter cited by Stovall in *Paris Noir,* 247–248, 266. *Paris Blues* cited ibid., 248.

36. Emerson cited by Harry Levin in "Introduction" to James, *Ambassadors,* 10.

37. Thomas Bender and Carl Schorske, eds., *Budapest and New York: Studies in Metropolitan Transformations, 1870–1930* (New York: Russell Sage Foundation, 1994), 25, 276. Bertolt Brecht, "Late Lamented Fame of the Giant City of New York," cited by James L. Wunsch in "Big Book, Big City," *Journal of Social History* 31, no. 1 (1997).

14. FROM MYTH TO PHANTASMAGORIA

1. Walter Benjamin, *Paris: Capitale du XIXe siècle* (Paris: Cerf, 1993), 425.

2. Dostoevsky, *Notes from the Underground* (New York: Dutton, 1960), 6. Benjamin, *Paris: Capitale,* 39, 802.

3. Emile Gigault de La Bédollière, *Publiciste au siècle,* cited by Jacques Gury in *Le Voyage outre-manche: Anthologie de voyageurs français de Voltaire à Mac Orlan* (Paris: Laffont, 1999), 210.

4. See Patricia Mainardi, *Art and Politics of the Second Empire: The Universal Expositions of 1855 and 1867* (New Haven: Yale University Press, 1987).

5. For this theme, see James Livesey, *Making Democracy in the French Revolution* (Cambridge, Mass.: Harvard University Press, 2001).

6. Edouard Drumont, "Les Expositions universelles d'autrefois," in *Mon vieux Paris* (Paris: Flammarion, 1893), 20–29.

7. Jean Favier, *Paris: 2000 ans d'histoire* (Paris: Fayard, 1997), 543.

8. Alfred Fierro, *Histoire et dictionnaire de Paris* (Paris: Laffont, 1996), 863.

9. Vigier cited by Pascal Ory in *Les Expositions universelles* (Paris: Ramsey, 1982), 100.

10. Jules and Edmond de Goncourt, May 27, 1867, *Journal* (Paris: Laffont, 1989), vol. 2, 86.

11. Houssaye cited by Benjamin in *Paris: Capitale,* 214.

12. Theodore Zeldin, *France, 1848–1945* (Oxford: Clarendon, 1973–1977), vol. 2, 710.

13. Abd el Kader cited by Ory in *Les Expositions universelles,* 27. Renan cited by Benjamin in *Paris: Capitale,* 199.

14. Du Camp, "Introduction," *Histoire de Paris* (Paris: Hachette, 1873), 14–15. "International Publication" cited by Benjamin in *Paris: Capitale*, 195.

15. Zeldin, *France, 1848–1945*, vol. 2, 162.

16. Ibid., 97.

17. Goncourts, Jan. 16, 1867, *Journal*, vol. 2, 64.

18. Gabriel Hanotaux, *Histoire de la nation française* (Paris: Plon Nourrit, 1920–1929), vol. 5, 609.

19. Charles Rearick, *Pleasures of the Belle Epoque: Entertainment and Festivity in Turn-of-the-Century France* (New Haven: Yale University Press, 1985), 130.

20. Jourdain cited by Jacques Chastenet in *La République des républicains, 1879–1893* (Paris: Hachette, 1960), 217. Jacques Benoist, *Le Sacré Coeur de Montmartre de 1870 à nos jours* (Paris: Editions ouvrières, 1992), 973.

21. Maurice Agulhon, "Concepts statufiés," in Geneviève Bresc-Bautier and Xavier Dectot, eds., *Art ou politique? Arcs, statues, et colonnes de Paris* (Paris: Action artistique de la ville de Paris, 1999), 164.

22. Lapparent cited by Walter Benjamin in *The Arcades Project* (Cambridge, Mass.: Harvard University Press, 1999), 167.

23. *Manifests of the Three Hundred* cited by Bernard Champigneule in *Paris: Architecture, sites, et jardins* (Paris: Seuil, 1973), 151.

24. Jourdain cited by Chastenet in *La République*, 216–217. Christophe [Georges Colomb], *La Famille Fenouillard* (Paris: Armand Colin, 1965), 26.

25. Charles-Robert Ageron, "L'Exposition coloniale de 1931," in Pierre Nora, ed., *Lieux de mémoire*, vol. 1, *La République* (Paris: Gallimard, 1984), 564.

26. Deborah Silverman, *Art Nouveau in Fin-de-Siècle France* (Berkeley: University of California Press, 1989), 5. Benjamin, *Paris: Capitale*, 41.

27. These trends are ably described in Silverman, *Art Nouveau*.

28. Morand cited by Julian Jackson in *France: The Dark Years* (Oxford: Oxford University Press, 2001), 40.

29. Deborah Silverman, "The 1889 Exhibition: The Crisis of Bourgeois Individualism," cited by Herman Lebovics in *True France: The Wars over Cultural Identity, 1900–1945* (Ithaca: Cornell University Press, 1992), 54n7.

30. Ageron, "L'Exposition coloniale," 564.

31. Paul Rabinow, *French Modern: Norms and Forms of the Social Environment* (Chicago: University of Chicago Press, 1995).

32. Lanza di Saclea cited by Lebovics in *True France*, 64.

33. Poster reproduced in Ageron, "L'Exposition coloniale," 582.

34. Ibid., 566.

35. *La Vie* cited ibid., 566.

36. Ibid., 570.

37. *Rapport général* (Paris: Imprimerie nationale, 1933), 422.

38. Marcel Ollivier, ibid., xii.

39. Anne Alter and Philippe Testard-Vaillant, *Guide du Paris savant* (Paris: Belin, 1997), 330.

40. *Candide,* May 14, 1931, cited by Catherine Hodeir in "Une Journée à l'exposition coloniale," *Histoire* 69 (1984).
41. Ageron, "L'Exposition coloniale," 568.
42. Ibid., 574. Maurois cited by Lebovics in *True France,* 59.
43. Lyautey was intent on minimizing the vulgarly touristic aspect of the event, but to do so completely would have been to undermine its success. A compromise was reached: women with distended lips, for example, were not to be seen, but there were folkloric native dances practiced by professional dancers who, quite properly, showed up for work in Western clothing.
44. Cited by Philippe Audouin in *Les Surréalistes* (Paris: Seuil, 1993), 76.
45. *Le Canard enchaîné,* March 11, 1931.
46. Tardieu and Romier cited by Ageron in "L'Exposition coloniale," 577, 578, 579.
47. *Rapport général,* 378.
48. Favier, *Paris,* 546. Paul Valéry, "Regards sur le monde actuel," in *Oeuvres* (Paris: Pléiade, 1957), 1156. Pascal Ory, "Une Cathédrale pour les temps nouveaux," in Régine Robin, *Masse et culture de masse* (Paris: Editions ouvrières, 1991), 187n40.
49. Laveillé cited by Ory in "Une Cathédrale," 186, 191. Labbé cited by Jean-Jacques Bloch in *Quand Paris allait "à l'Expo"* (Paris: Fayard, 1980), 11.

15. THE SURREALISTS' QUEST

1. I owe this idea—as I do so many others—to Margaret Randolph Higonnet.
2. Jean-Paul Crespelle, *La Vie quotidienne à Montparnasse, 1905–1930* (Paris: Hachette, 1976), 143.
3. Yves Duplessis, *Le Surréalisme* (Paris: PUF, 1950), 70.
4. André Breton, *Les Vases communicants,* in *Oeuvres* (Paris: Pléiade, 1992), 206–207. Marie-Claire Bancquart, *Le Paris des surréalistes* (Paris: Seghers, 1972), 17.
5. Breton, *La Clé des champs* (Paris: Pauvert, 1967), 280.
6. Aragon cited by Duplessis in *Le Surréalisme,* 29. On the relation between Aragon's formulation of the myth of Paris and Caillois's elaboration of that theme, see Karlheinz Stierle, *Der Mythos von Paris* (Munich, 1993), 24–28. Chirico cited by Maurizio Fagiolo in *Giorgio de Chirico: Parigi 1924–1929* (Milan, 1982), 71.
7. Duplessis, *Le Surréalisme,* 29. Bancquart, *Le Paris des surréalistes,* 7, 133, 106.
8. André Breton, *Nadja* (Paris: Gallimard, 1928), 150. Walter Benjamin, *Paris: Capitale du XIXe siècle* (Paris: Cerf, 1993), 426.
9. Bancquart, *Le Paris des surréalistes,* 73. Aragon, "Une Vaque de rêves," cited ibid., 72.
10. Paul Diels, *Le Symbolisme dans la mythologie grecque* (Paris: Zayyed, 1966), 40. Claude Lévi-Strauss, *L'Identité* (Paris: Grasset, 1977), 322.
11. Laurent cited by John Isbell in *The People's Voice: A Romantic Civilization, 1776–1848* (Bloomington: Indiana University Press, 1996), 84.
12. Baudelaire, *Salon de 1846,* in *Oeuvres complètes* (Paris: Pléiade, 1961). Sand cited

by René Dumesnil in his introduction to Flaubert, *L'Education sentimentale* (Paris: Pléiade, 1952), 30.

13. Jules and Edmond de Goncourt, *Journal* (Paris: Laffont, 1956), vol. 1, 406, 1010.

14. Baudelaire, "Le Peintre de la vie moderne," in *Oeuvres complètes* (Paris: Pléiade, 1961), 1155. Gautier cited by Judith Wechsler in *A Human Comedy: Physiognomy and Caricature in Nineteenth-Century Paris* (Chicago: University of Chicago Press, 1982), 42.

15. Whitney Chadwick, *Myth in Surrealist Painting, 1929–1939* (Ann Arbor: UMI Research Press, 1980), 19. Breton, *De la survivance de certains mythes* (Paris: Le Terrain Vague, 1988). Breton, "Comète surréaliste" (1947), in *La Clé des champs*. Audouin, *Les Surréalistes* (Paris: Le Seuil, 1993), 124.

16. Eluard cited by Audouin in *Les Surréalistes,* 91.

17. Masson, letter to Michel Leiris, Oct. 6, 1925, cited by Norbert Bandier in *Sociologie du surréalisme* (Paris: La Dispute, 1999), 259.

18. Bancquart, *Le Paris des surréalistes,* 123. Masson, *Cahiers d'art* (1939), cited by Bernard Ceysson in *L'Art dans les années 30 en France* (Saint-Etienne: Musée, 1979), 28.

19. Cited by Audouin in *Les Surréalistes,* 50.

20. Germaine Brée and Edouard Morot-Sir, *Du surréalisme à l'empire de la critique* (Paris: Artaud, 1984), 321.

21. Caillois, "Paris, mythe moderne," in *Le Mythe et l'homme* (Paris: Gallimard, 1938), 159–160.

22. Breton, *Les Vases communicants,* 205–206.

23. Soupault cited by Bancquart in *Le Paris des surréalistes,* 84.

24. Patrice Montcan and Christian Mahout, *Les Passages de Paris: Guide pratique, historique, et littéraire* (Paris: Sesam, 1991), 198. Aragon, *Le Paysan de Paris* (Paris: Gallimard, 1961), 21.

25. Aragon cited by Bancquart in *Le Paris des surréalistes,* 86.

26. Baudelaire cited by Paul Jarry in *Cénacles et vieux logis parisiens* (Paris: Tallandier, 1929), 49. Bancquart, *Le Paris des surréalistes,* 87. Aragon, *Le Paysan de Paris* (Paris: Gallimard, 1926), 148.

27. Soupault cited by Bancquart in *Le Paris des surréalistes,* 16.

28. Caillois and Breton cited ibid., 70, 195, 144.

29. Ibid., 129.

30. Aragon cited ibid., 9, 11. Breton, "Pont-Neuf" (1950), in *La Clé des champs,* 284.

31. Aragon cited by Bancquart in *Le Paris des surréalistes,* 87.

32. Breton cited by Audouin in *Les Surréalistes,* 30.

33. Breton cited by Bancquart in *Le Paris des surréalistes,* 67. Breton, *Nadja,* 166. Freud cited by Marcellin Pleynet in *Paris/New York 1908–1968* (Paris: Centre Pompidou, 1991), 190.

34. Bancquart, *Le Paris des surréalistes,* 77.

35. Ibid., 25, 71. Soupault, *Histoire d'un blanc,* cited ibid., 24, 25.

36. Ibid., 69.

37. Ibid., 50. Sontag cited by Marja Warehime in *Brassaï: Images of Culture and the Surrealist Observer* (Baton Rouge: Louisiana State University Press, 1996), 41.

38. Daniel Abadie, "L'Exposition internationale du surréalisme, Paris 1938," in *Paris 1937/Paris 1957* (Paris: Centre Pompidou, 1992), 119.

39. Bancquart, *Le Paris des surréalistes,* 12. Audouin, *Les Surréalistes,* 22. Crespelle, *La Vie quotidienne à Montparnasse,* 143.

40. Breton cited by Bancquart in *Le Paris des surréalistes,* 110. Ibid., 97. Julien Gracq, "André Breton," in Gracq, *Oeuvres complètes* (Paris: Pléiade, 1989), vol. 1, 416.

41. Bancquart, *Le Paris des surréalistes,* 109.

42. Ibid., 94.

43. Ibid., 138, 150, 151. Renée Hubert, "Femmes Dada, femmes surréalistes," in *La Femme s'entête: La Part du féminin dans le surréalisme,* ed. G. M. Colville and Katharine Conley (Paris: Lachenal and Ritter, 1998), 39.

44. Jean Favier, *Paris: 2000 mille ans d'histoire* (Paris: Fayard, 1997), 756.

45. Audouin, *Les Surréalistes,* 135.

16. CAPITAL OF ART

1. Valéry cited by Wolf Lepenies in "La Fin de l'utopie et le retour de la mélancolie," Leçon inaugurale au Collège de France, 15.

2. Jessica Gienow-Hecht, in a conference at Center for European Studies, Harvard University, Dec. 14, 1999.

3. Karl Marx, *The Eighteenth Brumaire of Louis Bonaparte* (1852; New York: International Publishers, 1963), 15. John Rewald, *The History of Impressionism* (New York: Museum of Modern Art, 1946), 9.

4. Marc Fumaroli, *L'Etat culturel: Une religion moderne* (Paris: Fallois, 1991), 11. Rolland cited by Esteban Buch in *La Neuvième de Beethoven: Une Histoire politique* (Paris: Gallimard, 1999), 11. Courbet cited by James Harding in *Artistes Pompiers: French Academic Art in the Nineteenth Century* (New York: Rizzoli, 1979), 13.

5. Denis Diderot, *Oeuvres esthétiques* (Paris: Garnier, 1968), 524.

6. Thomas Crow, *Painters and Public Life in Eighteenth-Century Paris* (New Haven: Yale University Press, 1985), 132.

7. Carmontelle cited ibid., 18–19.

8. Antoine Schnapper, "De Bélisaire à Brutus," in *David* (Paris: Réunion des Musées Nationaux, 1989), 115.

9. Grégoire cited by Paul Bénichou in *Le Sacre de l'écrivain, 1750–1830* (Paris: Librairie José Corti, 1973), 76.

10. Cited in Philippe Bordes and Regis Michel, eds., *Aux armes et aux arts* (Paris: Biro, 1988), 215.

11. Neufchâteau and Chaussard cited ibid., 196, 188.

12. M. T. Dremière cited by Daniel Roche in *France in the Enlightenment* (Cambridge, Mass.: Harvard University Press, 1998), 274.

13. Moulin, *Le Marché de l'art,* cited by Andrée Sfeir-Semler in *Die Maler am Pariser Salon, 1791–1880* (Frankfurt: Campus Verlag, 1992), 206.

14. Sfeir-Semler, *Die Maler,* 70. Léon Rosenthal, *Du romantisme au réalisme* (Paris: Laurens, 1914), 77. Blanc cited by Sfeir-Semler in *Die Maler,* 25.

15. Sfeir-Semler, *Die Maler,* 62. Peisse cited ibid., 37.

16. Ibid., 203.

17. Ibid., 212, 216, 215, 109, 108.

18. Courbet cited ibid., 213.

19. Ibid., 268. Michèle Perrot, ed., *A History of Private Life,* vol. 4 (Cambridge, Mass.: Harvard University Press, 1990), 644.

20. Taine in *Paris guide, 1867,* cited by Sfeir-Semler in *Die Maler,* 53. Lamartine cited by Rosenthal in *Du romantisme,* 77.

21. Rethel cited by Sfeir-Semler in *Die Maler,* 76.

22. Ibid., 65, 206, 218.

23. Joel-Marie Fauquet, *César Franck* (Paris: Fayard, 1999), 693. Sfeir-Semler, *Die Maler,* 185. Theodore Zeldin, *France, 1848–1945* (Oxford: Clarendon, 1973–1977).

24. Lois Fink, *American Art at the Nineteenth-Century Paris Salons* (Cambridge: Cambridge University Press, 1990), 58. Jules and Edmond de Goncourt, Dec. 17, 1860, *Journal* (Paris: Laffont, 1989), vol. 1, 644.

25. Sfeir-Semler, *Die Maler,* 189.

26. T. J. Clark, *The Absolute Bourgeois: Artists and Politics in France, 1848–1851* (Greenwich, Conn.: New York Graphic Society, 1973), 49.

27. Victor Fournel, *Ce qu'on voit dans les rues de Paris* (Paris: Delahays, 1858), 385. Chaumelin and the Goncourts cited by Sfeir-Semler in *Die Maler,* 297.

28. Zeldin, *France, 1848–1945,* 467.

29. Klaus Berger, *Japonisme in Western Painting from Whistler to Matisse* (Cambridge: Cambridge University Press, 1992), 8; Geneviève Lacambre, "Les Peintres japonais à Paris au XIXe siècle," in André Kaspi and Antoine Marès, eds., *Le Paris des étrangers* (Paris: Imprimerie nationale, 1989), 210. T. J. Clark, *The Painting of Modern Life* (Princeton: Princeton University Press, 1986), 272n19.

30. William M. Thackeray, *The Paris Sketch Book* (London, 1888), 53. Antoine Terrasse, *Bonnard* (Paris: Gallimard, 1988), 13.

31. *The Journal of Eugène Delacroix,* trans. Walter Pack (New York: Grove, 1961), 134.

32. Matisse cited in *Paris/New York 1908–1968* (Paris: Centre Pompidou, 1991), 398. Perhaps Matisse was attempting to distinguish himself from certain colleagues that an American magazine, the *Architectural Record,* had named, along with him, as "the wild men of Paris": Friesz, Derain, and above all Braque and Picasso. See *Paris/New York,* 431.

33. Rosenthal, *Du romantisme,* 355.

34. Angers cited by Sfeir-Semler in *Die Maler,* 365.

35. Charles Rosen and Henri Zerner, *Romanticism and Realism* (New York: Viking, 1984), 93.

36. Champfleury cited ibid., 22. Baudelaire, "Puisque réalisme il y a," in *Oeuvres complètes* (Paris: Pléiade, 1961), 634–635.

37. Goncourts, Oct. 6, 1861, *Journal,* vol. 1, 736. Zola, March 22, 1885, cited by Colette Becker in *Dictionnaire d'Emile Zola* (Paris: Laffont, 1993), 280.

38. Schurr cited by Sfeir-Semler in *Die Maler,* 325. Ibid., 364. Robert Herbert, *Impressionism* (New Haven: Yale University Press, 1988), ch. 2.

39. Fétis cited by Rosenthal in *Du romantisme,* 179. Champfleury, *Le Réalisme* (Paris: Lévy, 1857), 272. Baudelaire, "Richard Wagner et 'Tannhäuser' à Paris," in *Oeuvres complètes,* 1209, 1215. Thoré cited by Rosenthal in *Du romantisme,* 153n1, 118.

40. Rosen and Zerner, *Romanticism and Realism,* 151.

41. Breton, "Comète surréaliste" (1947), in *La Clé des champs* (Paris: Pauvert, 1979), 119.

42. Thackeray, *Paris Sketch Book,* 177.

43. Jean-Paul Crespelle, *La Vie quotidienne à Montparnasse, 1905–1930* (Paris: Hachette, 1976).

44. *Paris/New York,* 11.

45. Some French artists did understand the new importance of New York, especially Picabia, who insisted on the contrast between the concreteness of the city and the ineffability of its spirit.

46. Clement Greenberg, "Contribution to a Symposium," *Art and Culture* (1953), cited by Hubert Damisch in *Paris/New York,* 221.

47. Zeldin, *France 1848–1945,* 465. According to an article in the *New York Times* in 1910, 2,000 Rembrandts, both false and real, were found in America. A Parisian journal of the same epoch claimed that 2,849 Corots had recently been exported to the United States. Harvey Levenstein, *Seductive Journey: American Tourists in France from Jefferson to the Jazz Age* (Chicago: University of Chicago Press, 1998), 148.

48. Jean-Pierre cited by Alfred Pacquement in "Confrontations 1950–1953," in *Paris/New York,* 649.

17. A UNIVERSAL CITY

1. I owe this idea to Charles S. Maier.

Acknowledgments

This book began as sixteen lectures which I gave at the Collège de France in 1999. I am grateful to my sometime colleagues in that noble institution, and especially to Emmanuel Leroy-Ladurie, an old and much admired friend, for their invitation and their elegant courtesies.

As regards my home institution, I also wish to thank Henri Zerner and (would that it were truly possible!) the late John Clive, for our fruitful conversations about the life and times of Paris and London.

I learned a great deal from friends and readers who commented on some or all of these pages: Peter Beilharz, Ewa Lajer-Burcharth, John Gillies, Sudhir Hazareesingh, Barbara Rosenkranz, and Aurélie Thiria. In many different ways colleagues (and relations!) in Paris and Cambridge helped me to think about the history of this city, to structure my text, and finally, to write it: Maurice Agulhon, Sven Beckert, Jonathan Beecher, Guy Cardwell, Leslie Choquette, Margaret Cohen, Francois Delaporte, Marx Fumaroli, Patrice Gueniffey, Anne Higonnet, Ethel Higonnet, Fred Kameny, Kathleen Kete, David Leeming, Alain Salomon, Alex Schwartz, and Vanessa Schwartz.

The classes I have given at Harvard on the history of Paris have occasioned enriching conversations and much pleasure from exchange of thoughts and ideas, especially with Marcelline Block, Charlotte Houghteling, Laura Knoll, Elaine Kwok, Nora Morrison, Matthew Quirk, Miranda Richmond, Katherine Stirling, Naghmeh Sorabi, Daniel Sussner, and Matthew Yglesias.

ACKNOWL-
EDGMENTS

❧

Over the years I have learned to admire the skill and generosity of the staff at Widener and Houghton Libraries, the Bibliothèque de France, the British Museum, and the Bibliothèque Historique de la Ville de Paris, whose most able curator, Alfred Fierro, is often cited in these pages.

At Harvard University Press, I am grateful to Maria Ascher for her excellent editing of Chapter 1, to Kathi Drummy, who valiantly took on the daunting task of obtaining illustrations and permission to use them, and to Kathleen McDermott, who graciously oversaw the entire project. My thanks also to Aïda Donald—friend, mentor, and adviser—who nurtured this project when it was in its infancy. Arthur Goldhammer, with whom I have enjoyed for more than a decade long and engaging conversations, will find in this book not just his words but many of his ideas and observations as well. And particular thanks to my editor at the Press, Camille Smith, whose dedication and skill have amazed me from first to last. I am greatly in her debt.

Index

This book was set in Garamond No. 3 for the text
and Adobe Garamond for the captions, frontmatter, and endmatter
The display type was set in Castellar MT and Centaur MT Italics
with Swash Capitals, and the ornaments were set in
Type Embellishments One and
Schneidler Initials CS

Production of this book was coordinated by David Foss
The book and jacket were designed by Gwen Nefsky Frankfeldt
The text was typeset by Technologies 'N Typography

The book was printed and bound
by the Hamilton Printing Company on 60 pound
Opaque Cream Vellum made by the
Mohawk Paper Company

The color inserts, endpapers, and jacket were printed
by Henry N. Sawyer Company

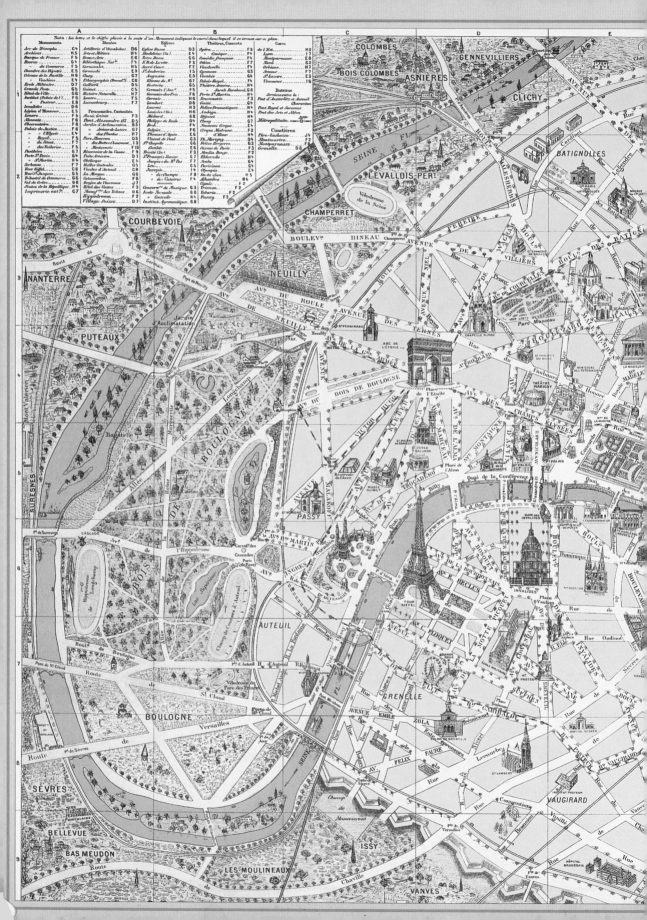